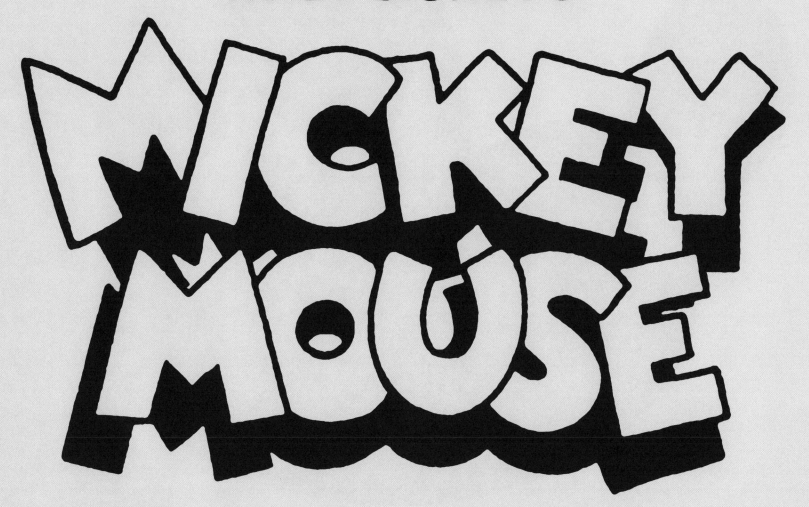

WALT DISNEY'S

MICKEY MOUSE

BY FLOYD GOTTFREDSON

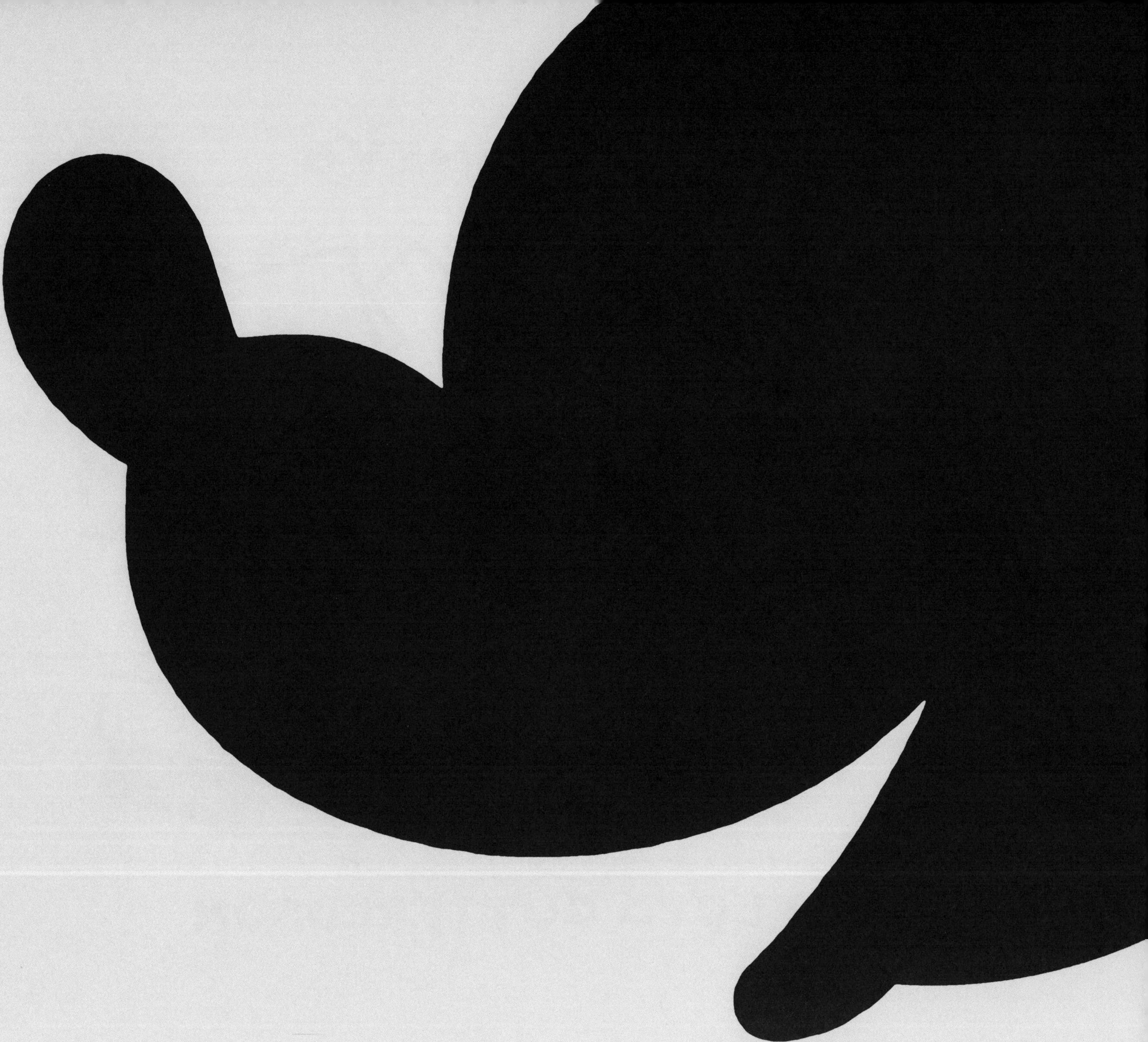

WALT DISNEY'S
MICKEY MOUSE
BY FLOYD GOTTFREDSON

VOLUME ONE

Color Sundays

"CALL OF THE WILD"

Series Editors: David Gerstein and Gary Groth

LEFT: when famed "Duck Man" Carl Barks (*Uncle Scrooge*) first applied for his job with Walt Disney in 1935, he submitted this drawing as one of several samples. Drawn with pen and ink and blue wash on board, it illustrates Floyd Gottfredson's "Lair of Wolf Barker," reprinted in this volume. Barks and Gottfredson would later become close friends.

The Floyd Gottfredson Library

Series Editors: DAVID GERSTEIN with GARY GROTH
Series Designers: JACOB COVEY and TONY ONG
Colorists: DIGIKORE STUDIOS with RICH TOMMASO
Production: PAUL BARESH
Associate Publisher: ERIC REYNOLDS
Publishers: GARY GROTH and KIM THOMPSON

To receive a free catalogue of graphic novels, newspaper strip reprints, prose novels, art books, cultural criticism and essays, and more, call 1-800-657-1100 or visit our website at Fantagraphics.com.

To receive a free catalogue of graphic novels, newspaper strip reprints, prose novels, art books, cultural criticism and essays, and more, call 1-800-657-1100 or visit our website at www.fantagraphics.com.

Distributed in the U.S. by W.W. Norton and Company, Inc. (800-233-4830)
Distributed in Canada by Canadian Manda Group (800-452-6642 x862)
Distributed in the U.K. by Turnaround Distribution (44 (0)20 8829-3002)
Distributed to comic stores by Diamond Comics Distributors (800-452-6642 x215)

ISBN 978-1-60699-643-0

Printed in Singapore.

FLOYD GOTTFREDSON'S MICKEY MOUSE enters every battle like a trouper. He tells desperados he'll "break ya with my naked hands"; almost as if, with just enough bluff, the fight might prove easy. But it's easier to *talk* about subduing tough guys than to *do* it. Mickey only soldiers through because his grit won't quit.

Remastering the *Mickey Mouse* Sunday strip was also easier to talk about than to do. Line art sometimes had to be reseparated from printed pages; compiling color stats for reference was an elephant of a job. But strip collectors Thomas Andrae and Thomas Jensen, and restoration master Paul Baresh, proved that an elephant could fly.

Many others also merit thanks for this book's contents. Ken Shue, Disney Publishing Worldwide's Vice President of Global Art and Design Development, and his Secretary Iliana Lopez, moved mountains to make surviving Gottfredson line art negs available. Danny Saeva, DPW's Director of Licensing, North America, aided us with further cross-studio connections.

Numerous other scholars contributed artwork, essays, knowledge, and archival items. We're grateful to Director Rebecca Cline, Archivist Michael Buckhoff, Contractor Kevin Kern, and Senior Secretary Alesha Reyes at the Walt Disney Archives; also to Creative Director Lella Smith, Research Manager Fox Carney, and Researchers Ann Hansen and Jackie Vasquez at the Walt Disney Animation Research Library. I'd also like to thank Paul F. Anderson, Gunnar Andreassen, Garry Apgar, Geoffrey Blum, Massimo Bonura, Paolo Castagno, Robert Cowan, Dale Dietzman, Diane Disney Miller, Shernaaz Engineer, Fabio Gadducci, Didier Ghez, Leonardo Gori, the Hake's Americana staff (including Alex Winter, Terence Kean, and Deak Stagemeyer), Kevin Huizenga, Lars Jensen, Mark and Cole Johnson, Diego Jourdan Pereira, Thad Komorowski, Jim Korkis, Kosta Labropoulos, Sergio Lama, Jens Lindell, Mike Matei, Stefano Priarone, Frank Stajano, Ricky Turner, Germund Von Wowern, and Dejan Zivkovic.

Others, too, have provided crucial support and encouragement. First and foremost come my parents, Susan and Larry Gerstein, and my brother Ben. Then come friends including Céline and Stefan Allirol-Molin, Christopher and Nicky Barat, Jerry Beck, John Clark, César Ferioli, Jonathan Gray, Joakim Gunnarsson, Andy Hershberger, Nelson Hughes, Vincent Joseph, Mark Kausler, Carl Keil, Raquel Lopez, Jean Marie Metauten, Geoffrey Moses, Floyd Norman, KaJuan Osborne, Tarkan Rosenberg, Travis Seitler, Warren Spector, Tom Stathes, Kwongmei To, Joe and Esther Torcivia, and Wilbert Watts.

A last, special thanks goes to scholar and friend J. B. Kaufman, who gave this volume its sparkling Foreword—and discovered that Mickey's vow to "break ya with my naked hands" actually references *The Spoilers* (1914), a pivotal early adventure film. J. B.'s grit, like Mickey's, won't quit.

—David Gerstein
January 2013

TABLE of CONTENTS

Setting the Stage

The Sundays: Floyd Gottfredson's Mickey Mouse Stories With Introductory Notes

TABLE *of* CONTENTS

THE GOTTFREDSON ARCHIVES: ESSAYS AND SPECIAL FEATURES

No "overnight" success ever really happens overnight; but to Mickey Mouse's many fans in the early 1930s, it must have seemed that their hero had burst into the public consciousness out of nowhere. Appearing sporadically on movie screens in 1928-29, elevated to greater national and international prominence by new distribution agreements in 1930, Mickey struck a responsive chord with audiences and quickly moved beyond the confines of the screen. By early 1932 he was everywhere: his grinning visage could be seen not only in the movies but in storybooks, on dolls and other toys—and in a daily black-and-white newspaper comic strip. A counterpart Sunday comic page in color must have seemed inevitable.

King Features, the comics syndicate handling the Mickey daily strip, evidently thought so. As comics legend Floyd Gottfredson later remembered it, the syndicate was eager for a Mickey Sunday page, and the feature might have started far earlier than it did if not for a simple lack of manpower. "King Features had been after Walt for, I guess, nearly a year to do a Sunday page," Gottfredson told Disney archivist Dave Smith. "Walt had thus been after me to do it, and I couldn't find the time."[1] In 1931 Gottfredson had his hands full writing and drawing the *Mickey* daily strip. But his department was gradually growing; and Earl Duvall, who had been hired to ink the dailies, had ambitions for bigger things. By the end of the year inker Al Taliaferro and scripter Ted Osborne had joined the team, relieving pressure on Gottfredson and Duvall and allowing them to devote some time to new projects. Early in 1932, Walt, King Features, and legions of Disney fans all got their wish: a fresh, delightful new Disney comics page in full color debuted in the Sunday papers.

RIGHT: Gottfredson self-caricature drawn for in-house use, c. 1933. Image courtesy The Walt Disney Company.

MICKEY'S SUNDAY BEST

FLOYD GOTTFREDSON AND THE DISNEY COLOR COMICS

1932-1935: *A New Arena*

» *FOREWORD BY J. B. KAUFMAN*

The new feature was an ambitious undertaking, occupying a full page in comic sections and offering *two* generous weekly servings of Disney art. The upper third of the page was devoted to a *Silly Symphony* top strip, initially written, drawn and inked by Duvall.[2] For the page's initial offering on 10 January 1932, Duvall was a true one-man show, performing all writing and artistic duties for both the *Silly Symphony* story *and* the *Mickey Mouse* episode—a somewhat odd one—that appeared on the bottom half of the page. Thereafter Gottfredson, the experienced hand, took over the *Mickey* series, launching what would become a long, rich body of work in its own right. The first four years of that remarkable series are collected in this volume for the first time in English.

In Fantagraphics' preceding *Mickey Mouse* daily strip books, David Gerstein and Thomas Andrae have already discussed the relationship between the Mickey theatrical cartoons and the daily newspaper comic strip—the fascinating process by which a central character, and a series of comic situations, were adapted from one medium into a very different medium with

different demands. By early 1932 the relationship between film and comic-strip worlds was well established, and Gottfredson had begun to explore it in depth. But the advent of the Sunday page represented a new arena: a form unlike either of the others, with new challenges and opportunities all its own. The creative team began to experiment in ways that are endlessly intriguing today. At the most basic level, the format of the Sundays differed from that of the dailies in three important ways: the stories were longer, they appeared at weekly intervals, and they were in color.

Today, in hindsight, the color may seem like a non-issue, but it's important to remember that in early 1932 Mickey and his friends were still appearing in the movies in black and white, and would continue to do so for another three years. In some instances, audiences knew them only in their monochrome incarnations, and King Features' colorists were charged with introducing them in color for the first time. The decision to render Mickey's shorts in red would seem a predetermined choice, since by January 1932 he had already appeared in books and merchandise with red shorts;

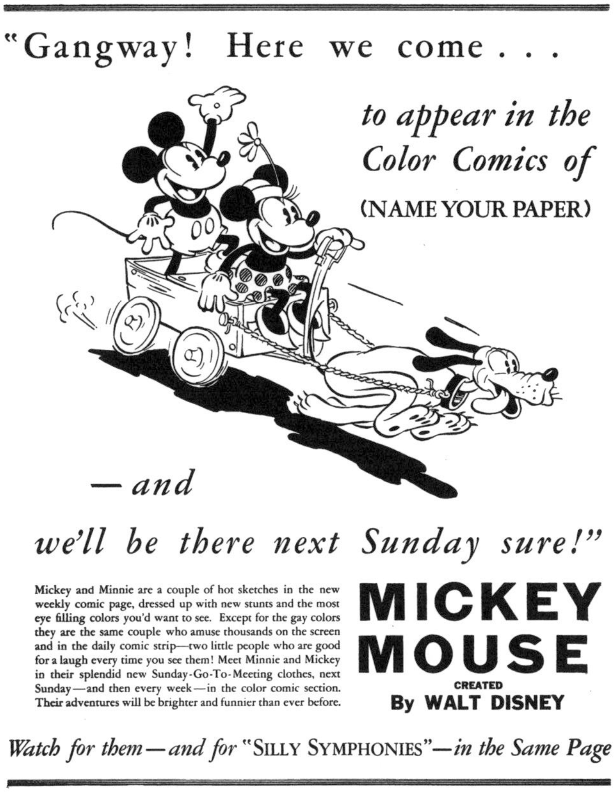
"Gangway! Here we come . . .
to appear in the Color Comics of (NAME YOUR PAPER)
— and we'll be there next Sunday sure!"
Mickey and Minnie are a couple of hot sketches in the new weekly comic page, dressed up with new stunts and the most eye filling colors you'd want to see. Except for the gay colors they are the same couple who amuse thousands on the screen and in the daily comic strip—two little people who are good for a laugh every time you see them! Meet Minnie and Mickey in their splendid new Sunday-Go-To-Meeting clothes, next Sunday—and then every week—in the color comic section. Their adventures will be brighter and funnier than ever before.
MICKEY MOUSE
CREATED
By WALT DISNEY
Watch for them—and for "SILLY SYMPHONIES"—in the Same Page

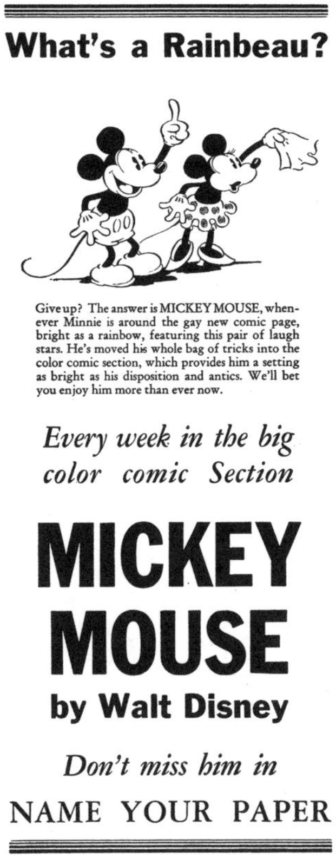
What's a Rainbeau?
Give up? The answer is MICKEY MOUSE, whenever Minnie is around the gay new comic page, bright as a rainbow, featuring this pair of laugh stars. He's moved his whole bag of tricks into the color comic section, which provides him a setting as bright as his disposition and antics. We'll bet you enjoy him more than ever now.
Every week in the big color comic Section
MICKEY MOUSE
by Walt Disney
Don't miss him in
NAME YOUR PAPER

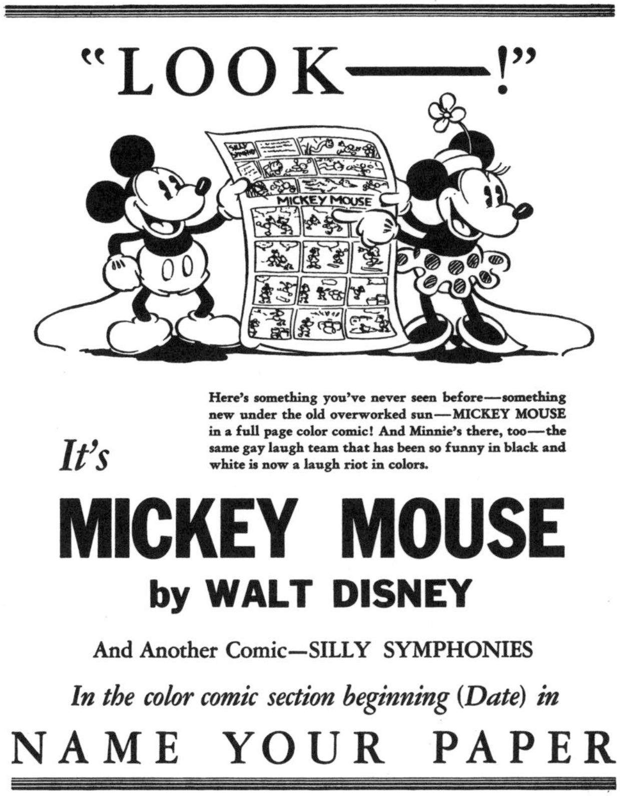
"LOOK——!"
MICKEY MOUSE
Here's something you've never seen before—something new under the old overworked sun—MICKEY MOUSE in a full page color comic! And Minnie's there, too—the same gay laugh team that has been so funny in black and white is now a laugh riot in colors.
It's
MICKEY MOUSE
by WALT DISNEY
And Another Comic—SILLY SYMPHONIES
In the color comic section beginning (Date) in
NAME YOUR PAPER

but even this was no certainty. In fact, the Mouse had sported *green* shorts in many early licensed items; and in November 1932, when he did first appear in a Technicolor cartoon—produced not for public consumption, but for the 1931-32 Academy Awards banquet—the shorts again were green.[3] No matter; the Sunday comics clothed Mickey in red from the beginning. By 1935, when the theatrical Mickey cartoons made their official jump to Technicolor, Mickey's red shorts had come to be accepted as the standard—thanks in no small part to the Sunday comics—and most later color films followed suit (no pun intended).

ABOVE: Three original ad drawings (and surrounding text copy) from Disney's and King Features' Sunday strip launch pack, 1932. Art by Floyd Gottfredson; images courtesy Walt Disney Archives.

Mickey's and Minnie's gloves proved likewise variable. Today we tend to picture the gloves in basic white, but in fact the yellow gloves in Gottfredson's comics reappeared in many of Mickey's earliest color films. Other anomalies of color, some more surprising than others, pop up in the Sunday pages as King's colorists—presumably with Walt's blessing—experiment with the form. Note Mickey's and Minnie's facial coloring during the first few months of the page, with a white area for the eyes set off by a pinkish "skin tone" below, and Pluto's startling "albino" appearance at various times in 1932. Donald Duck received yellow feathers throughout 1935; long enough for the trend to spread into locally produced European Disney comics.

Far more than color, the other inherent properties of the Sunday page—the dimensions of Gottfredson's canvas, and its appearance at weekly intervals—determined his approach to story material. We've already seen in Volume 1 of Fantagraphics' daily strip series how the nature of the daily—the steady recurrence of short bursts of action—lent itself to a continuing narrative. Scarcely two weeks into its run in January 1930, the daily had already launched a continuing story, its adventurous course plotted by Walt Disney himself. Gottfredson, taking over the writing duties in mid-1930, had built on this precedent with increasingly extended and thrill-packed plotlines, and by early 1932 had established the direction he would follow in the *Mouse* dailies for the rest of his career. But the Sunday page was a different matter. Continuity stories were not unheard of in Sunday comics, but Gottfredson seems to have felt from the beginning that this larger, colorful, intermittent format might be better suited to other kinds of story material—perhaps self-contained stories or gags that didn't depend on the reader's familiarity with earlier installments. For the first six months of its existence, and at frequent intervals thereafter, the *Mickey Mouse* Sunday page featured these self-contained "gag-a-day" stories.

And what sort of stories were they? Thanks to the increased length of the Sunday strip, Gottfredson was free to plot more extended narratives than in individual episodes of the daily—but he didn't always use that freedom. Sometimes the extra space was used for other purposes. Twice in July 1933, the *Mickey* page tells an exceedingly simple story, but one packed by Gottfredson with an overabundance of drawings. The result is a remarkable simulation of movement, reminding us that Gottfredson had begun his Disney career as an animator. By contrast, on other Sundays, Gottfredson *does* use the extra panels to build up the narrative substance of the story, filling them with incident, gags, and dialogue.

As with the daily strip, Gottfredson drew much of his basic inspiration from contemporary Mickey Mouse theatrical films. If anything, the Sunday Mickey remained closer to his cinematic roots than did his daily counterpart. Some examples are obvious enough: in February 1932 Gottfredson recycles a horse-anchor gag from *The Barn Dance* (1928), the fourth Mickey cartoon, more or less verbatim; and a month later Mickey shoots a literally explosive flash photo of a flock of prize hens—a memorable episode from *Musical Farmer* (1932), then in production. Elsewhere Gottfredson uses his source material in less obvious ways, creatively mixing gags and characters from more than one film. One Mickey-Pluto hunting story in February 1932 combines hunting gags from *The Moose Hunt* (1931) and *The Duck Hunt* (1932) with a Wild West bit player from *Pioneer Days* (1930).

Silly Symphonies
by Walt Disney
Bucky Bug wanders in Mother Goose Land, to the court of King Cole and his merry band!
OLD KING COLE, YOU'RE A MERRY OLD SOUL, WHILE I AM JUST ONE OF THE MOB... SAD AND BLUE AND HUNGRY, TOO... AND LOOKING FOR A JOB
HA! HA! HO! HO! A JOB FOR YOU; AND FOR ME, A SHOW! FOR MANY YEARS I'VE LAUGHED AND SUNG AND DANCED THE WHOLE DAY THROUGH, AND I'VE FORGOTTEN HOW IT FEELS TO BE FORLORN AND BLUE!
'TWOULD REALLY BE A NOVELTY IF I WERE FEELING BAD, SO ALL THAT YOU WILL HAVE TO DO IS TRY TO MAKE ME SAD!
HURRY! DRESS UP FOR THE PART, BUT PLEASE DON'T BE MIS-LED! FOR EITHER YOU MUST MAKE ME CRY OR...OFF WILL COME YOUR HEAD!
OLD KING COLE IS A MERRY OLD SOUL! YEAH! FAR TOO MERRY IS HE! HE MAY BE THE LIFE OF A PARTY, BUT HE'LL BE THE DEATH OF ME!
TO BE CONTINUED

FUNNY FILMS
BEGINNING
"DON POOCHO"
CUT OUT STAGE AND FILM — MAKE SLITS ALONG DOTTED LINES ON THE SCREEN-
CHANGE HEADS BY MOVING THEM THROUGH SLITS — A NEW SHOW -EVERY WEEK-
BEGINNING
THE "BOYS ABOUT TOWN"
MICKEY MOUSE MOVIES
END
END

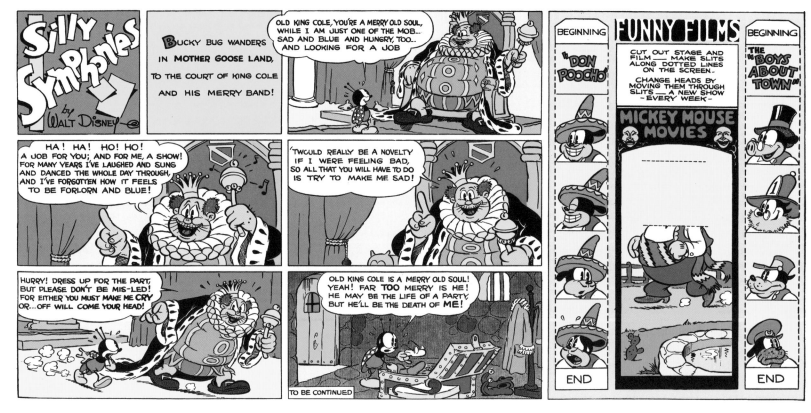

Sometimes, in fact, the relationship between the films and the comics became downright labyrinthine. In July 1933 the Disney story department circulated a story outline for a cartoon to be called "Spring Cleaning." This outline inspired so many gag and story ideas that it was split into two separate films, then three.[4] In the end "Spring Cleaning" kicked around the Disney studio for years without ever reaching the screen, although some of its component ideas did. In the meantime, three of those ideas—Mickey's attempt to patch a window screen, Pluto's misadventures with a garden hose, and Pluto's messy encounter with a package of flypaper—were borrowed for three separate installments of the Sunday comic strip in September-October 1933. By the following spring, all three of those gag ideas had also been absorbed into the theatrical short *Playful Pluto* (1934), and the last of the three would be forever enshrined in animation history as the legendary "flypaper sequence."

When the Sunday page did venture a continuing story, the results became even more fascinating. As a rule, the Sunday continuities were unlike those in the daily strip: less heroic adventure, more comedy and fantasy. Gottfredson set the tone in 1932 by plotting the page's first two continuities, filling them not with feats of derring-do but with gags, drama, and characters based loosely on two of the studio's current films. "Dan the Dogcatcher" starts with the last half of *The Mad Dog* (1932), then continues on a plot trajectory all its own. "Mickey's Nephews" may seem unconnected with any film, but Mickey's dream visions of wedding bells point unmistakably to *Mickey's Nightmare* (1932), which had climaxed with our hero's home overrun by mischievous little mice. In the strip—at Walt Disney's suggestion—Gottfredson singles out just two of those little hellions, personalizes them, and creates formative versions of two characters who will become familiar to later generations of comics fans.[5]

Early in 1933 Ted Osborne took over the writing duties for the Sunday page. As this volume demonstrates, Osborne's continuities followed Gottfredson's lead: stories based on current Disney pictures—with an offbeat twist. "Rumplewatt the Giant" pitted the giant from the Mickey short *Giantland* (1933) against the dwarfs from the Silly Symphony *Babes in the Woods* (1932), with Princess Minnie from *Ye Olden Days* (1933) thrown in for good measure. "Hoppy the Kangaroo," in 1935, starts like an obvious replay of that year's *Mickey's Kangaroo* (1935), then veers unexpectedly into story elements borrowed from the earlier *Mickey's Mechanical Man* (1933).

Even after surrendering the writing duties for the Sunday page, Gottfredson continued to plot the *Mickey* dailies. In effect, the daily and Sunday comics became two separate but parallel tracks, and Gottfredson seemed to revel in their relationship, creating a kind of subtle crosstalk between them. Sometimes this took the form of playful cross-references, inserted in the Sunday art as understated in-jokes. Readers of Fantagraphics' *Mickey* daily strip books will remember that, in April 1934, Gottfredson built a short daily serial around a character from an earlier Silly Symphony, *Just Dogs* (1932): an unnamed Boston terrier whom he dubbed "Terry." In *this* volume we can see that "Terry" had already been lurking around Gottfredson's Sunday comics for nearly two years by 1934—popping up unannounced as an occasional supporting character, as if to pave the way for his brief starring role in the dailies.

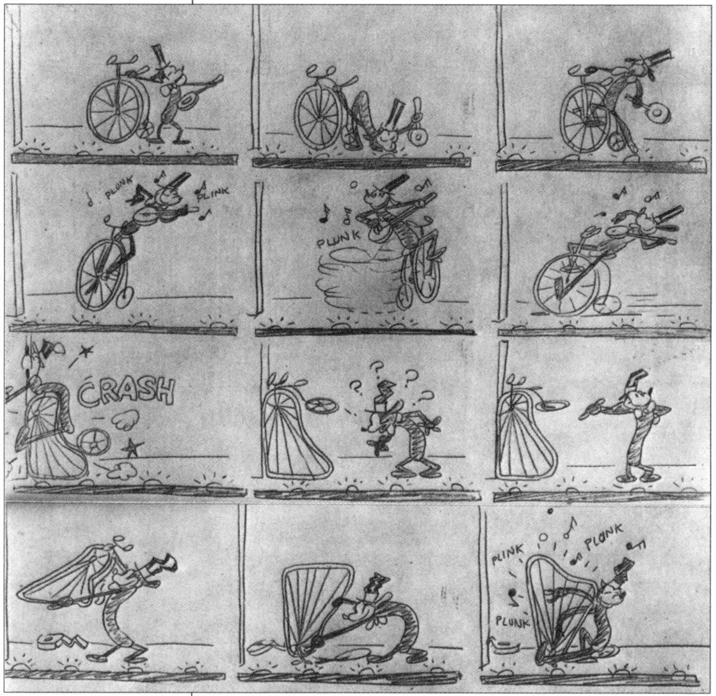
CRASH
PLUNK

Conversely, we've seen an extended daily continuity in June-October 1933 featuring "Mickey Mouse and His Horse Tanglefoot." Now we find that in the midst of that run, in August 1933, Tanglefoot made an unbilled guest appearance in the Sunday comics as well—testing the market, perhaps, before returning to Sundays the following spring in "Tanglefoot Pulls His Weight."

And what of the major characters? By and large, the world of the Sunday comics affected them

FACING PAGE: Sample *Silly Symphony* from September 24, 1933. By this time Al Taliaferro had supplanted Earl Duvall as sole artist on the strip. Taliaferro also drew the "Funny Films" extra feature, tied into Gottfredson's ongoing *Mickey* tales: the character of Don Jollio comes from this volume's "Lair of Wolf Barker" serial.

ABOVE: Gottfredson's strip for April 17, 1932 evolved from this unused storyboard sequence with Wienie the dachshund, perhaps intended at one time for *The Opry House* (1929). Art attributed to Ub Iwerks; image courtesy Walt Disney Archives.

SU

in varying ways. Horace Horsecollar and Clarabelle Cow, already well-established in early 1932 when the Sunday feature started, arrived in that world virtually unchanged. David Gerstein has written of an odd continuity lapse in the daily strips of 1932: the impending wedding of Horace and Clarabelle was announced, given an elaborate buildup, then apparently forgotten.[6] No matter; married or not, they behave like a stereotypical bickering married couple in Sunday continuities like "Dr. Oofgay's Secret Serum" and "Foray to Mt. Fishflake." Horace obnoxiously brags and brays; Clarabelle nags and criticizes. When Horace's life seems threatened by Dr. Oofgay's serum, Clarabelle calls him "the poor dear" and declares: "I always said there never was a finer character than old Horsecollar!" But no sooner is Horace cured than Clarabelle reverts to type, nagging him mercilessly.

Donald Duck, as introduced to movie audiences in *The Wise Little Hen* (1934), was notable for his laziness and greed—and a followup continuity in the *Silly Symphony* Sunday comics portrayed him in the same way.[7] But Donald soon migrated to the Mickey Mouse film series and to Mickey's half of the Sunday comics page, and now those traits were supplanted by a funnier one: his terrible temper. Osborne and Gottfredson were at pains to build up Donald's irascible nature: on his introduction in February 1935 Mickey comments that the Duck is "always scrappin' over somep'n," and in the last panel Donald assumes the fighting stance that he had introduced on the screen in *Orphans' Benefit* (1934).

Pluto, gradually introduced in both the movies and the daily strip during 1930-31, underwent an odd reentry process during the launch of the Sunday comics in 1932. In that first oddball Earl Duvall page, the hapless hound is unnamed, and Mickey seems never to have seen him before. It's not until Pluto's second appearance, a month later, that Mickey addresses him by name.

Dippy Dawg, the character who will evolve into Goofy, enters the Sunday page early in 1933—and, still being in a formative state, gives us a unique look at his early developmental process. (Note the "Dippy Dog" spelling in these earliest appearances, later replaced by the more familiar "Dawg.") Perhaps because the character was still so unformed and malleable, Osborne and Gottfredson felt free to take creative liberties with his personality. Dippy's outlandishly ingenious solutions to problems would become familiar on the screen soon enough, but his obsession with his "juice-harp," oblivious to the indifference or irritation of everyone around him, was an intriguing trait that could be found only in the comics.

It was Mickey himself, the star of the strip, who displayed the widest range of responses to its Sunday showcase. As the nature of the stories changed, Mickey's persona changed with it. For an adventure serial like "The Lair of Wolf Barker," he could be the same intrepid little daredevil as in the daily strip, but more benign settings and stories brought out

JOSEPH M. SCHENCK
PRESENTS
WALT DISNEY'S
MICKEY MOUSE
IN "MICKEY'S MECHANICAL MAN"
UNITED ARTISTS PICTURE
UMM-184

ABOVE: Some scenes in Gottfredson's "Rumplewatt the Giant" (1934) mimicked staging from the cartoon *Giantland* (1933): compare the film still with the Sunday strip for April 1, 1934. Animation by Hamilton Luske.

RIGHT: Gottfredson's "Hoppy the Kangaroo" (1935) featured the 'roo in a boxing match against a gorilla. On-screen, it was *Mickey's Mechanical Man* (1933) who fought the big ape in the ring.

FACING PAGE: Initial Sunday strip artist Earl Duvall also drew this 1930 box design for an unreleased card game. Image courtesy Hake's Americana; used with permission of the Walt Disney Family Foundation.

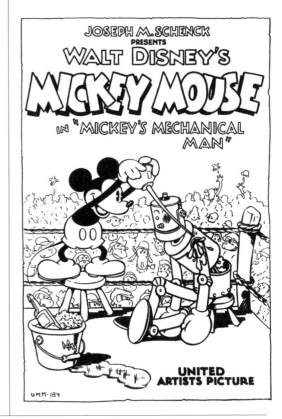

other facets of his personality. In some of the early Mickey films the Mouse had displayed a mischievous streak; in the Sunday page he became even more mischievous and was given to elaborate practical jokes. Sometimes, to be sure, those jokes backfired. In October 1934 Mickey pulls a prank on Minnie with a garden hose, only to be drenched himself; and in January 1933, after Minnie herself colludes with Mickey to throw a snowball at a top-hatted gent, both find themselves in frigid discomfort when their victim turns the tables on them. But just as often, Mickey's impish pranks are successful, and either way he usually prevails with a smile.

On and off the screen, the early Mickey loved music. In his films he occasionally sang, but more often was seen playing a piano or some other instrument. In the comics the proportions were reversed: Mickey might be seen playing instrumental music now and then, but was far more likely to lift his voice in song. "Minnie's Yoo Hoo," his theme song in the movies since 1929, was a favorite number in his comics repertoire as well; in one October 1932 page he performs a complete chorus—at intervals, pausing for various interruptions.

In the Sunday comics, in fact, Mickey takes his musical hobby a step further and tries his hand as a songwriter. Several installments find him actively endeavoring to write a love song for Minnie. On one of these occasions, in November 1932, his playful streak gets the better of him and he ends the song with a mischievous insult, bringing down Minnie's wrath and beating a retreat amidst a hail of cookware and other missiles. (In a later episode, playing Cyrano to Horace's Christian de Neuvillette, Mickey pulls a similar reversal on Clarabelle.) Elsewhere, in another variation, Mickey can sometimes be seen improvising a verse about events that have just taken place.

But Mickey is not always clever or mischievous. If the story calls for it, he can fill any number of other roles. In some pages he's simply a well-meaning good citizen whose earnest efforts to clean house, fix

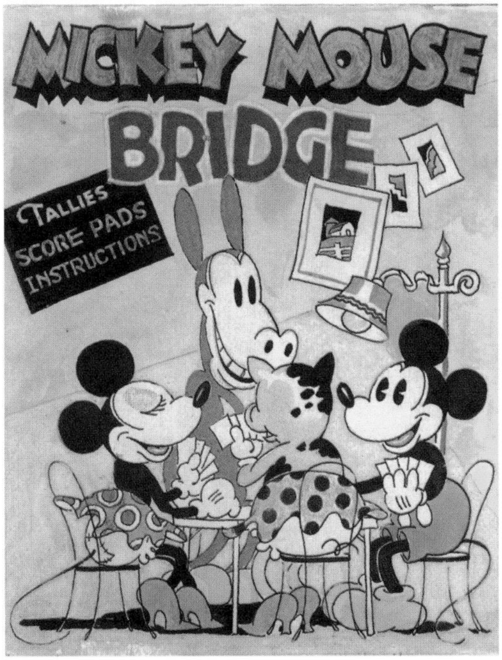
MICKEY MOUSE
BRIDGE
TALLIES
SCORE PADS
INSTRUCTIONS

a kitchen drain, or perform some other simple task lead to comic disaster. Yet again, even when he's not in a particularly mischievous mood, he may be simply a youngster bursting with energy and high spirits.

In his 1935 character analysis, Disney story department head Ted Sears would write: "Mickey is not a clown... he is neither silly nor dumb."[8] Not dumb, certainly, but in fact Mickey *had* already clowned around in a number of his films, indulging in silly hijinks just for the fun of it. Nor did this

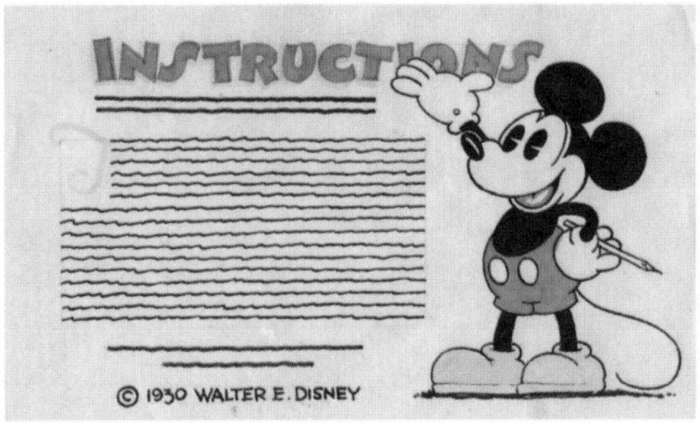
INSTRUCTIONS
© 1930 WALTER E. DISNEY

playful side disappear from Mickey's persona as he matured; his well-loved exploits in "The Sorcerer's Apprentice," appearing on the screen as late as 1940, were yet another expression of his boyish, unbounded enthusiasm. And that side of his persona continued to appear in the Sunday comics as well—sometimes with the same calamitous consequences.

Daring adventurer, hapless clown, songster, high-spirited mischief maker; these and other traits can easily be absorbed in Mickey Mouse's persona. It's a tribute to his versatility, and to the skill of Gottfredson and his collaborators, that one character can display all these facets and yet remain consistently a recognizable, distinct individual—a Mouse for all seasons. The early Sunday comics provide Mickey with a splendid stage; the years afterward, as we shall see in the next volume, will offer him a whole new set of challenges and innovations. •

1 Floyd Gottfredson to David R. Smith, *Mickey Mouse in Color* deluxe edition (Prescott: Another Rainbow, 1988), p. 159.

2 This and other credits information: Gottfredson to Smith, pp. 159-161.

3 See *Parade of the Award Nominees* (1932) on *Walt Disney Treasures: Mickey Mouse in Living Color* (Disney DVD, 2001).

4 The additional shorts were the "autumn cleaning" cartoon *Playful Pluto* (1934) and the unproduced "Interior Decorators" (in and out of production from 1936-38).

5 Gottfredson to Smith, p. 166. Gottfredson incorrectly recalled the source cartoon as *Orphans' Benefit* (1934), a much later appearance by the crowd of kids.

6 David Gerstein, "The Cast: Horace, Clarabelle... and Dippy," in *Walt Disney's Mickey Mouse: Trapped on Treasure Island* (Vol. 2 of Fantagraphics' companion daily strip series), p. 243.

7 "The Wise Little Hen" comics adaptation, September 16-December 16, 1934.

8 Ted Sears, "Mickey Mouse." Character analysis, 1935, p. 1.

A Brief Essay About FLOYD GOTTFREDSON

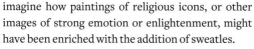

» Appreciation by Kevin Huizenga

I FIRST CAME ACROSS Floyd Gottfredson's work in *Mickey Mouse Best Comics*, the big white 1978 book that collected many of his 1930s strips in bright colors. I didn't know that the color wasn't original or that the stories were condensed. But I still checked the book out of the library many times as a teenager, back when reprints of old strips were much harder to come by.

Gottfredson's strips appealed to me in part because of the canonical 1930s cartoon style—that mix of pleasant liveliness and weirdly unsettling energy—but also because the storytelling was so straightforward. Mickey and the gang were mostly the same size from panel to panel, and the "camera angle" stayed sensibly steady. It was a breath of fresh air for me after all the "dynamic" layouts of modern superhero comics.

The other thing that amazed me about Gottfredson's work was his habit of drawing sweat droplets bursting from characters' heads. So many! Gottfredson drew *Mickey Mouse* for forty-five years, and some years are drier than others, but during the rainy seasons there are sometimes more panels with bursts of sweat (or tears) than not!

When I started work at a small design and illustration company, I learned to call these small droplets of liquid "sweatles" (pronounced "swet-tels"). The term first showed up in the comic strip *Bloom County* in 1987. But the sweatle itself is older, one of cartooning's great contributions to the vocabulary of art. Like a visual metaphor, the sweatle externalizes a subjective state; like the word balloon and the thought balloon, it is an intuitive and satisfying symbol that has passed into common use. One can imagine how paintings of religious icons, or other images of strong emotion or enlightenment, might have been enriched with the addition of sweatles.

Mickey and the gang are often surrounded by halos of water, shining from their heads like rays. It's clear Gottfredson knew that these droplets made a lot of subtle effects available to a cartoonist. One need only measure out the right amount of droplets, the right shape, and the trajectory which best fit not only the characters' internal states, but also the composition of each panel.

Other cartoonists—George Herriman (*Krazy Kat*), for instance—who also use a high volume of droplets often show gravity's curving effect on the water. Gottfredson's sweatles usually shoot off at a higher velocity, though there are a wide variety of forms and speeds for the connoisseur to find.

The effect of these thousands of sweatles is that Gottfredson's already-lively Mickey seems even more expressive and alive on the page. Not only do we see his expertly controlled expression and posture—but our glance picks up the sweatles in flight, signaling that this is the very moment that panic, or surprise, or joy is striking him. Mickey has feelings so strong that they actually produce a kind of kinetic energy. This is the same force that pushes cartoon hats up in the air. Gottfredson used it to open up shortcuts into our brains.

Some years ago I filled some space in my comic book *Or Else* with a visual tribute to Floyd Gottfredson (reprinted opposite)—and his supreme mastery of the sweatle. I also tried to answer the question: where do Mickey's sweatles *go*? •

જોયું કે મીની! આપુને છેક મુંબઈ માંબી યાદ કરેછ. આય જામે જમશેદ વાંચ.
Walt Disney

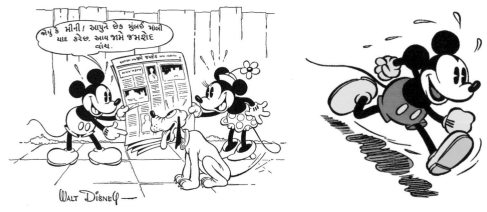

LEFT: Gottfredson's "sweatles" (detail from August 20, 1933) were such a trademark that his assistants mimicked them when creating ad art for the strip. Tom Wood drew the present example for a newspaper in India (March 21, 1934). Mickey's Gujarati voice balloon says, "Have you seen, Minnie? They know us all the way out in Mumbai! Read *Jam-e-Jamshed* and see for yourself!" Image from Walt Disney Archives; reprinted courtesy of Shernaaz Engineer, editor *Jam-e-Jamshed*.

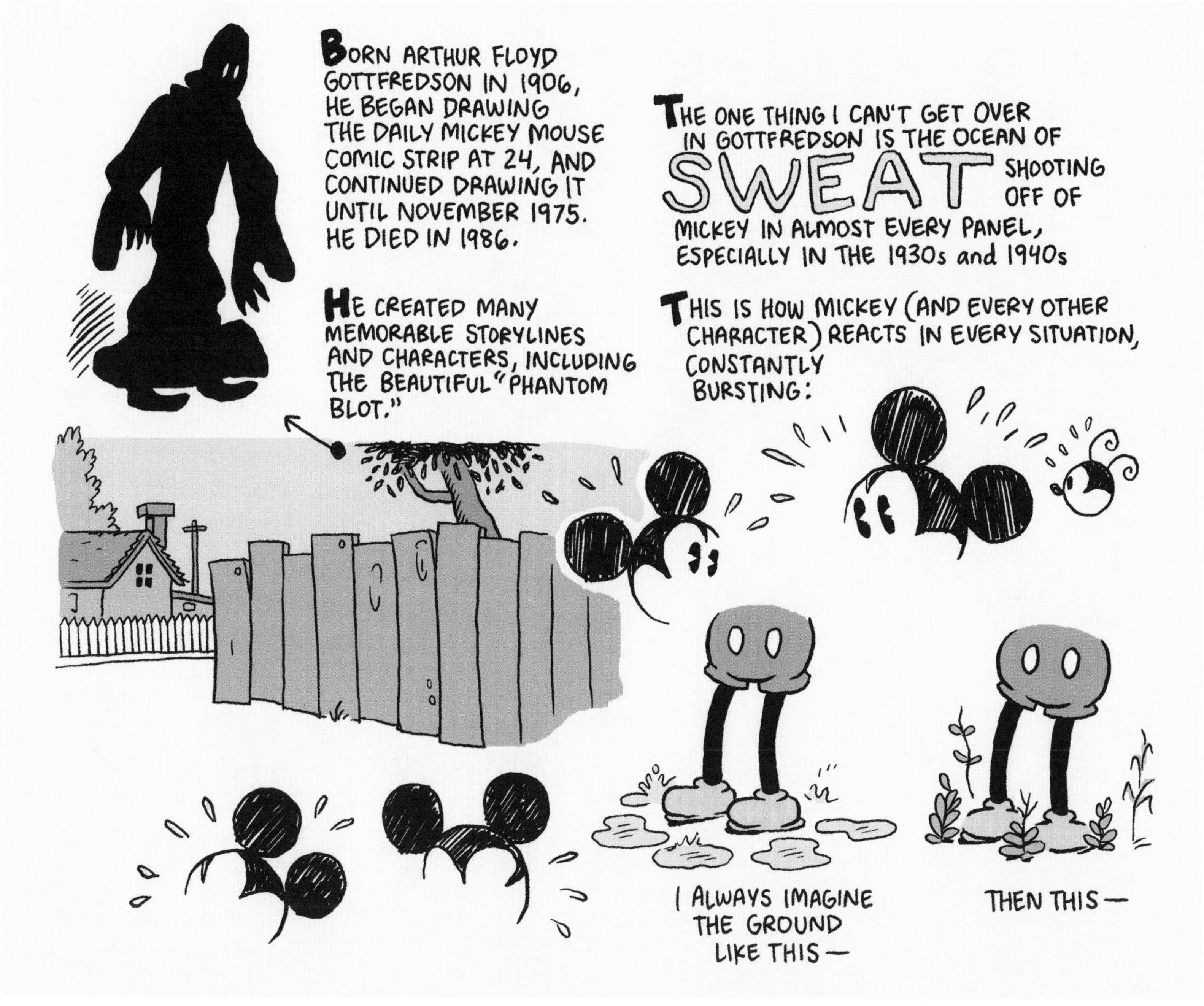
BORN ARTHUR FLOYD GOTTFREDSON IN 1906, HE BEGAN DRAWING THE DAILY MICKEY MOUSE COMIC STRIP AT 24, AND CONTINUED DRAWING IT UNTIL NOVEMBER 1975. HE DIED IN 1986.
HE CREATED MANY MEMORABLE STORYLINES AND CHARACTERS, INCLUDING THE BEAUTIFUL "PHANTOM BLOT."
THE ONE THING I CAN'T GET OVER IN GOTTFREDSON IS THE OCEAN OF SWEAT SHOOTING OFF OF MICKEY IN ALMOST EVERY PANEL, ESPECIALLY IN THE 1930s and 1940s
THIS IS HOW MICKEY (AND EVERY OTHER CHARACTER) REACTS IN EVERY SITUATION, CONSTANTLY BURSTING:
I ALWAYS IMAGINE THE GROUND LIKE THIS—
THEN THIS—

From *Or Else* 3 (1999). Art © and courtesy Kevin Huizenga.

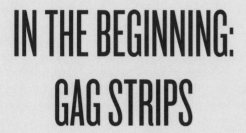

IN THE BEGINNING: GAG STRIPS

JANUARY 10, 1932
–
JULY 24, 1932

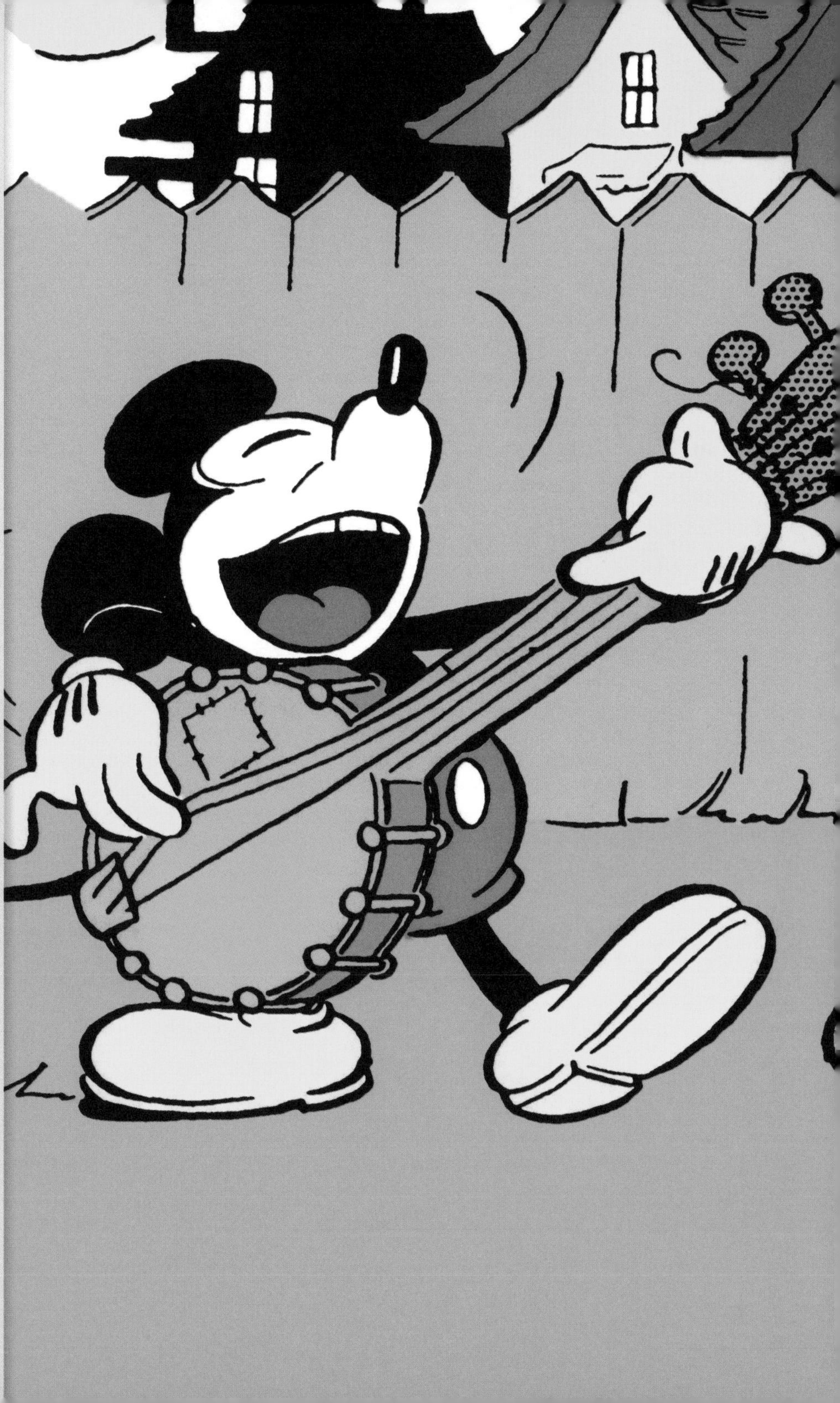

MICKEY MOUSE

REGISTERED U.S. PATENT OFFICE

SUNDAY STORYTELLING

While Mickey Mouse successfully entered comics in 1930, the tone of his animated shorts did not. The earliest *Mickey* daily gags tried to mimic cartoon slapstick; but the daily strip, limited to four or five panels per instalment, could only carry slapstick so far. At such a short length, the form felt simple and repetitive. Under Floyd Gottfredson's guiding hand, the daily soon evolved into an adventure serial—and rarely looked back at its cartoony origins.

But there was still a comics canvas where slapstick made sense; where intricate visual gags and extended cartoony situations had more breathing room to develop naturally. This canvas was the *Mickey* Sunday strip. In it, Gottfredson birthed an entirely different animal from the daily; but that in its difference, pioneered several classic storytelling techniques.

One technique involved more sophisticated pacing. Short daily strips had limited space per day to advance their plots; by contrast, Sunday strips had room to let the action stop and start. After setting up a plotline, Gottfredson could pause for comedic—or dramatic—tension as Mickey went about a task, unaware of what lay ahead. He could spend several panels happily stunting on ice, not noticing danger; he might be singing as he worked, unaware of an impending pratfall. The effect was fundamentally cartoonish; many a film short had used lulls to build up to a dramatic climax. But the effect also made for good comics storytelling; a kind that had been spatially impossible before.

A related Sunday-only technique was the gag that escalated. Prefigured, again, by similar structures in animation, the *Mickey* Sunday often involved an activity that got increasingly silly or comically frustrating as it continued; a hard concept to communicate in four panels, but easy to express in twelve. Mickey's setup of a farmyard photoshoot might involve increasing numbers of interfering animals. Mickey's effort to fix Minnie's pipes might extend to the point of enlisting wrench, plunger, pump and hose.

A third cartoon-like technique—often following on an escalating gag—was the final twist. Mickey or another character would attempt to accomplish some goal in an elaborate manner; multiple panels would show complex or frenzied action. But then, with victory or failure seemingly imminent, events would comically reverse themselves. Minnie's pipes might not have the problem Mickey thought they did. The photoshoot, after laborious prep work, might unexpectedly end in embarrassment.

Let's jump into the earliest Floyd Gottfredson Sunday strips—and Earl Duvall's one-time-only predecessor, with its taller aspect ratio–and see how these cartoonish techniques were explored.

(One final cartoonish technique we should note, by the way, is the occasional use of dated content: exaggerated ethnic characters, for instance, or gags about gunplay and smoking. Needless to say, Mickey wouldn't mix it up with these elements today; we include them here, as in our past volumes, with the understanding that they reflect a bygone era.) [DG]

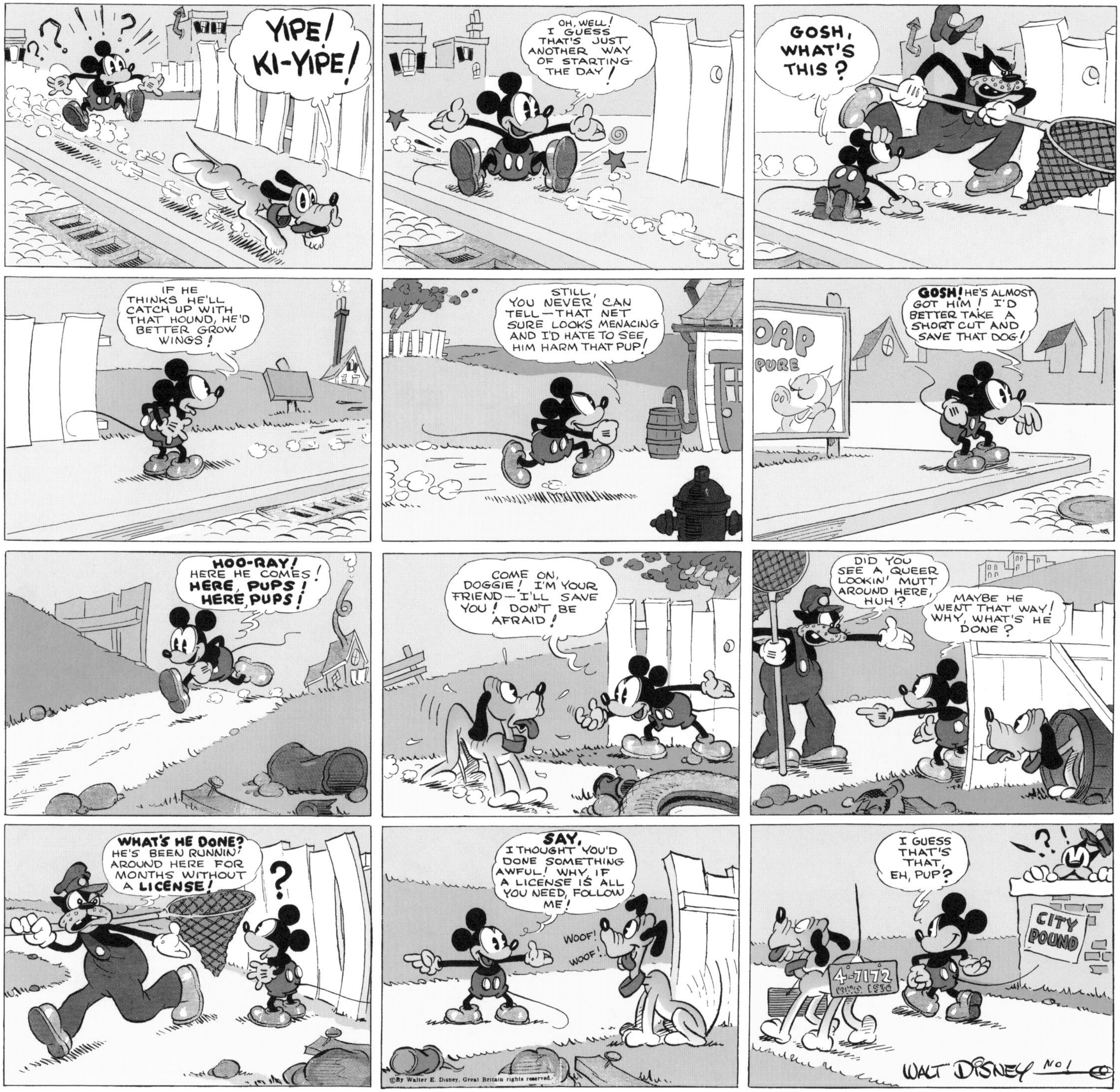

YIPE! KI-YIPE!
OH, WELL! I GUESS THAT'S JUST ANOTHER WAY OF STARTING THE DAY!
GOSH, WHAT'S THIS?
IF HE THINKS HE'LL CATCH UP WITH THAT HOUND, HE'D BETTER GROW WINGS!
STILL, YOU NEVER CAN TELL—THAT NET SURE LOOKS MENACING AND I'D HATE TO SEE HIM HARM THAT PUP!
OAP
PURE
GOSH! HE'S ALMOST GOT HIM! I'D BETTER TAKE A SHORT CUT AND SAVE THAT DOG!
HOO-RAY! HERE HE COMES! HERE, PUPS! HERE, PUPS!
COME ON, DOGGIE! I'M YOUR FRIEND—I'LL SAVE YOU! DON'T BE AFRAID!
DID YOU SEE A QUEER LOOKIN' MUTT AROUND HERE, HUH?
MAYBE HE WENT THAT WAY! WHY, WHAT'S HE DONE?
WHAT'S HE DONE? HE'S BEEN RUNNIN' AROUND HERE FOR MONTHS WITHOUT A LICENSE!
?
SAY, I THOUGHT YOU'D DONE SOMETHING AWFUL! WHY, IF A LICENSE IS ALL YOU NEED, FOLLOW ME!
WOOF! WOOF!
©By Walter E. Disney, Great Britain rights reserved.
I GUESS THAT'S THAT, EH, PUP?
CITY POUND
4-7172
WALT DISNEY

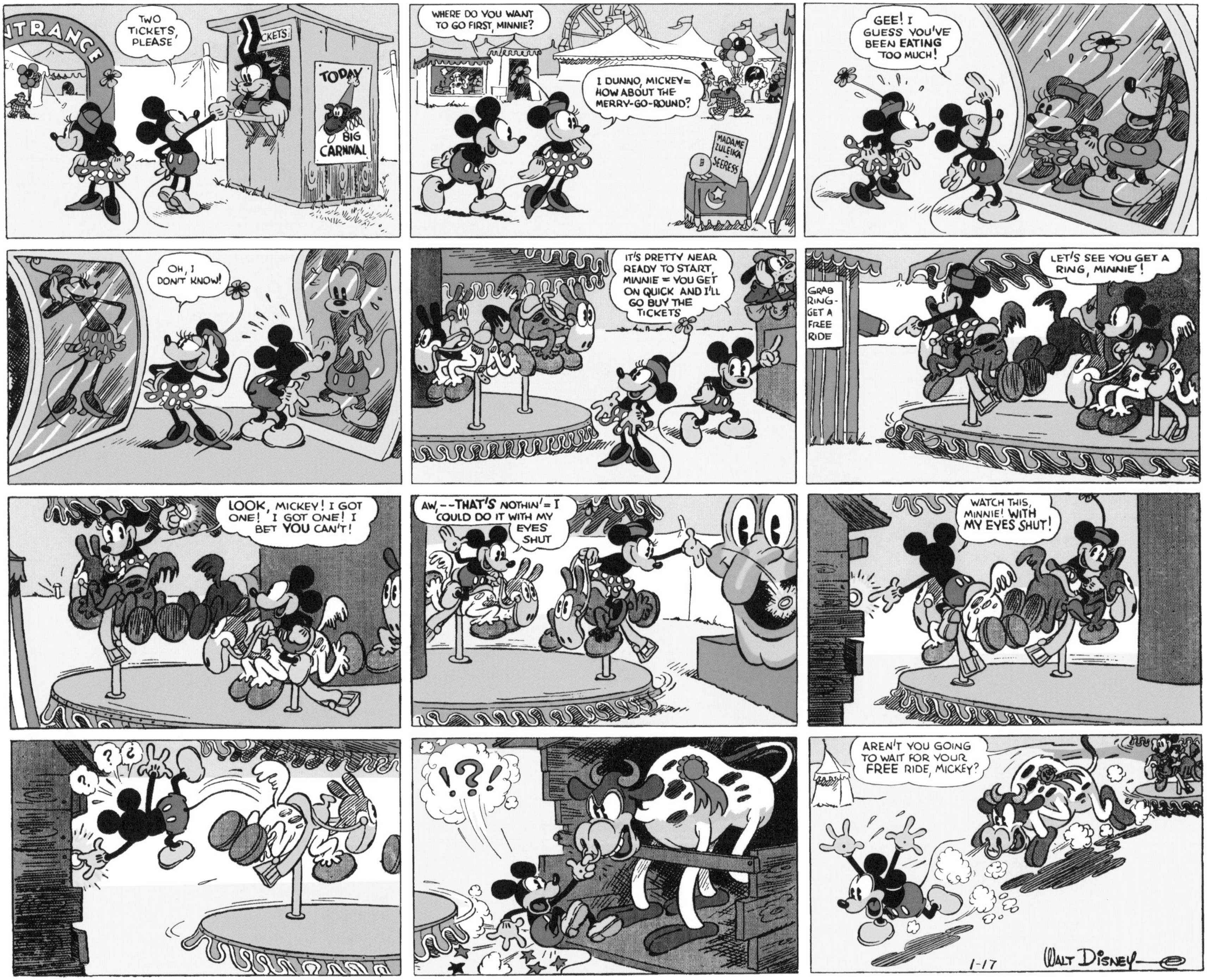
ENTRANCE
TWO TICKETS, PLEASE
TICKETS
TODAY BIG CARNIVAL
WHERE DO YOU WANT TO GO FIRST, MINNIE?
I DUNNO, MICKEY= HOW ABOUT THE MERRY-GO-ROUND?
MADAME ZULEIKA SEERESS
GEE! I GUESS YOU'VE BEEN EATING TOO MUCH!
OH, I DON'T KNOW!
IT'S PRETTY NEAR READY TO START, MINNIE = YOU GET ON QUICK AND I'LL GO BUY THE TICKETS
GRAB RING- GET A FREE RIDE
LET'S SEE YOU GET A RING, MINNIE!
LOOK, MICKEY! I GOT ONE! I GOT ONE! I BET YOU CAN'T!
AW, --THAT'S NOTHIN'= I COULD DO IT WITH MY EYES SHUT
WATCH THIS, MINNIE! WITH MY EYES SHUT!
!?!
AREN'T YOU GOING TO WAIT FOR YOUR FREE RIDE, MICKEY?
1-17
WALT DISNEY

20. THE COW'S HUSBAND

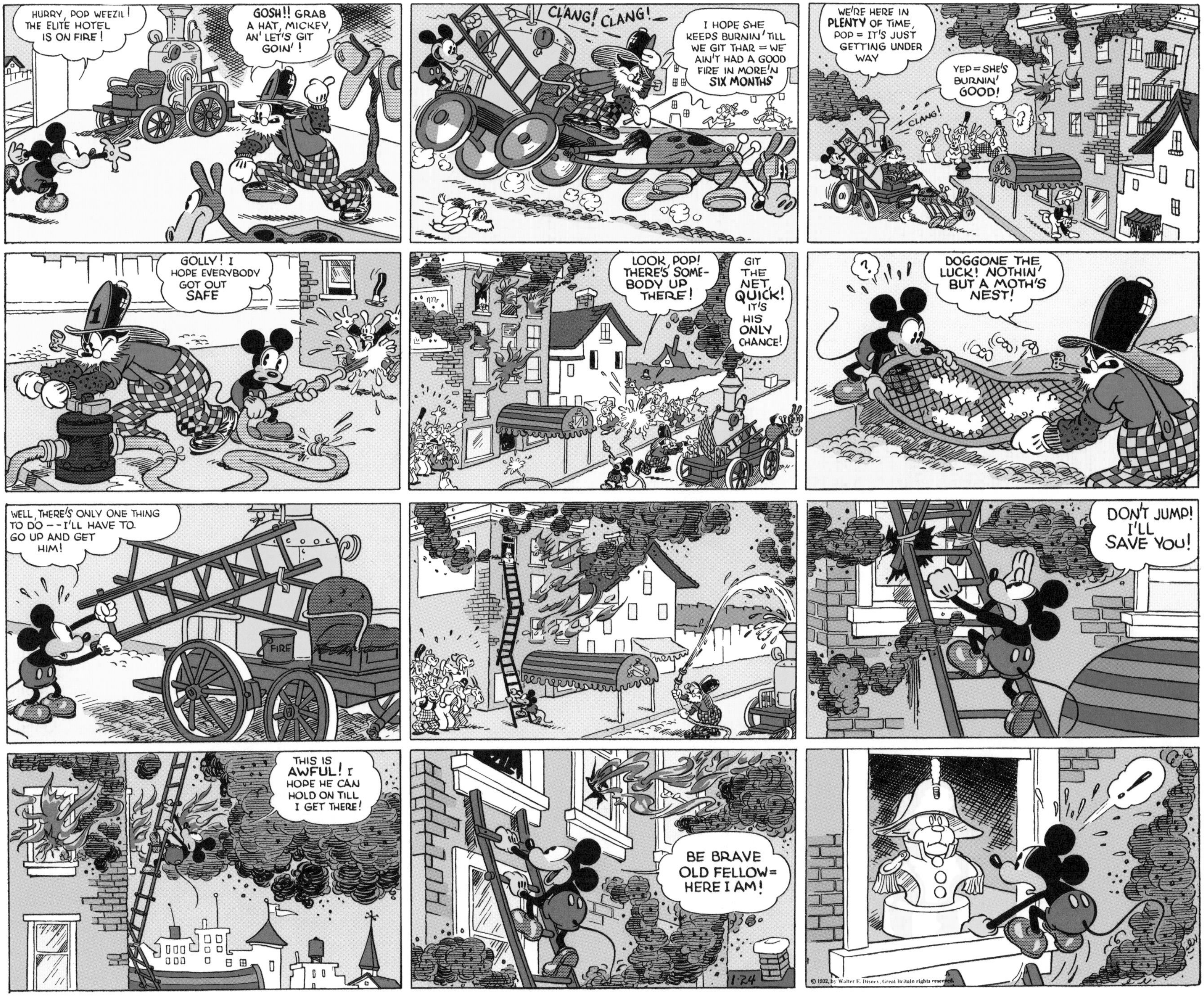
HURRY, POP WEEZIL! THE ELITE HOTEL IS ON FIRE!
GOSH!! GRAB A HAT, MICKEY, AN' LET'S GIT GOIN'!
CLANG! CLANG!
I HOPE SHE KEEPS BURNIN' TILL WE GIT THAR = WE AIN'T HAD A GOOD FIRE IN MORE'N **SIX MONTHS**
WE'RE HERE IN **PLENTY** OF TIME, POP = IT'S JUST GETTING UNDER WAY
CLANG!
YEP = SHE'S BURNIN' **GOOD!**
GOLLY! I HOPE EVERYBODY GOT OUT **SAFE**
LOOK, POP! THERE'S SOME-BODY UP THERE!
GIT THE NET, **QUICK!** IT'S HIS **ONLY** CHANCE!
?
DOGGONE THE LUCK! NOTHIN' BUT A MOTH'S NEST!
WELL, THERE'S ONLY ONE THING TO DO --I'LL HAVE TO GO UP AND GET HIM!
FIRE
DON'T JUMP! I'LL SAVE YOU!
THIS IS **AWFUL!** I HOPE HE CAN HOLD ON TILL I GET THERE!
BE BRAVE OLD FELLOW= HERE I AM!
1-24
© 1932, by Walter E. Disney, Great Britain rights reserved.
!

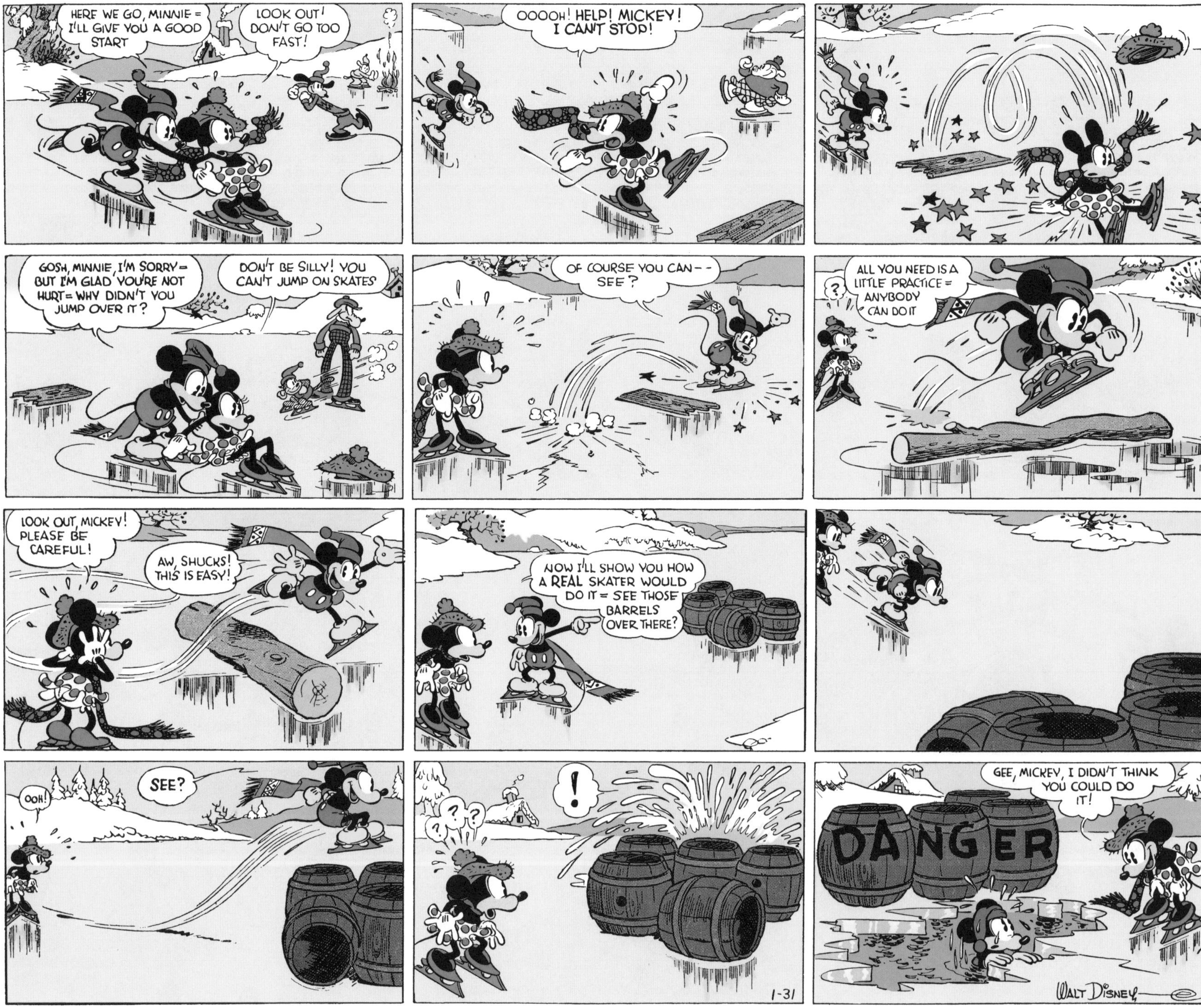
HERE WE GO, MINNIE = I'LL GIVE YOU A GOOD START
LOOK OUT! DON'T GO TOO FAST!
OOOOH! HELP! MICKEY! I CAN'T STOP!
GOSH, MINNIE, I'M SORRY= BUT I'M GLAD YOU'RE NOT HURT= WHY DIDN'T YOU JUMP OVER IT?
DON'T BE SILLY! YOU CAN'T JUMP ON SKATES
OF COURSE YOU CAN-- SEE?
?
ALL YOU NEED IS A LITTLE PRACTICE = ANYBODY CAN DO IT
LOOK OUT, MICKEY! PLEASE BE CAREFUL!
AW, SHUCKS! THIS IS EASY!
NOW I'LL SHOW YOU HOW A REAL SKATER WOULD DO IT = SEE THOSE BARRELS OVER THERE?
OOH!
SEE?
? ? ?
!
1-31
DANGER
GEE, MICKEY, I DIDN'T THINK YOU COULD DO IT!
WALT DISNEY

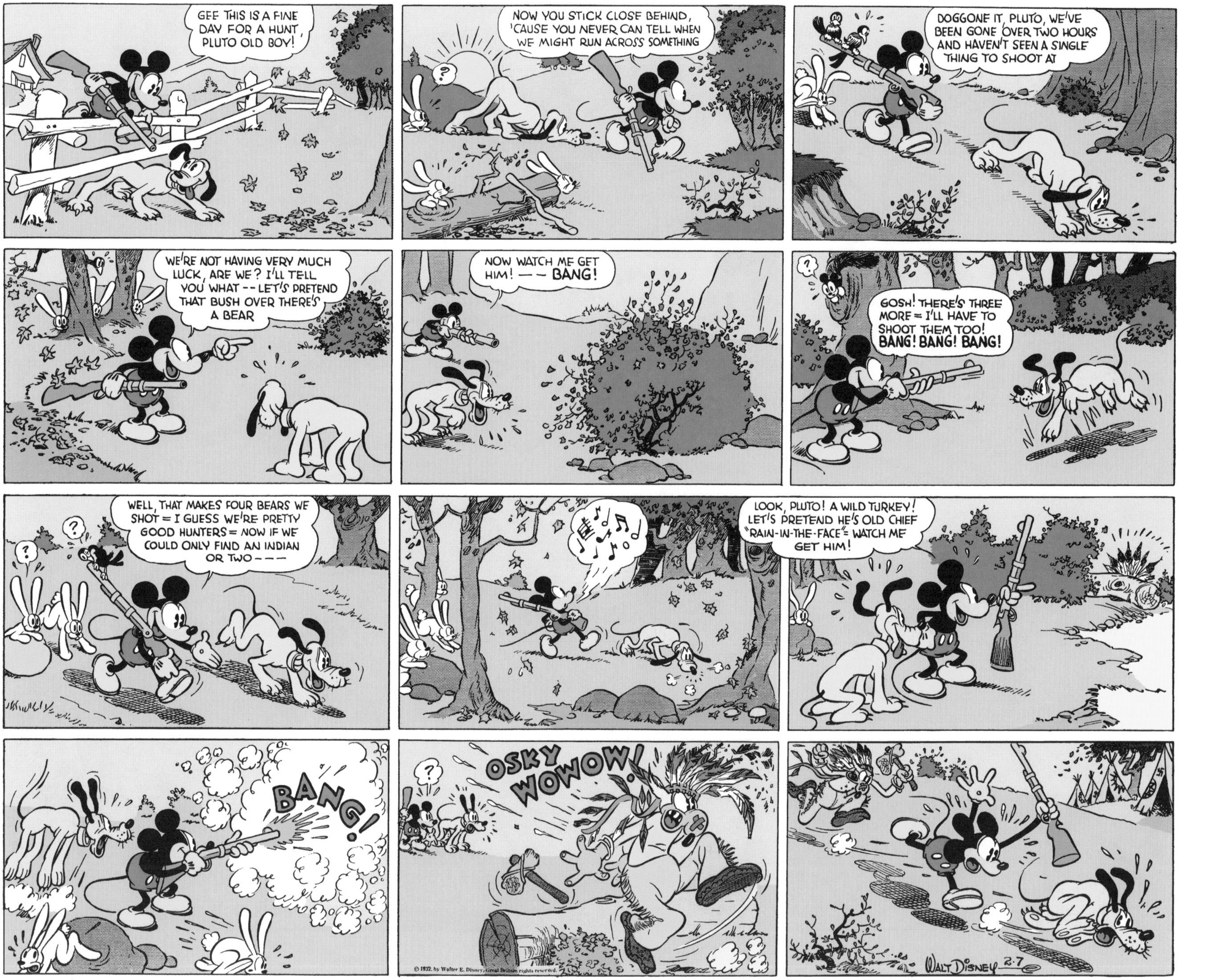
GEE THIS IS A FINE DAY FOR A HUNT, PLUTO OLD BOY!
NOW YOU STICK CLOSE BEHIND, 'CAUSE YOU NEVER CAN TELL WHEN WE MIGHT RUN ACROSS SOMETHING
DOGGONE IT, PLUTO, WE'VE BEEN GONE OVER TWO HOURS AND HAVEN'T SEEN A SINGLE THING TO SHOOT AT
WE'RE NOT HAVING VERY MUCH LUCK, ARE WE? I'LL TELL YOU WHAT -- LET'S PRETEND THAT BUSH OVER THERE'S A BEAR
NOW WATCH ME GET HIM! --- BANG!
GOSH! THERE'S THREE MORE = I'LL HAVE TO SHOOT THEM TOO! BANG! BANG! BANG!
WELL, THAT MAKES FOUR BEARS WE SHOT = I GUESS WE'RE PRETTY GOOD HUNTERS = NOW IF WE COULD ONLY FIND AN INDIAN OR TWO ---
LOOK, PLUTO! A WILD TURKEY! LET'S PRETEND HE'S OLD CHIEF "RAIN-IN-THE-FACE" = WATCH ME GET HIM!
BANG!
OSKY WOWOW!
WALT DISNEY 2-7

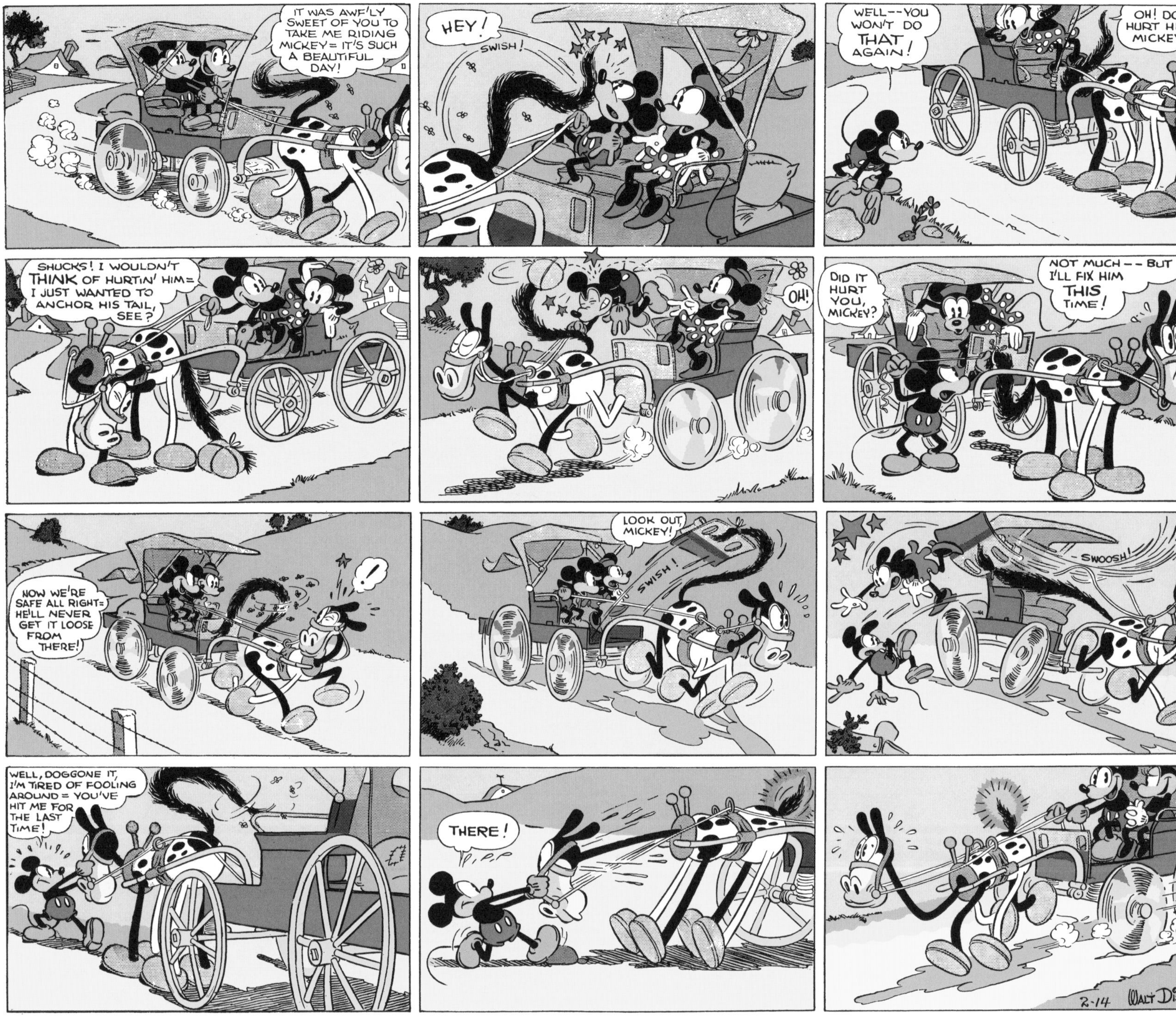
IT WAS AWF'LY SWEET OF YOU TO TAKE ME RIDING MICKEY= IT'S SUCH A BEAUTIFUL DAY!
HEY!
SWISH!
WELL--YOU WON'T DO THAT AGAIN!
OH! DON'T HURT HIM, MICKEY!
?
SHUCKS! I WOULDN'T THINK OF HURTIN' HIM= I JUST WANTED TO ANCHOR HIS TAIL, SEE?
OH!
DID IT HURT YOU, MICKEY?
NOT MUCH--BUT I'LL FIX HIM THIS TIME!
?
?
NOW WE'RE SAFE ALL RIGHT= HE'LL NEVER GET IT LOOSE FROM THERE!
!
LOOK OUT MICKEY!
SWISH!
SWOOSH!
WELL, DOGGONE IT, I'M TIRED OF FOOLING AROUND= YOU'VE HIT ME FOR THE LAST TIME!
THERE!
2-14
WALT DISNEY ©

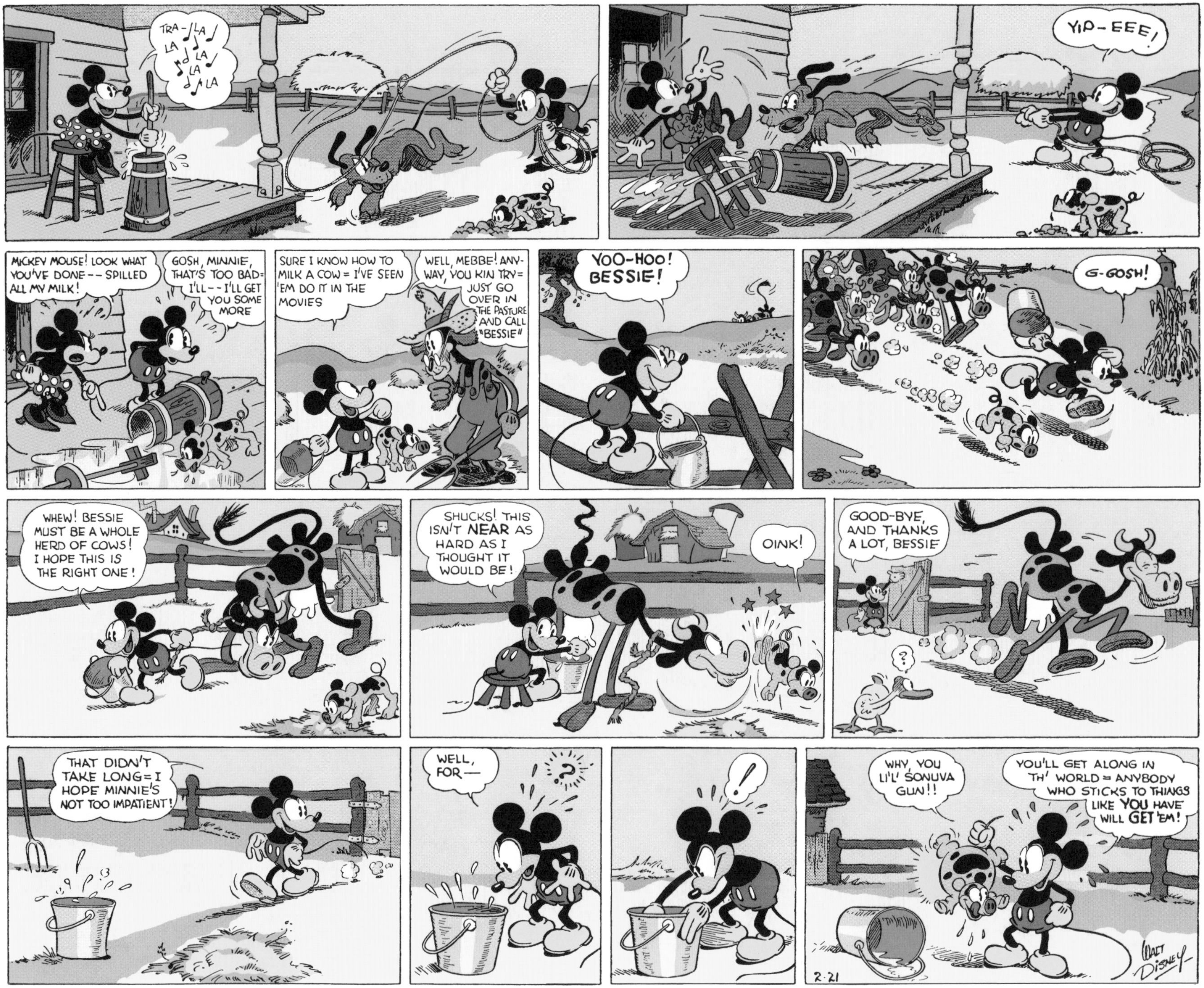
TRA-LA LA LA LA LA LA
YIP-EEE!
MICKEY MOUSE! LOOK WHAT YOU'VE DONE -- SPILLED ALL MY MILK!
GOSH, MINNIE, THAT'S TOO BAD= I'LL -- I'LL GET YOU SOME MORE
SURE I KNOW HOW TO MILK A COW = I'VE SEEN 'EM DO IT IN THE MOVIES
WELL, MEBBE! ANYWAY, YOU KIN TRY= JUST GO OVER IN THE PASTURE AND CALL "BESSIE"
YOO-HOO! BESSIE!
G-GOSH!
WHEW! BESSIE MUST BE A WHOLE HERD OF COWS! I HOPE THIS IS THE RIGHT ONE!
SHUCKS! THIS ISN'T NEAR AS HARD AS I THOUGHT IT WOULD BE!
OINK!
GOOD-BYE, AND THANKS A LOT, BESSIE
?
THAT DIDN'T TAKE LONG= I HOPE MINNIE'S NOT TOO IMPATIENT!
WELL, FOR—
?
!
WHY, YOU LI'L' SONUVA GUN!!
YOU'LL GET ALONG IN TH' WORLD = ANYBODY WHO STICKS TO THINGS LIKE YOU HAVE WILL GET 'EM!
2-21
WALT DISNEY

SWEEEET ROSIE O'GRAAAADY, SHEEEE'S MY LITTLE RO-O-OSE, TRAAAA LA LA-LA LAAAA LA MO-O-OST EV'RY ONE KNO-O-OWS=
HELLO, MINNIE! WHATCHA MAKIN'?
WHATCHA MAKIN', MINNIE?
DON'T BOTHER ME, MICKEY= I'M BUSY=
TAKE TWO CUPS OF SUGAR, HALF A CUP OF MILK---
WHERE DO YOU WANT ME TO TAKE 'EM?
BUTTER THE SIZE OF A WALNUT=
WHAT DO YOU MEAN, BUTTER THE SIDES OF A WALNUT? WHAT DO YOU WANT TO DO THAT FOR?
MICKEY, PULEEEZE! I'M BUSY!
WHATCHA MAKIN'?
NOTHING!
LET'S SEE--SIT ON A HOT STOVE AND STIR CONSTANTLY=
HUH! WHO WOULDN'T?
MICKEY MOUSE! YOU MAKE ME SO MAD! CAN'T YOU LEAVE ME ALONE?
SURE-- I CAN! BUT THAT WOULDN'T BE SO MUCH FUN!
LEMME LICK THE CROCK AND I'LL BET I CAN TELL YOU WHAT YOU'RE MAKIN'!
I WISH YOU'D GO ON HOME!
LOOK, MINNIE! I'LL BET YOU CAN'T DO THIS!
LOOK OUT!
YOO HOO!
UMMMM! NOW I KNOW WHAT YOU WERE MAKIN'= IT WAS UPSIDE DOWN CAKE=!
2-28 WALT DISNEY

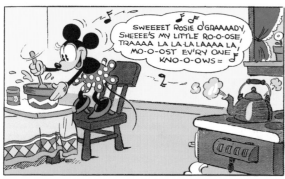

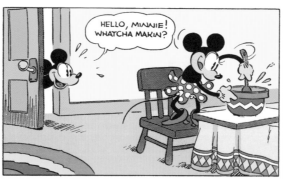

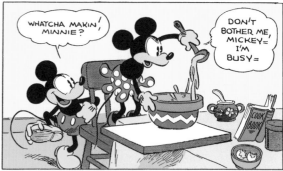

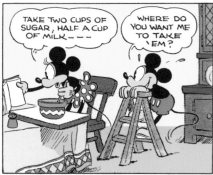

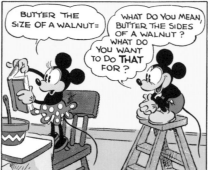

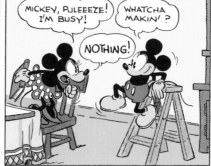

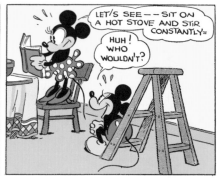

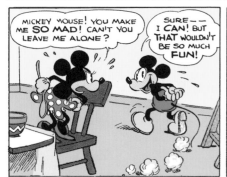

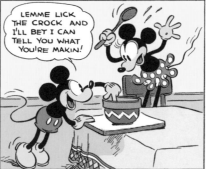

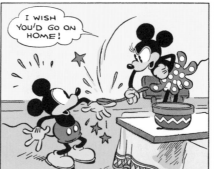

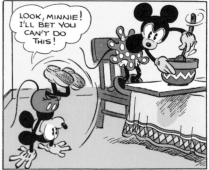

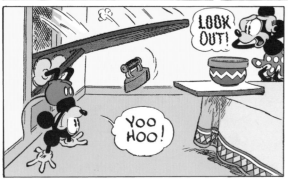

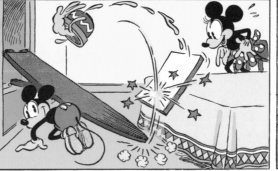

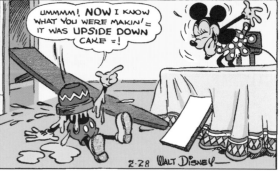

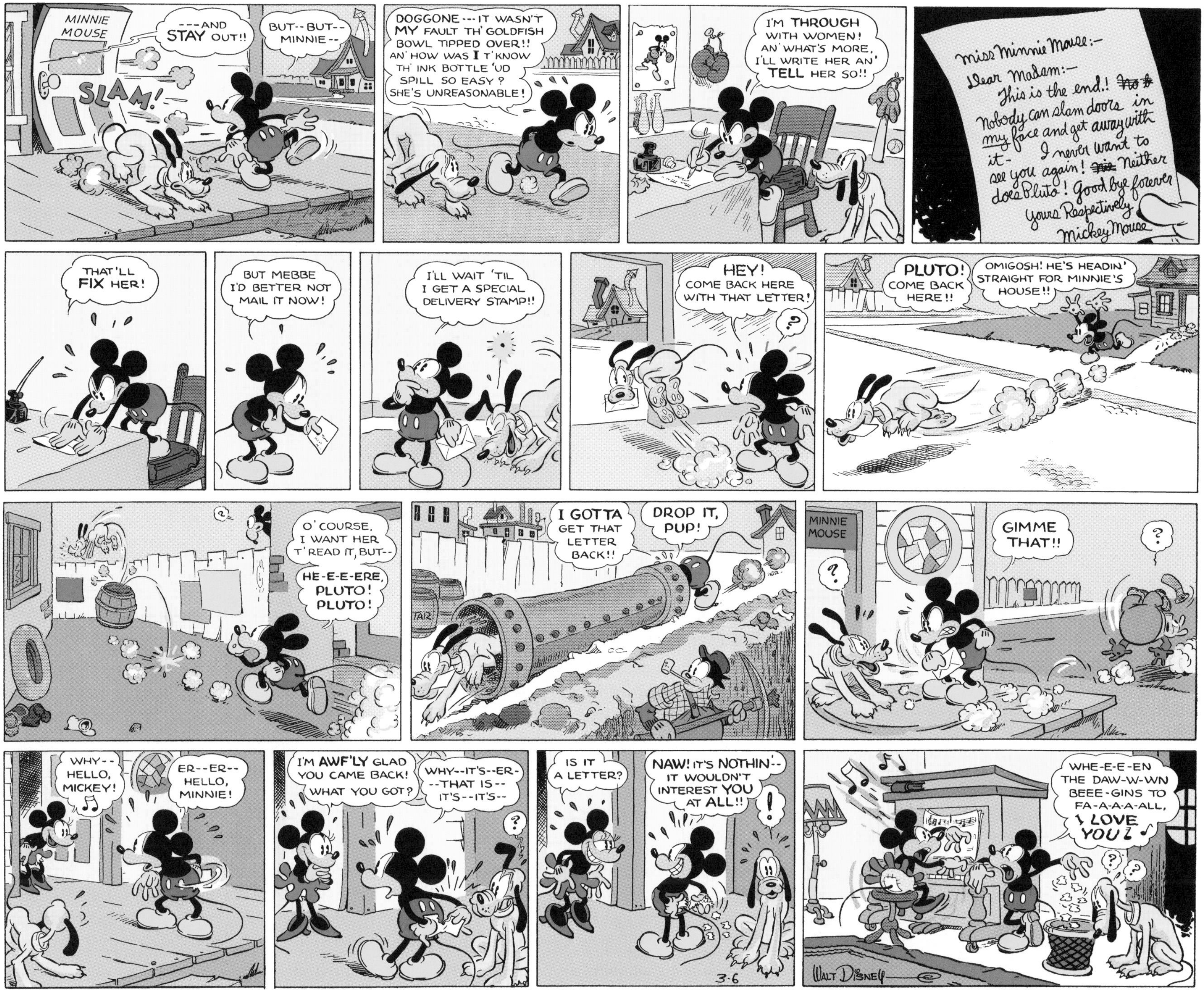
MINNIE MOUSE
---AND STAY OUT!!
SLAM!
BUT--BUT--MINNIE--
DOGGONE---IT WASN'T MY FAULT TH' GOLDFISH BOWL TIPPED OVER!! AN' HOW WAS I T'KNOW TH' INK BOTTLE 'UD SPILL SO EASY? SHE'S UNREASONABLE!
I'M THROUGH WITH WOMEN! AN' WHAT'S MORE, I'LL WRITE HER AN' TELL HER SO!!
Miss Minnie Mouse:—
Dear Madam:—
This is the end.! No
Nobody can slam doors in my face and get away with it- I never want to see you again! Neither does Pluto! Good bye forever
Yours Respectively
Mickey Mouse
THAT'LL FIX HER!
BUT MEBBE I'D BETTER NOT MAIL IT NOW!
I'LL WAIT 'TIL I GET A SPECIAL DELIVERY STAMP!!
HEY! COME BACK HERE WITH THAT LETTER!
PLUTO! COME BACK HERE!!
OMIGOSH! HE'S HEADIN' STRAIGHT FOR MINNIE'S HOUSE!!
O' COURSE, I WANT HER T' READ IT, BUT--
HE-E-E-ERE, PLUTO! PLUTO!
I GOTTA GET THAT LETTER BACK!!
DROP IT, PUP!
TAR
MINNIE MOUSE
GIMME THAT!!
WHY--HELLO, MICKEY!
ER--ER--HELLO, MINNIE!
I'M AWF'LY GLAD YOU CAME BACK! WHAT YOU GOT?
WHY--IT'S--ER--THAT IS--IT'S--IT'S--
IS IT A LETTER?
NAW! IT'S NOTHIN'--IT WOULDN'T INTEREST YOU AT ALL!!
3-6
WHE-E-E-EN THE DAW-W-WN BEEE-GINS TO FA-A-A-A-ALL, I LOVE YOU!
WALT DISNEY

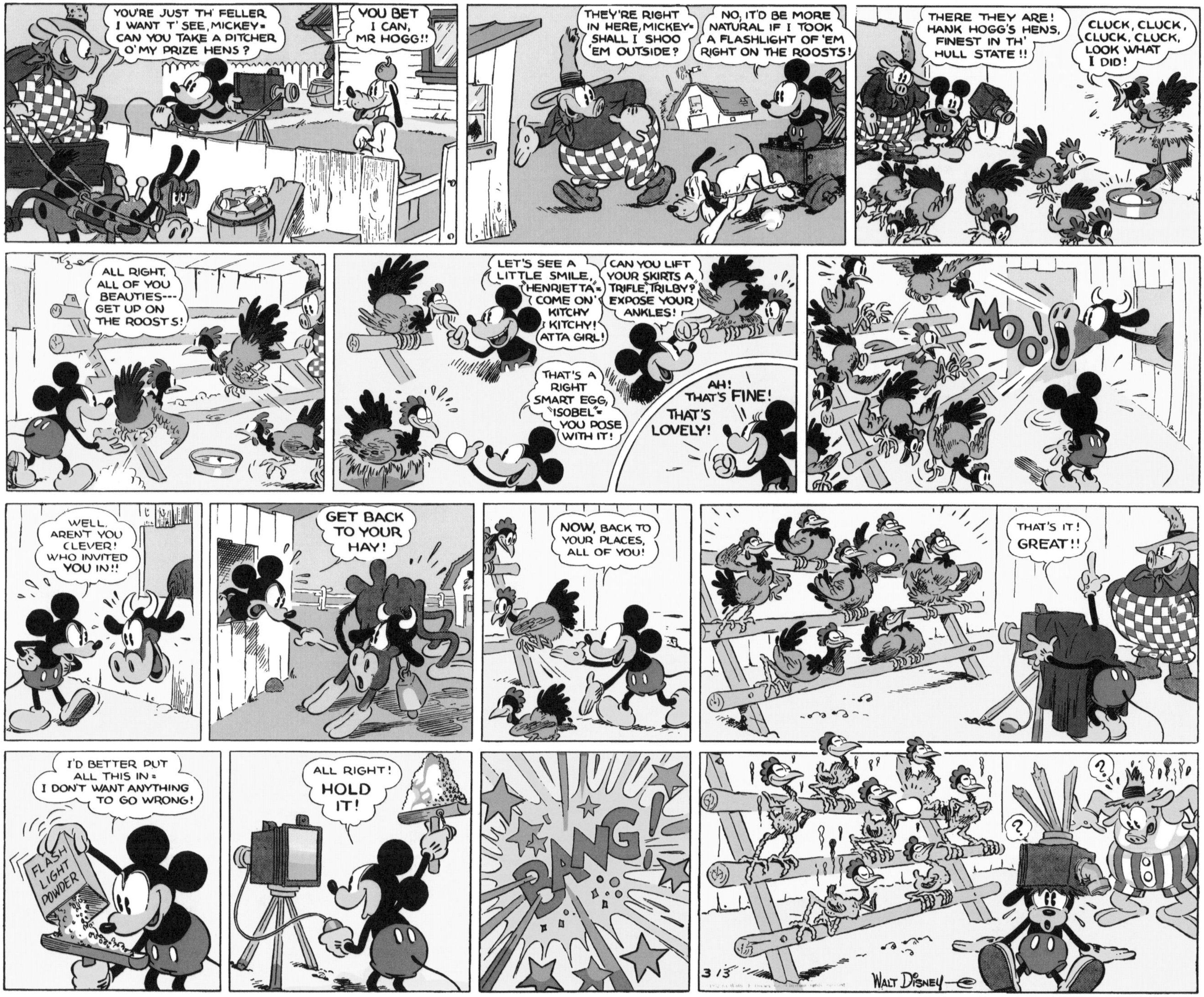

YOU'RE JUST TH' FELLER I WANT T' SEE, MICKEY= CAN YOU TAKE A PITCHER O' MY PRIZE HENS?
YOU BET I CAN, MR HOGG!!
THEY'RE RIGHT IN HERE, MICKEY= SHALL I SHOO 'EM OUTSIDE?
NO, IT'D BE MORE NATURAL IF I TOOK A FLASHLIGHT OF 'EM RIGHT ON THE ROOSTS!
THERE THEY ARE! HANK HOGG'S HENS, FINEST IN TH' HULL STATE!!
CLUCK, CLUCK, CLUCK, CLUCK, LOOK WHAT I DID!
ALL RIGHT, ALL OF YOU BEAUTIES--- GET UP ON THE ROOSTS!
LET'S SEE A LITTLE SMILE, "HENRIETTA"= COME ON' KITCHY KITCHY! ATTA GIRL!
CAN YOU LIFT YOUR SKIRTS A TRIFLE, TRILBY? EXPOSE YOUR ANKLES!
THAT'S A RIGHT SMART EGG, "ISOBEL"= YOU POSE WITH IT!
AH! THAT'S FINE!
THAT'S LOVELY!
MOO!
WELL, AREN'T YOU CLEVER! WHO INVITED YOU IN!!
GET BACK TO YOUR HAY!
NOW, BACK TO YOUR PLACES, ALL OF YOU!
THAT'S IT! GREAT!!
I'D BETTER PUT ALL THIS IN= I DON'T WANT ANYTHING TO GO WRONG!
FLASH LIGHT POWDER
ALL RIGHT! HOLD IT!
BANG!
3/13
WALT DISNEY

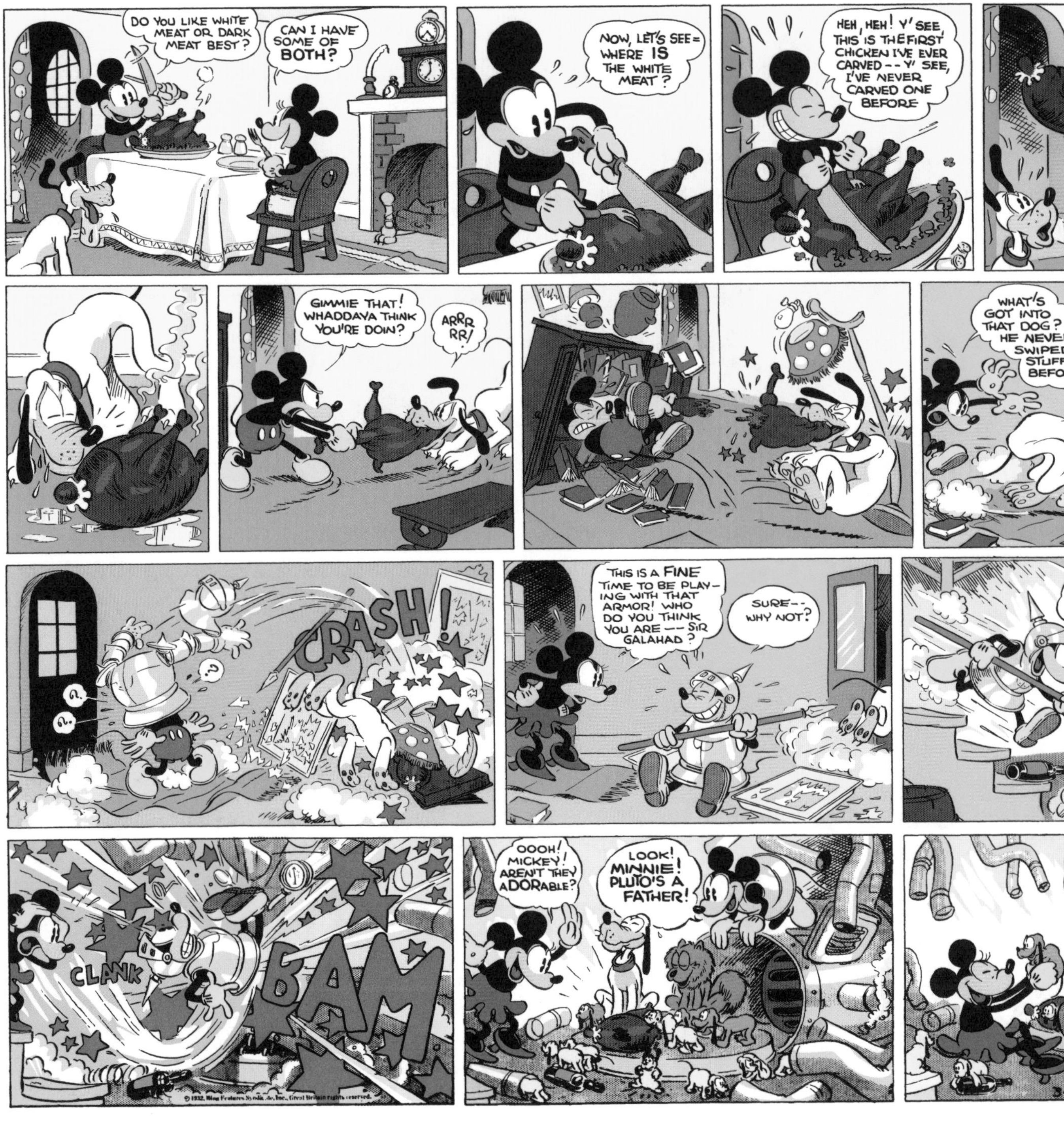
DO YOU LIKE WHITE MEAT OR DARK MEAT BEST?
CAN I HAVE SOME OF BOTH?
NOW, LET'S SEE = WHERE IS THE WHITE MEAT?
HEH, HEH! Y' SEE, THIS IS THE FIRST CHICKEN I'VE EVER CARVED - - Y' SEE, I'VE NEVER CARVED ONE BEFORE
GOOD GOSH! WHAT A SLIPPERY BIRD!
SWEEESHH
GIMMIE THAT! WHADDAYA THINK YOU'RE DOIN?
ARRR RR!
WHAT'S GOT INTO THAT DOG? HE NEVER SWIPED STUFF BEFORE!
CRASH!
THIS IS A FINE TIME TO BE PLAYING WITH THAT ARMOR! WHO DO YOU THINK YOU ARE - - SIR GALAHAD?
SURE - - WHY NOT?
I'LL CAPTURE YON TENDER MORSEL OF FOOD FOR PRINCESS MINNIE = AN' WHAT'S MORE, I'M GONNA SOCK YON PLUTO, TOO
CLANK
BAM
OOOH! MICKEY! AREN'T THEY ADORABLE?
LOOK! MINNIE! PLUTO'S A FATHER!
SO THAT'S WHY YOU WERE OUT RUSTLIN' FOOD, YOU OLD RASCAL = I DIDN'T KNOW YOU HAD A FAMILY TO SUPPORT
3-20 WALT DISNEY

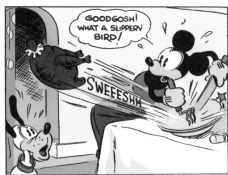

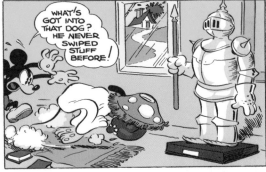

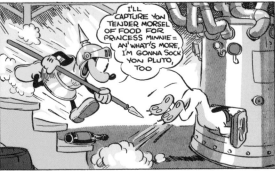

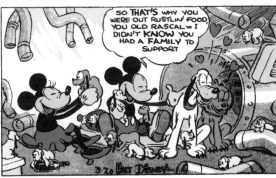

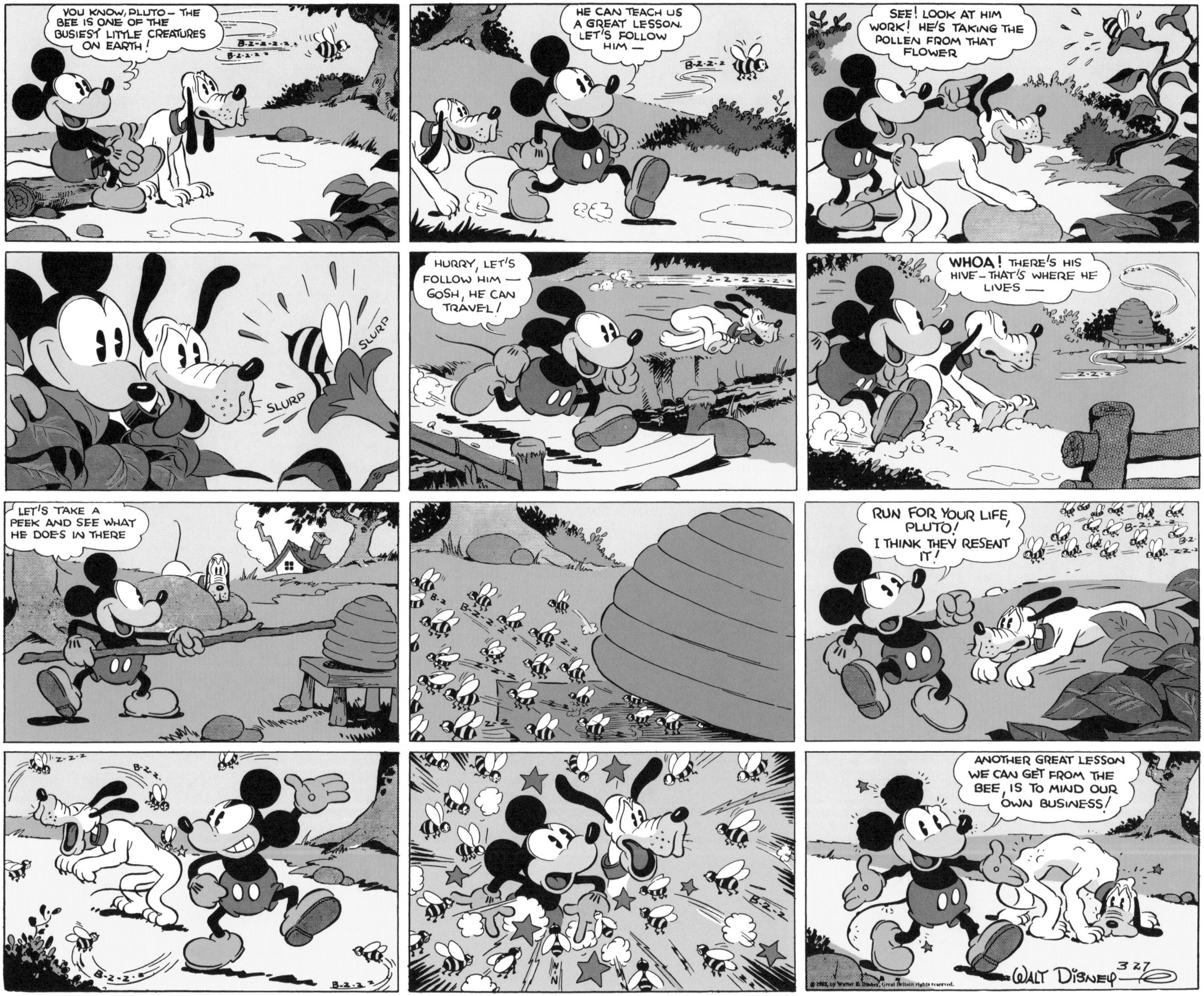
YOU KNOW, PLUTO – THE BEE IS ONE OF THE BUSIEST LITTLE CREATURES ON EARTH!
HE CAN TEACH US A GREAT LESSON. LET'S FOLLOW HIM –
SEE! LOOK AT HIM WORK! HE'S TAKING THE POLLEN FROM THAT FLOWER
SLURP
SLURP
SLURP
HURRY, LET'S FOLLOW HIM – GOSH, HE CAN TRAVEL!
WHOA! THERE'S HIS HIVE – THAT'S WHERE HE LIVES –
LET'S TAKE A PEEK AND SEE WHAT HE DOES IN THERE
RUN FOR YOUR LIFE, PLUTO! I THINK THEY RESENT IT!
ANOTHER GREAT LESSON WE CAN GET FROM THE BEE, IS TO MIND OUR OWN BUSINESS!
WALT DISNEY 3 27

30. TO BEE OR NOT TO BEE

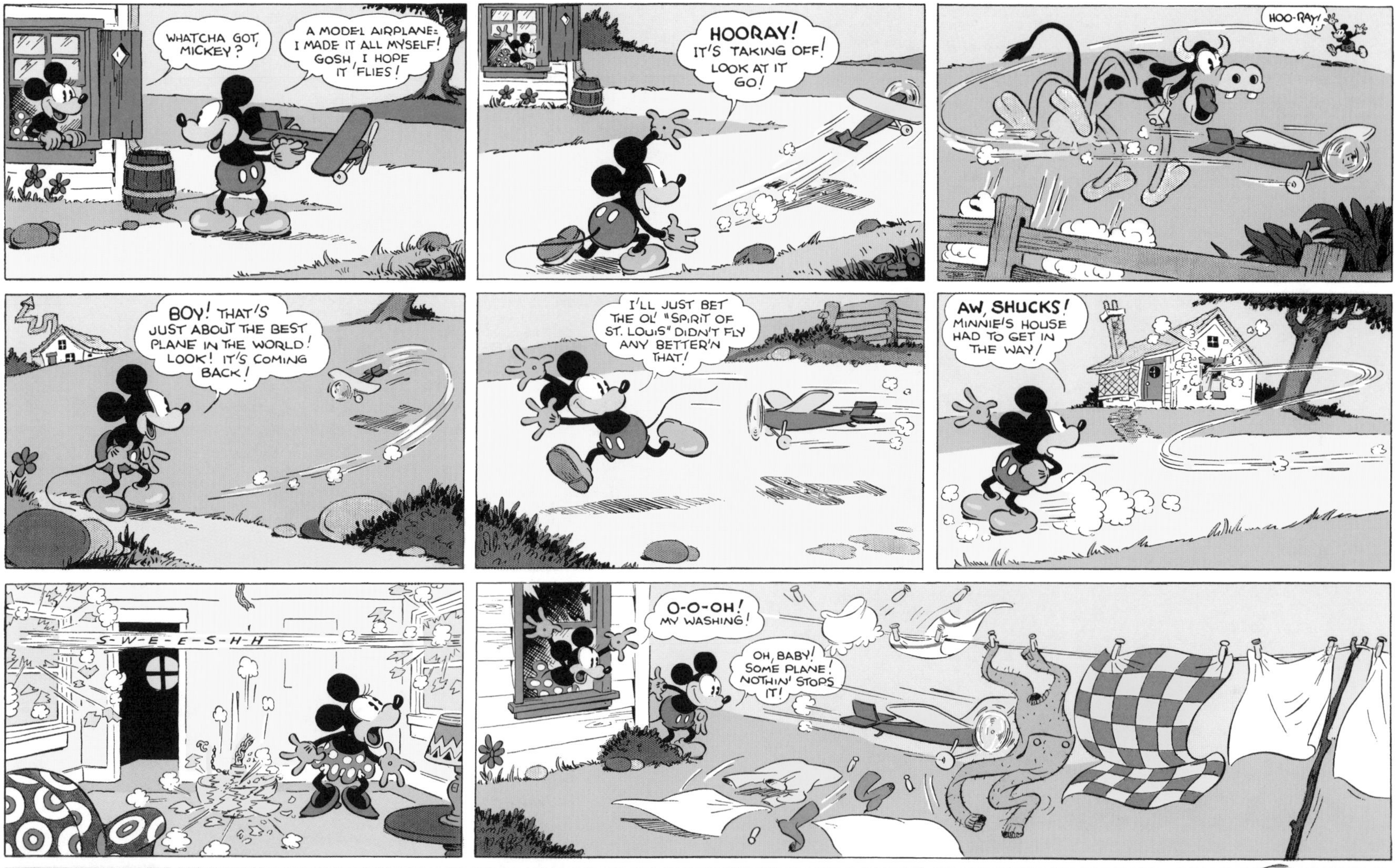
WHATCHA GOT, MICKEY?
A MODEL AIRPLANE- I MADE IT ALL MYSELF! GOSH, I HOPE IT FLIES!
HOORAY! IT'S TAKING OFF! LOOK AT IT GO!
HOO-RAY!
BOY! THAT'S JUST ABOUT THE BEST PLANE IN THE WORLD! LOOK! IT'S COMING BACK!
I'LL JUST BET THE OL' "SPIRIT OF ST. LOUIS" DIDN'T FLY ANY BETTER'N THAT!
AW, SHUCKS! MINNIE'S HOUSE HAD TO GET IN THE WAY!
S-W-E-E-S-H-H
O-O-OH! MY WASHING!
OH, BABY! SOME PLANE! NOTHIN' STOPS IT!
HEY, WHERE'D IT GO?
ANYWAY, I'M GONNA BE A GREAT FLIER SOME DAY!
WELL, YOU'D BETTER START RIGHT NOW!
4-3
WALT DISNEY

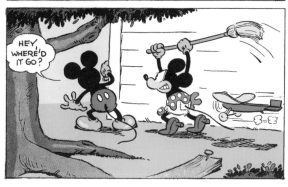

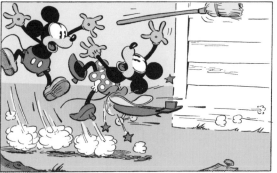

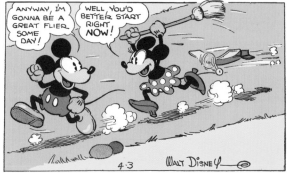

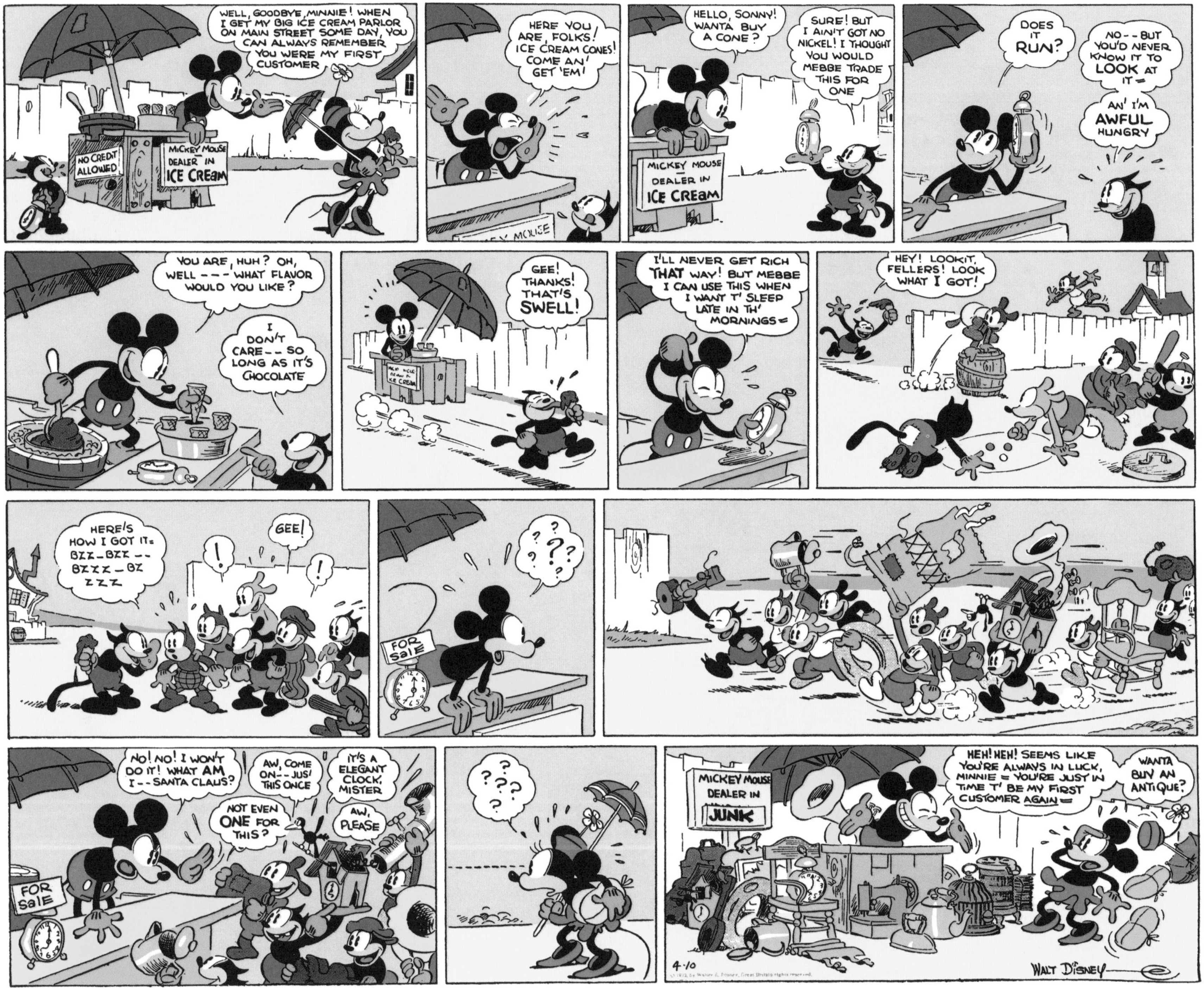
WELL, GOODBYE, MINNIE! WHEN I GET MY BIG ICE CREAM PARLOR ON MAIN STREET SOME DAY, YOU CAN ALWAYS REMEMBER YOU WERE MY FIRST CUSTOMER
NO CREDIT ALLOWED
MICKEY MOUSE DEALER IN ICE CREAM
HERE YOU ARE, FOLKS! ICE CREAM CONES! COME AN' GET 'EM!
HELLO, SONNY! WANTA BUY A CONE?
SURE! BUT I AIN'T GOT NO NICKEL! I THOUGHT YOU WOULD MEBBE TRADE THIS FOR ONE
MICKEY MOUSE DEALER IN ICE CREAM
DOES IT RUN?
NO--BUT YOU'D NEVER KNOW IT TO LOOK AT IT=
AN' I'M AWFUL HUNGRY
YOU ARE, HUH? OH, WELL --- WHAT FLAVOR WOULD YOU LIKE?
I DON'T CARE -- SO LONG AS IT'S CHOCOLATE
GEE! THANKS! THAT'S SWELL!
I'LL NEVER GET RICH THAT WAY! BUT MEBBE I CAN USE THIS WHEN I WANT T' SLEEP LATE IN TH' MORNINGS=
HEY! LOOKIT, FELLERS! LOOK WHAT I GOT!
HERE'S HOW I GOT IT= BZZ-BZZ -- BZZZ-BZ ZZZ
GEE!
!
!
FOR SALE
? ? ? ?? ? ?
NO! NO! I WON'T DO IT! WHAT AM I--SANTA CLAUS?
AW, COME ON--JUS' THIS ONCE
IT'S A ELEGANT CLOCK, MISTER
NOT EVEN ONE FOR THIS?
AW, PLEASE
FOR SALE
? ? ? ? ? ?
MICKEY MOUSE DEALER IN JUNK
HEH! HEH! SEEMS LIKE YOU'RE ALWAYS IN LUCK, MINNIE = YOU'RE JUST IN TIME T' BE MY FIRST CUSTOMER AGAIN =
WANTA BUY AN ANTIQUE?
4-10
WALT DISNEY

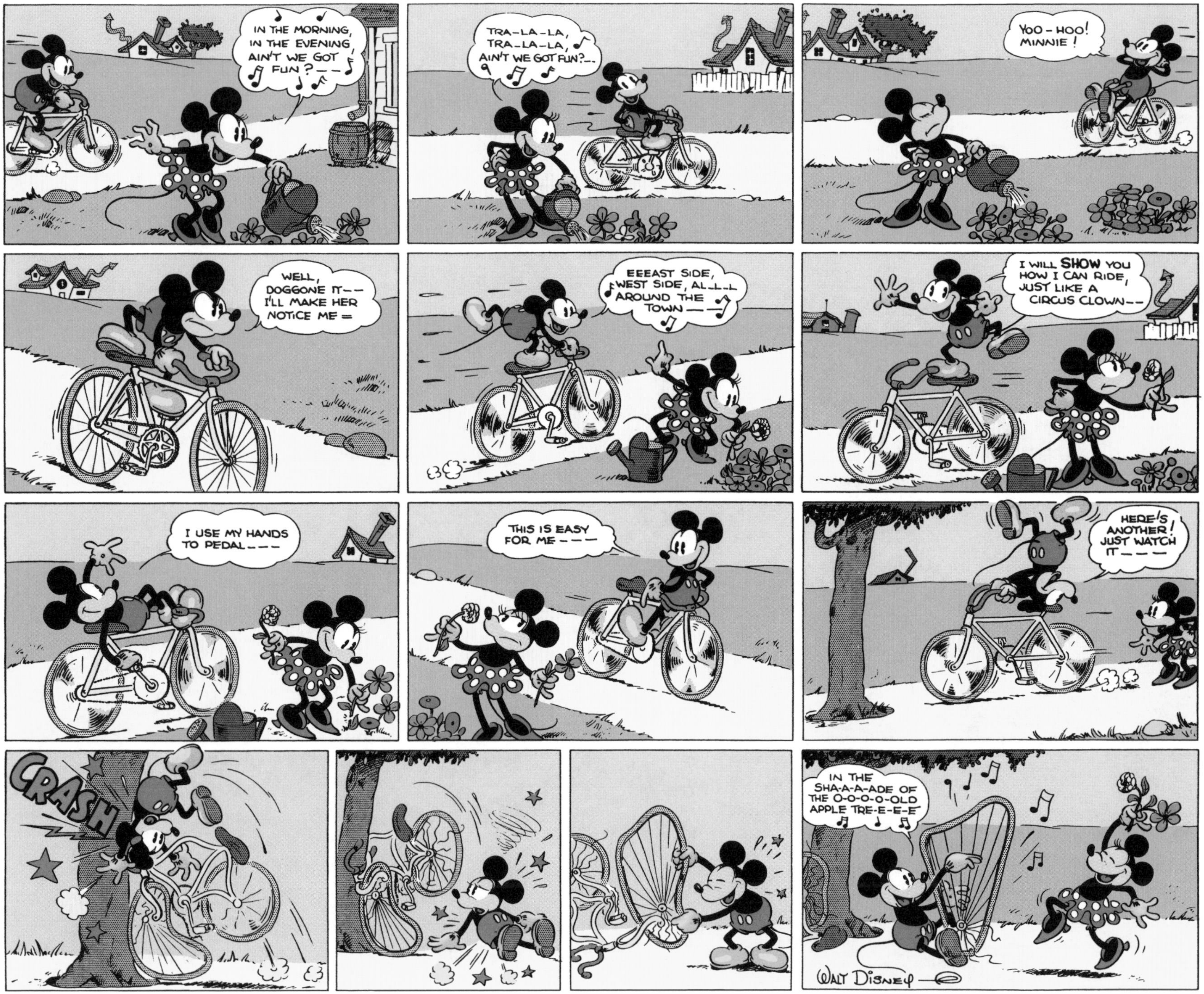
IN THE MORNING, IN THE EVENING AIN'T WE GOT FUN?---
TRA-LA-LA, TRA-LA-LA, AIN'T WE GOT FUN?--
YOO-HOO! MINNIE!
WELL, DOGGONE IT-- I'LL MAKE HER NOTICE ME=
EEEAST SIDE, WEST SIDE, AL-L-L AROUND THE TOWN---
I WILL SHOW YOU HOW I CAN RIDE, JUST LIKE A CIRCUS CLOWN--
I USE MY HANDS TO PEDAL---
THIS IS EASY FOR ME---
HERE'S ANOTHER! JUST WATCH IT---
CRASH
IN THE SHA-A-A-ADE OF THE O-O-O-O-OLD APPLE TRE-E-E-E
WALT DISNEY

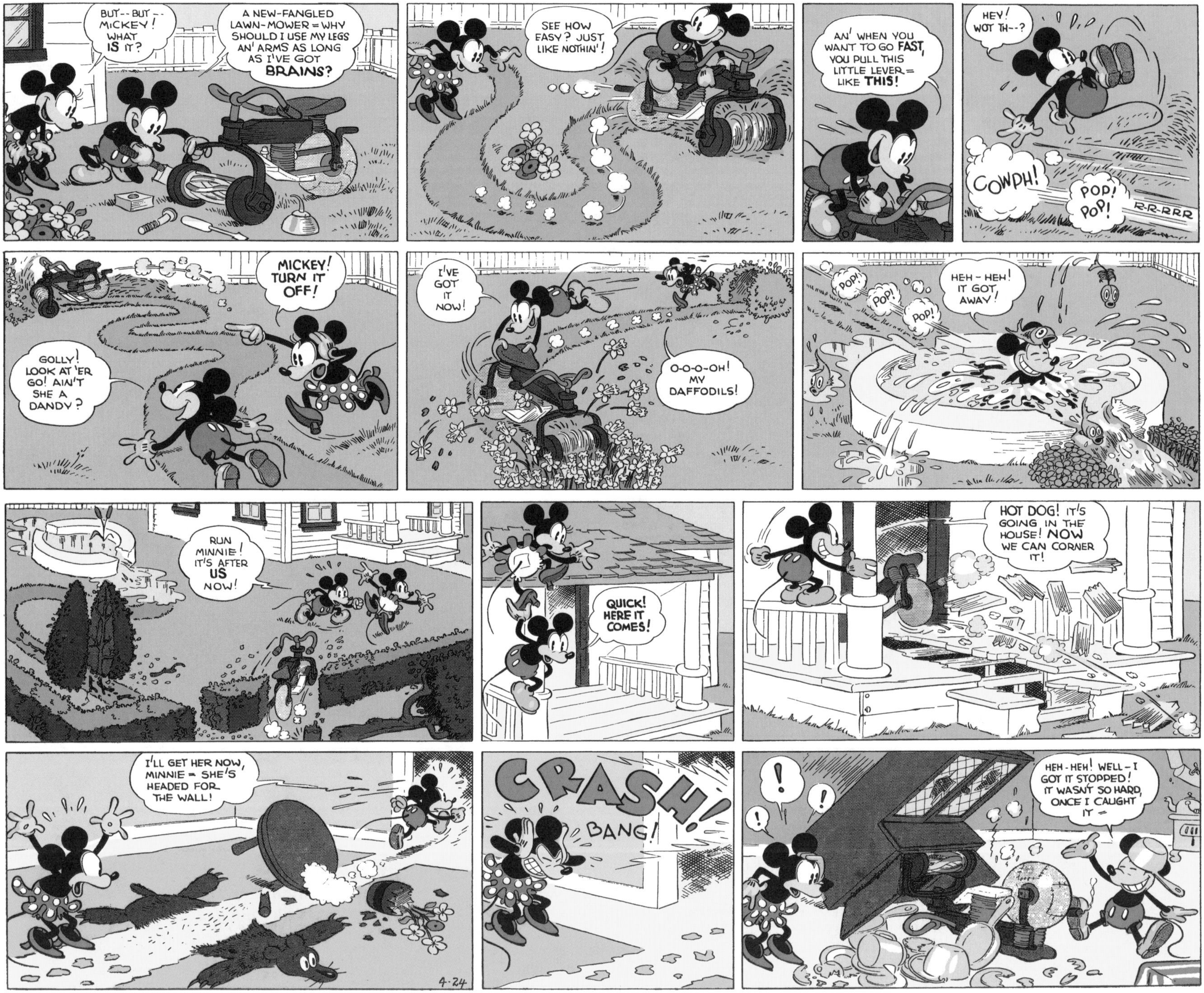
BUT-- BUT-- MICKEY! WHAT IS IT?
A NEW-FANGLED LAWN-MOWER = WHY SHOULD I USE MY LEGS AN' ARMS AS LONG AS I'VE GOT BRAINS?
SEE HOW EASY? JUST LIKE NOTHIN'!
AN' WHEN YOU WANT TO GO FAST, YOU PULL THIS LITTLE LEVER = LIKE THIS!
HEY! WOT TH--?
COWPH!
POP! POP!
R-R-RRR
MICKEY! TURN IT OFF!
GOLLY! LOOK AT 'ER GO! AIN'T SHE A DANDY?
I'VE GOT IT NOW!
O-O-O-OH! MY DAFFODILS!
POP!
POP!
POP!
HEH-HEH! IT GOT AWAY!
RUN MINNIE! IT'S AFTER US NOW!
QUICK! HERE IT COMES!
HOT DOG! IT'S GOING IN THE HOUSE! NOW WE CAN CORNER IT!
I'LL GET HER NOW, MINNIE = SHE'S HEADED FOR THE WALL!
4·24
CRASH!
BANG!
!
!
!
HEH-HEH! WELL- I GOT IT STOPPED! IT WASN'T SO HARD, ONCE I CAUGHT IT =

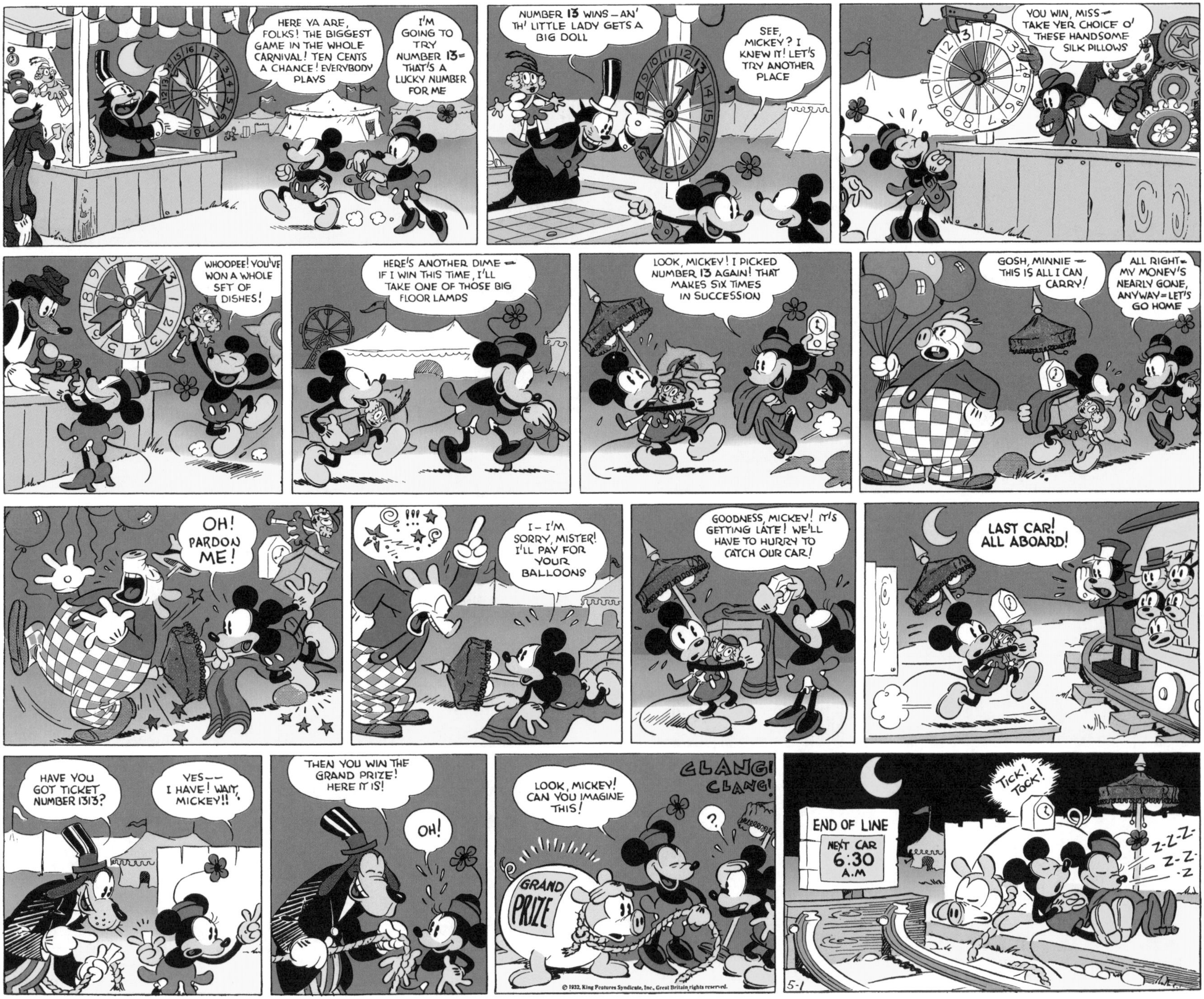
HERE YA ARE, FOLKS! THE BIGGEST GAME IN THE WHOLE CARNIVAL! TEN CENTS A CHANCE! EVERYBODY PLAYS
I'M GOING TO TRY NUMBER 13= THAT'S A LUCKY NUMBER FOR ME
NUMBER 13 WINS—AN' TH' LITTLE LADY GETS A BIG DOLL
SEE, MICKEY? I KNEW IT! LET'S TRY ANOTHER PLACE
YOU WIN, MISS— TAKE YER CHOICE O' THESE HANDSOME SILK PILLOWS
WHOOPEE! YOU'VE WON A WHOLE SET OF DISHES!
HERE'S ANOTHER DIME— IF I WIN THIS TIME, I'LL TAKE ONE OF THOSE BIG FLOOR LAMPS
LOOK, MICKEY! I PICKED NUMBER 13 AGAIN! THAT MAKES SIX TIMES IN SUCCESSION
GOSH, MINNIE— THIS IS ALL I CAN CARRY!
ALL RIGHT— MY MONEY'S NEARLY GONE, ANYWAY= LET'S GO HOME
OH! PARDON ME!
I—I'M SORRY, MISTER! I'LL PAY FOR YOUR BALLOONS
GOODNESS, MICKEY! IT'S GETTING LATE! WE'LL HAVE TO HURRY TO CATCH OUR CAR!
LAST CAR! ALL ABOARD!
HAVE YOU GOT TICKET NUMBER 1313?
YES— I HAVE! WAIT, MICKEY!!
THEN YOU WIN THE GRAND PRIZE! HERE IT IS!
OH!
CLANG! CLANG!
LOOK, MICKEY! CAN YOU IMAGINE THIS!
GRAND PRIZE
TICK! TOCK!
END OF LINE
NEXT CAR 6:30 A.M
Z-Z-Z- Z-Z- -Z
5-1

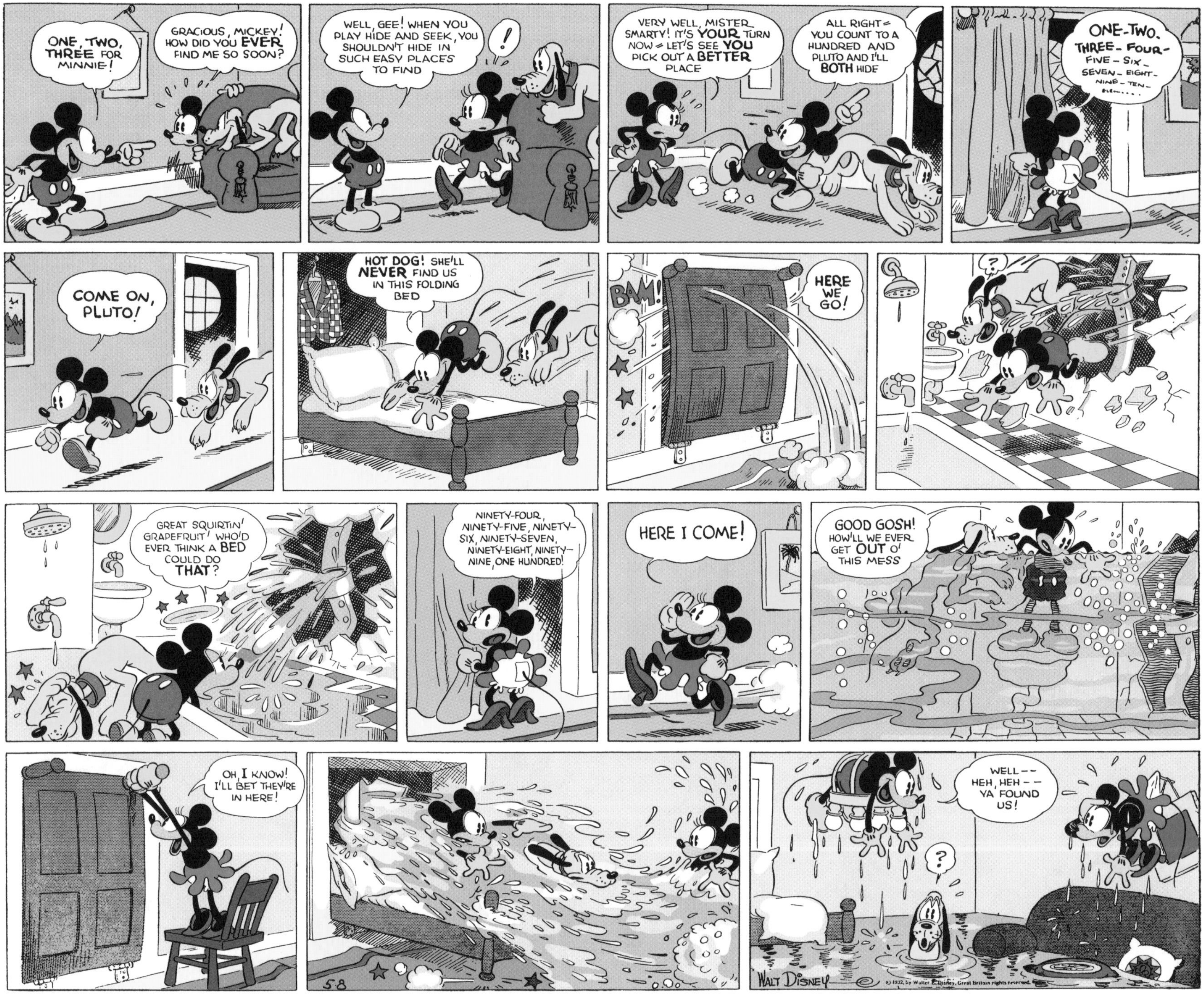

ONE, TWO, THREE FOR MINNIE!
GRACIOUS, MICKEY! HOW DID YOU EVER FIND ME SO SOON?
WELL, GEE! WHEN YOU PLAY HIDE AND SEEK, YOU SHOULDN'T HIDE IN SUCH EASY PLACES TO FIND
!
VERY WELL, MISTER SMARTY! IT'S YOUR TURN NOW = LET'S SEE YOU PICK OUT A BETTER PLACE
ALL RIGHT = YOU COUNT TO A HUNDRED AND PLUTO AND I'LL BOTH HIDE
ONE-TWO-THREE-FOUR-FIVE-SIX-SEVEN-EIGHT-NINE-TEN-
COME ON, PLUTO!
HOT DOG! SHE'LL NEVER FIND US IN THIS FOLDING BED
BAM!
HERE WE GO!
?
GREAT SQUIRTIN' GRAPEFRUIT! WHO'D EVER THINK A BED COULD DO THAT?
NINETY-FOUR, NINETY-FIVE, NINETY-SIX, NINETY-SEVEN, NINETY-EIGHT, NINETY-NINE, ONE HUNDRED!
HERE I COME!
GOOD GOSH! HOW'LL WE EVER GET OUT O' THIS MESS
OH, I KNOW! I'LL BET THEY'RE IN HERE!
5-8
WELL-- HEH, HEH -- YA' FOUND US!
?
WALT DISNEY
© 1932, by Walter E. Disney, Great Britain rights reserved.

36. HIDE AND FOUND

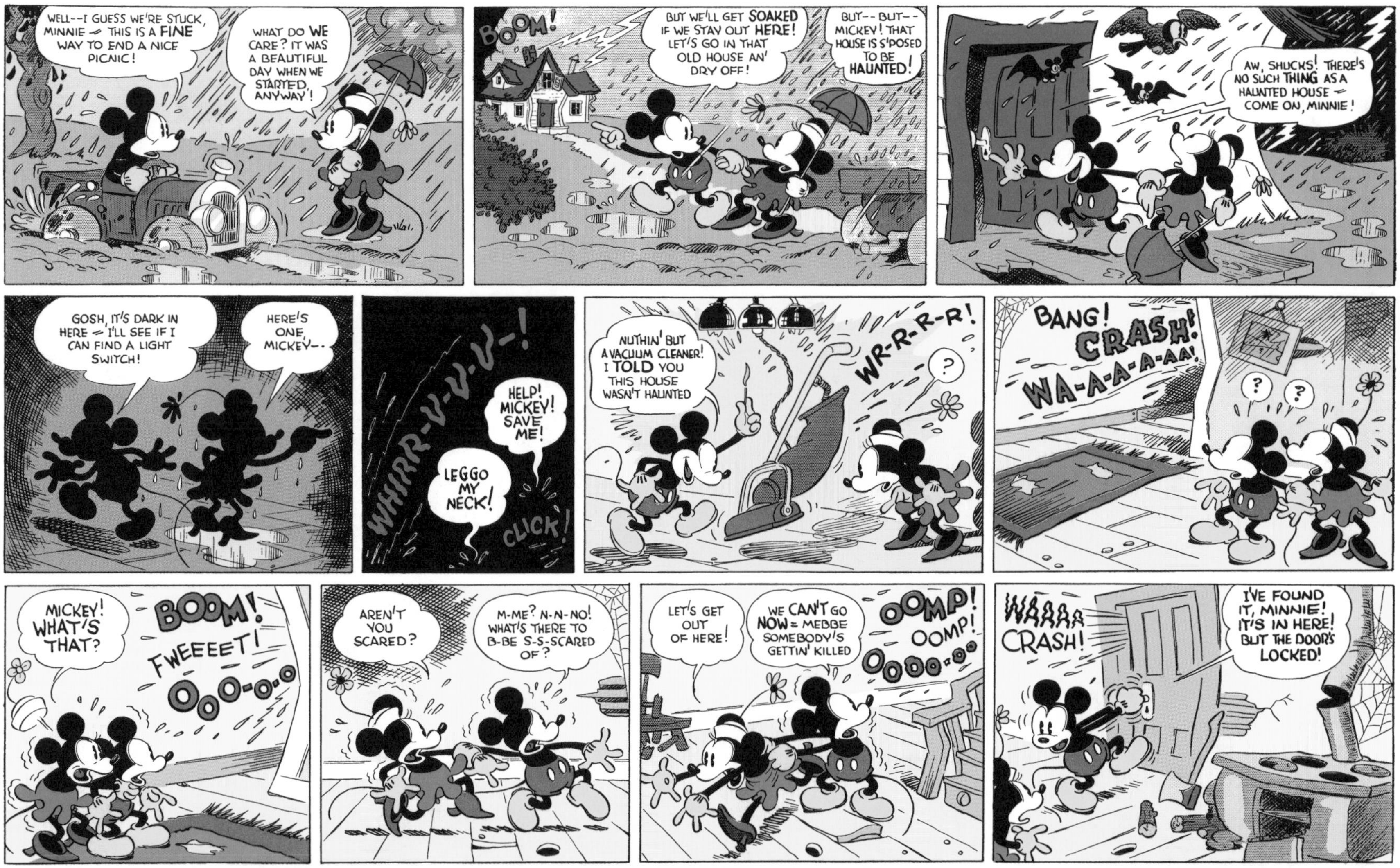
WELL--I GUESS WE'RE STUCK, MINNIE — THIS IS A FINE WAY TO END A NICE PICNIC!
WHAT DO WE CARE? IT WAS A BEAUTIFUL DAY WHEN WE STARTED, ANYWAY!
BOOM!
BUT WE'LL GET SOAKED IF WE STAY OUT HERE! LET'S GO IN THAT OLD HOUSE AN' DRY OFF!
BUT-- BUT-- MICKEY! THAT HOUSE IS S'POSED TO BE HAUNTED!
AW, SHUCKS! THERE'S NO SUCH THING AS A HAUNTED HOUSE — COME ON, MINNIE!
GOSH, IT'S DARK IN HERE — I'LL SEE IF I CAN FIND A LIGHT SWITCH!
HERE'S ONE, MICKEY--
WHIRR-V-V-V-V-!
HELP! MICKEY! SAVE ME!
LEGGO MY NECK!
CLICK!
NUTHIN' BUT A VACUUM CLEANER! I TOLD YOU THIS HOUSE WASN'T HAUNTED
WR-R-R-R-R!
?
BANG!
CRASH!
WA-A-A-A-AA!
? ?
MICKEY! WHAT'S THAT?
BOOM!
FWEEEET!
OOO-o-o
AREN'T YOU SCARED?
M-ME? N-N-NO! WHAT'S THERE TO B-BE S-S-SCARED OF?
LET'S GET OUT OF HERE!
WE CAN'T GO NOW = MEBBE SOMEBODY'S GETTIN' KILLED
OOMP!
OOMP!
OOOO-oo
WAAAA
CRASH!
I'VE FOUND IT, MINNIE! IT'S IN HERE! BUT THE DOOR'S LOCKED!
G-G-GOSH, MINNIE = I CAN'T STAND IT ANY LONGER = I'VE GOTTA SEE WHAT'S IN THERE
BAM
HORACE! WHAT TH' HECK-?
YEAH! I HAD T' COME OUT HERE = TH' NEIGHBORS WON'T LET ME PRACTISE AROUND MY OWN HOUSE
WALT DISNEY
OHHH-HO-HO-HO-HO-HO! AN'--WE THOUGHT--HO-HO-HO--IT WAS — — — GHO-HO-HO-HO-HOSTS!
WAAAA!
BOOM!
CRASH!
5-15

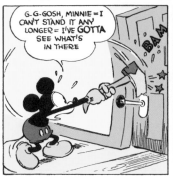

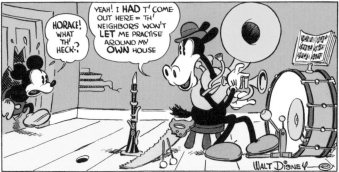

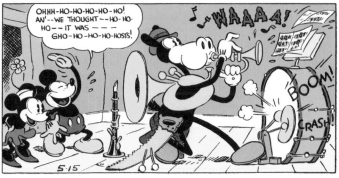

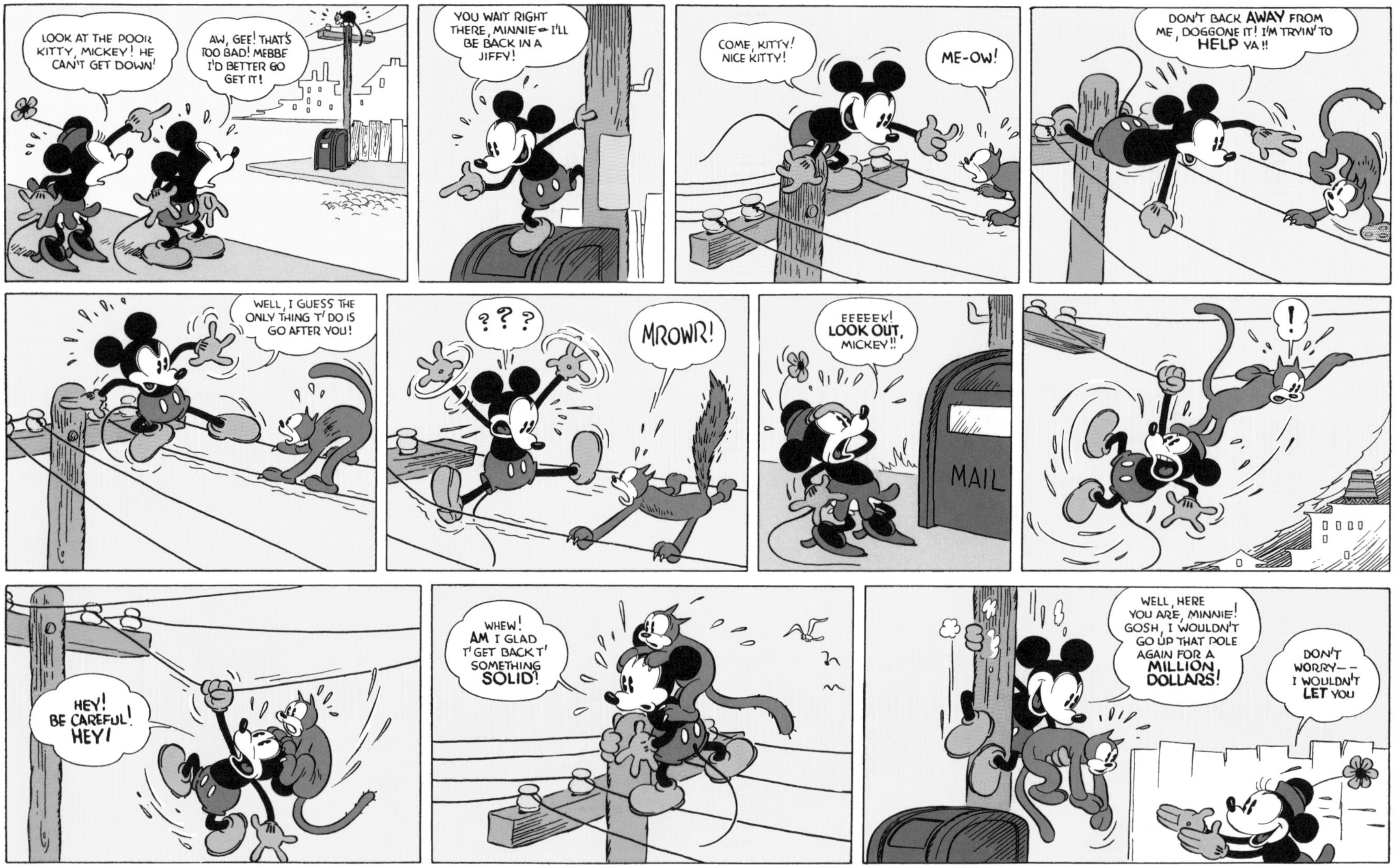
LOOK AT THE POOR KITTY, MICKEY! HE CAN'T GET DOWN!
AW, GEE! THAT'S TOO BAD! MEBBE I'D BETTER GO GET IT!
YOU WAIT RIGHT THERE, MINNIE—I'LL BE BACK IN A JIFFY!
COME, KITTY! NICE KITTY!
ME-OW!
DON'T BACK AWAY FROM ME, DOGGONE IT! I'M TRYIN' TO HELP YA!!
WELL, I GUESS THE ONLY THING T' DO IS GO AFTER YOU!
???
MROWR!
EEEEEK! LOOK OUT, MICKEY!!
MAIL
!
HEY! BE CAREFUL! HEY!
WHEW! AM I GLAD T' GET BACK T' SOMETHING SOLID!
WELL, HERE YOU ARE, MINNIE! GOSH, I WOULDN'T GO UP THAT POLE AGAIN FOR A MILLION DOLLARS!
DON'T WORRY-- I WOULDN'T LET YOU
?
HEY! WHAT TH' HECK?
MRRAWW-SISSS! SPT-SPT-SP-
PLUTO! GET AWAY! KEEP OUT O' HERE, PLUTO!
ARF! ARF!
WALT DISNEY 5·22
MEOWRR!
OW!
WURFF!

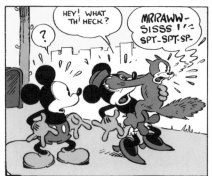

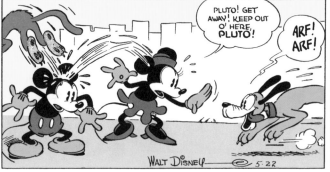

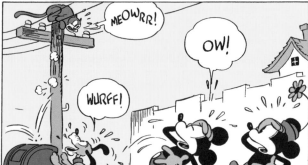

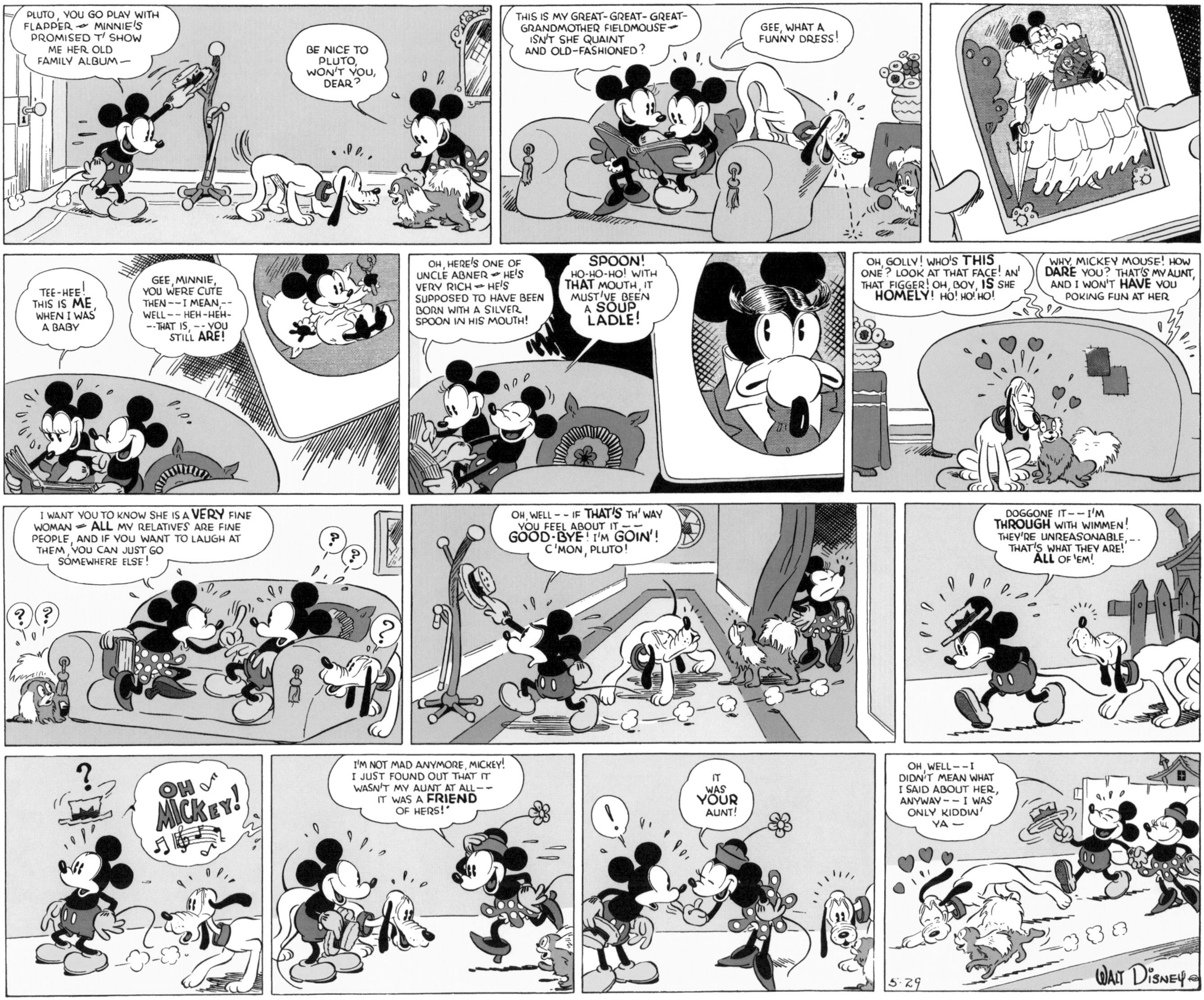
PLUTO, YOU GO PLAY WITH FLAPPER — MINNIE'S PROMISED T' SHOW ME HER OLD FAMILY ALBUM —
BE NICE TO PLUTO, WON'T YOU, DEAR?
THIS IS MY GREAT-GREAT-GREAT-GRANDMOTHER FIELDMOUSE — ISN'T SHE QUAINT AND OLD-FASHIONED?
GEE, WHAT A FUNNY DRESS!
TEE-HEE! THIS IS ME, WHEN I WAS A BABY
GEE, MINNIE, YOU WERE CUTE THEN -- I MEAN, -- WELL -- HEH-HEH- -- THAT IS, -- YOU STILL ARE!
OH, HERE'S ONE OF UNCLE ABNER — HE'S VERY RICH — HE'S SUPPOSED TO HAVE BEEN BORN WITH A SILVER SPOON IN HIS MOUTH!
SPOON! HO-HO-HO! WITH THAT MOUTH, IT MUST'VE BEEN A SOUP LADLE!
OH, GOLLY! WHO'S THIS ONE? LOOK AT THAT FACE! AN' THAT FIGGER! OH, BOY, IS SHE HOMELY! HO! HO! HO!
WHY, MICKEY MOUSE! HOW DARE YOU? THAT'S MY AUNT, AND I WON'T HAVE YOU POKING FUN AT HER
I WANT YOU TO KNOW SHE IS A VERY FINE WOMAN — ALL MY RELATIVES ARE FINE PEOPLE, AND IF YOU WANT TO LAUGH AT THEM, YOU CAN JUST GO SOMEWHERE ELSE!
OH, WELL -- IF THAT'S TH' WAY YOU FEEL ABOUT IT -- GOOD-BYE! I'M GOIN'! C'MON, PLUTO!
DOGGONE IT -- I'M THROUGH WITH WIMMEN! THEY'RE UNREASONABLE, -- THAT'S WHAT THEY ARE! ALL OF 'EM!
OH MICKEY!
I'M NOT MAD ANYMORE, MICKEY! I JUST FOUND OUT THAT IT WASN'T MY AUNT AT ALL -- IT WAS A FRIEND OF HERS!
IT WAS YOUR AUNT!
OH, WELL -- I DIDN'T MEAN WHAT I SAID ABOUT HER, ANYWAY -- I WAS ONLY KIDDIN' YA —
5-29
WALT DISNEY

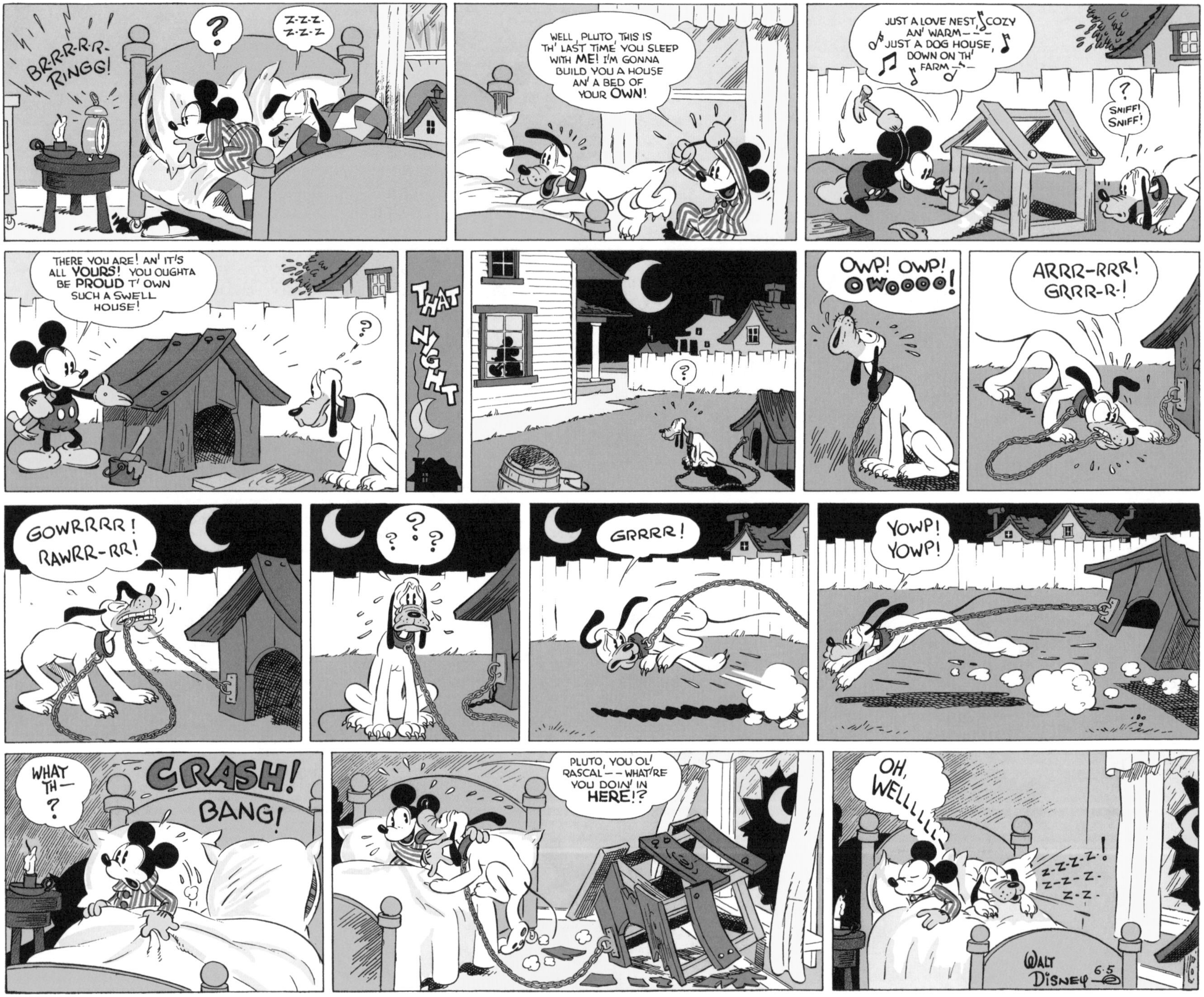
BR-R-R-R-R-RINGG!
?
Z-Z-Z-
Z-Z-Z
WELL, PLUTO, THIS IS TH' LAST TIME YOU SLEEP WITH ME! I'M GONNA BUILD YOU A HOUSE AN' A BED OF YOUR OWN!
JUST A LOVE NEST, COZY AN' WARM— — JUST A DOG HOUSE, DOWN ON TH' FARM—
?
SNIFF! SNIFF!
THERE YOU ARE! AN' IT'S ALL YOURS! YOU OUGHTA BE PROUD T' OWN SUCH A SWELL HOUSE!
?
THAT NIGHT
?
OWP! OWP! OWOOOO!
ARRR-RRR! GRRR-R-!
GOWRRRR! RAWRR-RR!
? ? ?
GRRRR!
YOWP! YOWP!
WHAT TH— ?
CRASH!
BANG!
PLUTO, YOU OL' RASCAL— — WHAT'RE YOU DOIN' IN HERE!?
OH, WELLLLLL
Z-Z-Z-Z-Z-! Z-Z-Z- Z-Z-
WALT DISNEY 6-5

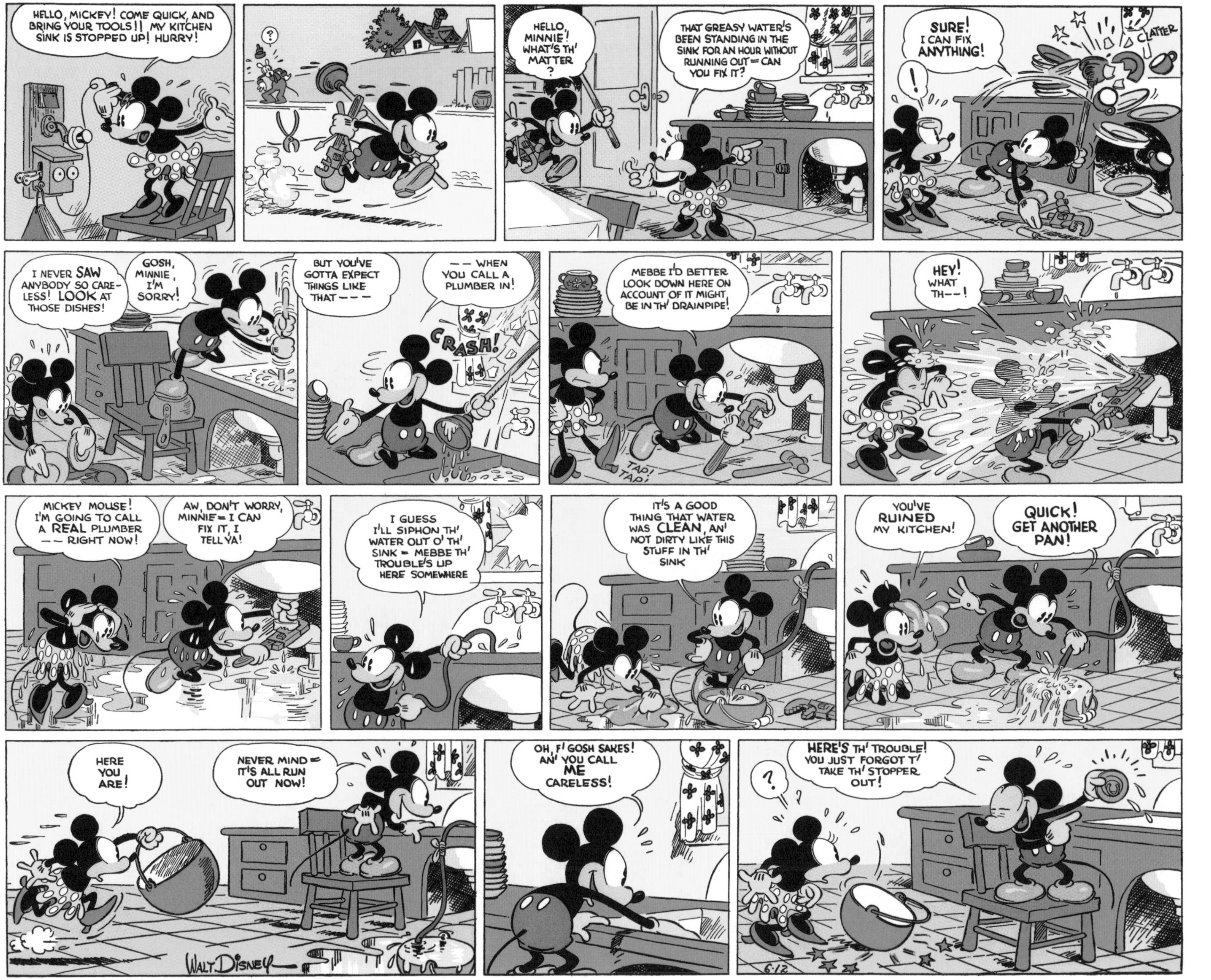
HELLO, MICKEY! COME QUICK, AND BRING YOUR TOOLS!! MY KITCHEN SINK IS STOPPED UP! HURRY!
?
HELLO, MINNIE! WHAT'S TH' MATTER ?
THAT GREASY WATER'S BEEN STANDING IN THE SINK FOR AN HOUR WITHOUT RUNNING OUT= CAN YOU FIX IT?
SURE! I CAN FIX ANYTHING!
!
CLATTER
I NEVER SAW ANYBODY SO CARE-LESS! LOOK AT THOSE DISHES!
GOSH, MINNIE, I'M SORRY!
BUT YOU'VE GOTTA EXPECT THINGS LIKE THAT---
-- WHEN YOU CALL A PLUMBER IN!
CRASH!
MEBBE I'D BETTER LOOK DOWN HERE ON ACCOUNT OF IT MIGHT BE IN TH' DRAINPIPE!
TAP! TAP!
HEY! WHAT TH--!
MICKEY MOUSE! I'M GOING TO CALL A REAL PLUMBER -- RIGHT NOW!
AW, DON'T WORRY, MINNIE= I CAN FIX IT, I TELL YA!
I GUESS I'LL SIPHON TH' WATER OUT O' TH' SINK = MEBBE TH' TROUBLE'S UP HERE SOMEWHERE
IT'S A GOOD THING THAT WATER WAS CLEAN, AN' NOT DIRTY LIKE THIS STUFF IN TH' SINK
YOU'VE RUINED MY KITCHEN!
QUICK! GET ANOTHER PAN!
HERE YOU ARE!
NEVER MIND= IT'S ALL RUN OUT NOW!
WALT DISNEY
OH, F' GOSH SAKES! AN' YOU CALL ME CARELESS!
HERE'S TH' TROUBLE! YOU JUST FORGOT T' TAKE TH' STOPPER OUT!
?
6-12

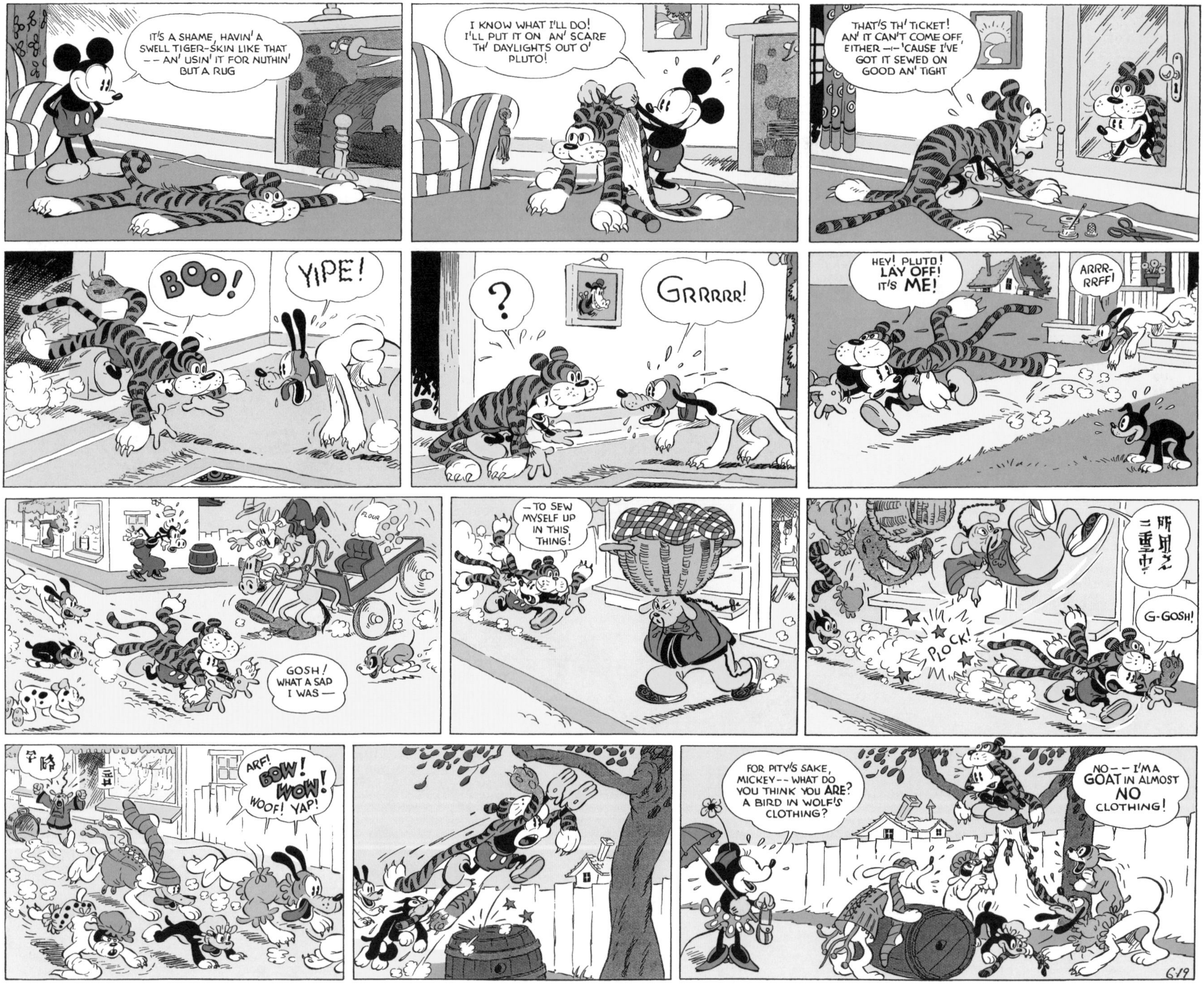
IT'S A SHAME, HAVIN' A SWELL TIGER-SKIN LIKE THAT -- AN' USIN' IT FOR NUTHIN' BUT A RUG
I KNOW WHAT I'LL DO! I'LL PUT IT ON AN' SCARE TH' DAYLIGHTS OUT O' PLUTO!
THAT'S TH' TICKET! AN' IT CAN'T COME OFF, EITHER —I— 'CAUSE I'VE GOT IT SEWED ON GOOD AN' TIGHT
BOO!
YIPE!
?
GRRRRRR!
HEY! PLUTO! LAY OFF! IT'S ME!
ARRR-RRFF!
FLOUR
GOSH! WHAT A SAD I WAS —
— TO SEW MYSELF UP IN THIS THING!
PLOCK!
G-GOSH!
ARF! BOW! WOW! WOOF! YAP!
FOR PITY'S SAKE, MICKEY-- WHAT DO YOU THINK YOU ARE? A BIRD IN WOLF'S CLOTHING?
NO-- I'M A GOAT IN ALMOST NO CLOTHING!
6-19

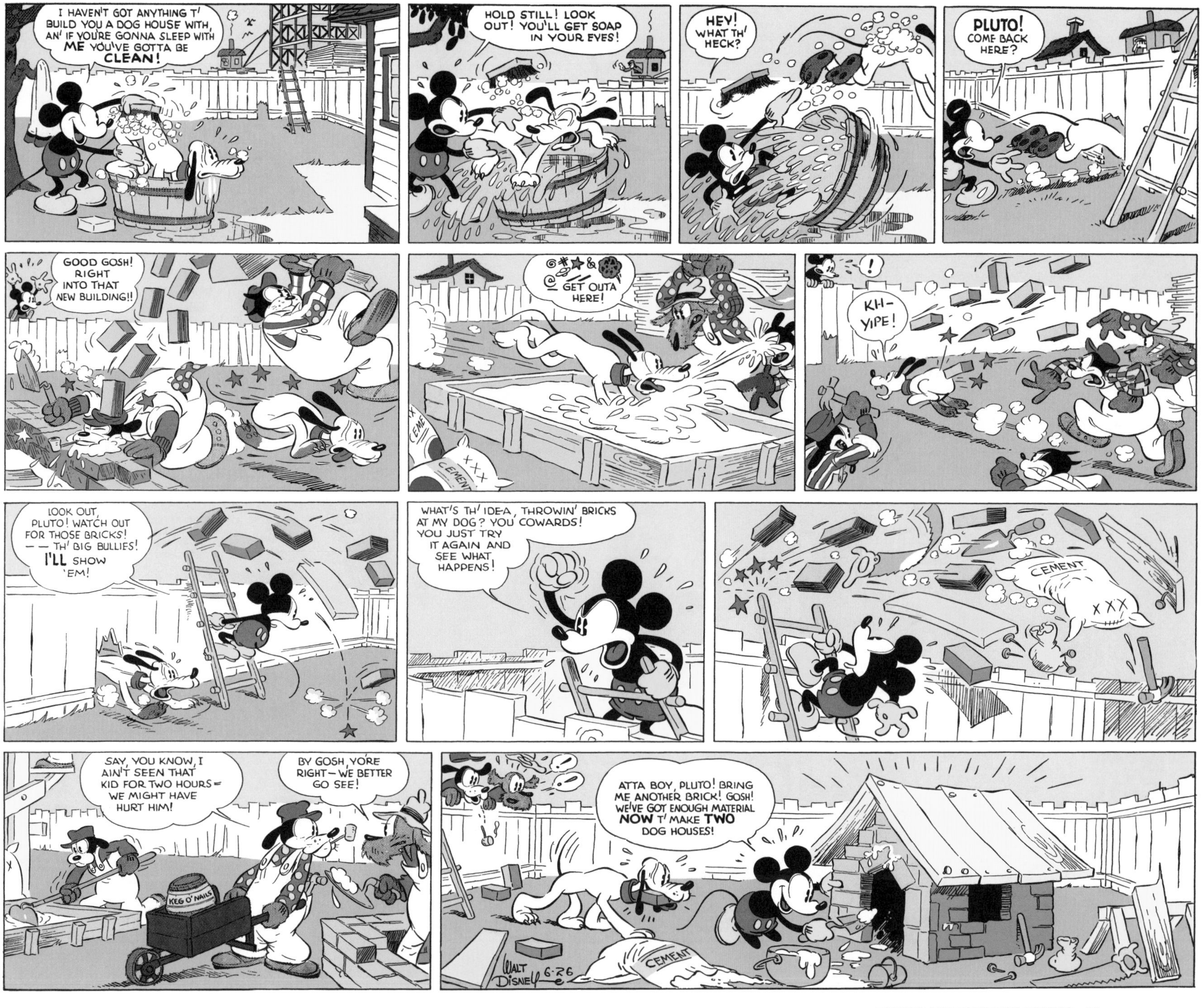
I HAVEN'T GOT ANYTHING T' BUILD YOU A DOG HOUSE WITH, AN' IF YOU'RE GONNA SLEEP WITH ME YOU'VE GOTTA BE CLEAN!
HOLD STILL! LOOK OUT! YOU'LL GET SOAP IN YOUR EYES!
HEY! WHAT TH' HECK?
PLUTO! COME BACK HERE?
GOOD GOSH! RIGHT INTO THAT NEW BUILDING!!
GET OUTA HERE!
CEMENT
KH-YIPE!
LOOK OUT, PLUTO! WATCH OUT FOR THOSE BRICKS! — — TH' BIG BULLIES! I'LL SHOW 'EM!
WHAT'S TH' IDE-A, THROWIN' BRICKS AT MY DOG? YOU COWARDS! YOU JUST TRY IT AGAIN AND SEE WHAT HAPPENS!
CEMENT
SAY, YOU KNOW, I AIN'T SEEN THAT KID FOR TWO HOURS = WE MIGHT HAVE HURT HIM!
BY GOSH, YO'RE RIGHT — WE BETTER GO SEE!
KEG O' NAILS
ATTA BOY, PLUTO! BRING ME ANOTHER BRICK! GOSH! WE'VE GOT ENOUGH MATERIAL NOW T' MAKE TWO DOG HOUSES!
CEMENT
WALT DISNEY 6-26

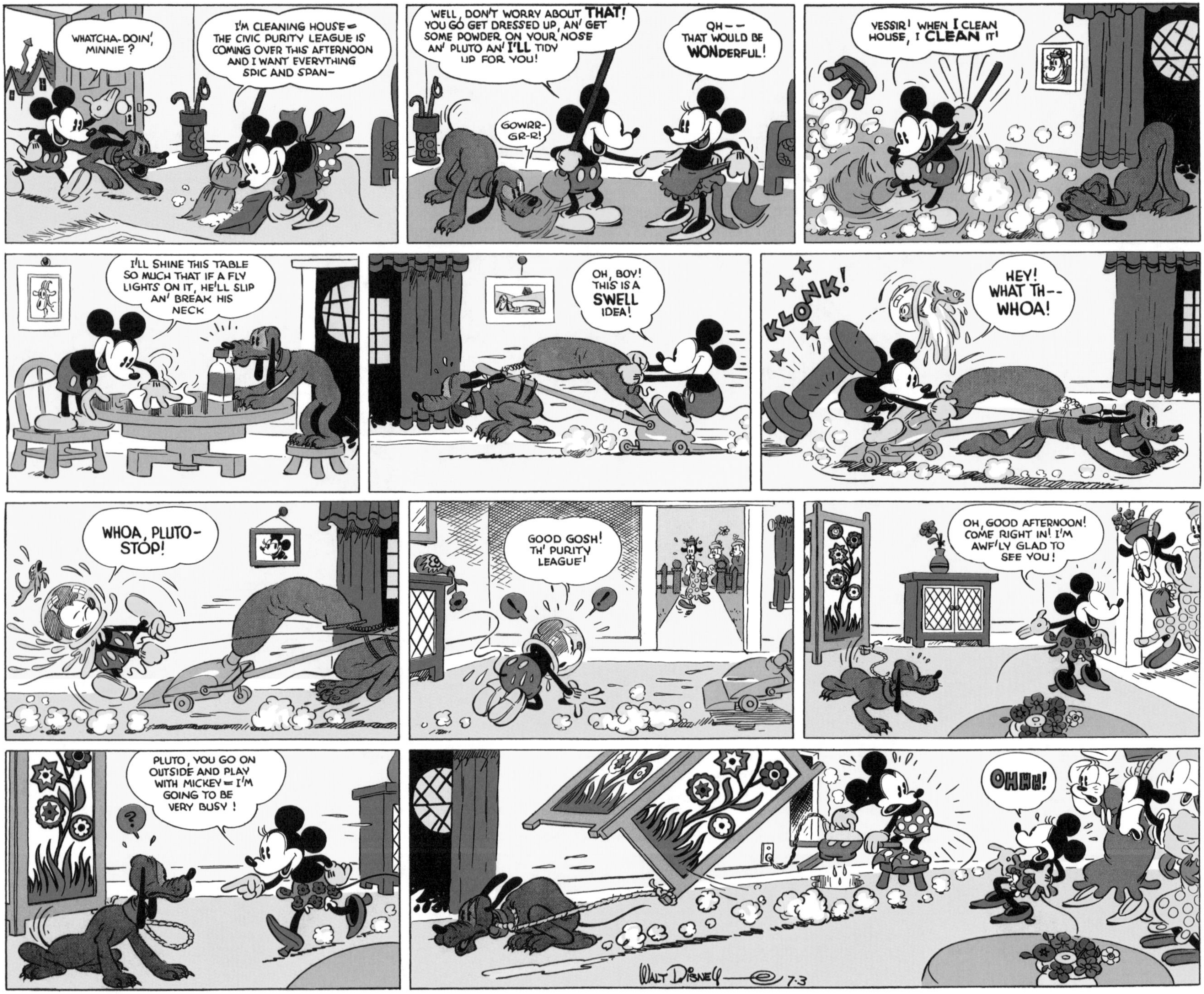
WHATCHA-DOIN', MINNIE ?
I'M CLEANING HOUSE = THE CIVIC PURITY LEAGUE IS COMING OVER THIS AFTERNOON AND I WANT EVERYTHING SPIC AND SPAN—
WELL, DON'T WORRY ABOUT THAT! YOU GO GET DRESSED UP, AN' GET SOME POWDER ON YOUR NOSE AN' PLUTO AN' I'LL TIDY UP FOR YOU!
GOWRR-GR-R!
OH— — THAT WOULD BE WONDERFUL!
YESSIR! WHEN I CLEAN HOUSE, I CLEAN IT!
I'LL SHINE THIS TABLE SO MUCH THAT IF A FLY LIGHTS ON IT, HE'LL SLIP AN' BREAK HIS NECK
OH, BOY! THIS IS A SWELL IDEA!
KLONK!
HEY! WHAT TH-- WHOA!
WHOA, PLUTO-STOP!
GOOD GOSH! TH' PURITY LEAGUE!
OH, GOOD AFTERNOON! COME RIGHT IN! I'M AWF'LY GLAD TO SEE YOU!
PLUTO, YOU GO ON OUTSIDE AND PLAY WITH MICKEY = I'M GOING TO BE VERY BUSY !
OHHH!
WALT DISNEY
7-3

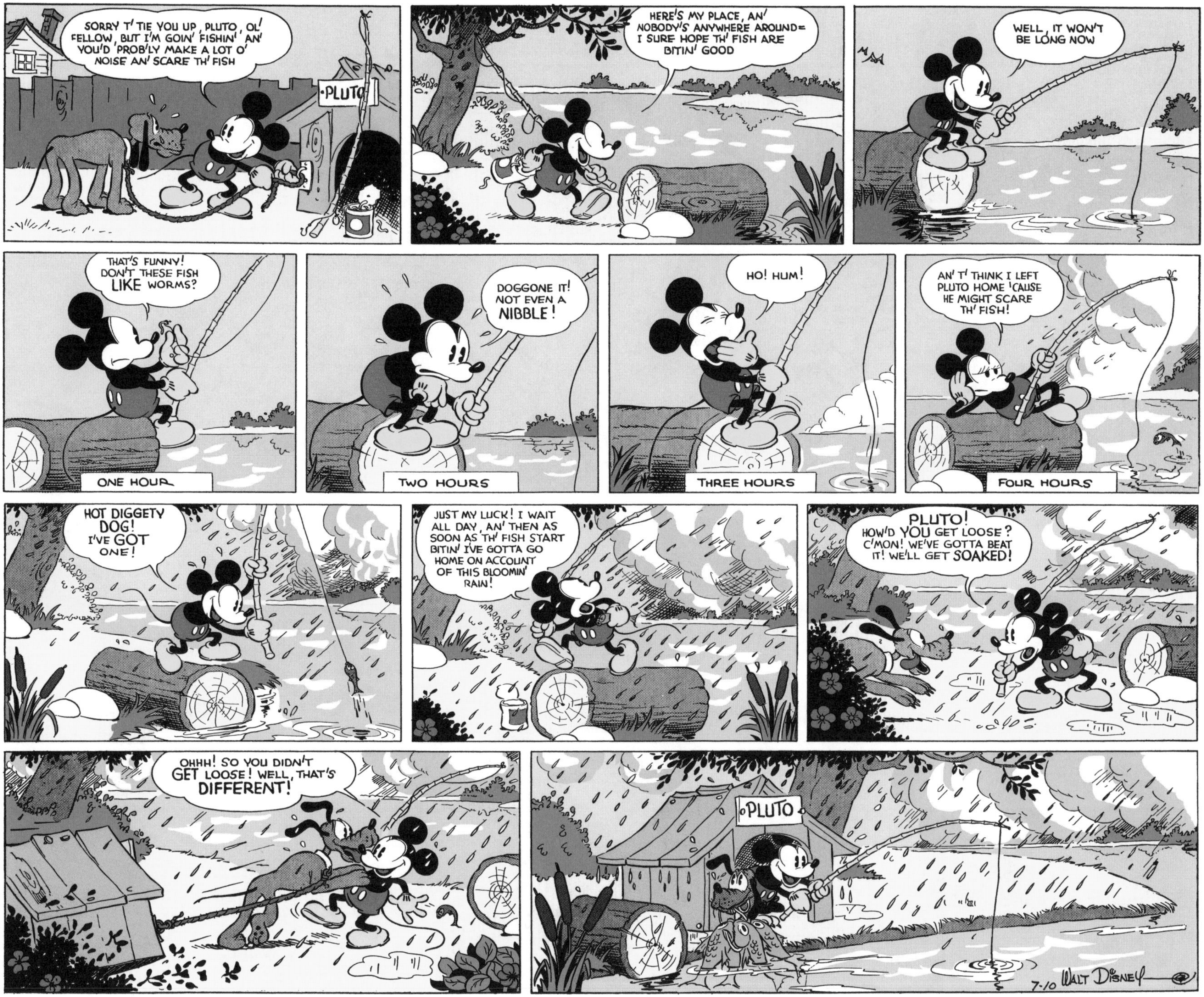
SORRY T' TIE YOU UP, PLUTO, OL' FELLOW, BUT I'M GOIN' FISHIN' AN' YOU'D PROB'LY MAKE A LOT O' NOISE AN' SCARE TH' FISH
PLUTO
HERE'S MY PLACE, AN' NOBODY'S ANYWHERE AROUND= I SURE HOPE TH' FISH ARE BITIN' GOOD
WELL, IT WON'T BE LONG NOW
THAT'S FUNNY! DON'T THESE FISH LIKE WORMS?
ONE HOUR
DOGGONE IT! NOT EVEN A NIBBLE!
TWO HOURS
HO! HUM!
THREE HOURS
AN' T' THINK I LEFT PLUTO HOME 'CAUSE HE MIGHT SCARE TH' FISH!
FOUR HOURS
HOT DIGGETY DOG! I'VE GOT ONE!
JUST MY LUCK! I WAIT ALL DAY, AN' THEN AS SOON AS TH' FISH START BITIN' I'VE GOTTA GO HOME ON ACCOUNT OF THIS BLOOMIN' RAIN!
PLUTO! HOW'D YOU GET LOOSE? C'MON! WE'VE GOTTA BEAT IT! WE'LL GET SOAKED!
OHHH! SO YOU DIDN'T GET LOOSE! WELL, THAT'S DIFFERENT!
PLUTO
7-10 WALT DISNEY

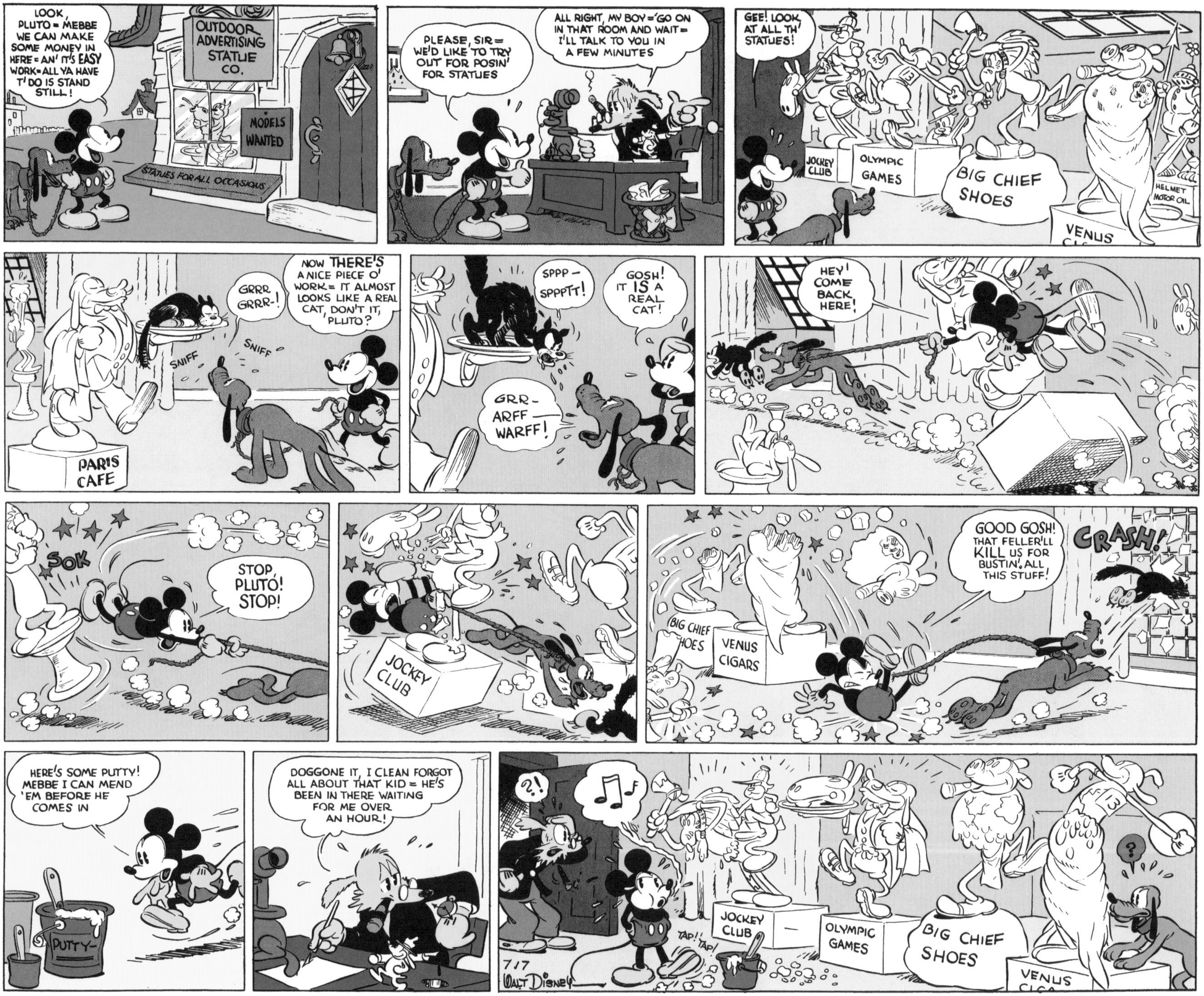
LOOK, PLUTO = MEBBE WE CAN MAKE SOME MONEY IN HERE = AN' IT'S EASY WORK = ALL YA HAVE T' DO IS STAND STILL!
OUTDOOR ADVERTISING STATUE CO.
MODELS WANTED
STATUES FOR ALL OCCASIONS
PLEASE, SIR = WE'D LIKE TO TRY OUT FOR POSIN' FOR STATUES
ALL RIGHT, MY BOY = GO ON IN THAT ROOM AND WAIT = I'LL TALK TO YOU IN A FEW MINUTES
GEE! LOOK AT ALL TH' STATUES!
JOCKEY CLUB
OLYMPIC GAMES
BIG CHIEF SHOES
HELMET MOTOR OIL
VENUS
NOW THERE'S A NICE PIECE O' WORK = IT ALMOST LOOKS LIKE A REAL CAT, DON'T IT, PLUTO?
GRRR GRRR-!
SNIFF
SNIFF
PARIS CAFE
SPPP - SPPPTT!
GOSH! IT IS A REAL CAT!
GRR- ARFF - WARFF!
HEY! COME BACK HERE!
SOK
STOP, PLUTO! STOP!
JOCKEY CLUB
GOOD GOSH! THAT FELLER'LL KILL US FOR BUSTIN' ALL THIS STUFF!
CRASH!
BIG CHIEF SHOES
VENUS CIGARS
HERE'S SOME PUTTY! MEBBE I CAN MEND 'EM BEFORE HE COMES IN
PUTTY
DOGGONE IT, I CLEAN FORGOT ALL ABOUT THAT KID = HE'S BEEN IN THERE WAITING FOR ME OVER AN HOUR!
?!
TAP! TAP!
JOCKEY CLUB
OLYMPIC GAMES
BIG CHIEF SHOES
VENUS
?
7/7
WALT DISNEY

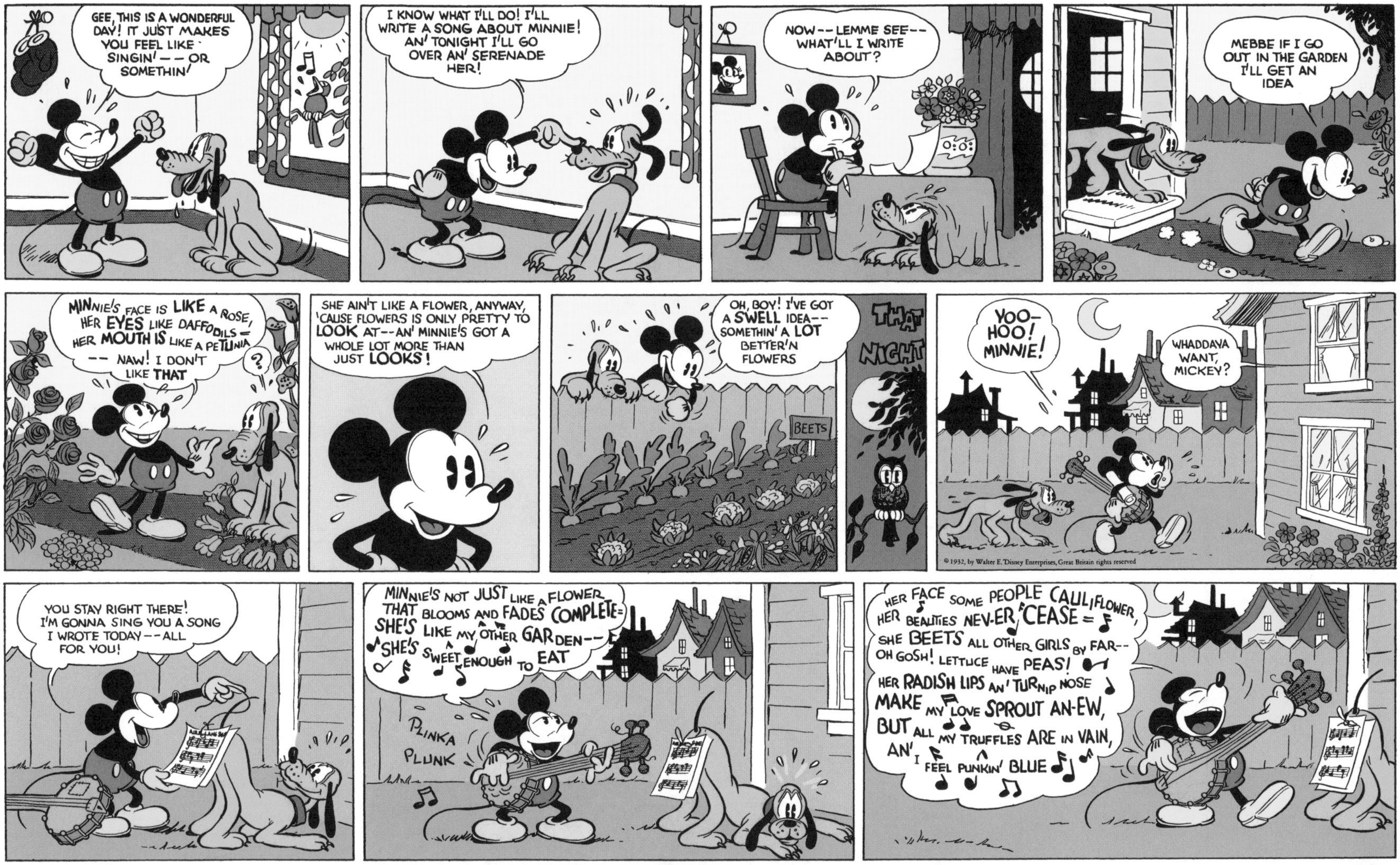
GEE, THIS IS A WONDERFUL DAY! IT JUST MAKES YOU FEEL LIKE SINGIN' -- OR SOMETHIN'
I KNOW WHAT I'LL DO! I'LL WRITE A SONG ABOUT MINNIE! AN' TONIGHT I'LL GO OVER AN' SERENADE HER!
NOW -- LEMME SEE -- WHAT'LL I WRITE ABOUT?
MEBBE IF I GO OUT IN THE GARDEN I'LL GET AN IDEA
MINNIE'S FACE IS LIKE A ROSE, HER EYES LIKE DAFFODILS = HER MOUTH IS LIKE A PETUNIA -- NAW! I DON'T LIKE THAT
?
SHE AIN'T LIKE A FLOWER, ANYWAY, 'CAUSE FLOWERS IS ONLY PRETTY TO LOOK AT -- AN' MINNIE'S GOT A WHOLE LOT MORE THAN JUST LOOKS!
OH, BOY! I'VE GOT A SWELL IDEA -- SOMETHIN' A LOT BETTER'N FLOWERS
BEETS
THAT NIGHT
YOO-HOO! MINNIE!
WHADDAYA WANT, MICKEY?
© 1932, by Walter E. Disney Enterprises, Great Britain rights reserved
YOU STAY RIGHT THERE! I'M GONNA SING YOU A SONG I WROTE TODAY -- ALL FOR YOU!
MINNIE'S NOT JUST LIKE A FLOWER THAT BLOOMS AND FADES COMPLETE = SHE'S LIKE MY OTHER GARDEN -- SHE'S SWEET ENOUGH TO EAT
PLINKA
PLUNK
HER FACE SOME PEOPLE CAULIFLOWER, HER BEAUTIES NEV-ER CEASE = SHE BEETS ALL OTHER GIRLS BY FAR -- OH GOSH! LETTUCE HAVE PEAS! HER RADISH LIPS AN' TURNIP NOSE MAKE MY LOVE SPROUT AN-EW, BUT ALL MY TRUFFLES ARE IN VAIN, AN' I FEEL PUNKIN' BLUE
TH' TROUBLE IS I HAVE NO KALE -- MY CELERY'S TOO SMALL = I ARTICHOKE HER HALF TO DEATH, AN' THEN PERHAPS SHE'D FALL = I'D GIVE A LOT IF SHE COULD SEE, BUT SQUASH! GOES EVERY HOPE — SHE DOESN'T CARROT ALL FOR ME -- AN' SO WE CANTELOUPE
WELL, THE VERY IDEA! I WAS NEVER SO INSULTED IN MY LIFE!
?
?
—MAKING FUN OF ME, JUST 'CAUSE MY FACE IS ALL SWELLED UP! SAYIN' I LOOK LIKE A VEGETABLE!
DOGGONE IT, PLUTO! HOW'D I KNOW SHE HAD TH' MUMPS?
WALT DISNEY 7-24

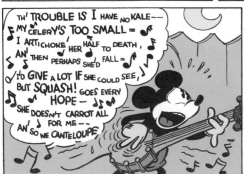

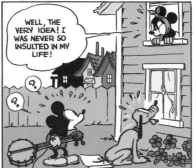

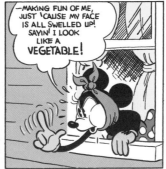

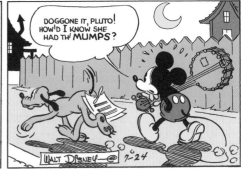

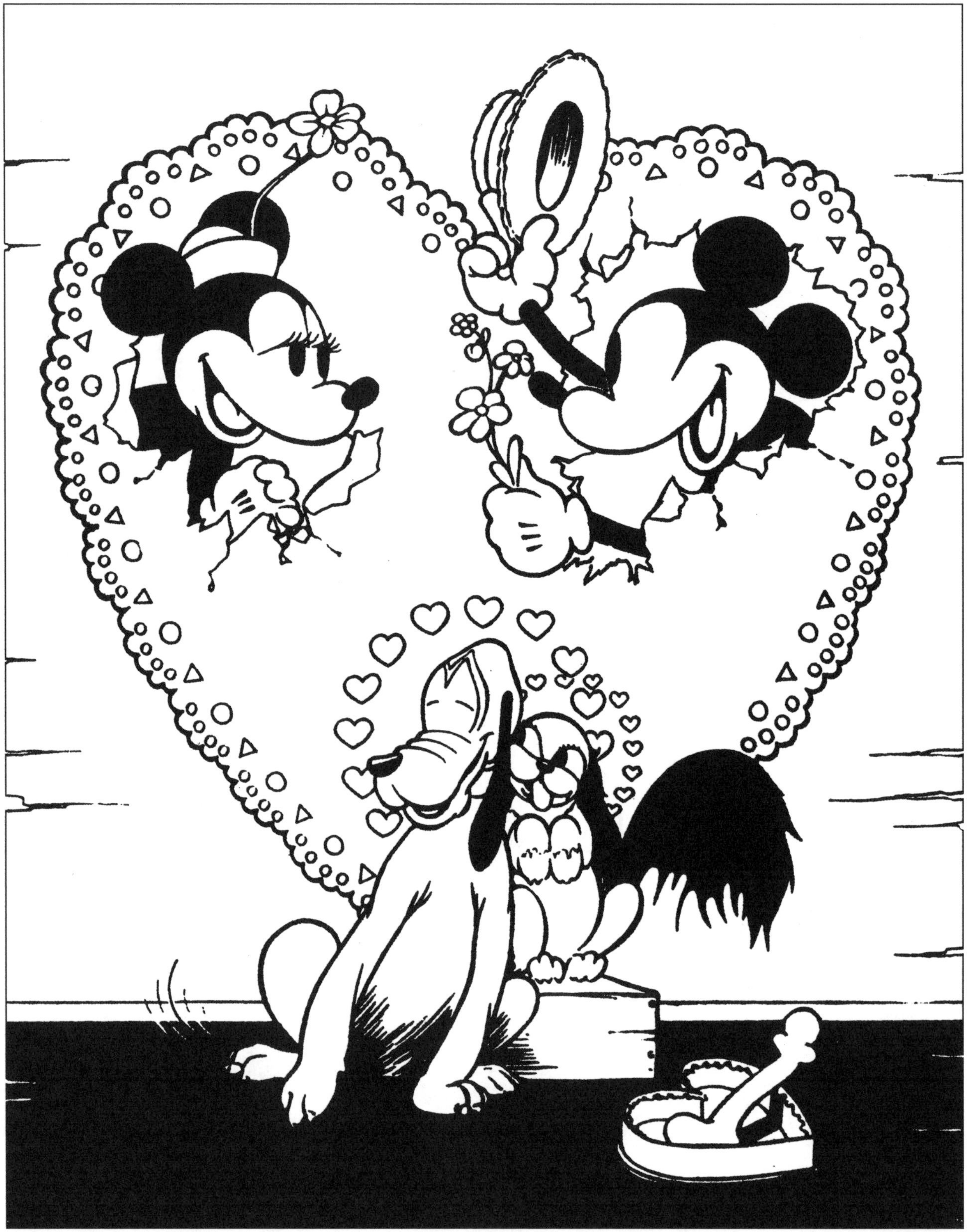

Yowp! Pluto and Mickey would a-wooing go in *Puppy Love* (1933), a classic cartoon short adapted roughly from Gottfredson's May 29, 1932 Sunday strip. Poster art from theatrical release; artist unknown. Image courtesy Walt Disney Archives.

DAN THE DOGCATCHER

AND

MICKEY'S NEPHEWS

AND

GAG STRIPS

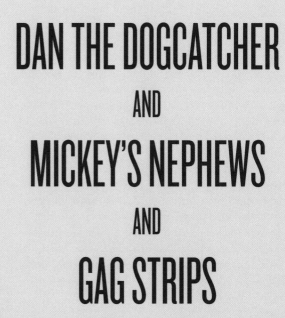

JULY 31, 1932

–

JANUARY 22, 1933

MICKEY MOUSE

REGISTERED U.S. PATENT OFFICE

THE PETER PRINCIPLE

Floyd Gottfredson was not one to rest on his laurels. After mastering several kinds of Sunday gag strip storytelling, how else could he improve his new feature? Perhaps by introducing continuity—though not yet the semi-serious, high adventure continuity that characterized the *Mickey* daily strip.

Gottfredson's first Sunday serials were firmly comedies, often loosely inspired by concurrent cartoons. But this didn't make them lightweight in Gottfredson's mind. He evidently took care to make sure that they integrated sensibly with the continuity of their daily counterparts.

What did this mean in practice? It meant that when *The Mad Dog* (1932), a new Mickey cartoon short, featured a comedy storyline that begged for Sunday adaptation, Gottfredson hopped right to it. Action-packed battles between Mickey and a misunderstanding dogcatcher—as shown in the cartoon—were obvious fodder for a long-form, multi-week scenario. But there was a problem: in the cartoon, this dogcatcher—the voice of law and order—was "played" by Pegleg Pete. And in Gottfredson's ongoing daily strip serials, Pegleg Pete was consistently a crook: "the most perennial heavy of all time," as Gottfredson described him.[1] Could *Mickey Mouse* comics fans make sense of seeing Pete as a lawbreaker during the week, and a law-and-order city official on Sunday? Perhaps not. So how to avoid confusion?

Gottfredson's "out" seems to have been the fact that in *The Mad Dog* cartoon, Pete's physique differed slightly from past incarnations. *Dog* gave Pete a fatter figure and more slovenly demeanor than in earlier *Mickey* shorts—and earlier Gottfredson strips. At the time, Gottfredson drew Pete as a top-heavy, barrel-chested strongman, not a fat slob; and Gottfredson decided to continue that way for the moment. The *Mad Dog* slob design could instead become a somewhat Petelike, but ultimately different peg-legged cat. Exit Pete; enter "Dan the Dogcatcher," fat feline lawman, who starred in both the eponymous 1932 Sunday story and the short 1933 daily serial, "Pluto and the Dogcatcher" (see Volume 2 of our daily strip series).

Of course, time wounds all heels. Several cartoons later, it became clear that Disney's Animation Department would be *keeping* the animated Pete in his new fatter form. What to do now? Gottfredson's cast numbered a Pete who no longer looked like the cartoon Pete—and a Dan who did.

The answer was to blubber up the comics Pete, which Gottfredson did in 1934, and surreptitiously remove Dan from the cast for awhile. In much later 1940s strips, the catfaced dogcatcher eventually reappeared, fat figure and all. But in a nod to perfectionism, Dan now had gray fur or a shaven chin, just to make sure readers still knew he wasn't Pete.

Continuity makes perfect. [DG]

1 Floyd Gottfredson, *Walt Disney Best Comics—Mickey Mouse* (New York: Abbeville Press, Inc., 1978), p. 12.

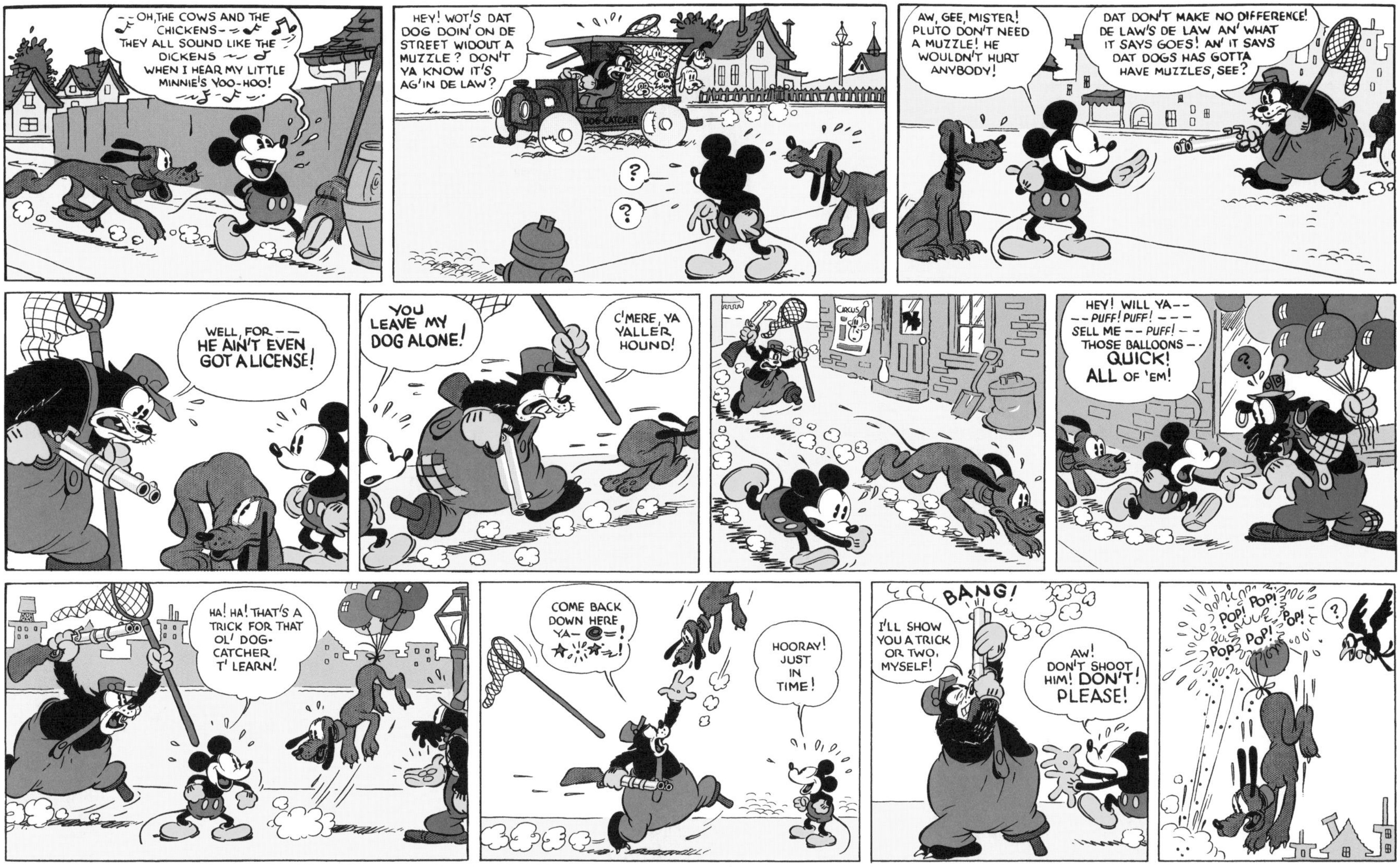
--OH, THE COWS AND THE CHICKENS-- THEY ALL SOUND LIKE THE DICKENS WHEN I HEAR MY LITTLE MINNIE'S YOO-HOO!
HEY! WOT'S DAT DOG DOIN' ON DE STREET WIDOUT A MUZZLE? DON'T YA KNOW IT'S AG'IN DE LAW?
DOG-CATCHER
?
?
AW, GEE, MISTER! PLUTO DON'T NEED A MUZZLE! HE WOULDN'T HURT ANYBODY!
DAT DON'T MAKE NO DIFFERENCE! DE LAW'S DE LAW AN' WHAT IT SAYS GOES! AN' IT SAYS DAT DOGS HAS GOTTA HAVE MUZZLES, SEE?
WELL, FOR-- HE AIN'T EVEN GOT A LICENSE!
YOU LEAVE MY DOG ALONE!
C'MERE, YA YALLER HOUND!
CIRCUS
HEY! WILL YA-- --PUFF! PUFF! --- SELL ME --PUFF!-- THOSE BALLOONS-- QUICK! ALL OF 'EM!
?
HA! HA! THAT'S A TRICK FOR THAT OL' DOG-CATCHER T' LEARN!
COME BACK DOWN HERE YA--
HOORAY! JUST IN TIME!
BANG!
I'LL SHOW YOU A TRICK OR TWO, MYSELF!
AW! DON'T SHOOT HIM! DON'T! PLEASE!
POP! POP! POP! POP! POP! POP!
?
HE'S TH' FIRST GUY YOU EVER HURT, AN' YOU DIDN'T BITE HIM! SO IF HE WANTS YOU SHOULD HAVE A MUZZLE, I'M GONNA PUT IT WHERE IT BELONGS
?
CITY DUMP
WALT DISNEY

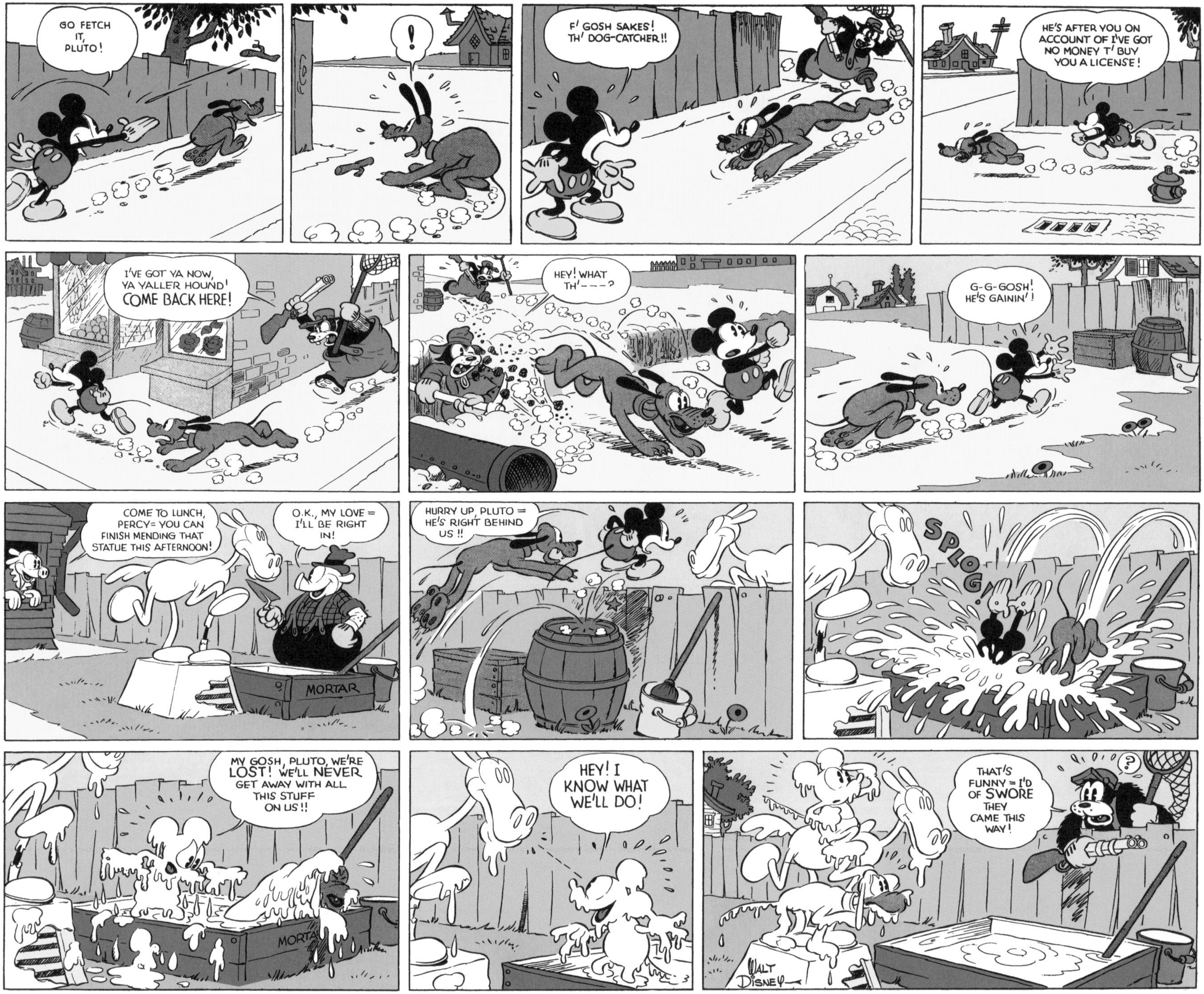
GO FETCH IT, PLUTO!
!
F' GOSH SAKES! TH' DOG-CATCHER!!
HE'S AFTER YOU ON ACCOUNT OF I'VE GOT NO MONEY T' BUY YOU A LICENSE!
I'VE GOT YA NOW, YA YALLER HOUND! COME BACK HERE!
HEY! WHAT TH'---?
G-G-GOSH! HE'S GAININ'!
COME TO LUNCH, PERCY= YOU CAN FINISH MENDING THAT STATUE THIS AFTERNOON!
O.K., MY LOVE = I'LL BE RIGHT IN!
MORTAR
HURRY UP, PLUTO = HE'S RIGHT BEHIND US!!
SPLOG!
MY GOSH, PLUTO, WE'RE LOST! WE'LL NEVER GET AWAY WITH ALL THIS STUFF ON US!!
MORTA
HEY! I KNOW WHAT WE'LL DO!
THAT'S FUNNY = I'D OF SWORE THEY CAME THIS WAY!
?
WALT DISNEY

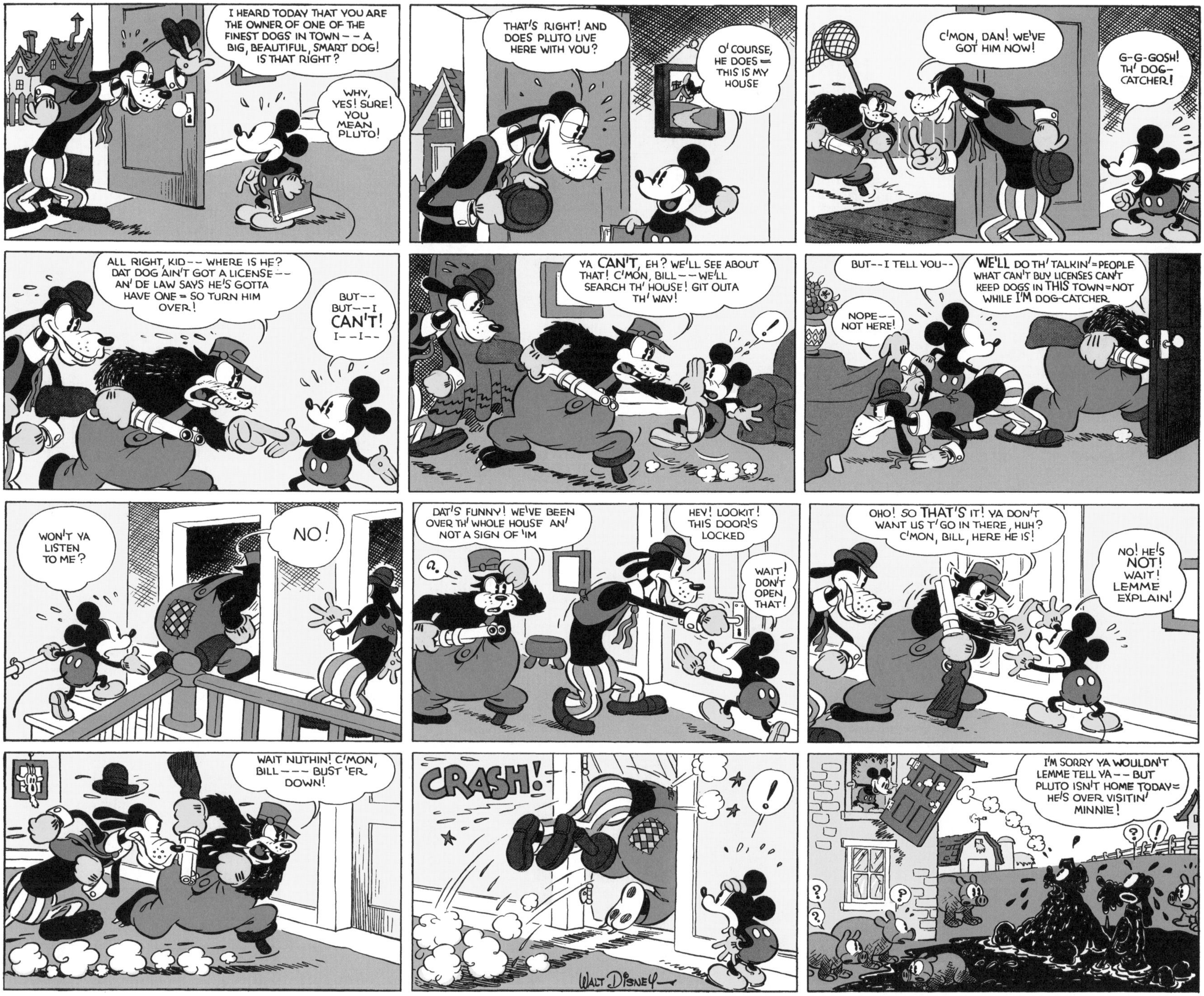
I HEARD TODAY THAT YOU ARE THE OWNER OF ONE OF THE FINEST DOGS IN TOWN -- A BIG, BEAUTIFUL, SMART DOG! IS THAT RIGHT?
WHY, YES! SURE! YOU MEAN PLUTO!
THAT'S RIGHT! AND DOES PLUTO LIVE HERE WITH YOU?
O' COURSE, HE DOES = THIS IS MY HOUSE
C'MON, DAN! WE'VE GOT HIM NOW!
G-G-GOSH! TH' DOG-CATCHER!
ALL RIGHT, KID -- WHERE IS HE? DAT DOG AIN'T GOT A LICENSE -- AN' DE LAW SAYS HE'S GOTTA HAVE ONE = SO TURN HIM OVER!
BUT -- BUT -- I CAN'T! I -- I --
YA CAN'T, EH? WE'LL SEE ABOUT THAT! C'MON, BILL -- WE'LL SEARCH TH' HOUSE! GIT OUTA TH' WAY!
!
BUT -- I TELL YOU --
WE'LL DO TH' TALKIN' = PEOPLE WHAT CAN'T BUY LICENSES CAN'T KEEP DOGS IN THIS TOWN = NOT WHILE I'M DOG-CATCHER
NOPE -- NOT HERE!
WON'T YA LISTEN TO ME?
NO!
DAT'S FUNNY! WE'VE BEEN OVER TH' WHOLE HOUSE AN' NOT A SIGN OF 'IM
HEY! LOOKIT! THIS DOOR'S LOCKED
WAIT! DON'T OPEN THAT!
OHO! SO THAT'S IT! YA DON'T WANT US T' GO IN THERE, HUH? C'MON, BILL, HERE HE IS!
NO! HE'S NOT! WAIT! LEMME EXPLAIN!
WAIT NUTHIN! C'MON, BILL --- BUST 'ER DOWN!
CRASH!
!
WALT DISNEY
I'M SORRY YA WOULDN'T LEMME TELL YA -- BUT PLUTO ISN'T HOME TODAY = HE'S OVER VISITIN' MINNIE!

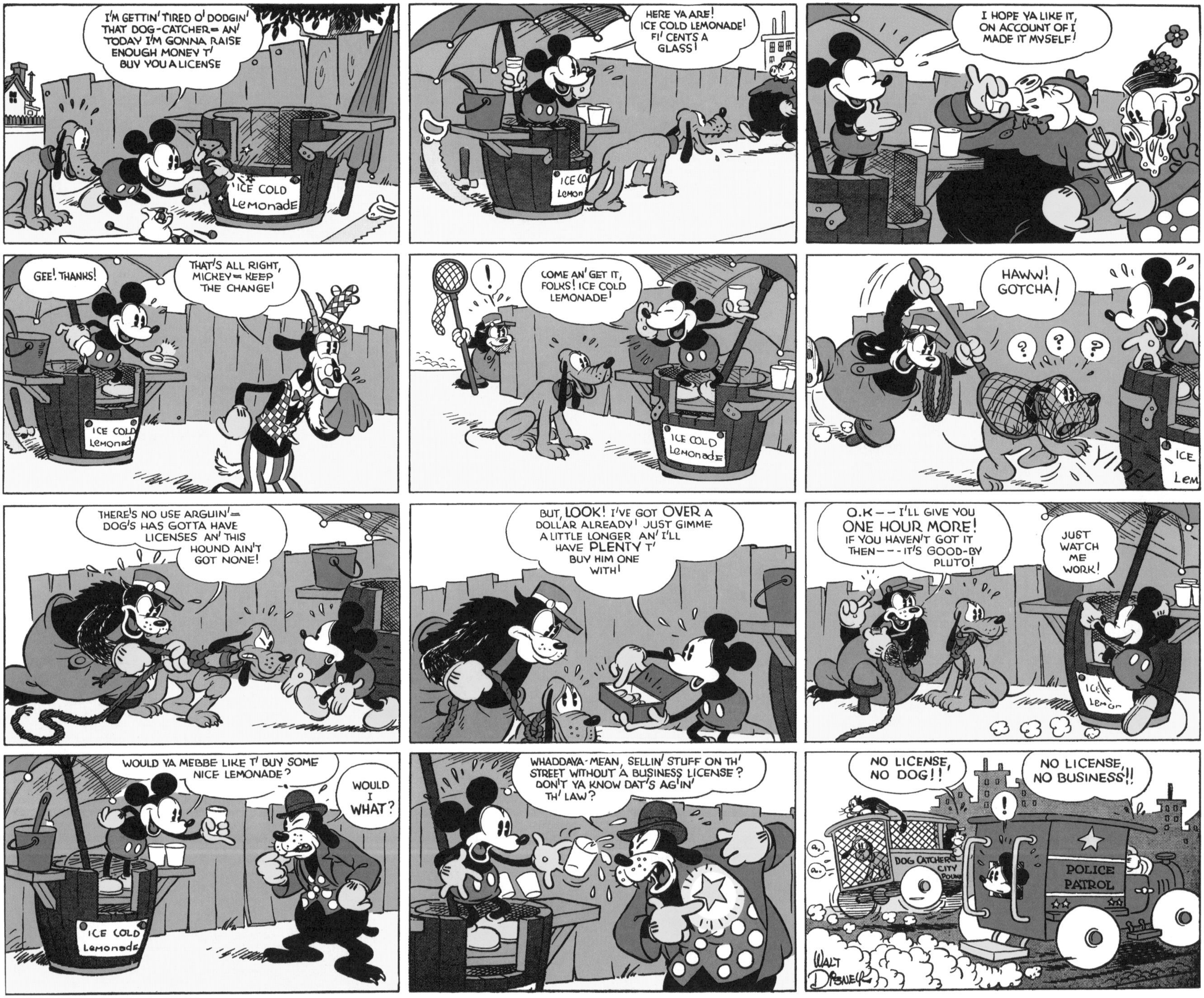
I'M GETTIN' TIRED O' DODGIN' THAT DOG-CATCHER— AN' TODAY I'M GONNA RAISE ENOUGH MONEY T' BUY YOU A LICENSE
ICE COLD Lemonade
HERE YA ARE! ICE COLD LEMONADE! FI' CENTS A GLASS!
ICE COLD Lemon
I HOPE YA LIKE IT, ON ACCOUNT OF I MADE IT MYSELF!
GEE! THANKS!
THAT'S ALL RIGHT, MICKEY— KEEP THE CHANGE!
ICE COLD Lemonade
!
COME AN' GET IT, FOLKS! ICE COLD LEMONADE!
ICE COLD Lemonade
HAWW! GOTCHA!
? ? ?
YIPE!
ICE Lem
THERE'S NO USE ARGUIN'— DOG'S HAS GOTTA HAVE LICENSES AN' THIS HOUND AIN'T GOT NONE!
BUT, LOOK! I'VE GOT OVER A DOLLAR ALREADY! JUST GIMME A LITTLE LONGER AN' I'LL HAVE PLENTY T' BUY HIM ONE WITH!
O.K— I'LL GIVE YOU ONE HOUR MORE! IF YOU HAVEN'T GOT IT THEN— IT'S GOOD-BY PLUTO!
JUST WATCH ME WORK!
WOULD YA MEBBE LIKE T' BUY SOME NICE LEMONADE?
WOULD I WHAT?
ICE COLD Lemonade
WHADDAYA-MEAN, SELLIN' STUFF ON TH' STREET WITHOUT A BUSINESS LICENSE? DON'T YA KNOW DAT'S AG'IN' TH' LAW?
NO LICENSE, NO DOG!!
NO LICENSE, NO BUSINESS!!
DOG CATCHER CITY POUND
POLICE PATROL
WALT DISNEY

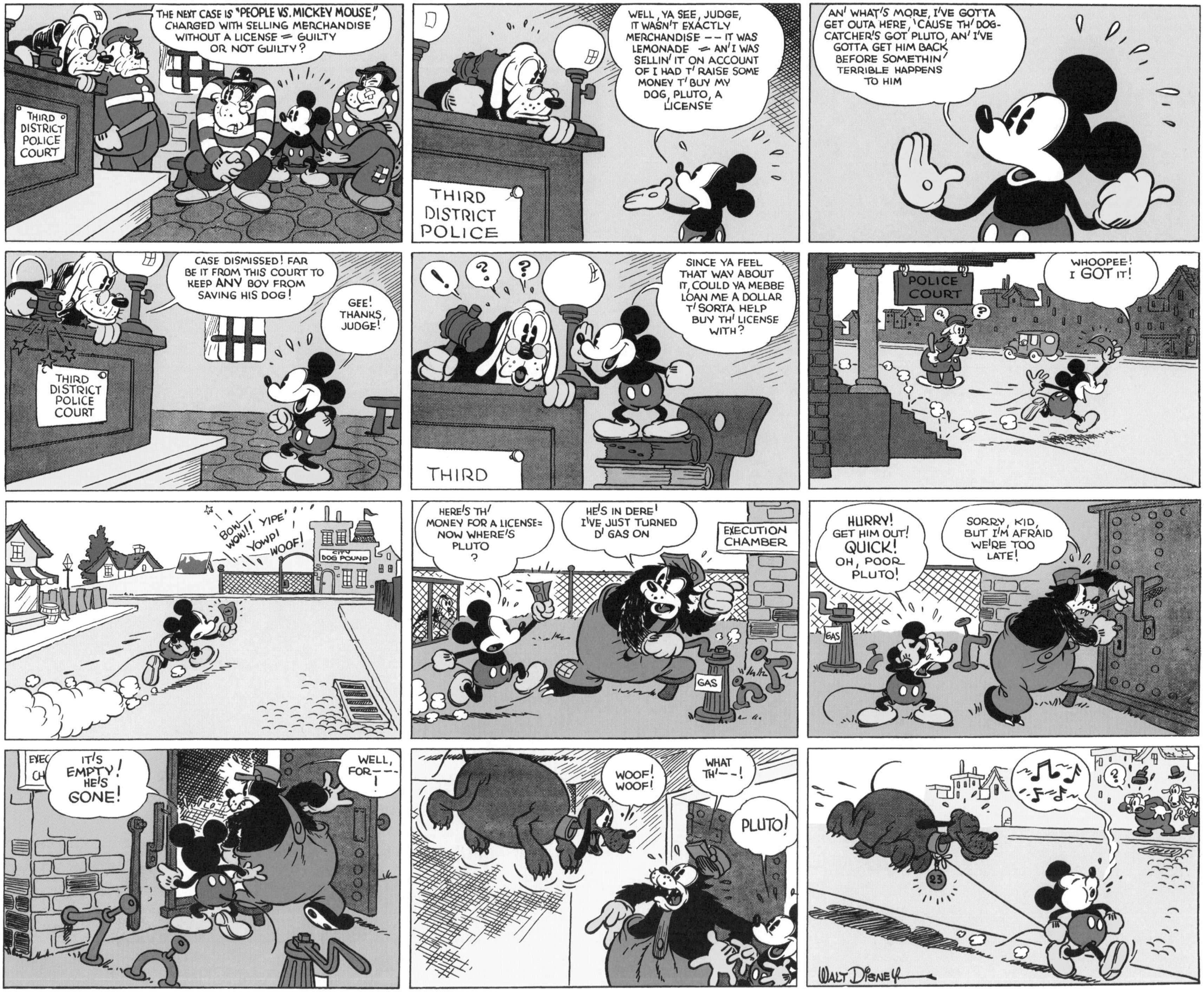
THE NEXT CASE IS "PEOPLE VS. MICKEY MOUSE," CHARGED WITH SELLING MERCHANDISE WITHOUT A LICENSE = GUILTY OR NOT GUILTY?
THIRD DISTRICT POLICE COURT
WELL, YA SEE, JUDGE, IT WASN'T EXACTLY MERCHANDISE -- IT WAS LEMONADE = AN' I WAS SELLIN' IT ON ACCOUNT OF I HAD T' RAISE SOME MONEY T' BUY MY DOG, PLUTO, A LICENSE
THIRD DISTRICT POLICE
AN' WHAT'S MORE, I'VE GOTTA GET OUTA HERE, 'CAUSE TH' DOG-CATCHER'S GOT PLUTO, AN' I'VE GOTTA GET HIM BACK BEFORE SOMETHIN' TERRIBLE HAPPENS TO HIM
CASE DISMISSED! FAR BE IT FROM THIS COURT TO KEEP ANY BOY FROM SAVING HIS DOG!
THIRD DISTRICT POLICE COURT
GEE! THANKS, JUDGE!
!
?
?
SINCE YA FEEL THAT WAY ABOUT IT, COULD YA MEBBE LOAN ME A DOLLAR T' SORTA HELP BUY TH' LICENSE WITH?
THIRD
POLICE COURT
WHOOPEE! I GOT IT!
BOW-WOW!! YIPE! YOWP! WOOF!
CITY DOG POUND
HERE'S TH' MONEY FOR A LICENSE= NOW WHERE'S PLUTO?
HE'S IN DERE! I'VE JUST TURNED D' GAS ON
EXECUTION CHAMBER
GAS
HURRY! GET HIM OUT! QUICK! OH, POOR PLUTO!
SORRY, KID, BUT I'M AFRAID WE'RE TOO LATE!
GAS
IT'S EMPTY! HE'S GONE!
WELL, FOR---!
WOOF! WOOF!
WHAT TH'--!
PLUTO!
23
WALT DISNEY

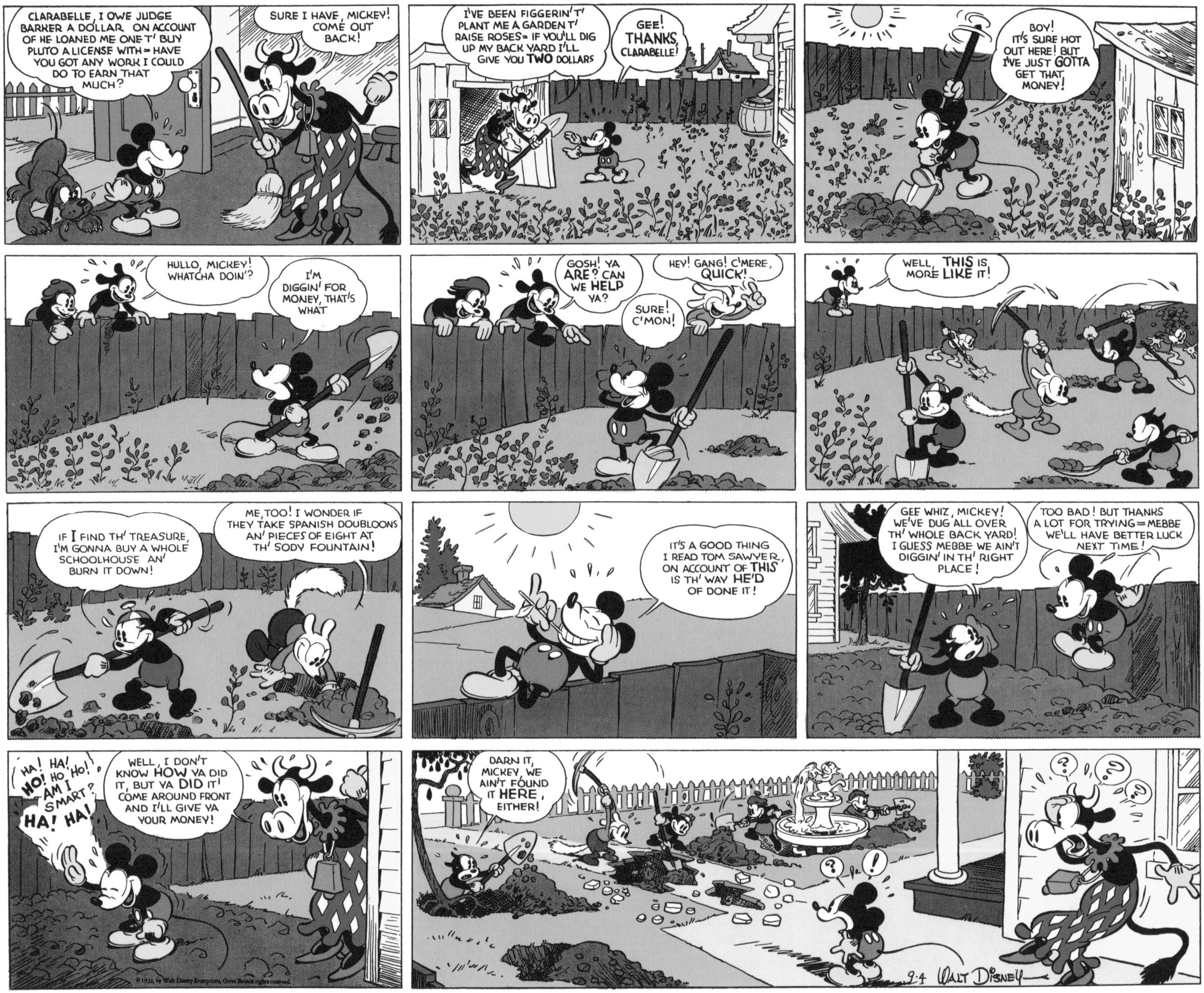
CLARABELLE, I OWE JUDGE BARKER A DOLLAR ON ACCOUNT OF HE LOANED ME ONE T' BUY PLUTO A LICENSE WITH = HAVE YOU GOT ANY WORK I COULD DO TO EARN THAT MUCH?
SURE I HAVE, MICKEY! COME OUT BACK!
I'VE BEEN FIGGERIN' T' PLANT ME A GARDEN T' RAISE ROSES = IF YOU'LL DIG UP MY BACK YARD I'LL GIVE YOU TWO DOLLARS
GEE! THANKS, CLARABELLE!
BOY! IT'S SURE HOT OUT HERE! BUT I'VE JUST GOTTA GET THAT MONEY!
HULLO, MICKEY! WHATCHA DOIN'?
I'M DIGGIN' FOR MONEY, THAT'S WHAT
GOSH! YA ARE? CAN WE HELP YA?
HEY! GANG! C'MERE, QUICK!
SURE! C'MON!
WELL, THIS IS MORE LIKE IT!
IF I FIND TH' TREASURE, I'M GONNA BUY A WHOLE SCHOOLHOUSE AN' BURN IT DOWN!
ME, TOO! I WONDER IF THEY TAKE SPANISH DOUBLOONS AN' PIECES OF EIGHT AT TH' SODY FOUNTAIN!
IT'S A GOOD THING I READ TOM SAWYER, ON ACCOUNT OF THIS IS TH' WAY HE'D OF DONE IT!
GEE WHIZ, MICKEY! WE'VE DUG ALL OVER TH' WHOLE BACK YARD! I GUESS MEBBE WE AIN'T DIGGIN' IN TH' RIGHT PLACE!
TOO BAD! BUT THANKS A LOT FOR TRYING = MEBBE WE'LL HAVE BETTER LUCK NEXT TIME!
HA! HA! HO! HO! HO! AM I SMART? HA! HA!
WELL, I DON'T KNOW HOW YA DID IT, BUT YA DID IT! COME AROUND FRONT AND I'LL GIVE YA YOUR MONEY!
DARN IT, MICKEY, WE AIN'T FOUND IT HERE, EITHER!
9-4 WALT DISNEY

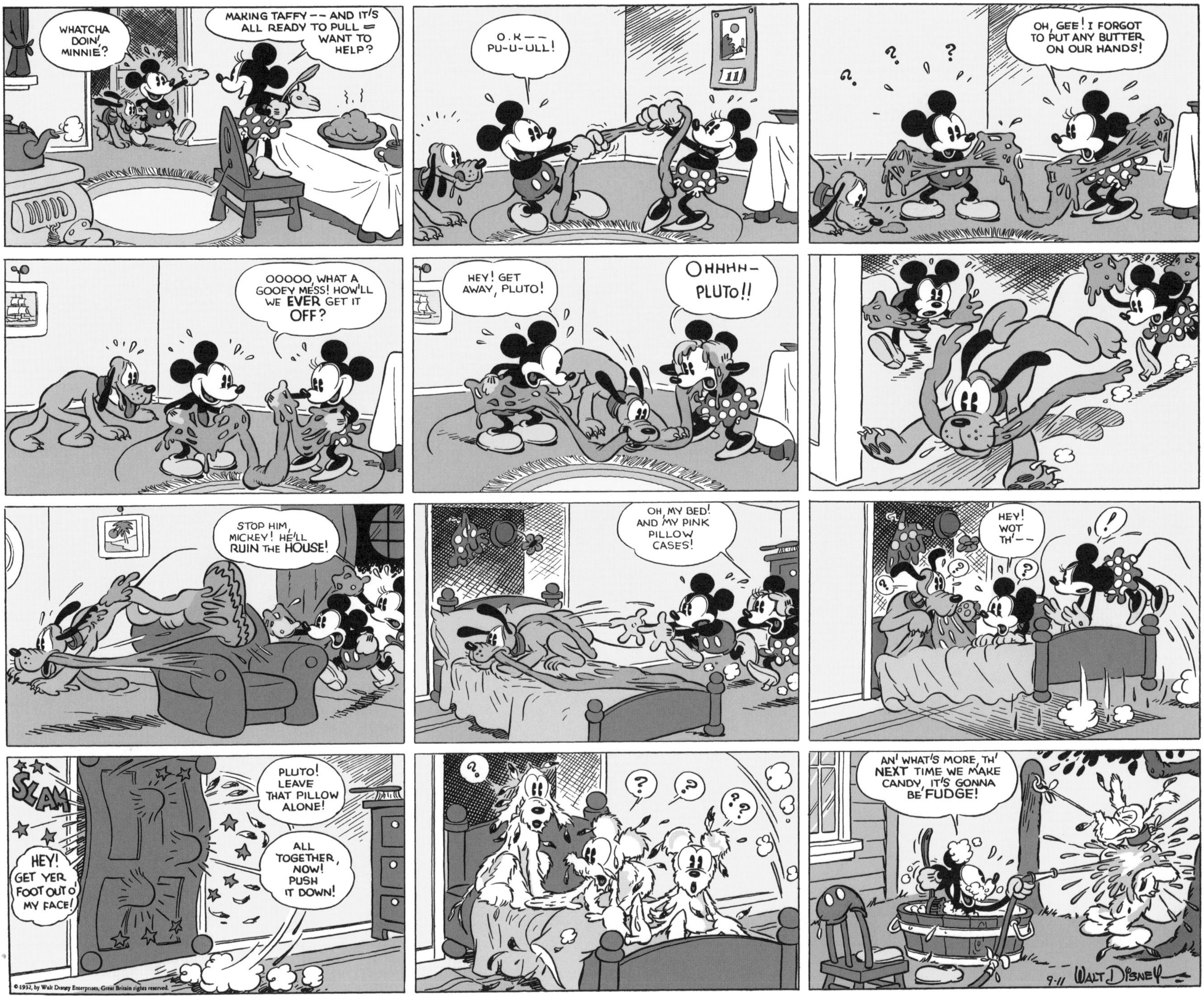
WHATCHA DOIN', MINNIE?
MAKING TAFFY -- AND IT'S ALL READY TO PULL = WANT TO HELP?
11
O.K -- PU-U-ULL!
OH, GEE! I FORGOT TO PUT ANY BUTTER ON OUR HANDS!
OOOOO, WHAT A GOOEY MESS! HOW'LL WE EVER GET IT OFF?
HEY! GET AWAY, PLUTO!
OHHHH- PLUTO!!
STOP HIM, MICKEY! HE'LL RUIN THE HOUSE!
OH, MY BED! AND MY PINK PILLOW CASES!
HEY! WOT TH'--
SLAM
PLUTO! LEAVE THAT PILLOW ALONE!
ALL TOGETHER, NOW! PUSH IT DOWN!
HEY! GET YER FOOT OUT O' MY FACE!
AN' WHAT'S MORE, TH' NEXT TIME WE MAKE CANDY, IT'S GONNA BE FUDGE!
9-11 WALT DISNEY
© 1932, by Walt Disney Enterprises, Great Britain rights reserved.

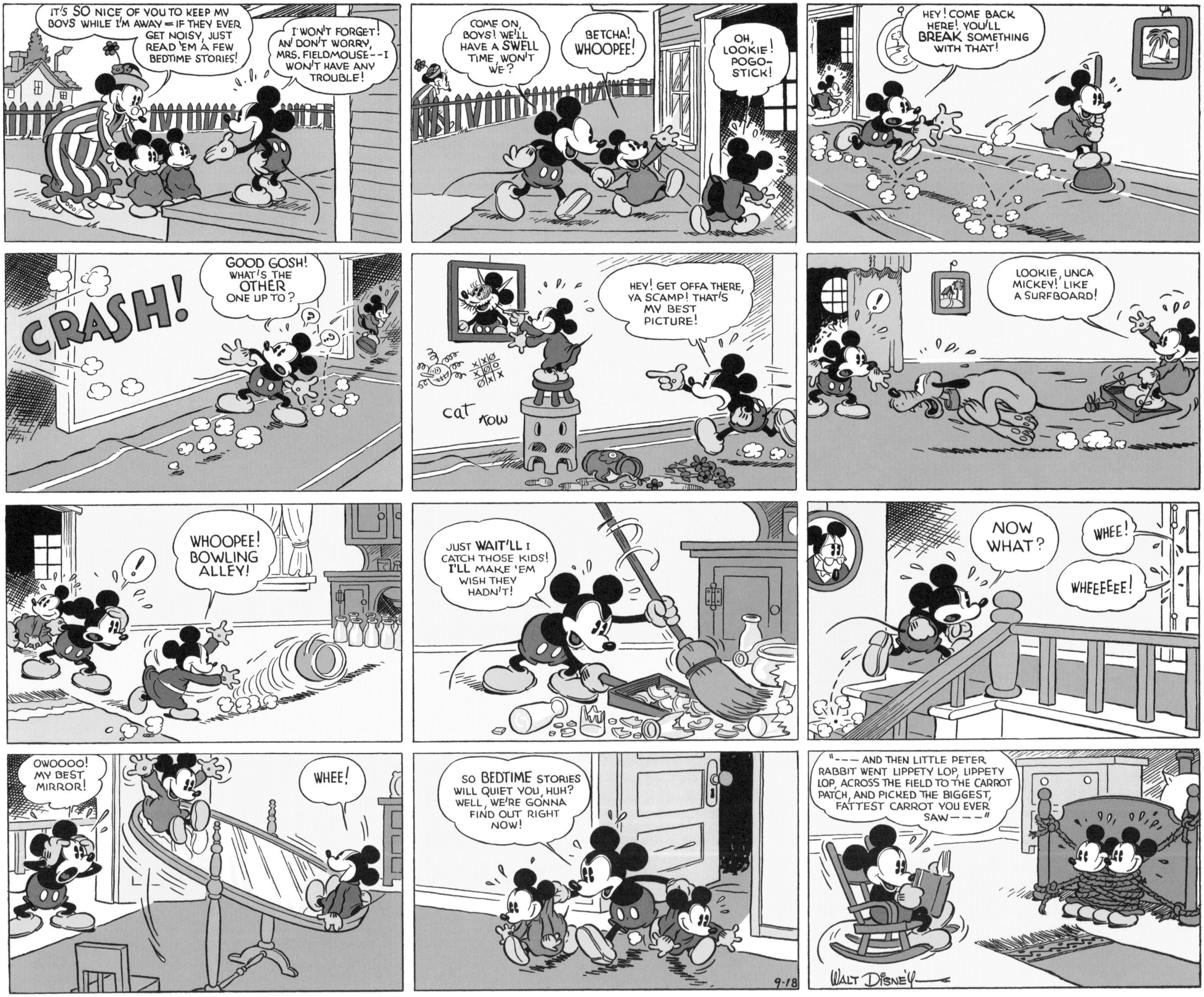
IT'S SO NICE OF YOU TO KEEP MY BOYS WHILE I'M AWAY = IF THEY EVER GET NOISY, JUST READ 'EM A FEW BEDTIME STORIES!
I WON'T FORGET! AN' DON'T WORRY, MRS. FIELDMOUSE--I WON'T HAVE ANY TROUBLE!
COME ON, BOYS! WE'LL HAVE A SWELL TIME, WON'T WE?
BETCHA! WHOOPEE!
OH, LOOKIE! POGO-STICK!
HEY! COME BACK HERE! YOU'LL BREAK SOMETHING WITH THAT!
CRASH!
GOOD GOSH! WHAT'S THE OTHER ONE UP TO?
HEY! GET OFFA THERE, YA SCAMP! THAT'S MY BEST PICTURE!
CAT
LOOKIE, UNCA MICKEY! LIKE A SURFBOARD!
WHOOPEE! BOWLING ALLEY!
JUST WAIT'LL I CATCH THOSE KIDS! I'LL MAKE 'EM WISH THEY HADN'T!
NOW WHAT?
WHEE!
WHEEEEEE!
OWOOOO! MY BEST MIRROR!
WHEE!
SO BEDTIME STORIES WILL QUIET YOU, HUH? WELL, WE'RE GONNA FIND OUT RIGHT NOW!
9-18
"--- AND THEN LITTLE PETER RABBIT WENT LIPPETY LOP, LIPPETY LOP, ACROSS THE FIELD TO THE CARROT PATCH, AND PICKED THE BIGGEST, FATTEST CARROT YOU EVER SAW---"
WALT DISNEY

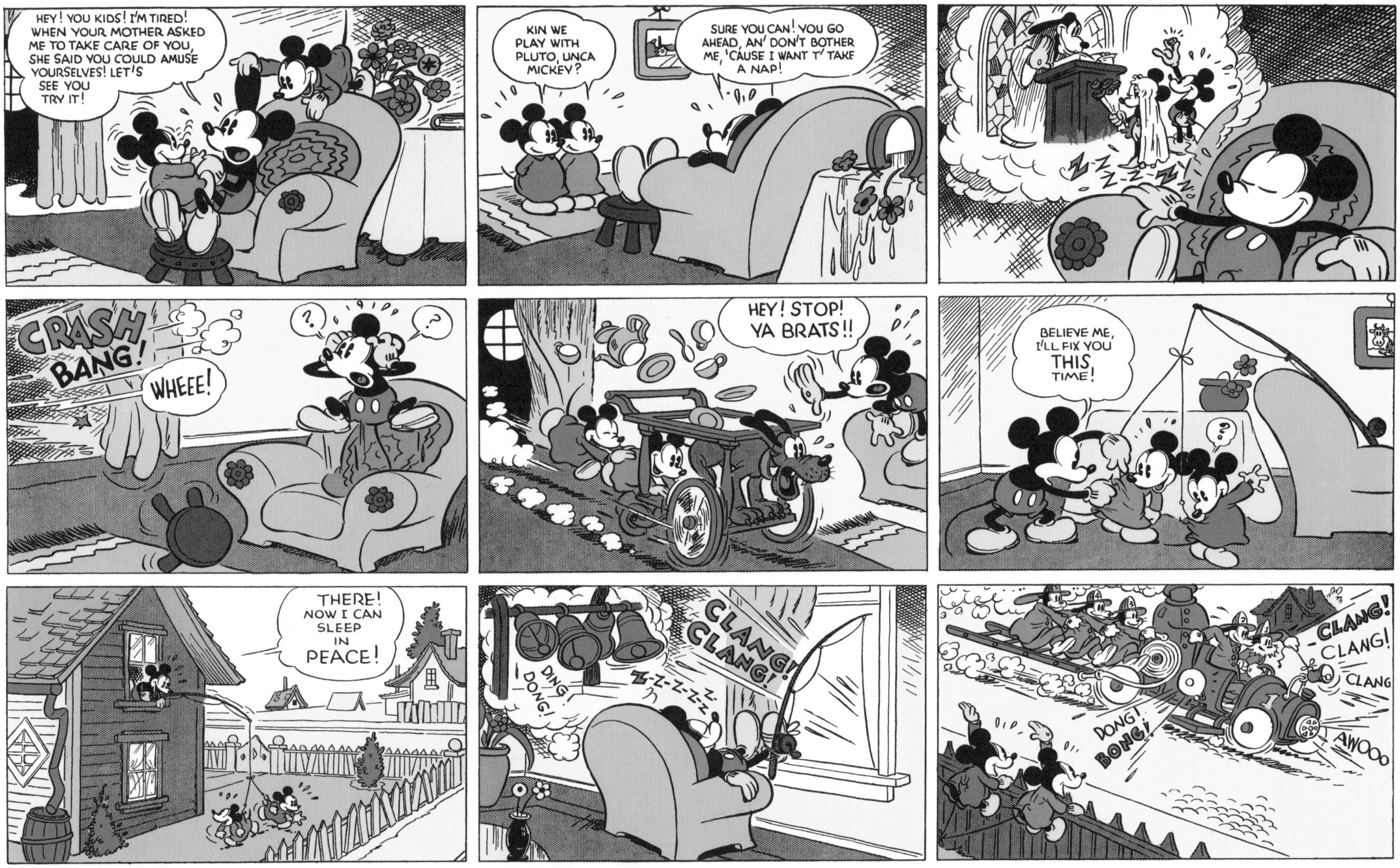
HEY! YOU KIDS! I'M TIRED! WHEN YOUR MOTHER ASKED ME TO TAKE CARE OF YOU, SHE SAID YOU COULD AMUSE YOURSELVES! LET'S SEE YOU TRY IT!
KIN WE PLAY WITH PLUTO, UNCA MICKEY?
SURE YOU CAN! YOU GO AHEAD, AN' DON'T BOTHER ME, 'CAUSE I WANT T' TAKE A NAP!
Z-Z-Z-Z-Z
CRASH BANG!
WHEEE!
?
?
HEY! STOP! YA BRATS!!
BELIEVE ME, I'LL FIX YOU THIS TIME!
?
THERE! NOW I CAN SLEEP IN PEACE!
CLANG! CLANG!
DING! DONG!
Z-Z-Z-Z-Z
CLANG! CLANG! CLANG
DONG! BONG!
AWOOO
HEY—WHAT TH—???
?
?
?
?
WALT DISNEY
9-25

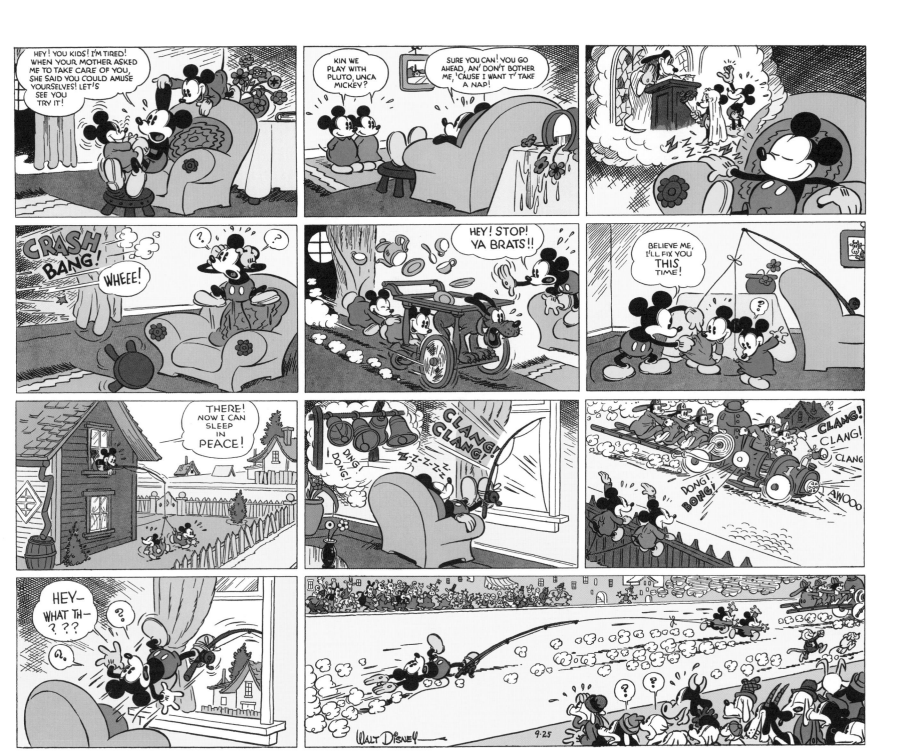

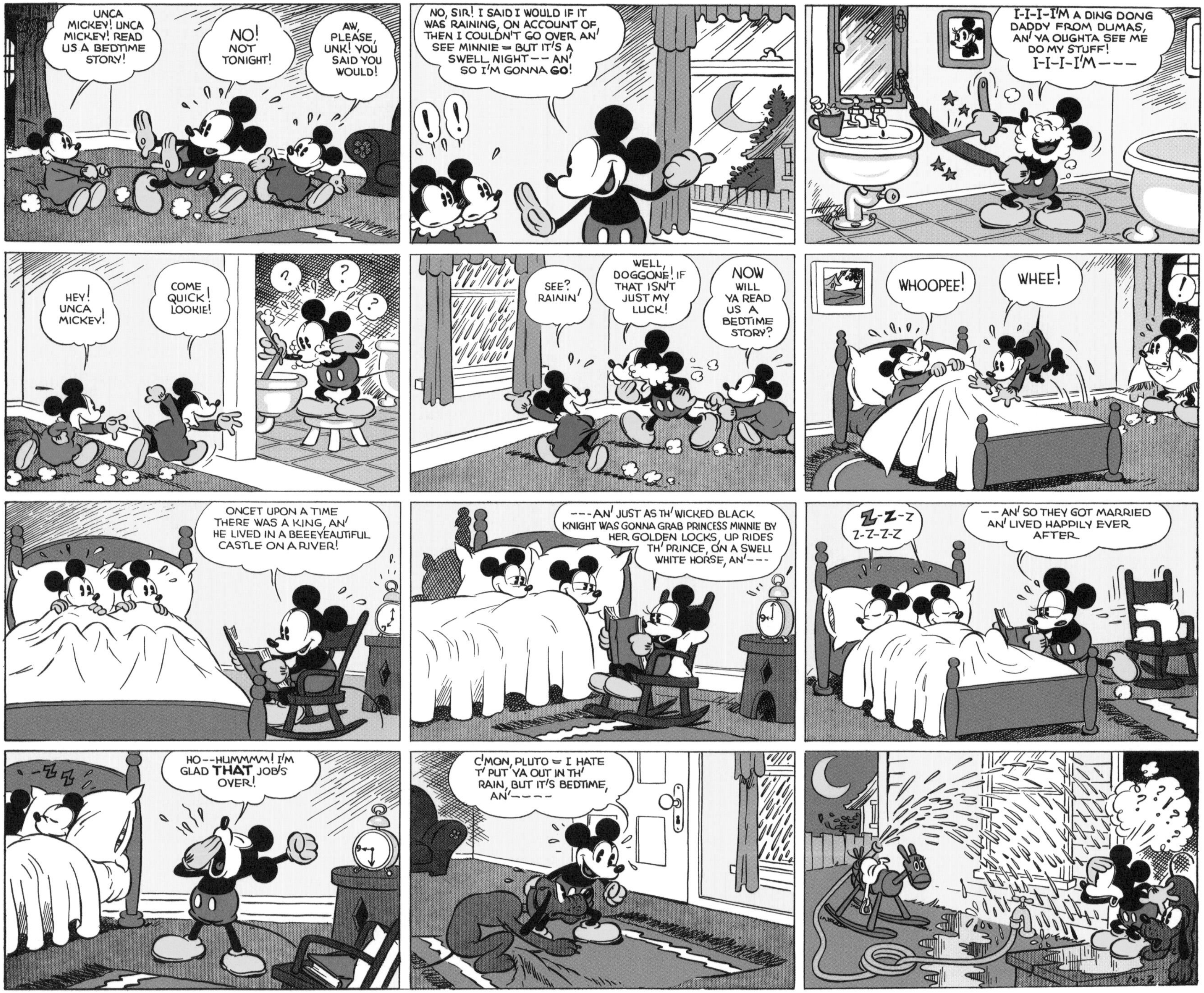
UNCA MICKEY! UNCA MICKEY! READ US A BEDTIME STORY!
NO! NOT TONIGHT!
AW, PLEASE, UNK! YOU SAID YOU WOULD!
NO, SIR! I SAID I WOULD IF IT WAS RAINING, ON ACCOUNT OF THEN I COULDN'T GO OVER AN' SEE MINNIE = BUT IT'S A SWELL NIGHT -- AN' SO I'M GONNA GO!
!!
I-I-I-I'M A DING DONG DADDY FROM DUMAS, AN' YA OUGHTA SEE ME DO MY STUFF! I-I-I-I'M ---
HEY! UNCA MICKEY!
COME QUICK! LOOKIE!
? ? ?
SEE? RAININ'
WELL, DOGGONE! IF THAT ISN'T JUST MY LUCK!
NOW WILL YA READ US A BEDTIME STORY?
WHOOPEE!
WHEE!
!
ONCET UPON A TIME THERE WAS A KING, AN' HE LIVED IN A BEEEYEAUTIFUL CASTLE ON A RIVER!
---AN' JUST AS TH' WICKED BLACK KNIGHT WAS GONNA GRAB PRINCESS MINNIE BY HER GOLDEN LOCKS, UP RIDES TH' PRINCE, ON A SWELL WHITE HORSE, AN'---
Z-Z-Z Z-Z-Z-Z
--AN' SO THEY GOT MARRIED AN' LIVED HAPPILY EVER AFTER
HO--HUMMMM! I'M GLAD THAT JOB'S OVER!
C'MON, PLUTO = I HATE T' PUT YA OUT IN TH' RAIN, BUT IT'S BEDTIME, AN'----

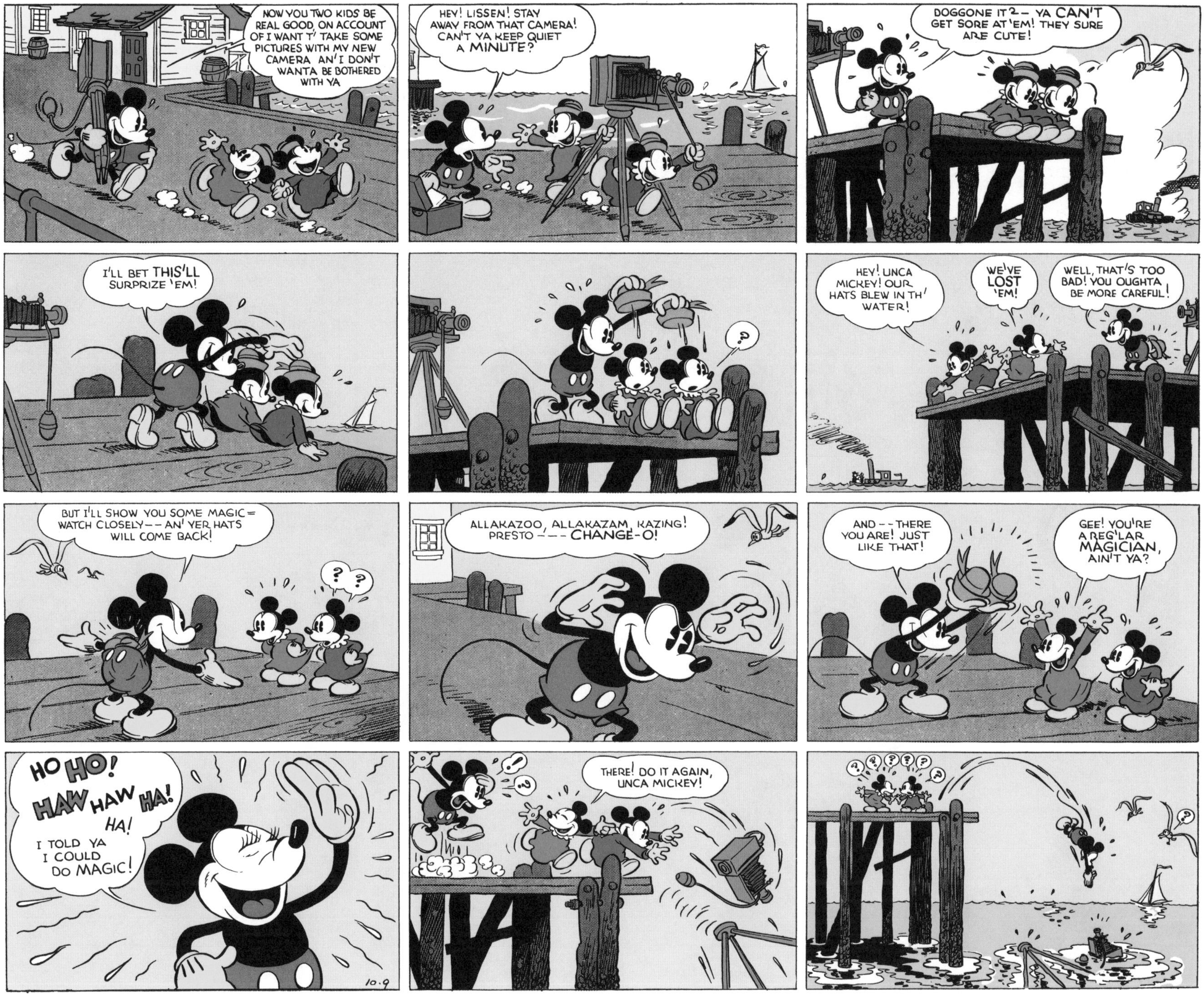
NOW YOU TWO KIDS BE REAL GOOD, ON ACCOUNT OF I WANT T' TAKE SOME PICTURES WITH MY NEW CAMERA AN' I DON'T WANTA BE BOTHERED WITH YA
HEY! LISSEN! STAY AWAY FROM THAT CAMERA! CAN'T YA KEEP QUIET A MINUTE?
DOGGONE IT?-- YA CAN'T GET SORE AT 'EM! THEY SURE ARE CUTE!
I'LL BET THIS'LL SURPRIZE 'EM!
?
HEY! UNCA MICKEY! OUR HATS BLEW IN TH' WATER!
WE'VE LOST 'EM!
WELL, THAT'S TOO BAD! YOU OUGHTA BE MORE CAREFUL!
BUT I'LL SHOW YOU SOME MAGIC= WATCH CLOSELY-- AN' YER HATS WILL COME BACK!
? ?
ALLAKAZOO, ALLAKAZAM, KAZING! PRESTO --- CHANGE-O!
AND -- THERE YOU ARE! JUST LIKE THAT!
GEE! YOU'RE A REG'LAR MAGICIAN, AIN'T YA?
HO HO! HAW HAW HA! HA!
I TOLD YA I COULD DO MAGIC!
10.9
THERE! DO IT AGAIN, UNCA MICKEY!

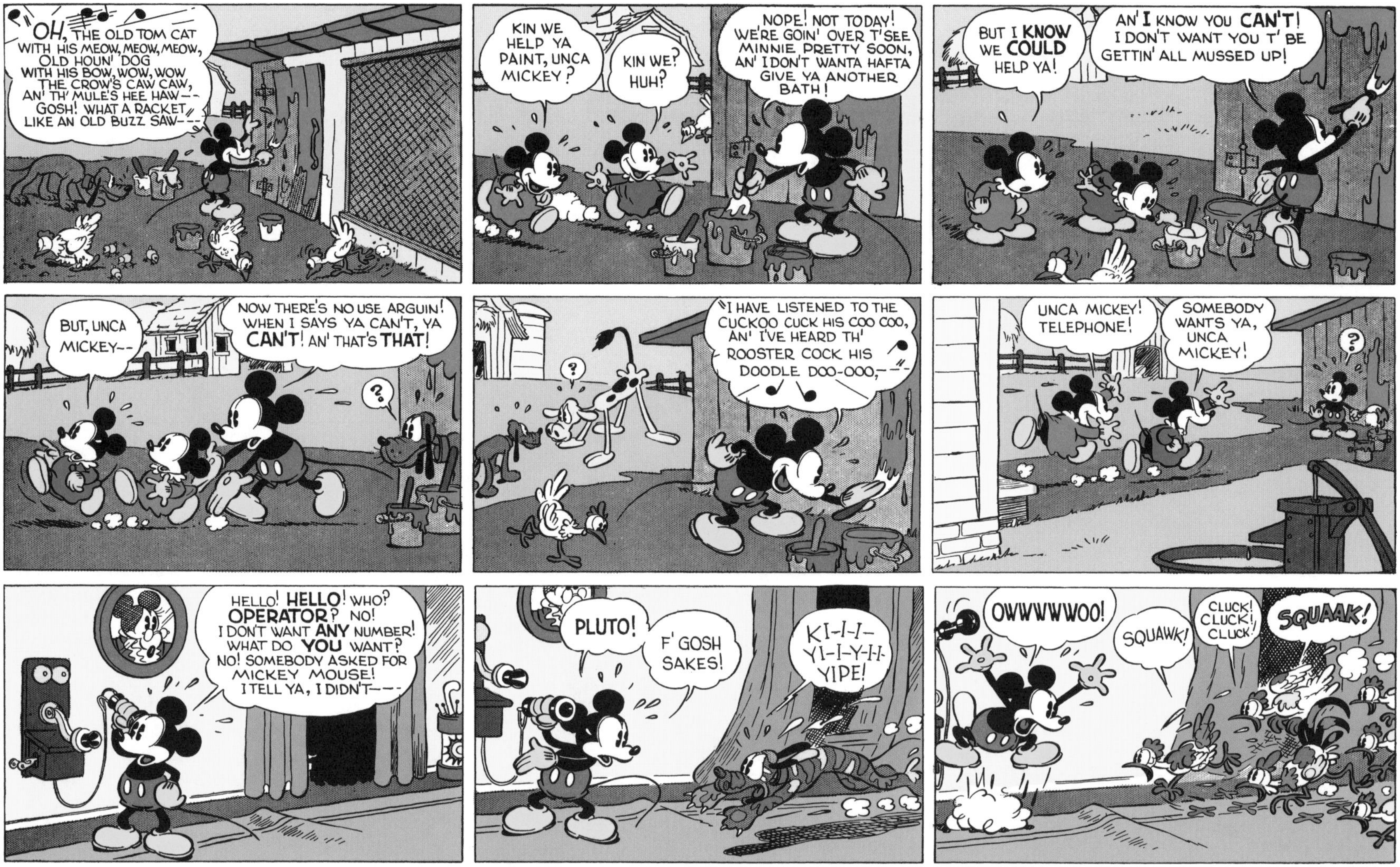
OH, THE OLD TOM CAT WITH HIS MEOW, MEOW, MEOW, OLD HOUN' DOG WITH HIS BOW, WOW, WOW THE CROW'S CAW CAW, AN' TH' MULE'S HEE HAW-- GOSH! WHAT A RACKET LIKE AN OLD BUZZ SAW---
KIN WE HELP YA PAINT, UNCA MICKEY?
KIN WE? HUH?
NOPE! NOT TODAY! WE'RE GOIN' OVER T'SEE MINNIE PRETTY SOON, AN' I DON'T WANTA HAFTA GIVE YA ANOTHER BATH!
BUT I KNOW WE COULD HELP YA!
AN' I KNOW YOU CAN'T! I DON'T WANT YOU T' BE GETTIN' ALL MUSSED UP!
BUT, UNCA MICKEY--
NOW THERE'S NO USE ARGUIN! WHEN I SAYS YA CAN'T, YA CAN'T! AN' THAT'S THAT!
?
?
I HAVE LISTENED TO THE CUCKOO CUCK HIS COO COO, AN' I'VE HEARD TH' ROOSTER COCK HIS DOODLE DOO-OOO,--
UNCA MICKEY! TELEPHONE!
SOMEBODY WANTS YA, UNCA MICKEY!
?
HELLO! HELLO! WHO? OPERATOR? NO! I DON'T WANT ANY NUMBER! WHAT DO YOU WANT? NO! SOMEBODY ASKED FOR MICKEY MOUSE! I TELL YA, I DIDN'T---
PLUTO!
F' GOSH SAKES!
KI-I-I-YI-I-Y-I-I-YIPE!
OWWWWWOO!
SQUAWK!
CLUCK! CLUCK! CLUCK!
SQUAAK!
THOSE DOGGONE KIDS!
WHEEE!
SEE, UNCLE MICKEY? I TOLD YA WE COULD HELP YA!
10-16
BUT TH' COWS AN' TH' CHICKENS, THEY ALL SOUND LIKE TH' DICKENS WHEN I HEAR MY LITTLE MINNIE'S YOO-HOO!
WALT DISNEY

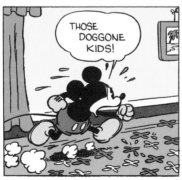

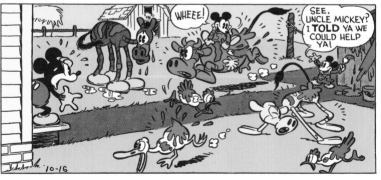

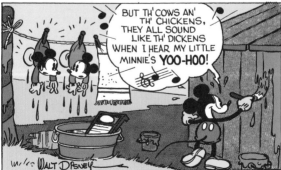

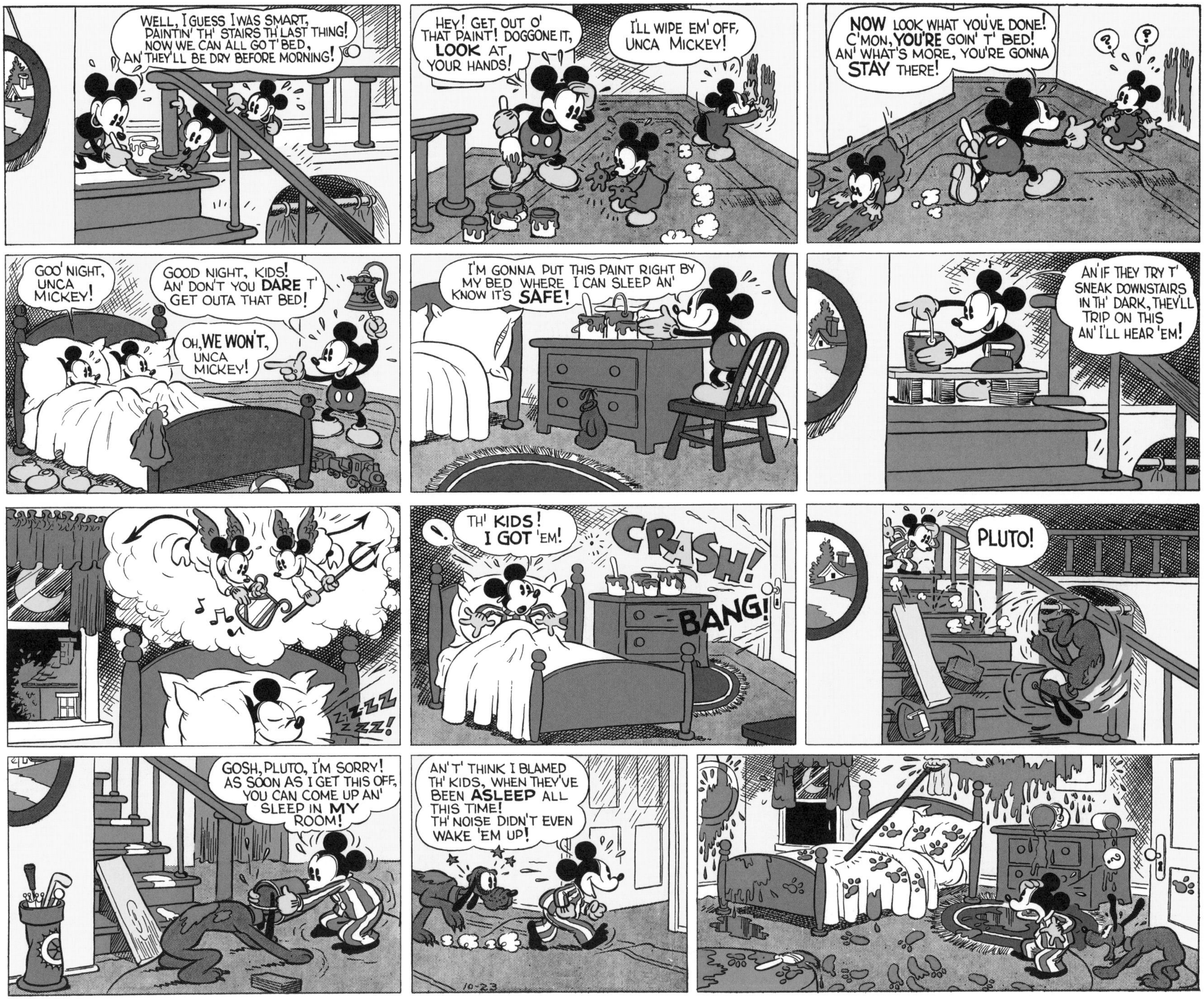
WELL, I GUESS I WAS SMART, PAINTIN' TH' STAIRS TH' LAST THING! NOW WE CAN ALL GO T' BED, AN' THEY'LL BE DRY BEFORE MORNING!
HEY! GET OUT O' THAT PAINT! DOGGONE IT, LOOK AT YOUR HANDS!
I'LL WIPE EM' OFF, UNCA MICKEY!
NOW LOOK WHAT YOU'VE DONE! C'MON, YOU'RE GOIN' T' BED! AN' WHAT'S MORE, YOU'RE GONNA STAY THERE!
?
?
GOO' NIGHT, UNCA MICKEY!
GOOD NIGHT, KIDS! AN' DON'T YOU DARE T' GET OUTA THAT BED!
OH, WE WON'T, UNCA MICKEY!
I'M GONNA PUT THIS PAINT RIGHT BY MY BED WHERE I CAN SLEEP AN' KNOW IT'S SAFE!
AN' IF THEY TRY T' SNEAK DOWNSTAIRS IN TH' DARK, THEY'LL TRIP ON THIS AN' I'LL HEAR 'EM!
ZZZZ ZZZZ!
!
TH' KIDS! I GOT 'EM!
CRASH!
BANG!
PLUTO!
GOSH, PLUTO, I'M SORRY! AS SOON AS I GET THIS OFF, YOU CAN COME UP AN' SLEEP IN MY ROOM!
AN' T' THINK I BLAMED TH' KIDS, WHEN THEY'VE BEEN ASLEEP ALL THIS TIME! TH' NOISE DIDN'T EVEN WAKE 'EM UP!
10-23

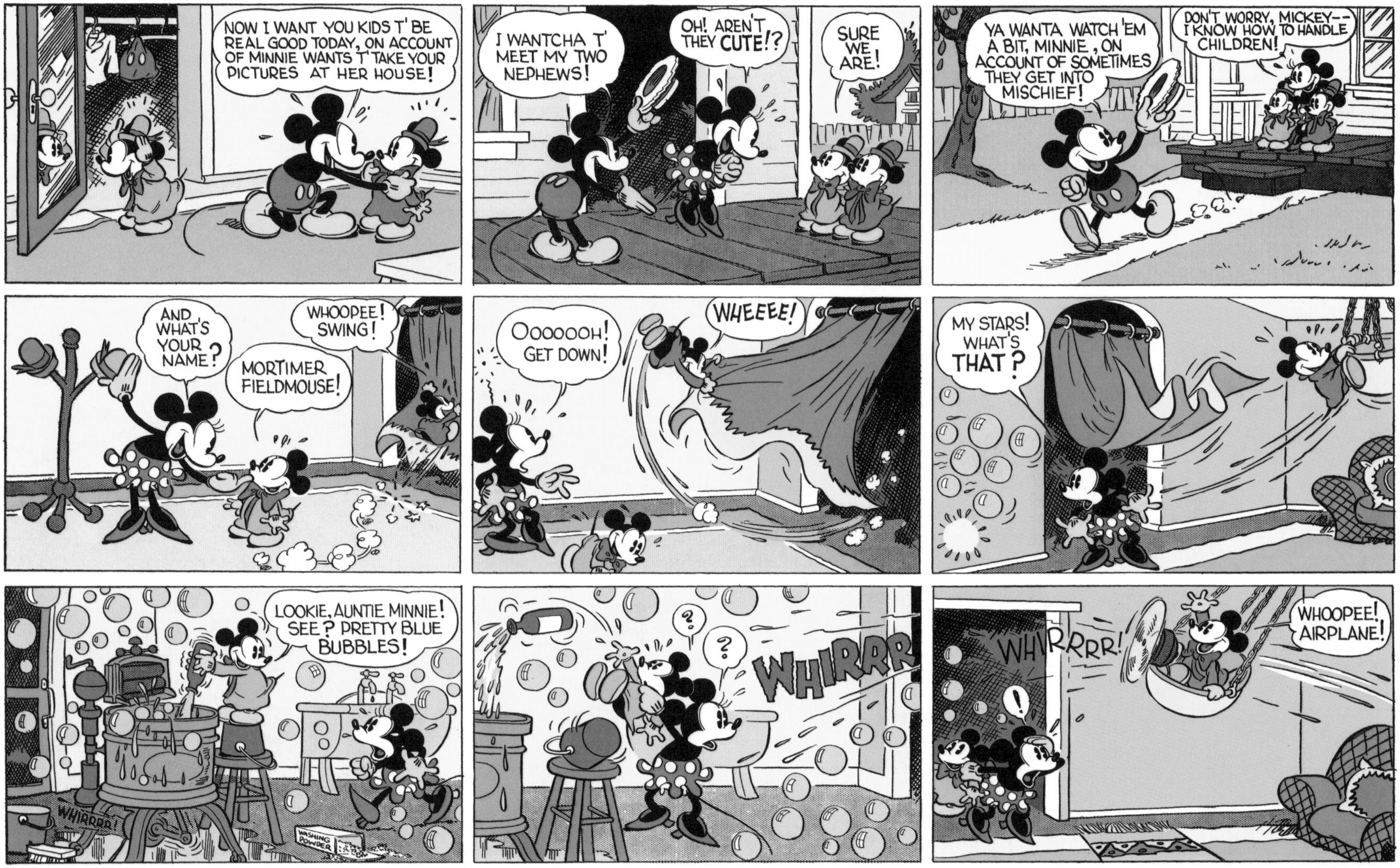
NOW I WANT YOU KIDS T' BE REAL GOOD TODAY, ON ACCOUNT OF MINNIE WANTS T' TAKE YOUR PICTURES AT HER HOUSE!
I WANTCHA T' MEET MY TWO NEPHEWS!
OH! AREN'T THEY CUTE!?
SURE WE ARE!
YA WANTA WATCH 'EM A BIT, MINNIE, ON ACCOUNT OF SOMETIMES THEY GET INTO MISCHIEF!
DON'T WORRY, MICKEY-- I KNOW HOW TO HANDLE CHILDREN!
AND WHAT'S YOUR NAME?
MORTIMER FIELDMOUSE!
WHOOPEE! SWING!
OOOOOOH! GET DOWN!
WHEEEE!
MY STARS! WHAT'S THAT?
LOOKIE, AUNTIE MINNIE! SEE? PRETTY BLUE BUBBLES!
WASHING POWDER
?
?
WHIRRR
WHIRRRR!
!
WHOOPEE! AIRPLANE!
YOU COME WITH ME! WE'RE GOING TO TAKE THAT PICTURE RIGHT NOW! AND NO MORE MONKEY BUSINESS!
THE NEXT DAY
MINNIE MOUSE ASKED ME T' GET A PICTURE SHE LEFT HERE YESTERDAY!
YES, SIR! HERE IT IS!
10-30
WALT DISNEY

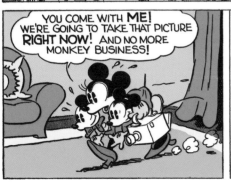

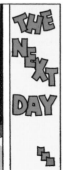

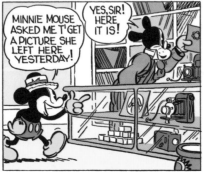

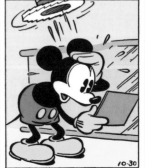

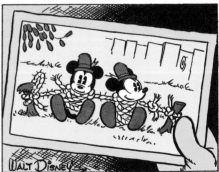

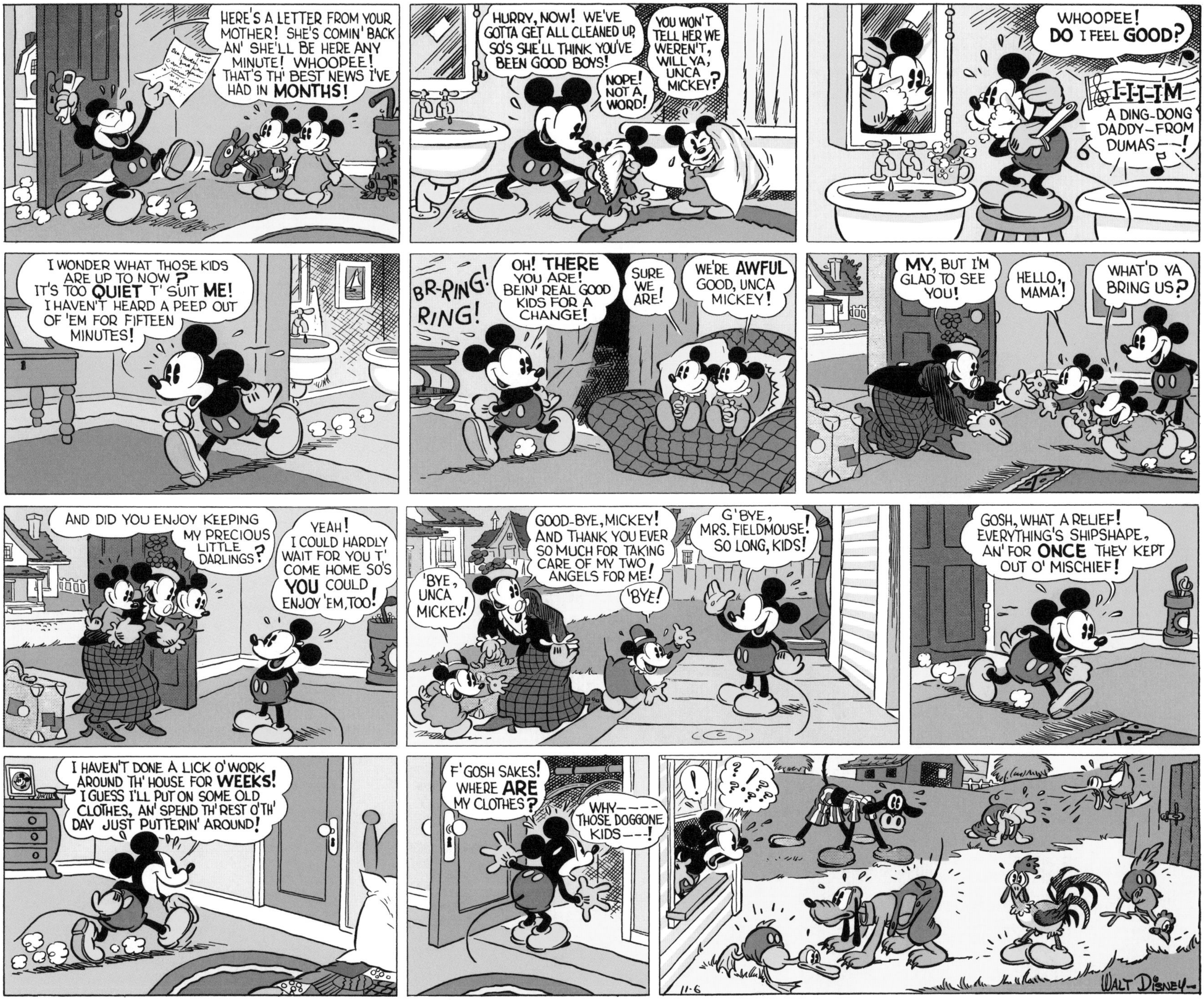
HERE'S A LETTER FROM YOUR MOTHER! SHE'S COMIN' BACK AN' SHE'LL BE HERE ANY MINUTE! WHOOPEE! THAT'S TH' BEST NEWS I'VE HAD IN MONTHS!
HURRY, NOW! WE'VE GOTTA GET ALL CLEANED UP, SO'S SHE'LL THINK YOU'VE BEEN GOOD BOYS!
YOU WON'T TELL HER WE WEREN'T, WILL YA, UNCA MICKEY?
NOPE! NOT A WORD!
WHOOPEE! DO I FEEL GOOD?
I-I-I-I'M A DING-DONG DADDY-FROM DUMAS---!
I WONDER WHAT THOSE KIDS ARE UP TO NOW? IT'S TOO QUIET T' SUIT ME! I HAVEN'T HEARD A PEEP OUT OF 'EM FOR FIFTEEN MINUTES!
BR-RING! RING!
OH! THERE YOU ARE! BEIN' REAL GOOD KIDS FOR A CHANGE!
SURE WE ARE!
WE'RE AWFUL GOOD, UNCA MICKEY!
MY, BUT I'M GLAD TO SEE YOU!
HELLO, MAMA!
WHAT'D YA BRING US?
AND DID YOU ENJOY KEEPING MY PRECIOUS LITTLE DARLINGS?
YEAH! I COULD HARDLY WAIT FOR YOU T' COME HOME SO'S YOU COULD ENJOY 'EM, TOO!
GOOD-BYE, MICKEY! AND THANK YOU EVER SO MUCH FOR TAKING CARE OF MY TWO ANGELS FOR ME!
'BYE, UNCA MICKEY!
'BYE!
G'BYE, MRS. FIELDMOUSE! SO LONG, KIDS!
GOSH, WHAT A RELIEF! EVERYTHING'S SHIPSHAPE, AN' FOR ONCE THEY KEPT OUT O' MISCHIEF!
I HAVEN'T DONE A LICK O' WORK AROUND TH' HOUSE FOR WEEKS! I GUESS I'LL PUT ON SOME OLD CLOTHES, AN' SPEND TH' REST O' TH' DAY JUST PUTTERIN' AROUND!
F' GOSH SAKES! WHERE ARE MY CLOTHES?
WHY---- THOSE DOGGONE KIDS---!
!
11-6
WALT DISNEY

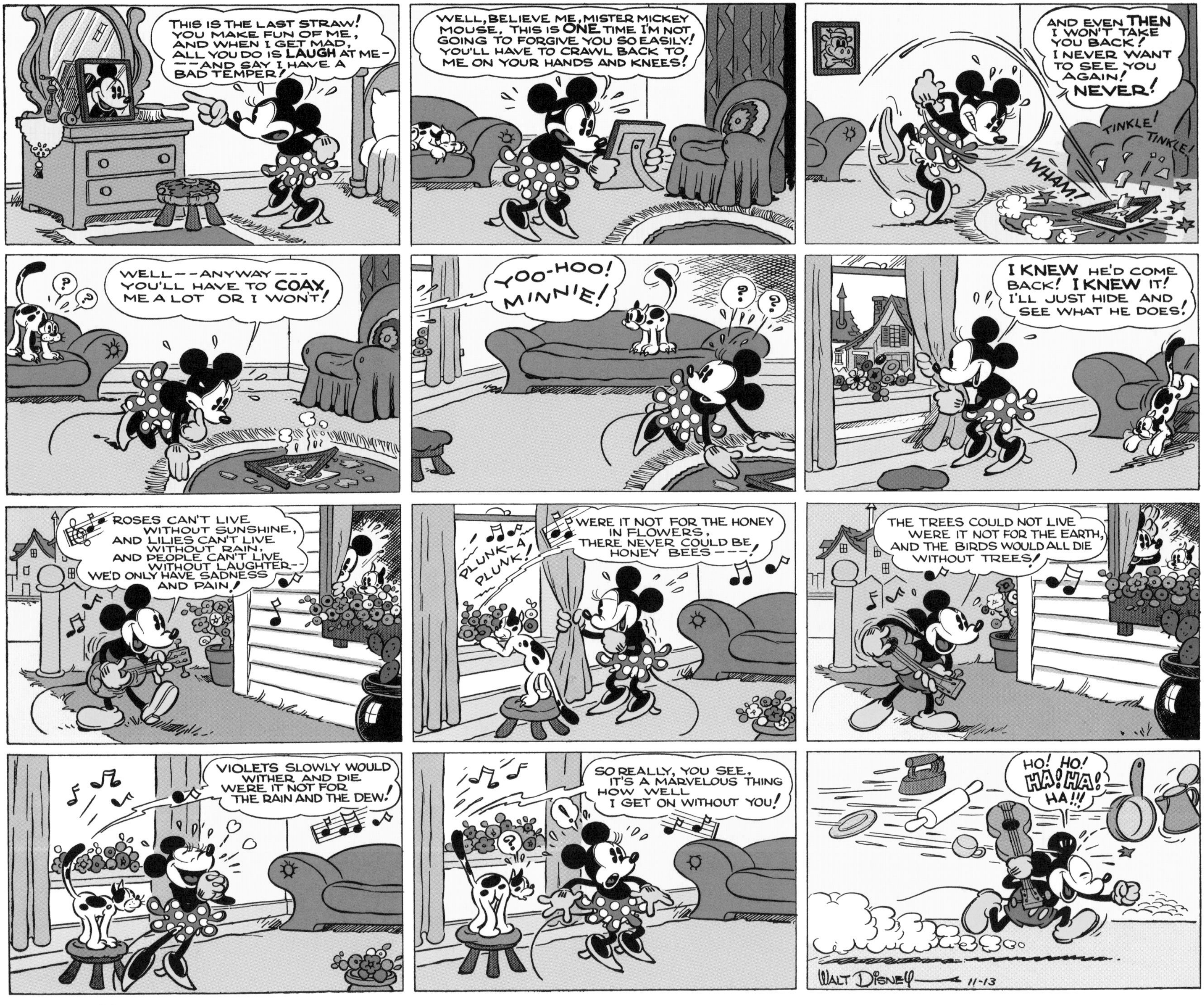
THIS IS THE LAST STRAW! YOU MAKE FUN OF ME, AND WHEN I GET MAD, ALL YOU DO IS LAUGH AT ME---AND SAY I HAVE A BAD TEMPER!
WELL, BELIEVE ME, MISTER MICKEY MOUSE, THIS IS ONE TIME I'M NOT GOING TO FORGIVE YOU SO EASILY! YOU'LL HAVE TO CRAWL BACK TO ME ON YOUR HANDS AND KNEES!
AND EVEN THEN I WON'T TAKE YOU BACK! I NEVER WANT TO SEE YOU AGAIN! NEVER!
TINKLE! TINKLE!
WHAM!
WELL--ANYWAY--- YOU'LL HAVE TO COAX ME A LOT OR I WON'T!
YOO-HOO! MINNIE!
I KNEW HE'D COME BACK! I KNEW IT! I'LL JUST HIDE AND SEE WHAT HE DOES!
ROSES CAN'T LIVE WITHOUT SUNSHINE, AND LILIES CAN'T LIVE WITHOUT RAIN, AND PEOPLE CAN'T LIVE WITHOUT LAUGHTER-- WE'D ONLY HAVE SADNESS AND PAIN!
PLUNK-A PLUNK!
WERE IT NOT FOR THE HONEY IN FLOWERS, THERE NEVER COULD BE HONEY BEES---!
THE TREES COULD NOT LIVE WERE IT NOT FOR THE EARTH, AND THE BIRDS WOULD ALL DIE WITHOUT TREES!
VIOLETS SLOWLY WOULD WITHER AND DIE WERE IT NOT FOR THE RAIN AND THE DEW!
SO REALLY, YOU SEE, IT'S A MARVELOUS THING HOW WELL I GET ON WITHOUT YOU!
HO! HO! HA! HA! HA!!!
WALT DISNEY 11-13

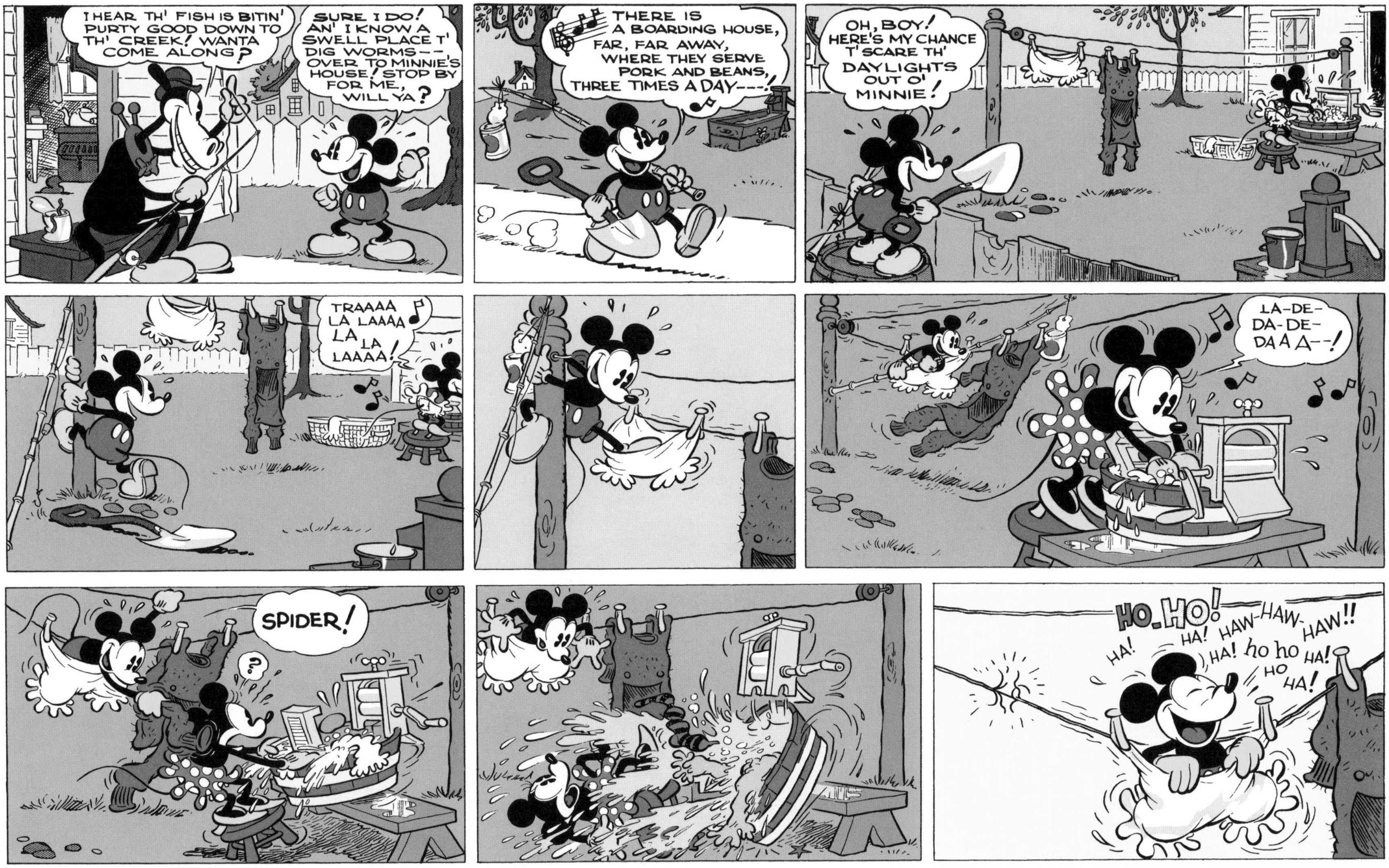
I HEAR TH' FISH IS BITIN' PURTY GOOD DOWN TO TH' CREEK! WANTA COME ALONG?
SURE I DO! AN' I KNOW A SWELL PLACE T' DIG WORMS-- OVER TO MINNIE'S HOUSE! STOP BY FOR ME, WILL YA?
THERE IS A BOARDING HOUSE, FAR, FAR AWAY, WHERE THEY SERVE PORK AND BEANS, THREE TIMES A DAY---!
OH, BOY! HERE'S MY CHANCE T' SCARE TH' DAYLIGHTS OUT O' MINNIE!
TRAAAA LA LAAAA LA LA LAAAA!
LA-DE-DA-DE-DA A A--!
SPIDER!
?
HO-HO! HA! HA! HAW-HAW-HAW!! HA! ho ho HA! HO HA!
HEY! WHAT TH!--!
!
SMACK!
!!!
???
11·20
???
TAP! TAP!

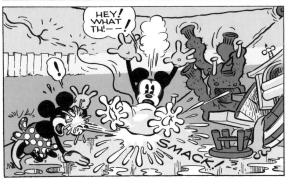

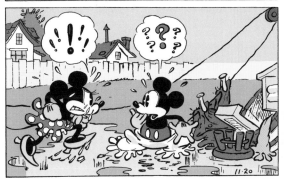

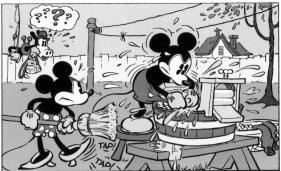

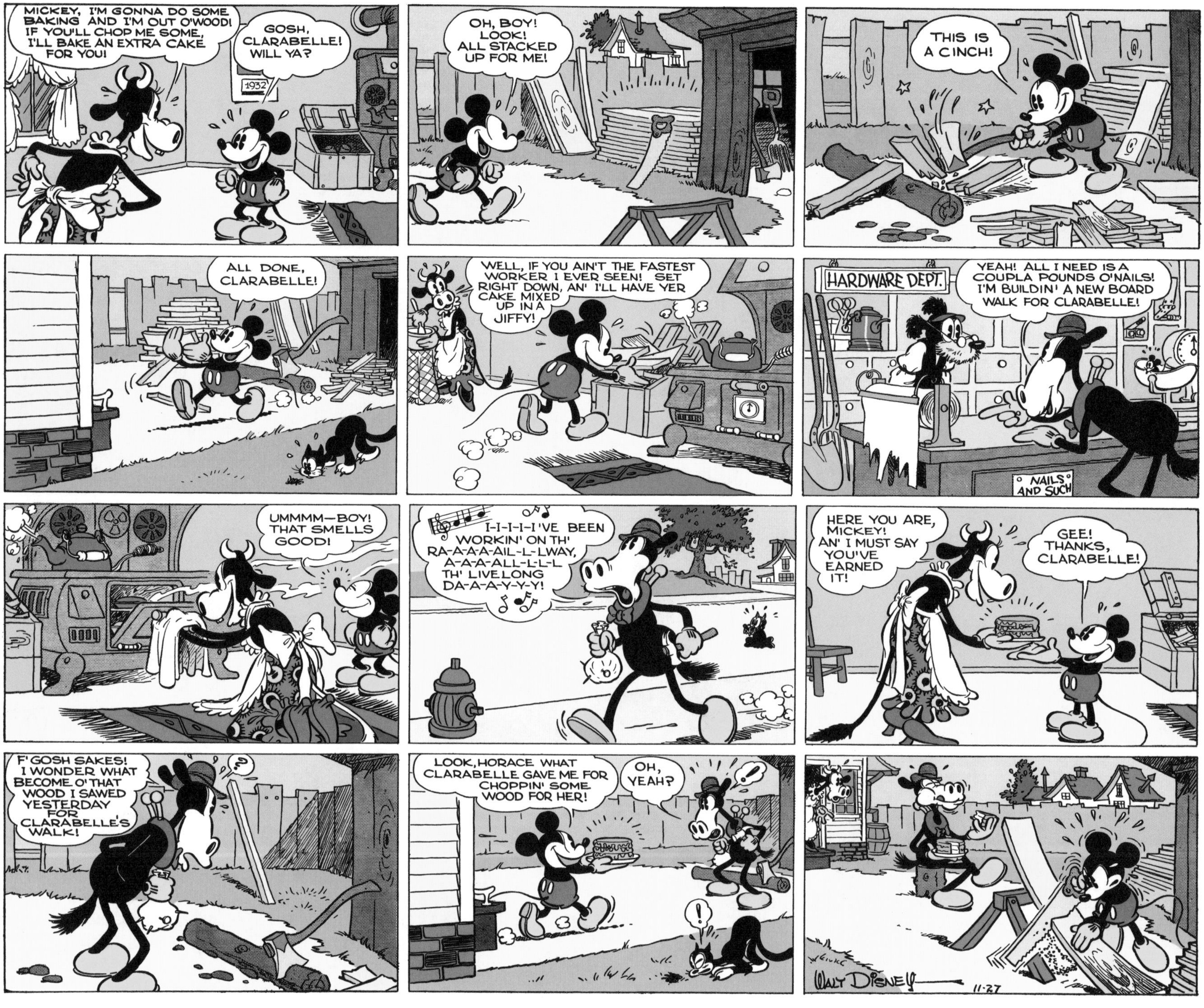
MICKEY, I'M GONNA DO SOME BAKING AND I'M OUT O'WOOD! IF YOU'LL CHOP ME SOME, I'LL BAKE AN EXTRA CAKE FOR YOU!
GOSH, CLARABELLE! WILL YA?
1932
OH, BOY! LOOK! ALL STACKED UP FOR ME!
THIS IS A CINCH!
ALL DONE, CLARABELLE!
WELL, IF YOU AIN'T THE FASTEST WORKER I EVER SEEN! SET RIGHT DOWN, AN' I'LL HAVE YER CAKE MIXED UP IN A JIFFY!
HARDWARE DEPT.
YEAH! ALL I NEED IS A COUPLA POUNDS O'NAILS! I'M BUILDIN' A NEW BOARD WALK FOR CLARABELLE!
NAILS AND SUCH
UMMMM—BOY! THAT SMELLS GOOD!
I-I-I-I-I'VE BEEN WORKIN' ON TH' RA-A-A-A-AIL-L-LWAY, A-A-A-ALL-L-L-L TH' LIVELONG DA-A-A-Y-Y-Y!
HERE YOU ARE, MICKEY! AN' I MUST SAY YOU'VE EARNED IT!
GEE! THANKS, CLARABELLE!
F'GOSH SAKES! I WONDER WHAT BECOME O' THAT WOOD I SAWED YESTERDAY FOR CLARABELLE'S WALK!
LOOK, HORACE WHAT CLARABELLE GAVE ME FOR CHOPPIN' SOME WOOD FOR HER!
OH, YEAH?
WALT DISNEY
11-27

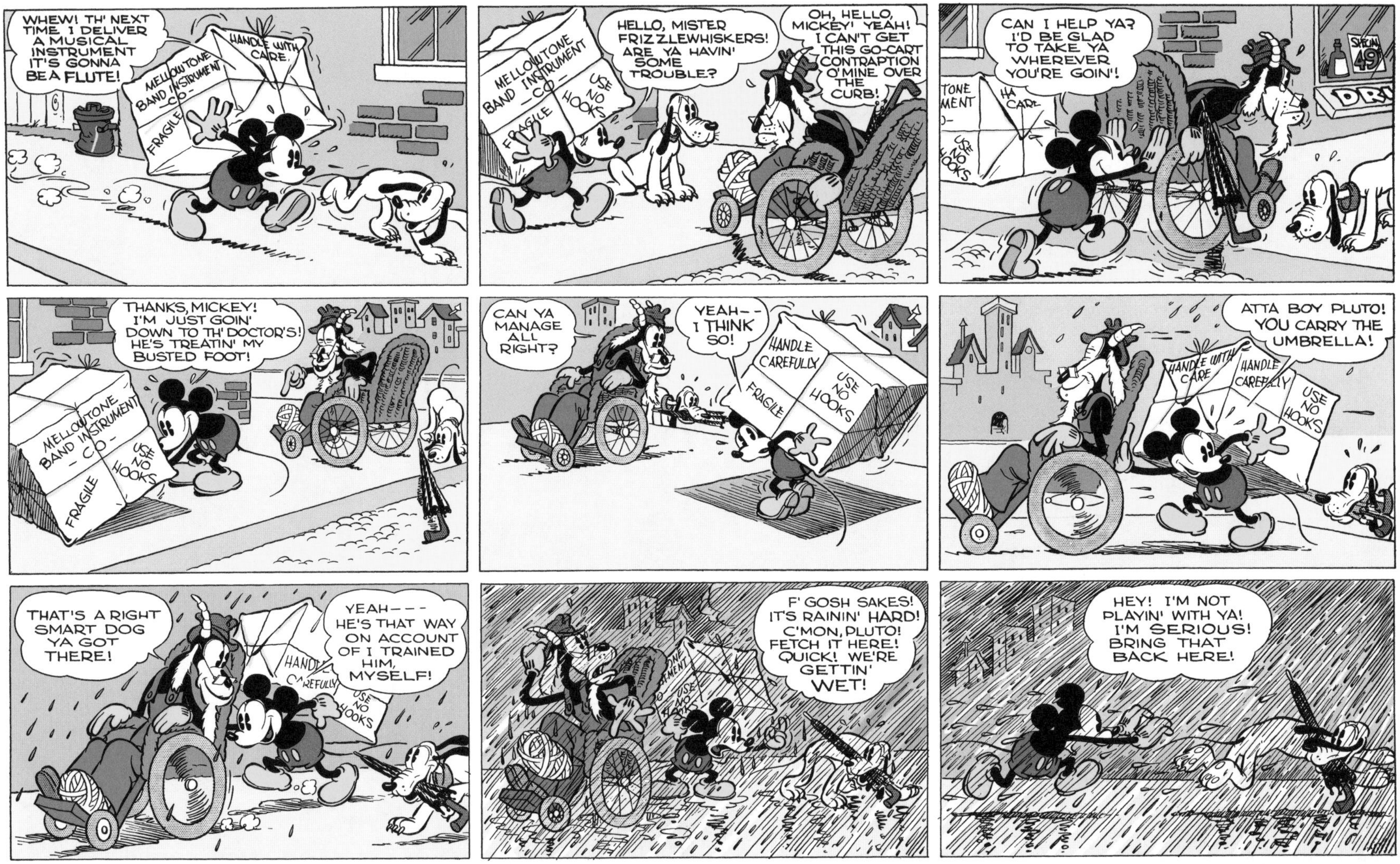
WHEW! TH' NEXT TIME I DELIVER A MUSICAL INSTRUMENT IT'S GONNA BE A FLUTE!
MELLOWTONE BAND INSTRUMENT — CO — FRAGILE
HANDLE WITH CARE.
HELLO, MISTER FRIZZLEWHISKERS! ARE YA HAVIN' SOME TROUBLE?
OH, HELLO, MICKEY! YEAH! I CAN'T GET THIS GO-CART CONTRAPTION O'MINE OVER THE CURB!
CAN I HELP YA? I'D BE GLAD TO TAKE YA WHEREVER YOU'RE GOIN'!
THANKS, MICKEY! I'M JUST GOIN' DOWN TO TH' DOCTOR'S! HE'S TREATIN' MY BUSTED FOOT!
CAN YA MANAGE ALL RIGHT?
YEAH-- I THINK SO!
ATTA BOY PLUTO! YOU CARRY THE UMBRELLA!
THAT'S A RIGHT SMART DOG YA GOT THERE!
YEAH--- HE'S THAT WAY ON ACCOUNT OF I TRAINED HIM, MYSELF!
F' GOSH SAKES! IT'S RAININ' HARD! C'MON, PLUTO! FETCH IT HERE! QUICK! WE'RE GETTIN' WET!
HEY! I'M NOT PLAYIN' WITH YA! I'M SERIOUS! BRING THAT BACK HERE!
HE WON'T DO IT! HE THINKS I'M JUST KIDDIN!
BUT HOW ABOUT ME? IF I GET WET, I'LL GET TH' RHEU-MATIZ!
DON'T WORRY! I'LL FIX IT FOR YA!
I'M A RED HOT BO, FULL O' VO-DE-O-DO, AN MY SONG IS HOT-CHA-CHA--!
©1932, by Walt Disney Enterprises, Great Britain rights reserved
WALT DISNEY 12-4

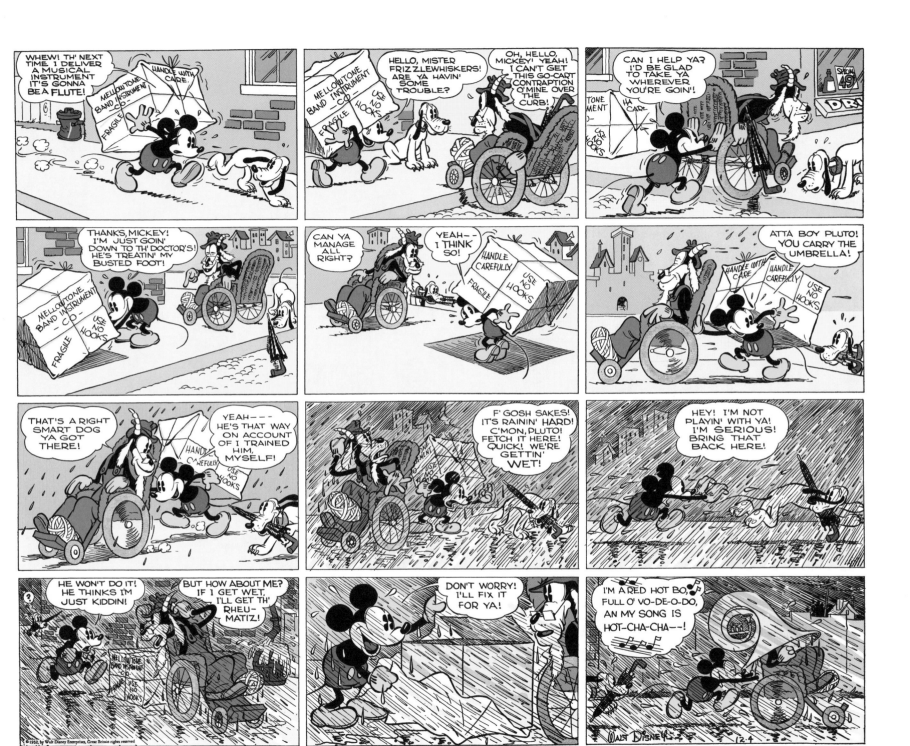

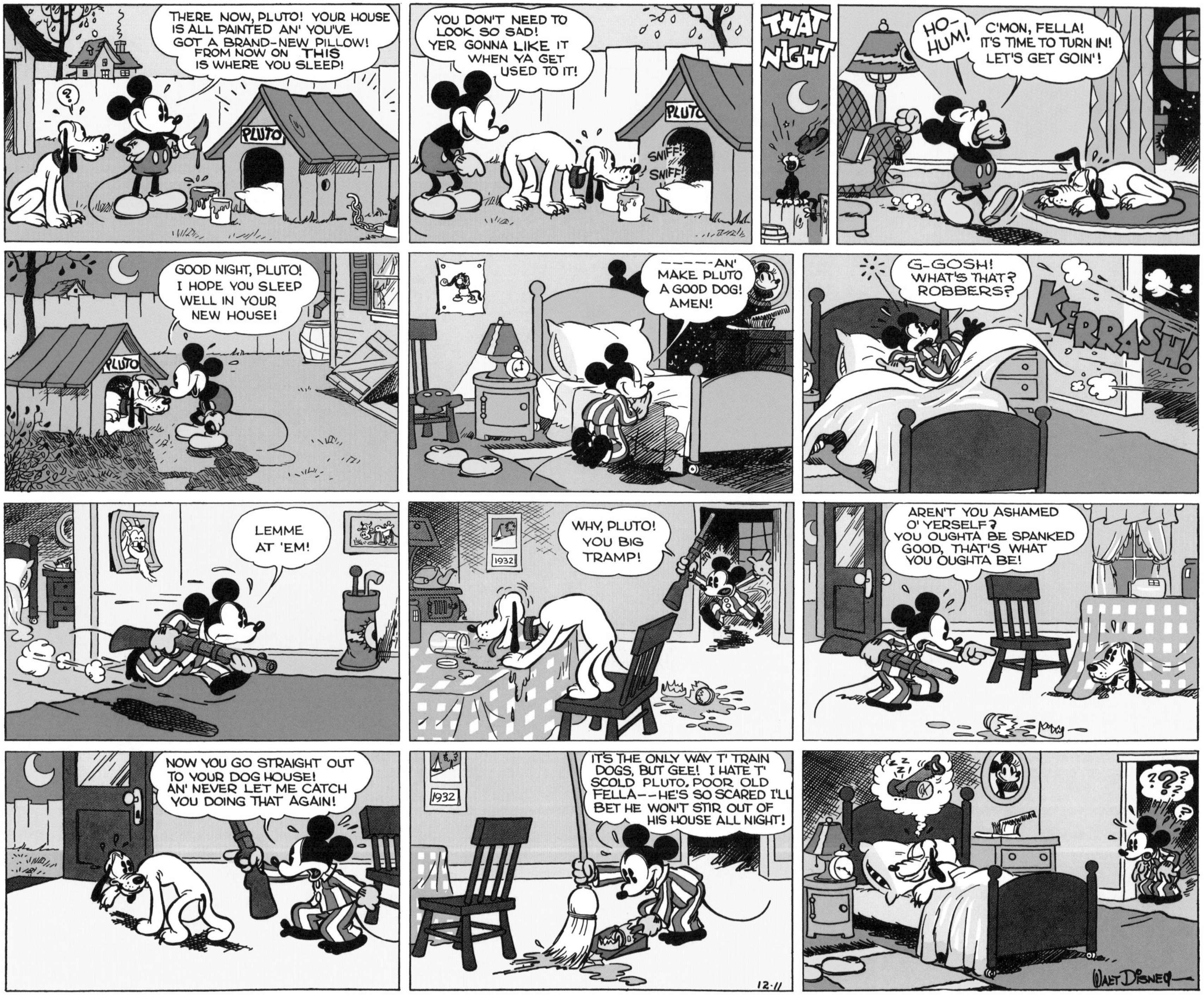
THERE NOW, PLUTO! YOUR HOUSE IS ALL PAINTED AN' YOU'VE GOT A BRAND-NEW PILLOW! FROM NOW ON THIS IS WHERE YOU SLEEP!
PLUTO
YOU DON'T NEED TO LOOK SO SAD! YER GONNA LIKE IT WHEN YA GET USED TO IT!
SNIFF! SNIFF!
THAT NIGHT
HO-HUM!
C'MON, FELLA! IT'S TIME TO TURN IN! LET'S GET GOIN'!
GOOD NIGHT, PLUTO! I HOPE YOU SLEEP WELL IN YOUR NEW HOUSE!
-----AN' MAKE PLUTO A GOOD DOG! AMEN!
G-GOSH! WHAT'S THAT? ROBBERS?
KERRASH!
LEMME AT 'EM!
1932
WHY, PLUTO! YOU BIG TRAMP!
AREN'T YOU ASHAMED O' YERSELF? YOU OUGHTA BE SPANKED GOOD, THAT'S WHAT YOU OUGHTA BE!
NOW YOU GO STRAIGHT OUT TO YOUR DOG HOUSE! AN' NEVER LET ME CATCH YOU DOING THAT AGAIN!
IT'S THE ONLY WAY T' TRAIN DOGS, BUT GEE! I HATE T' SCOLD PLUTO, POOR OLD FELLA--HE'S SO SCARED I'LL BET HE WON'T STIR OUT OF HIS HOUSE ALL NIGHT!
12-11
WALT DISNEY

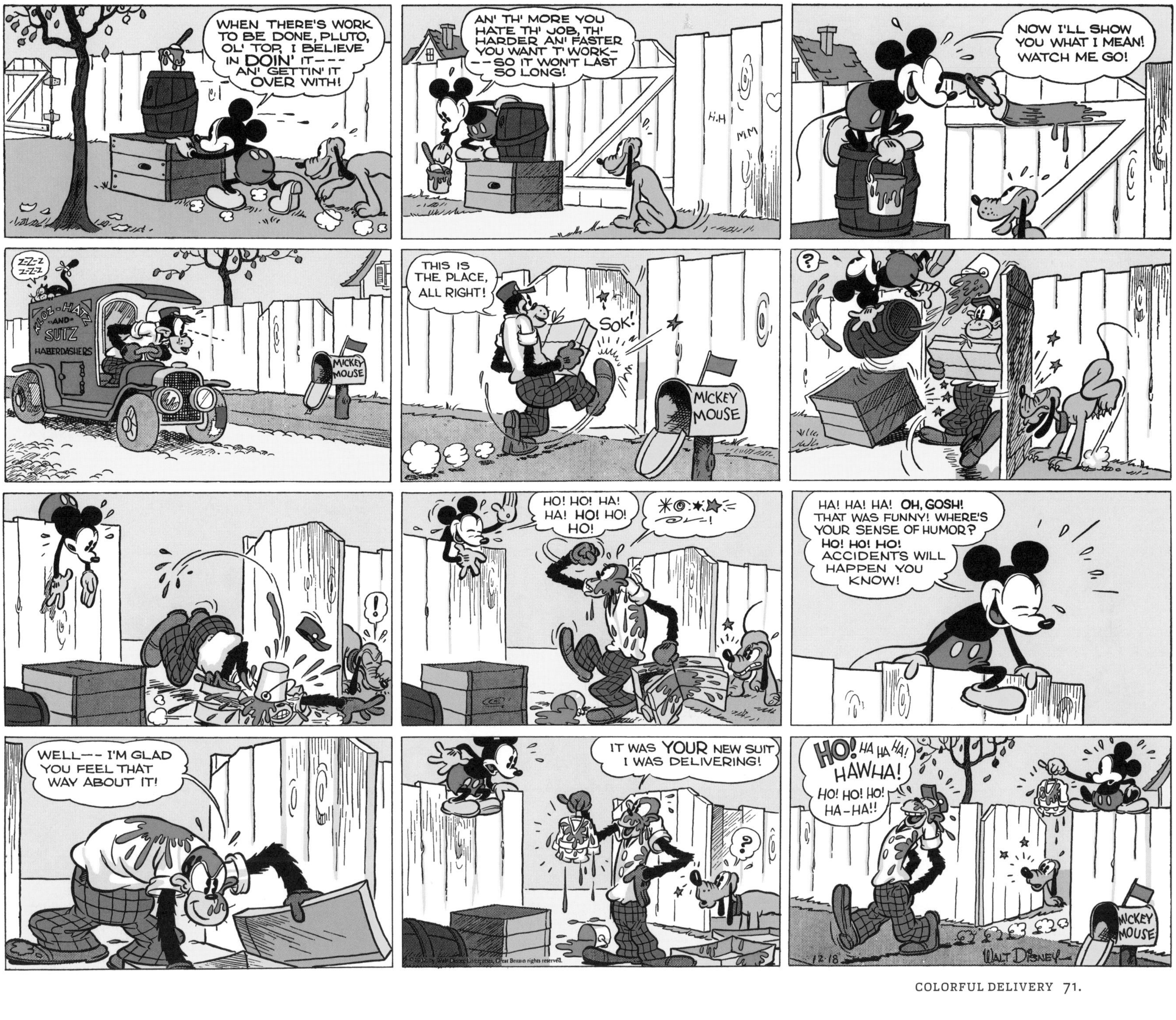
WHEN THERE'S WORK TO BE DONE, PLUTO, OL' TOP, I BELIEVE IN DOIN' IT--- AN' GETTIN' IT OVER WITH!
AN' TH' MORE YOU HATE TH' JOB, TH' HARDER AN' FASTER YOU WANT T' WORK--- SO IT WON'T LAST SO LONG!
H.H
M.M
NOW I'LL SHOW YOU WHAT I MEAN! WATCH ME GO!
Z-Z-Z Z-Z-Z
KLOZ-HATZ -AND- SUTZ HABERDASHERS
MICKEY MOUSE
THIS IS THE PLACE, ALL RIGHT!
SOK!
MICKEY MOUSE
?
!
HO! HO! HA! HA! HO! HO! HO!
HA! HA! HA! OH, GOSH! THAT WAS FUNNY! WHERE'S YOUR SENSE OF HUMOR? HO! HO! HO! ACCIDENTS WILL HAPPEN YOU KNOW!
WELL-- I'M GLAD YOU FEEL THAT WAY ABOUT IT!
IT WAS YOUR NEW SUIT I WAS DELIVERING!
?
HO! HA HA HA! HAWHA! HO! HO! HO! HA-HA!!
MICKEY MOUSE
12/18
WALT DISNEY

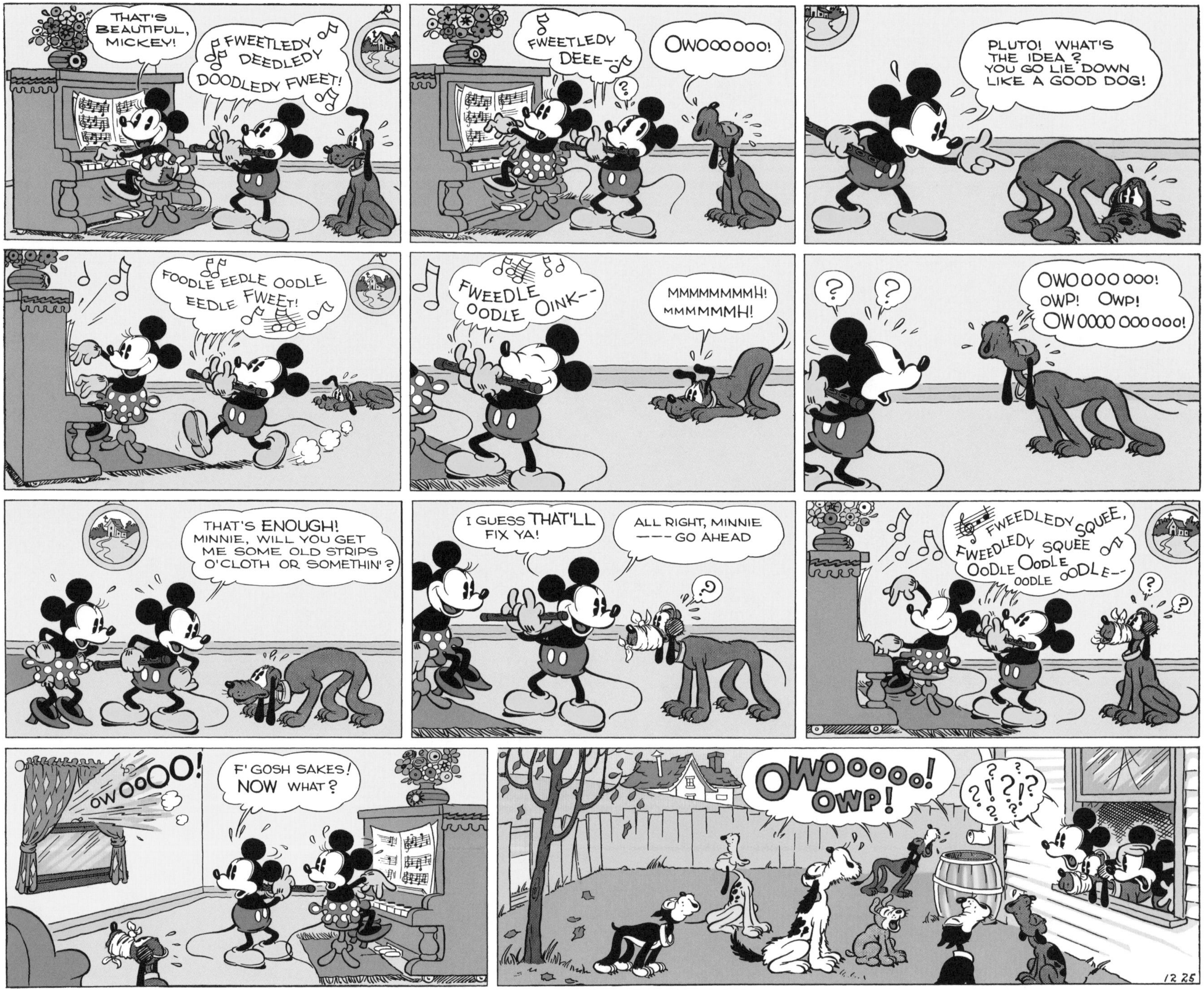
THAT'S BEAUTIFUL, MICKEY!
FWEETLEDY DEEDLEDY DOODLEDY FWEET!
FWEETLEDY DEEE--
OWOOOOOO!
PLUTO! WHAT'S THE IDEA ? YOU GO LIE DOWN LIKE A GOOD DOG!
FOODLE EEDLE OODLE EEDLE FWEET!
FWEEDLE OODLE OINK--
MMMMMMMMH! MMMMMMH!
OWO OOO OOO! OWP! OWP! OW OOOO OOO OOO!
THAT'S ENOUGH! MINNIE, WILL YOU GET ME SOME OLD STRIPS O'CLOTH OR SOMETHIN'?
I GUESS THAT'LL FIX YA!
ALL RIGHT, MINNIE --- GO AHEAD
FWEEDLEDY SQUEE, FWEEDLEDY SQUEE OODLE OODLE OODLE OODLE--
OW OOOO!
F' GOSH SAKES! NOW WHAT?
OWOOOOOO! OWP!
12 25

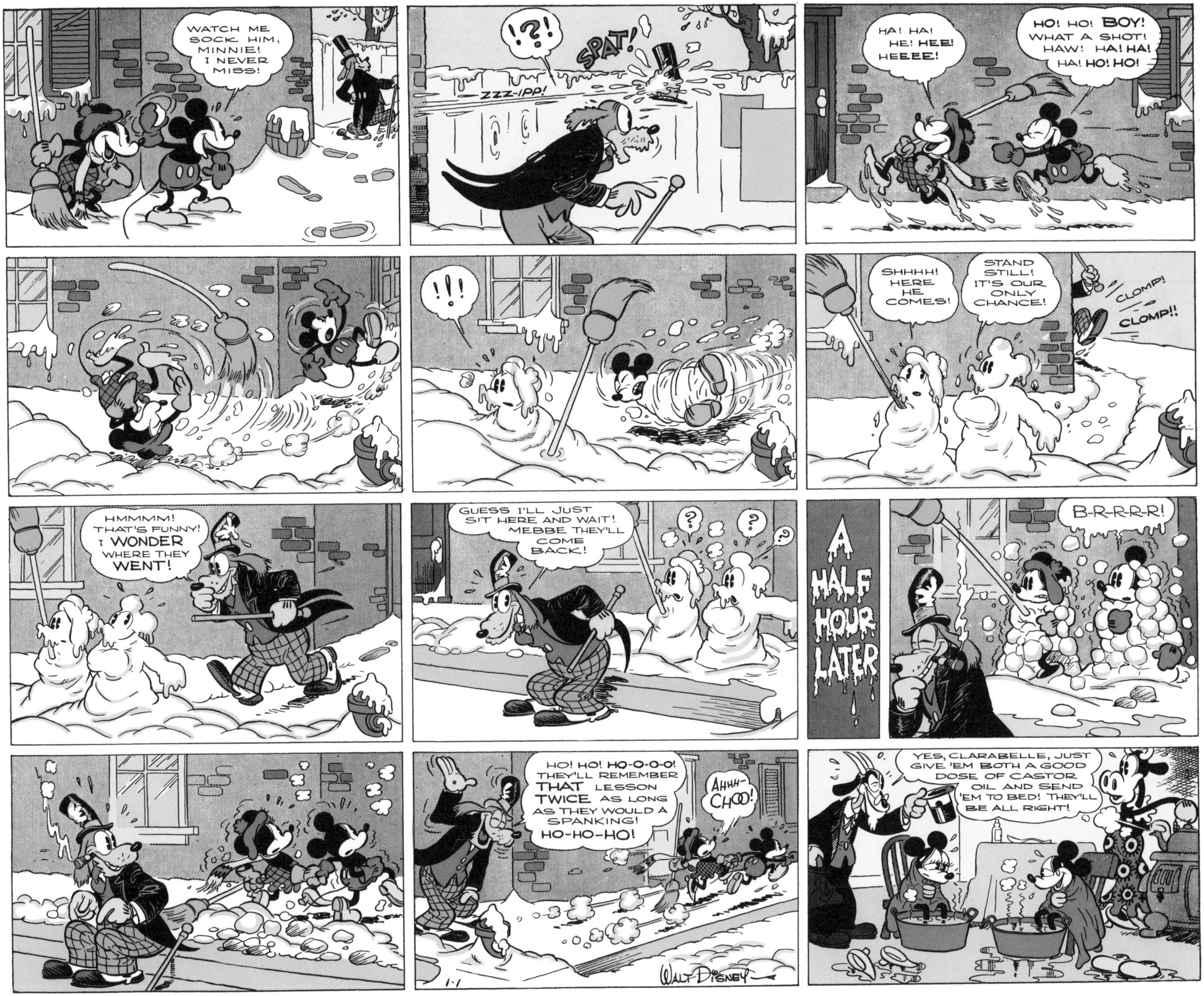
WATCH ME SOCK HIM, MINNIE! I NEVER MISS!
!?!
SPAT!
ZZZ-IPP!
HA! HA! HE! HEE! HEEEE!
HO! HO! BOY! WHAT A SHOT! HAW! HA! HA! HA! HO! HO!
!!!
SHHHH! HERE HE COMES!
STAND STILL! IT'S OUR ONLY CHANCE!
CLOMP!
CLOMP!!
HMMMM! THAT'S FUNNY! I WONDER WHERE THEY WENT!
GUESS I'LL JUST SIT HERE AND WAIT! MEBBE THEY'LL COME BACK!
?
?
?
A HALF HOUR LATER
B-R-R-R-R!
HO! HO! HO-O-O-O! THEY'LL REMEMBER THAT LESSON TWICE AS LONG AS THEY WOULD A SPANKING! HO-HO-HO!
AHHH-CHOO!
1-1
WALT DISNEY
YES, CLARABELLE, JUST GIVE 'EM BOTH A GOOD DOSE OF CASTOR OIL AND SEND 'EM TO BED! THEY'LL BE ALL RIGHT!

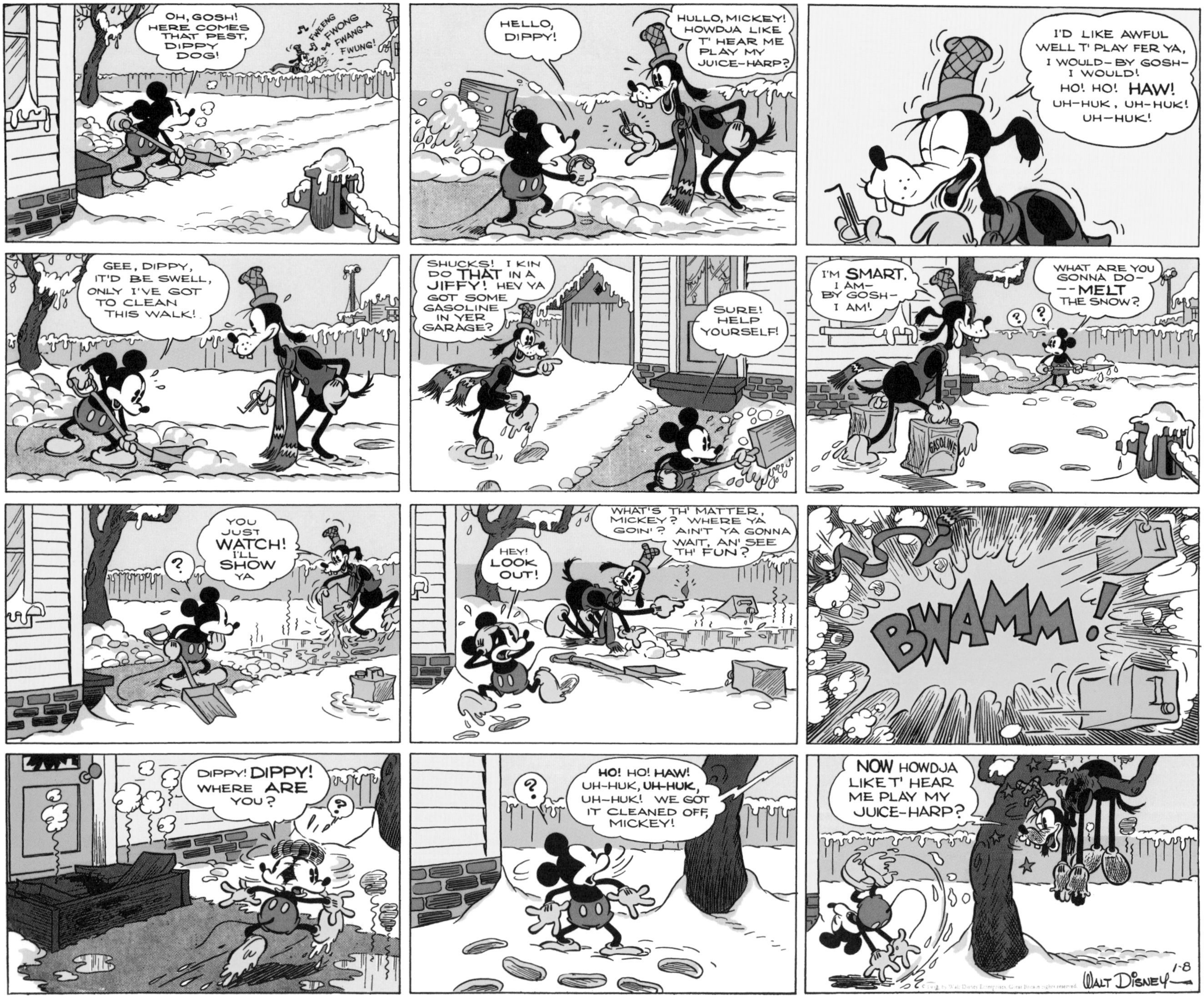
OH, GOSH! HERE COMES THAT PEST, DIPPY DOG!
FWEENG FWONG FWANG-A FWUNG!
HELLO, DIPPY!
HULLO, MICKEY! HOWDJA LIKE T' HEAR ME PLAY MY JUICE-HARP?
I'D LIKE AWFUL WELL T' PLAY FER YA, I WOULD–BY GOSH–I WOULD! HO! HO! HAW! UH-HUK, UH-HUK! UH-HUK!
GEE, DIPPY, IT'D BE SWELL, ONLY I'VE GOT TO CLEAN THIS WALK!
SHUCKS! I KIN DO THAT IN A JIFFY! HEV YA GOT SOME GASOLINE IN YER GARAGE?
SURE! HELP YOURSELF!
I'M SMART, I AM–BY GOSH–I AM!
WHAT ARE YOU GONNA DO– –MELT THE SNOW?
GASOLINE
?
YOU JUST WATCH! I'LL SHOW YA
WHAT'S TH' MATTER, MICKEY? WHERE YA GOIN'? AIN'T YA GONNA WAIT, AN' SEE TH' FUN?
HEY! LOOK OUT!
BWAMM!
DIPPY! DIPPY! WHERE ARE YOU?
?
HO! HO! HAW! UH-HUK, UH-HUK, UH-HUK! WE GOT IT CLEANED OFF, MICKEY!
NOW HOWDJA LIKE T' HEAR ME PLAY MY JUICE-HARP?
1-8
WALT DISNEY

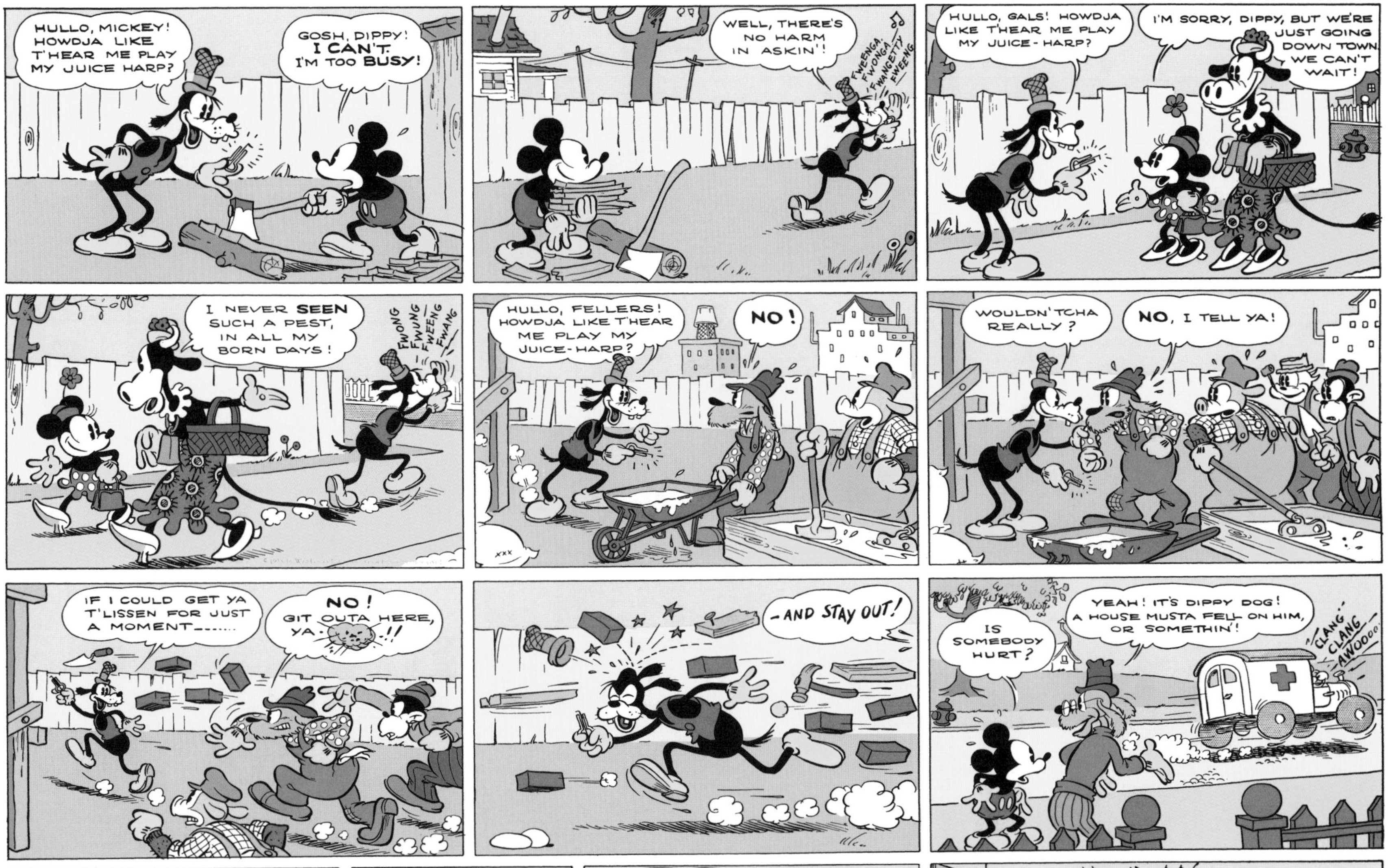
HULLO, MICKEY! HOWDJA LIKE T'HEAR ME PLAY MY JUICE HARP?
GOSH, DIPPY! I CAN'T. I'M TOO BUSY!
WELL, THERE'S NO HARM IN ASKIN'!
FWEENGA, FWONGA, FWANGETTY FWEENG
HULLO, GALS! HOWDJA LIKE T'HEAR ME PLAY MY JUICE-HARP?
I'M SORRY, DIPPY, BUT WE'RE JUST GOING DOWN TOWN. WE CAN'T WAIT!
I NEVER SEEN SUCH A PEST, IN ALL MY BORN DAYS!
FWONG FWUNG FWEENG FWANG
HULLO, FELLERS! HOWDJA LIKE T'HEAR ME PLAY MY JUICE-HARP?
NO!
WOULDN'TCHA REALLY?
NO, I TELL YA!
IF I COULD GET YA T'LISSEN FOR JUST A MOMENT—.......
NO! GIT OUTA HERE, YA
—AND STAY OUT!
IS SOMEBODY HURT?
YEAH! IT'S DIPPY DOG! A HOUSE MUSTA FELL ON HIM, OR SOMETHIN'!
CLANG CLANG AWOOO
HE'LL PULL THROUGH ALL RIGHT. LET'S GO AWAY, AND LET HIM SLEEP.
M.D.
HOWDJA LIKE T'HEAR ME PLAY MY JUICE-HARP?
THAT'S EVER SO KIND OF YOU!
UMPH! GLOPH! OLPH!
FWING FWANG FWANGA FWONG
WALT DISNEY 1-15

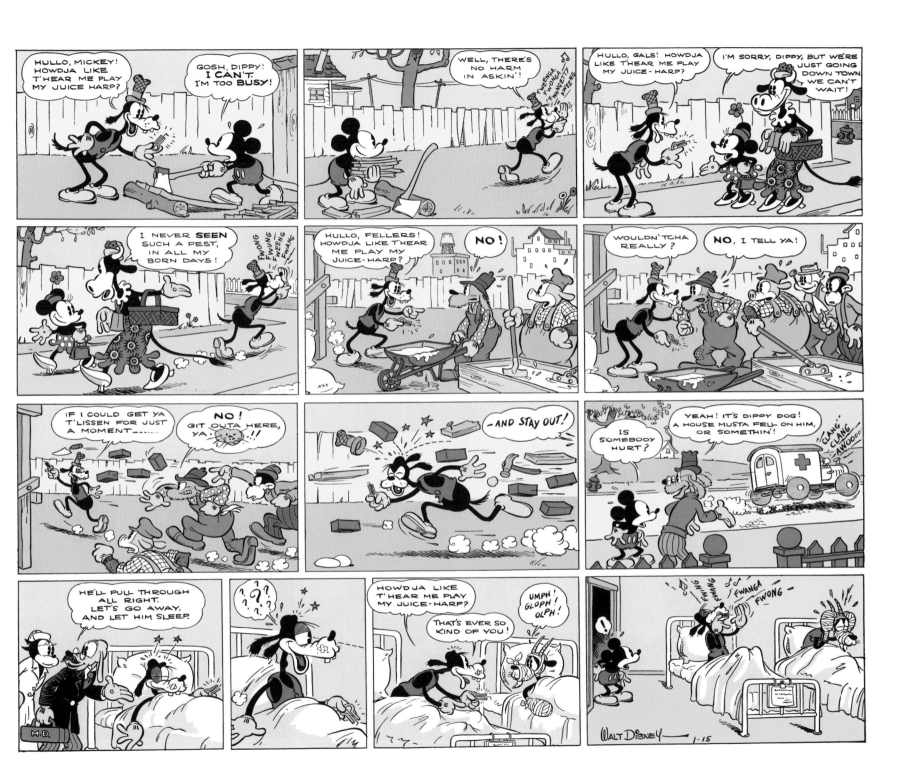

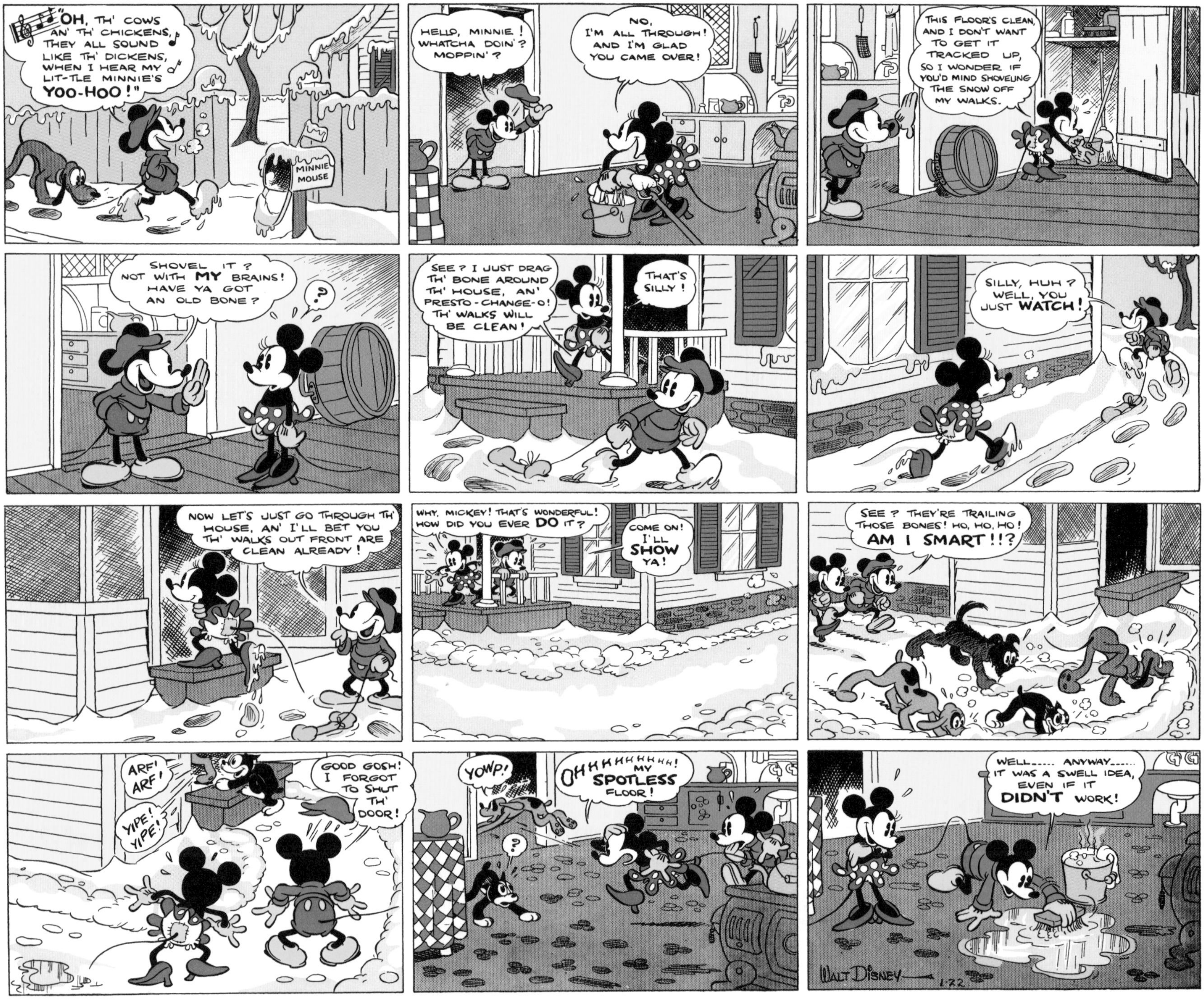
"OH, TH' COWS AN' TH' CHICKENS, THEY ALL SOUND LIKE TH' DICKENS, WHEN I HEAR MY LIT-TLE MINNIE'S YOO-HOO!"
MINNIE MOUSE
HELLO, MINNIE! WHATCHA DOIN'? MOPPIN'?
NO, I'M ALL THROUGH! AND I'M GLAD YOU CAME OVER!
THIS FLOOR'S CLEAN, AND I DON'T WANT TO GET IT TRACKED UP, SO I WONDER IF YOU'D MIND SHOVELING THE SNOW OFF MY WALKS.
SHOVEL IT? NOT WITH MY BRAINS! HAVE YA GOT AN OLD BONE?
?
SEE? I JUST DRAG TH' BONE AROUND TH' HOUSE, AN' PRESTO-CHANGE-O! TH' WALKS WILL BE CLEAN!
THAT'S SILLY!
SILLY, HUH? WELL, YOU JUST WATCH!
NOW LET'S JUST GO THROUGH TH' HOUSE, AN' I'LL BET YOU TH' WALKS OUT FRONT ARE CLEAN ALREADY!
WHY, MICKEY! THAT'S WONDERFUL! HOW DID YOU EVER DO IT?
COME ON! I'LL SHOW YA!
SEE? THEY'RE TRAILING THOSE BONES! HO, HO, HO! AM I SMART!!?
ARF! ARF!
YIPE! YIPE!
GOOD GOSH! I FORGOT TO SHUT TH' DOOR!
YOWP!
?
OHHHHHHHHH! MY SPOTLESS FLOOR!
WELL..... ANYWAY..... IT WAS A SWELL IDEA, EVEN IF IT DIDN'T WORK!
WALT DISNEY 1-22

THE LAIR OF WOLF BARKER AND GAG STRIPS

JANUARY 29, 1933
–
MARCH 4, 1934

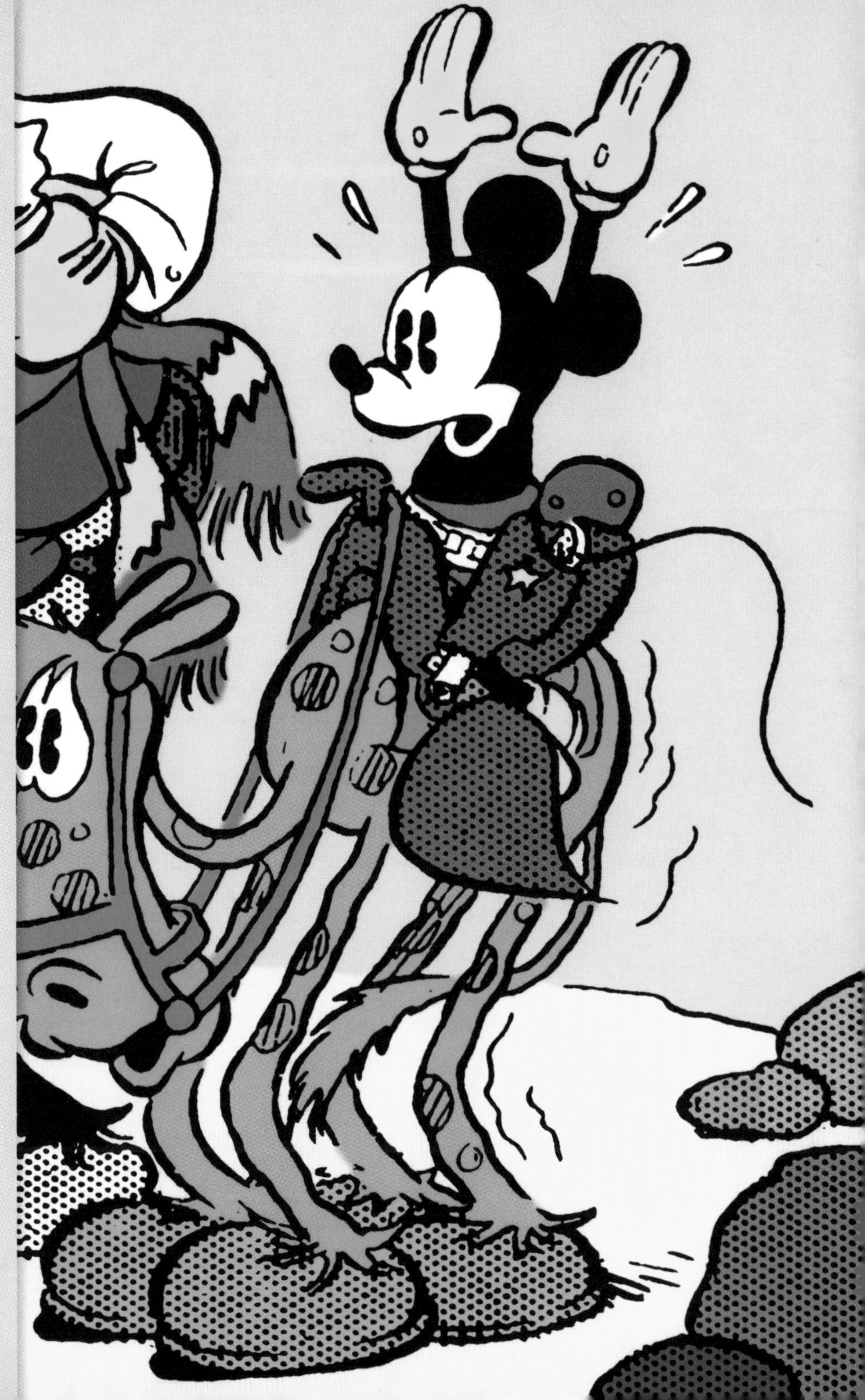

MICKEY MOUSE

REGISTERED U.S. PATENT OFFICE

MICKEY'S DELAYED DRAMA

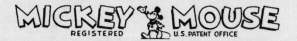

Once again, a letter with a plea for help calls Mickey and friends to action. But this time the "action" is not quite a grand adventure in some exotic locale. It's merely a task, looking after Uncle Mortimer's cattle ranch in his absence—and, despite a definite change of scenery, this particular "Far West" doesn't actually feel that far from home; certainly not when compared to, say, Treasure Island or other daily strip locales.

The first few scene-setting weeks of "Wolf Barker" are full of cartoon-like humor. Dippy Dog continues to upset everyone with his noisy juice-harp. Horace attempts to look cool in his cowboy outfit, but his misplaced pride hilariously backfires. Don Poocho, the fat foreman with the Hispanic accent, is instantly made funny by his plump looks and overly laidback attitude—and funnier still when a mouthful of Tabasco sauce puts an abrupt stop to his musical performance. We also smile at Poocho's quick wits, as when he tricks and deters Wolf Barker's bandits by demonstrating Mickey's alleged sharpshooting prowess.

It's all a laugh; especially when Minnie, not to be outdone by Mickey's tracking skill, discovers a "cow's nest" with delightful naïveté. Even the gangsters that stop the stagecoach—with the intention of robbing the passengers and kidnapping the girl—cannot be taken too seriously; they are scared away by a walking luggage-trunk.

In the end, though, our suspension of disbelief gets turned up a couple of notches—from a "Sunday strip mood" to a "daily strip mood," one might say—and we do get our dose of proper adventure. Once again we see Gottfredson's classic Mickey leitmotivs: the glorious Horatio Alger hero; the conflict between David and Goliath; and the victory of intelligence over brute force, particularly at the climax of the fight between Mickey and Wolf Barker in a dilapidated cabin.

It is fascinating to note the evolution of Mickey's partners in his escapades. In 1933, Dippy has yet to morph into the more well-rounded character of Goofy: he is not merely simpleminded—as when he hands over his friends' luggage to a junk dealer—but peskily mischievous, as when he stows away in Clarabelle's trunk, throwing out her clothes in the process. Dippy is mostly part of the story for comic relief: it is still Horace who plays the role of Mickey's buddy during the actual rustler-chasing adventure, as he did in the contemporary daily serial "Blaggard Castle" (1932-33). The resourceful Horace Horsecollar can serenade his girl (albeit with dubious results) and is capable of wielding a revolver (well, almost), while the dimwitted Dippy Dog is not capable of handling much more than his annoying juice-harp.

But just give it a few more years. Once Dippy matures into Goofy, he will take over Horace's buddy role, causing the humanized horse to all but disappear from the strip.

—LEONARDO GORI AND FRANCESCO STAJANO

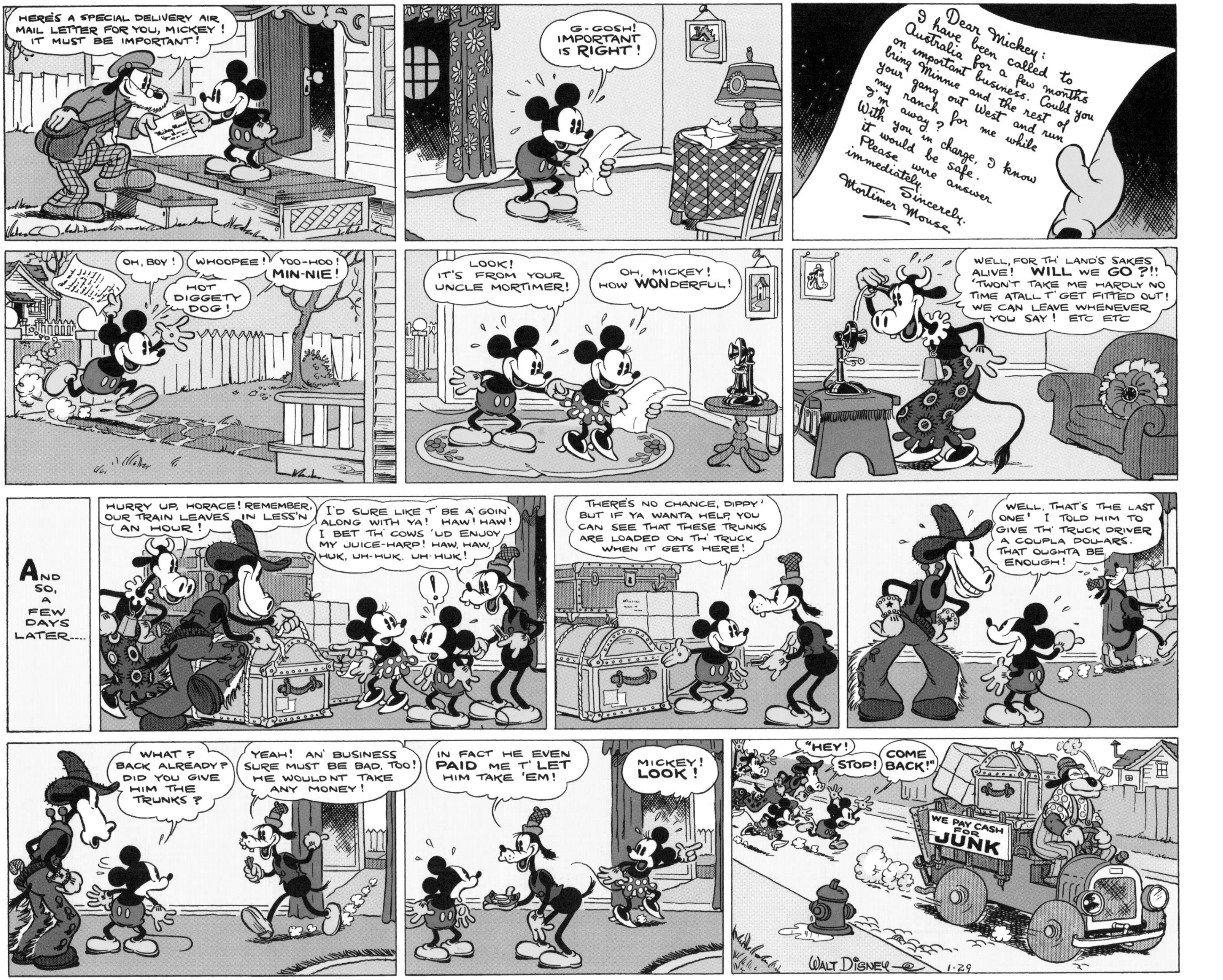
HERE'S A SPECIAL DELIVERY AIR MAIL LETTER FOR YOU, MICKEY! IT MUST BE IMPORTANT!
G-GOSH! IMPORTANT IS RIGHT!
Dear Mickey:
I have been called to Australia for a few months on important business. Could you bring Minnie and the rest of your gang out West and run my ranch for me while I'm away? With you in charge, I know it would be safe. Please wire answer immediately.
Sincerely,
Mortimer Mouse
OH, BOY!
WHOOPEE!
YOO-HOO! MIN-NIE!
HOT DIGGETY DOG!
LOOK! IT'S FROM YOUR UNCLE MORTIMER!
OH, MICKEY! HOW WONDERFUL!
WELL, FOR TH' LAND'S SAKES ALIVE! WILL WE GO?!! 'TWON'T TAKE ME HARDLY NO TIME ATALL T' GET FITTED OUT! WE CAN LEAVE WHENEVER YOU SAY! ETC ETC
AND SO, A FEW DAYS LATER....
HURRY UP, HORACE! REMEMBER, OUR TRAIN LEAVES IN LESS'N AN HOUR!
I'D SURE LIKE T' BE A GOIN' ALONG WITH YA! HAW! HAW! I BET TH' COWS 'UD ENJOY MY JUICE-HARP! HAW, HAW, HUK, UH-HUK, UH-HUK!
!
THERE'S NO CHANCE, DIPPY! BUT IF YA WANTA HELP, YOU CAN SEE THAT THESE TRUNKS ARE LOADED ON TH' TRUCK WHEN IT GETS HERE!
WELL, THAT'S THE LAST ONE! I TOLD HIM TO GIVE TH' TRUCK DRIVER A COUPLA DOLLARS. THAT OUGHTA BE ENOUGH!
WHAT? BACK ALREADY? DID YOU GIVE HIM THE TRUNKS?
YEAH! AN' BUSINESS SURE MUST BE BAD, TOO! HE WOULDN'T TAKE ANY MONEY!
IN FACT HE EVEN PAID ME T' LET HIM TAKE 'EM!
MICKEY! LOOK!
"HEY!
STOP!
COME BACK!"
WE PAY CASH FOR JUNK
WALT DISNEY
1-29

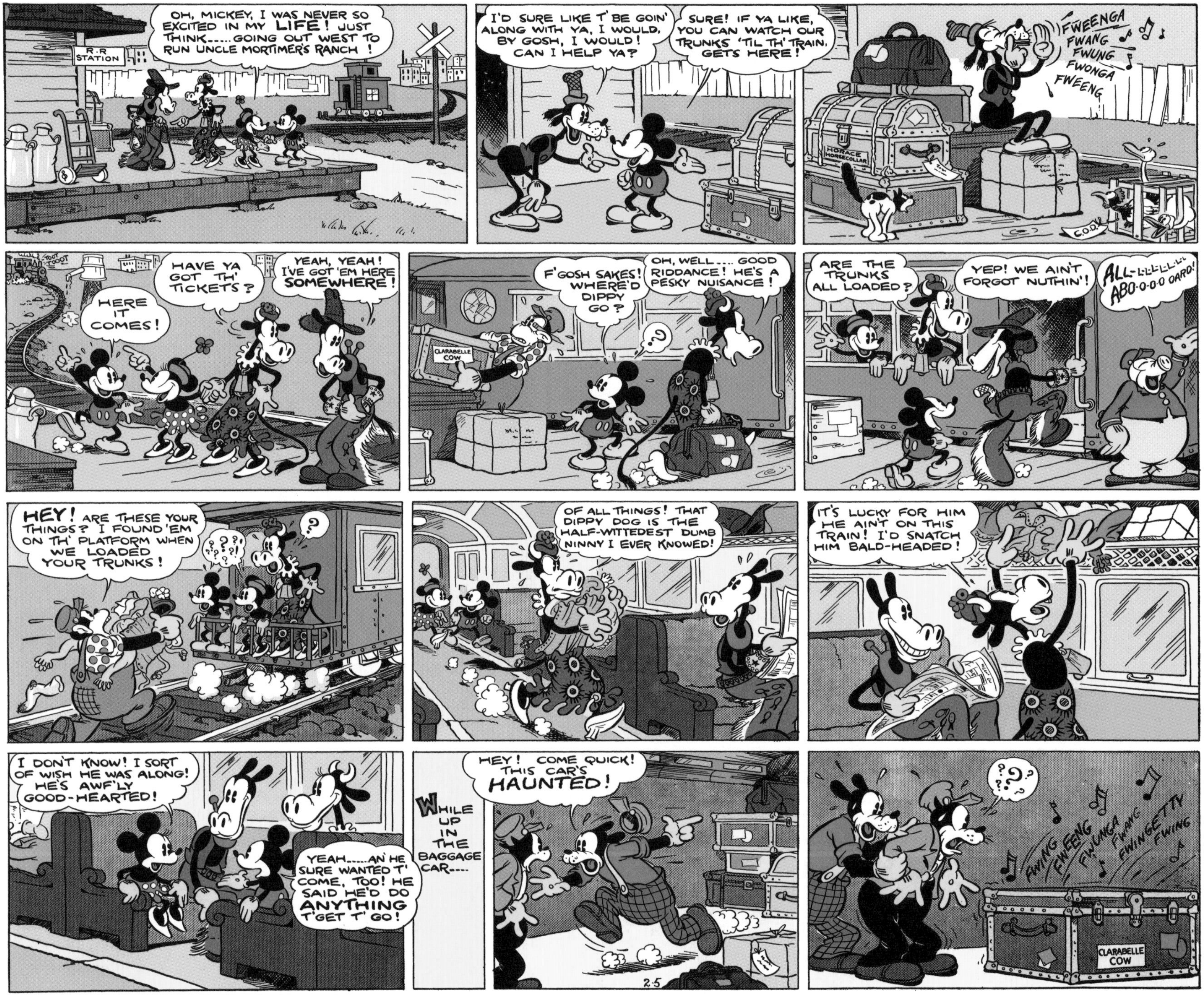
R.R STATION
OH, MICKEY, I WAS NEVER SO EXCITED IN MY LIFE! JUST THINK.....GOING OUT WEST TO RUN UNCLE MORTIMER'S RANCH!
I'D SURE LIKE T' BE GOIN' ALONG WITH YA, I WOULD, BY GOSH, I WOULD! CAN I HELP YA?
SURE! IF YA LIKE, YOU CAN WATCH OUR TRUNKS 'TIL TH' TRAIN GETS HERE!
HORACE HORSECOLLAR
FWEENGA FWANG FWUNG FWONGA FWEENG
C.O.D.
TOOT TOOOT
HERE IT COMES!
HAVE YA GOT TH' TICKETS?
YEAH, YEAH! I'VE GOT 'EM HERE SOMEWHERE!
F'GOSH SAKES! WHERE'D DIPPY GO?
OH, WELL.... GOOD RIDDANCE! HE'S A PESKY NUISANCE!
CLARABELLE COW
?
ARE THE TRUNKS ALL LOADED?
YEP! WE AIN'T FORGOT NUTHIN'!
ALL-LLLLLLL ABO-O-O-O OARD!
HEY! ARE THESE YOUR THINGS? I FOUND 'EM ON TH' PLATFORM WHEN WE LOADED YOUR TRUNKS!
?
OF ALL THINGS! THAT DIPPY DOG IS THE HALF-WITTEDEST DUMB NINNY I EVER KNOWED!
IT'S LUCKY FOR HIM HE AIN'T ON THIS TRAIN! I'D SNATCH HIM BALD-HEADED!
I DON'T KNOW! I SORT OF WISH HE WAS ALONG! HE'S AWF'LY GOOD-HEARTED!
YEAH.....AN' HE SURE WANTED T' COME, TOO! HE SAID HE'D DO ANYTHING T' GET T' GO!
WHILE UP IN THE BAGGAGE CAR....
HEY! COME QUICK! THIS CAR'S HAUNTED!
2.5
?
FWING FWEENG FWUNGA FWANG FWINGETTY FWING
CLARABELLE COW

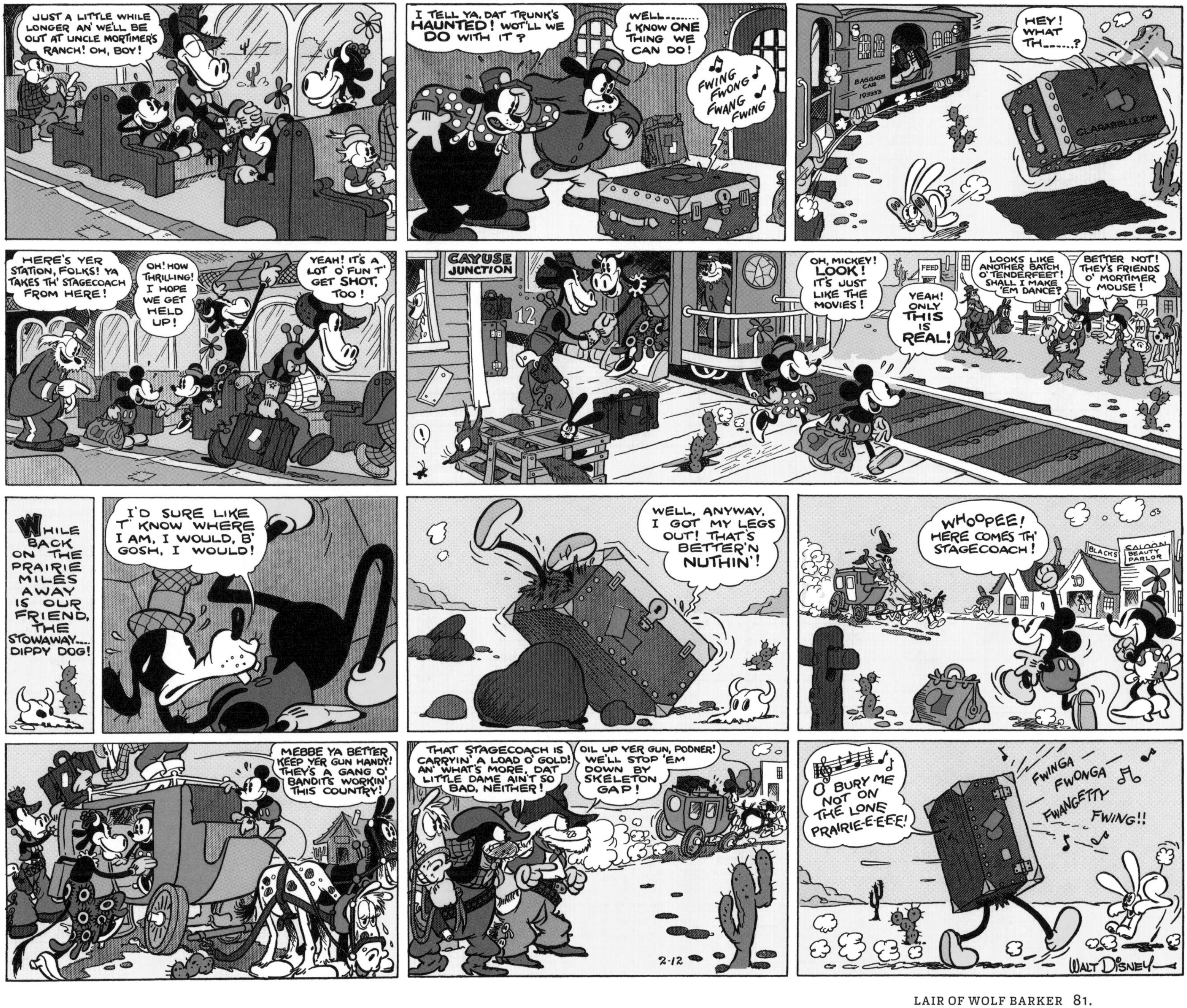
JUST A LITTLE WHILE LONGER AN' WE'LL BE OUT AT UNCLE MORTIMER'S RANCH! OH, BOY!
I TELL YA, DAT TRUNK'S HAUNTED! WOT'LL WE DO WITH IT?
WELL....... I KNOW ONE THING WE CAN DO!
FWING FWONG FWANG FWING
BAGGAGE CAR 193333
HEY! WHAT TH.....?
CLARABELLE COW
HERE'S YER STATION, FOLKS! YA TAKES TH' STAGECOACH FROM HERE!
OH! HOW THRILLING! I HOPE WE GET HELD UP!
YEAH! IT'S A LOT O' FUN T' GET SHOT, TOO!
CAYUSE JUNCTION
12
FEED
OH, MICKEY! LOOK! IT'S JUST LIKE THE MOVIES!
YEAH! ONLY THIS IS REAL!
LOOKS LIKE ANOTHER BATCH O' TENDERFEET! SHALL I MAKE 'EM DANCE?
BETTER NOT! THEY'S FRIENDS O' MORTIMER MOUSE!
WHILE BACK ON THE PRAIRIE MILES AWAY IS OUR FRIEND, THE STOWAWAY.... DIPPY DOG!
I'D SURE LIKE T' KNOW WHERE I AM, I WOULD, B' GOSH, I WOULD!
WELL, ANYWAY, I GOT MY LEGS OUT! THAT'S BETTER'N NUTHIN'!
WHOOPEE! HERE COMES TH' STAGECOACH!
SALOON
BEAUTY PARLOR
MEBBE YA BETTER KEEP YER GUN HANDY! THEY'S A GANG O' BANDITS WORKIN' THIS COUNTRY!
THAT STAGECOACH IS CARRYIN' A LOAD O' GOLD! AN' WHAT'S MORE, DAT LITTLE DAME AIN'T SO BAD, NEITHER!
OIL UP YER GUN, PODNER! WE'LL STOP 'EM DOWN BY SKELETON GAP!
2-12
O BURY ME NOT ON THE LONE PRAIRIE-E-E-E-E!
FWINGA FWONGA FWANGETTY FWING!!
WALT DISNEY

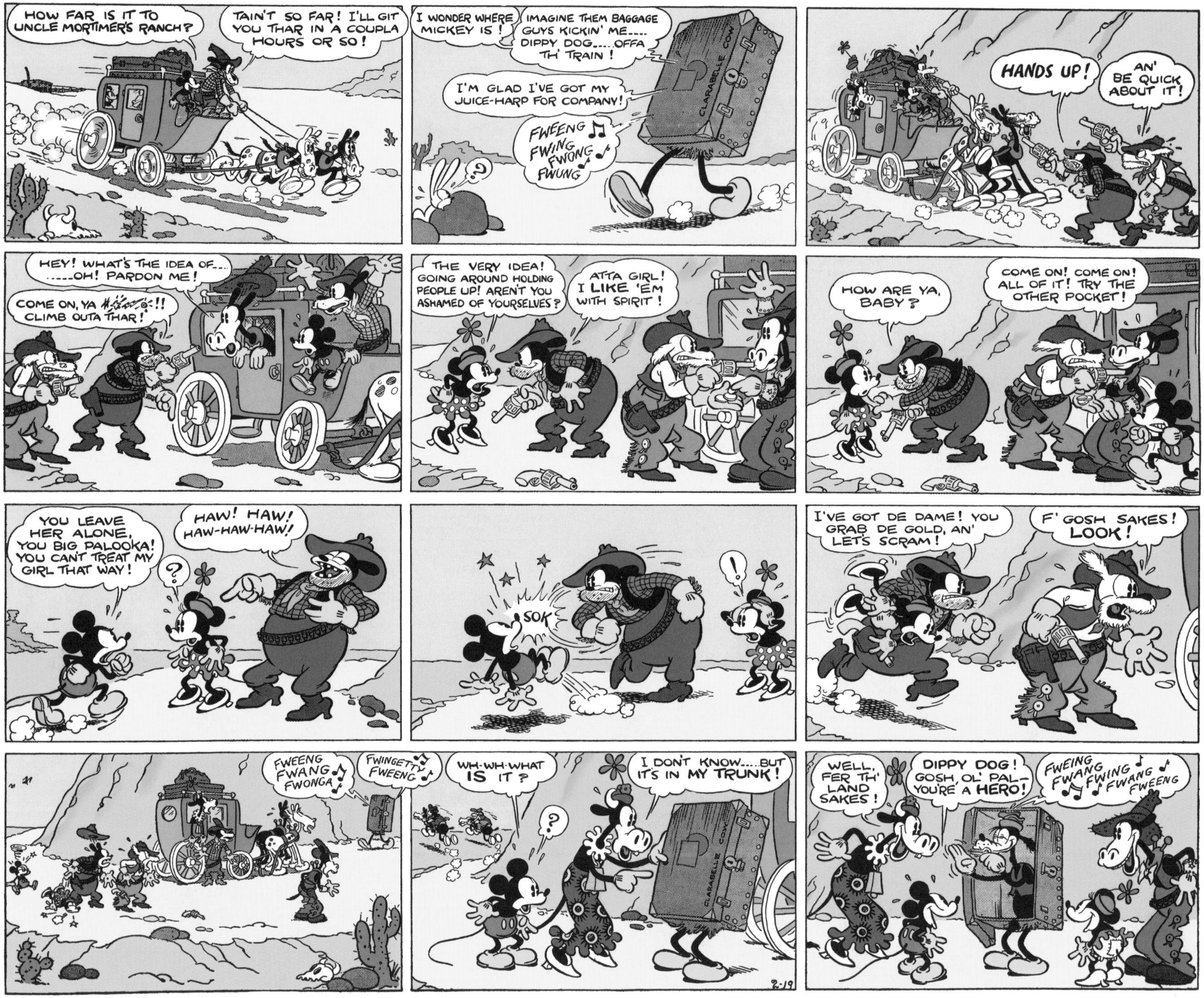
HOW FAR IS IT TO UNCLE MORTIMER'S RANCH?
TAIN'T SO FAR! I'LL GIT YOU THAR IN A COUPLA HOURS OR SO!
I WONDER WHERE MICKEY IS!
IMAGINE THEM BAGGAGE GUYS KICKIN' ME.... DIPPY DOG.....OFFA TH' TRAIN!
I'M GLAD I'VE GOT MY JUICE-HARP FOR COMPANY!
FWEENG FWING FWONG FWUNG
CLARABELLE COW
HANDS UP!
AN' BE QUICK ABOUT IT!
HEY! WHAT'S THE IDEA OF..... ......OH! PARDON ME!
COME ON, YA !! CLIMB OUTA THAR!
THE VERY IDEA! GOING AROUND HOLDING PEOPLE UP! AREN'T YOU ASHAMED OF YOURSELVES?
ATTA GIRL! I LIKE 'EM WITH SPIRIT!
HOW ARE YA, BABY?
COME ON! COME ON! ALL OF IT! TRY THE OTHER POCKET!
YOU LEAVE HER ALONE, YOU BIG PALOOKA! YOU CAN'T TREAT MY GIRL THAT WAY!
HAW! HAW! HAW-HAW-HAW!
SOK
I'VE GOT DE DAME! YOU GRAB DE GOLD, AN' LET'S SCRAM!
F' GOSH SAKES! LOOK!
FWEENG FWANG FWONGA
FWINGETTY FWEENG
WH-WH-WHAT IS IT?
I DON'T KNOW.....BUT IT'S IN MY TRUNK!
CLARABELLE COW
2-19
WELL, FER TH' LAND SAKES!
DIPPY DOG! GOSH, OL' PAL-YOU'RE A HERO!
FWEING FWANG FWING FWANG FWEENG

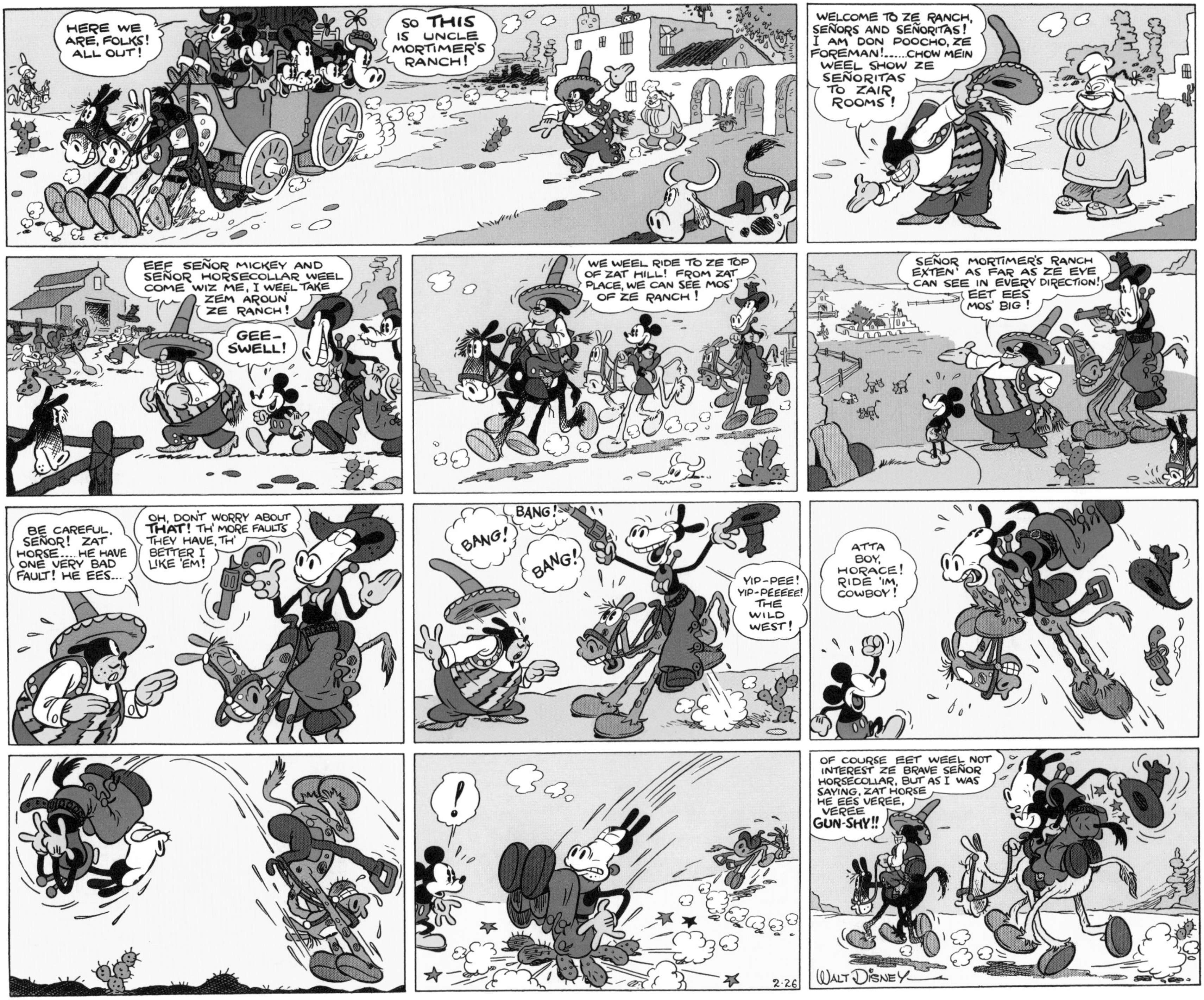
HERE WE ARE, FOLKS! ALL OUT!
SO THIS IS UNCLE MORTIMER'S RANCH!
WELCOME TO ZE RANCH, SEÑORS AND SEÑORITAS! I AM DON POOCHO, ZE FOREMAN!......CHOW MEIN WEEL SHOW ZE SEÑORITAS TO ZAIR ROOMS!
EEF SEÑOR MICKEY AND SEÑOR HORSECOLLAR WEEL COME WIZ ME, I WEEL TAKE ZEM AROUN' ZE RANCH!
GEE-SWELL!
WE WEEL RIDE TO ZE TOP OF ZAT HILL! FROM ZAT PLACE, WE CAN SEE MOS' OF ZE RANCH!
SEÑOR MORTIMER'S RANCH EXTEN' AS FAR AS ZE EYE CAN SEE IN EVERY DIRECTION! EET EES MOS' BIG!
BE CAREFUL, SEÑOR! ZAT HORSE.... HE HAVE ONE VERY BAD FAULT! HE EES...
OH, DON'T WORRY ABOUT THAT! TH' MORE FAULTS THEY HAVE, TH' BETTER I LIKE 'EM!
BANG!
BANG!
BANG!
YIP-PEE! YIP-PEEEEE! THE WILD WEST!
ATTA BOY, HORACE! RIDE 'IM, COWBOY!
!
2·26
OF COURSE EET WEEL NOT INTEREST ZE BRAVE SEÑOR HORSECOLLAR, BUT AS I WAS SAYING, ZAT HORSE HE EES VEREE, VEREE GUN-SHY!!
WALT DISNEY

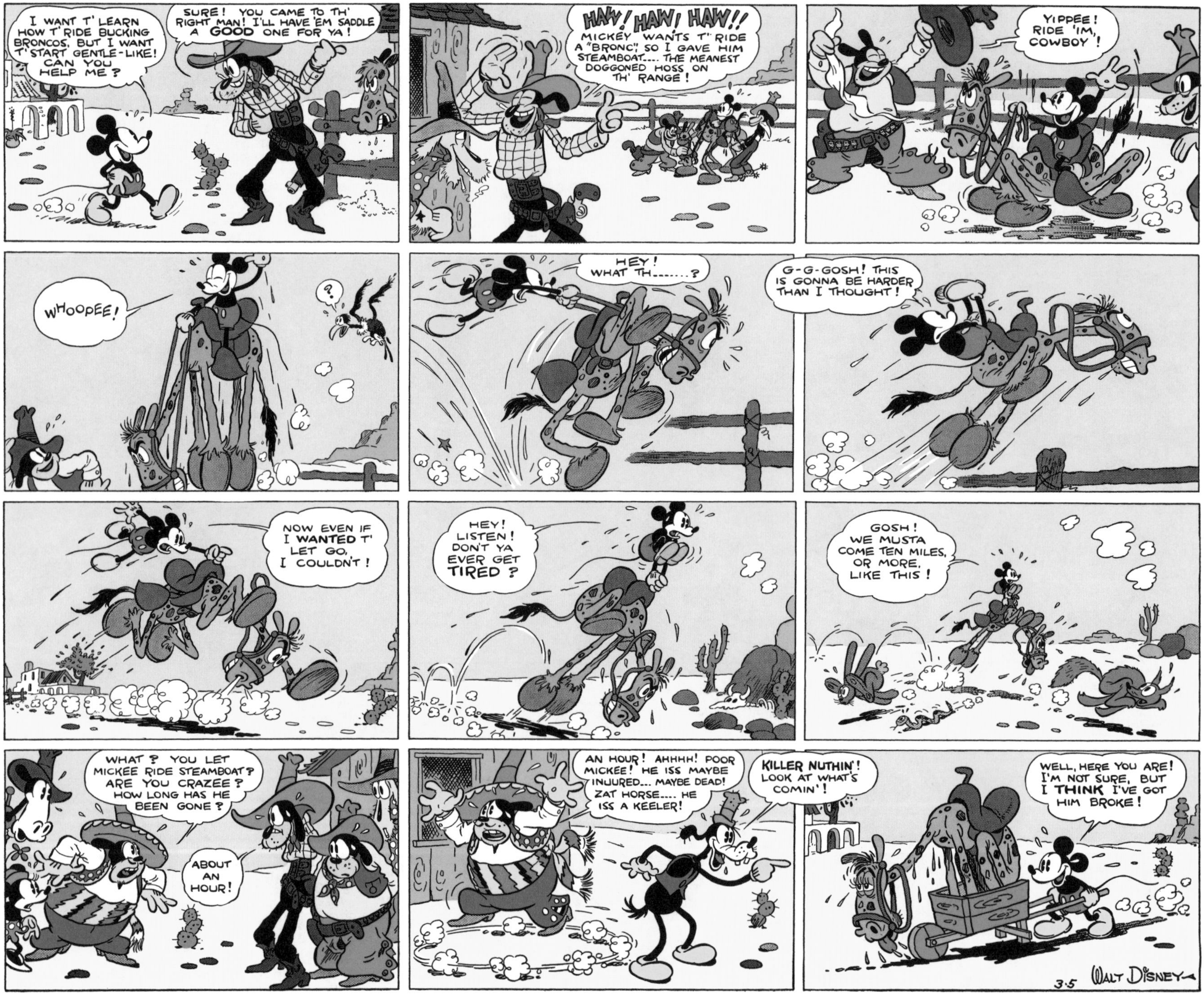
I WANT T' LEARN HOW T' RIDE BUCKING BRONCOS, BUT I WANT T' START GENTLE-LIKE! CAN YOU HELP ME?
SURE! YOU CAME TO TH' RIGHT MAN! I'LL HAVE 'EM SADDLE A GOOD ONE FOR YA!
HAW! HAW! HAW!!
MICKEY WANTS T' RIDE A "BRONC," SO I GAVE HIM STEAMBOAT.... THE MEANEST DOGGONED HOSS ON TH' RANGE!
YIPPEE! RIDE 'IM, COWBOY!
WHOOPEE!
?
HEY! WHAT TH.......?
G-G-GOSH! THIS IS GONNA BE HARDER THAN I THOUGHT!
NOW EVEN IF I WANTED T' LET GO, I COULDN'T!
HEY! LISTEN! DON'T YA EVER GET TIRED?
GOSH! WE MUSTA COME TEN MILES, OR MORE, LIKE THIS!
WHAT? YOU LET MICKEE RIDE STEAMBOAT? ARE YOU CRAZEE? HOW LONG HAS HE BEEN GONE?
ABOUT AN HOUR!
AN HOUR! AHHHH! POOR MICKEE! HE ISS MAYBE INJURED... MAYBE DEAD! ZAT HORSE.... HE ISS A KEELER!
KILLER NUTHIN'! LOOK AT WHAT'S COMIN'!
WELL, HERE YOU ARE! I'M NOT SURE, BUT I THINK I'VE GOT HIM BROKE!
3·5
WALT DISNEY

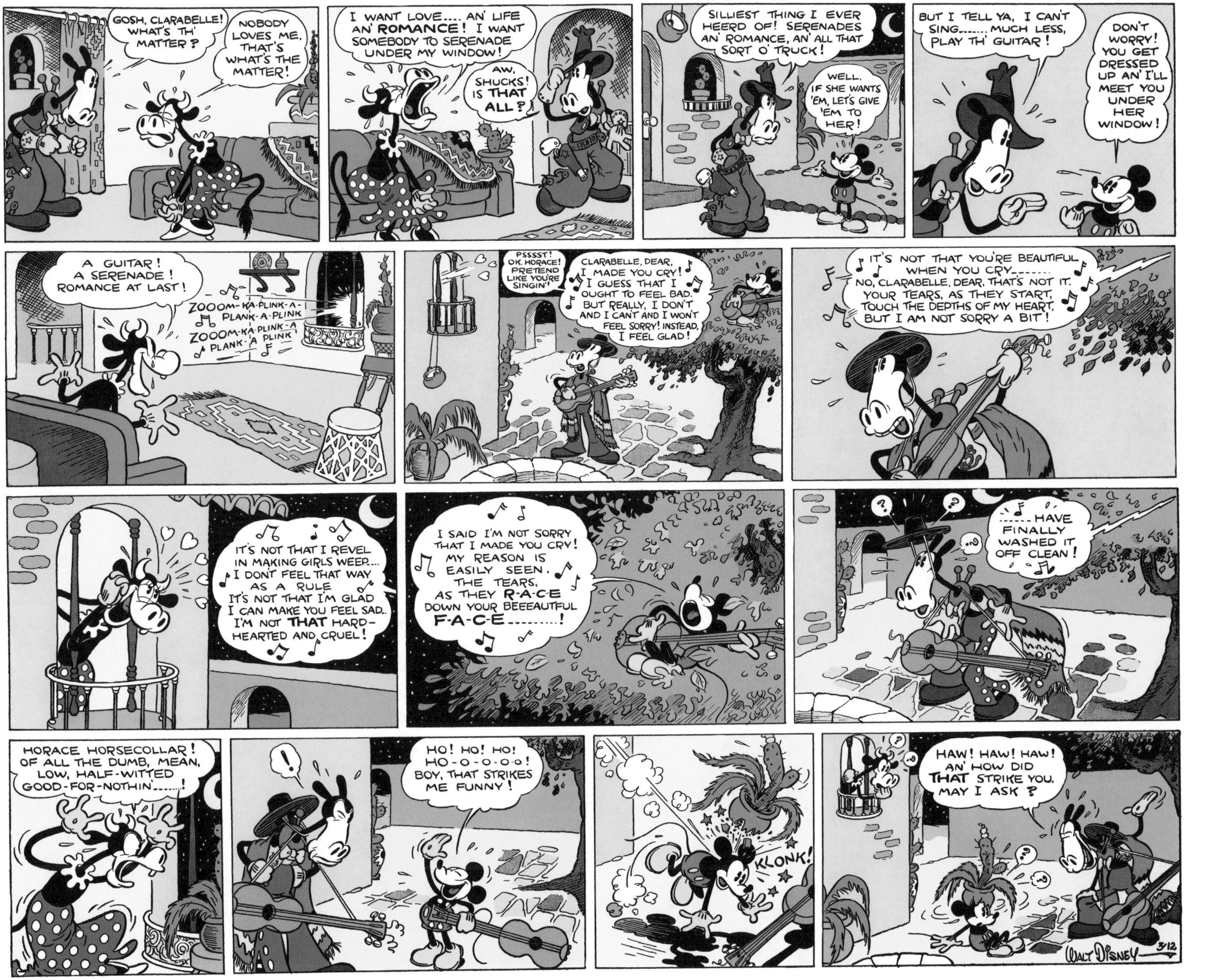

GOSH, CLARABELLE! WHAT'S TH' MATTER?
NOBODY LOVES ME. THAT'S WHAT'S THE MATTER!
I WANT LOVE.... AN' LIFE AN' ROMANCE! I WANT SOMEBODY TO SERENADE UNDER MY WINDOW!
AW, SHUCKS! IS THAT ALL?
SILLIEST THING I EVER HEERD OF! SERENADES AN' ROMANCE, AN' ALL THAT SORT O' TRUCK!
WELL, IF SHE WANTS 'EM, LET'S GIVE 'EM TO HER!
BUT I TELL YA, I CAN'T SING....... MUCH LESS, PLAY TH' GUITAR!
DON'T WORRY! YOU GET DRESSED UP AN' I'LL MEET YOU UNDER HER WINDOW!
A GUITAR! A SERENADE! ROMANCE AT LAST!
ZOOOM-KA-PLINK-A-PLANK-A-PLINK
ZOOOM-KA-PLINK-A-PLANK-A PLINK
PSSSST! OK, HORACE! PRETEND LIKE YOU'RE SINGIN'!
CLARABELLE, DEAR, I MADE YOU CRY! I GUESS THAT I OUGHT TO FEEL BAD. BUT REALLY, I DON'T AND I CAN'T AND I WON'T FEEL SORRY! INSTEAD, I FEEL GLAD!
IT'S NOT THAT YOU'RE BEAUTIFUL WHEN YOU CRY...... NO, CLARABELLE, DEAR, THAT'S NOT IT. YOUR TEARS, AS THEY START, TOUCH THE DEPTHS OF MY HEART, BUT I AM NOT SORRY A BIT!
IT'S NOT THAT I REVEL IN MAKING GIRLS WEEP.... I DON'T FEEL THAT WAY AS A RULE. IT'S NOT THAT I'M GLAD I CAN MAKE YOU FEEL SAD.. I'M NOT THAT HARD-HEARTED AND CRUEL!
I SAID I'M NOT SORRY THAT I MADE YOU CRY! MY REASON IS EASILY SEEN. THE TEARS, AS THEY R-A-C-E DOWN YOUR BEEEAUTFUL F-A-C-E.........!
......HAVE FINALLY WASHED IT OFF CLEAN!
HORACE HORSECOLLAR! OF ALL THE DUMB, MEAN, LOW, HALF-WITTED GOOD-FOR-NOTHIN'.......!
!
HO! HO! HO! HO-O-O-O-O! BOY, THAT STRIKES ME FUNNY!
KLONK!
HAW! HAW! HAW! AN' HOW DID THAT STRIKE YOU, MAY I ASK?
WALT DISNEY
3/12

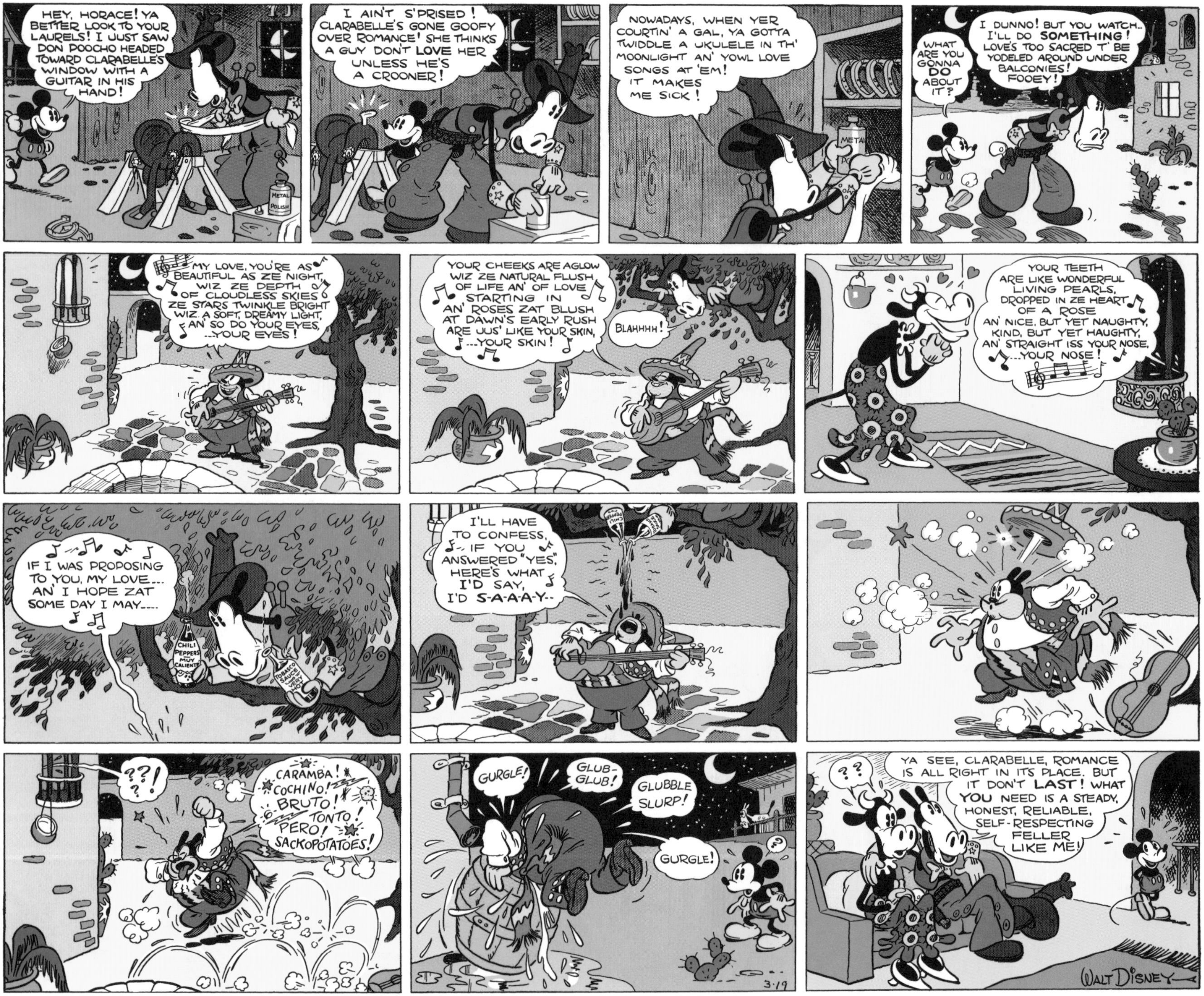
HEY, HORACE! YA BETTER LOOK TO YOUR LAURELS! I JUST SAW DON POOCHO HEADED TOWARD CLARABELLE'S WINDOW WITH A GUITAR IN HIS HAND!
METAL POLISH
I AIN'T S'PRISED! CLARABELLE'S GONE GOOFY OVER ROMANCE! SHE THINKS A GUY DON'T **LOVE** HER UNLESS HE'S A CROONER!
NOWADAYS, WHEN YER COURTIN' A GAL, YA GOTTA TWIDDLE A UKULELE IN TH' MOONLIGHT AN' YOWL LOVE SONGS AT 'EM! IT MAKES ME SICK!
WHAT ARE YOU GONNA **DO** ABOUT IT?
I DUNNO! BUT YOU WATCH.. I'LL DO **SOMETHING**! LOVE'S TOO SACRED T' BE YODELED AROUND UNDER BALCONIES! FOOEY!
MY LOVE, YOU'RE AS BEAUTIFUL AS ZE NIGHT, WIZ ZE DEPTH OF CLOUDLESS SKIES ZE STARS TWINKLE BRIGHT WIZ A SOFT, DREAMY LIGHT, AN' SO DO YOUR EYES, ...YOUR EYES!
YOUR CHEEKS ARE AGLOW WIZ ZE NATURAL FLUSH OF LIFE AN' OF LOVE STARTING IN AN' ROSES ZAT BLUSH AT DAWN'S EARLY RUSH ARE JUS' LIKE YOUR SKIN, ...YOUR SKIN!
BLAHHHH!
YOUR TEETH ARE LIKE WONDERFUL LIVING PEARLS, DROPPED IN ZE HEART OF A ROSE AN' NICE, BUT YET NAUGHTY, KIND, BUT YET HAUGHTY, AN' STRAIGHT ISS YOUR NOSE, ...YOUR NOSE!
IF I WAS PROPOSING TO YOU, MY LOVE... AN' I HOPE ZAT SOME DAY I MAY....
CHILI PEPPERS MUY CALIENTE
TOBASCO SAUCE
I'LL HAVE TO CONFESS, IF YOU ANSWERED "YES," HERE'S WHAT **I'D** SAY, I'D **S-A-A-A-Y**--
??!
CARAMBA! COCHINO! BRUTO! TONTO! PERO! SACKOPOTATOES!
GURGLE!
GLUB-GLUB!
GLUBBLE SLURP!
GURGLE!
3·19
??
YA SEE, CLARABELLE, ROMANCE IS ALL RIGHT IN ITS PLACE. BUT IT DON'T **LAST**! WHAT **YOU** NEED IS A STEADY, HONEST, RELIABLE, SELF-RESPECTING FELLER LIKE ME!
WALT DISNEY

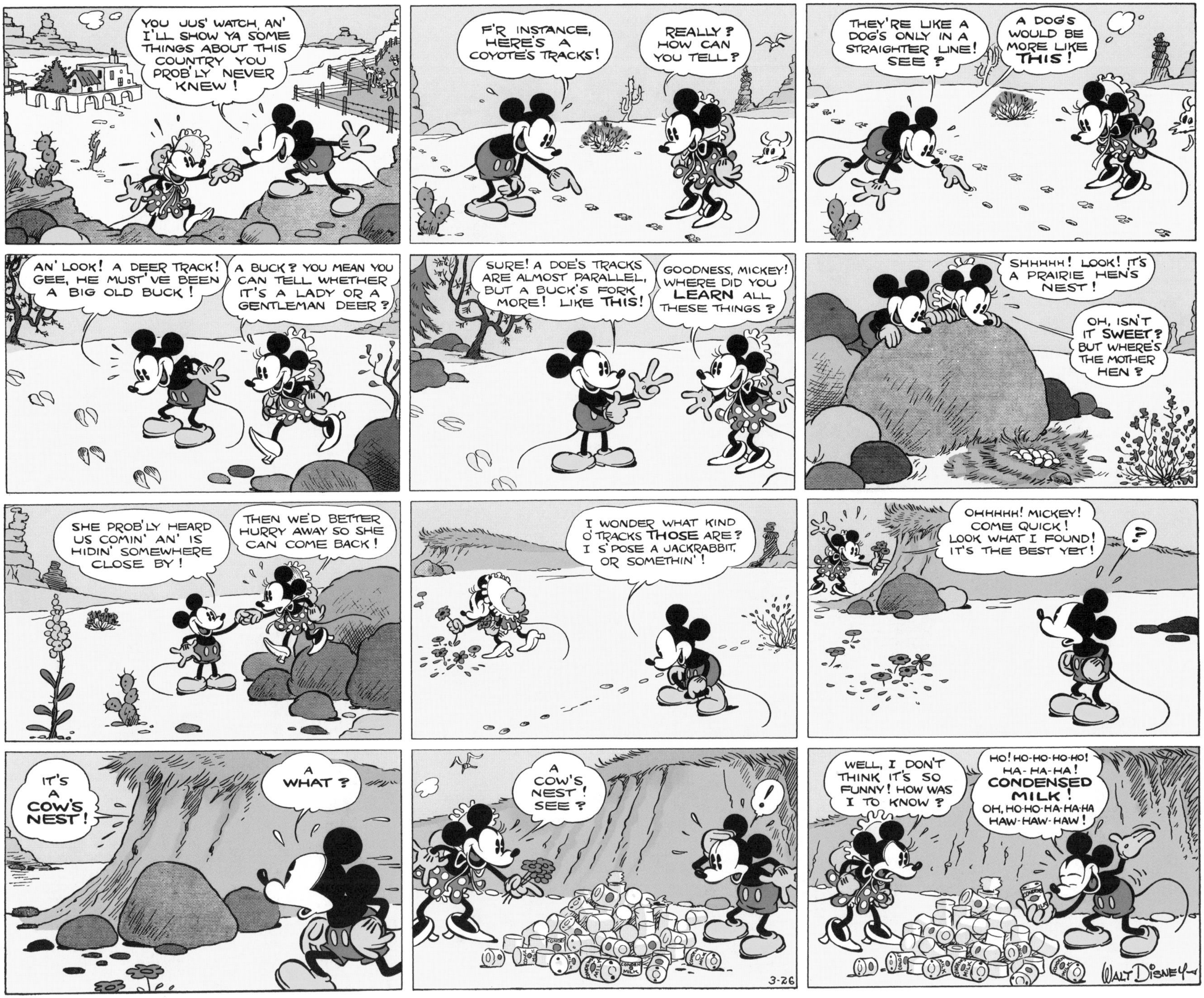
YOU JUS' WATCH, AN' I'LL SHOW YA SOME THINGS ABOUT THIS COUNTRY YOU PROB'LY NEVER KNEW!
F'R INSTANCE, HERE'S A COYOTE'S TRACKS!
REALLY? HOW CAN YOU TELL?
THEY'RE LIKE A DOG'S ONLY IN A STRAIGHTER LINE! SEE?
A DOG'S WOULD BE MORE LIKE THIS!
AN' LOOK! A DEER TRACK! GEE, HE MUST'VE BEEN A BIG OLD BUCK!
A BUCK? YOU MEAN YOU CAN TELL WHETHER IT'S A LADY OR A GENTLEMAN DEER?
SURE! A DOE'S TRACKS ARE ALMOST PARALLEL, BUT A BUCK'S FORK MORE! LIKE THIS!
GOODNESS, MICKEY! WHERE DID YOU LEARN ALL THESE THINGS?
SHHHHH! LOOK! IT'S A PRAIRIE HEN'S NEST!
OH, ISN'T IT SWEET? BUT WHERE'S THE MOTHER HEN?
SHE PROB'LY HEARD US COMIN' AN' IS HIDIN' SOMEWHERE CLOSE BY!
THEN WE'D BETTER HURRY AWAY SO SHE CAN COME BACK!
I WONDER WHAT KIND O' TRACKS THOSE ARE? I S'POSE A JACKRABBIT, OR SOMETHIN'!
OHHHHH! MICKEY! COME QUICK! LOOK WHAT I FOUND! IT'S THE BEST YET!
?
IT'S A COW'S NEST!
A WHAT?
A COW'S NEST! SEE?
!
WELL, I DON'T THINK IT'S SO FUNNY! HOW WAS I TO KNOW?
HO! HO-HO-HO-HO! HA-HA-HA! CONDENSED MILK! OH, HO-HO-HA-HA-HA HAW-HAW-HAW!
3-26
WALT DISNEY

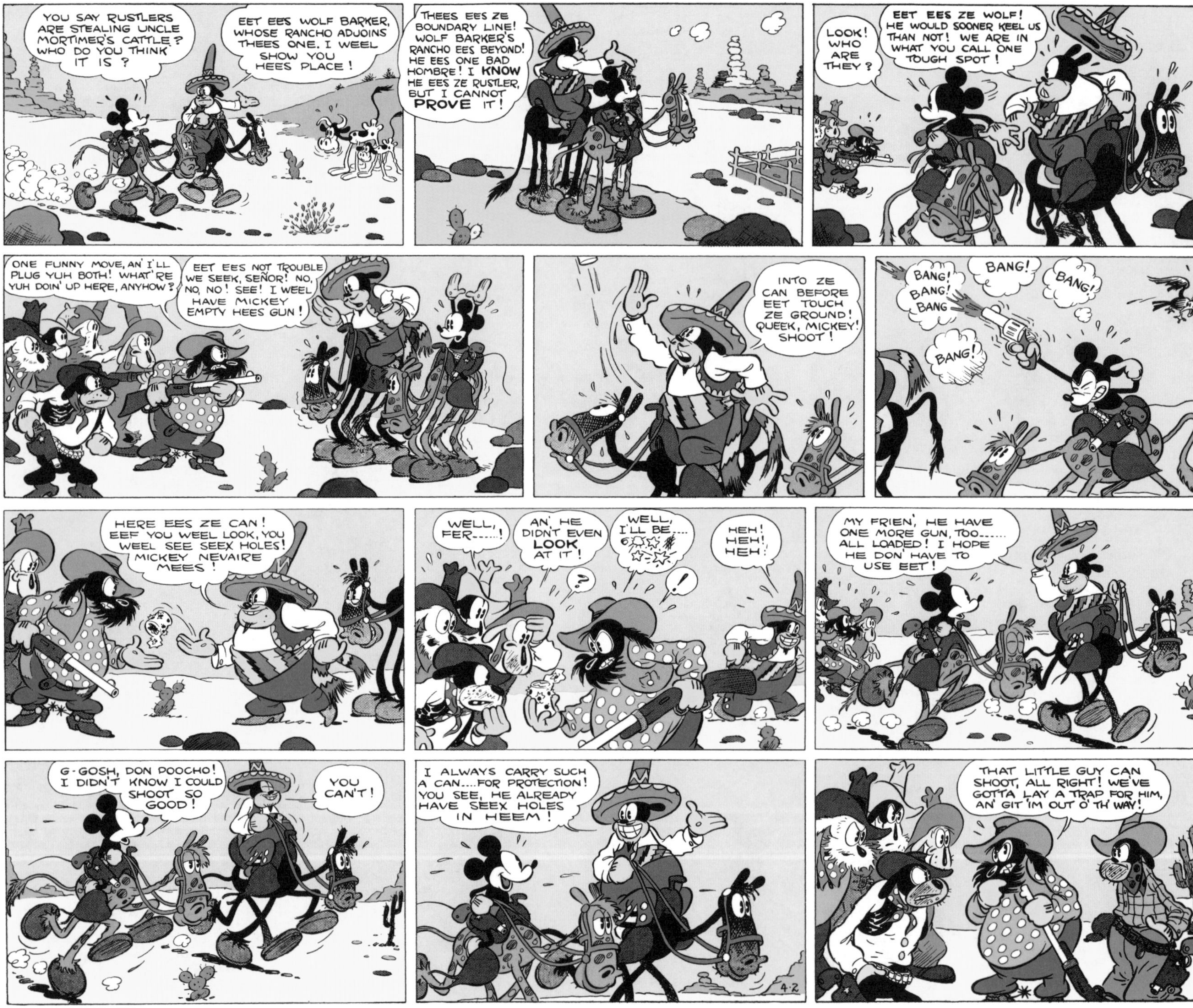
YOU SAY RUSTLERS ARE STEALING UNCLE MORTIMER'S CATTLE? WHO DO YOU THINK IT IS?
EET EES WOLF BARKER, WHOSE RANCHO ADJOINS THEES ONE. I WEEL SHOW YOU HEES PLACE!
THEES EES ZE BOUNDARY LINE! WOLF BARKER'S RANCHO EES BEYOND! HE EES ONE BAD HOMBRE! I KNOW HE EES ZE RUSTLER, BUT I CANNOT PROVE IT!
LOOK! WHO ARE THEY?
EET EES ZE WOLF! HE WOULD SOONER KEEL US THAN NOT! WE ARE IN WHAT YOU CALL ONE TOUGH SPOT!
ONE FUNNY MOVE, AN' I'LL PLUG YUH BOTH! WHAT'RE YUH DOIN' UP HERE, ANYHOW?
EET EES NOT TROUBLE WE SEEK, SEÑOR! NO, NO, NO! SEE! I WEEL HAVE MICKEY EMPTY HEES GUN!
INTO ZE CAN BEFORE EET TOUCH ZE GROUND! QUEEK, MICKEY! SHOOT!
BANG! BANG! BANG
BANG!
BANG!
BANG!
HERE EES ZE CAN! EEF YOU WEEL LOOK, YOU WEEL SEE SEEX HOLES! MICKEY NEVAIRE MEES!
WELL, FER.....!
AN' HE DIDN'T EVEN LOOK AT IT!
WELL, I'LL BE....
HEH! HEH! HEH!
MY FRIEN', HE HAVE ONE MORE GUN, TOO...... ALL LOADED! I HOPE HE DON' HAVE TO USE EET!
G-GOSH, DON POOCHO! I DIDN'T KNOW I COULD SHOOT SO GOOD!
YOU CAN'T!
I ALWAYS CARRY SUCH A CAN....FOR PROTECTION! YOU SEE, HE ALREADY HAVE SEEX HOLES IN HEEM!
THAT LITTLE GUY CAN SHOOT, ALL RIGHT! WE'VE GOTTA LAY A TRAP FOR HIM, AN' GIT 'IM OUT O' TH' WAY!

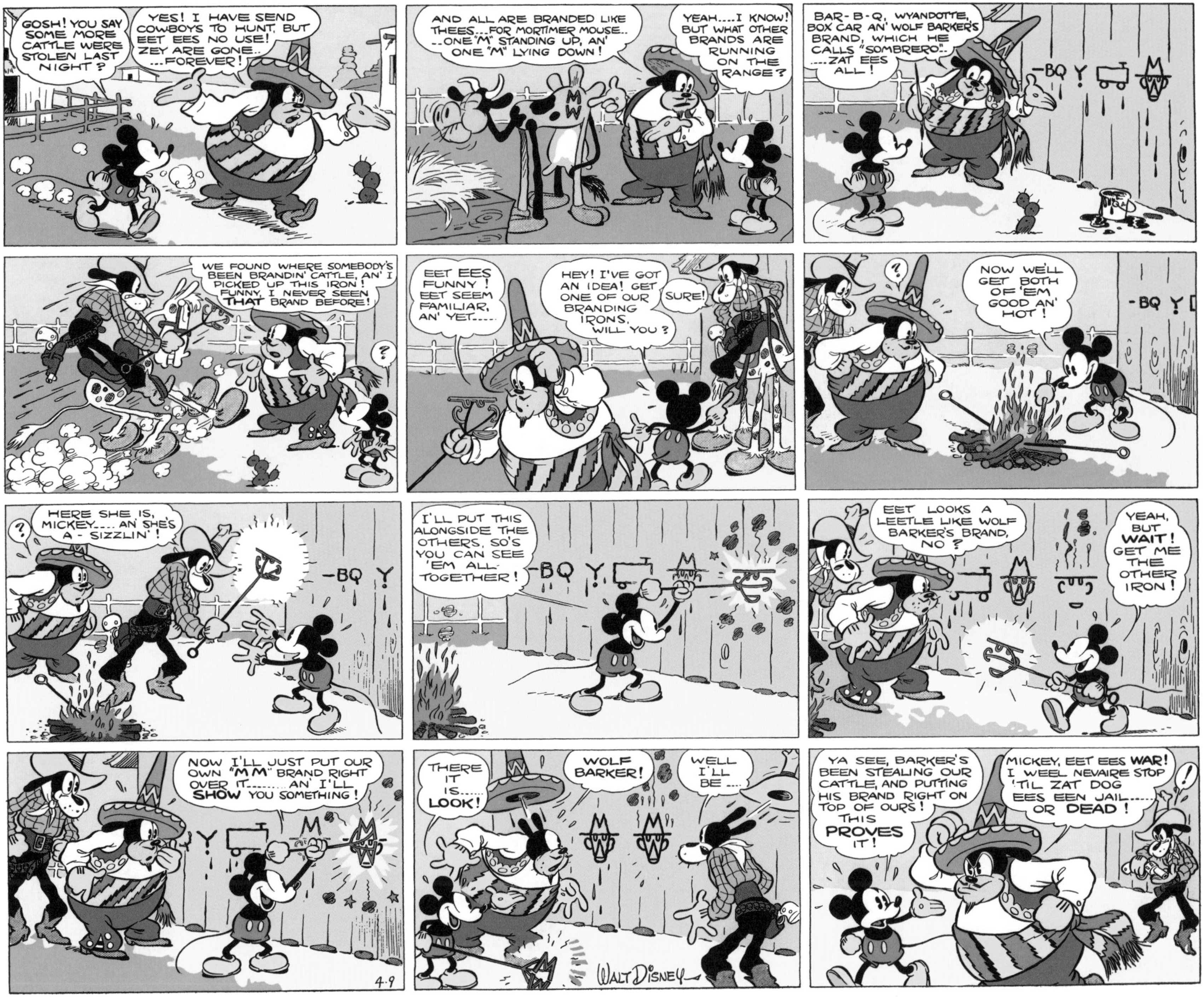

GOSH! YOU SAY SOME MORE CATTLE WERE STOLEN LAST NIGHT?
YES! I HAVE SEND COWBOYS TO HUNT, BUT EET EES NO USE! ZEY ARE GONE.. ...FOREVER!
AND ALL ARE BRANDED LIKE THEES...FOR MORTIMER MOUSE.. ..ONE "M" STANDING UP, AN' ONE "M" LYING DOWN!
YEAH....I KNOW! BUT WHAT OTHER BRANDS ARE RUNNING ON THE RANGE?
BAR-B-Q, WYANDOTTE, BOX CAR AN' WOLF BARKER'S BRAND, WHICH HE CALLS "SOMBRERO".. ....ZAT EES ALL!
-BQ
WE FOUND WHERE SOMEBODY'S BEEN BRANDIN' CATTLE, AN' I PICKED UP THIS IRON! FUNNY, I NEVER SEEN THAT BRAND BEFORE!
?
EET EES FUNNY! EET SEEM FAMILIAR, AN' YET.....
HEY! I'VE GOT AN IDEA! GET ONE OF OUR BRANDING IRONS, WILL YOU?
SURE!
?
NOW WE'LL GET BOTH OF 'EM GOOD AN' HOT!
-BQ
?
HERE SHE IS, MICKEY.... AN' SHE'S A-SIZZLIN'!
-BQ
I'LL PUT THIS ALONGSIDE THE OTHERS, SO'S YOU CAN SEE 'EM ALL TOGETHER!
-BQ
EET LOOKS A LEETLE LIKE WOLF BARKER'S BRAND, NO?
YEAH, BUT WAIT! GET ME THE OTHER IRON!
NOW I'LL JUST PUT OUR OWN "MM" BRAND RIGHT OVER IT........ AN' I'LL SHOW YOU SOMETHING!
4-9
THERE IT IS...... LOOK!
WOLF BARKER!
WELL I'LL BE....
WALT DISNEY
YA SEE, BARKER'S BEEN STEALING OUR CATTLE, AND PUTTING HIS BRAND RIGHT ON TOP OF OURS! THIS PROVES IT!
MICKEY, EET EES WAR! I WEEL NEVAIRE STOP 'TIL ZAT DOG EES EEN JAIL...... OR DEAD!
!

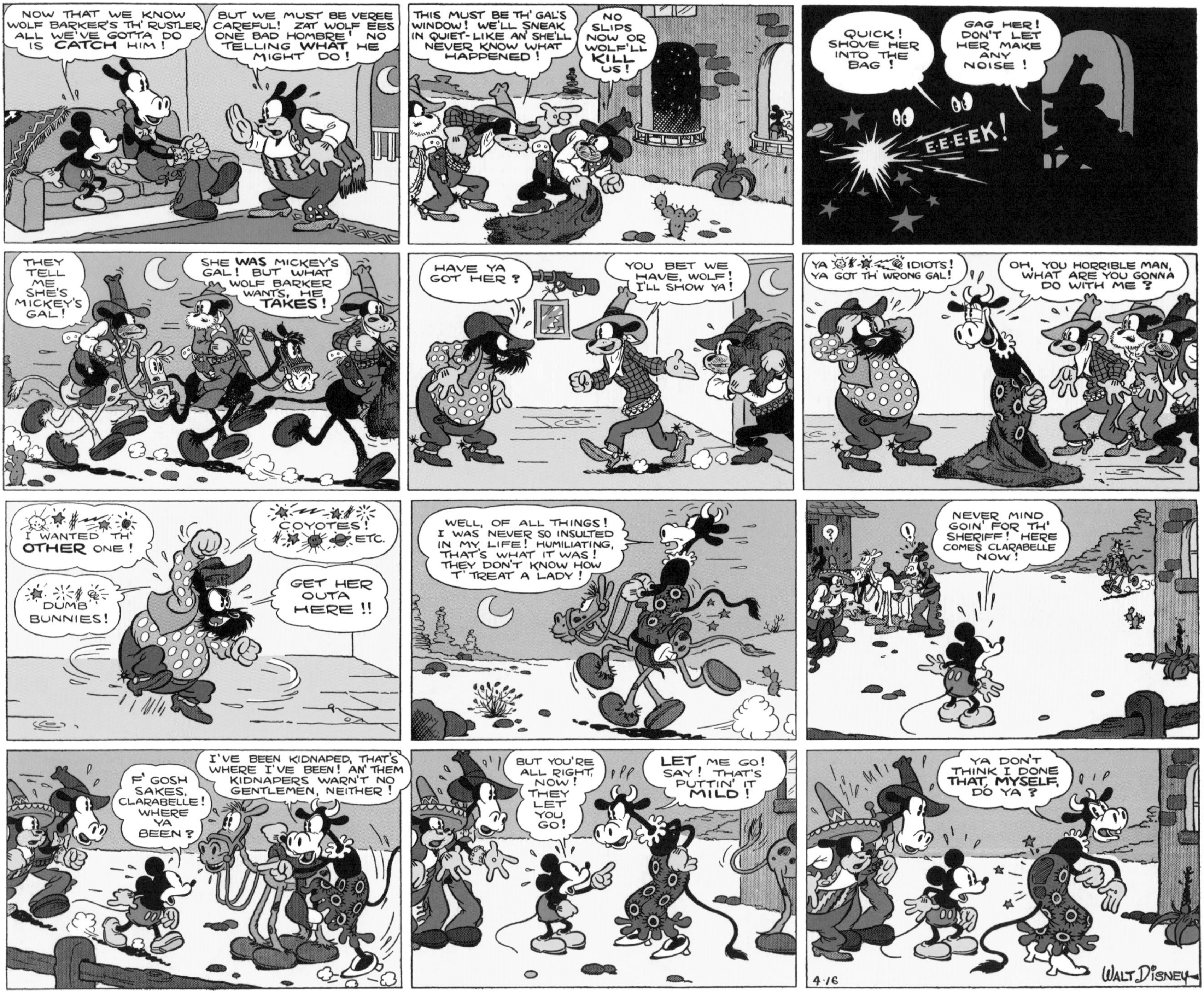
NOW THAT WE KNOW WOLF BARKER'S TH' RUSTLER, ALL WE'VE GOTTA DO IS CATCH HIM!
BUT WE MUST BE VEREE CAREFUL! ZAT WOLF EES ONE BAD HOMBRE! NO TELLING WHAT HE MIGHT DO!
THIS MUST BE TH' GAL'S WINDOW! WE'LL SNEAK IN QUIET-LIKE AN' SHE'LL NEVER KNOW WHAT HAPPENED!
NO SLIPS NOW OR WOLF'LL KILL US!
QUICK! SHOVE HER INTO THE BAG!
GAG HER! DON'T LET HER MAKE ANY NOISE!
E-E-E-EK!
THEY TELL ME SHE'S MICKEY'S GAL!
SHE WAS MICKEY'S GAL! BUT WHAT WOLF BARKER WANTS, HE TAKES!
HAVE YA GOT HER?
YOU BET WE HAVE, WOLF! I'LL SHOW YA!
YA IDIOTS! YA GOT TH' WRONG GAL!
OH, YOU HORRIBLE MAN, WHAT ARE YOU GONNA DO WITH ME?
I WANTED TH' OTHER ONE!
COYOTES! ETC.
DUMB BUNNIES!
GET HER OUTA HERE!!
WELL, OF ALL THINGS! I WAS NEVER SO INSULTED IN MY LIFE! HUMILIATING, THAT'S WHAT IT WAS! THEY DON'T KNOW HOW T' TREAT A LADY!
?
!
NEVER MIND GOIN' FOR TH' SHERIFF! HERE COMES CLARABELLE NOW!
F' GOSH SAKES, CLARABELLE! WHERE YA BEEN?
I'VE BEEN KIDNAPED, THAT'S WHERE I'VE BEEN! AN' THEM KIDNAPERS WARN'T NO GENTLEMEN, NEITHER!
BUT YOU'RE ALL RIGHT, NOW! THEY LET YOU GO!
LET ME GO! SAY! THAT'S PUTTIN' IT MILD!
YA DON'T THINK I DONE THAT, MYSELF, DO YA?
4·16
WALT DISNEY

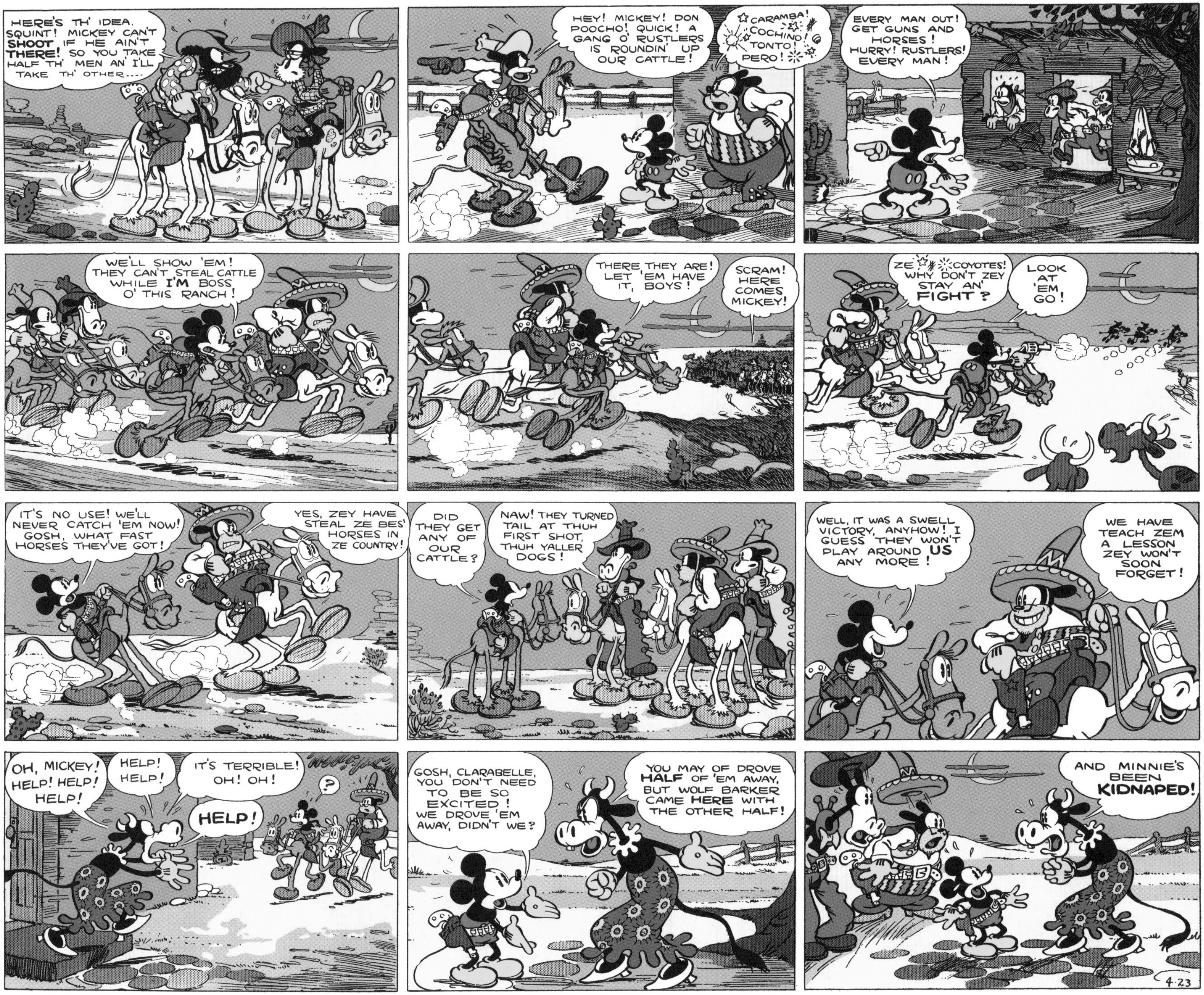
HERE'S TH' IDEA. SQUINT! MICKEY CAN'T **SHOOT** IF HE AIN'T **THERE!** SO YOU TAKE HALF TH' MEN AN' I'LL TAKE TH' OTHER....
HEY! MICKEY! DON POOCHO! QUICK! A GANG O' RUSTLERS IS ROUNDIN' UP OUR CATTLE!
CARAMBA! COCHINO! TONTO PERO!
EVERY MAN OUT! GET GUNS AND HORSES! HURRY! RUSTLERS! EVERY MAN!
WE'LL SHOW 'EM! THEY CAN'T STEAL CATTLE WHILE **I'M** BOSS O' THIS RANCH!
THERE THEY ARE! LET 'EM HAVE IT, BOYS!
SCRAM! HERE COMES MICKEY!
ZE COYOTES! WHY DON'T ZEY STAY AN' **FIGHT?**
LOOK AT 'EM GO!
IT'S NO USE! WE'LL NEVER CATCH 'EM NOW! GOSH, WHAT FAST HORSES THEY'VE GOT!
YES, ZEY HAVE STEAL ZE BES' HORSES IN ZE COUNTRY!
DID THEY GET ANY OF OUR CATTLE?
NAW! THEY TURNED TAIL AT THUH FIRST SHOT, THUH YALLER DOGS!
WELL, IT WAS A SWELL VICTORY, ANYHOW! I GUESS THEY WON'T PLAY AROUND **US** ANY MORE!
WE HAVE TEACH ZEM A LESSON ZEY WON'T SOON FORGET!
OH, MICKEY! HELP! HELP! HELP!
HELP! HELP!
IT'S TERRIBLE! OH! OH!
HELP!
?
GOSH, CLARABELLE, YOU DON'T NEED TO BE SO EXCITED! WE DROVE 'EM AWAY, DIDN'T WE?
YOU MAY OF DROVE **HALF** OF 'EM AWAY, BUT WOLF BARKER CAME **HERE** WITH THE OTHER HALF!
AND MINNIE'S BEEN **KIDNAPED!**
4.23

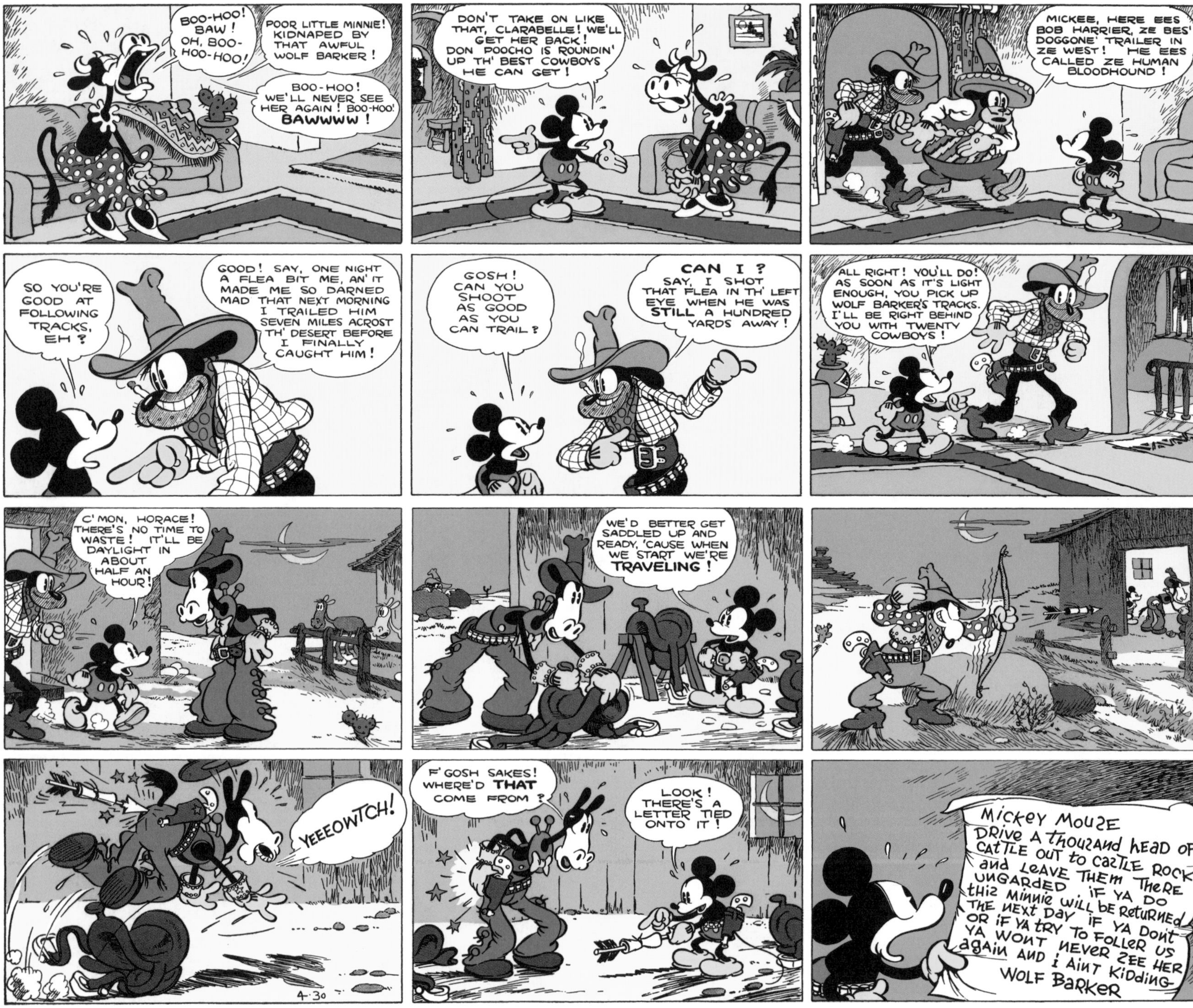
BOO-HOO! BAW! OH, BOO-HOO-HOO!
POOR LITTLE MINNIE! KIDNAPED BY THAT AWFUL WOLF BARKER!
BOO-HOO! WE'LL NEVER SEE HER AGAIN! BOO-HOO! BAWWWW!
DON'T TAKE ON LIKE THAT, CLARABELLE! WE'LL GET HER BACK! DON POOCHO IS ROUNDIN' UP TH' BEST COWBOYS HE CAN GET!
MICKEE, HERE EES BOB HARRIER, ZE BES' DOGGONE' TRAILER IN ZE WEST! HE EES CALLED ZE HUMAN BLOODHOUND!
SO YOU'RE GOOD AT FOLLOWING TRACKS, EH?
GOOD! SAY, ONE NIGHT A FLEA BIT ME, AN' IT MADE ME SO DARNED MAD THAT NEXT MORNING I TRAILED HIM SEVEN MILES ACROST TH' DESERT BEFORE I FINALLY CAUGHT HIM!
GOSH! CAN YOU SHOOT AS GOOD AS YOU CAN TRAIL?
CAN I? SAY, I SHOT THAT FLEA IN TH' LEFT EYE WHEN HE WAS STILL A HUNDRED YARDS AWAY!
ALL RIGHT! YOU'LL DO! AS SOON AS IT'S LIGHT ENOUGH, YOU PICK UP WOLF BARKER'S TRACKS. I'LL BE RIGHT BEHIND YOU WITH TWENTY COWBOYS!
C'MON, HORACE! THERE'S NO TIME TO WASTE! IT'LL BE DAYLIGHT IN ABOUT HALF AN HOUR!
WE'D BETTER GET SADDLED UP AND READY, 'CAUSE WHEN WE START WE'RE TRAVELING!
YEEEOWTCH!
4-30
F' GOSH SAKES! WHERE'D THAT COME FROM?
LOOK! THERE'S A LETTER TIED ONTO IT!
MICKEY MOUZE DRIVE A THOUZAND HEAD OF CATTLE OUT TO CAZTLE ROCK AND LEAVE THEM THERE UNGARDED. IF YA DO THIZ MINNIE WILL BE RETURNED THE NEXT DAY IF YA DONT OR IF YA TRY TO FOLLER US YA WONT NEVER ZEE HER AGAIN AND I AINT KIDDING — WOLF BARKER

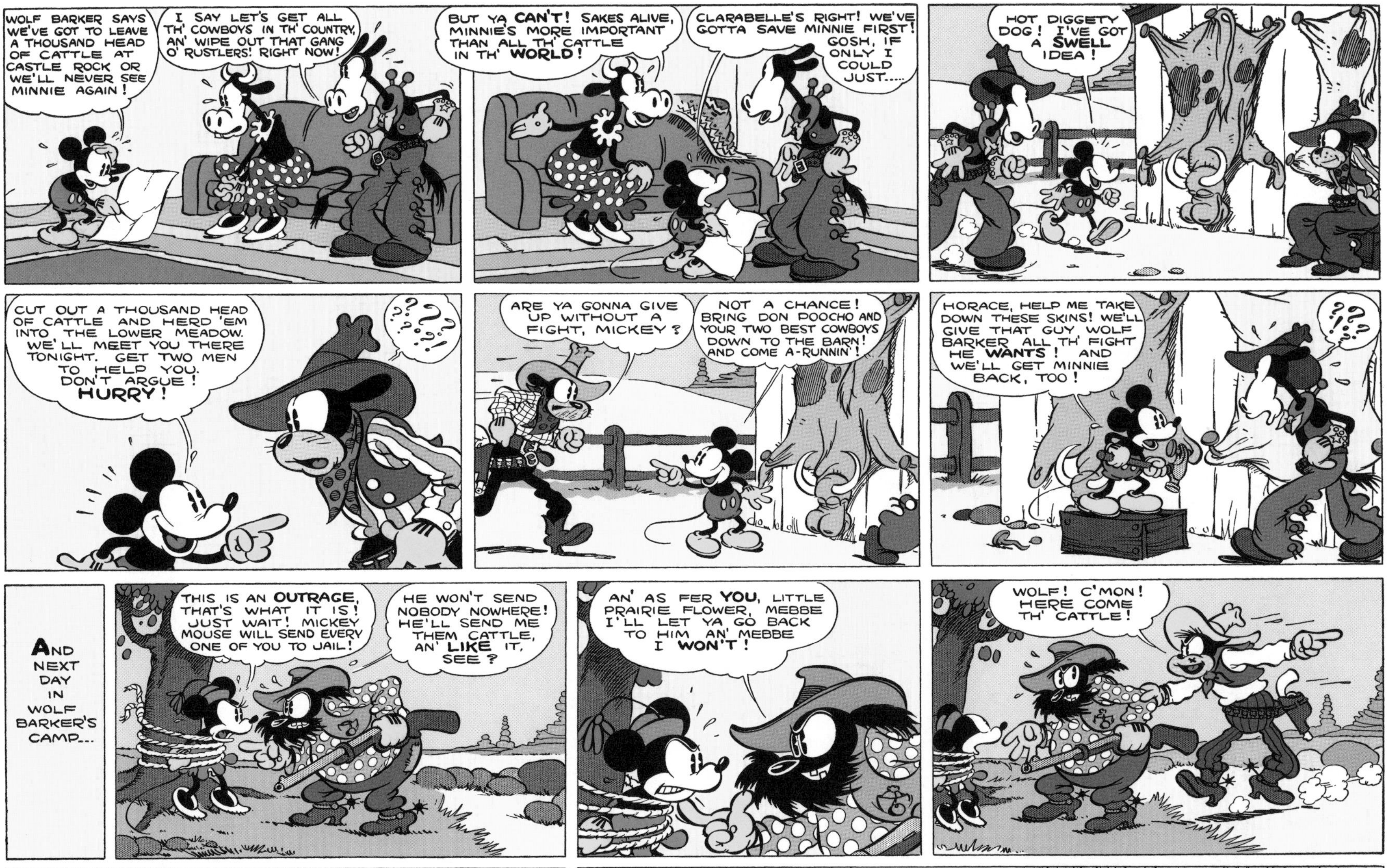
WOLF BARKER SAYS WE'VE GOT TO LEAVE A THOUSAND HEAD OF CATTLE AT CASTLE ROCK OR WE'LL NEVER SEE MINNIE AGAIN!
I SAY LET'S GET ALL TH' COWBOYS IN TH' COUNTRY, AN' WIPE OUT THAT GANG O' RUSTLERS! RIGHT NOW!
BUT YA CAN'T! SAKES ALIVE, MINNIE'S MORE IMPORTANT THAN ALL TH' CATTLE IN TH' WORLD!
CLARABELLE'S RIGHT! WE'VE GOTTA SAVE MINNIE FIRST!
GOSH, IF ONLY I COULD JUST.....
HOT DIGGETY DOG! I'VE GOT A SWELL IDEA!
CUT OUT A THOUSAND HEAD OF CATTLE AND HERD 'EM INTO THE LOWER MEADOW. WE'LL MEET YOU THERE TONIGHT. GET TWO MEN TO HELP YOU. DON'T ARGUE! HURRY!
??
ARE YA GONNA GIVE UP WITHOUT A FIGHT, MICKEY?
NOT A CHANCE! BRING DON POOCHO AND YOUR TWO BEST COWBOYS DOWN TO THE BARN! AND COME A-RUNNIN'!
HORACE, HELP ME TAKE DOWN THESE SKINS! WE'LL GIVE THAT GUY WOLF BARKER ALL TH' FIGHT HE WANTS! AND WE'LL GET MINNIE BACK, TOO!
??
AND NEXT DAY IN WOLF BARKER'S CAMP...
THIS IS AN OUTRAGE, THAT'S WHAT IT IS! JUST WAIT! MICKEY MOUSE WILL SEND EVERY ONE OF YOU TO JAIL!
HE WON'T SEND NOBODY NOWHERE! HE'LL SEND ME THEM CATTLE, AN' LIKE IT, SEE?
AN' AS FER YOU, LITTLE PRAIRIE FLOWER, MEBBE I'LL LET YA GO BACK TO HIM AN' MEBBE I WON'T!
WOLF! C'MON! HERE COME TH' CATTLE!
SEE, GAL? YER LITTLE HERO DIDN'T EVEN HAVE TH' NERVE T' COME HISSELF! HE AIN'T NOWHERE IN SIGHT!
GET YOUR GUNS READY, HORACE! WE'RE PRETTY NEAR THERE!
THANK GOODNESS! I'M DURNED NEAR SUFFOCATIN' IN THIS BLAMED COWSKIN!

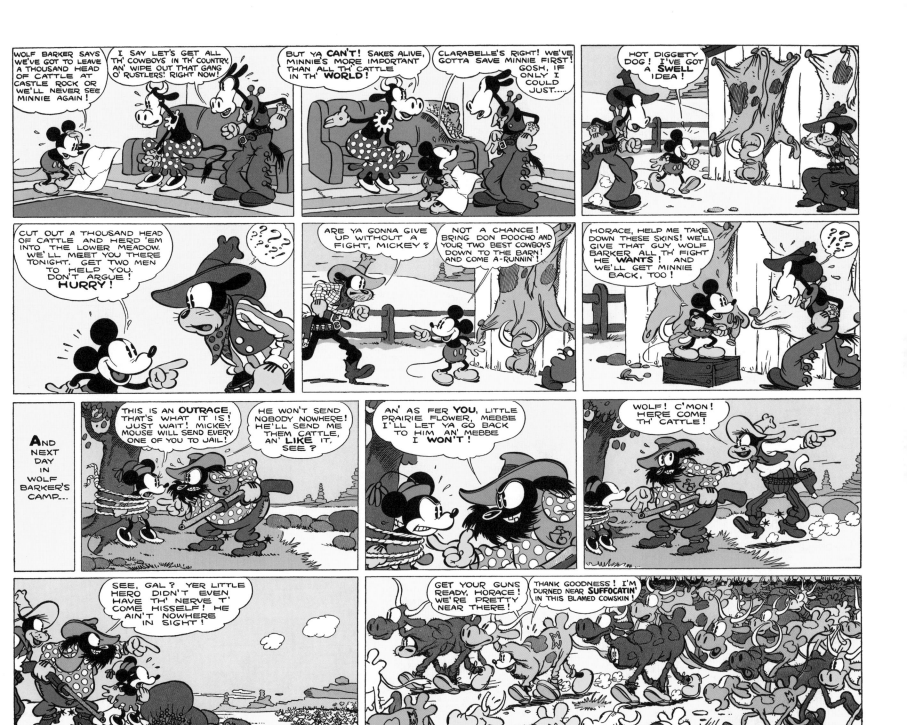

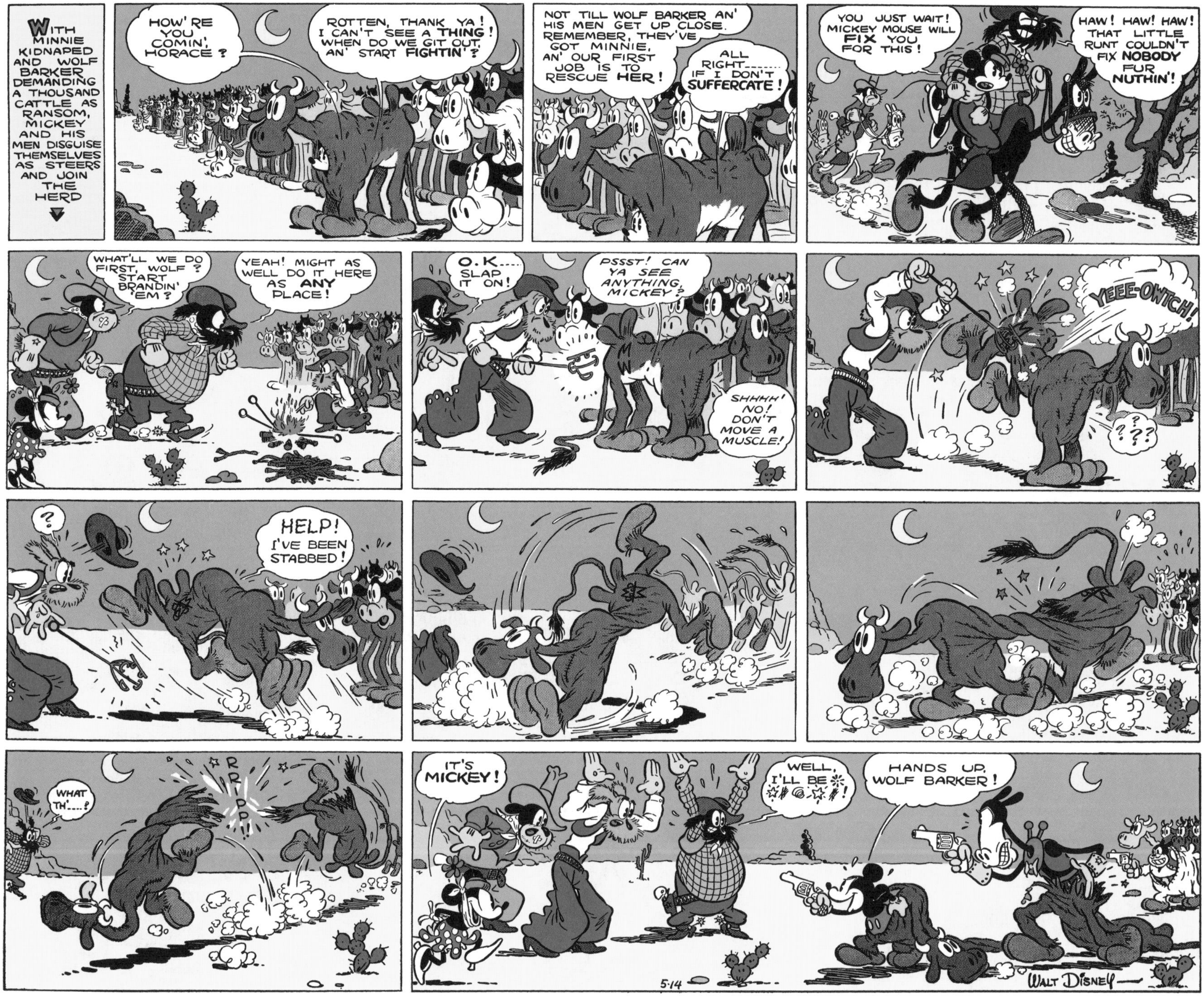

WITH MINNIE KIDNAPED AND WOLF BARKER DEMANDING A THOUSAND CATTLE AS RANSOM, MICKEY AND HIS MEN DISGUISE THEMSELVES AS STEERS AND JOIN THE HERD
HOW'RE YOU COMIN', HORACE?
ROTTEN, THANK YA! I CAN'T SEE A THING! WHEN DO WE GIT OUT, AN' START FIGHTIN'?
NOT TILL WOLF BARKER AN' HIS MEN GET UP CLOSE. REMEMBER, THEY'VE GOT MINNIE, AN' OUR FIRST JOB IS TO RESCUE HER!
ALL RIGHT------ IF I DON'T SUFFERCATE!
YOU JUST WAIT! MICKEY MOUSE WILL FIX YOU FOR THIS!
HAW! HAW! HAW! THAT LITTLE RUNT COULDN'T FIX NOBODY FUR NUTHIN'!
WHAT'LL WE DO FIRST, WOLF? START BRANDIN' 'EM?
YEAH! MIGHT AS WELL DO IT HERE AS ANY PLACE!
O.K.---- SLAP IT ON!
PSSST! CAN YA SEE ANYTHING, MICKEY?
SHHHH! NO! DON'T MOVE A MUSCLE!
YEEE-OWTCH!
???
?
HELP! I'VE BEEN STABBED!
WHAT TH'----?
RRIPP!!
IT'S MICKEY!
WELL, I'LL BE
HANDS UP, WOLF BARKER!
5-14
WALT DISNEY

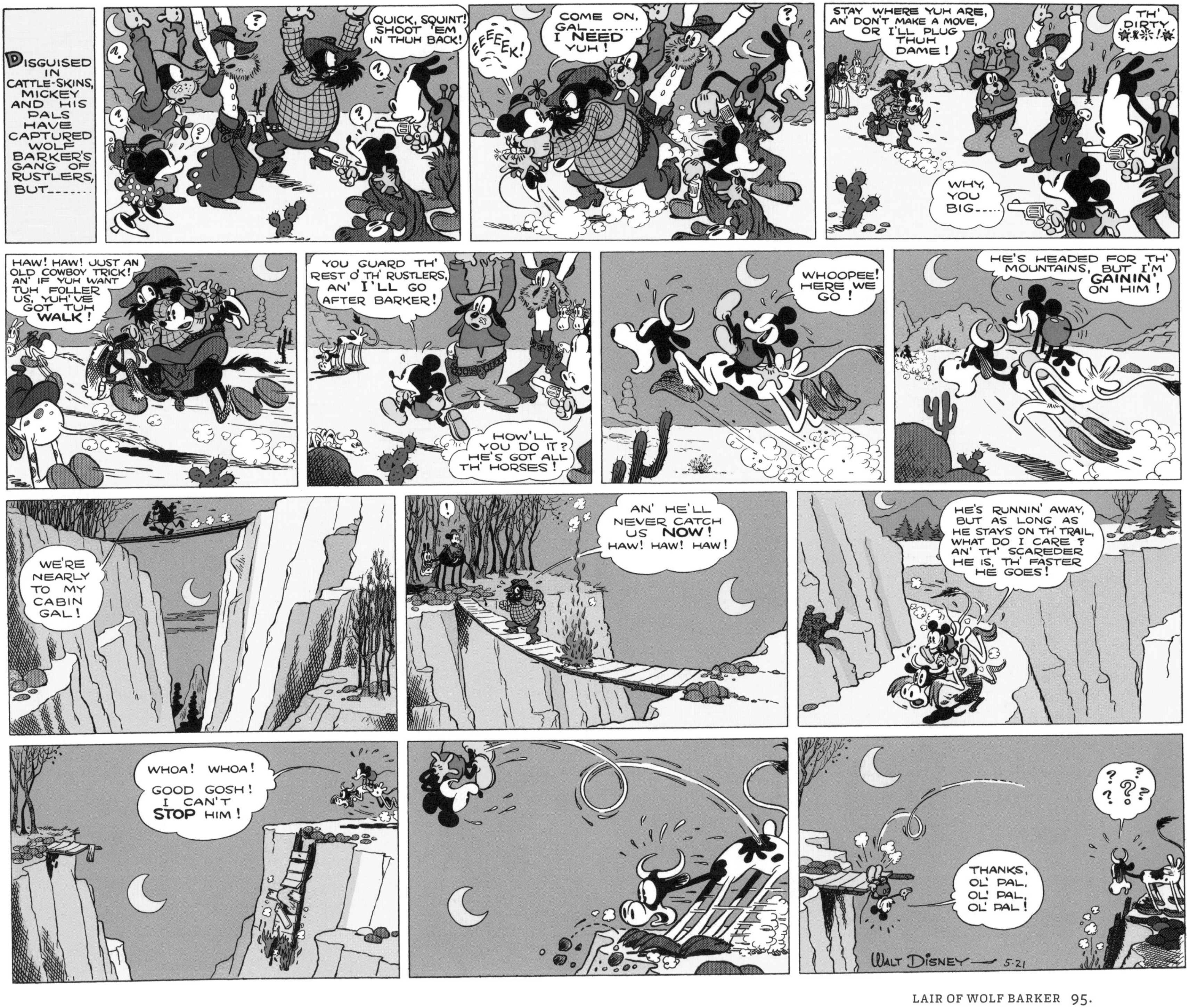

DISGUISED IN CATTLE-SKINS, MICKEY AND HIS PALS HAVE CAPTURED WOLF BARKER'S GANG OF RUSTLERS, BUT.......
QUICK, SQUINT! SHOOT 'EM IN THUH BACK!
EEEEEEK!
COME ON, GAL......... I NEED YUH!
STAY WHERE YUH ARE, AN' DON'T MAKE A MOVE, OR I'LL PLUG THUH DAME!
TH' DIRTY !
WHY, YOU BIG.....
HAW! HAW! JUST AN OLD COWBOY TRICK! AN' IF YUH WANT TUH FOLLER US, YUH'VE GOT TUH WALK!
YOU GUARD TH' REST O' TH' RUSTLERS, AN' I'LL GO AFTER BARKER!
HOW'LL YOU DO IT? HE'S GOT ALL TH' HORSES!
WHOOPEE! HERE WE GO!
HE'S HEADED FOR TH' MOUNTAINS, BUT I'M GAININ' ON HIM!
WE'RE NEARLY TO MY CABIN GAL!
AN' HE'LL NEVER CATCH US NOW! HAW! HAW! HAW!
HE'S RUNNIN' AWAY, BUT AS LONG AS HE STAYS ON TH' TRAIL, WHAT DO I CARE? AN' TH' SCAREDER HE IS, TH' FASTER HE GOES!
WHOA! WHOA! GOOD GOSH! I CAN'T STOP HIM!
THANKS, OL' PAL, OL' PAL, OL' PAL!
WALT DISNEY 5.21

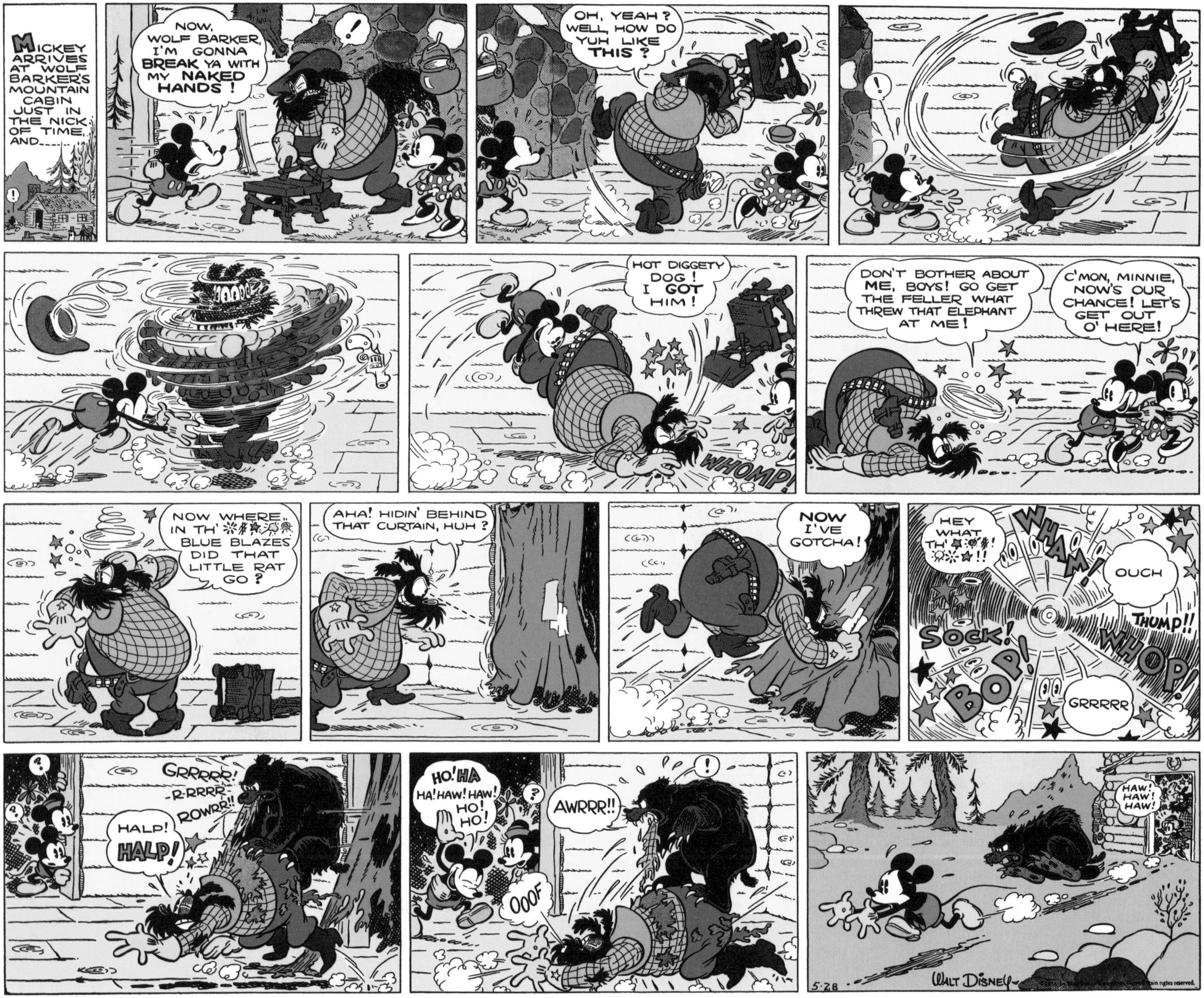

MICKEY ARRIVES AT WOLF BARKER'S MOUNTAIN CABIN JUST IN THE NICK OF TIME, AND-------
!
NOW, WOLF BARKER, I'M GONNA BREAK YA WITH MY NAKED HANDS!
!
OH, YEAH? WELL, HOW DO YUH LIKE THIS?
!
HOT DIGGETY DOG! I GOT HIM!
WHOMP!
DON'T BOTHER ABOUT ME, BOYS! GO GET THE FELLER WHAT THREW THAT ELEPHANT AT ME!
C'MON, MINNIE, NOW'S OUR CHANCE! LET'S GET OUT O' HERE!
NOW WHERE IN TH'
BLUE BLAZES DID THAT LITTLE RAT GO?
AHA! HIDIN' BEHIND THAT CURTAIN, HUH?
NOW I'VE GOTCHA!
HEY WHAT TH'
WHAM!
OUCH
THUMP!!
SOCK!
BOP!
WHOP!
GRRRRR
?
GRRRRR!
-R-RRRR
ROWRR!!
HALP!
HALP!
HO! HA
HA! HAW! HAW! HO! HO!
?
!
AWRRR!!
OOOF
HAW! HAW! HAW!
5-28
WALT DISNEY

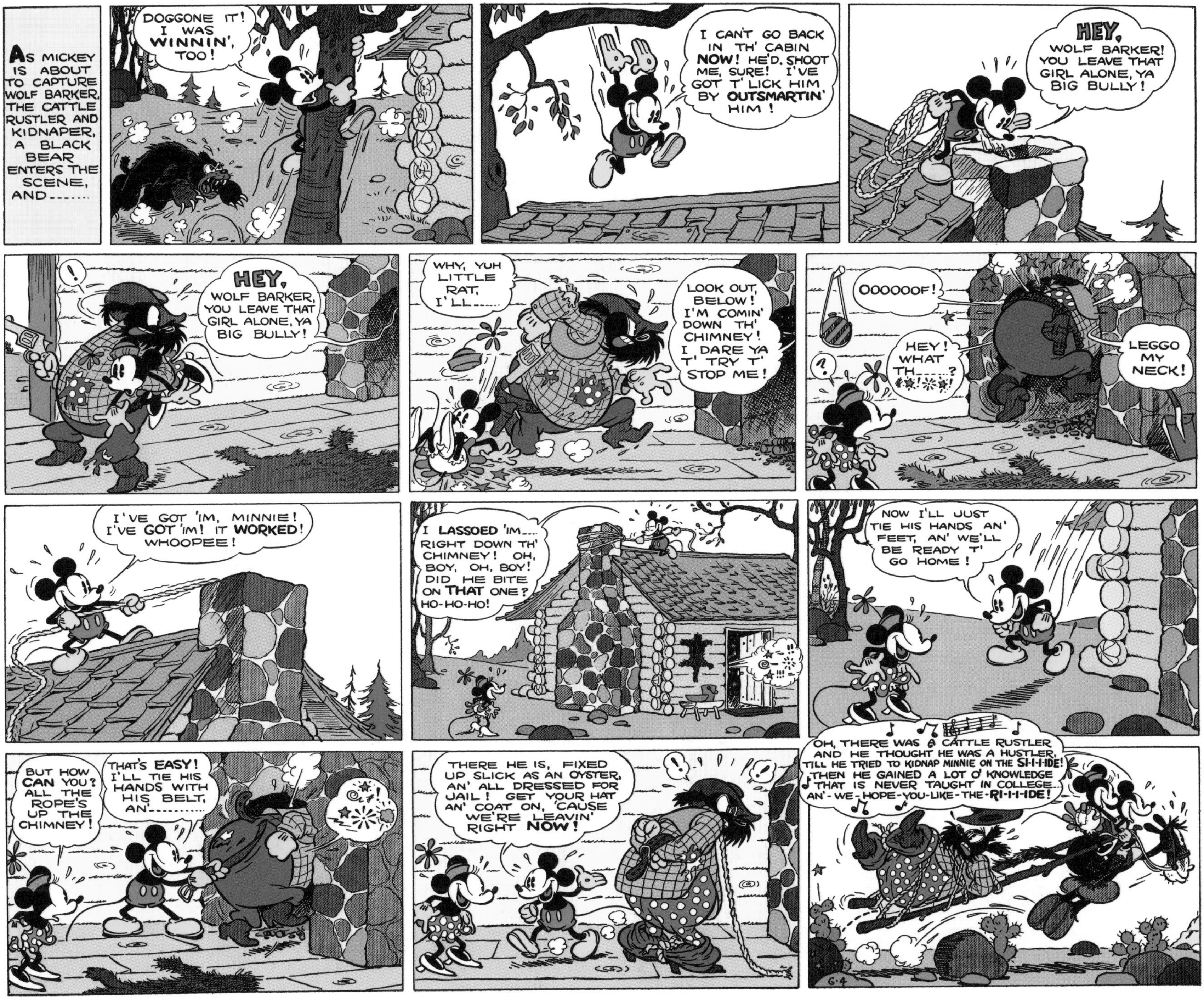
AS MICKEY IS ABOUT TO CAPTURE WOLF BARKER, THE CATTLE RUSTLER AND KIDNAPER, A BLACK BEAR ENTERS THE SCENE, AND-------
DOGGONE IT! I WAS WINNIN', TOO!
I CAN'T GO BACK IN TH' CABIN NOW! HE'D SHOOT ME, SURE! I'VE GOT T' LICK HIM BY OUTSMARTIN' HIM!
HEY, WOLF BARKER! YOU LEAVE THAT GIRL ALONE, YA BIG BULLY!
!
HEY, WOLF BARKER, YOU LEAVE THAT GIRL ALONE, YA BIG BULLY!
WHY, YUH LITTLE RAT, I'LL------
LOOK OUT, BELOW! I'M COMIN' DOWN TH' CHIMNEY! I DARE YA T' TRY T' STOP ME!
OOOOOOF!
?
HEY! WHAT TH------?
LEGGO MY NECK!
I'VE GOT 'IM, MINNIE! I'VE GOT 'IM! IT WORKED! WHOOPEE!
I LASSOED 'IM--- RIGHT DOWN TH' CHIMNEY! OH, BOY, OH, BOY! DID HE BITE ON THAT ONE? HO-HO-HO!
NOW I'LL JUST TIE HIS HANDS AN' FEET, AN' WE'LL BE READY T' GO HOME!
BUT HOW CAN YOU? ALL THE ROPE'S UP THE CHIMNEY!
THAT'S EASY! I'LL TIE HIS HANDS WITH HIS BELT, AN'----------
THERE HE IS, FIXED UP SLICK AS AN OYSTER, AN' ALL DRESSED FOR JAIL! GET YOUR HAT AN' COAT ON, 'CAUSE WE'RE LEAVIN' RIGHT NOW!
!
OH, THERE WAS A CATTLE RUSTLER AND HE THOUGHT HE WAS A HUSTLER, TILL HE TRIED TO KIDNAP MINNIE ON THE SI-I-I-IDE! THEN HE GAINED A LOT O' KNOWLEDGE THAT IS NEVER TAUGHT IN COLLEGE-- AN'-WE-HOPE-YOU-LIKE-THE-RI-I-I-IDE!
6-4

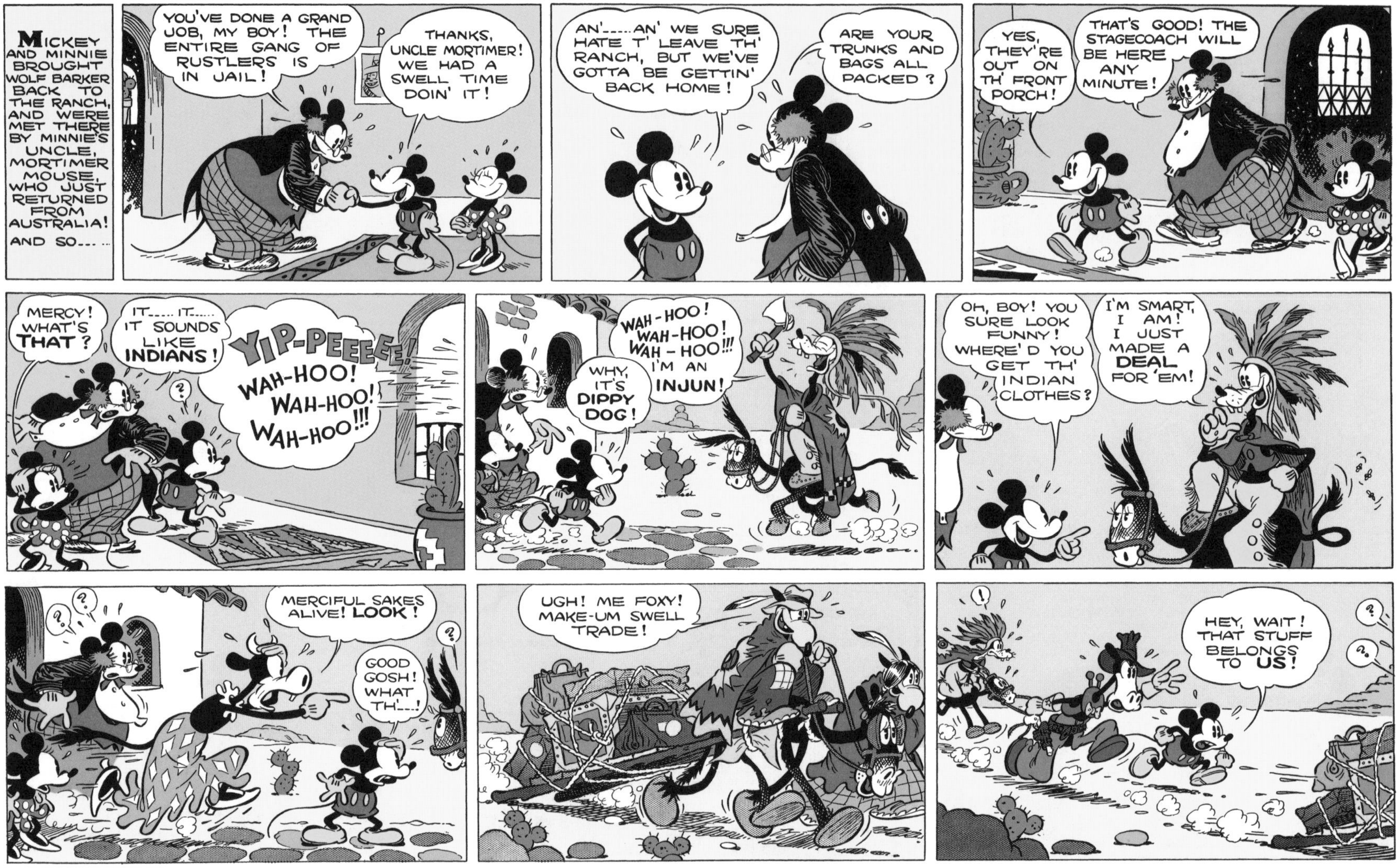
MICKEY AND MINNIE BROUGHT WOLF BARKER BACK TO THE RANCH, AND WERE MET THERE BY MINNIE'S UNCLE, MORTIMER MOUSE, WHO JUST RETURNED FROM AUSTRALIA! AND SO......
YOU'VE DONE A GRAND JOB, MY BOY! THE ENTIRE GANG OF RUSTLERS IS IN JAIL!
THANKS, UNCLE MORTIMER! WE HAD A SWELL TIME DOIN' IT!
AN'.....AN' WE SURE HATE T' LEAVE TH' RANCH, BUT WE'VE GOTTA BE GETTIN' BACK HOME!
ARE YOUR TRUNKS AND BAGS ALL PACKED?
YES, THEY'RE OUT ON TH' FRONT PORCH!
THAT'S GOOD! THE STAGECOACH WILL BE HERE ANY MINUTE!
MERCY! WHAT'S THAT?
IT..... IT..... IT SOUNDS LIKE INDIANS!
YIP-PEEEEEE! WAH-HOO! WAH-HOO! WAH-HOO!!!
WAH-HOO! WAH-HOO! WAH-HOO!!! I'M AN INJUN!
WHY, IT'S DIPPY DOG!
OH, BOY! YOU SURE LOOK FUNNY! WHERE'D YOU GET TH' INDIAN CLOTHES?
I'M SMART, I AM! I JUST MADE A DEAL FOR 'EM!
MERCIFUL SAKES ALIVE! LOOK!
GOOD GOSH! WHAT TH'...!
UGH! ME FOXY! MAKE-UM SWELL TRADE!
HEY, WAIT! THAT STUFF BELONGS TO US!
UGH! WHITE MAN NO GOOD! SAY YES .....SAY NO! BAHHHHHHH!
OF ALL THE DUMB, NIT-WITTED, HALF-BAKED.....OHHHHH! ANOTHER MINUTE, AN' WE'D OF HAD NO CLOTHES AT ALL! NO, SIR! I WON'T RIDE WITH HIM! I'LL STAY HERE FIRST!
SHUCKS! DARN! HECK! CONSARN IT!
6-11
WALT DISNEY

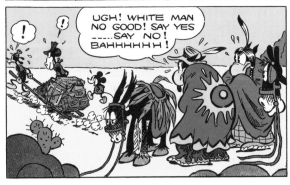

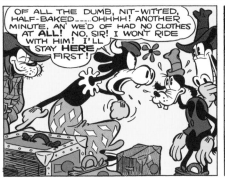

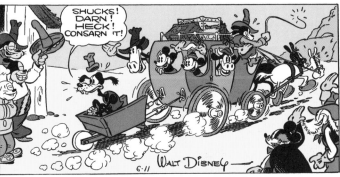

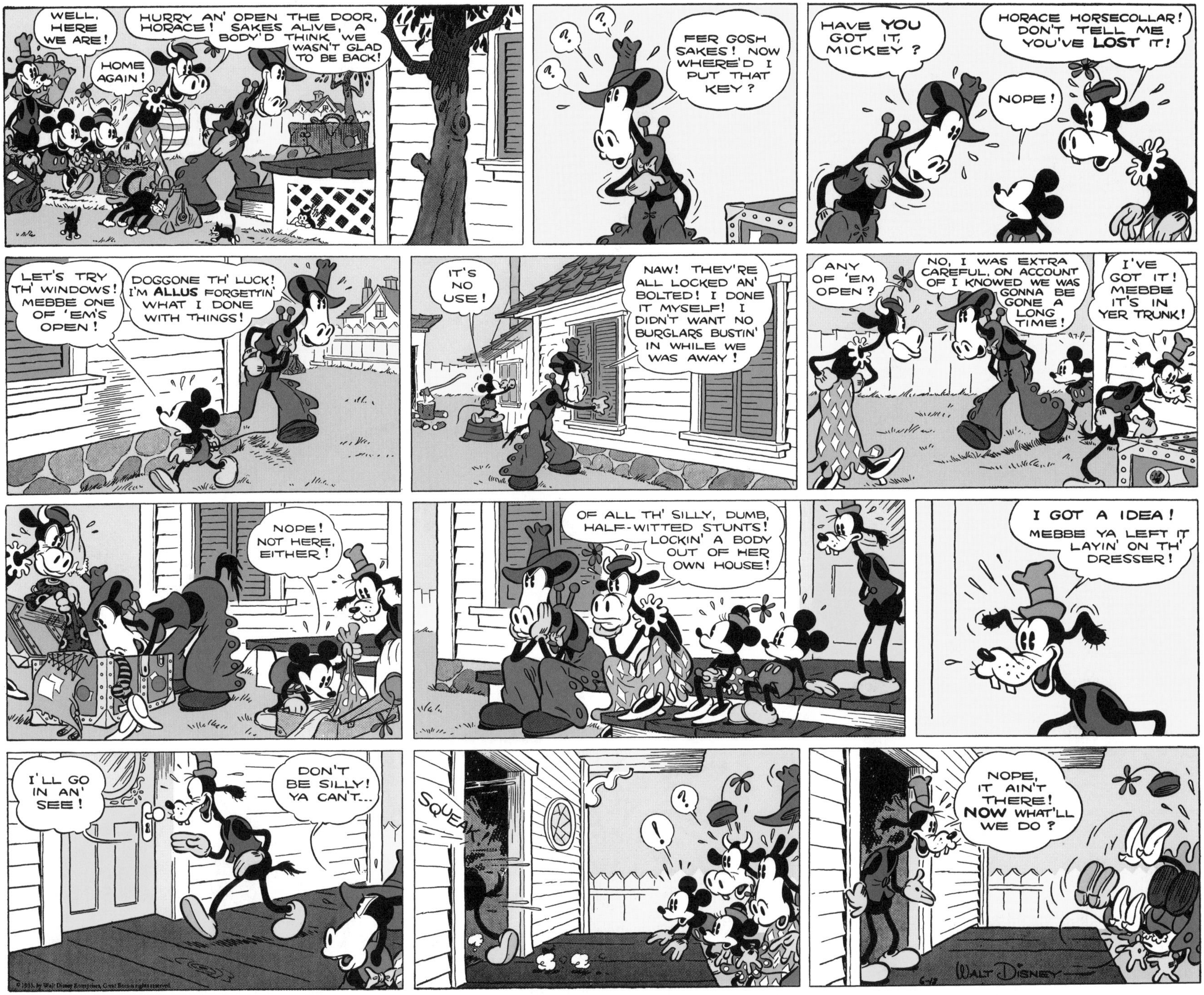
WELL, HERE WE ARE!
HURRY AN' OPEN THE DOOR, HORACE! SAKES ALIVE, A BODY'D THINK WE WASN'T GLAD TO BE BACK!
HOME AGAIN!
?
?
?
FER GOSH SAKES! NOW WHERE'D I PUT THAT KEY?
HAVE **YOU** GOT IT, MICKEY?
HORACE HORSECOLLAR! DON'T TELL ME YOU'VE **LOST** IT!
NOPE!
LET'S TRY TH' WINDOWS! MEBBE ONE OF 'EM'S OPEN!
DOGGONE TH' LUCK! I'M **ALLUS** FORGETTIN' WHAT I DONE WITH THINGS!
IT'S NO USE!
NAW! THEY'RE ALL LOCKED AN' BOLTED! I DONE IT MYSELF! I DIDN'T WANT NO BURGLARS BUSTIN' IN WHILE WE WAS AWAY!
ANY OF 'EM OPEN?
NO, I WAS EXTRA CAREFUL, ON ACCOUNT OF I KNOWED WE WAS GONNA BE GONE A LONG TIME!
I'VE GOT IT! MEBBE IT'S IN YER TRUNK!
NOPE! NOT HERE, EITHER!
OF ALL TH' SILLY, DUMB, HALF-WITTED STUNTS! LOCKIN' A BODY OUT OF HER OWN HOUSE!
I GOT A IDEA! MEBBE YA LEFT IT LAYIN' ON TH' DRESSER!
I'LL GO IN AN' SEE!
DON'T BE SILLY! YA CAN'T...
SQUEAK
?
!
NOPE, IT AIN'T THERE! **NOW** WHAT'LL WE DO?
WALT DISNEY

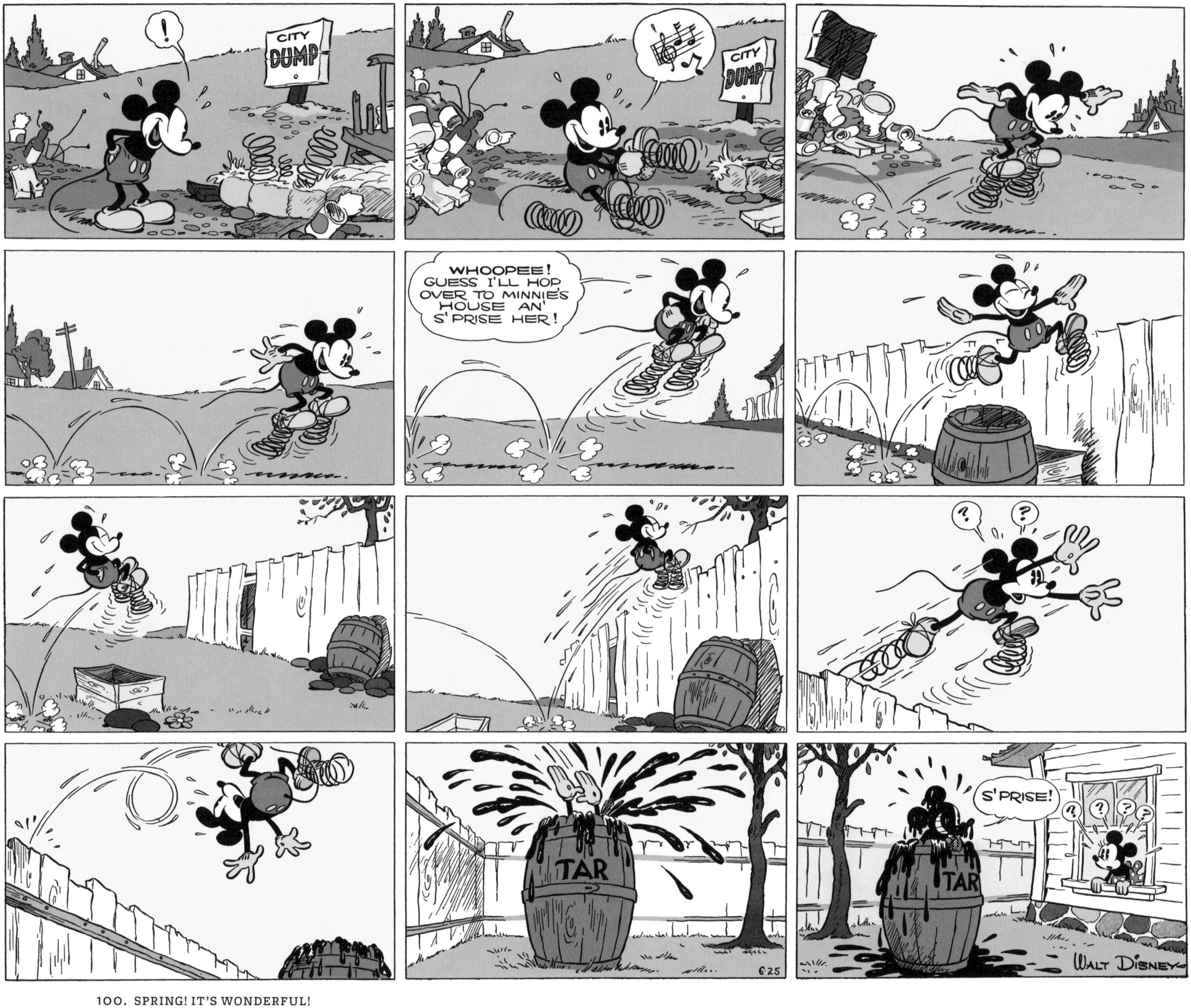
CITY DUMP
CITY DUMP
WHOOPEE! GUESS I'LL HOP OVER TO MINNIE'S HOUSE AN' S'PRISE HER!
TAR
6-25
S'PRISE!
TAR
WALT DISNEY

100. SPRING! IT'S WONDERFUL!

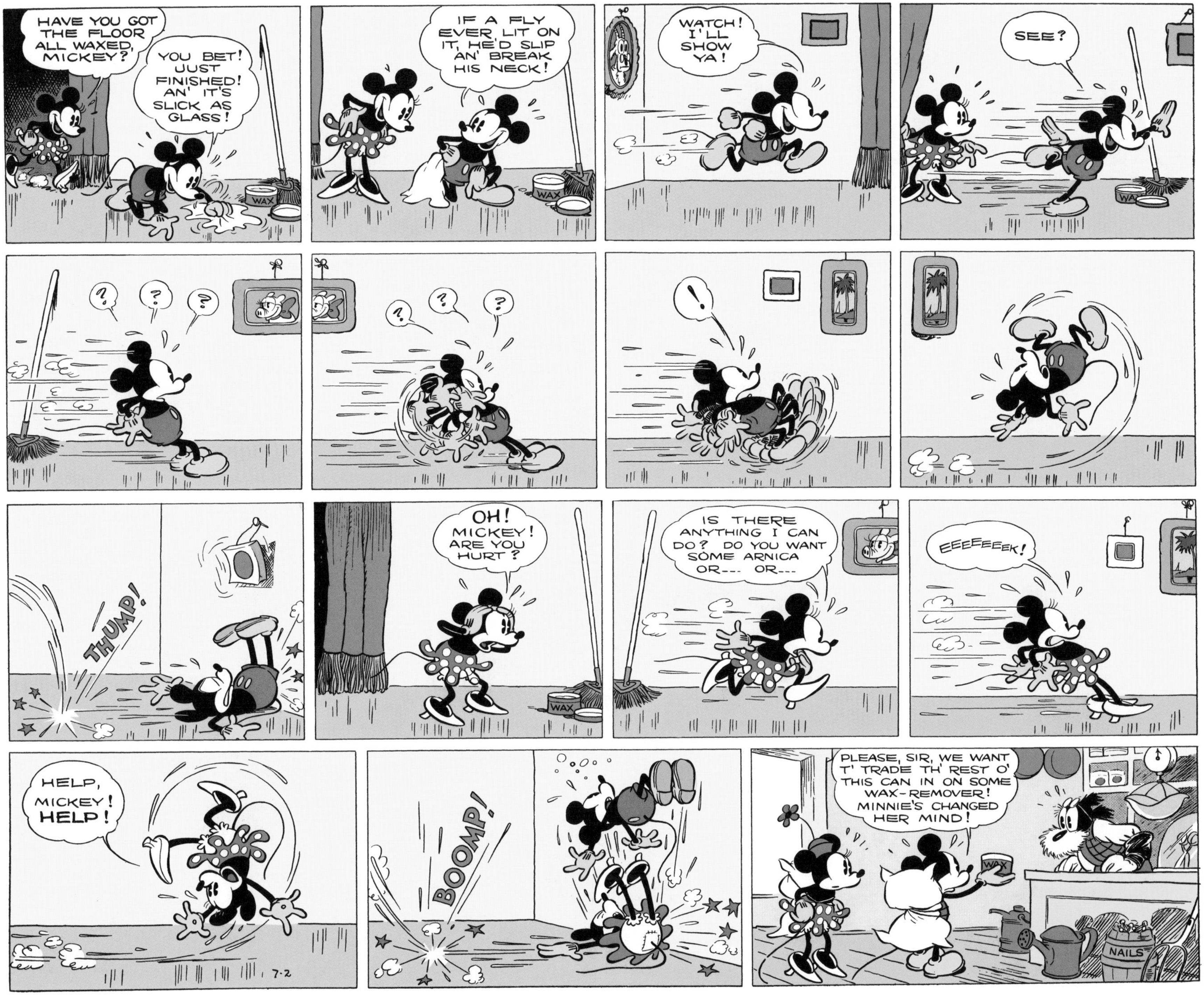
HAVE YOU GOT THE FLOOR ALL WAXED, MICKEY?
YOU BET! JUST FINISHED! AN' IT'S SLICK AS GLASS!
WAX
IF A FLY EVER LIT ON IT, HE'D SLIP AN' BREAK HIS NECK!
WAX
WATCH! I'LL SHOW YA!
SEE?
?
?
?
?
?
?
!
THUMP!
OH! MICKEY! ARE YOU HURT?
WAX
IS THERE ANYTHING I CAN DO? DO YOU WANT SOME ARNICA OR--- OR---
EEEEEEEEK!
HELP, MICKEY! HELP!
7·2
BOOMP!
PLEASE, SIR, WE WANT T' TRADE TH' REST O' THIS CAN IN ON SOME WAX-REMOVER! MINNIE'S CHANGED HER MIND!
WAX
NAILS

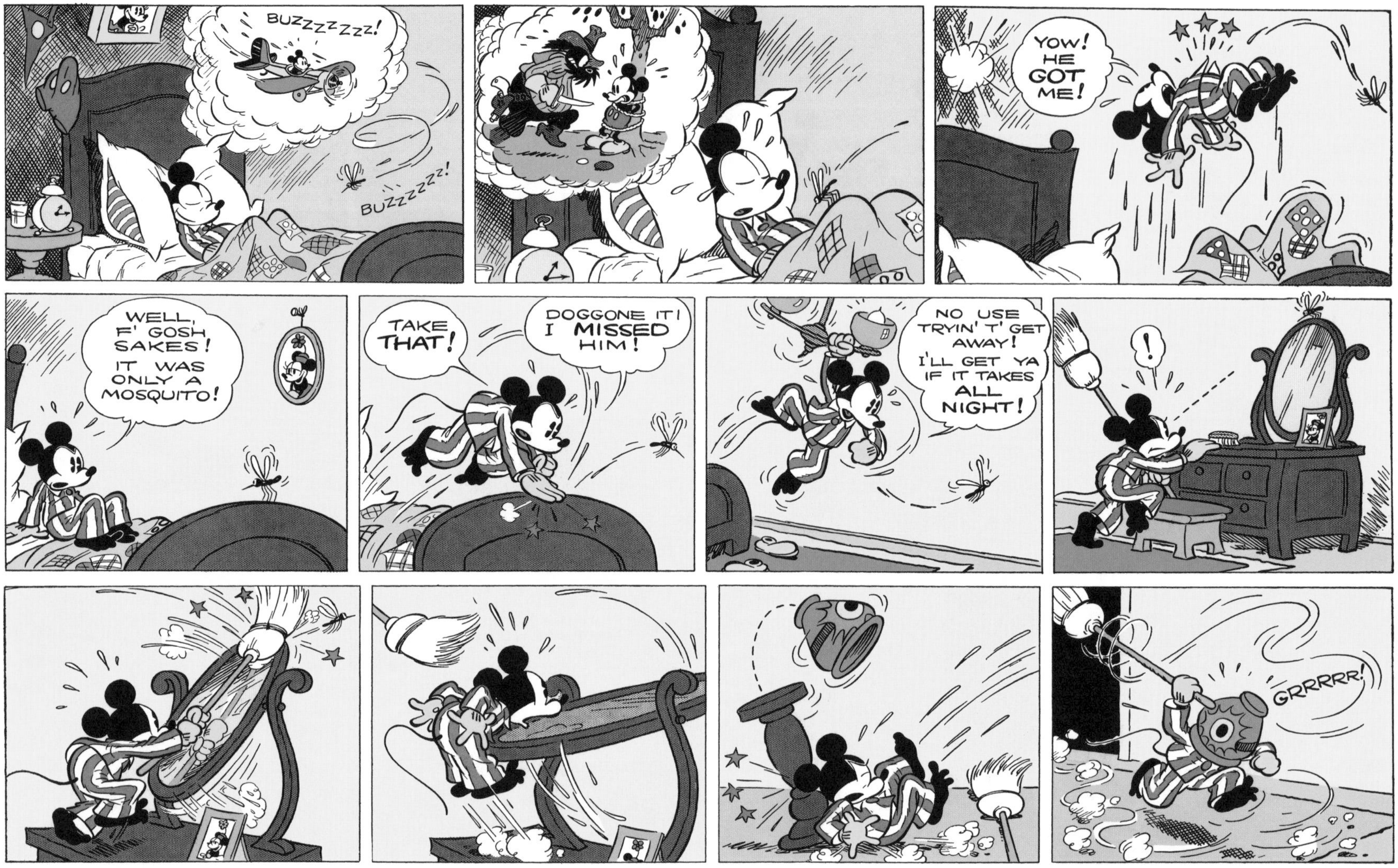
BUZZZZZZZ!
BUZZZZZZ!
YOW! HE GOT ME!
WELL, F' GOSH SAKES! IT WAS ONLY A MOSQUITO!
TAKE THAT!
DOGGONE IT! I MISSED HIM!
NO USE TRYIN' T' GET AWAY! I'LL GET YA IF IT TAKES ALL NIGHT!
!
GRRRRR!
NOW, WHERE'D THAT LITTLE PEST GO?
AH! THERE HE IS!
!
?
WALT DISNEY

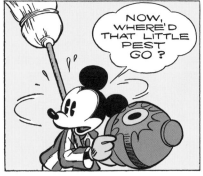

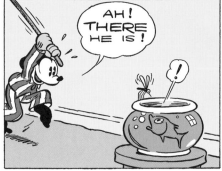

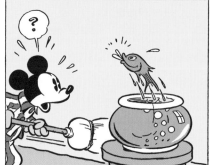

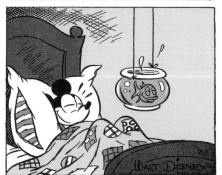

102. THE MOSQUITOES' PARADE

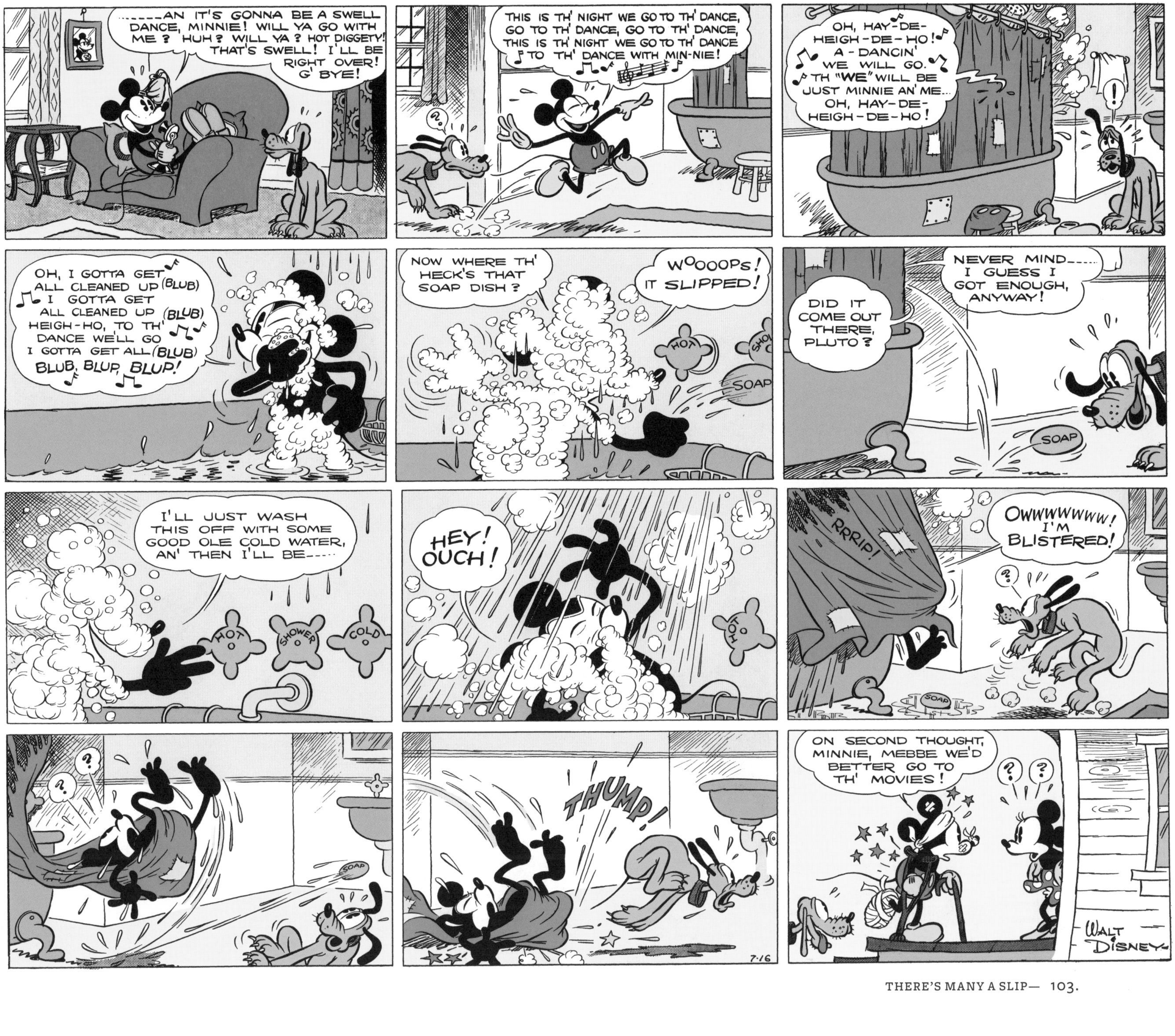

......AN IT'S GONNA BE A SWELL DANCE, MINNIE! WILL YA GO WITH ME? HUH? WILL YA? HOT DIGGETY! THAT'S SWELL! I'LL BE RIGHT OVER! G' BYE!
THIS IS TH' NIGHT WE GO TO TH' DANCE, GO TO TH' DANCE, GO TO TH' DANCE, THIS IS TH' NIGHT WE GO TO TH' DANCE TO TH' DANCE WITH MIN-NIE!
OH, HAY-DE-HEIGH-DE-HO! A-DANCIN' WE WILL GO. TH "WE" WILL BE JUST MINNIE AN' ME... OH, HAY-DE-HEIGH-DE-HO!
OH, I GOTTA GET ALL CLEANED UP (BLUB) I GOTTA GET ALL CLEANED UP (BLUB) HEIGH-HO, TO TH' DANCE WE'LL GO I GOTTA GET ALL (BLUB) BLUB, BLUP, BLUP!
NOW WHERE TH' HECK'S THAT SOAP DISH?
WOOOOPS! IT SLIPPED!
HOT
SOAP
DID IT COME OUT THERE, PLUTO?
NEVER MIND..... I GUESS I GOT ENOUGH, ANYWAY!
SOAP
I'LL JUST WASH THIS OFF WITH SOME GOOD OLE COLD WATER, AN' THEN I'LL BE-----
HOT
SHOWER
COLD
HEY! OUCH!
HOT
RRRIP!
OWWWWWWW! I'M BLISTERED!
SOAP
SOAP
THUMP!
7-16
ON SECOND THOUGHT, MINNIE, MEBBE WE'D BETTER GO TO TH' MOVIES!
WALT DISNEY

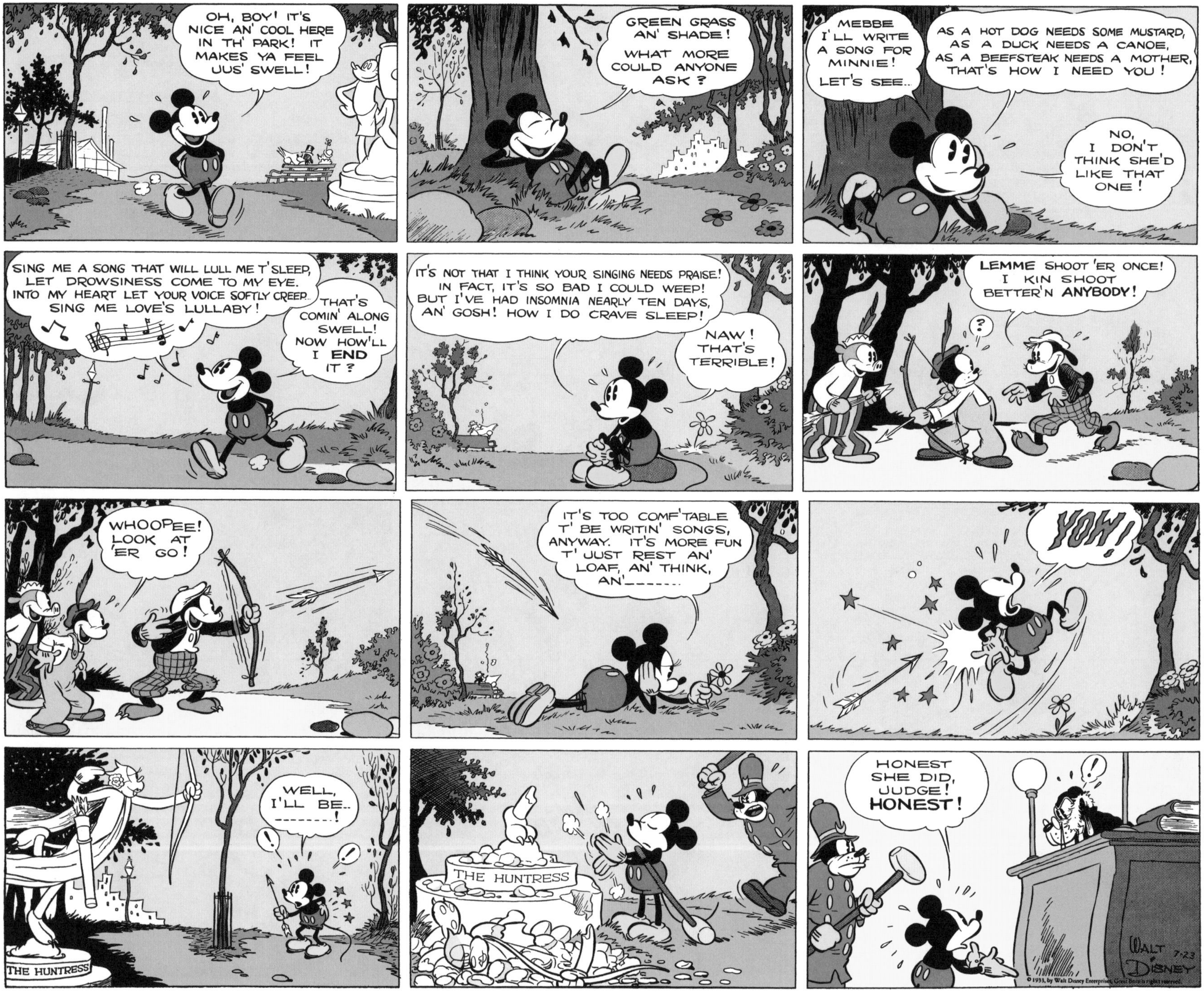
OH, BOY! IT'S NICE AN' COOL HERE IN TH' PARK! IT MAKES YA FEEL UUS' SWELL!
GREEN GRASS AN' SHADE! WHAT MORE COULD ANYONE ASK?
MEBBE I'LL WRITE A SONG FOR MINNIE! LET'S SEE...
AS A HOT DOG NEEDS SOME MUSTARD, AS A DUCK NEEDS A CANOE, AS A BEEFSTEAK NEEDS A MOTHER, THAT'S HOW I NEED YOU!
NO, I DON'T THINK SHE'D LIKE THAT ONE!
SING ME A SONG THAT WILL LULL ME T'SLEEP, LET DROWSINESS COME TO MY EYE. INTO MY HEART LET YOUR VOICE SOFTLY CREEP... SING ME LOVE'S LULLABY!
THAT'S COMIN' ALONG SWELL! NOW HOW'LL I END IT?
IT'S NOT THAT I THINK YOUR SINGING NEEDS PRAISE! IN FACT, IT'S SO BAD I COULD WEEP! BUT I'VE HAD INSOMNIA NEARLY TEN DAYS, AN' GOSH! HOW I DO CRAVE SLEEP!
NAW! THAT'S TERRIBLE!
LEMME SHOOT 'ER ONCE! I KIN SHOOT BETTER'N ANYBODY!
WHOOPEE! LOOK AT 'ER GO!
IT'S TOO COMF'TABLE T' BE WRITIN' SONGS, ANYWAY. IT'S MORE FUN T' JUST REST AN' LOAF, AN' THINK, AN'-------
YOW!
THE HUNTRESS
WELL, I'LL BE.. -------!
THE HUNTRESS
HONEST SHE DID, JUDGE! HONEST!
WALT DISNEY 7-23
1933, by Walt Disney Enterprises, Great Britain rights reserved.

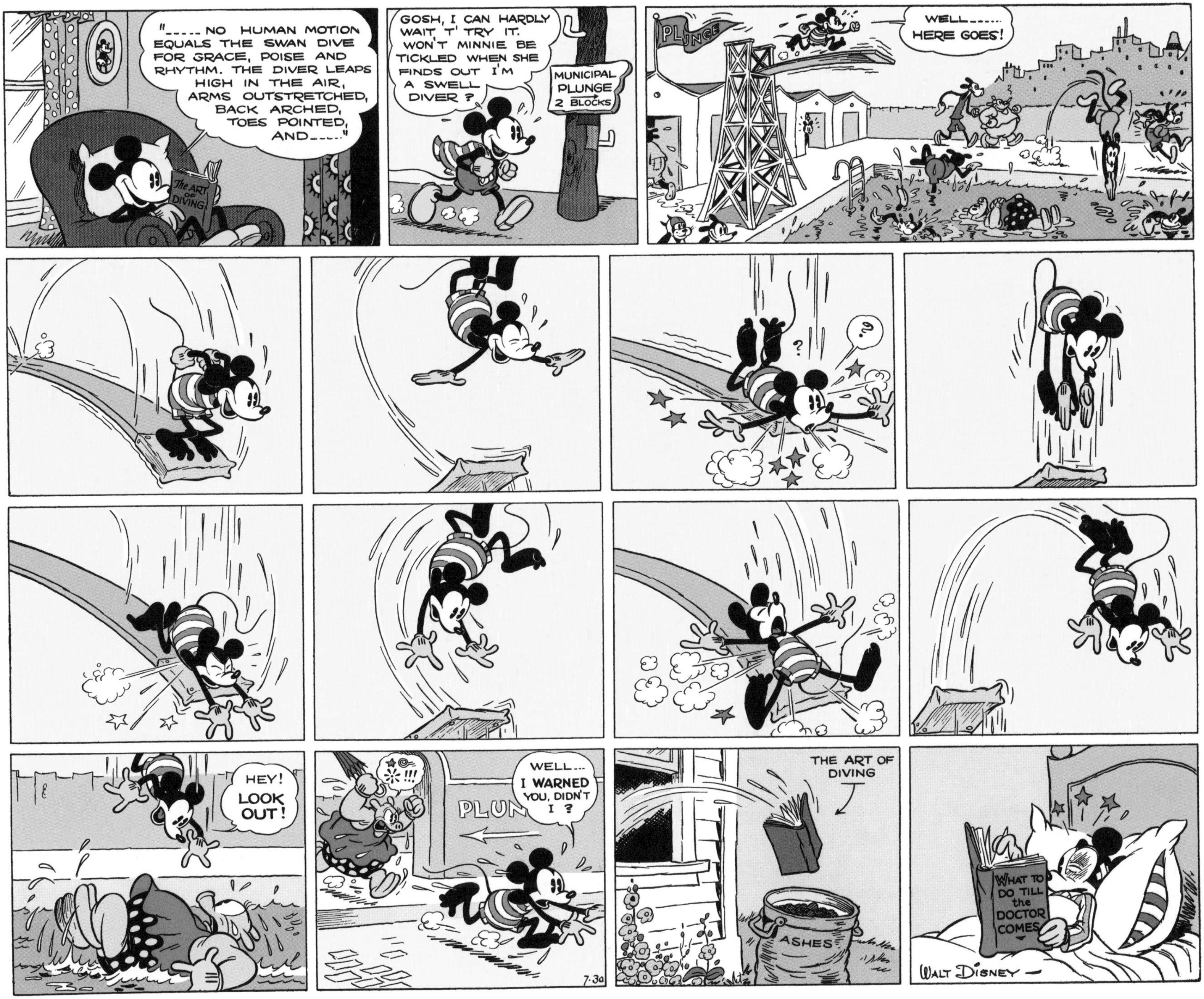
"----- NO HUMAN MOTION EQUALS THE SWAN DIVE FOR GRACE, POISE AND RHYTHM. THE DIVER LEAPS HIGH IN THE AIR, ARMS OUTSTRETCHED, BACK ARCHED, TOES POINTED, AND----."
The ART of DIVING
GOSH, I CAN HARDLY WAIT T' TRY IT. WON'T MINNIE BE TICKLED WHEN SHE FINDS OUT I'M A SWELL DIVER ?
MUNICIPAL PLUNGE 2 BLOCKS
PLUNGE
WELL----- HERE GOES!
HEY! LOOK OUT!
WELL... I WARNED YOU, DIDN'T I ?
PLUN
7-30
THE ART OF DIVING
ASHES
WHAT TO DO TILL the DOCTOR COMES
WALT DISNEY

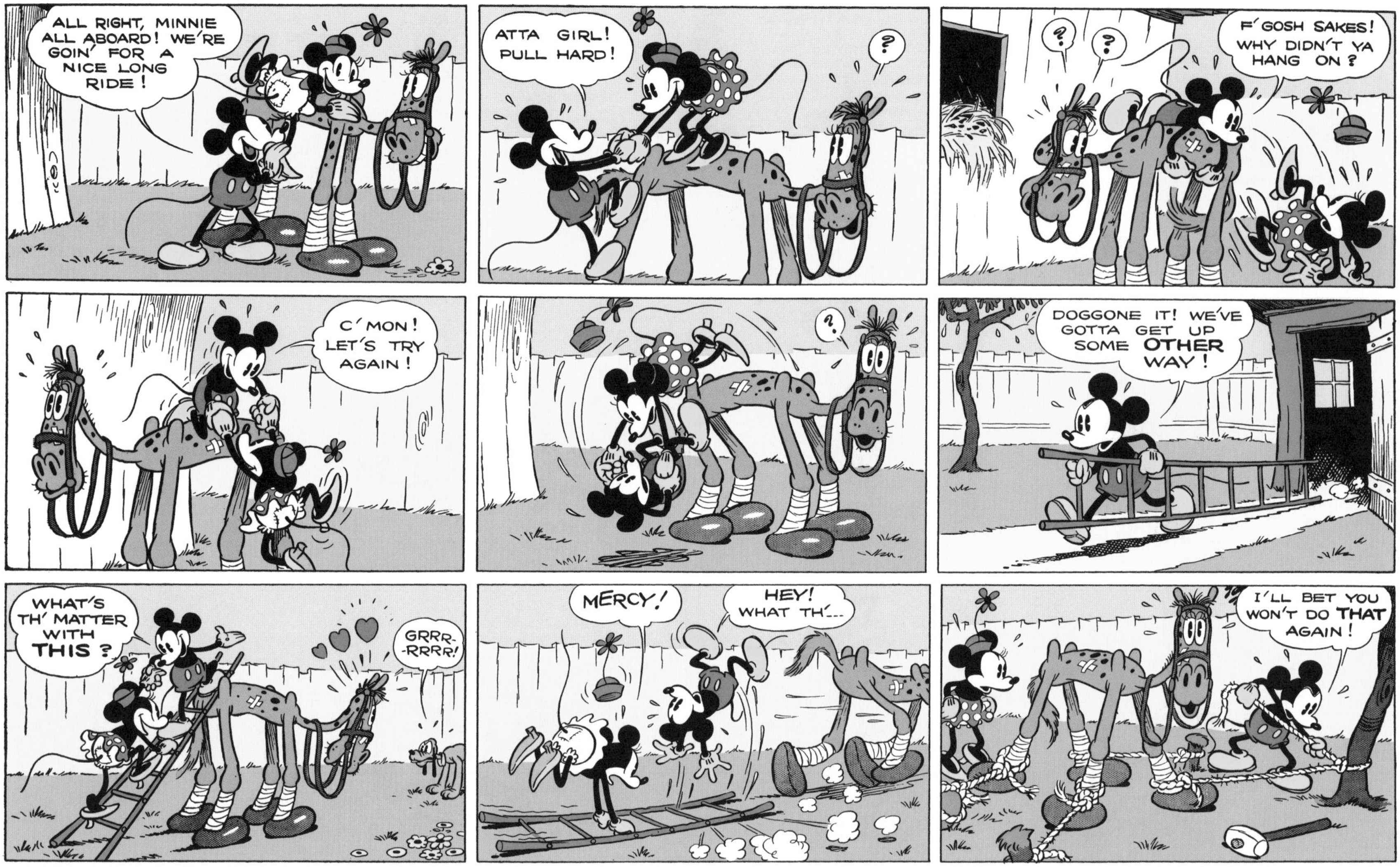
ALL RIGHT, MINNIE ALL ABOARD! WE'RE GOIN' FOR A NICE LONG RIDE!
ATTA GIRL! PULL HARD!
?
??
?
F' GOSH SAKES! WHY DIDN'T YA HANG ON?
C'MON! LET'S TRY AGAIN!
?
DOGGONE IT! WE'VE GOTTA GET UP SOME OTHER WAY!
WHAT'S TH' MATTER WITH THIS?
GRRR-RRRR!
MERCY!
HEY! WHAT TH'---
I'LL BET YOU WON'T DO THAT AGAIN!
STEP RIGHT THIS WAY, MADAM!
I GUESS I AIN'T SO DUMB!
WELL------ HERE WE ARE!
YES, BUT, MICKEY----
!
HOW ARE YOU GOING TO UNTIE HIM?
8-6
WALT DISNEY

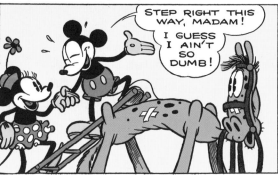

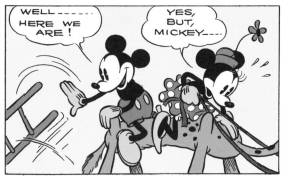

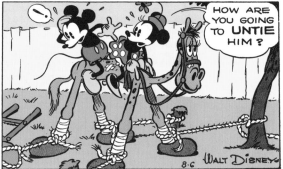

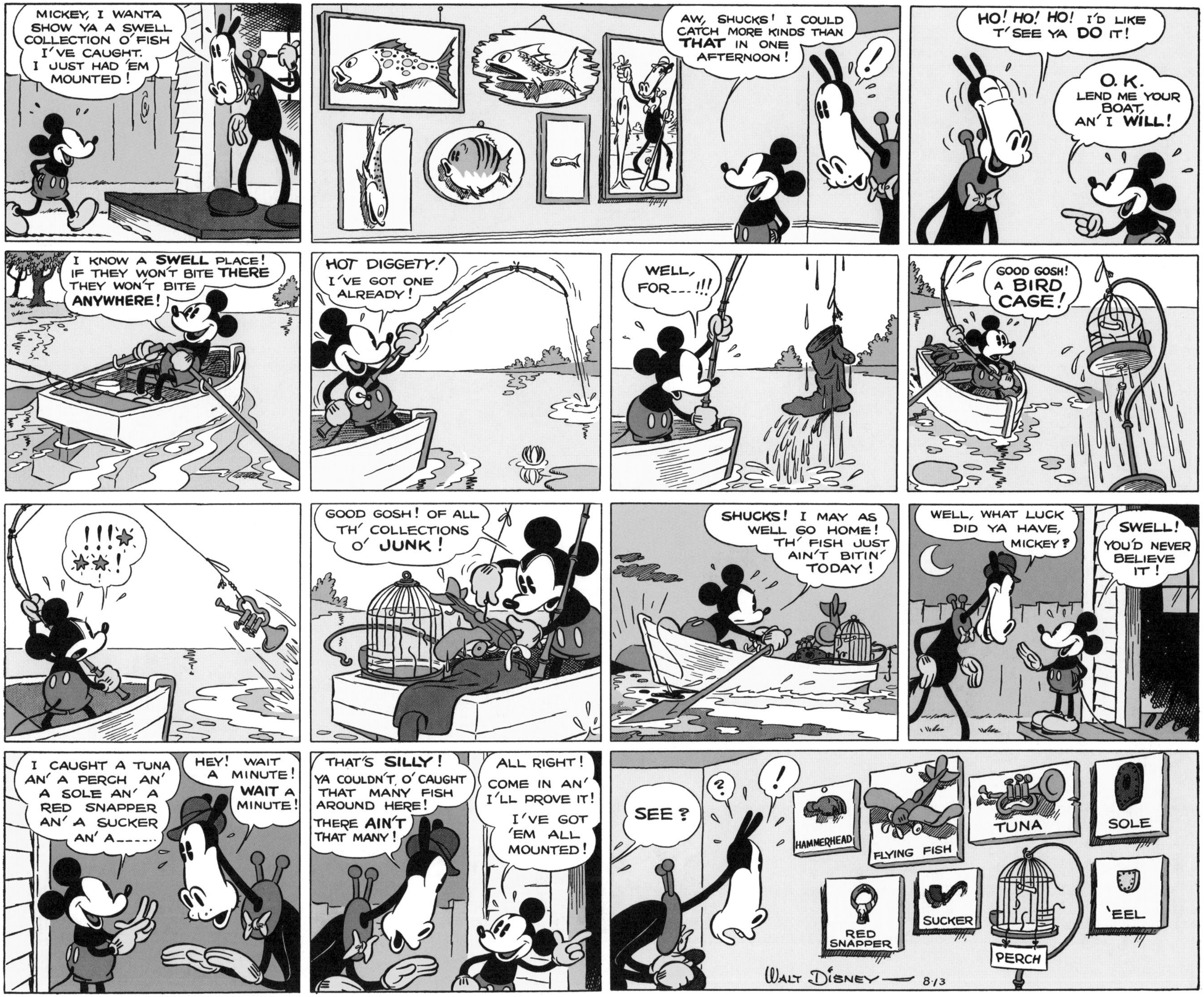
MICKEY, I WANTA SHOW YA A SWELL COLLECTION O' FISH I'VE CAUGHT. I JUST HAD 'EM MOUNTED!
AW, SHUCKS! I COULD CATCH MORE KINDS THAN THAT IN ONE AFTERNOON!
!
HO! HO! HO! I'D LIKE T' SEE YA DO IT!
O.K. LEND ME YOUR BOAT, AN' I WILL!
I KNOW A SWELL PLACE! IF THEY WON'T BITE THERE THEY WON'T BITE ANYWHERE!
HOT DIGGETY! I'VE GOT ONE ALREADY!
WELL, FOR---!!!
GOOD GOSH! A BIRD CAGE!
!!!!
GOOD GOSH! OF ALL TH' COLLECTIONS O' JUNK!
SHUCKS! I MAY AS WELL GO HOME! TH' FISH JUST AIN'T BITIN' TODAY!
WELL, WHAT LUCK DID YA HAVE, MICKEY?
SWELL! YOU'D NEVER BELIEVE IT!
I CAUGHT A TUNA AN' A PERCH AN' A SOLE AN' A RED SNAPPER AN' A SUCKER AN' A-----
HEY! WAIT A MINUTE! WAIT A MINUTE!
THAT'S SILLY! YA COULDN'T O' CAUGHT THAT MANY FISH AROUND HERE! THERE AIN'T THAT MANY!
ALL RIGHT! COME IN AN' I'LL PROVE IT! I'VE GOT 'EM ALL MOUNTED!
SEE?
?
!
HAMMERHEAD
FLYING FISH
TUNA
SOLE
RED SNAPPER
SUCKER
'EEL
PERCH
WALT DISNEY 8-13

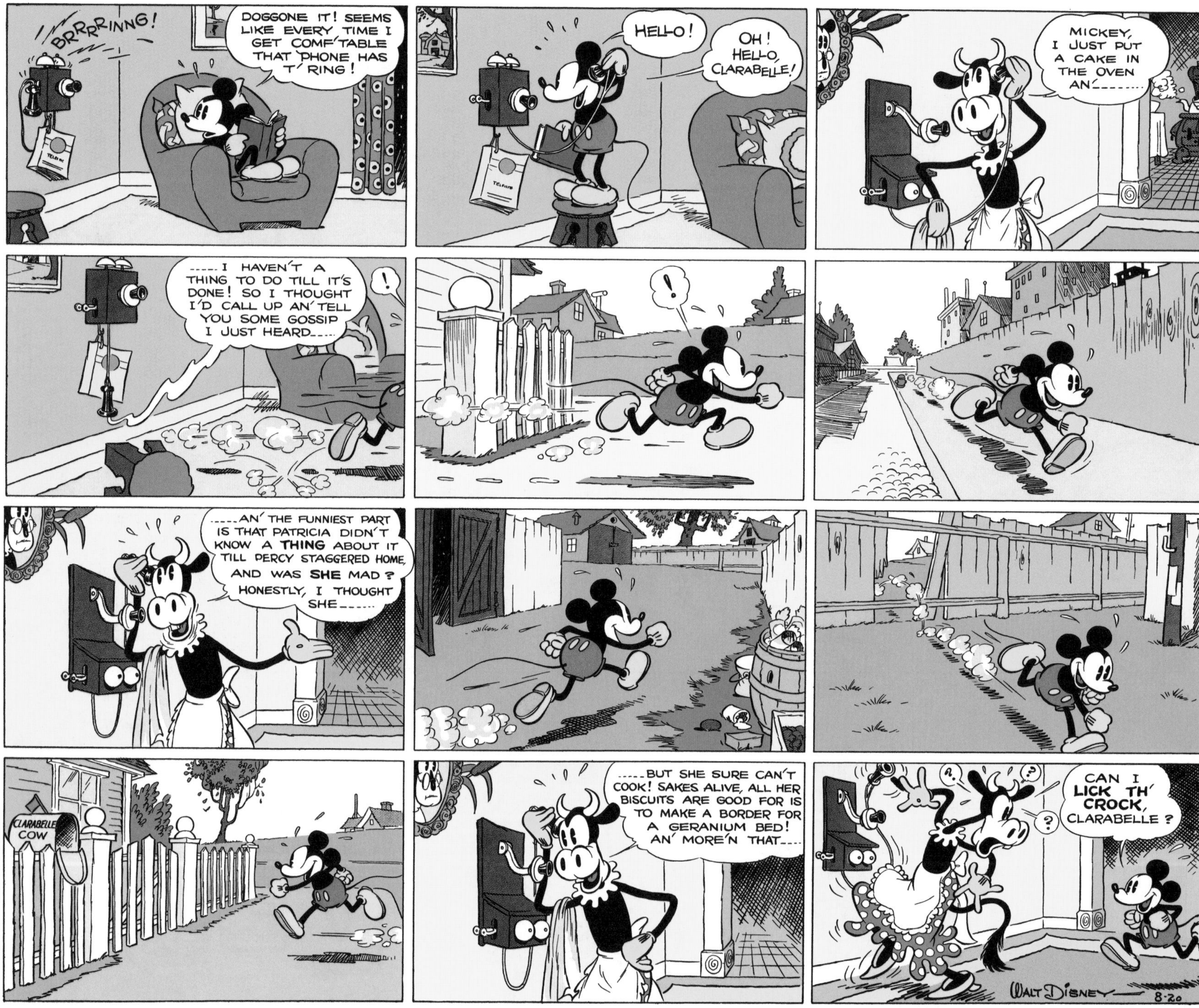
BRRRRINNG!
DOGGONE IT! SEEMS LIKE EVERY TIME I GET COMF'TABLE THAT 'PHONE HAS T' RING!
HELLO!
OH! HELLO, CLARABELLE!
MICKEY, I JUST PUT A CAKE IN THE OVEN AN'------
-----I HAVEN'T A THING TO DO TILL IT'S DONE! SO I THOUGHT I'D CALL UP AN' TELL YOU SOME GOSSIP I JUST HEARD-----
!
!
-----AN' THE FUNNIEST PART IS THAT PATRICIA DIDN'T KNOW A THING ABOUT IT TILL PERCY STAGGERED HOME, AND WAS SHE MAD? HONESTLY, I THOUGHT SHE------
CLARABELLE COW
-----BUT SHE SURE CAN'T COOK! SAKES ALIVE, ALL HER BISCUITS ARE GOOD FOR IS TO MAKE A BORDER FOR A GERANIUM BED! AN' MORE'N THAT-----
?
?
?
CAN I LICK TH' CROCK, CLARABELLE?
WALT DISNEY
8-20

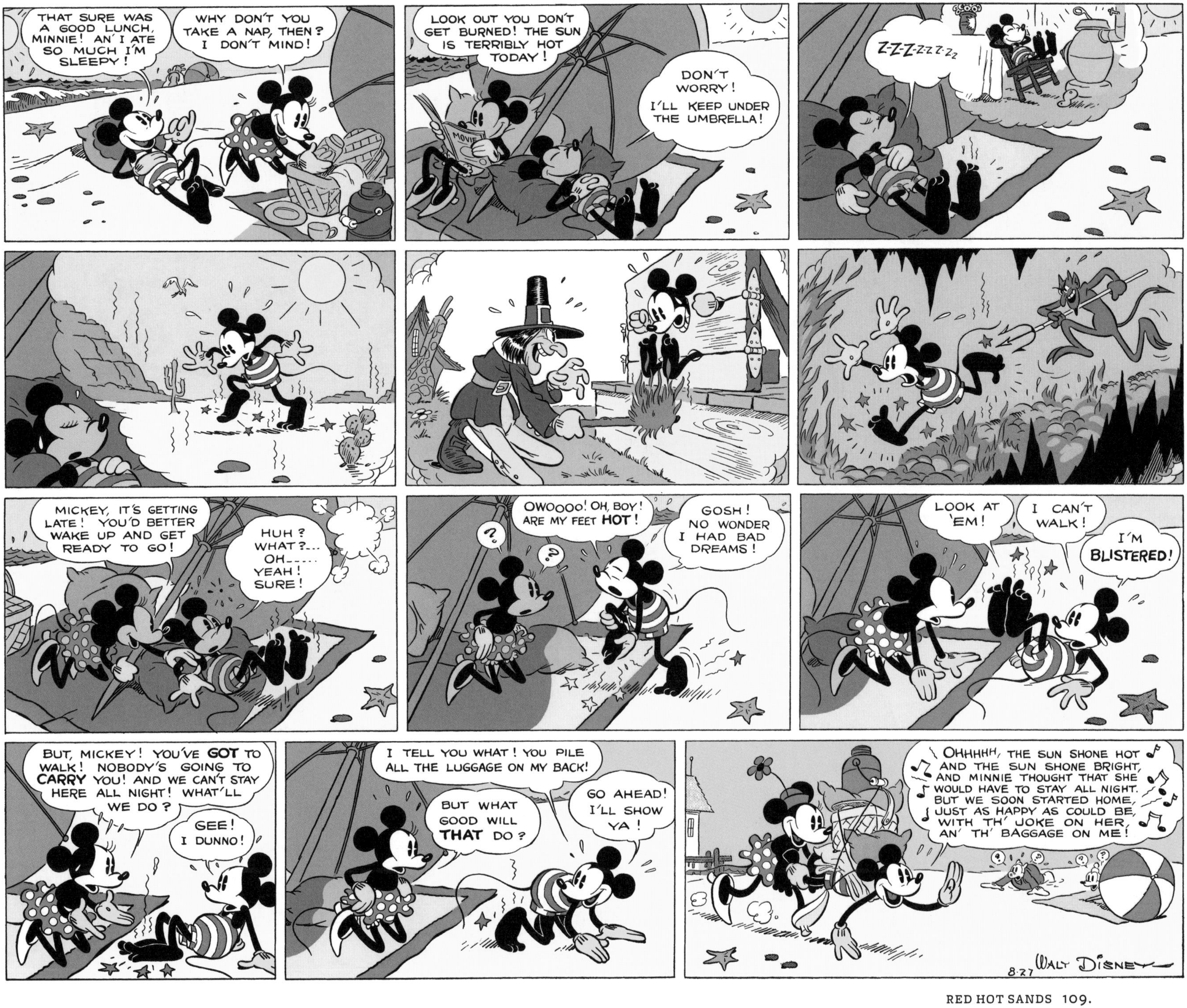
THAT SURE WAS A GOOD LUNCH, MINNIE! AN' I ATE SO MUCH I'M SLEEPY!
WHY DON'T YOU TAKE A NAP, THEN? I DON'T MIND!
LOOK OUT YOU DON'T GET BURNED! THE SUN IS TERRIBLY HOT TODAY!
MOVIE
DON'T WORRY! I'LL KEEP UNDER THE UMBRELLA!
Z-Z-Z-Z-Z-Z-Z-Z
MICKEY, IT'S GETTING LATE! YOU'D BETTER WAKE UP AND GET READY TO GO!
HUH? WHAT?... OH..... YEAH! SURE!
OWOOOO! OH, BOY! ARE MY FEET HOT!
GOSH! NO WONDER I HAD BAD DREAMS!
LOOK AT 'EM!
I CAN'T WALK!
I'M BLISTERED!
BUT, MICKEY! YOU'VE GOT TO WALK! NOBODY'S GOING TO CARRY YOU! AND WE CAN'T STAY HERE ALL NIGHT! WHAT'LL WE DO?
GEE! I DUNNO!
I TELL YOU WHAT! YOU PILE ALL THE LUGGAGE ON MY BACK!
BUT WHAT GOOD WILL THAT DO?
GO AHEAD! I'LL SHOW YA!
OHHHHH, THE SUN SHONE HOT AND THE SUN SHONE BRIGHT, AND MINNIE THOUGHT THAT SHE WOULD HAVE TO STAY ALL NIGHT. BUT WE SOON STARTED HOME, JUST AS HAPPY AS COULD BE, WITH TH' JOKE ON HER, AN' TH' BAGGAGE ON ME!
8-27 WALT DISNEY

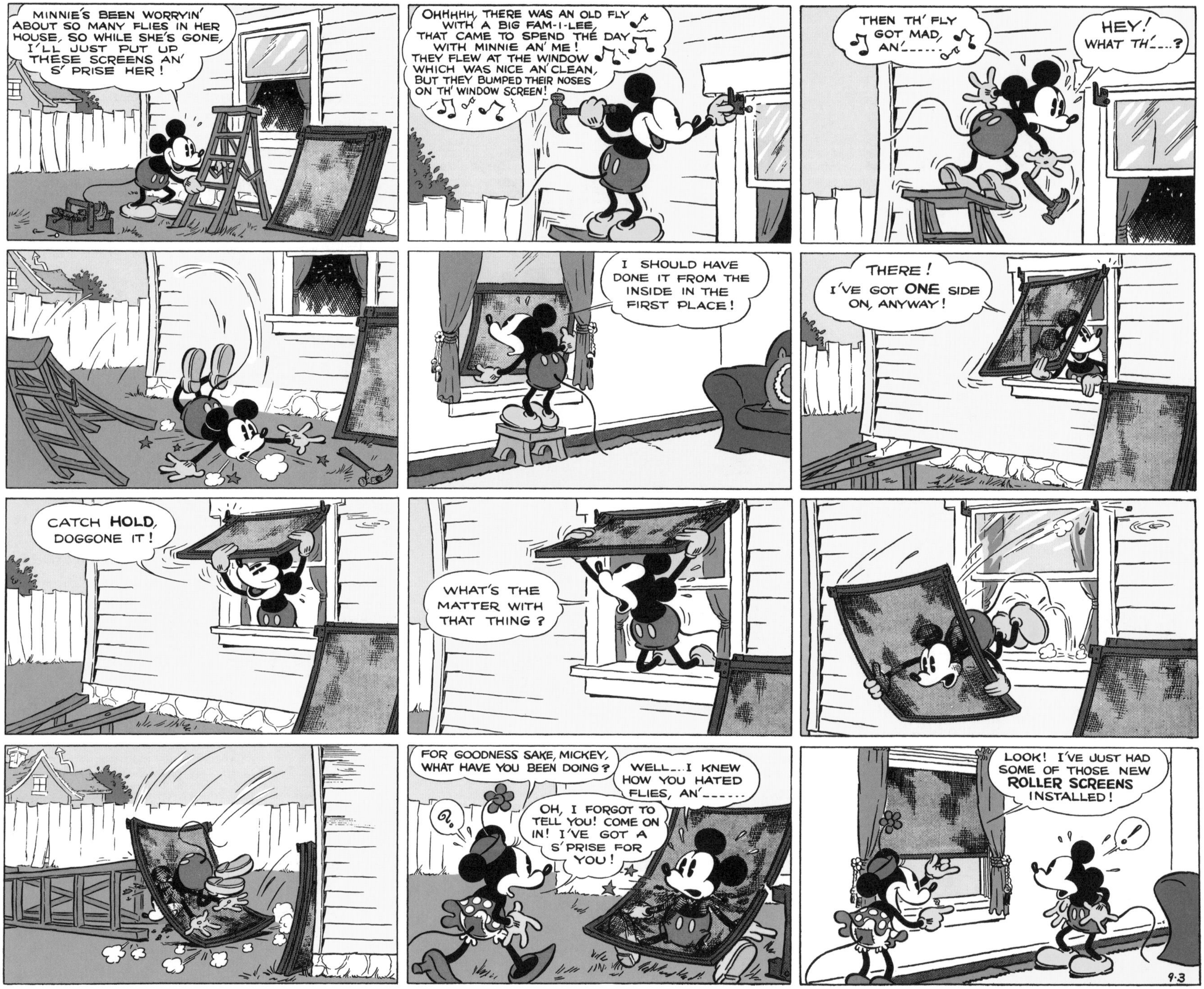

MINNIE'S BEEN WORRYIN' ABOUT SO MANY FLIES IN HER HOUSE, SO WHILE SHE'S GONE, I'LL JUST PUT UP THESE SCREENS AN' S'PRISE HER!
OHHHHH, THERE WAS AN OLD FLY WITH A BIG FAM-I-LEE, THAT CAME TO SPEND THE DAY WITH MINNIE AN' ME! THEY FLEW AT THE WINDOW WHICH WAS NICE AN' CLEAN, BUT THEY BUMPED THEIR NOSES ON TH' WINDOW SCREEN!
THEN TH' FLY GOT MAD, AN'------
HEY! WHAT TH'---?
I SHOULD HAVE DONE IT FROM THE INSIDE IN THE FIRST PLACE!
THERE! I'VE GOT ONE SIDE ON, ANYWAY!
CATCH HOLD, DOGGONE IT!
WHAT'S THE MATTER WITH THAT THING?
FOR GOODNESS SAKE, MICKEY, WHAT HAVE YOU BEEN DOING?
WELL---I KNEW HOW YOU HATED FLIES, AN'------
OH, I FORGOT TO TELL YOU! COME ON IN! I'VE GOT A S'PRISE FOR YOU!
LOOK! I'VE JUST HAD SOME OF THOSE NEW ROLLER SCREENS INSTALLED!
9-3

110. WINDOW PAIN

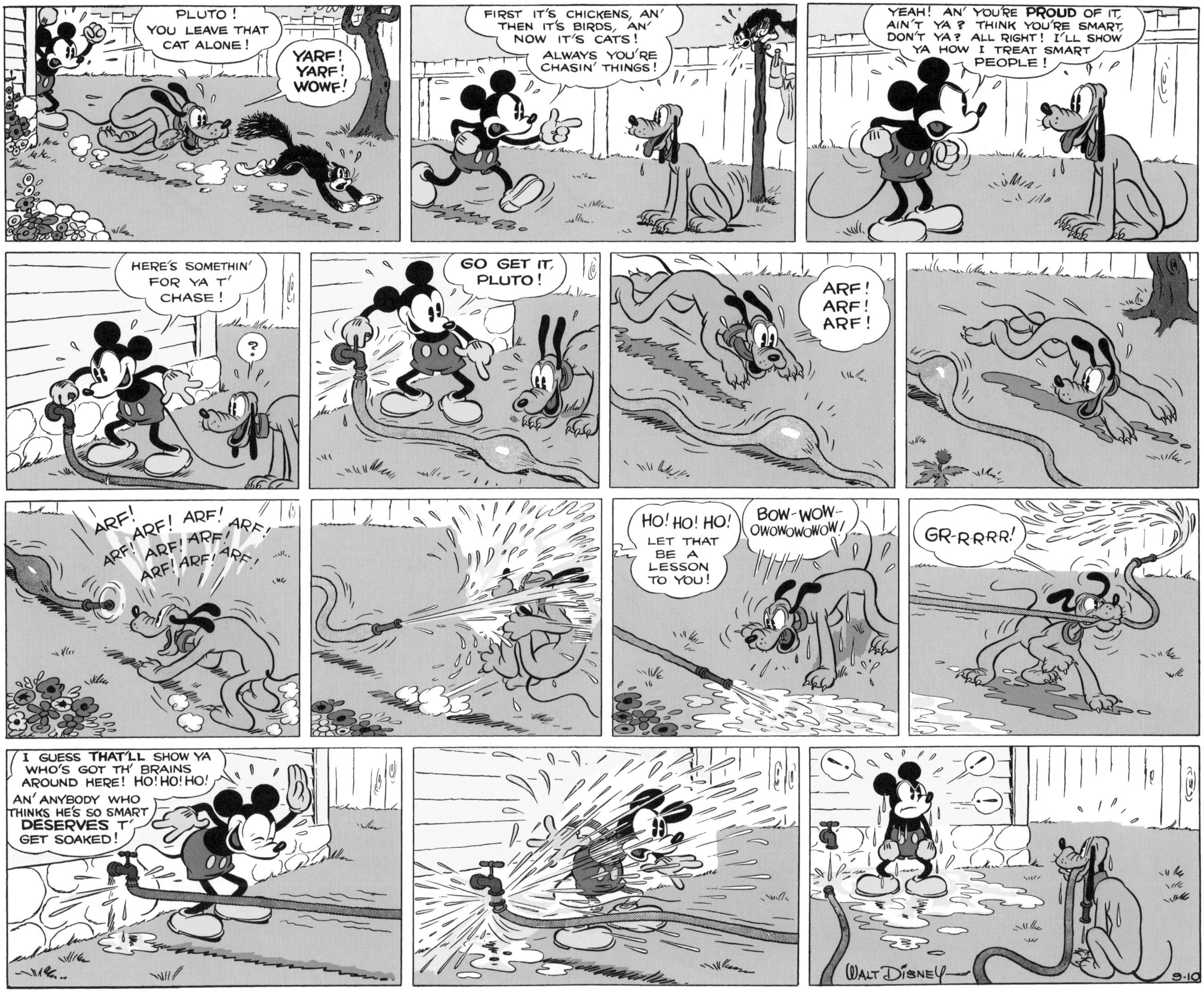
PLUTO! YOU LEAVE THAT CAT ALONE!
YARF! YARF! WOWF!
FIRST IT'S CHICKENS, AN' THEN IT'S BIRDS, AN' NOW IT'S CATS!
ALWAYS YOU'RE CHASIN' THINGS!
YEAH! AN' YOU'RE PROUD OF IT, AIN'T YA? THINK YOU'RE SMART, DON'T YA? ALL RIGHT! I'LL SHOW YA HOW I TREAT SMART PEOPLE!
HERE'S SOMETHIN' FOR YA T' CHASE!
?
GO GET IT, PLUTO!
ARF! ARF! ARF!
ARF! ARF! ARF! ARF! ARF! ARF! ARF! ARF! ARF! ARF!
HO! HO! HO! LET THAT BE A LESSON TO YOU!
BOW-WOW-OWOWOWOWOW!
GR-R-R-R-R!
I GUESS THAT'LL SHOW YA WHO'S GOT TH' BRAINS AROUND HERE! HO! HO! HO!
AN' ANYBODY WHO THINKS HE'S SO SMART DESERVES T' GET SOAKED!
!
!
!
WALT DISNEY
9-10

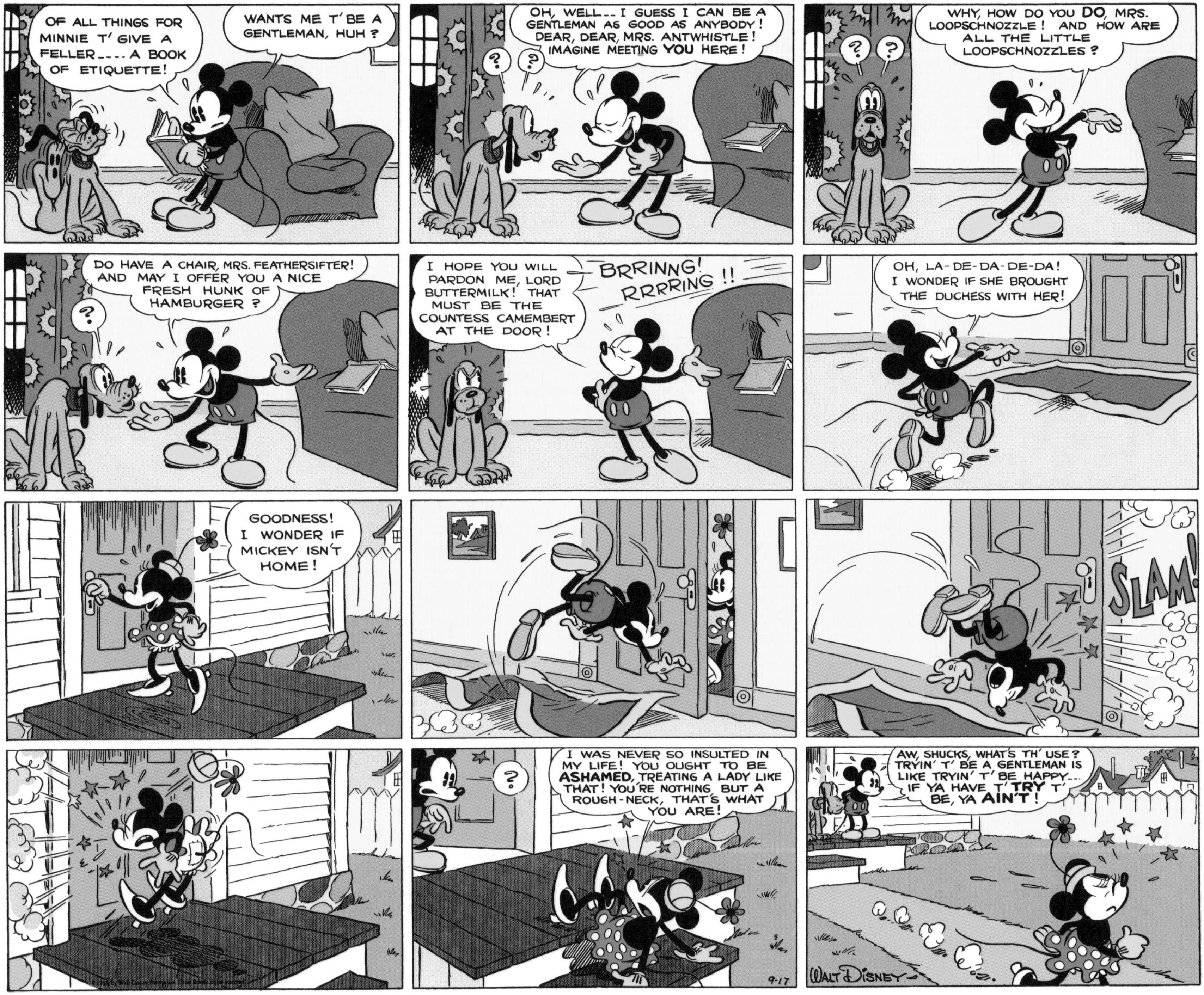

OF ALL THINGS FOR MINNIE T' GIVE A FELLER---- A BOOK OF ETIQUETTE!
WANTS ME T' BE A GENTLEMAN, HUH ?
?
?
OH, WELL-- I GUESS I CAN BE A GENTLEMAN AS GOOD AS ANYBODY! DEAR, DEAR, MRS. ANTWHISTLE! IMAGINE MEETING YOU HERE!
?
?
WHY, HOW DO YOU DO, MRS. LOOPSCHNOZZLE! AND HOW ARE ALL THE LITTLE LOOPSCHNOZZLES ?
?
DO HAVE A CHAIR, MRS. FEATHERSIFTER! AND MAY I OFFER YOU A NICE FRESH HUNK OF HAMBURGER ?
I HOPE YOU WILL PARDON ME, LORD BUTTERMILK! THAT MUST BE THE COUNTESS CAMEMBERT AT THE DOOR!
BRRINNG! RRRRING !!
OH, LA-DE-DA-DE-DA! I WONDER IF SHE BROUGHT THE DUCHESS WITH HER!
GOODNESS! I WONDER IF MICKEY ISN'T HOME!
SLAM!
?
I WAS NEVER SO INSULTED IN MY LIFE! YOU OUGHT TO BE ASHAMED, TREATING A LADY LIKE THAT! YOU'RE NOTHING BUT A ROUGH-NECK, THAT'S WHAT YOU ARE!
9-17
AW, SHUCKS, WHAT'S TH' USE? TRYIN' T' BE A GENTLEMAN IS LIKE TRYIN' T' BE HAPPY... IF YA HAVE T' TRY T' BE, YA AIN'T!
WALT DISNEY

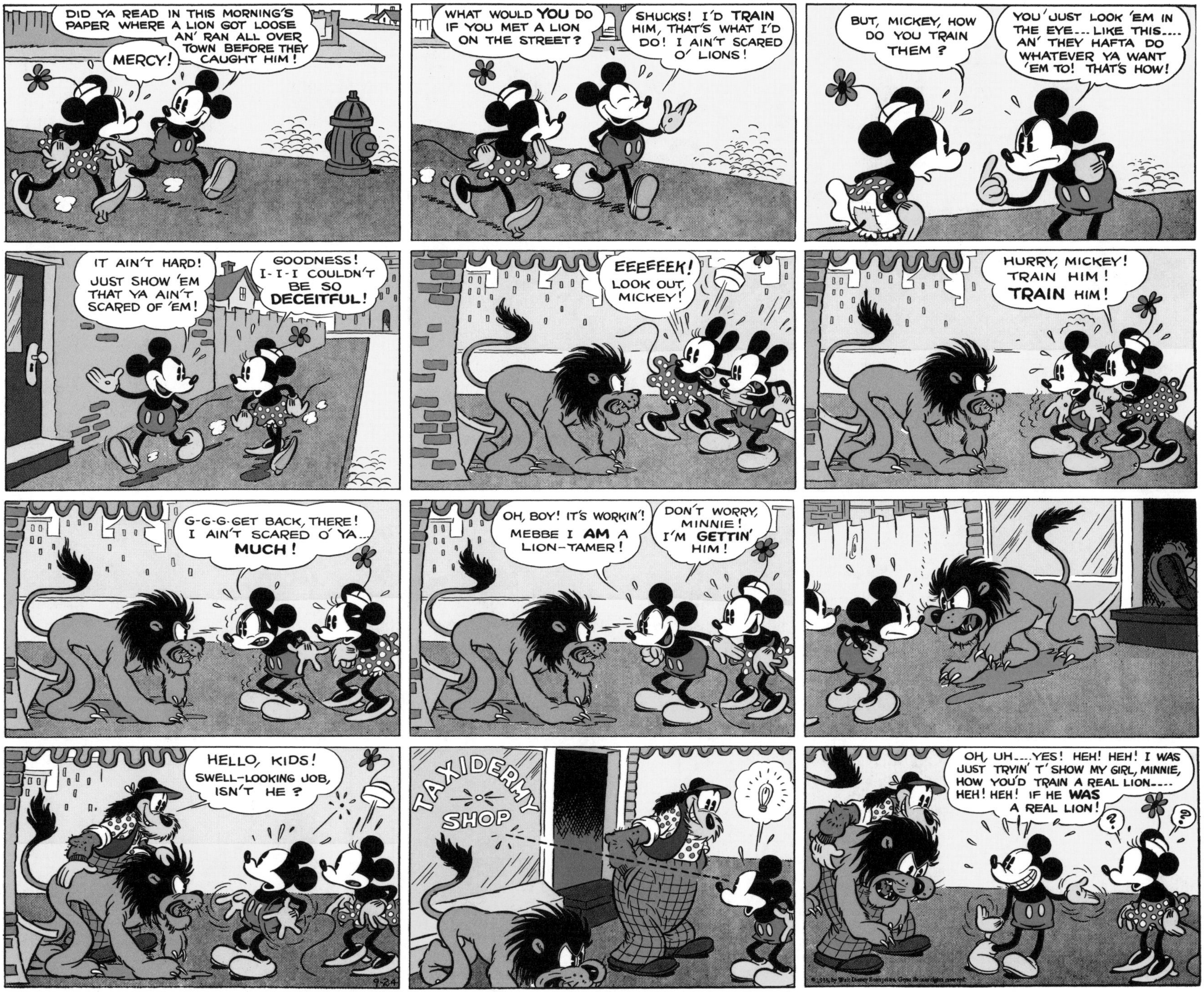
DID YA READ IN THIS MORNING'S PAPER WHERE A LION GOT LOOSE AN' RAN ALL OVER TOWN BEFORE THEY CAUGHT HIM!
MERCY!
WHAT WOULD **YOU** DO IF YOU MET A LION ON THE STREET?
SHUCKS! I'D **TRAIN** HIM, THAT'S WHAT I'D DO! I AIN'T SCARED O' LIONS!
BUT, MICKEY, HOW DO YOU TRAIN THEM?
YOU JUST LOOK 'EM IN THE EYE.... LIKE THIS.... AN' THEY HAFTA DO WHATEVER YA WANT 'EM TO! THAT'S HOW!
IT AIN'T HARD! JUST SHOW 'EM THAT YA AIN'T SCARED OF 'EM!
GOODNESS! I-I-I COULDN'T BE SO **DECEITFUL!**
EEEEEEK! LOOK OUT, MICKEY!
HURRY, MICKEY! TRAIN HIM! **TRAIN** HIM!
G-G-G-GET BACK, THERE! I AIN'T SCARED O' YA... **MUCH!**
OH, BOY! IT'S WORKIN'! MEBBE I **AM** A LION-TAMER!
DON'T WORRY, MINNIE! I'M **GETTIN'** HIM!
HELLO, KIDS! SWELL-LOOKING JOB, ISN'T HE?
TAXIDERMY SHOP
OH, UH.... YES! HEH! HEH! I WAS JUST TRYIN' T' SHOW MY GIRL, MINNIE, HOW YOU'D TRAIN A REAL LION.... HEH! HEH! IF HE **WAS** A REAL LION!

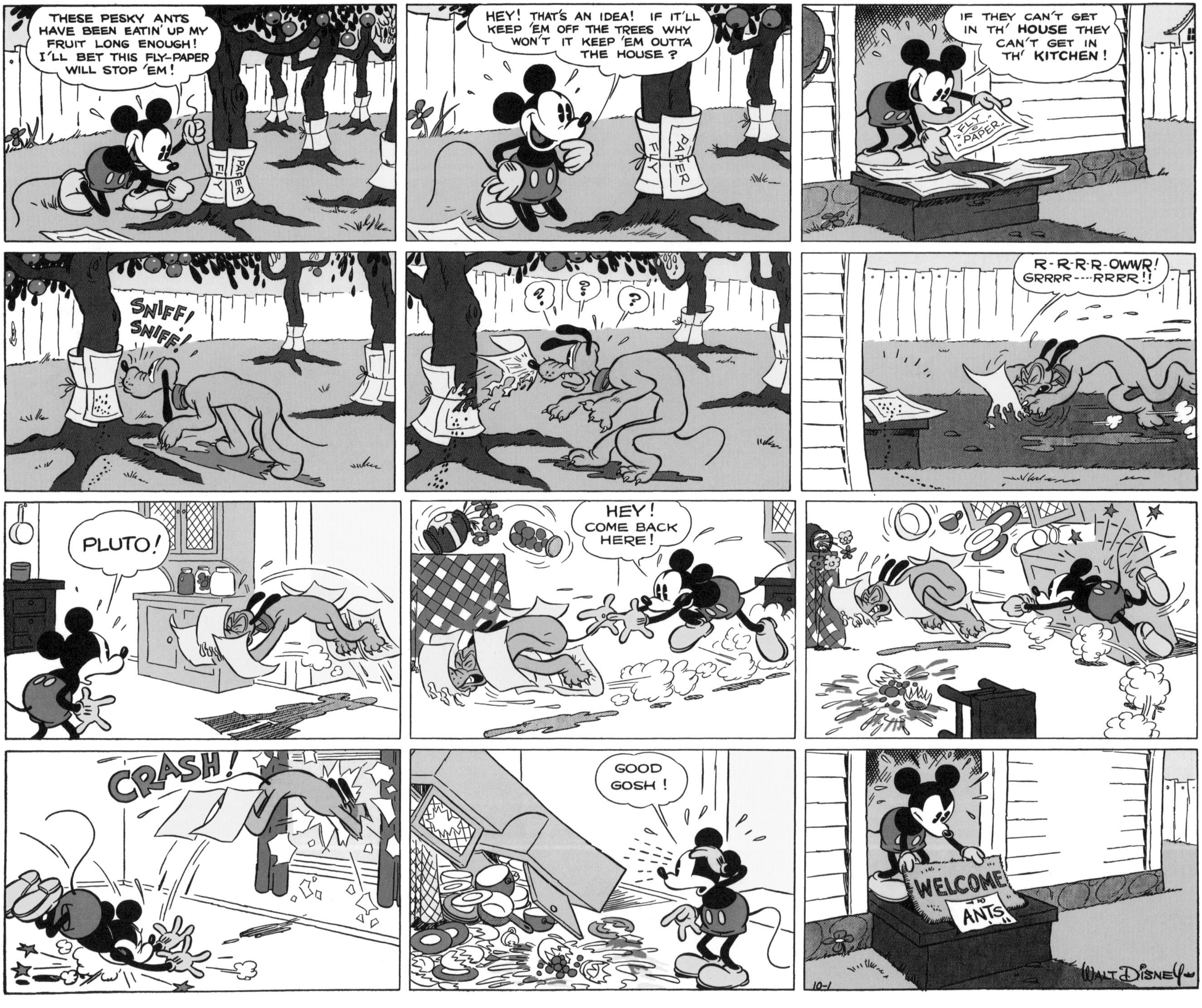
THESE PESKY ANTS HAVE BEEN EATIN' UP MY FRUIT LONG ENOUGH! I'LL BET THIS FLY-PAPER WILL STOP 'EM!
FLY PAPER
HEY! THAT'S AN IDEA! IF IT'LL KEEP 'EM OFF THE TREES WHY WON'T IT KEEP 'EM OUTTA THE HOUSE?
FLY PAPER
IF THEY CAN'T GET IN TH' HOUSE THEY CAN'T GET IN TH' KITCHEN!
FLY PAPER
SNIFF! SNIFF!
?
?
?
R-R-R-R-OWWR! GRRRR----RRRR!!
PLUTO!
HEY! COME BACK HERE!
CRASH!
GOOD GOSH!
WELCOME
ANTS
10-1
WALT DISNEY

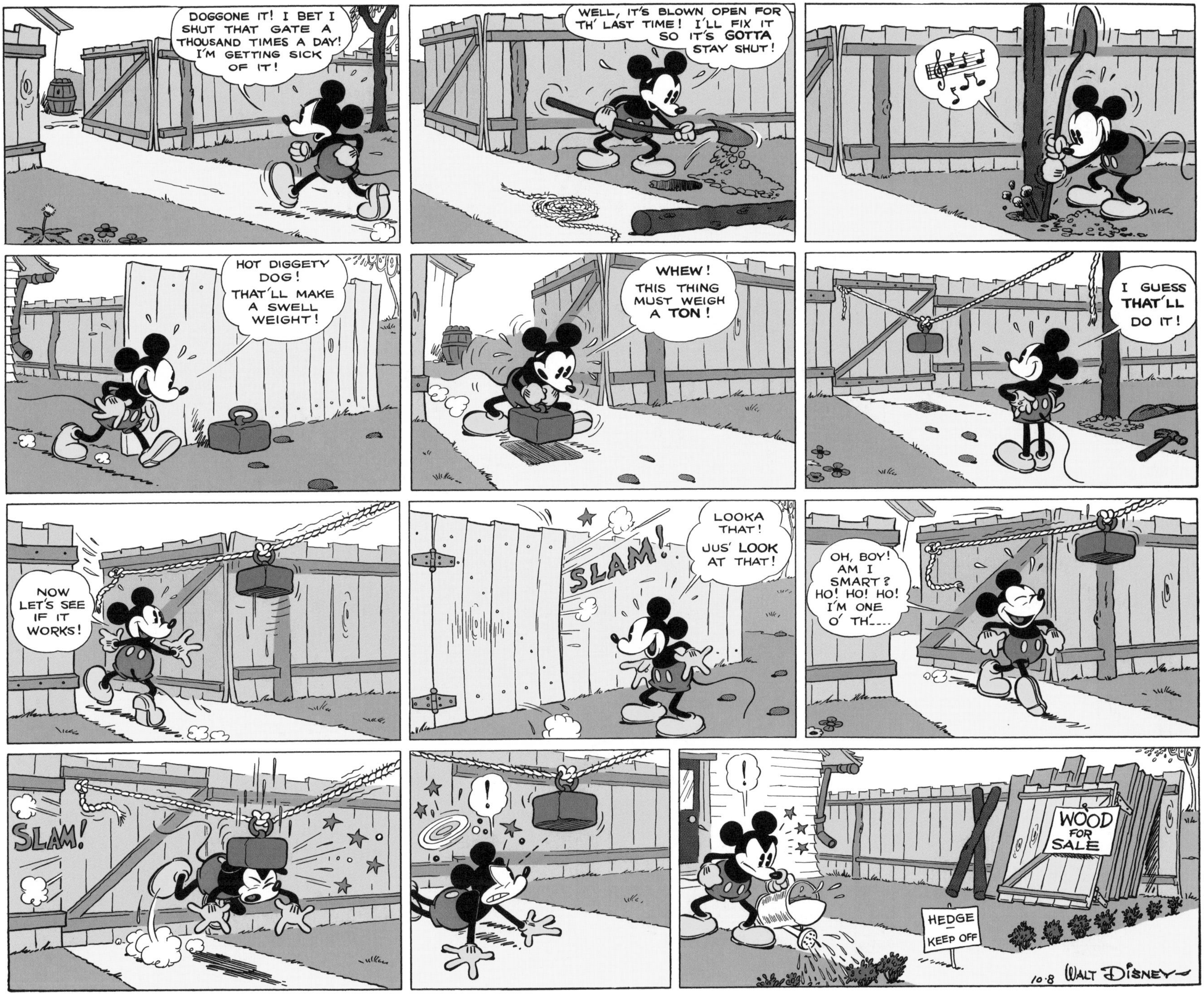
DOGGONE IT! I BET I SHUT THAT GATE A THOUSAND TIMES A DAY! I'M GETTING SICK OF IT!
WELL, IT'S BLOWN OPEN FOR TH' LAST TIME! I'LL FIX IT SO IT'S GOTTA STAY SHUT!
HOT DIGGETY DOG! THAT'LL MAKE A SWELL WEIGHT!
WHEW! THIS THING MUST WEIGH A TON!
I GUESS THAT'LL DO IT!
NOW LET'S SEE IF IT WORKS!
SLAM!
LOOKA THAT! JUS' LOOK AT THAT!
OH, BOY! AM I SMART? HO! HO! HO! I'M ONE O' TH'...
SLAM!
!
!
WOOD FOR SALE
HEDGE — KEEP OFF
10·8 WALT DISNEY

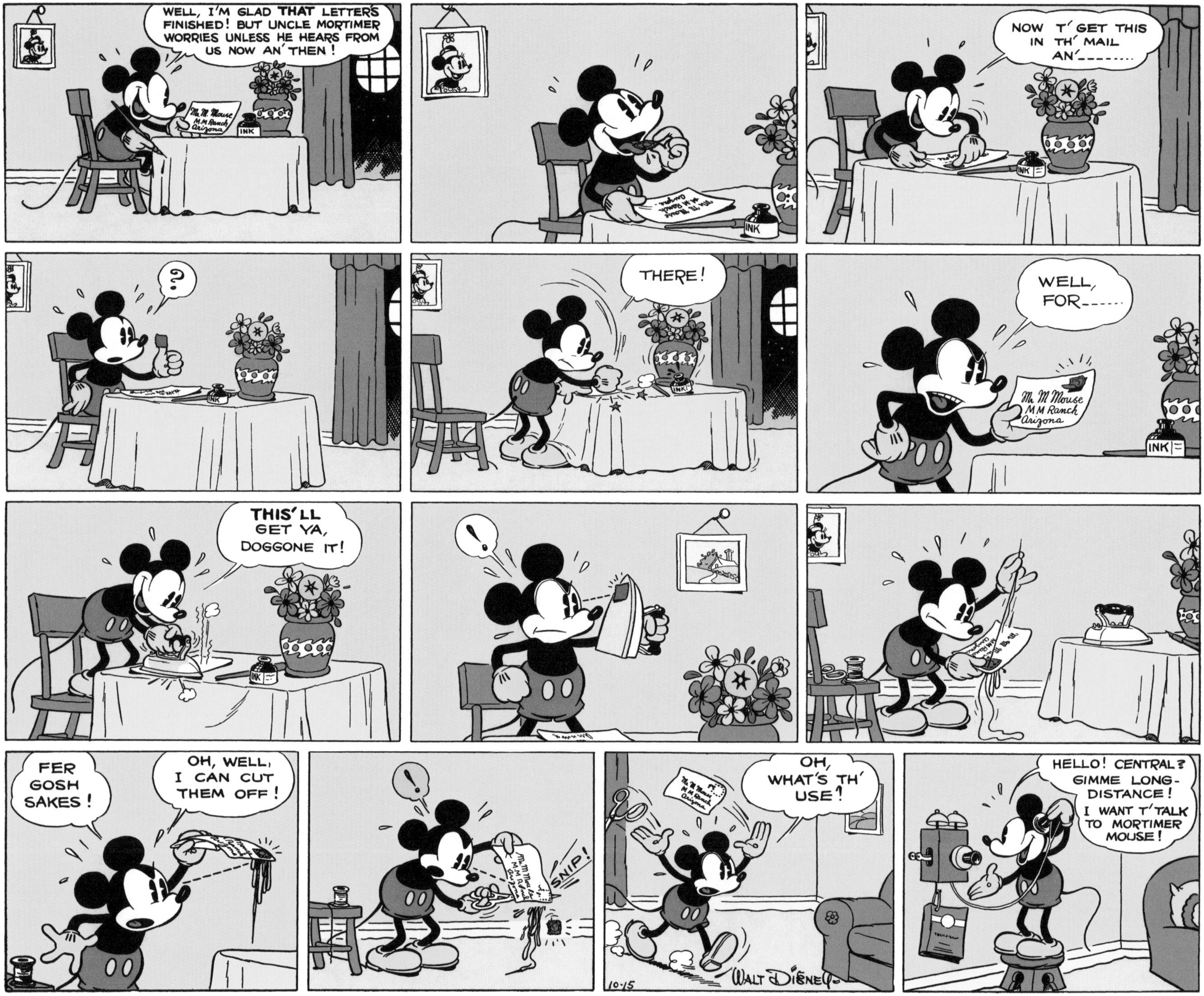
WELL, I'M GLAD THAT LETTER'S FINISHED! BUT UNCLE MORTIMER WORRIES UNLESS HE HEARS FROM US NOW AN' THEN!
Mr. M. Mouse
M.M Ranch
Arizona
INK
INK
NOW T' GET THIS IN TH' MAIL AN'-------
INK
?
INK
THERE!
INK
WELL, FOR------
Mr. M Mouse
M M Ranch
Arizona
INK
THIS'LL GET YA, DOGGONE IT!
INK
!
FER GOSH SAKES!
OH, WELL, I CAN CUT THEM OFF!
!
SNIP!
OH, WHAT'S TH' USE!
10-15
WALT DISNEY
HELLO! CENTRAL? GIMME LONG-DISTANCE!
I WANT T' TALK TO MORTIMER MOUSE!

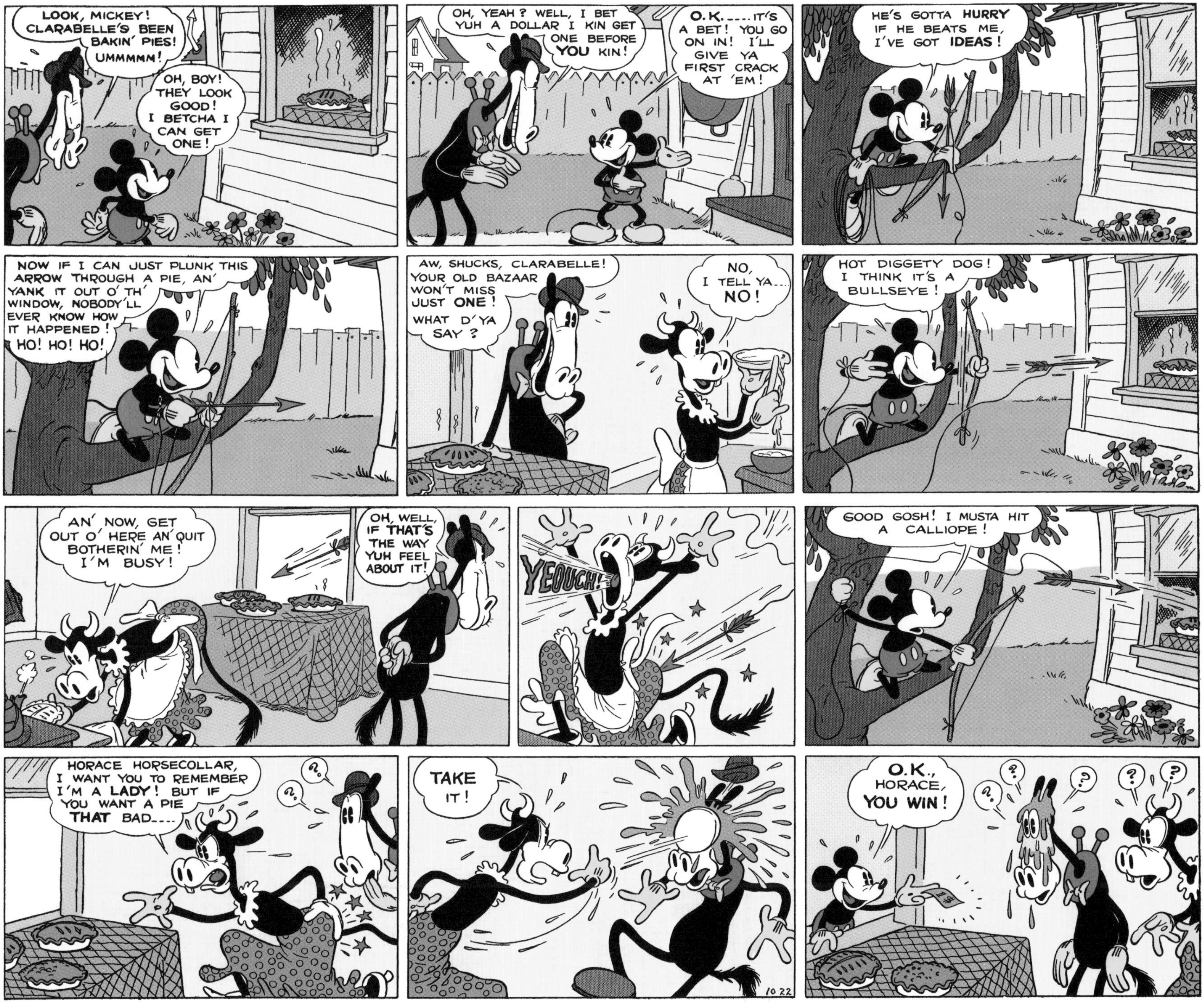

LOOK, MICKEY! CLARABELLE'S BEEN BAKIN' PIES! UMMMMM!
OH, BOY! THEY LOOK GOOD! I BETCHA I CAN GET ONE!
OH, YEAH? WELL, I BET YUH A DOLLAR I KIN GET ONE BEFORE YOU KIN!
O.K.---- IT'S A BET! YOU GO ON IN! I'LL GIVE YA FIRST CRACK AT 'EM!
HE'S GOTTA HURRY IF HE BEATS ME, I'VE GOT IDEAS!
NOW IF I CAN JUST PLUNK THIS ARROW THROUGH A PIE, AN' YANK IT OUT O' TH' WINDOW, NOBODY'LL EVER KNOW HOW IT HAPPENED! HO! HO! HO!
AW, SHUCKS, CLARABELLE! YOUR OLD BAZAAR WON'T MISS JUST ONE! WHAT D'YA SAY?
NO, I TELL YA--- NO!
HOT DIGGETY DOG! I THINK IT'S A BULLSEYE!
AN' NOW, GET OUT O' HERE AN' QUIT BOTHERIN' ME! I'M BUSY!
OH, WELL, IF THAT'S THE WAY YUH FEEL ABOUT IT!
YEOUCH!
GOOD GOSH! I MUSTA HIT A CALLIOPE!
HORACE HORSECOLLAR, I WANT YOU TO REMEMBER I'M A LADY! BUT IF YOU WANT A PIE THAT BAD----
TAKE IT!
O.K., HORACE, YOU WIN!
10 22

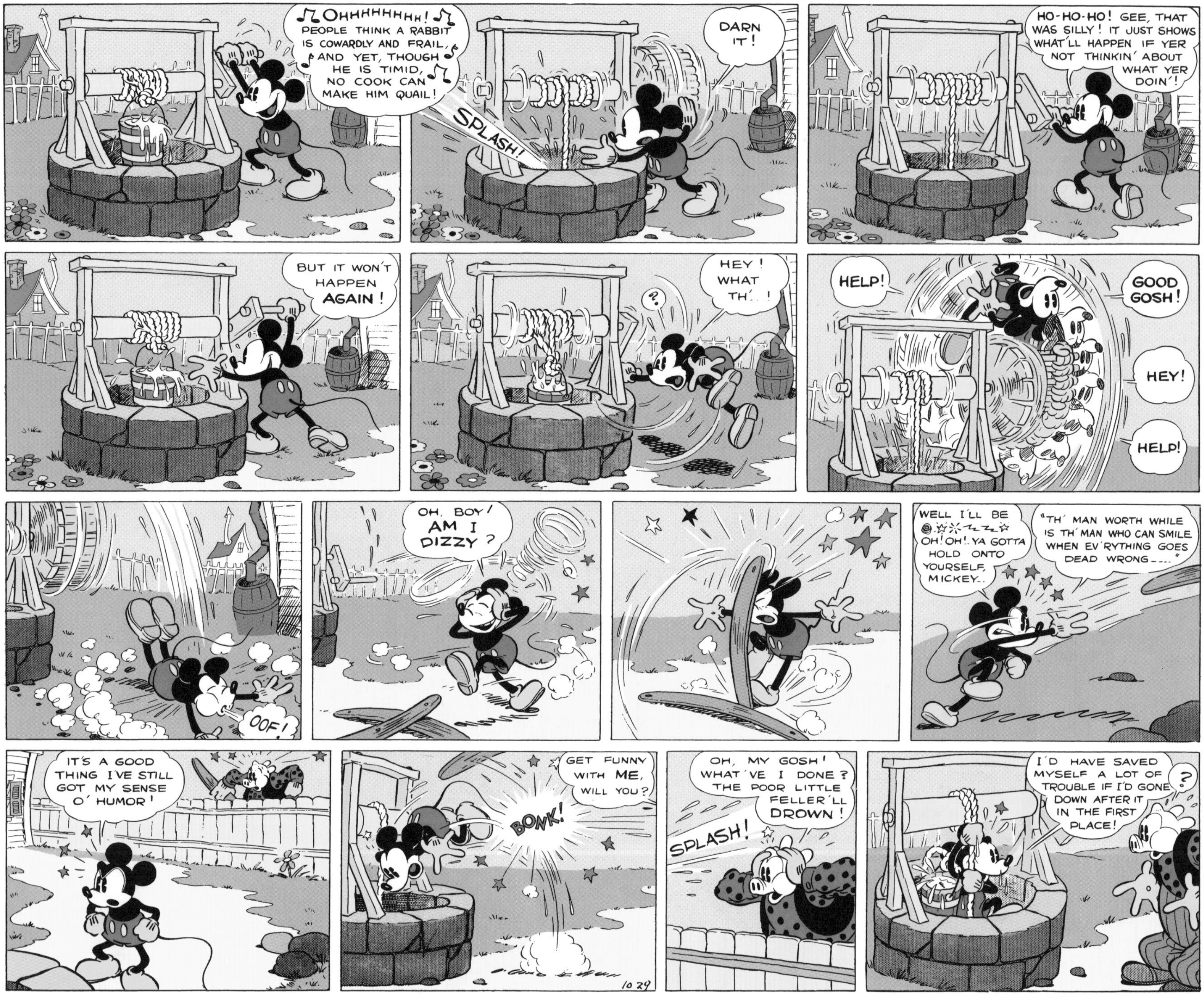
OHHHHHHHH! PEOPLE THINK A RABBIT IS COWARDLY AND FRAIL, AND YET, THOUGH HE IS TIMID, NO COOK CAN MAKE HIM QUAIL!
SPLASH!
DARN IT!
HO-HO-HO! GEE, THAT WAS SILLY! IT JUST SHOWS WHAT'LL HAPPEN IF YER NOT THINKIN' ABOUT WHAT YER DOIN'!
BUT IT WON'T HAPPEN AGAIN!
?
HEY! WHAT TH'...!
HELP!
GOOD GOSH!
HEY!
HELP!
OOF!
OH, BOY! AM I DIZZY?
WELL I'LL BE OH! OH!.. YA GOTTA HOLD ONTO YOURSELF, MICKEY..
"TH' MAN WORTH WHILE IS TH' MAN WHO CAN SMILE WHEN EV'RYTHING GOES DEAD WRONG ...."
IT'S A GOOD THING I'VE STILL GOT MY SENSE O' HUMOR!
GET FUNNY WITH ME, WILL YOU?
BONK!
OH, MY GOSH! WHAT'VE I DONE? THE POOR LITTLE FELLER'LL DROWN!
SPLASH!
I'D HAVE SAVED MYSELF A LOT OF TROUBLE IF I'D GONE DOWN AFTER IT IN THE FIRST PLACE!
?

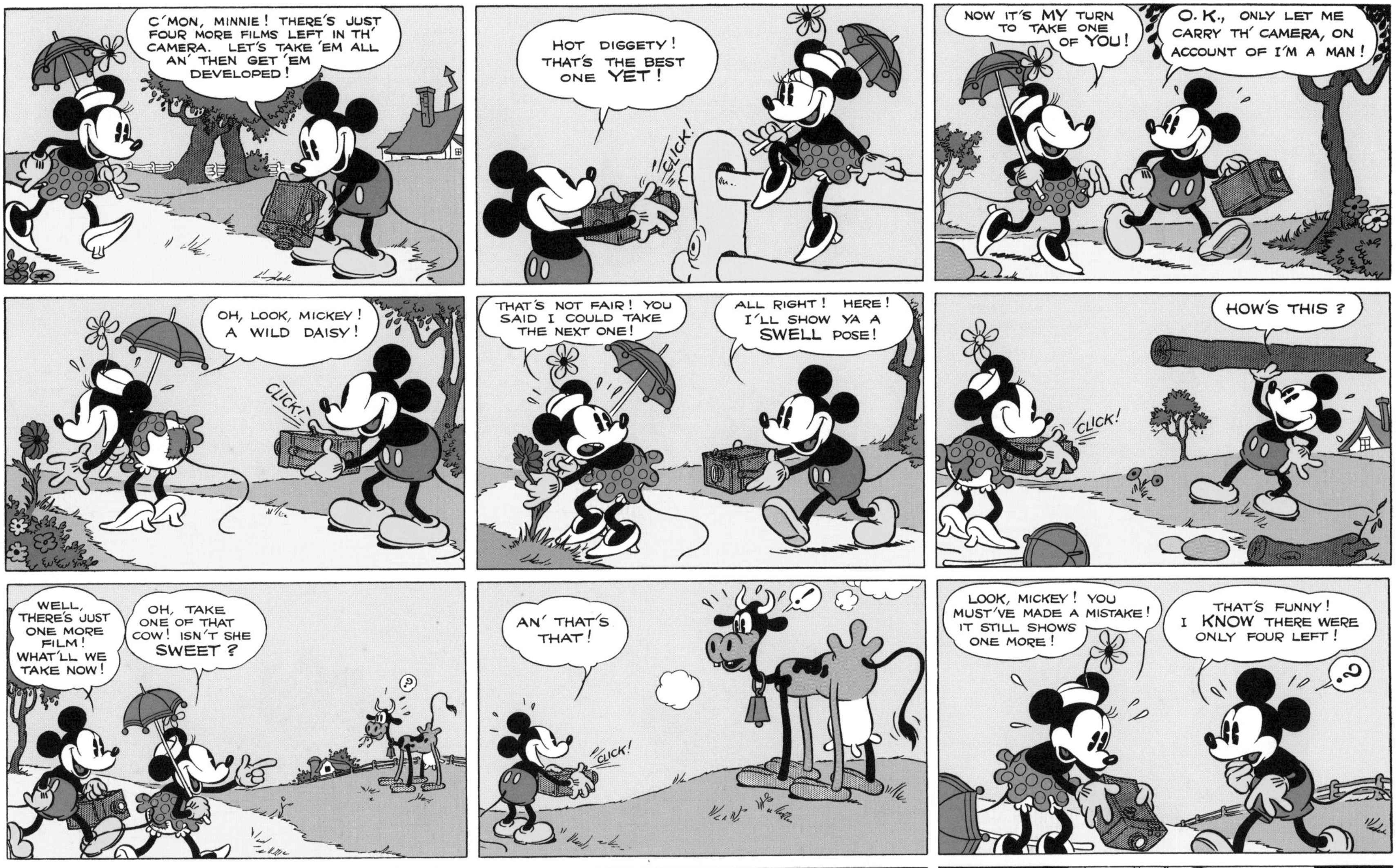
C'MON, MINNIE! THERE'S JUST FOUR MORE FILMS LEFT IN TH' CAMERA. LET'S TAKE 'EM ALL AN' THEN GET 'EM DEVELOPED!
HOT DIGGETY! THAT'S THE BEST ONE YET!
CLICK!
NOW IT'S MY TURN TO TAKE ONE OF YOU!
O.K., ONLY LET ME CARRY TH' CAMERA, ON ACCOUNT OF I'M A MAN!
OH, LOOK, MICKEY! A WILD DAISY!
CLICK!
THAT'S NOT FAIR! YOU SAID I COULD TAKE THE NEXT ONE!
ALL RIGHT! HERE! I'LL SHOW YA A SWELL POSE!
HOW'S THIS?
CLICK!
WELL, THERE'S JUST ONE MORE FILM! WHAT'LL WE TAKE NOW!
OH, TAKE ONE OF THAT COW! ISN'T SHE SWEET?
AN' THAT'S THAT!
CLICK!
LOOK, MICKEY! YOU MUST'VE MADE A MISTAKE! IT STILL SHOWS ONE MORE!
THAT'S FUNNY! I KNOW THERE WERE ONLY FOUR LEFT!
GOSH! I HOPE WE DIDN'T TAKE TWO PICTURES ON TH' SAME FILM!
PHOTO SHOP • FILMS • DEVELOPED
THE NEXT DAY---
HERE YOU ARE, SIR! AND I MUST SAY THAT YOU'RE THE STRONGEST MAN OF YOUR SIZE I EVER SAW!
YEAH! I'M PRETTY STR---- WELL, FER---!!
WALT DISNEY
11-5

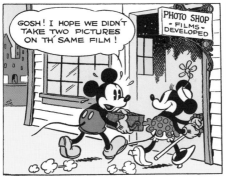

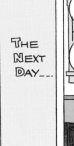

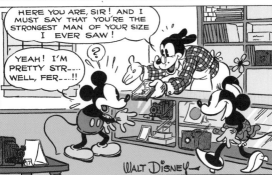

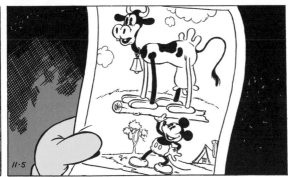

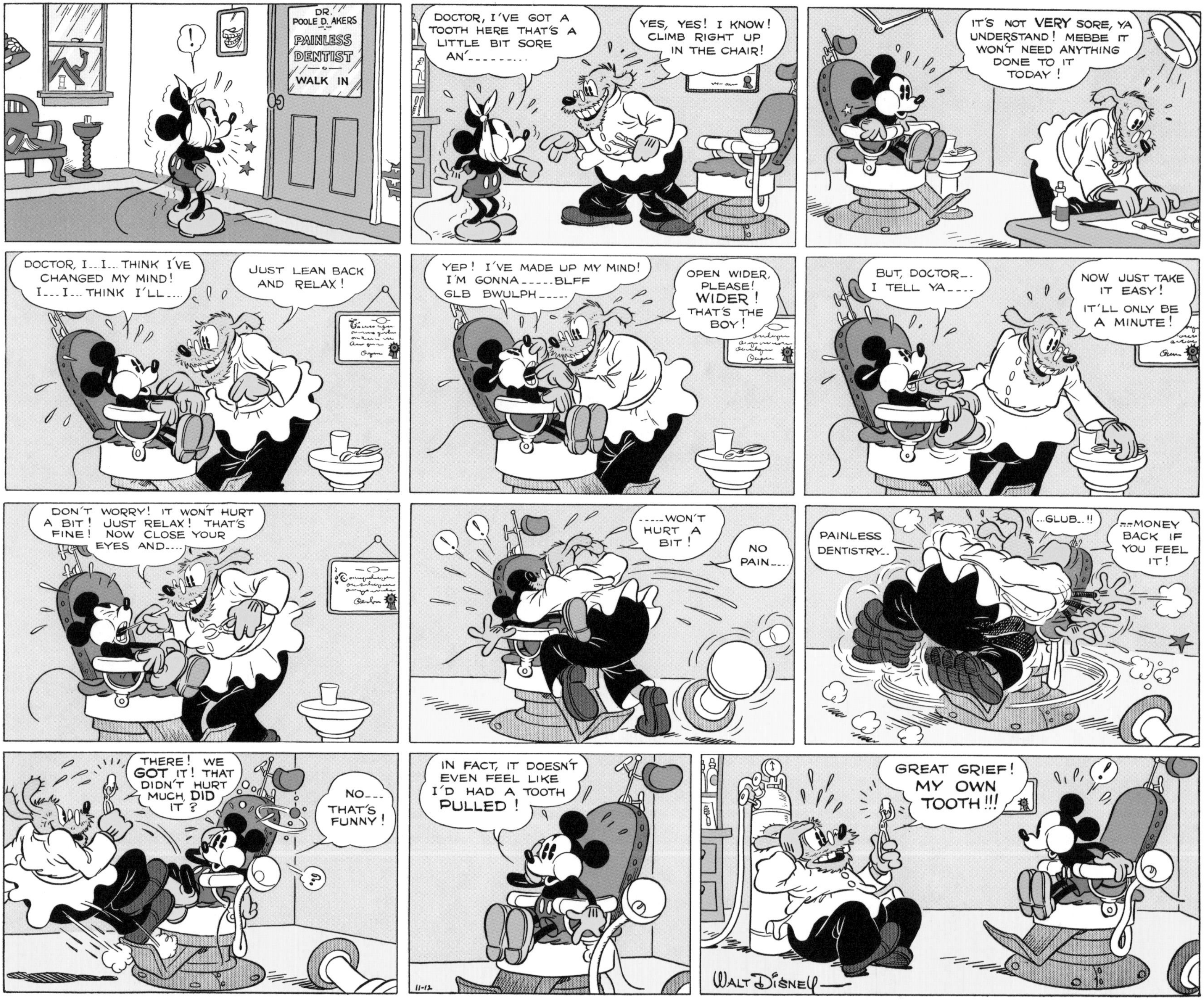
DR. POOLE D. AKERS
PAINLESS DENTIST
WALK IN
!
DOCTOR, I'VE GOT A TOOTH HERE THAT'S A LITTLE BIT SORE AN'.........
YES, YES! I KNOW! CLIMB RIGHT UP IN THE CHAIR!
IT'S NOT VERY SORE, YA UNDERSTAND! MEBBE IT WON'T NEED ANYTHING DONE TO IT TODAY!
DOCTOR, I...I... THINK I'VE CHANGED MY MIND! I...I... THINK I'LL....
JUST LEAN BACK AND RELAX!
YEP! I'VE MADE UP MY MIND! I'M GONNA.....BLFF GLB BWULPH.....
OPEN WIDER, PLEASE! WIDER! THAT'S THE BOY!
BUT, DOCTOR... I TELL YA....
NOW JUST TAKE IT EASY! IT'LL ONLY BE A MINUTE!
DON'T WORRY! IT WON'T HURT A BIT! JUST RELAX! THAT'S FINE! NOW CLOSE YOUR EYES AND....
.....WON'T HURT A BIT!
NO PAIN....
PAINLESS DENTISTRY..
...GLUB..!!
...MONEY BACK IF YOU FEEL IT!
THERE! WE GOT IT! THAT DIDN'T HURT MUCH, DID IT?
NO... THAT'S FUNNY!
IN FACT, IT DOESN'T EVEN FEEL LIKE I'D HAD A TOOTH PULLED!
GREAT GRIEF! MY OWN TOOTH!!!
WALT DISNEY

120. A TOUGH PULL

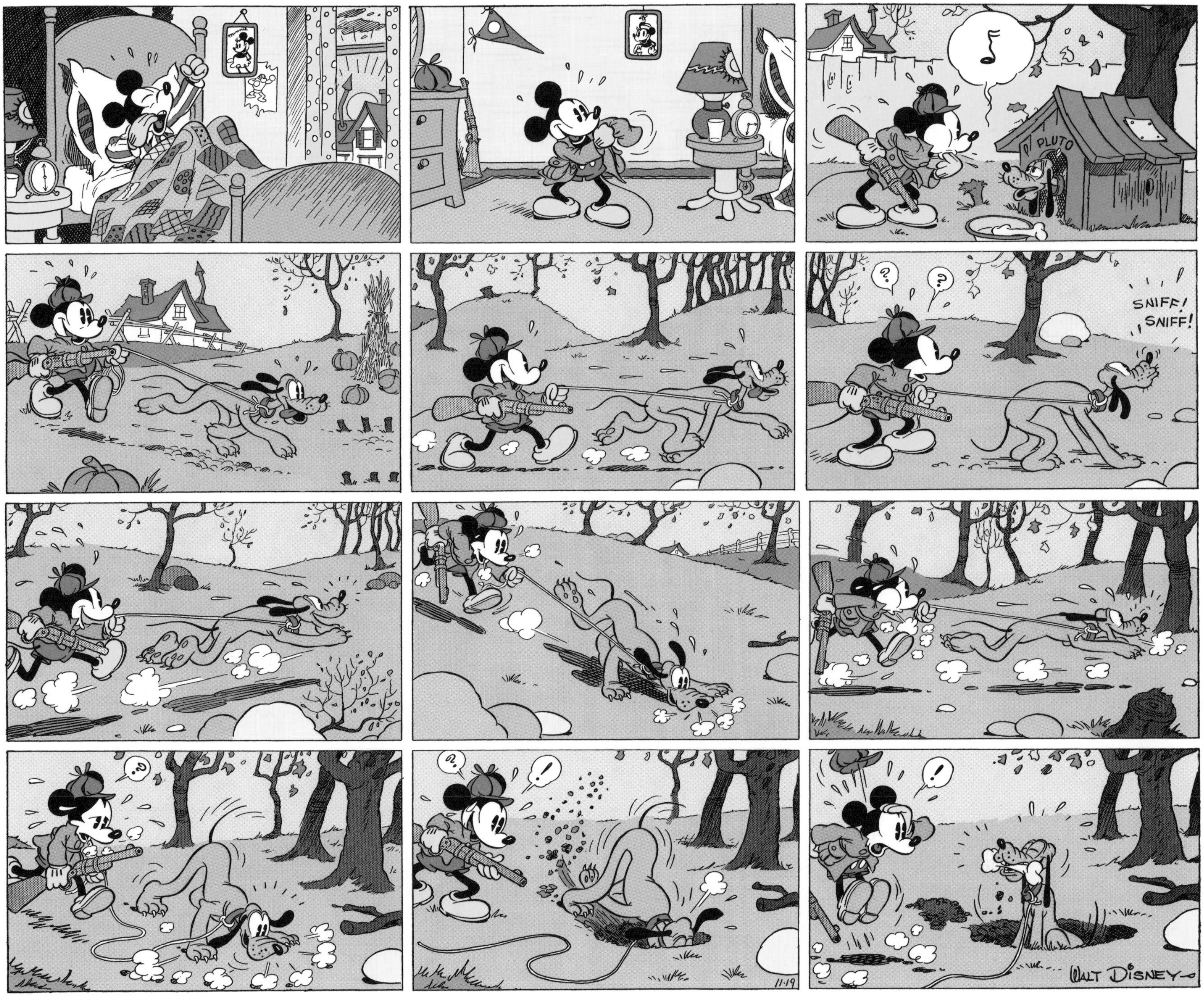
PLUTO
?
?
SNIFF!
SNIFF!
?
?
!
!
11-19
WALT DISNEY

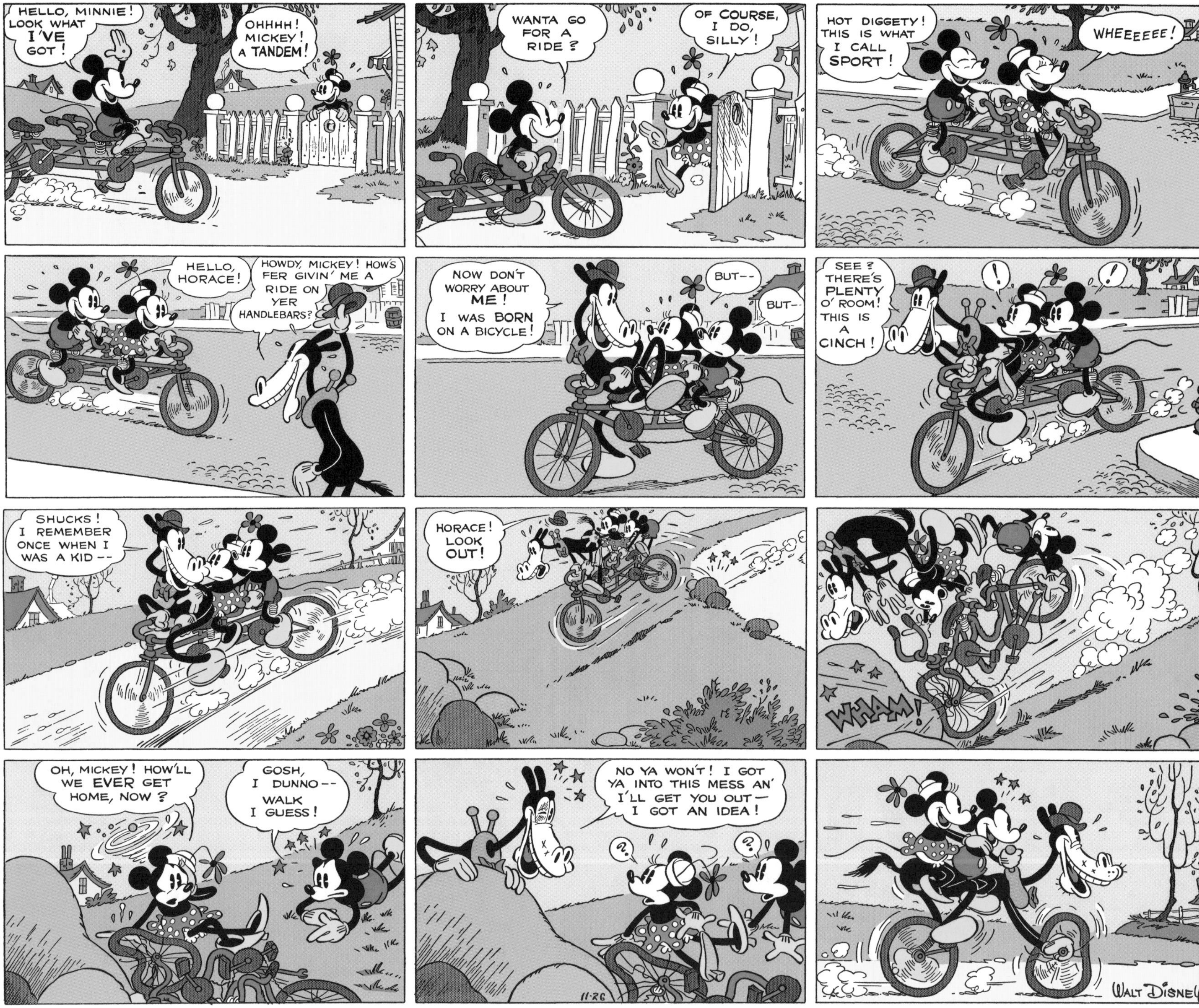
HELLO, MINNIE! LOOK WHAT I'VE GOT!
OHHHH! MICKEY! A TANDEM!
WANTA GO FOR A RIDE?
OF COURSE, I DO, SILLY!
HOT DIGGETY! THIS IS WHAT I CALL SPORT!
WHEEEEEE!
HELLO, HORACE!
HOWDY, MICKEY! HOW'S FER GIVIN' ME A RIDE ON YER HANDLEBARS?
NOW DON'T WORRY ABOUT ME! I WAS BORN ON A BICYCLE!
BUT--
BUT--
SEE? THERE'S PLENTY O' ROOM! THIS IS A CINCH!
SHUCKS! I REMEMBER ONCE WHEN I WAS A KID--
HORACE! LOOK OUT!
WHAM!
OH, MICKEY! HOW'LL WE EVER GET HOME, NOW?
GOSH, I DUNNO-- WALK I GUESS!
NO YA WON'T! I GOT YA INTO THIS MESS AN' I'LL GET YOU OUT— I GOT AN IDEA!
11-26
WALT DISNEY

122. A BICYCLE BUILT FOR THREE

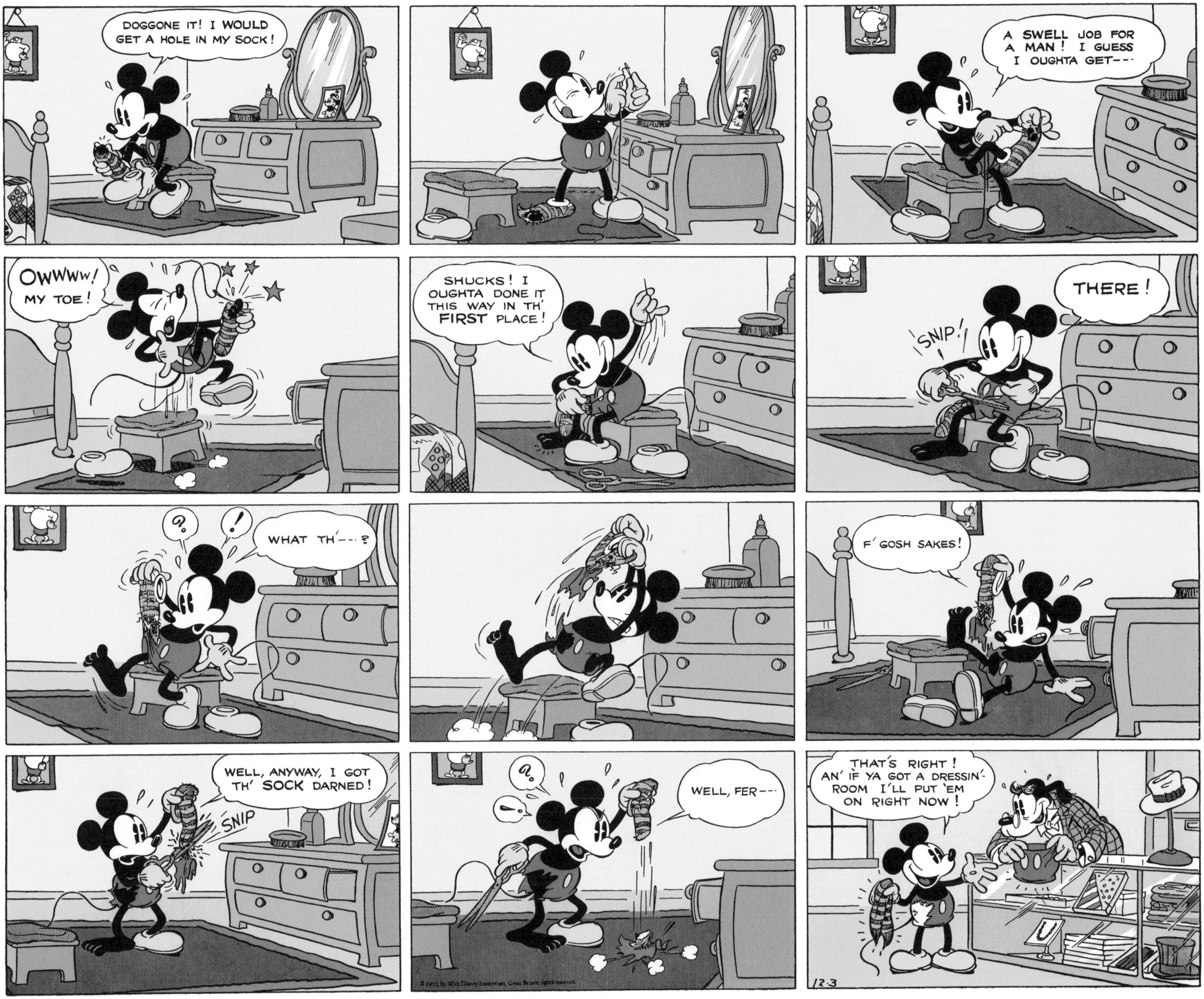
DOGGONE IT! I WOULD GET A HOLE IN MY SOCK!
A SWELL JOB FOR A MAN! I GUESS I OUGHTA GET---
OWWWW! MY TOE!
SHUCKS! I OUGHTA DONE IT THIS WAY IN TH' FIRST PLACE!
SNIP!
THERE!
?
!
WHAT TH'---?
F' GOSH SAKES!
WELL, ANYWAY, I GOT TH' SOCK DARNED!
SNIP
?
!
WELL, FER---
THAT'S RIGHT! AN' IF YA GOT A DRESSIN' ROOM I'LL PUT 'EM ON RIGHT NOW!
12-3

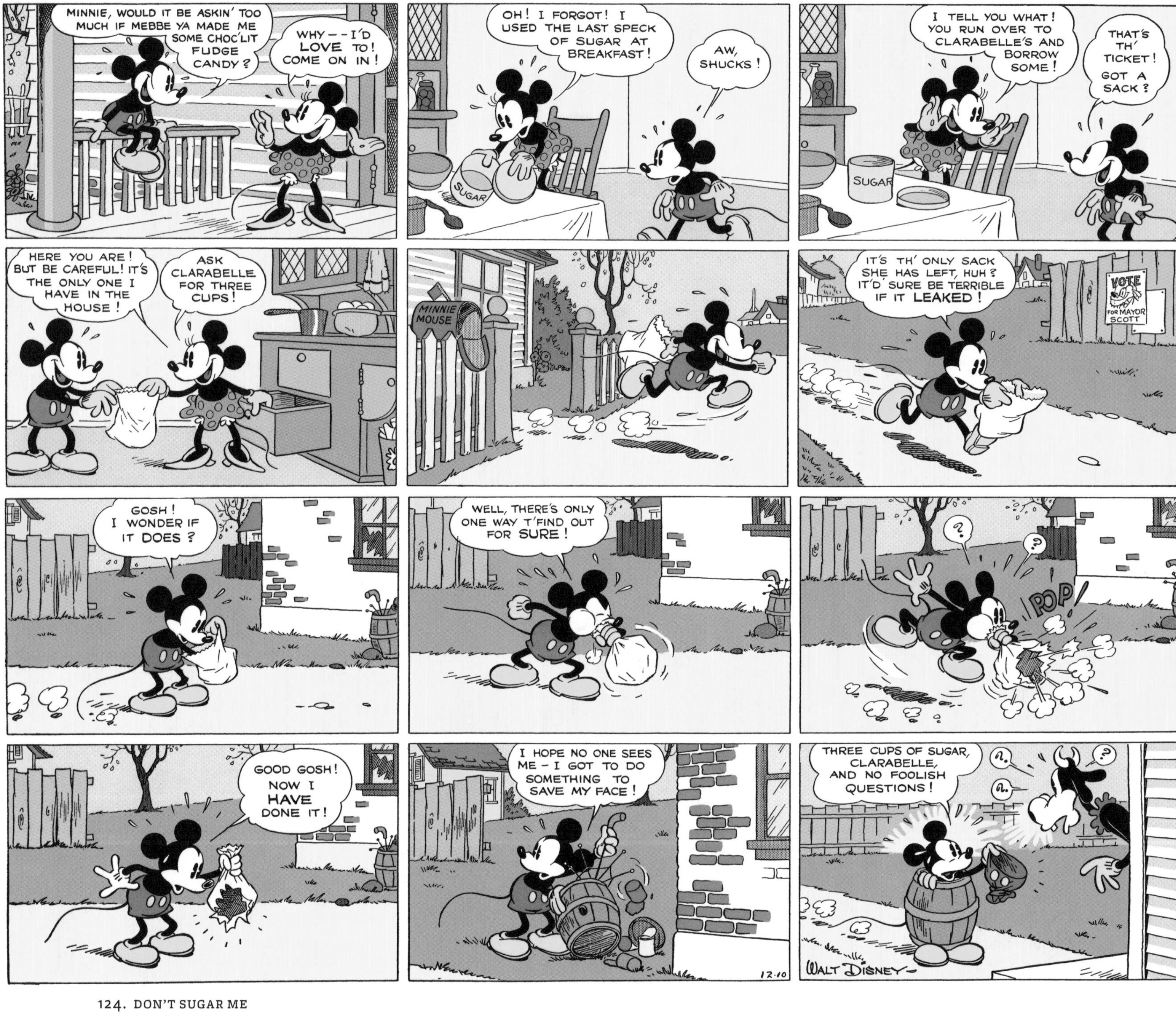
MINNIE, WOULD IT BE ASKIN' TOO MUCH IF MEBBE YA MADE ME SOME CHOC'LIT FUDGE CANDY?
WHY--I'D LOVE TO! COME ON IN!
OH! I FORGOT! I USED THE LAST SPECK OF SUGAR AT BREAKFAST!
SUGAR
AW, SHUCKS!
I TELL YOU WHAT! YOU RUN OVER TO CLARABELLE'S AND BORROW SOME!
THAT'S TH' TICKET! GOT A SACK?
SUGAR
HERE YOU ARE! BUT BE CAREFUL! IT'S THE ONLY ONE I HAVE IN THE HOUSE!
ASK CLARABELLE FOR THREE CUPS!
MINNIE MOUSE
IT'S TH' ONLY SACK SHE HAS LEFT, HUH? IT'D SURE BE TERRIBLE IF IT LEAKED!
VOTE
FOR MAYOR SCOTT
GOSH! I WONDER IF IT DOES?
WELL, THERE'S ONLY ONE WAY T'FIND OUT FOR SURE!
POP!
GOOD GOSH! NOW I HAVE DONE IT!
I HOPE NO ONE SEES ME - I GOT TO DO SOMETHING TO SAVE MY FACE!
12-10
THREE CUPS OF SUGAR, CLARABELLE, AND NO FOOLISH QUESTIONS!
WALT DISNEY

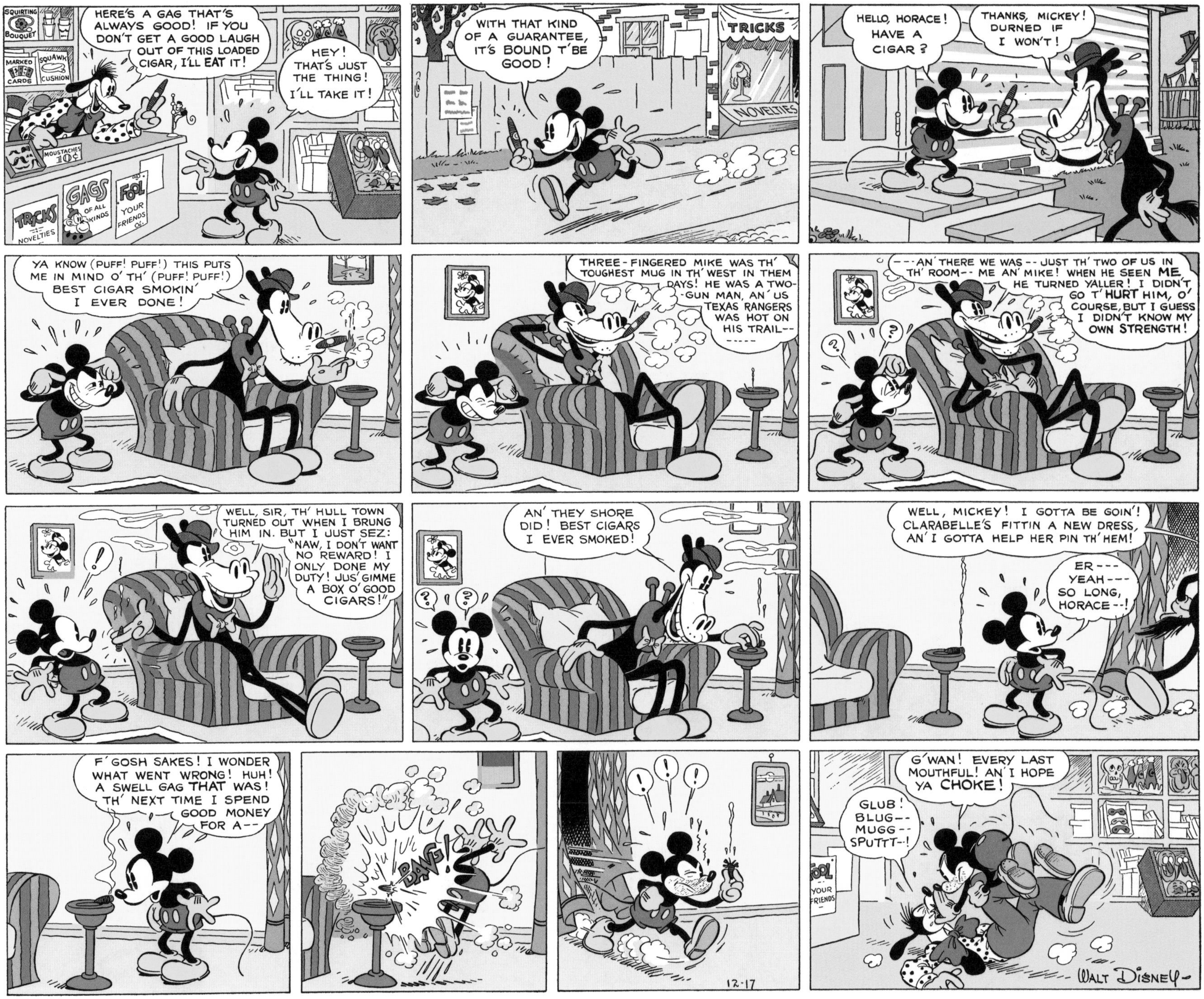
SQUIRTING BOUQUET
MARKED CARDS
SQUAWK CUSHION
MOUSTACHES 10¢
TRICKS NOVELTIES
GAGS OF ALL KINDS
FOOL YOUR FRIENDS
HERE'S A GAG THAT'S ALWAYS GOOD! IF YOU DON'T GET A GOOD LAUGH OUT OF THIS LOADED CIGAR, I'LL EAT IT!
HEY! THAT'S JUST THE THING! I'LL TAKE IT!
TRICKS
NOVELTIES
WITH THAT KIND OF A GUARANTEE, IT'S BOUND T'BE GOOD!
HELLO, HORACE! HAVE A CIGAR?
THANKS, MICKEY! DURNED IF I WON'T!
YA KNOW (PUFF! PUFF!) THIS PUTS ME IN MIND O' TH' (PUFF! PUFF!) BEST CIGAR SMOKIN' I EVER DONE!
THREE-FINGERED MIKE WAS TH' TOUGHEST MUG IN TH' WEST IN THEM DAYS! HE WAS A TWO-GUN MAN, AN' US TEXAS RANGERS WAS HOT ON HIS TRAIL-- -----
---AN' THERE WE WAS--JUST TH' TWO OF US IN TH' ROOM--ME AN' MIKE! WHEN HE SEEN ME, HE TURNED YALLER! I DIDN'T GO T' HURT HIM, O' COURSE, BUT I GUESS I DIDN'T KNOW MY OWN STRENGTH!
WELL, SIR, TH' HULL TOWN TURNED OUT WHEN I BRUNG HIM IN. BUT I JUST SEZ: "NAW, I DON'T WANT NO REWARD! I ONLY DONE MY DUTY! JUS' GIMME A BOX O' GOOD CIGARS!"
AN' THEY SHORE DID! BEST CIGARS I EVER SMOKED!
WELL, MICKEY! I GOTTA BE GOIN'! CLARABELLE'S FITTIN A NEW DRESS, AN' I GOTTA HELP HER PIN TH' HEM!
ER--- YEAH--- SO LONG, HORACE--!
F'GOSH SAKES! I WONDER WHAT WENT WRONG! HUH! A SWELL GAG THAT WAS! TH' NEXT TIME I SPEND GOOD MONEY FOR A--
BANG!
12-17
G'WAN! EVERY LAST MOUTHFUL! AN' I HOPE YA CHOKE!
GLUB! BLUG-- MUGG-- SPUTTT--!
FOOL YOUR FRIENDS
WALT DISNEY

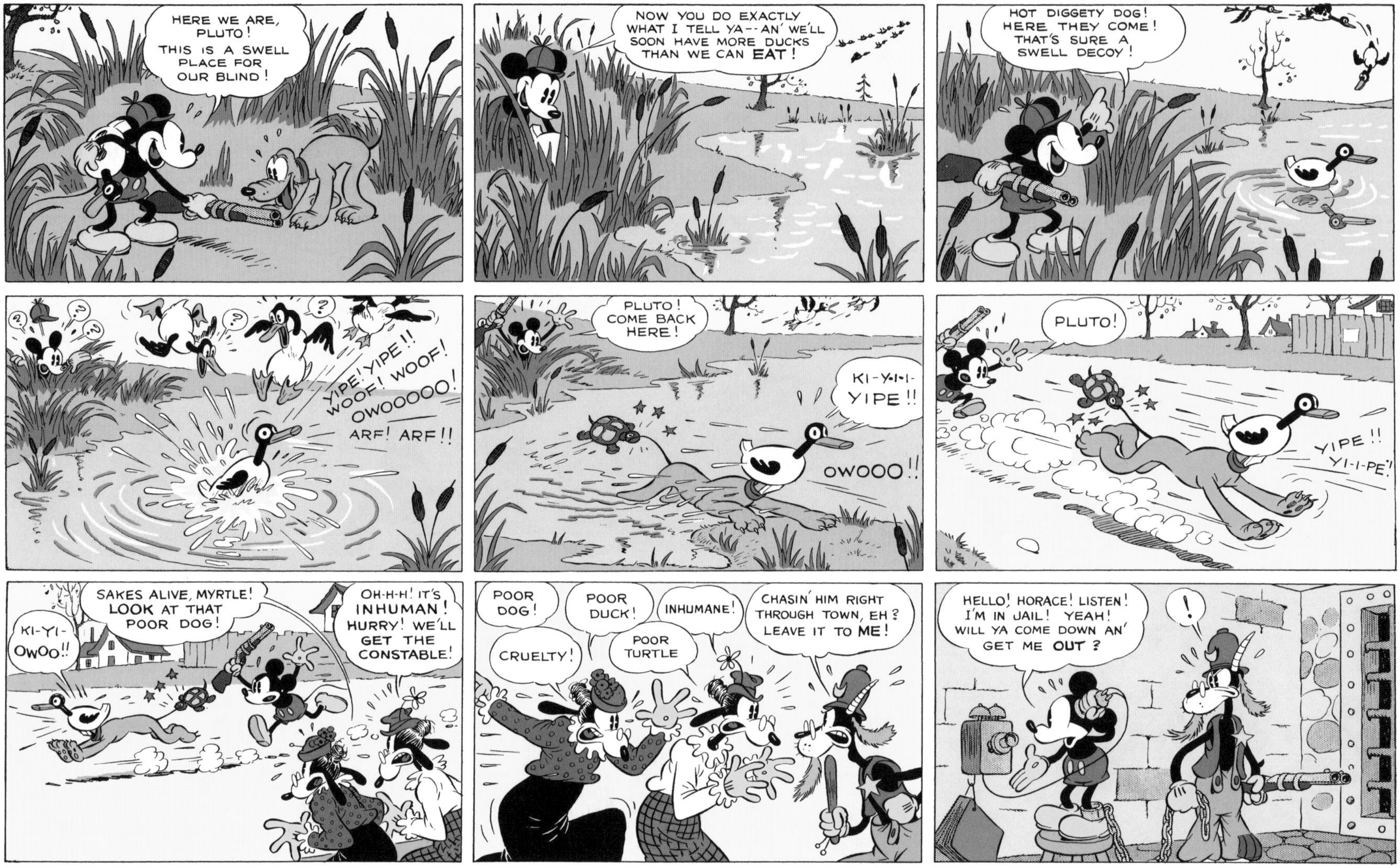
HERE WE ARE, PLUTO! THIS IS A SWELL PLACE FOR OUR BLIND!
NOW YOU DO EXACTLY WHAT I TELL YA--AN' WE'LL SOON HAVE MORE DUCKS THAN WE CAN EAT!
HOT DIGGETY DOG! HERE THEY COME! THAT'S SURE A SWELL DECOY!
YIPE! YIPE!! WOOF! WOOF! OWOOOOO!
ARF! ARF!!
PLUTO! COME BACK HERE!
KI-Y-I-I- YIPE!!
OWOOO!!
PLUTO!
YIPE!! YI-I-PE!
KI-YI- OWOO!!
SAKES ALIVE, MYRTLE! LOOK AT THAT POOR DOG!
OH-H-H! IT'S INHUMAN! HURRY! WE'LL GET THE CONSTABLE!
POOR DOG!
CRUELTY!
POOR DUCK!
POOR TURTLE
INHUMANE!
CHASIN' HIM RIGHT THROUGH TOWN, EH? LEAVE IT TO ME!
HELLO, HORACE! LISTEN! I'M IN JAIL! YEAH! WILL YA COME DOWN AN' GET ME OUT?
!
WHY, SURE, MICKEY! I'M GLAD T' KNOW WHERE YA ARE! I'VE BEEN LOOKIN' FOR YA! I'VE GOT A SWELL IDEA! YA SEE PLUTO JUST BRUNG HOME A BRAND-NEW DECOY!
---AN I THINK MEBBE YA'D LIKE T'GO DUCK HUNTIN'!
WHAT???
BR-R-R-R-PPP!!! THAT FOR YOU!
?
?
?
WALT DISNEY
12-24

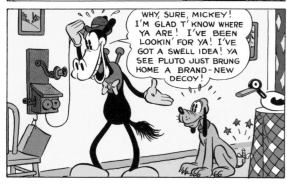

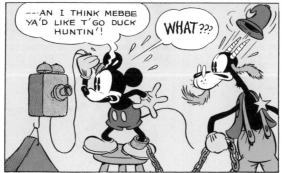

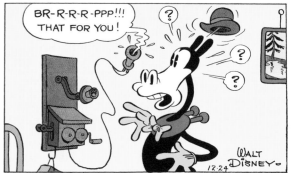

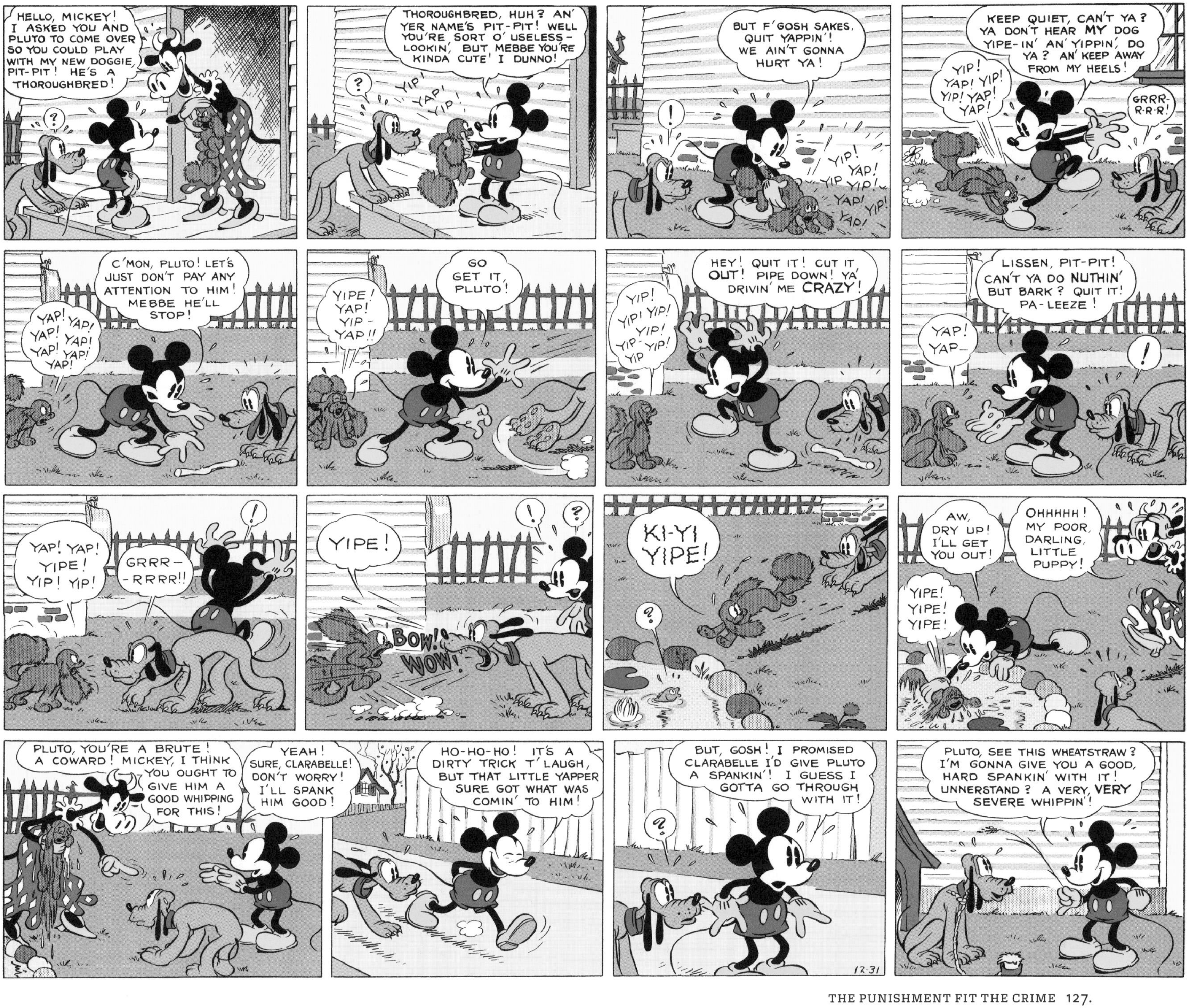
HELLO, MICKEY! I ASKED YOU AND PLUTO TO COME OVER SO YOU COULD PLAY WITH MY NEW DOGGIE, PIT-PIT! HE'S A THOROUGHBRED!
?
THOROUGHBRED, HUH? AN' YER NAME'S PIT-PIT! WELL YOU'RE SORT O' USELESS-LOOKIN', BUT MEBBE YOU'RE KINDA CUTE! I DUNNO!
?
YIP! YAP! YIP!
BUT F'GOSH SAKES, QUIT YAPPIN'! WE AIN'T GONNA HURT YA!
!
YIP! YAP! YIP YIP! YAP! YIP! YAP!
KEEP QUIET, CAN'T YA? YA DON'T HEAR MY DOG YIPE-IN' AN' YIPPIN', DO YA? AN' KEEP AWAY FROM MY HEELS!
YIP! YAP! YIP! YIP! YAP! YAP!
GRRR-R-R-R!
C'MON, PLUTO! LET'S JUST DON'T PAY ANY ATTENTION TO HIM! MEBBE HE'LL STOP!
YAP! YAP! YAP! YAP! YAP! YAP! YAP!
GO GET IT, PLUTO!
YIPE! YAP! YIP-YAP!!
HEY! QUIT IT! CUT IT OUT! PIPE DOWN! YA' DRIVIN' ME CRAZY!
YIP! YIP! YIP! YIP! YIP-YIP YIP!
LISSEN, PIT-PIT! CAN'T YA DO NUTHIN' BUT BARK? QUIT IT! PA-LEEZE!
YAP! YAP-
!
YAP! YAP! YIPE! YIP! YIP!
GRRR--RRRR!!
!
YIPE!
BOW! WOW!
!
?
KI-YI YIPE!
?
AW, DRY UP! I'LL GET YOU OUT!
OHHHHH! MY POOR, DARLING, LITTLE PUPPY!
YIPE! YIPE! YIPE!
PLUTO, YOU'RE A BRUTE! A COWARD! MICKEY, I THINK YOU OUGHT TO GIVE HIM A GOOD WHIPPING FOR THIS!
YEAH! SURE, CLARABELLE! DON'T WORRY! I'LL SPANK HIM GOOD!
HO-HO-HO! IT'S A DIRTY TRICK T' LAUGH, BUT THAT LITTLE YAPPER SURE GOT WHAT WAS COMIN' TO HIM!
BUT, GOSH! I PROMISED CLARABELLE I'D GIVE PLUTO A SPANKIN'! I GUESS I GOTTA GO THROUGH WITH IT!
?
12·31
PLUTO, SEE THIS WHEATSTRAW? I'M GONNA GIVE YOU A GOOD, HARD SPANKIN' WITH IT! UNNERSTAND? A VERY, VERY SEVERE WHIPPIN'!

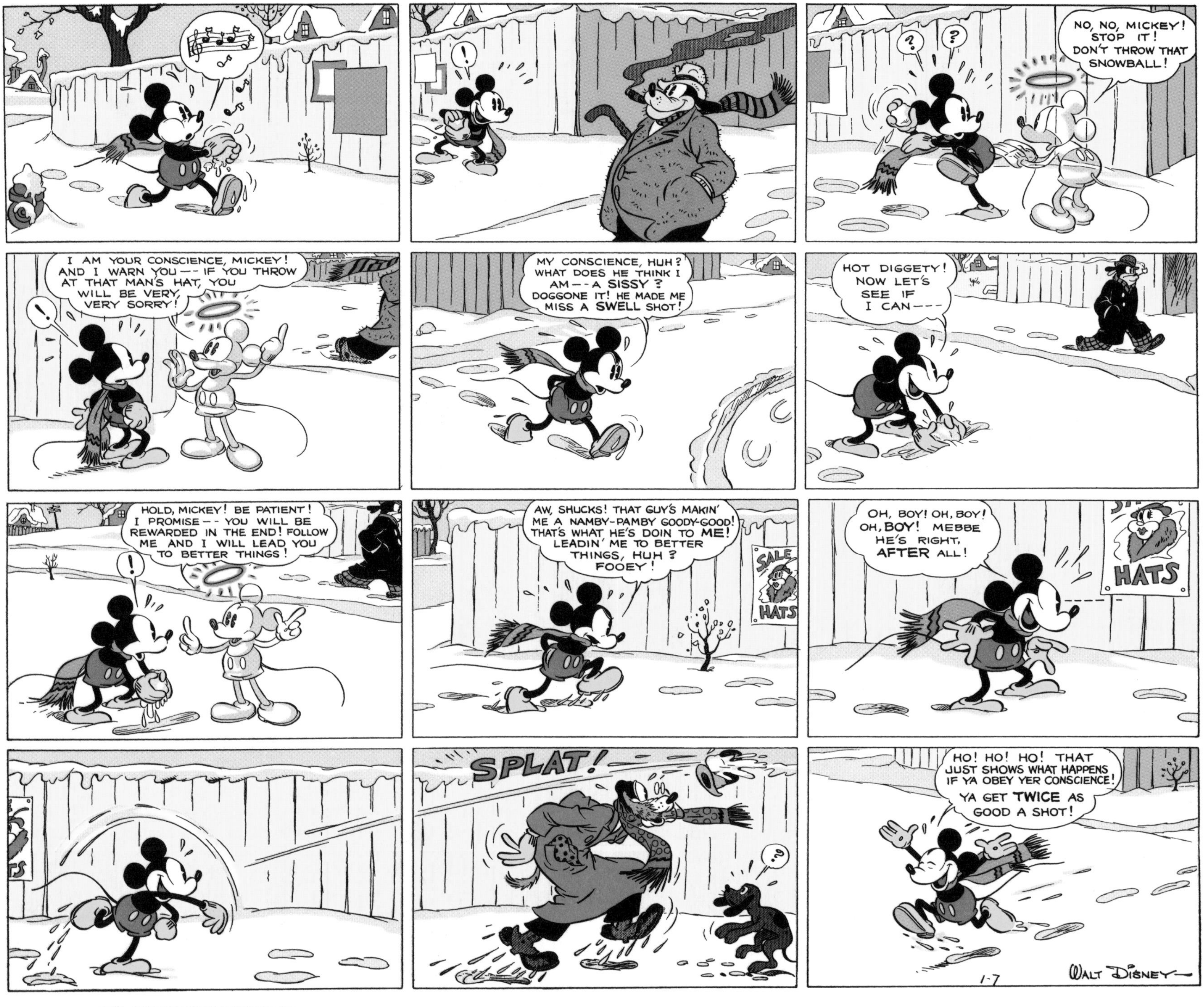
NO, NO, MICKEY! STOP IT! DON'T THROW THAT SNOWBALL!
I AM YOUR CONSCIENCE, MICKEY! AND I WARN YOU -- IF YOU THROW AT THAT MAN'S HAT, YOU WILL BE VERY, VERY SORRY!
MY CONSCIENCE, HUH? WHAT DOES HE THINK I AM -- A SISSY? DOGGONE IT! HE MADE ME MISS A SWELL SHOT!
HOT DIGGETY! NOW LET'S SEE IF I CAN ---
HOLD, MICKEY! BE PATIENT! I PROMISE -- YOU WILL BE REWARDED IN THE END! FOLLOW ME AND I WILL LEAD YOU TO BETTER THINGS!
AW, SHUCKS! THAT GUY'S MAKIN' ME A NAMBY-PAMBY GOODY-GOOD! THAT'S WHAT HE'S DOIN TO ME! LEADIN' ME TO BETTER THINGS, HUH? FOOEY!
SALE HATS
OH, BOY! OH, BOY! OH, BOY! MEBBE HE'S RIGHT, AFTER ALL!
HATS
SPLAT!
HO! HO! HO! THAT JUST SHOWS WHAT HAPPENS IF YA OBEY YER CONSCIENCE! YA GET TWICE AS GOOD A SHOT!
1-7
WALT DISNEY

128. PATIENCE IS REWARDED

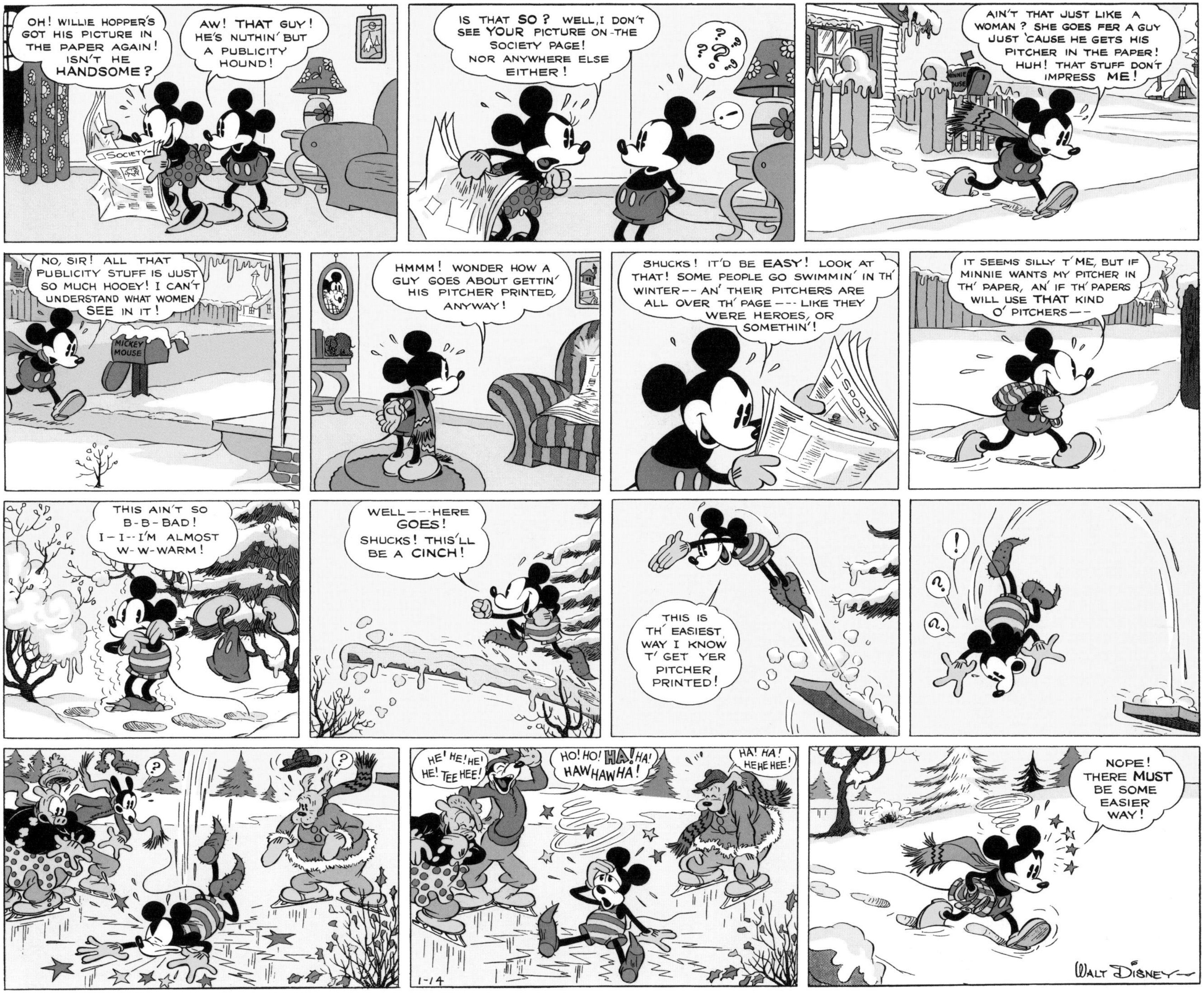
OH! WILLIE HOPPER'S GOT HIS PICTURE IN THE PAPER AGAIN! ISN'T HE HANDSOME?
SOCIETY
AW! THAT GUY! HE'S NUTHIN' BUT A PUBLICITY HOUND!
IS THAT SO? WELL, I DON'T SEE YOUR PICTURE ON THE SOCIETY PAGE! NOR ANYWHERE ELSE EITHER!
AIN'T THAT JUST LIKE A WOMAN? SHE GOES FER A GUY JUST 'CAUSE HE GETS HIS PITCHER IN THE PAPER! HUH! THAT STUFF DON'T IMPRESS ME!
MINNIE MOUSE
NO, SIR! ALL THAT PUBLICITY STUFF IS JUST SO MUCH HOOEY! I CAN'T UNDERSTAND WHAT WOMEN SEE IN IT!
MICKEY MOUSE
HMMM! WONDER HOW A GUY GOES ABOUT GETTIN' HIS PITCHER PRINTED, ANYWAY!
SHUCKS! IT'D BE EASY! LOOK AT THAT! SOME PEOPLE GO SWIMMIN' IN TH' WINTER-- AN' THEIR PITCHERS ARE ALL OVER TH' PAGE--- LIKE THEY WERE HEROES, OR SOMETHIN'!
SPORTS
IT SEEMS SILLY T'ME, BUT IF MINNIE WANTS MY PITCHER IN TH' PAPER, AN' IF TH' PAPERS WILL USE THAT KIND O' PITCHERS--
THIS AIN'T SO B-B-BAD! I-I--I'M ALMOST W-W-WARM!
WELL---HERE GOES! SHUCKS! THIS'LL BE A CINCH!
THIS IS TH' EASIEST WAY I KNOW T' GET YER PITCHER PRINTED!
HE! HE! HE! HE! TEE HEE!
HO! HO! HA! HA! HAW HAW HA!
HA! HA! HE HE HEE!
NOPE! THERE MUST BE SOME EASIER WAY!
1-14
WALT DISNEY

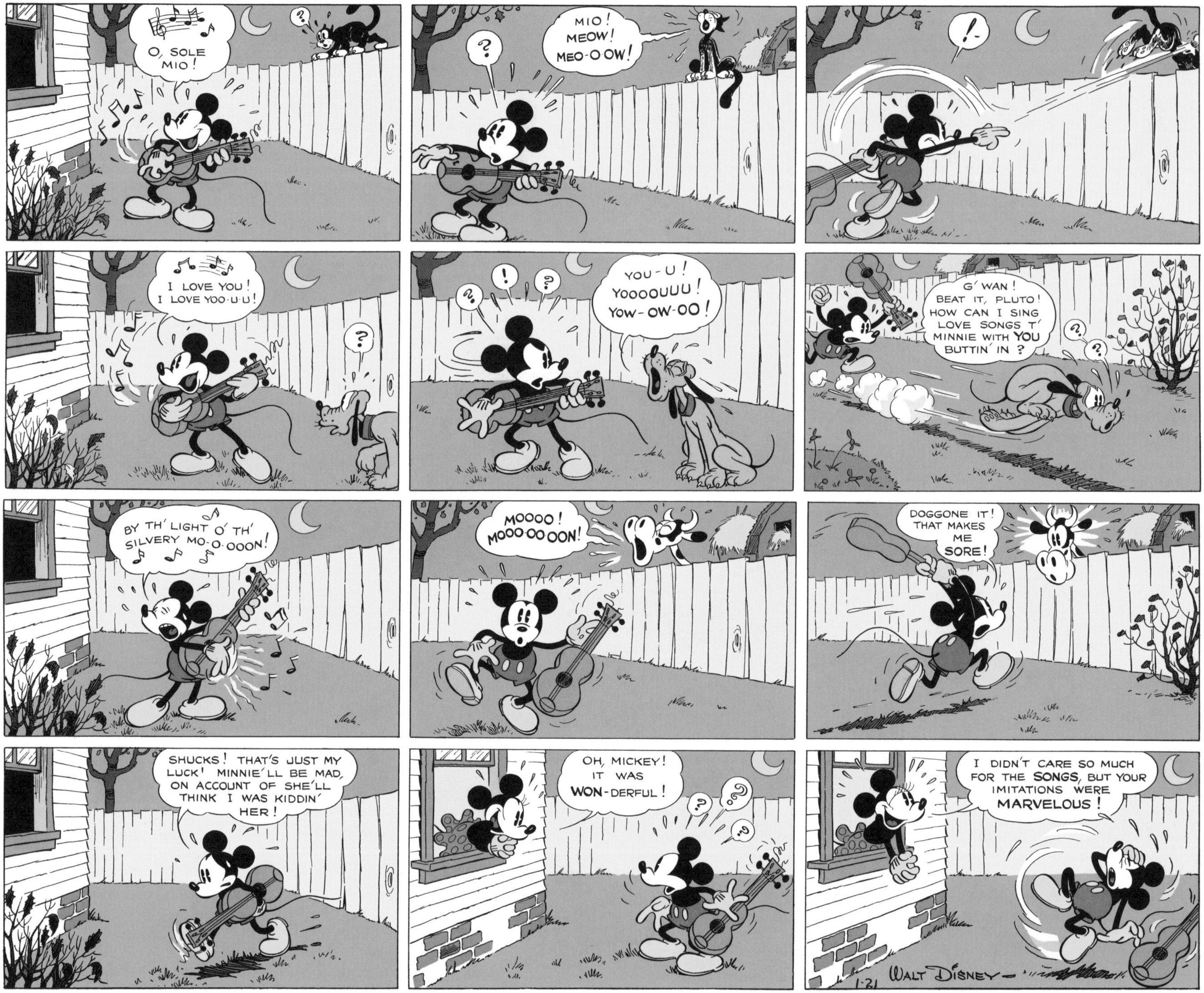
O, SOLE MIO!
MIO! MEOW! MEO-O-OW!
I LOVE YOU! I LOVE YOO-U-U!
YOU-U! YOOOOUUU! YOW-OW-OO!
G' WAN! BEAT IT, PLUTO! HOW CAN I SING LOVE SONGS T' MINNIE WITH YOU BUTTIN' IN?
BY TH' LIGHT O' TH' SILVERY MO-O-OOON!
MOOOO! MOOO-OO-OON!
DOGGONE IT! THAT MAKES ME SORE!
SHUCKS! THAT'S JUST MY LUCK! MINNIE'LL BE MAD, ON ACCOUNT OF SHE'LL THINK I WAS KIDDIN' HER!
OH, MICKEY! IT WAS WON-DERFUL!
I DIDN'T CARE SO MUCH FOR THE SONGS, BUT YOUR IMITATIONS WERE MARVELOUS!
1-21
WALT DISNEY

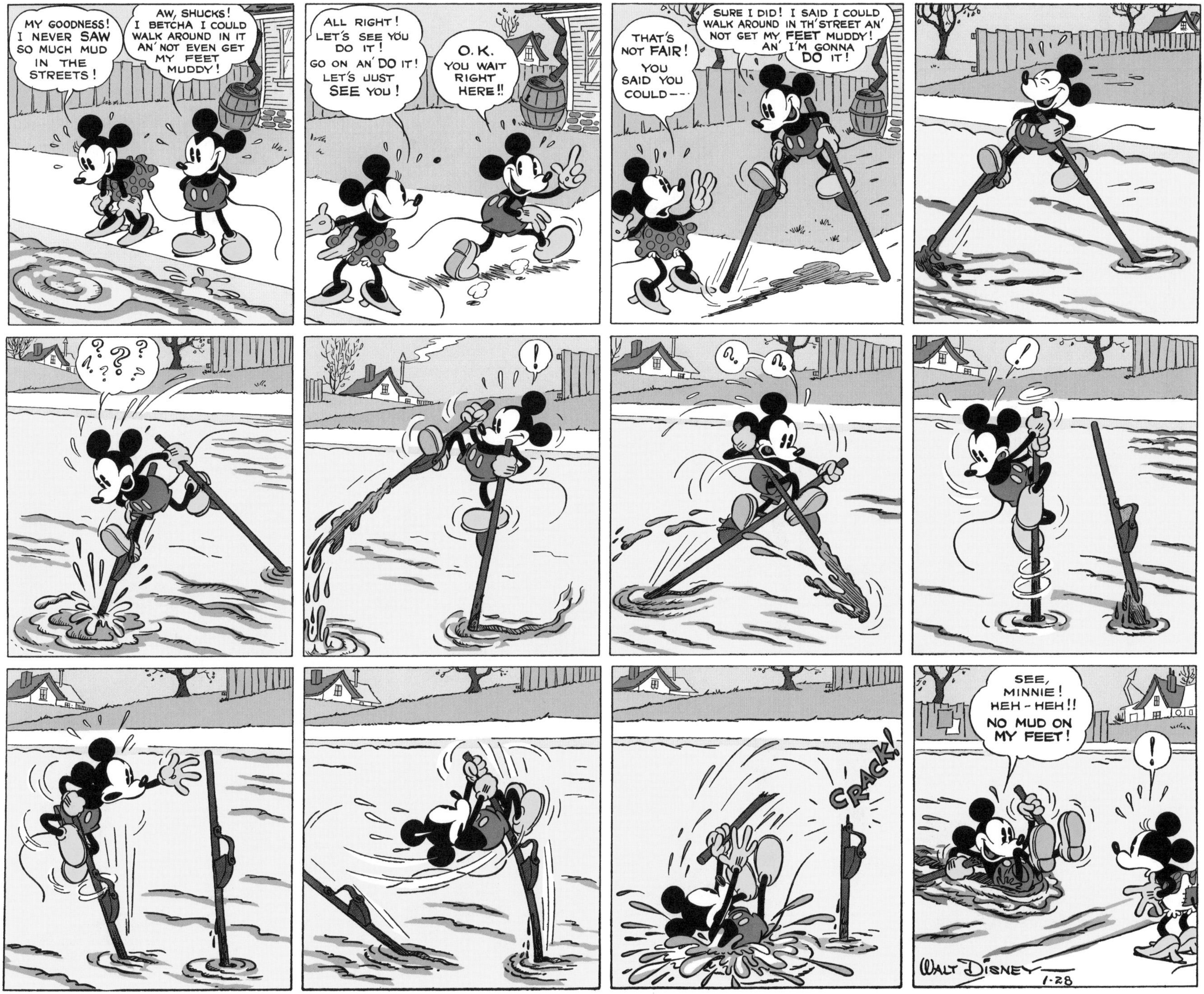
MY GOODNESS! I NEVER SAW SO MUCH MUD IN THE STREETS!
AW, SHUCKS! I BETCHA I COULD WALK AROUND IN IT AN' NOT EVEN GET MY FEET MUDDY!
ALL RIGHT! LET'S SEE YOU DO IT! GO ON AN' DO IT! LET'S JUST SEE YOU!
O.K. YOU WAIT RIGHT HERE!!
THAT'S NOT FAIR! YOU SAID YOU COULD---
SURE I DID! I SAID I COULD WALK AROUND IN TH' STREET AN' NOT GET MY FEET MUDDY! AN' I'M GONNA DO IT!
CRACK!
SEE, MINNIE! HEH-HEH!! NO MUD ON MY FEET!
WALT DISNEY
1-28

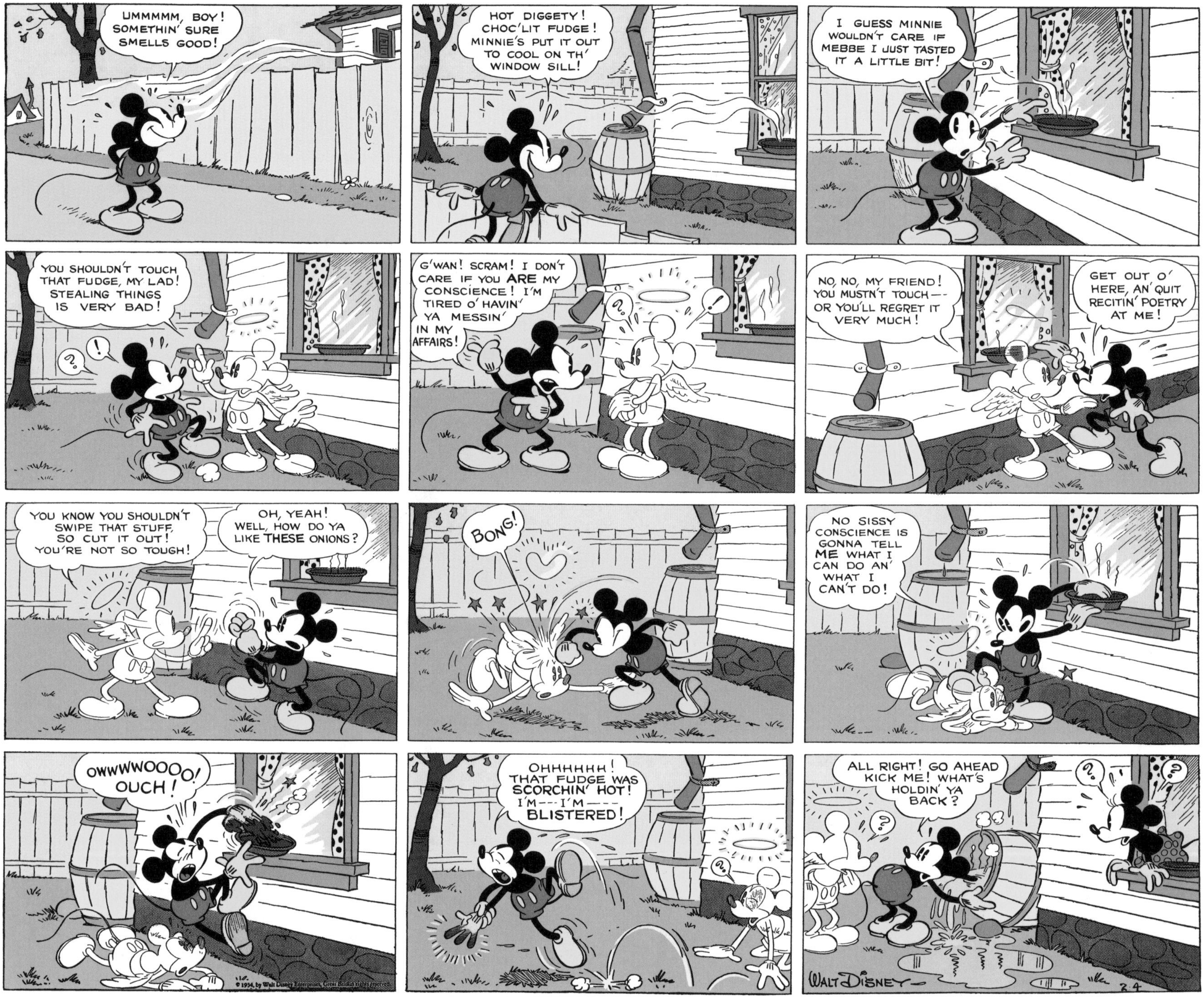
UMMMMM, BOY! SOMETHIN' SURE SMELLS GOOD!
HOT DIGGETY! CHOC'LIT FUDGE! MINNIE'S PUT IT OUT TO COOL ON TH' WINDOW SILL!
I GUESS MINNIE WOULDN'T CARE IF MEBBE I JUST TASTED IT A LITTLE BIT!
YOU SHOULDN'T TOUCH THAT FUDGE, MY LAD! STEALING THINGS IS VERY BAD!
G'WAN! SCRAM! I DON'T CARE IF YOU **ARE** MY CONSCIENCE! I'M TIRED O' HAVIN' YA MESSIN' IN MY AFFAIRS!
NO, NO, MY FRIEND! YOU MUSTN'T TOUCH—OR YOU'LL REGRET IT VERY MUCH!
GET OUT O' HERE, AN' QUIT RECITIN' POETRY AT ME!
YOU KNOW YOU SHOULDN'T SWIPE THAT STUFF, SO CUT IT OUT! YOU'RE NOT SO TOUGH!
OH, YEAH! WELL, HOW DO YA LIKE **THESE** ONIONS?
BONG!
NO SISSY CONSCIENCE IS GONNA TELL **ME** WHAT I CAN DO AN' WHAT I CAN'T DO!
OWWWWOOOO! OUCH!
© 1934, by Walt Disney Enterprises. Great Britain rights reserved
OHHHHHH! THAT FUDGE WAS **SCORCHIN' HOT!** I'M—I'M— **BLISTERED!**
ALL RIGHT! GO AHEAD KICK ME! WHAT'S HOLDIN' YA BACK?
WALT DISNEY
3-4

132. AW, FUDGE

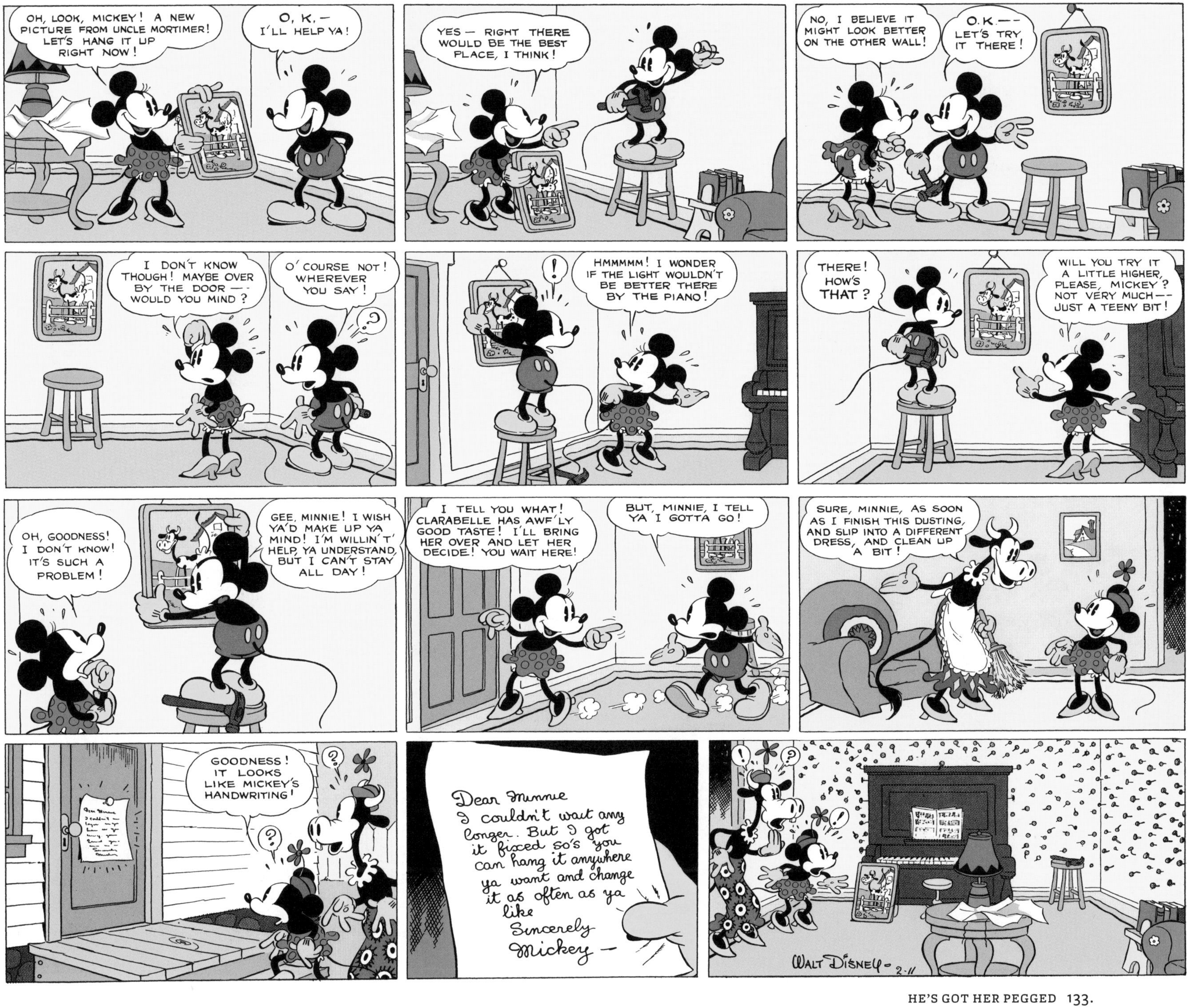
OH, LOOK, MICKEY! A NEW PICTURE FROM UNCLE MORTIMER! LET'S HANG IT UP RIGHT NOW!
O. K. — I'LL HELP YA!
YES — RIGHT THERE WOULD BE THE BEST PLACE, I THINK!
NO, I BELIEVE IT MIGHT LOOK BETTER ON THE OTHER WALL!
O.K.— — LET'S TRY IT THERE!
I DON'T KNOW THOUGH! MAYBE OVER BY THE DOOR — - WOULD YOU MIND?
O' COURSE NOT! WHEREVER YOU SAY!
HMMMMM! I WONDER IF THE LIGHT WOULDN'T BE BETTER THERE BY THE PIANO!
THERE! HOW'S THAT?
WILL YOU TRY IT A LITTLE HIGHER, PLEASE, MICKEY? NOT VERY MUCH— — JUST A TEENY BIT!
OH, GOODNESS! I DON'T KNOW! IT'S SUCH A PROBLEM!
GEE, MINNIE! I WISH YA'D MAKE UP YA MIND! I'M WILLIN' T' HELP, YA UNDERSTAND, BUT I CAN'T STAY ALL DAY!
I TELL YOU WHAT! CLARABELLE HAS AWF'LY GOOD TASTE! I'LL BRING HER OVER AND LET HER DECIDE! YOU WAIT HERE!
BUT, MINNIE, I TELL YA I GOTTA GO!
SURE, MINNIE, AS SOON AS I FINISH THIS DUSTING, AND SLIP INTO A DIFFERENT DRESS, AND CLEAN UP A BIT!
GOODNESS! IT LOOKS LIKE MICKEY'S HANDWRITING!
Dear Minnie
I couldn't wait any longer. But I got it fixed so's you can hang it anywhere ya want and change it as often as ya like
Sincerely
Mickey —
WALT DISNEY — 2-11

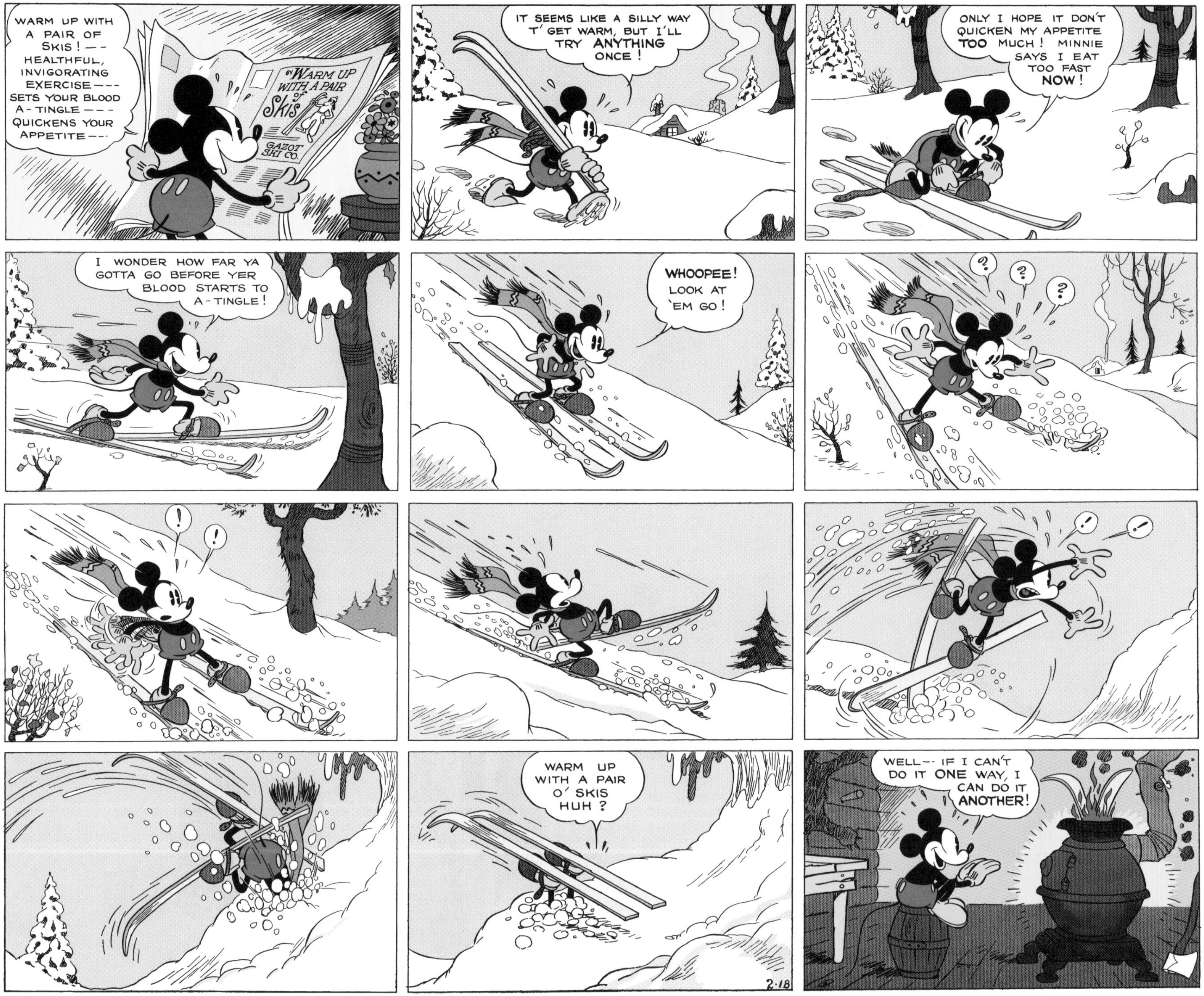
WARM UP WITH A PAIR OF SKIS! —— HEALTHFUL, INVIGORATING EXERCISE——— SETS YOUR BLOOD A-TINGLE——— QUICKENS YOUR APPETITE———
WARM UP WITH A PAIR of SKIS
GAZOT SKI CO.
IT SEEMS LIKE A SILLY WAY T' GET WARM, BUT I'LL TRY ANYTHING ONCE!
ONLY I HOPE IT DON'T QUICKEN MY APPETITE TOO MUCH! MINNIE SAYS I EAT TOO FAST NOW!
I WONDER HOW FAR YA GOTTA GO BEFORE YER BLOOD STARTS TO A-TINGLE!
WHOOPEE! LOOK AT 'EM GO!
WARM UP WITH A PAIR O' SKIS HUH?
2-18
WELL-- IF I CAN'T DO IT ONE WAY, I CAN DO IT ANOTHER!

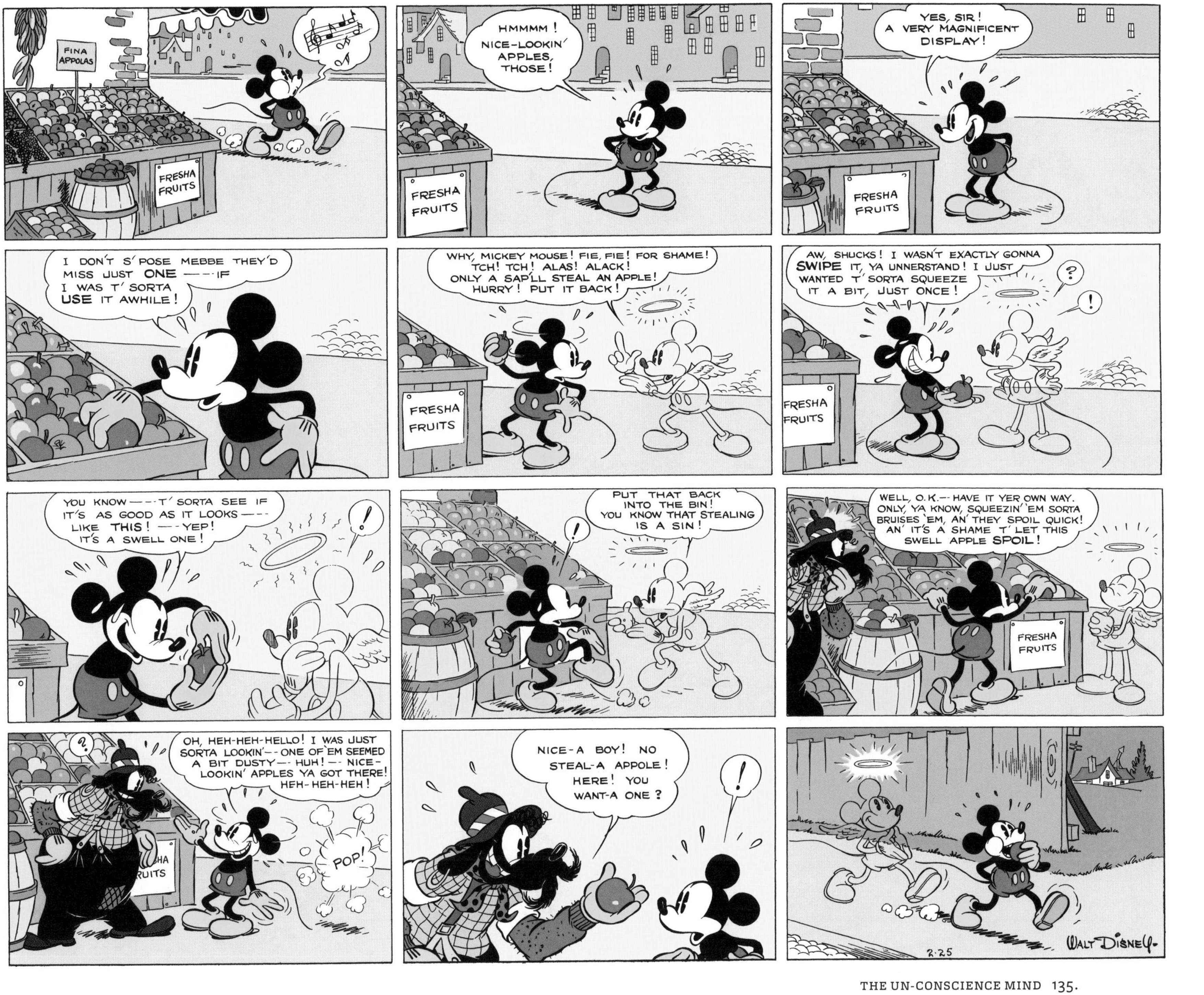
FINA APPOLAS
FRESHA FRUITS
HMMMM! NICE-LOOKIN' APPLES, THOSE!
FRESHA FRUITS
YES, SIR! A VERY MAGNIFICENT DISPLAY!
FRESHA FRUITS
I DON'T S'POSE MEBBE THEY'D MISS JUST ONE --- IF I WAS T' SORTA USE IT AWHILE!
WHY, MICKEY MOUSE! FIE, FIE! FOR SHAME! TCH! TCH! ALAS! ALACK! ONLY A SAP'LL STEAL AN APPLE! HURRY! PUT IT BACK!
FRESHA FRUITS
AW, SHUCKS! I WASN'T EXACTLY GONNA SWIPE IT, YA UNNERSTAND! I JUST WANTED T' SORTA SQUEEZE IT A BIT, JUST ONCE!
?
!
FRESHA FRUITS
YOU KNOW --- T' SORTA SEE IF IT'S AS GOOD AS IT LOOKS --- LIKE THIS! --- YEP! IT'S A SWELL ONE!
!
PUT THAT BACK INTO THE BIN! YOU KNOW THAT STEALING IS A SIN!
!
WELL, O.K.-- HAVE IT YER OWN WAY. ONLY, YA KNOW, SQUEEZIN' 'EM SORTA BRUISES 'EM, AN' THEY SPOIL QUICK! AN' IT'S A SHAME T' LET THIS SWELL APPLE SPOIL!
FRESHA FRUITS
?
OH, HEH-HEH-HELLO! I WAS JUST SORTA LOOKIN'-- ONE OF 'EM SEEMED A BIT DUSTY-- HUH! -- NICE-LOOKIN' APPLES YA GOT THERE! HEH-HEH-HEH!
POP!
NICE-A BOY! NO STEAL-A APPOLE! HERE! YOU WANT-A ONE?
!
2·25
WALT DISNEY

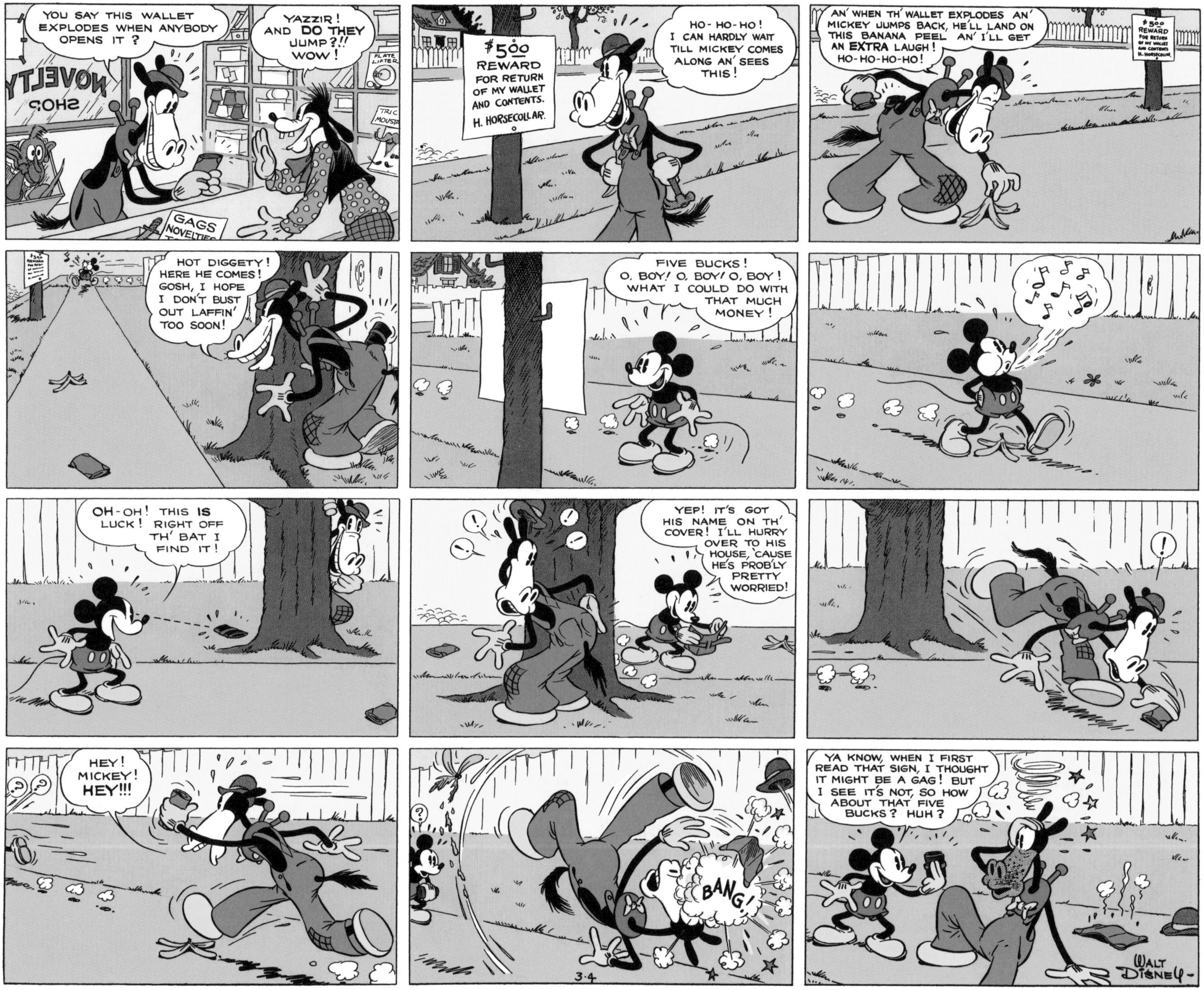
YOU SAY THIS WALLET EXPLODES WHEN ANYBODY OPENS IT ?
YAZZIR! AND DO THEY JUMP?!! WOW!
PLATE LIFTER
GAGS
$5.00 REWARD FOR RETURN OF MY WALLET AND CONTENTS. H. HORSECOLLAR.
HO-HO-HO! I CAN HARDLY WAIT TILL MICKEY COMES ALONG AN' SEES THIS!
AN' WHEN TH' WALLET EXPLODES AN' MICKEY JUMPS BACK, HE'LL LAND ON THIS BANANA PEEL AN' I'LL GET AN EXTRA LAUGH! HO-HO-HO-HO!
HOT DIGGETY! HERE HE COMES! GOSH, I HOPE I DON'T BUST OUT LAFFIN' TOO SOON!
FIVE BUCKS! O, BOY! O, BOY! O, BOY! WHAT I COULD DO WITH THAT MUCH MONEY!
OH-OH! THIS IS LUCK! RIGHT OFF TH' BAT I FIND IT!
YEP! IT'S GOT HIS NAME ON TH' COVER! I'LL HURRY OVER TO HIS HOUSE, 'CAUSE HE'S PROB'LY PRETTY WORRIED!
HEY! MICKEY! HEY!!!
BANG!
3-4
YA KNOW, WHEN I FIRST READ THAT SIGN, I THOUGHT IT MIGHT BE A GAG! BUT I SEE IT'S NOT, SO HOW ABOUT THAT FIVE BUCKS? HUH?
WALT DISNEY

RUMPLEWATT THE GIANT

AND

TANGLEFOOT PULLS HIS WEIGHT

MARCH 11, 1934

–

JUNE 10, 1934

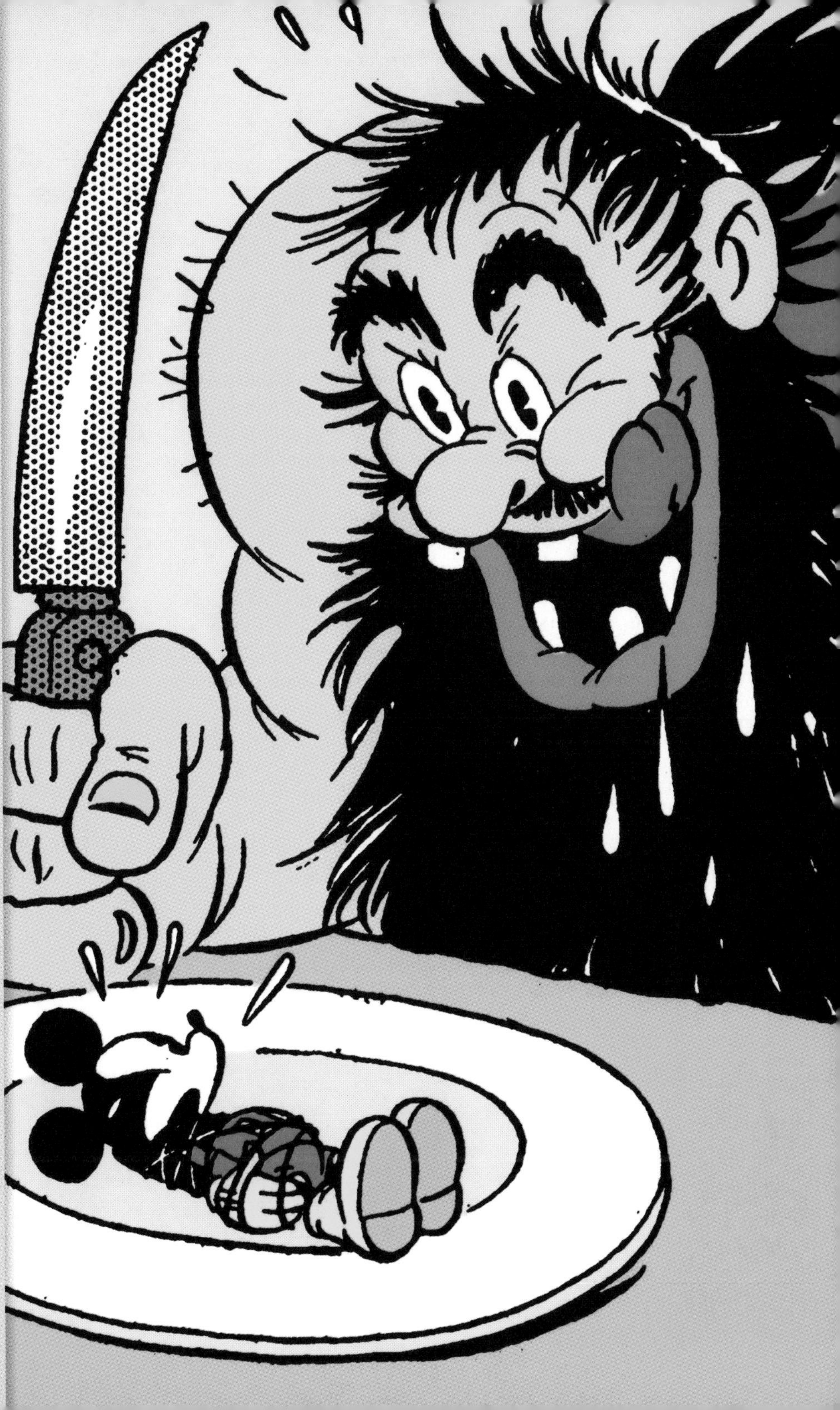

MICKEY MOUSE

REGISTERED U.S. PATENT OFFICE

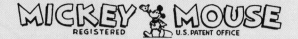

THE LONGEST SHORT STORY EVER TOLD!

The Mickey Mouse of the comics is known for being many things: brave, scrappy, determined, spunky, empathetic—and possessing an extraordinary amount of what bygone generations once called "moxie."

Yes, Mickey embodies many endearing character traits... but long-windedness has never been one of them. At least not until Mickey was provided with a receptive audience of about a dozen identical, night-shirted mouselings to hang on his every word. The Sunday continuity now known as "Rumplewatt the Giant" was based upon the Mickey Mouse cartoon short *Giantland* (1933). The crowd of young listeners was carried over from the cartoon—but the seven-minute runtime was not.

Vastly expanded for comics, Mickey's tall-tale of a tall adversary now unfolded over eight Sunday strips. Encountering it in one "dose," without weekly gaps between installments, the modern reader might fail to grasp exactly how long-winded Mickey's wily whopper actually is. But our "munchausing" Mouse acknowledges the epic length of the tale to come—and comes close to breaking the fourth wall (truly a rarity for a 1930s Disney strip)—when he ends the first installment with: "Th' story's too long t' finish now! You come back next week, an' I'll tell ya more!" Clearly, Mickey's announcement is intended for *us* as well as the mini-mice.

True to his word, Mickey does indeed continue the story "next week" with the March 18 installment. Three more Sundays are spent in Mickey's living room as the tale unfolds. But by April 15, we find Mickey continuing his epic adventure tale as a *bedtime* story—meaning that he has likely gone on *all day* and into the evening with his giant-sized saga! Even if all previous installments are to be considered as taking place over the course of a single day, we have the inescapable "overnight aspect" to consider, when measuring the windy effort from start to finish.

April 22 finds our tale-teller and his tell-ees back in the living room. Finally, on April 29, Mickey wraps up a lengthy storytelling effort that would shame Scheherazade—perhaps making "Rumplewatt" the longest short story ever told!

With Mickey suddenly given to so much talk, we might jokingly claim to have uncovered the reason why the busy Mr. Disney eventually ceased voicing his creation on-screen... he might have worried that one day he would be required to tell a story as lengthy as this! After all, more giants—in both *The Brave Little Tailor* (1938) and the "Mickey and the Beanstalk" segment of *Fun and Fancy Free* (1947)—were still to come, each rife with the possibility of its own embellished comics adaptation.

—JOE TORCIVIA

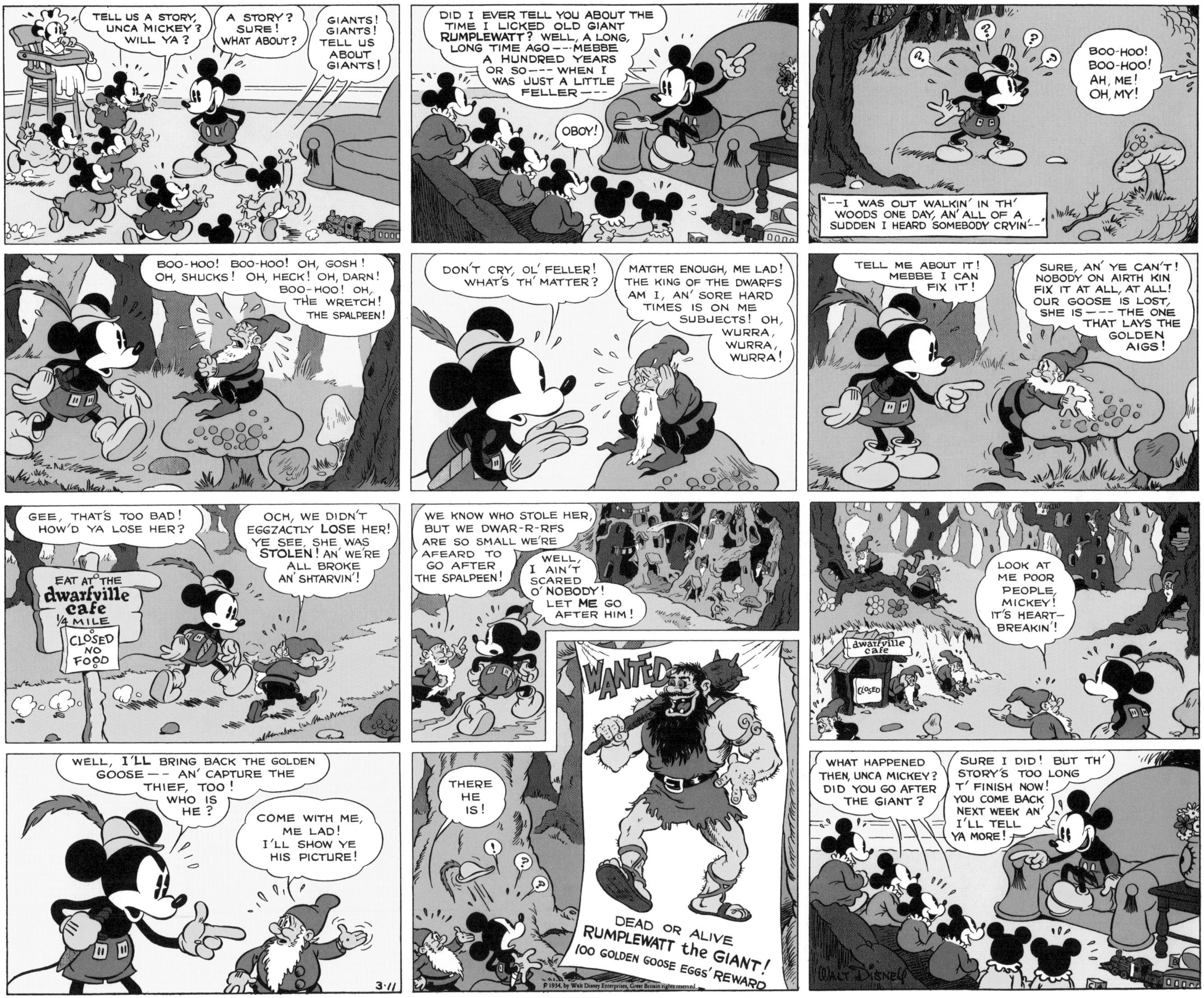
TELL US A STORY, UNCA MICKEY? WILL YA?
A STORY? SURE! WHAT ABOUT?
GIANTS! GIANTS! TELL US ABOUT GIANTS!
DID I EVER TELL YOU ABOUT THE TIME I LICKED OLD GIANT RUMPLEWATT? WELL, A LONG, LONG TIME AGO---MEBBE A HUNDRED YEARS OR SO--- WHEN I WAS JUST A LITTLE FELLER---
OBOY!
"--I WAS OUT WALKIN' IN TH' WOODS ONE DAY, AN' ALL OF A SUDDEN I HEARD SOMEBODY CRYIN'--"
BOO-HOO! BOO-HOO! AH, ME! OH, MY!
BOO-HOO! BOO-HOO! OH, GOSH! OH, SHUCKS! OH, HECK! OH, DARN! BOO-HOO! OH, THE WRETCH! THE SPALPEEN!
DON'T CRY, OL' FELLER! WHAT'S TH' MATTER?
MATTER ENOUGH, ME LAD! THE KING OF THE DWARFS AM I, AN' SORE HARD TIMES IS ON ME SUBJECTS! OH, WURRA, WURRA, WURRA!
TELL ME ABOUT IT! MEBBE I CAN FIX IT!
SURE, AN' YE CAN'T! NOBODY ON AIRTH KIN FIX IT AT ALL, AT ALL! OUR GOOSE IS LOST, SHE IS--- THE ONE THAT LAYS THE GOLDEN AIGS!
GEE, THAT'S TOO BAD! HOW'D YA LOSE HER?
OCH, WE DIDN'T EGGZACTLY LOSE HER! YE SEE, SHE WAS STOLEN! AN' WE'RE ALL BROKE AN' SHTARVIN'!
EAT AT THE dwarfville cafe 1/4 MILE
CLOSED NO FOOD
WE KNOW WHO STOLE HER, BUT WE DWAR-R-RFS ARE SO SMALL WE'RE AFEARD TO GO AFTER THE SPALPEEN!
WELL, I AIN'T SCARED O' NOBODY! LET ME GO AFTER HIM!
LOOK AT ME POOR PEOPLE, MICKEY! IT'S HEART-BREAKIN'!
dwarfville cafe
CLOSED
WELL, I'LL BRING BACK THE GOLDEN GOOSE-- AN' CAPTURE THE THIEF, TOO! WHO IS HE?
COME WITH ME, ME LAD! I'LL SHOW YE HIS PICTURE!
3·11
THERE HE IS!
WANTED
DEAD OR ALIVE
RUMPLEWATT the GIANT!
100 GOLDEN GOOSE EGGS' REWARD
© 1934, by Walt Disney Enterprises, Great Britain rights reserved
WHAT HAPPENED THEN, UNCA MICKEY? DID YOU GO AFTER THE GIANT?
SURE I DID! BUT TH' STORY'S TOO LONG T' FINISH NOW! YOU COME BACK NEXT WEEK AN' I'LL TELL YA MORE!
WALT DISNEY

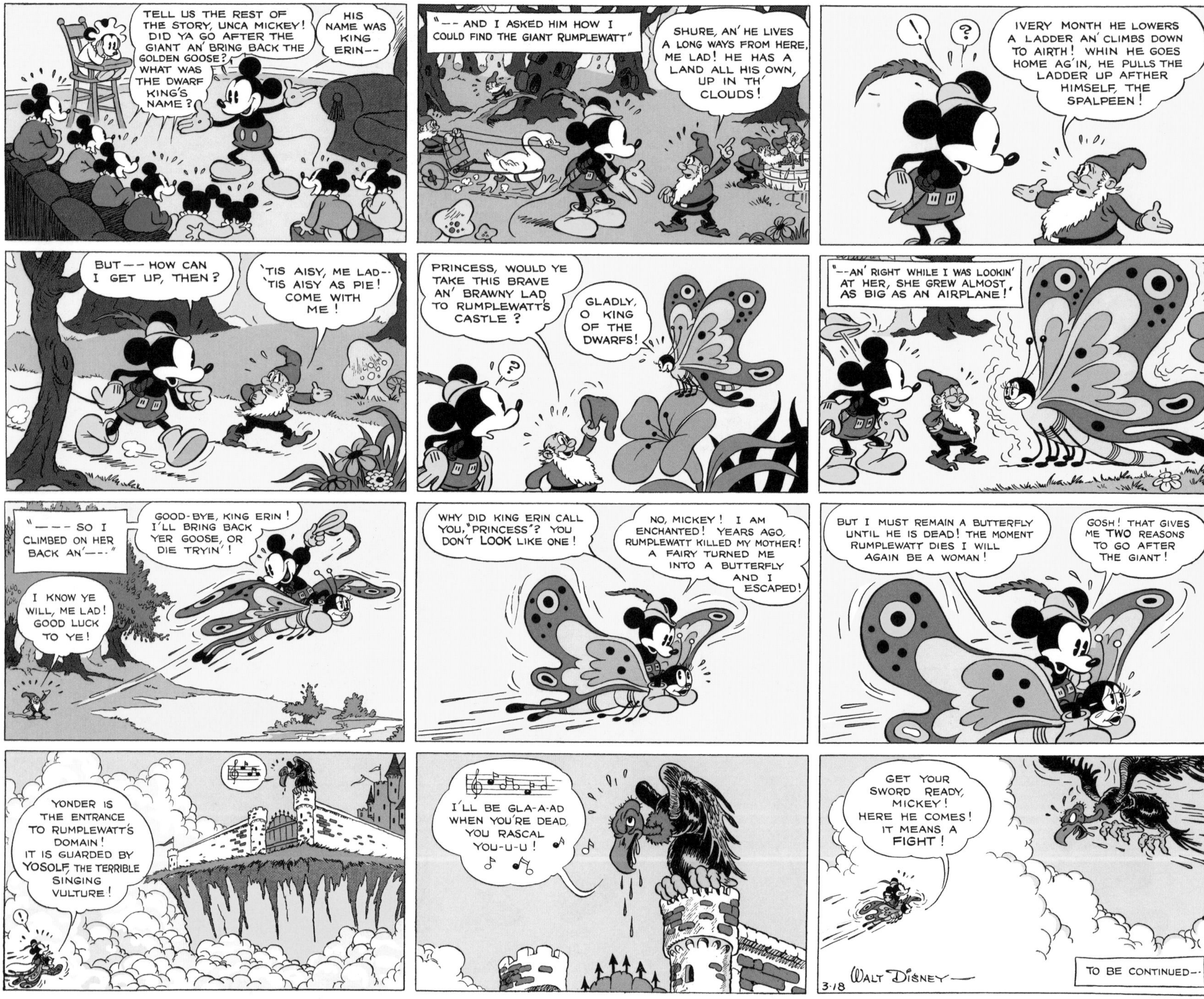
TELL US THE REST OF THE STORY, UNCA MICKEY! DID YA GO AFTER THE GIANT AN' BRING BACK THE GOLDEN GOOSE? WHAT WAS THE DWARF KING'S NAME?
HIS NAME WAS KING ERIN--
"-- AND I ASKED HIM HOW I COULD FIND THE GIANT RUMPLEWATT"
SHURE, AN' HE LIVES A LONG WAYS FROM HERE, ME LAD! HE HAS A LAND ALL HIS OWN, UP IN TH' CLOUDS!
!
?
IVERY MONTH HE LOWERS A LADDER AN' CLIMBS DOWN TO AIRTH! WHIN HE GOES HOME AG'IN, HE PULLS THE LADDER UP AFTHER HIMSELF, THE SPALPEEN!
BUT -- HOW CAN I GET UP, THEN?
'TIS AISY, ME LAD-- 'TIS AISY AS PIE! COME WITH ME!
PRINCESS, WOULD YE TAKE THIS BRAVE AN' BRAWNY LAD TO RUMPLEWATT'S CASTLE?
?
GLADLY, O KING OF THE DWARFS!
"--AN' RIGHT WHILE I WAS LOOKIN' AT HER, SHE GREW ALMOST AS BIG AS AN AIRPLANE!"
"--- SO I CLIMBED ON HER BACK AN'---"
GOOD-BYE, KING ERIN! I'LL BRING BACK YER GOOSE, OR DIE TRYIN'!
I KNOW YE WILL, ME LAD! GOOD LUCK TO YE!
WHY DID KING ERIN CALL YOU, "PRINCESS"? YOU DON'T LOOK LIKE ONE!
NO, MICKEY! I AM ENCHANTED! YEARS AGO, RUMPLEWATT KILLED MY MOTHER! A FAIRY TURNED ME INTO A BUTTERFLY AND I ESCAPED!
BUT I MUST REMAIN A BUTTERFLY UNTIL HE IS DEAD! THE MOMENT RUMPLEWATT DIES I WILL AGAIN BE A WOMAN!
GOSH! THAT GIVES ME TWO REASONS TO GO AFTER THE GIANT!
YONDER IS THE ENTRANCE TO RUMPLEWATT'S DOMAIN! IT IS GUARDED BY YOSOLF, THE TERRIBLE SINGING VULTURE!
!
I'LL BE GLA-A-AD WHEN YOU'RE DEAD, YOU RASCAL YOU-U-U!
GET YOUR SWORD READY, MICKEY! HERE HE COMES! IT MEANS A FIGHT!
3-18
WALT DISNEY
TO BE CONTINUED--

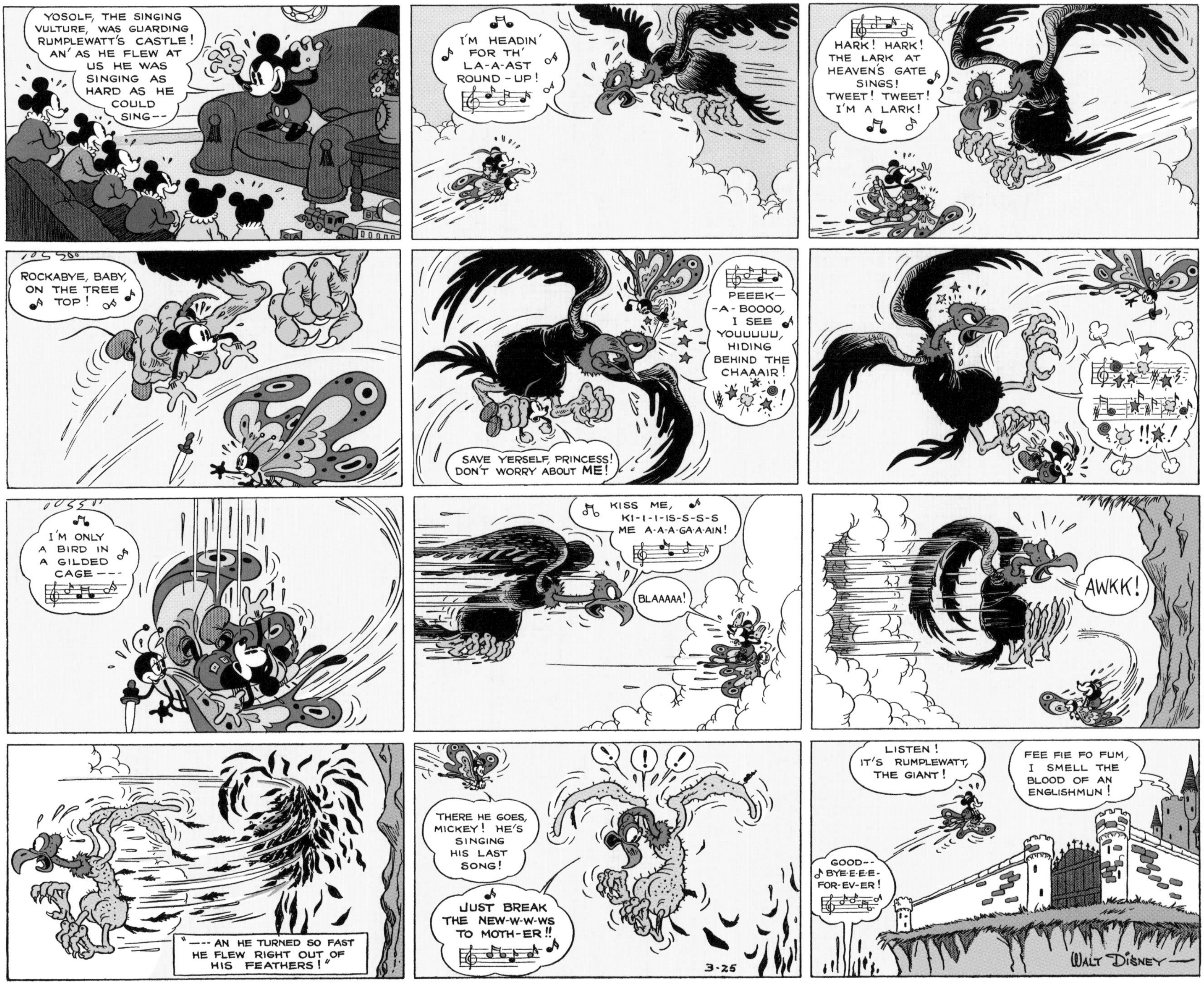
YOSOLF, THE SINGING VULTURE, WAS GUARDING RUMPLEWATT'S CASTLE! AN' AS HE FLEW AT US HE WAS SINGING AS HARD AS HE COULD SING--
I'M HEADIN' FOR TH' LA-A-AST ROUND-UP!
HARK! HARK! THE LARK AT HEAVEN'S GATE SINGS! TWEET! TWEET! I'M A LARK!
ROCKABYE, BABY, ON THE TREE TOP!
PEEEK--A-BOOOO, I SEE YOUUUUU, HIDING BEHIND THE CHAAAIR!
SAVE YERSELF, PRINCESS! DON'T WORRY ABOUT ME!
I'M ONLY A BIRD IN A GILDED CAGE---
KISS ME, KI-I-I-IS-S-S-S ME A-A-GA-A-AIN!
BLAAAAA!
AWKK!
"---AN HE TURNED SO FAST HE FLEW RIGHT OUT OF HIS FEATHERS!"
THERE HE GOES, MICKEY! HE'S SINGING HIS LAST SONG!
JUST BREAK THE NEW-W-WS TO MOTH-ER!!
3-25
LISTEN! IT'S RUMPLEWATT, THE GIANT!
FEE FIE FO FUM, I SMELL THE BLOOD OF AN ENGLISHMUN!
GOOD--BYE-E-E-E-FOR-EV-ER!
WALT DISNEY

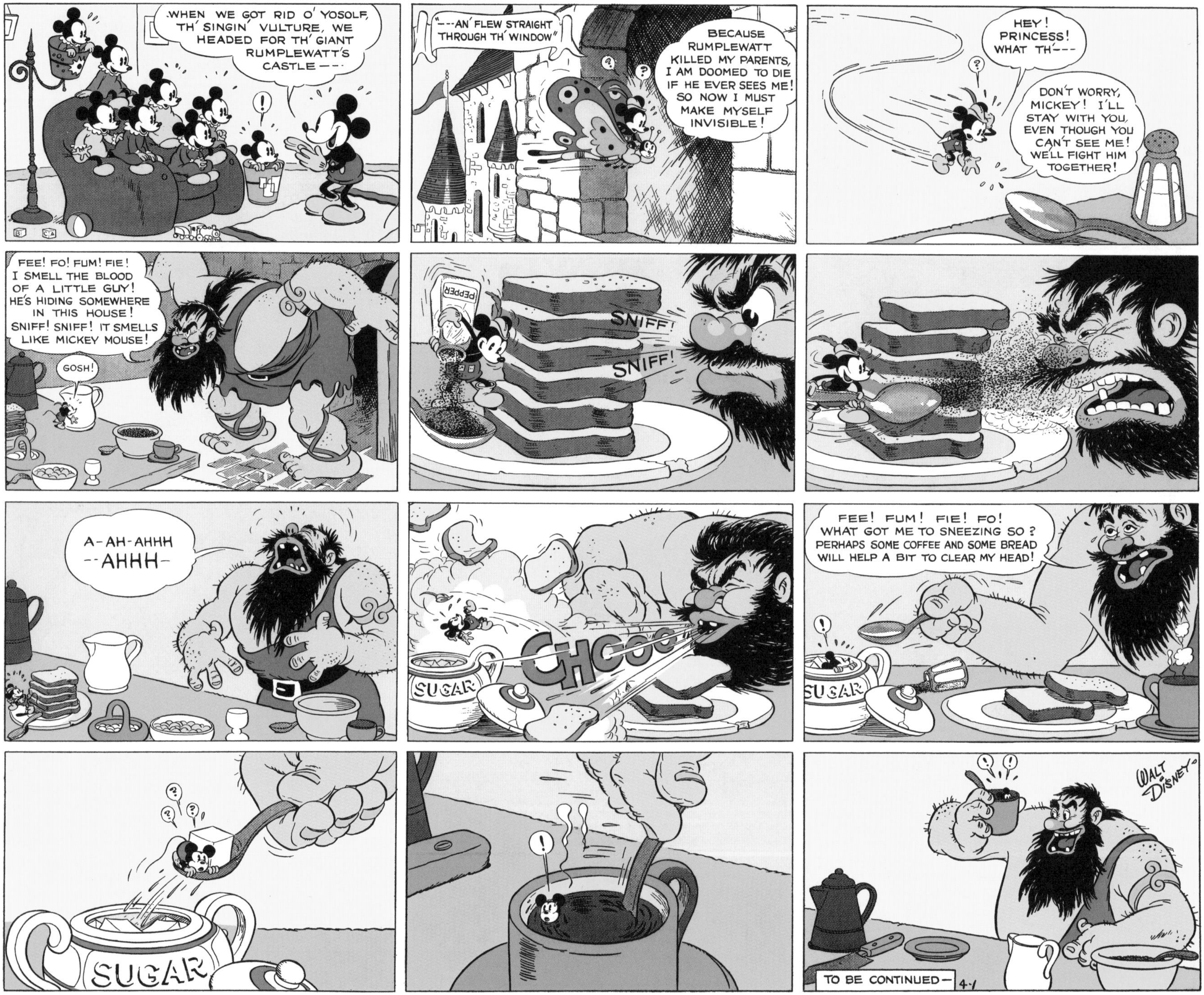
WHEN WE GOT RID O' YOSOLF, TH' SINGIN' VULTURE, WE HEADED FOR TH' GIANT RUMPLEWATT'S CASTLE ---
"---AN' FLEW STRAIGHT THROUGH TH' WINDOW"
BECAUSE RUMPLEWATT KILLED MY PARENTS, I AM DOOMED TO DIE IF HE EVER SEES ME! SO NOW I MUST MAKE MYSELF INVISIBLE!
HEY! PRINCESS! WHAT TH'---
DON'T WORRY, MICKEY! I'LL STAY WITH YOU, EVEN THOUGH YOU CAN'T SEE ME! WE'LL FIGHT HIM TOGETHER!
FEE! FO! FUM! FIE! I SMELL THE BLOOD OF A LITTLE GUY! HE'S HIDING SOMEWHERE IN THIS HOUSE! SNIFF! SNIFF! IT SMELLS LIKE MICKEY MOUSE!
GOSH!
PEPPER
SNIFF!
SNIFF!
A-AH-AHHH --AHHH-
CHOOO
SUGAR
FEE! FUM! FIE! FO! WHAT GOT ME TO SNEEZING SO? PERHAPS SOME COFFEE AND SOME BREAD WILL HELP A BIT TO CLEAR MY HEAD!
SUGAR
SUGAR
WALT DISNEY
TO BE CONTINUED— 4-1

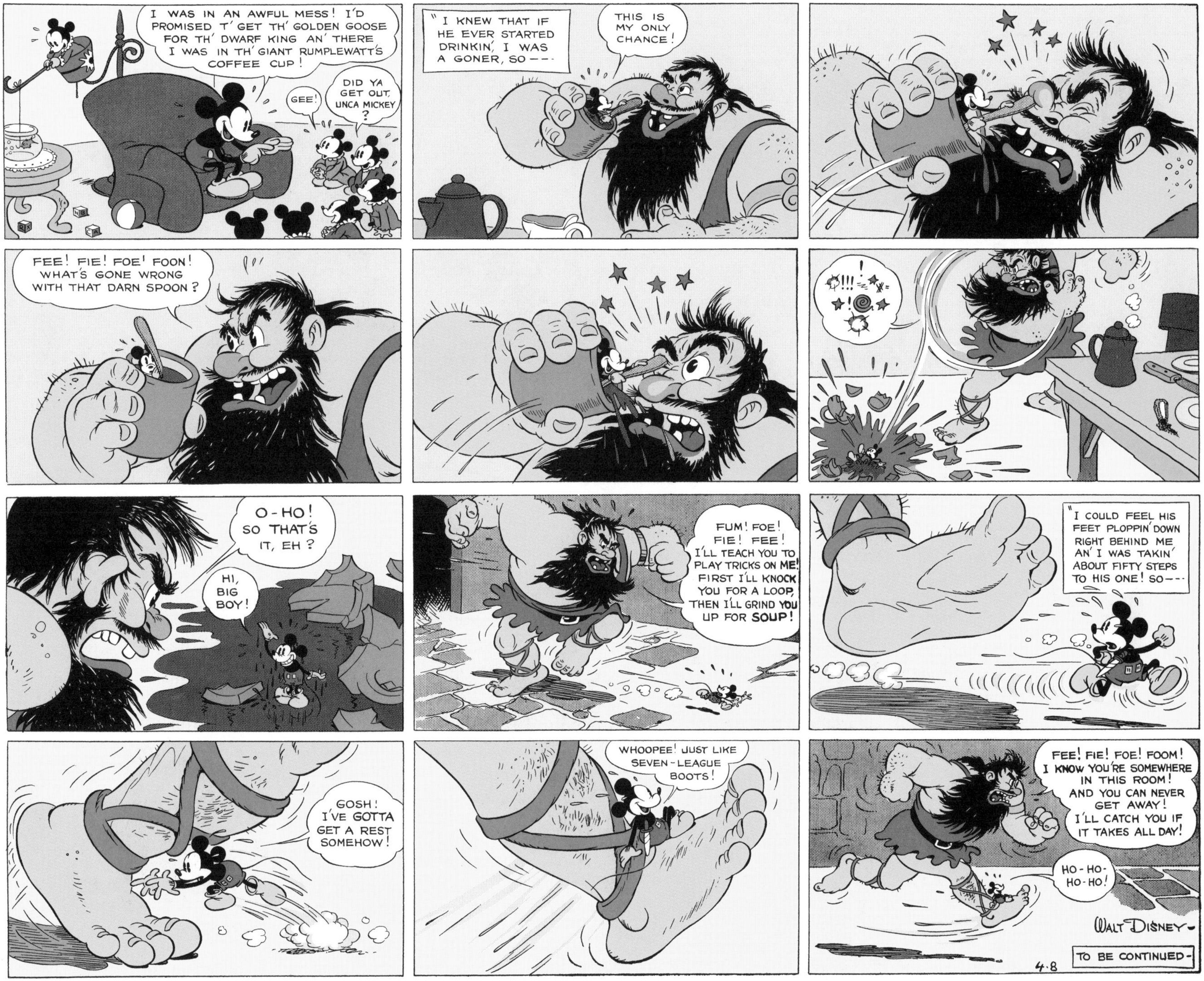

I WAS IN AN AWFUL MESS! I'D PROMISED T' GET TH' GOLDEN GOOSE FOR TH' DWARF KING AN' THERE I WAS IN TH' GIANT RUMPLEWATT'S COFFEE CUP!
GEE!
DID YA GET OUT, UNCA MICKEY?
"I KNEW THAT IF HE EVER STARTED DRINKIN', I WAS A GONER, SO---
THIS IS MY ONLY CHANCE!
FEE! FIE! FOE! FOON! WHAT'S GONE WRONG WITH THAT DARN SPOON?
O-HO! SO THAT'S IT, EH?
HI, BIG BOY!
FUM! FOE! FIE! FEE! I'LL TEACH YOU TO PLAY TRICKS ON ME! FIRST I'LL KNOCK YOU FOR A LOOP, THEN I'LL GRIND YOU UP FOR SOUP!
"I COULD FEEL HIS FEET PLOPPIN' DOWN RIGHT BEHIND ME AN' I WAS TAKIN' ABOUT FIFTY STEPS TO HIS ONE! SO---
GOSH! I'VE GOTTA GET A REST SOMEHOW!
WHOOPEE! JUST LIKE SEVEN-LEAGUE BOOTS!
FEE! FIE! FOE! FOOM! I KNOW YOU'RE SOMEWHERE IN THIS ROOM! AND YOU CAN NEVER GET AWAY! I'LL CATCH YOU IF IT TAKES ALL DAY!
HO-HO-HO-HO!
WALT DISNEY
TO BE CONTINUED
4·8

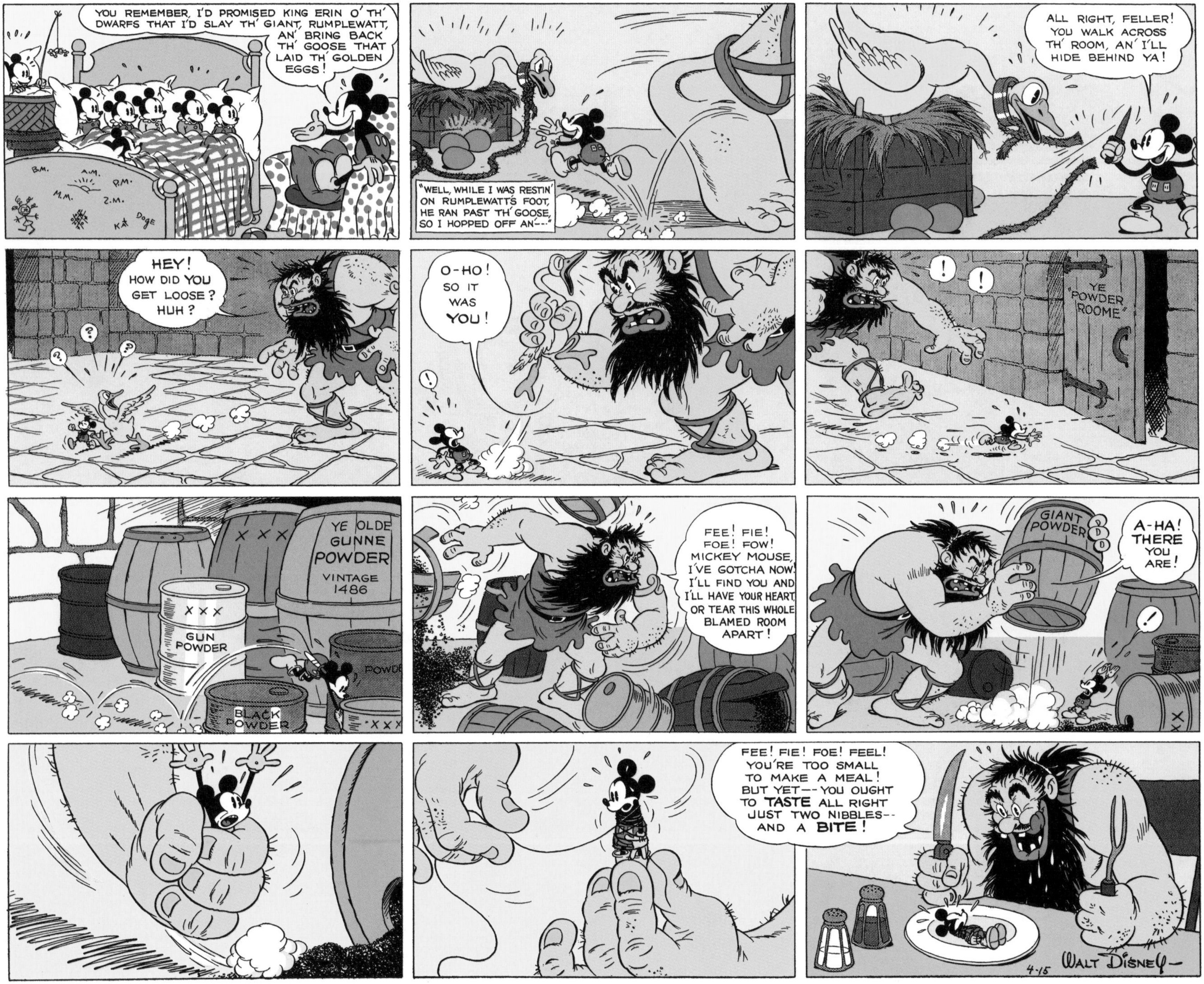
YOU REMEMBER, I'D PROMISED KING ERIN O' TH' DWARFS THAT I'D SLAY TH' GIANT, RUMPLEWATT, AN' BRING BACK TH' GOOSE THAT LAID TH' GOLDEN EGGS!
"WELL, WHILE I WAS RESTIN' ON RUMPLEWATT'S FOOT, HE RAN PAST TH' GOOSE, SO I HOPPED OFF AN'--"
ALL RIGHT, FELLER! YOU WALK ACROSS TH' ROOM, AN' I'LL HIDE BEHIND YA!
HEY! HOW DID YOU GET LOOSE? HUH?
O-HO! SO IT WAS YOU!
YE POWDER ROOME
YE OLDE GUNNE POWDER VINTAGE 1486
XXX
XXX GUN POWDER
BLACK POWDER
FEE! FIE! FOE! FOW! MICKEY MOUSE, I'VE GOTCHA NOW! I'LL FIND YOU AND I'LL HAVE YOUR HEART, OR TEAR THIS WHOLE BLAMED ROOM APART!
GIANT POWDER
A-HA! THERE YOU ARE!
FEE! FIE! FOE! FEEL! YOU'RE TOO SMALL TO MAKE A MEAL! BUT YET-- YOU OUGHT TO TASTE ALL RIGHT JUST TWO NIBBLES-- AND A BITE!
4-15
WALT DISNEY

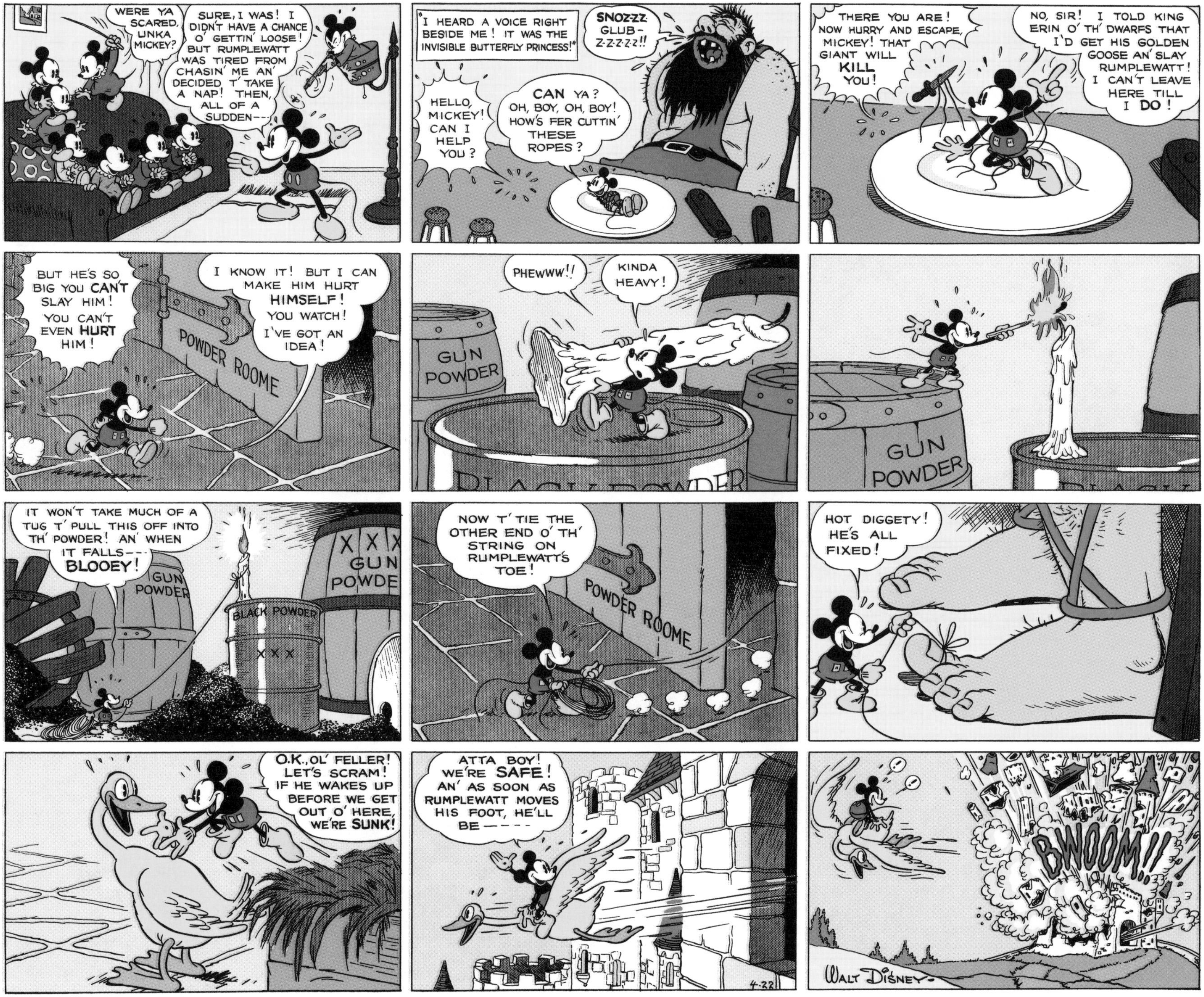
WERE YA SCARED, UNKA MICKEY?
SURE, I WAS! I DIDN'T HAVE A CHANCE O' GETTIN' LOOSE! BUT RUMPLEWATT WAS TIRED FROM CHASIN' ME AN' DECIDED T' TAKE A NAP! THEN, ALL OF A SUDDEN---
"I HEARD A VOICE RIGHT BESIDE ME! IT WAS THE INVISIBLE BUTTERFLY PRINCESS!"
SNOZ-ZZ GLUB-Z-Z-Z-Z-Z!!
HELLO, MICKEY! CAN I HELP YOU?
CAN YA? OH, BOY, OH, BOY! HOW'S FER CUTTIN' THESE ROPES?
THERE YOU ARE! NOW HURRY AND ESCAPE, MICKEY! THAT GIANT WILL KILL YOU!
NO, SIR! I TOLD KING ERIN O' TH' DWARFS THAT I'D GET HIS GOLDEN GOOSE AN' SLAY RUMPLEWATT! I CAN'T LEAVE HERE TILL I DO!
BUT HE'S SO BIG YOU CAN'T SLAY HIM! YOU CAN'T EVEN HURT HIM!
I KNOW IT! BUT I CAN MAKE HIM HURT HIMSELF! YOU WATCH! I'VE GOT AN IDEA!
POWDER ROOME
PHEWWW!!
KINDA HEAVY!
GUN POWDER
GUN POWDER
IT WON'T TAKE MUCH OF A TUG T' PULL THIS OFF INTO TH' POWDER! AN' WHEN IT FALLS--- BLOOEY!
GUN POWDER
BLACK POWDER
X X X
X X X GUN POWDE
NOW T' TIE THE OTHER END O' TH' STRING ON RUMPLEWATT'S TOE!
POWDER ROOME
HOT DIGGETY! HE'S ALL FIXED!
O.K., OL' FELLER! LET'S SCRAM! IF HE WAKES UP BEFORE WE GET OUT O' HERE, WE'RE SUNK!
ATTA BOY! WE'RE SAFE! AN' AS SOON AS RUMPLEWATT MOVES HIS FOOT, HE'LL BE-----
4-22
BWOOM!!
WALT DISNEY

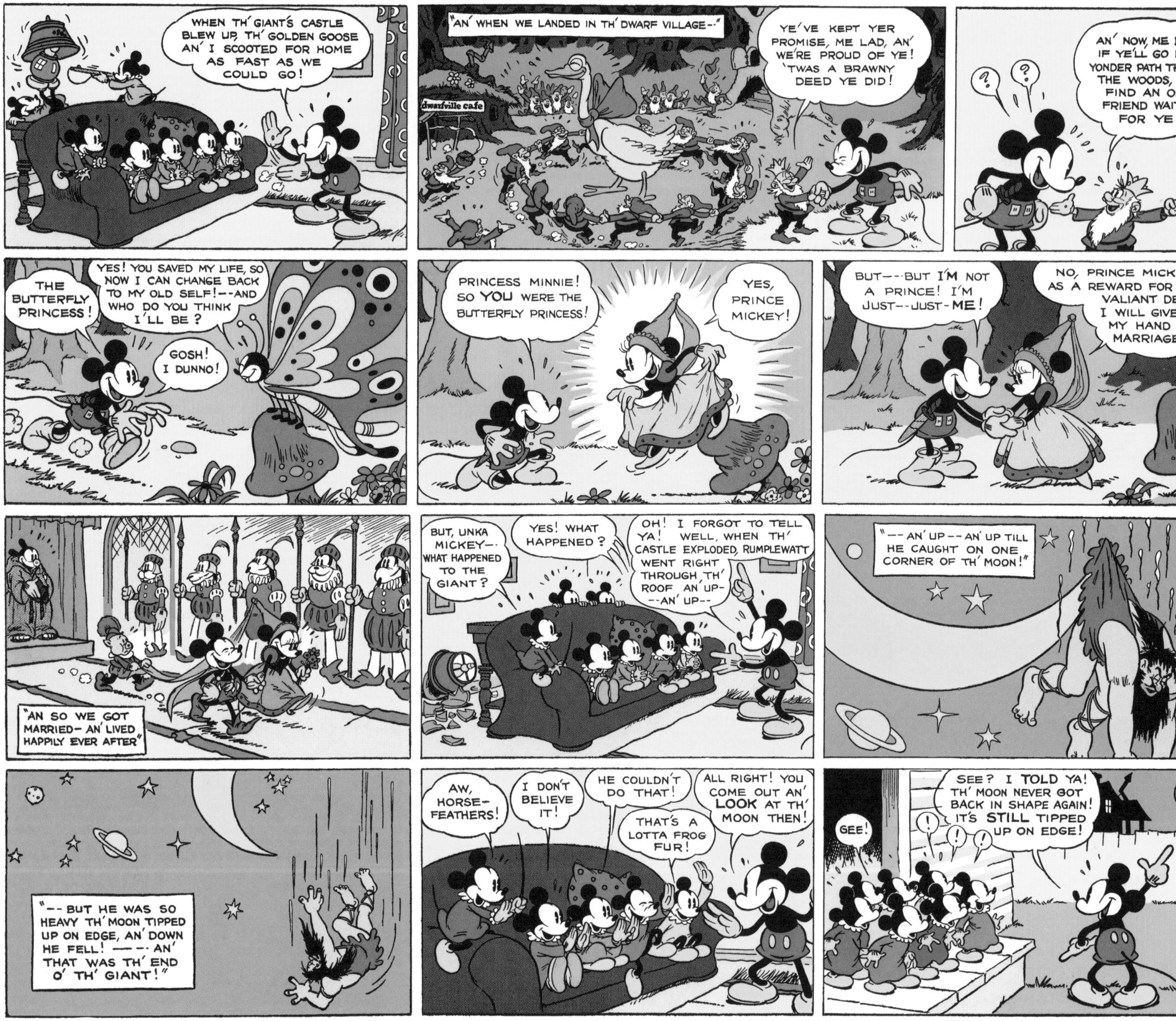
WHEN TH' GIANT'S CASTLE BLEW UP, TH' GOLDEN GOOSE AN' I SCOOTED FOR HOME AS FAST AS WE COULD GO!
"AN' WHEN WE LANDED IN TH' DWARF VILLAGE--"
dwarfville cafe
YE'VE KEPT YER PROMISE, ME LAD, AN' WE'RE PROUD OF YE! 'TWAS A BRAWNY DEED YE DID!
?
?
AN' NOW, ME BHOY, IF YE'LL GO DOWN YONDER PATH THROUGH THE WOODS, YE'LL FIND AN OLD FRIEND WAITIN' FOR YE!
THE BUTTERFLY PRINCESS!
YES! YOU SAVED MY LIFE, SO NOW I CAN CHANGE BACK TO MY OLD SELF!--AND WHO DO YOU THINK I'LL BE?
GOSH! I DUNNO!
PRINCESS MINNIE! SO YOU WERE THE BUTTERFLY PRINCESS!
YES, PRINCE MICKEY!
BUT---BUT I'M NOT A PRINCE! I'M JUST--JUST--ME!
NO, PRINCE MICKEY! AS A REWARD FOR YOUR VALIANT DEEDS, I WILL GIVE YOU MY HAND IN MARRIAGE!
"AN SO WE GOT MARRIED— AN' LIVED HAPPILY EVER AFTER"
BUT, UNKA MICKEY-- WHAT HAPPENED TO THE GIANT?
YES! WHAT HAPPENED?
OH! I FORGOT TO TELL YA! WELL, WHEN TH' CASTLE EXPLODED, RUMPLEWATT WENT RIGHT THROUGH TH' ROOF AN' UP--AN' UP--
"--AN' UP--AN' UP TILL HE CAUGHT ON ONE CORNER OF TH' MOON!"
"--BUT HE WAS SO HEAVY TH' MOON TIPPED UP ON EDGE, AN' DOWN HE FELL! ---AN' THAT WAS TH' END O' TH' GIANT!"
AW, HORSE-FEATHERS!
I DON'T BELIEVE IT!
HE COULDN'T DO THAT!
ALL RIGHT! YOU COME OUT AN' LOOK AT TH' MOON THEN!
THAT'S A LOTTA FROG FUR!
GEE!
!
!
!
SEE? I TOLD YA! TH' MOON NEVER GOT BACK IN SHAPE AGAIN! IT'S STILL TIPPED UP ON EDGE!

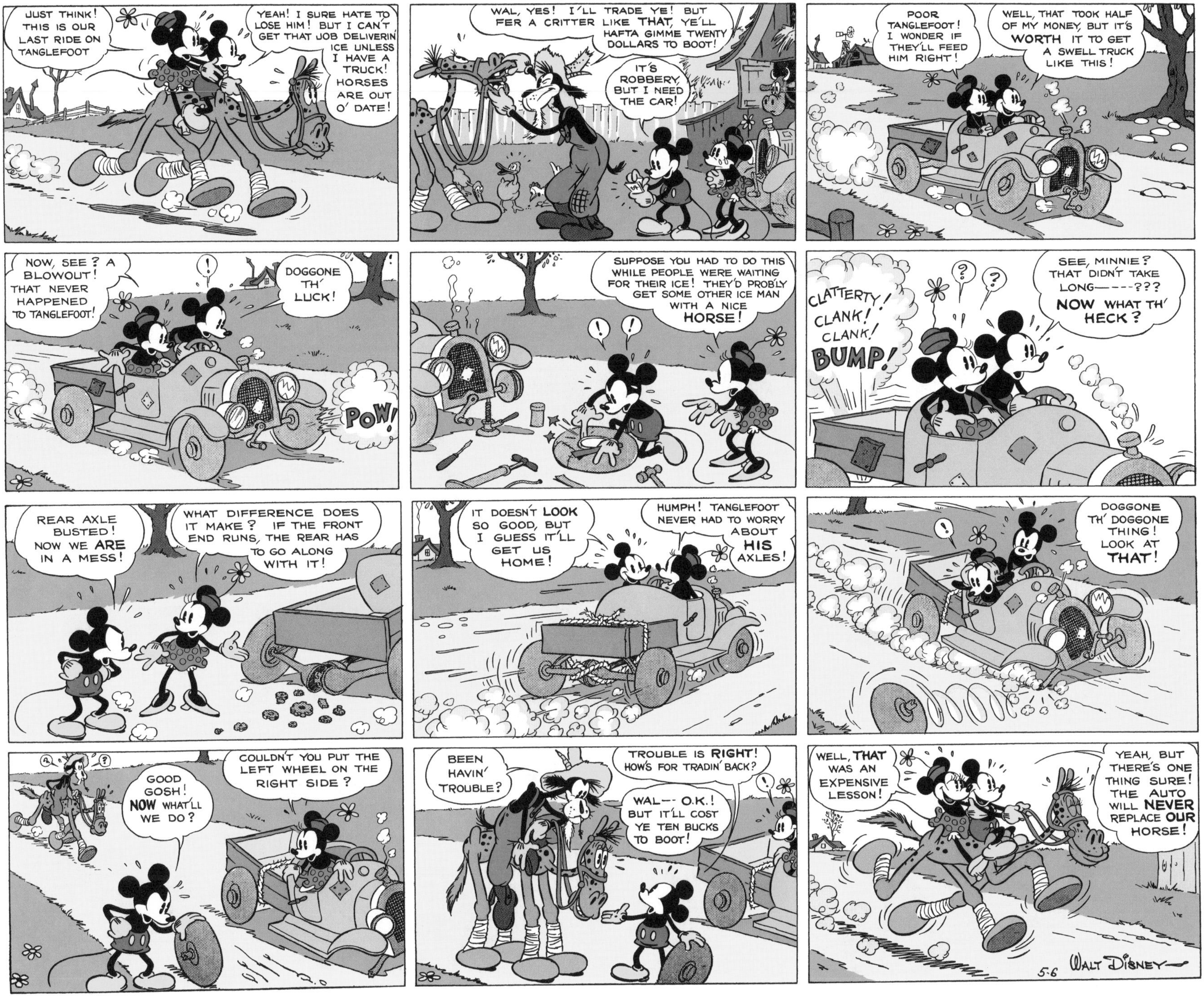
JUST THINK! THIS IS OUR LAST RIDE ON TANGLEFOOT
YEAH! I SURE HATE TO LOSE HIM! BUT I CAN'T GET THAT JOB DELIVERIN' ICE UNLESS I HAVE A TRUCK! HORSES ARE OUT O' DATE!
WAL, YES! I'LL TRADE YE! BUT FER A CRITTER LIKE THAT, YE'LL HAFTA GIMME TWENTY DOLLARS TO BOOT!
IT'S ROBBERY, BUT I NEED THE CAR!
POOR TANGLEFOOT! I WONDER IF THEY'LL FEED HIM RIGHT!
WELL, THAT TOOK HALF OF MY MONEY, BUT IT'S WORTH IT TO GET A SWELL TRUCK LIKE THIS!
NOW, SEE? A BLOWOUT! THAT NEVER HAPPENED TO TANGLEFOOT!
DOGGONE TH' LUCK!
POW!
SUPPOSE YOU HAD TO DO THIS WHILE PEOPLE WERE WAITING FOR THEIR ICE! THEY'D PROB'LY GET SOME OTHER ICE MAN WITH A NICE HORSE!
CLATTERTY! CLANK! CLANK! BUMP!
SEE, MINNIE? THAT DIDN'T TAKE LONG----??? NOW WHAT TH' HECK?
REAR AXLE BUSTED! NOW WE ARE IN A MESS!
WHAT DIFFERENCE DOES IT MAKE? IF THE FRONT END RUNS, THE REAR HAS TO GO ALONG WITH IT!
IT DOESN'T LOOK SO GOOD, BUT I GUESS IT'LL GET US HOME!
HUMPH! TANGLEFOOT NEVER HAD TO WORRY ABOUT HIS AXLES!
DOGGONE TH' DOGGONE THING! LOOK AT THAT!
GOOD GOSH! NOW WHAT'LL WE DO?
COULDN'T YOU PUT THE LEFT WHEEL ON THE RIGHT SIDE?
BEEN HAVIN' TROUBLE?
TROUBLE IS RIGHT! HOW'S FOR TRADIN' BACK?
WAL-- O.K.! BUT IT'LL COST YE TEN BUCKS TO BOOT!
WELL, THAT WAS AN EXPENSIVE LESSON!
YEAH, BUT THERE'S ONE THING SURE! THE AUTO WILL NEVER REPLACE OUR HORSE!
5-6
WALT DISNEY

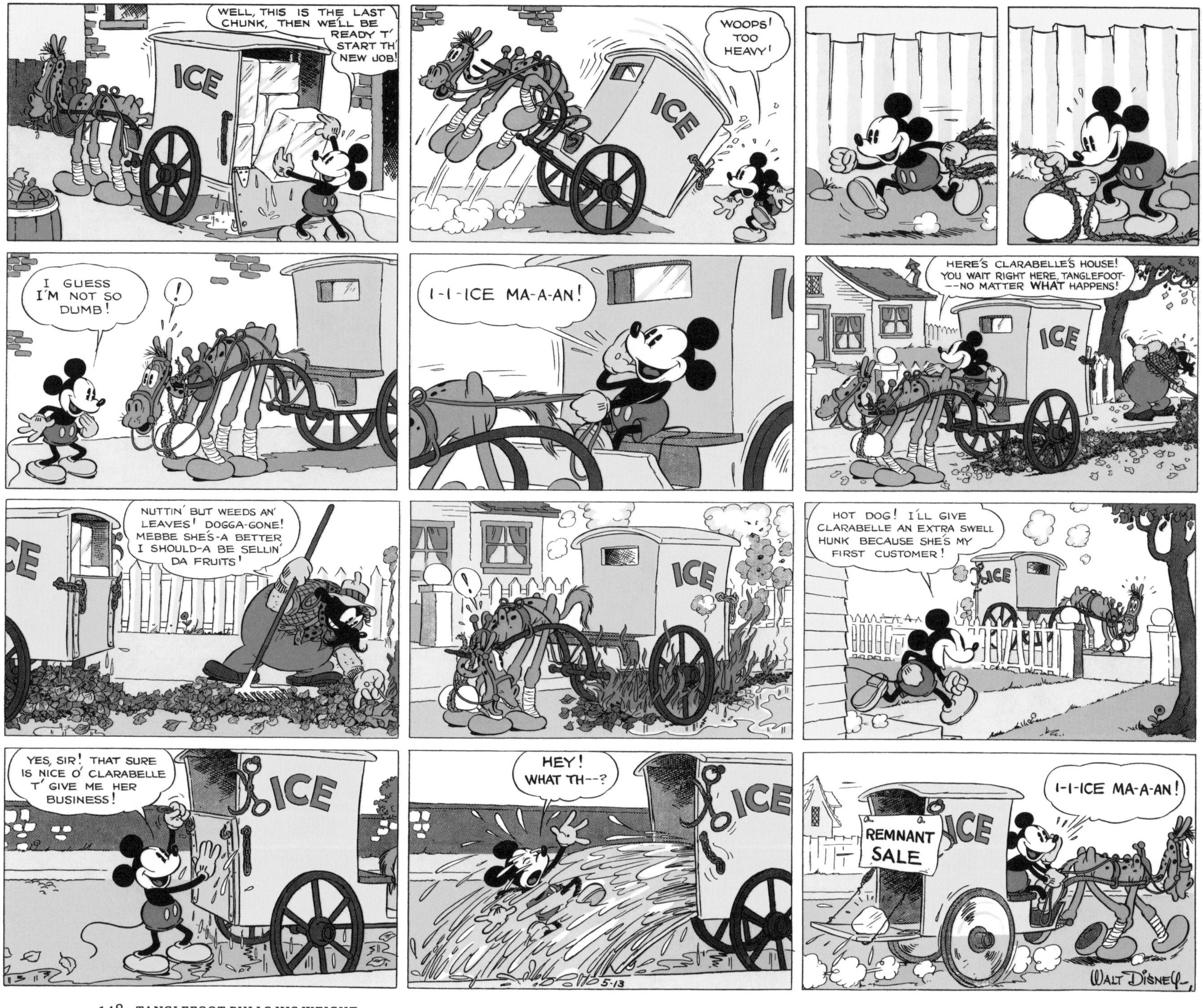
WELL, THIS IS THE LAST CHUNK, THEN WE'LL BE READY T' START TH' NEW JOB!
ICE
WOOPS! TOO HEAVY!
I GUESS I'M NOT SO DUMB!
!
I-I-ICE MA-A-AN!
HERE'S CLARABELLE'S HOUSE! YOU WAIT RIGHT HERE, TANGLEFOOT--NO MATTER WHAT HAPPENS!
NUTTIN' BUT WEEDS AN' LEAVES! DOGGA-GONE! MEBBE SHE'S-A BETTER I SHOULD-A BE SELLIN' DA FRUITS!
!
HOT DOG! I'LL GIVE CLARABELLE AN EXTRA SWELL HUNK BECAUSE SHE'S MY FIRST CUSTOMER!
YES, SIR! THAT SURE IS NICE O' CLARABELLE T' GIVE ME HER BUSINESS!
HEY! WHAT TH--?
5-13
REMNANT SALE
I-I-ICE MA-A-AN!
WALT DISNEY

148. TANGLEFOOT PULLS HIS WEIGHT

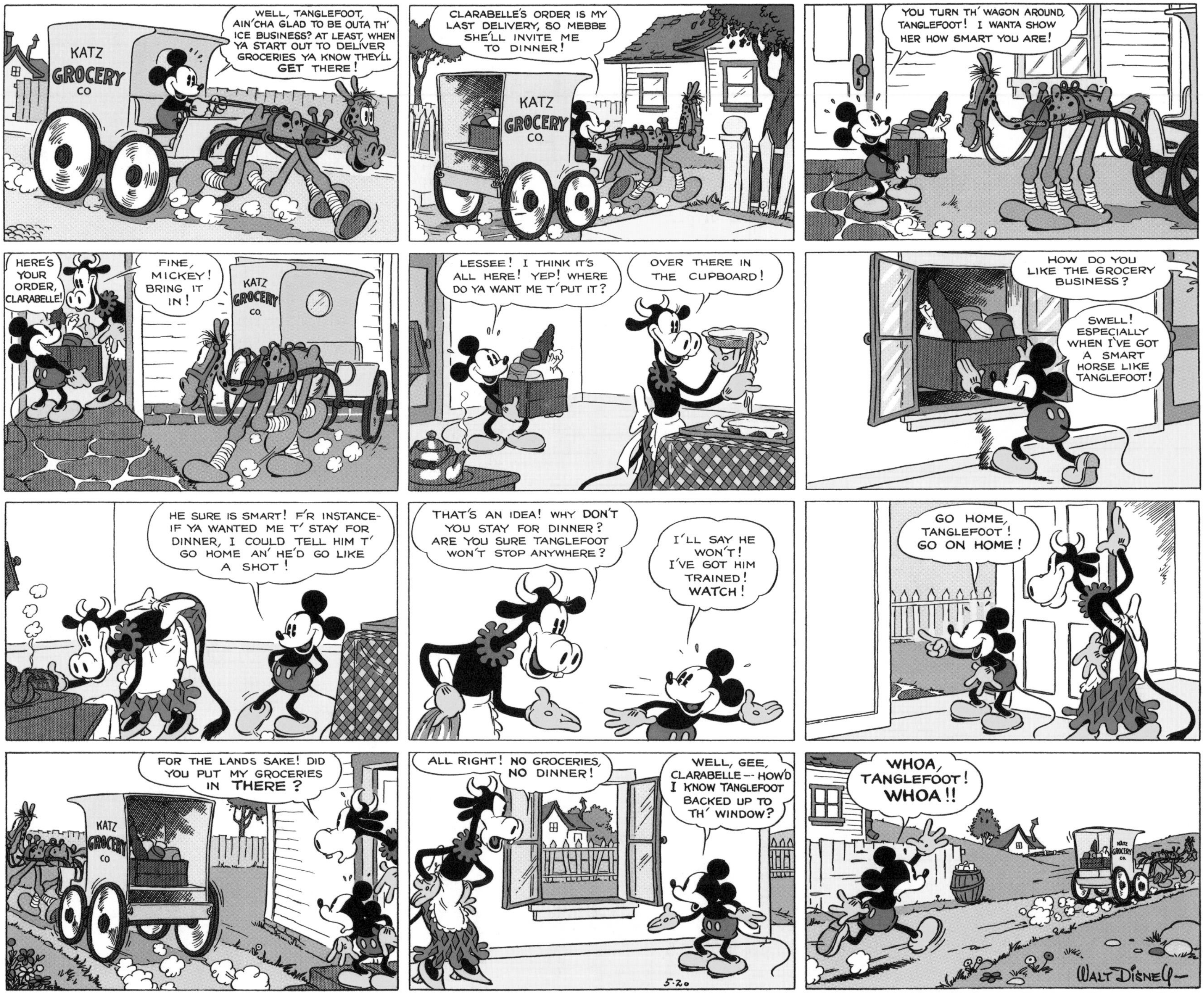
KATZ GROCERY CO
WELL, TANGLEFOOT, AIN'CHA GLAD TO BE OUTA TH' ICE BUSINESS? AT LEAST, WHEN YA START OUT TO DELIVER GROCERIES YA KNOW THEY'LL GET THERE!
CLARABELLE'S ORDER IS MY LAST DELIVERY, SO MEBBE SHE'LL INVITE ME TO DINNER!
KATZ GROCERY CO.
YOU TURN TH' WAGON AROUND, TANGLEFOOT! I WANTA SHOW HER HOW SMART YOU ARE!
HERE'S YOUR ORDER, CLARABELLE!
FINE, MICKEY! BRING IT IN!
KATZ GROCERY CO.
LESSEE! I THINK IT'S ALL HERE! YEP! WHERE DO YA WANT ME T'PUT IT?
OVER THERE IN THE CUPBOARD!
HOW DO YOU LIKE THE GROCERY BUSINESS?
SWELL! ESPECIALLY WHEN I'VE GOT A SMART HORSE LIKE TANGLEFOOT!
HE SURE IS SMART! F'R INSTANCE- IF YA WANTED ME T' STAY FOR DINNER, I COULD TELL HIM T' GO HOME AN' HE'D GO LIKE A SHOT!
THAT'S AN IDEA! WHY DON'T YOU STAY FOR DINNER? ARE YOU SURE TANGLEFOOT WON'T STOP ANYWHERE?
I'LL SAY HE WON'T! I'VE GOT HIM TRAINED! WATCH!
GO HOME, TANGLEFOOT! GO ON HOME!
FOR THE LANDS SAKE! DID YOU PUT MY GROCERIES IN THERE?
KATZ GROCERY CO
ALL RIGHT! NO GROCERIES, NO DINNER!
WELL, GEE, CLARABELLE-- HOW'D I KNOW TANGLEFOOT BACKED UP TO TH' WINDOW?
5-20
WHOA, TANGLEFOOT! WHOA!!
KATZ GROCERY CO.
WALT DISNEY

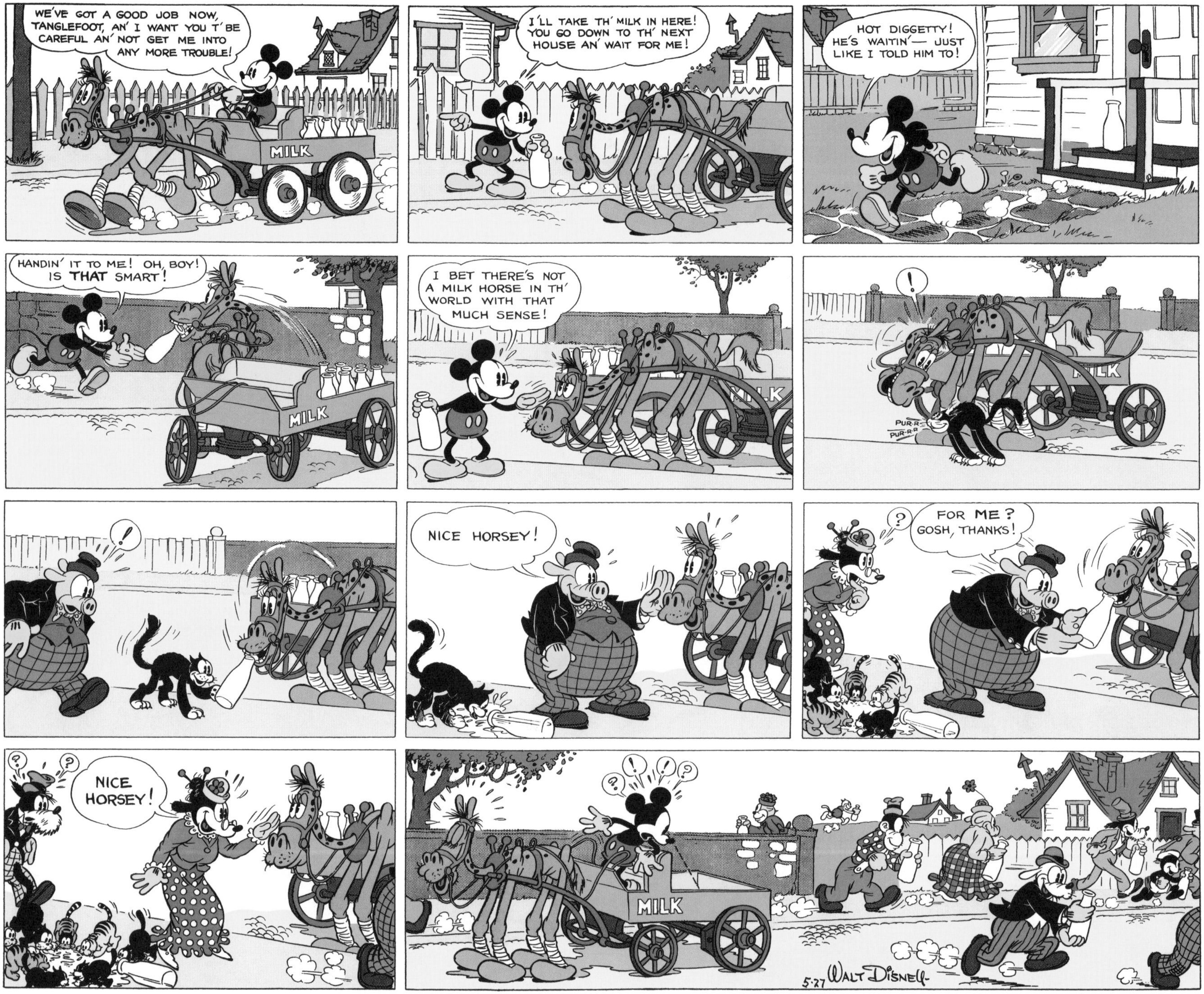
WE'VE GOT A GOOD JOB NOW, TANGLEFOOT, AN' I WANT YOU T' BE CAREFUL AN' NOT GET ME INTO ANY MORE TROUBLE!
MILK
I'LL TAKE TH' MILK IN HERE! YOU GO DOWN TO TH' NEXT HOUSE AN' WAIT FOR ME!
HOT DIGGETTY! HE'S WAITIN'— JUST LIKE I TOLD HIM TO!
HANDIN' IT TO ME! OH, BOY! IS THAT SMART!
MILK
I BET THERE'S NOT A MILK HORSE IN TH' WORLD WITH THAT MUCH SENSE!
MILK
!
PUR-R PUR-R-R
MILK
!
NICE HORSEY!
?
FOR ME? GOSH, THANKS!
? ?
NICE HORSEY!
? ! ! ?
MILK
5-27 WALT DISNEY

150. TANGLEFOOT PULLS HIS WEIGHT

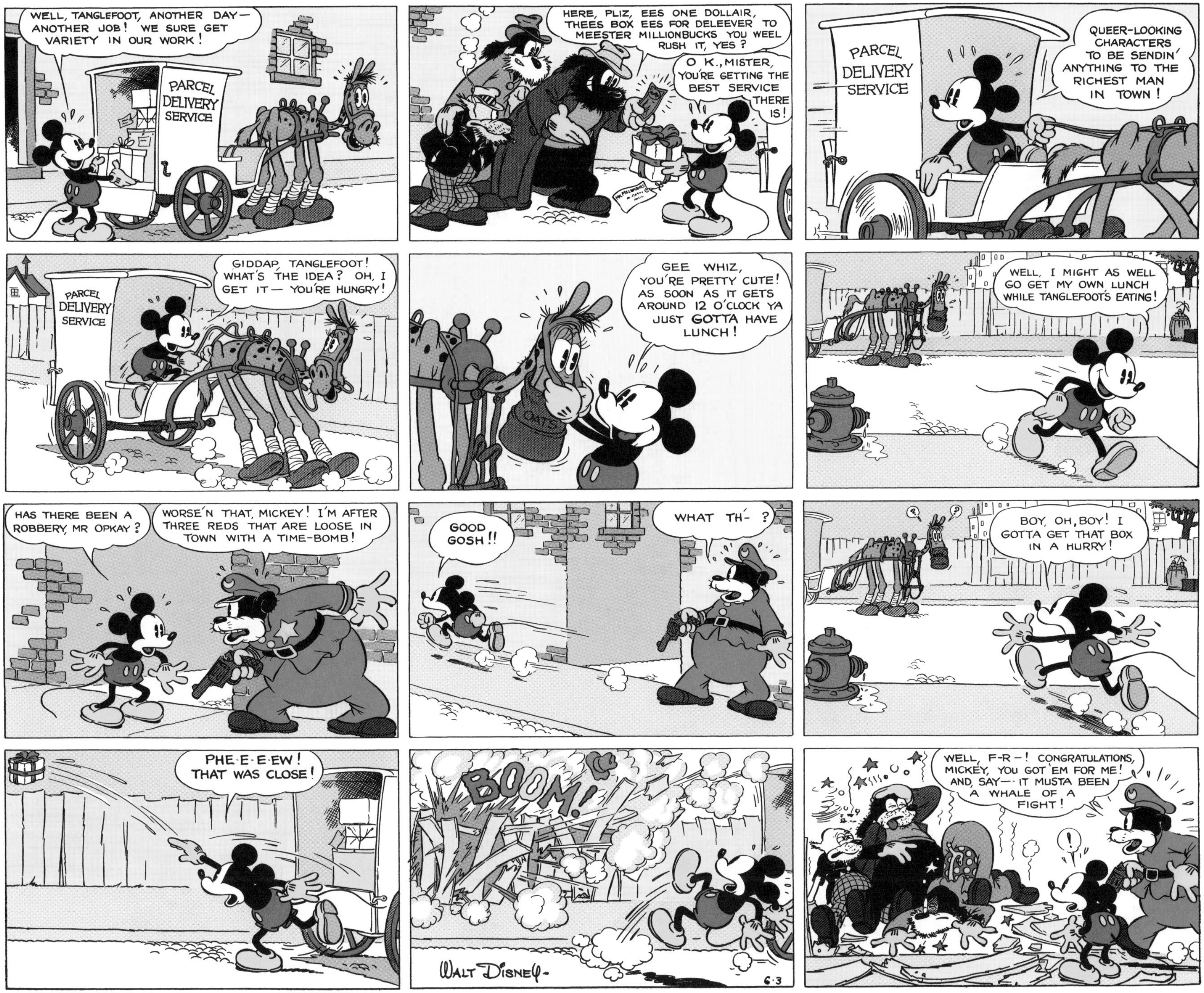

WELL, TANGLEFOOT, ANOTHER DAY— ANOTHER JOB! WE SURE GET VARIETY IN OUR WORK!
PARCEL DELIVERY SERVICE
HERE, PLIZ, EES ONE DOLLAIR, THEES BOX EES FOR DELEEVER TO MEESTER MILLIONBUCKS YOU WEEL RUSH IT, YES?
O K., MISTER, YOU'RE GETTING THE BEST SERVICE THERE IS!
PARCEL DELIVERY SERVICE
QUEER-LOOKING CHARACTERS TO BE SENDIN' ANYTHING TO THE RICHEST MAN IN TOWN!
PARCEL DELIVERY SERVICE
GIDDAP, TANGLEFOOT! WHAT'S THE IDEA? OH, I GET IT— YOU'RE HUNGRY!
GEE WHIZ, YOU'RE PRETTY CUTE! AS SOON AS IT GETS AROUND 12 O'CLOCK YA JUST GOTTA HAVE LUNCH!
OATS
WELL, I MIGHT AS WELL GO GET MY OWN LUNCH WHILE TANGLEFOOT'S EATING!
HAS THERE BEEN A ROBBERY, MR OPKAY?
WORSE'N THAT, MICKEY! I'M AFTER THREE REDS THAT ARE LOOSE IN TOWN WITH A TIME-BOMB!
GOOD GOSH!!
WHAT TH'-?
BOY, OH, BOY! I GOTTA GET THAT BOX IN A HURRY!
PHE-E-E-EW! THAT WAS CLOSE!
BOOM!
WALT DISNEY
6·3
WELL, F-R-! CONGRATULATIONS, MICKEY, YOU GOT 'EM FOR ME! AND, SAY— IT MUSTA BEEN A WHALE OF A FIGHT!

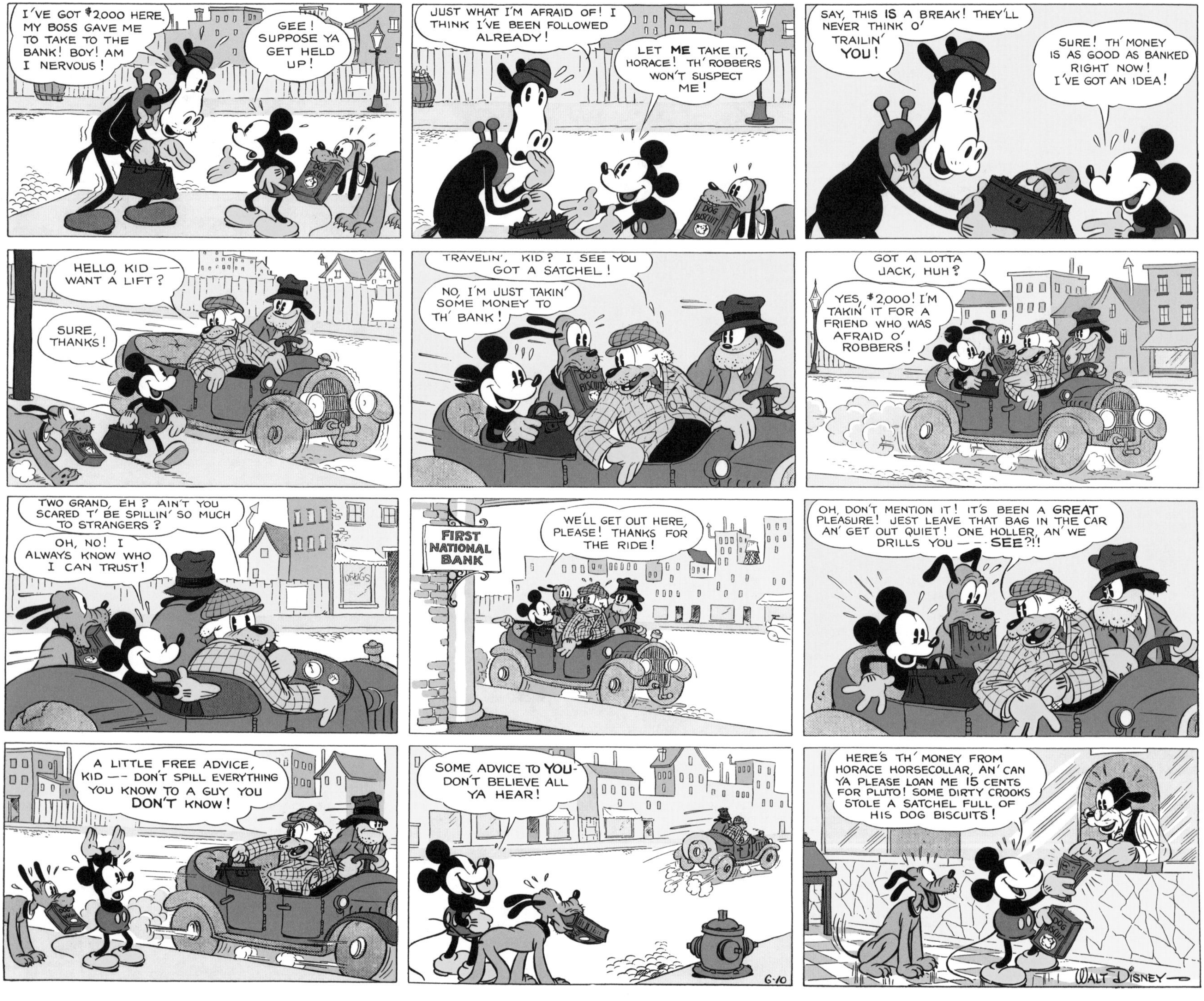
I'VE GOT $2000 HERE. MY BOSS GAVE ME TO TAKE TO THE BANK! BOY! AM I NERVOUS!
GEE! SUPPOSE YA GET HELD UP!
DOG BISCUIT
JUST WHAT I'M AFRAID OF! I THINK I'VE BEEN FOLLOWED ALREADY!
LET ME TAKE IT, HORACE! TH' ROBBERS WON'T SUSPECT ME!
DOG BISCUIT
SAY, THIS IS A BREAK! THEY'LL NEVER THINK O' TRAILIN' YOU!
SURE! TH' MONEY IS AS GOOD AS BANKED RIGHT NOW! I'VE GOT AN IDEA!
HELLO, KID —— WANT A LIFT?
SURE, THANKS!
TRAVELIN', KID? I SEE YOU GOT A SATCHEL!
NO, I'M JUST TAKIN' SOME MONEY TO TH' BANK!
GOT A LOTTA JACK, HUH?
YES, $2,000! I'M TAKIN' IT FOR A FRIEND WHO WAS AFRAID O' ROBBERS!
TWO GRAND, EH? AIN'T YOU SCARED T' BE SPILLIN' SO MUCH TO STRANGERS?
OH, NO! I ALWAYS KNOW WHO I CAN TRUST!
DRUGS
FIRST NATIONAL BANK
WE'LL GET OUT HERE, PLEASE! THANKS FOR THE RIDE!
OH, DON'T MENTION IT! IT'S BEEN A GREAT PLEASURE! JEST LEAVE THAT BAG IN THE CAR AN' GET OUT QUIET! ONE HOLLER, AN' WE DRILLS YOU——SEE?!!
A LITTLE FREE ADVICE, KID —— DON'T SPILL EVERYTHING YOU KNOW TO A GUY YOU DON'T KNOW!
SOME ADVICE TO YOU-DON'T BELIEVE ALL YA HEAR!
6-10
HERE'S TH' MONEY FROM HORACE HORSECOLLAR, AN' CAN YA PLEASE LOAN ME 15 CENTS FOR PLUTO! SOME DIRTY CROOKS STOLE A SATCHEL FULL OF HIS DOG BISCUITS!
DOG BISCUIT
WALT DISNEY

DR. OOFGAY'S SECRET SERUM

AND

GAG STRIPS

JUNE 17, 1934
–
DECEMBER 2, 1934

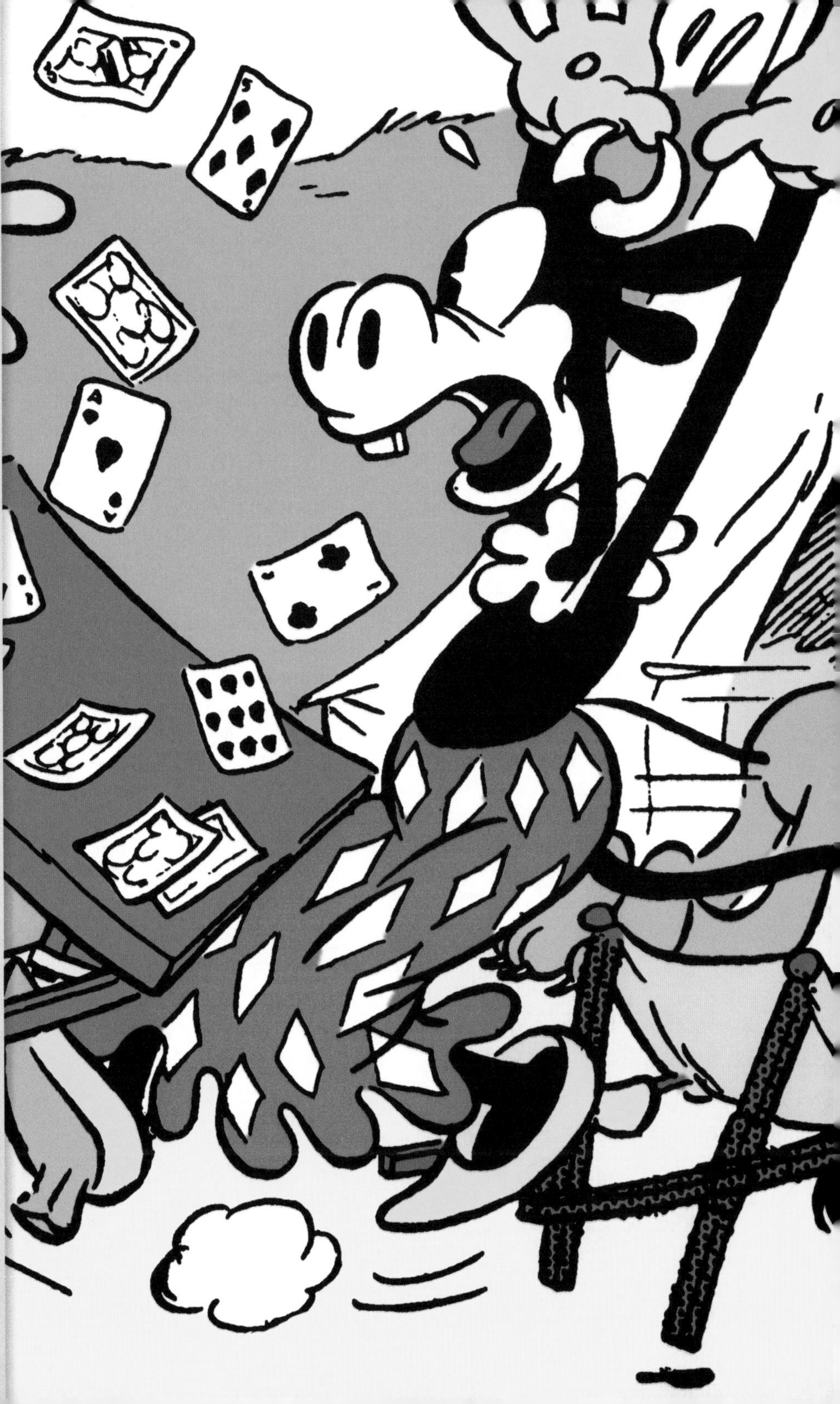

MICKEY MOUSE

REGISTERED U.S. PATENT OFFICE

CALL OF THE WILD

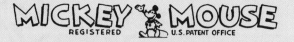

Ah, anthropomorphism; how we take you for granted! The attribution of human characteristics to animals far predates the art of print and animated cartooning, but perhaps found its greatest sanctuary at the Walt Disney Studio. How many times have you heard people questioning why Mickey *Mouse* owns Pluto, a full-sized dog? Or: “Why does Goofy get to drive a car, while Pluto has to sleep outside, if they’re both dogs?” To paraphrase *Mystery Science Theater 3000*, the answer is: “It’s just a cartoon—relax.”

Our cover story would not dare be so blasé. In “Dr. Oofgay’s Secret Serum,” we are only introduced to the titular mad scientist deep into the thirteen-week continuity. During the gang’s camping trip to Dusty Lake, Mickey and Minnie stumble upon a mountain lion who is mysteriously “gentle as a lamb.” After seven weeks of gags involving genuine, often dangerous wild animals, the reader would not be satisfied with simple cartoon license as an explanation. Enter Dr. Oofgay, who reveals that the lion has been given one of his marvelous serums. One chemical compound will tame even the wildest animal; the other will revert the beast to its wild state. Horace Horsecollar accidentally sits on the doctor’s “wild” needle and becomes a rowdy, uncivilized brute. Of course, Clarabelle Cow—depending on her mood—might argue that there is little difference either way.

And that brings us to the real centerpiece of this very funny story: the dynamic between Horace and Clarabelle, a couple whose everyday routine normally involves a feigned damsel-in-distress act and an inept rescue attempt. The Horace-Clarabelle relationship was one of Floyd Gottfredson’s funnier creations in the first half of the 1930s, a time when he helmed a strong supporting cast that would later prove interesting and workable in stories sans Mickey.

While in later years, Goofy has often posed as a suitor for Clarabelle, it has always been clear that the pompous, know-it-all “jackass” Horsecollar was made for the vain, gossipy bovine. During their darkest hours—as when Horace, hypnotized by Oofgay’s serum, is howling at the moon—Clarabelle is the only person to voice genuine concern about her “poor Horace” and what a “noble character” he once was.

One might say Clarabelle and Horace are Ethel and Fred to Minnie and Mickey’s Lucy and Desi, if the mice ever exhibited such rowdiness and energy. But doesn’t Horace and Clarabelle’s sheer instability more than make up for anyone else’s normalcy?

— THAD KOMOROWSKI

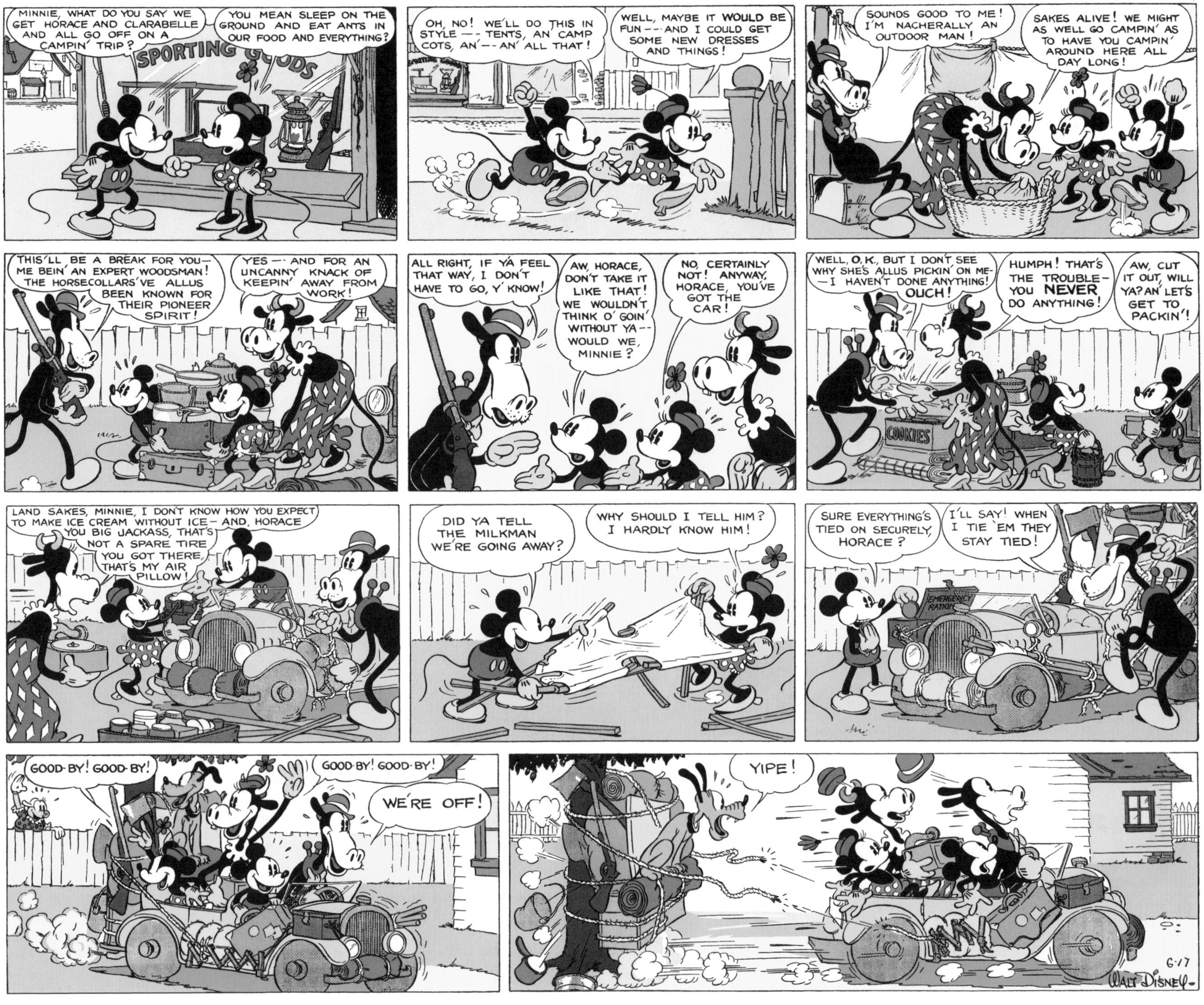
MINNIE, WHAT DO YOU SAY WE GET HORACE AND CLARABELLE AND ALL GO OFF ON A CAMPIN' TRIP?
YOU MEAN SLEEP ON THE GROUND AND EAT ANTS IN OUR FOOD AND EVERYTHING?
SPORTING GOODS
OH, NO! WE'LL DO THIS IN STYLE -- TENTS, AN CAMP COTS, AN'-- AN' ALL THAT!
WELL, MAYBE IT WOULD BE FUN -- AND I COULD GET SOME NEW DRESSES AND THINGS!
SOUNDS GOOD TO ME! I'M NACHERALLY AN OUTDOOR MAN!
SAKES ALIVE! WE MIGHT AS WELL GO CAMPIN' AS TO HAVE YOU CAMPIN' AROUND HERE ALL DAY LONG!
THIS'LL BE A BREAK FOR YOU— ME BEIN' AN EXPERT WOODSMAN! THE HORSECOLLARS'VE ALLUS BEEN KNOWN FOR THEIR PIONEER SPIRIT!
YES -- AND FOR AN UNCANNY KNACK OF KEEPIN' AWAY FROM WORK!
ALL RIGHT, IF YA FEEL THAT WAY, I DON'T HAVE TO GO, Y'KNOW!
AW, HORACE, DON'T TAKE IT LIKE THAT! WE WOULDN'T THINK O' GOIN' WITHOUT YA -- WOULD WE, MINNIE?
NO, CERTAINLY NOT! ANYWAY, HORACE, YOU'VE GOT THE CAR!
WELL, O.K., BUT I DON'T SEE WHY SHE'S ALLUS PICKIN' ON ME— I HAVEN'T DONE ANYTHING! OUCH!
HUMPH! THAT'S THE TROUBLE— YOU NEVER DO ANYTHING!
AW, CUT IT OUT, WILL YA? AN' LET'S GET TO PACKIN'!
COOKIES
LAND SAKES, MINNIE, I DON'T KNOW HOW YOU EXPECT TO MAKE ICE CREAM WITHOUT ICE— AND, HORACE YOU BIG JACKASS, THAT'S NOT A SPARE TIRE YOU GOT THERE, THAT'S MY AIR PILLOW!
DID YA TELL THE MILKMAN WE'RE GOING AWAY?
WHY SHOULD I TELL HIM? I HARDLY KNOW HIM!
SURE EVERYTHING'S TIED ON SECURELY, HORACE?
I'LL SAY! WHEN I TIE 'EM THEY STAY TIED!
EMERGENCY RATION
GOOD-BY! GOOD-BY!
GOOD-BY! GOOD-BY!
WE'RE OFF!
YIPE!
6-17
WALT DISNEY

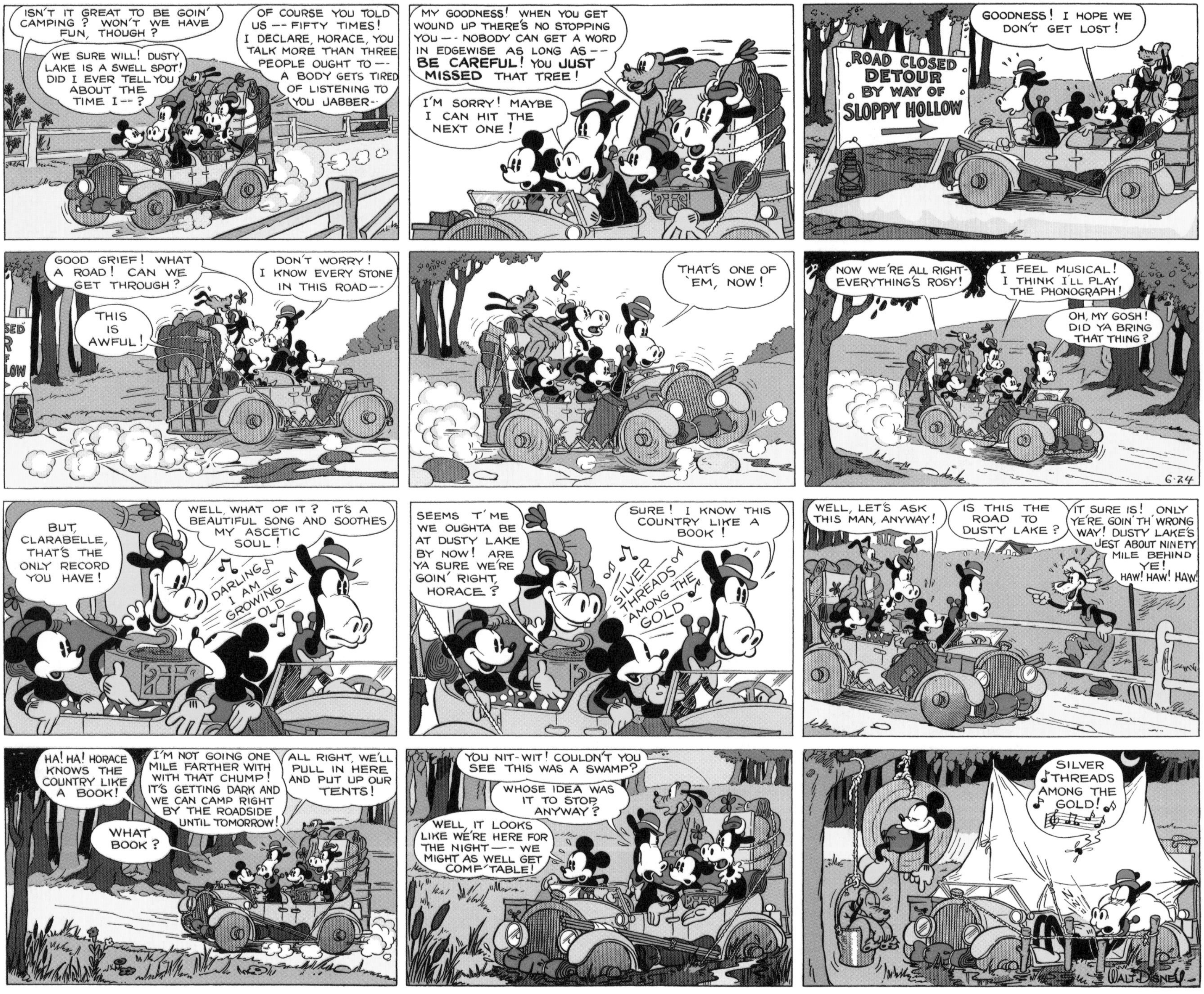
ISN'T IT GREAT TO BE GOIN' CAMPING? WON'T WE HAVE FUN, THOUGH?
WE SURE WILL! DUSTY LAKE IS A SWELL SPOT! DID I EVER TELL YOU ABOUT THE TIME I--?
OF COURSE YOU TOLD US -- FIFTY TIMES! I DECLARE, HORACE, YOU TALK MORE THAN THREE PEOPLE OUGHT TO -- A BODY GETS TIRED OF LISTENING TO YOU JABBER--
MY GOODNESS! WHEN YOU GET WOUND UP THERE'S NO STOPPING YOU -- NOBODY CAN GET A WORD IN EDGEWISE AS LONG AS -- BE CAREFUL! YOU JUST MISSED THAT TREE!
I'M SORRY! MAYBE I CAN HIT THE NEXT ONE!
GOODNESS! I HOPE WE DON'T GET LOST!
ROAD CLOSED DETOUR BY WAY OF SLOPPY HOLLOW
GOOD GRIEF! WHAT A ROAD! CAN WE GET THROUGH?
DON'T WORRY! I KNOW EVERY STONE IN THIS ROAD--
THIS IS AWFUL!
THAT'S ONE OF 'EM, NOW!
NOW WE'RE ALL RIGHT-EVERYTHING'S ROSY!
I FEEL MUSICAL! I THINK I'LL PLAY THE PHONOGRAPH!
OH, MY GOSH! DID YA BRING THAT THING?
6-24
BUT, CLARABELLE, THAT'S THE ONLY RECORD YOU HAVE!
WELL, WHAT OF IT? IT'S A BEAUTIFUL SONG AND SOOTHES MY ASCETIC SOUL!
DARLING I AM GROWING OLD
SEEMS T'ME WE OUGHTA BE AT DUSTY LAKE BY NOW! ARE YA SURE WE'RE GOIN' RIGHT, HORACE?
SURE! I KNOW THIS COUNTRY LIKE A BOOK!
SILVER THREADS AMONG THE GOLD
WELL, LET'S ASK THIS MAN, ANYWAY!
IS THIS THE ROAD TO DUSTY LAKE?
IT SURE IS! ONLY YE'RE GOIN' TH' WRONG WAY! DUSTY LAKE'S JEST ABOUT NINETY MILE BEHIND YE! HAW! HAW! HAW!
HA! HA! HORACE KNOWS THE COUNTRY LIKE A BOOK!
I'M NOT GOING ONE MILE FARTHER WITH WITH THAT CHUMP! IT'S GETTING DARK AND WE CAN CAMP RIGHT BY THE ROADSIDE UNTIL TOMORROW!
ALL RIGHT, WE'LL PULL IN HERE AND PUT UP OUR TENTS!
WHAT BOOK?
YOU NIT-WIT! COULDN'T YOU SEE THIS WAS A SWAMP?
WHOSE IDEA WAS IT TO STOP ANYWAY?
WELL, IT LOOKS LIKE WE'RE HERE FOR THE NIGHT -- WE MIGHT AS WELL GET COMF'TABLE!
SILVER THREADS AMONG THE GOLD!
WALT DISNEY

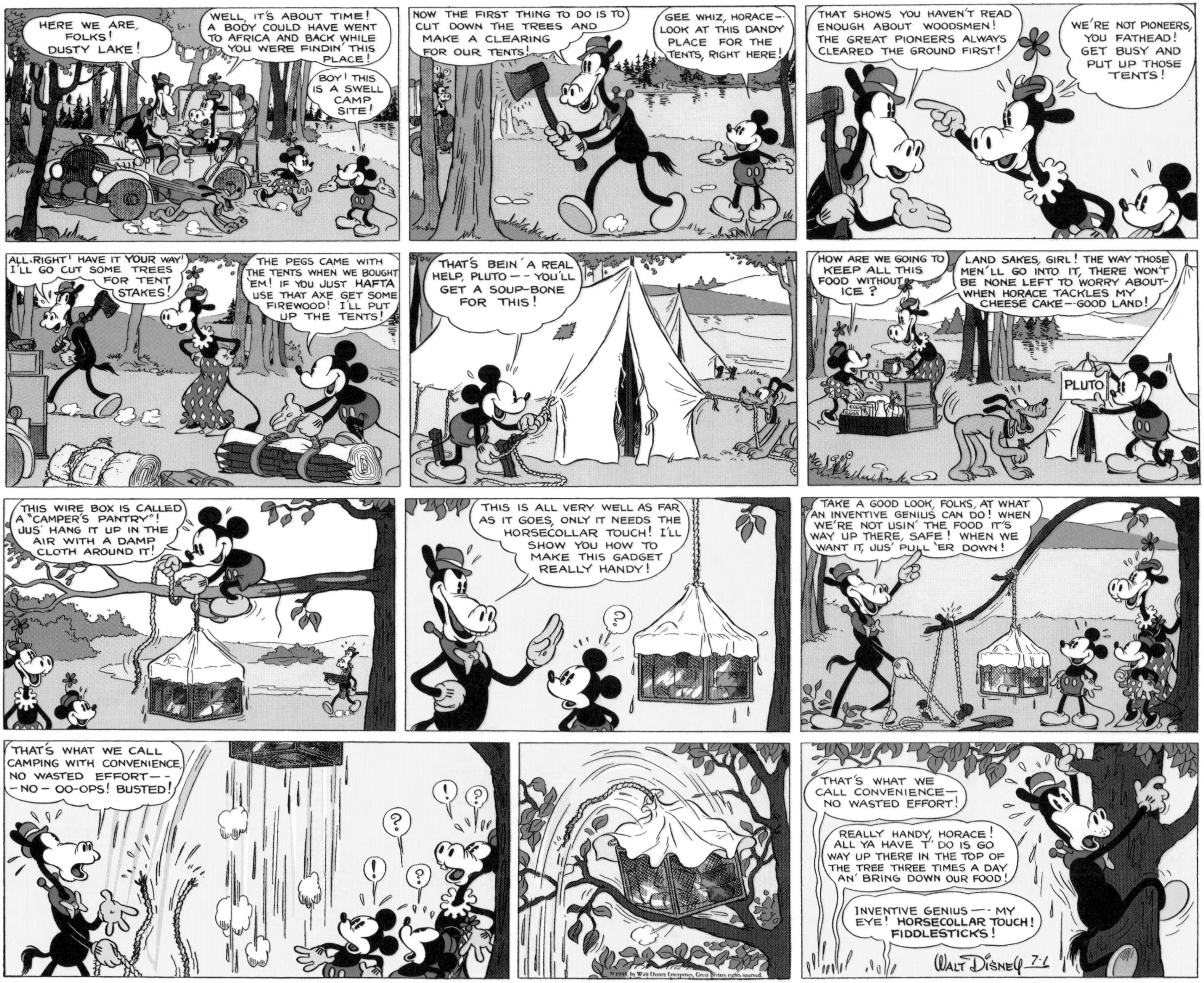
HERE WE ARE, FOLKS! DUSTY LAKE!
WELL, IT'S ABOUT TIME! A BODY COULD HAVE WENT TO AFRICA AND BACK WHILE YOU WERE FINDIN' THIS PLACE!
BOY! THIS IS A SWELL CAMP SITE!
NOW THE FIRST THING TO DO IS TO CUT DOWN THE TREES AND MAKE A CLEARING FOR OUR TENTS!
GEE WHIZ, HORACE-- LOOK AT THIS DANDY PLACE FOR THE TENTS, RIGHT HERE!
THAT SHOWS YOU HAVEN'T READ ENOUGH ABOUT WOODSMEN! THE GREAT PIONEERS ALWAYS CLEARED THE GROUND FIRST!
WE'RE NOT PIONEERS, YOU FATHEAD! GET BUSY AND PUT UP THOSE TENTS!
ALL RIGHT! HAVE IT YOUR WAY! I'LL GO CUT SOME TREES FOR TENT STAKES!
THE PEGS CAME WITH THE TENTS WHEN WE BOUGHT 'EM! IF YOU JUST HAFTA USE THAT AXE GET SOME FIREWOOD! I'LL PUT UP THE TENTS!
THAT'S BEIN' A REAL HELP, PLUTO -- YOU'LL GET A SOUP-BONE FOR THIS!
HOW ARE WE GOING TO KEEP ALL THIS FOOD WITHOUT ICE?
LAND SAKES, GIRL! THE WAY THOSE MEN'LL GO INTO IT, THERE WON'T BE NONE LEFT TO WORRY ABOUT-- WHEN HORACE TACKLES MY CHEESE CAKE -- GOOD LAND!
PLUTO
THIS WIRE BOX IS CALLED A "CAMPER'S PANTRY"! JUS' HANG IT UP IN THE AIR WITH A DAMP CLOTH AROUND IT!
THIS IS ALL VERY WELL AS FAR AS IT GOES, ONLY IT NEEDS THE HORSECOLLAR TOUCH! I'LL SHOW YOU HOW TO MAKE THIS GADGET REALLY HANDY!
TAKE A GOOD LOOK, FOLKS, AT WHAT AN INVENTIVE GENIUS CAN DO! WHEN WE'RE NOT USIN' THE FOOD IT'S WAY UP THERE, SAFE! WHEN WE WANT IT, JUS' PULL 'ER DOWN!
THAT'S WHAT WE CALL CAMPING WITH CONVENIENCE, NO WASTED EFFORT-- --NO -- OO-OPS! BUSTED!
THAT'S WHAT WE CALL CONVENIENCE-- NO WASTED EFFORT!
REALLY HANDY, HORACE! ALL YA HAVE T' DO IS GO WAY UP THERE IN THE TOP OF THE TREE THREE TIMES A DAY AN' BRING DOWN OUR FOOD!
INVENTIVE GENIUS -- MY EYE! HORSECOLLAR TOUCH! FIDDLESTICKS!
WALT DISNEY 7-1

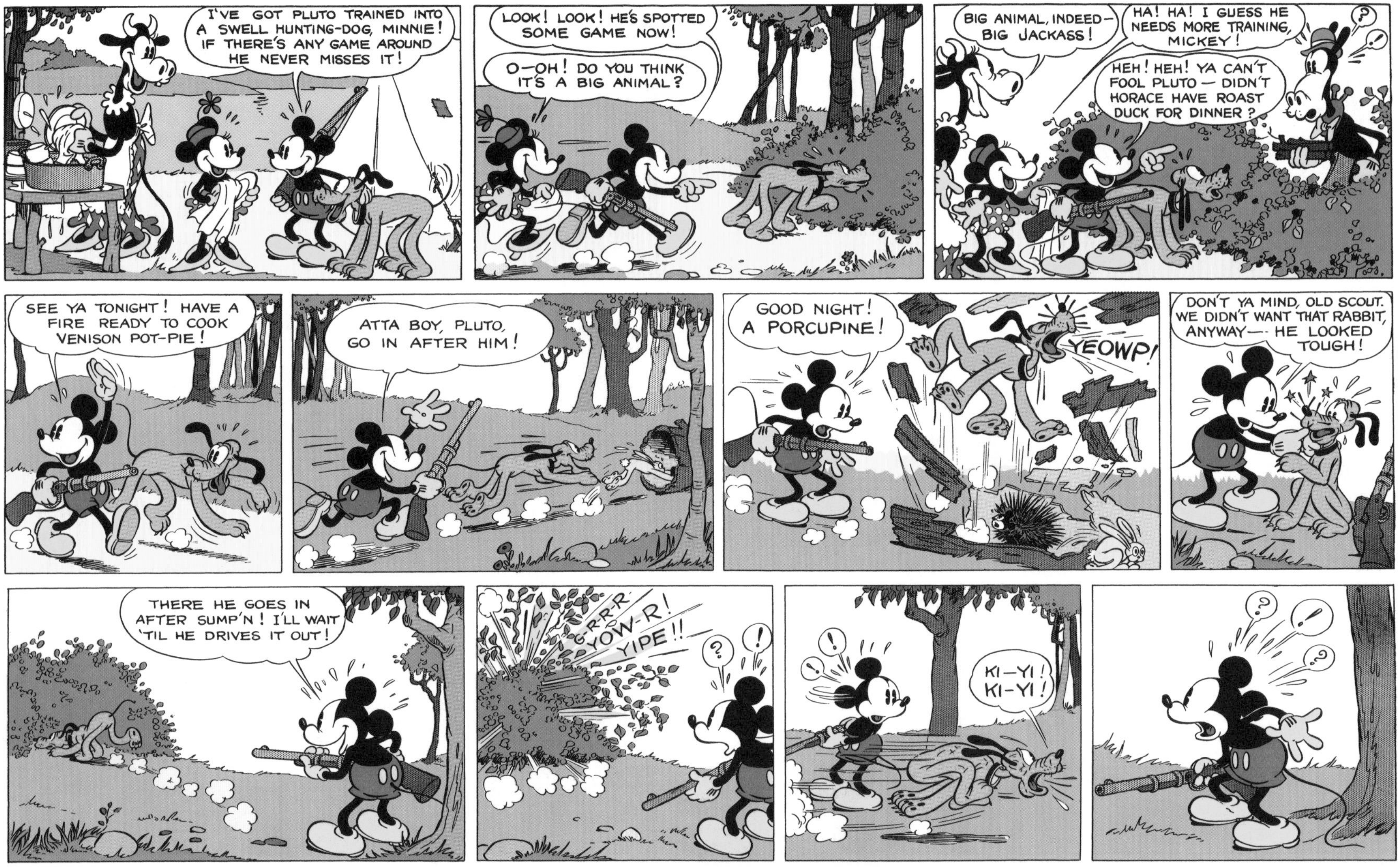
I'VE GOT PLUTO TRAINED INTO A SWELL HUNTING-DOG, MINNIE! IF THERE'S ANY GAME AROUND HE NEVER MISSES IT!
LOOK! LOOK! HE'S SPOTTED SOME GAME NOW!
O-OH! DO YOU THINK IT'S A BIG ANIMAL?
BIG ANIMAL, INDEED— BIG JACKASS!
HA! HA! I GUESS HE NEEDS MORE TRAINING, MICKEY!
HEH! HEH! YA CAN'T FOOL PLUTO — DIDN'T HORACE HAVE ROAST DUCK FOR DINNER?
?
!
SEE YA TONIGHT! HAVE A FIRE READY TO COOK VENISON POT-PIE!
ATTA BOY, PLUTO, GO IN AFTER HIM!
GOOD NIGHT! A PORCUPINE!
YEOWP!
DON'T YA MIND, OLD SCOUT. WE DIDN'T WANT THAT RABBIT, ANYWAY—- HE LOOKED TOUGH!
THERE HE GOES IN AFTER SUMP'N! I'LL WAIT 'TIL HE DRIVES IT OUT!
G-R-R-R
YOW-R!
YIPE!!
?
!
!
!
KI-YI! KI-YI!
?
!
?
!
!
CAMP AHOY! CAMP, AHOY! GET THE FIRE AND PAN READY—-!
?
!
?
?
--BUT CHANGE THE ORDER TO BEAR STEAKS-- --I HOPE!
© 1934, by Walt Disney Enterprises, Great Britain rights reserved.
WALT DISNEY — 7·8

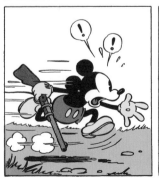

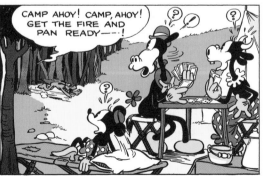

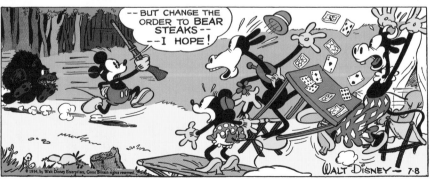

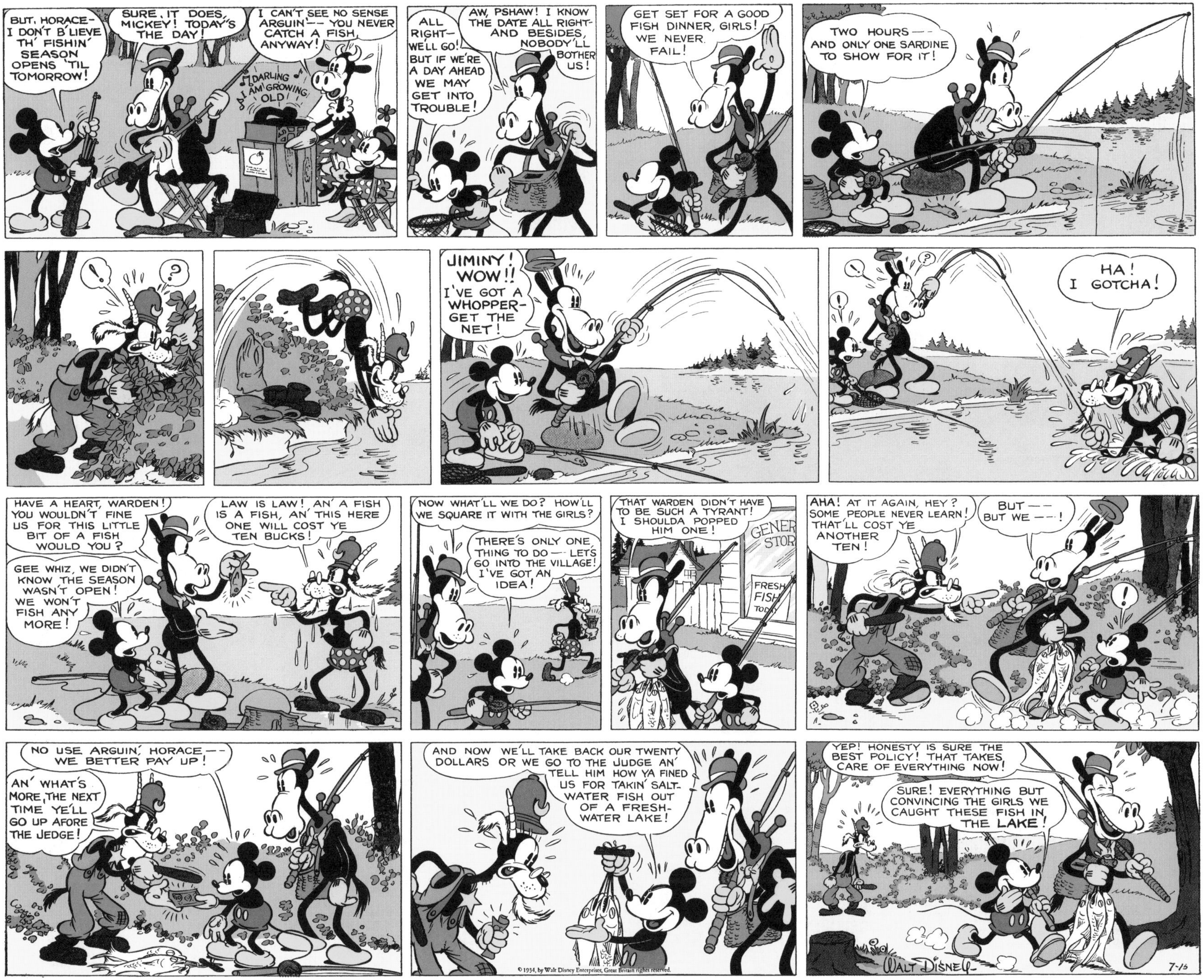
BUT, HORACE- I DON'T B'LIEVE TH' FISHIN' SEASON OPENS 'TIL TOMORROW!
SURE, IT DOES, MICKEY! TODAY'S THE DAY!
I CAN'T SEE NO SENSE ARGUIN'-- YOU NEVER CATCH A FISH ANYWAY!
♫DARLING I AM GROWING OLD!
ALL RIGHT-- WE'LL GO! BUT IF WE'RE A DAY AHEAD WE MAY GET INTO TROUBLE!
AW, PSHAW! I KNOW THE DATE ALL RIGHT- AND BESIDES, NOBODY'LL BOTHER US!
GET SET FOR A GOOD FISH DINNER, GIRLS! WE NEVER FAIL!
TWO HOURS--- AND ONLY ONE SARDINE TO SHOW FOR IT!
!
?
JIMINY! WOW!! I'VE GOT A WHOPPER- GET THE NET!
!
?
!
HA! I GOTCHA!
HAVE A HEART, WARDEN! YOU WOULDN'T FINE US FOR THIS LITTLE BIT OF A FISH WOULD YOU?
LAW IS LAW! AN' A FISH IS A FISH, AN' THIS HERE ONE WILL COST YE TEN BUCKS!
GEE WHIZ, WE DIDN'T KNOW THE SEASON WASN'T OPEN! WE WON'T FISH ANY MORE!
NOW WHAT'LL WE DO? HOW'LL WE SQUARE IT WITH THE GIRLS?
THERE'S ONLY ONE THING TO DO -- LET'S GO INTO THE VILLAGE! I'VE GOT AN IDEA!
THAT WARDEN DIDN'T HAVE TO BE SUCH A TYRANT! I SHOULDA POPPED HIM ONE!
GENER STOR
FRESH FISH TOD
AHA! AT IT AGAIN, HEY? SOME PEOPLE NEVER LEARN! THAT'LL COST YE ANOTHER TEN!
BUT --- BUT WE ---!
!
NO USE ARGUIN', HORACE--- WE BETTER PAY UP!
AN' WHAT'S MORE, THE NEXT TIME YE'LL GO UP AFORE THE JEDGE!
AND NOW WE'LL TAKE BACK OUR TWENTY DOLLARS OR WE GO TO THE JUDGE AN' TELL HIM HOW YA FINED US FOR TAKIN' SALT-WATER FISH OUT OF A FRESH-WATER LAKE!
© 1934, by Walt Disney Enterprises, Great Britain rights reserved.
YEP! HONESTY IS SURE THE BEST POLICY! THAT TAKES CARE OF EVERYTHING NOW!
SURE! EVERYTHING BUT CONVINCING THE GIRLS WE CAUGHT THESE FISH IN THE LAKE!
WALT DISNEY
7-15

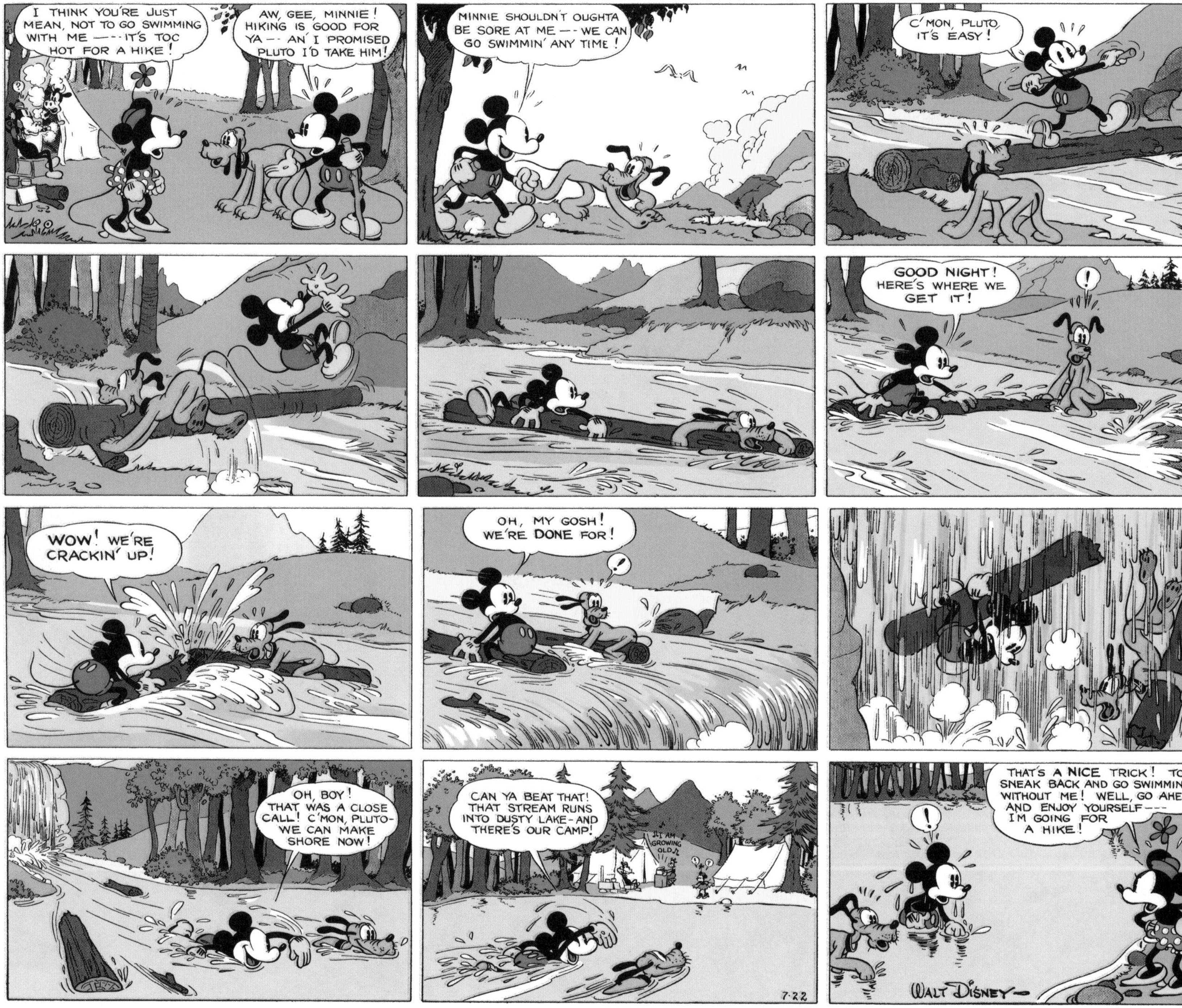
I THINK YOU'RE JUST MEAN, NOT TO GO SWIMMING WITH ME ---IT'S TOO HOT FOR A HIKE!
AW, GEE, MINNIE! HIKING IS GOOD FOR YA -- AN' I PROMISED PLUTO I'D TAKE HIM!
MINNIE SHOULDN'T OUGHTA BE SORE AT ME -- WE CAN GO SWIMMIN' ANY TIME!
C'MON, PLUTO, IT'S EASY!
GOOD NIGHT! HERE'S WHERE WE GET IT!
!
WOW! WE'RE CRACKIN' UP!
OH, MY GOSH! WE'RE DONE FOR!
!
OH, BOY! THAT WAS A CLOSE CALL! C'MON, PLUTO-WE CAN MAKE SHORE NOW!
CAN YA BEAT THAT! THAT STREAM RUNS INTO DUSTY LAKE-AND THERE'S OUR CAMP!
I AM GROWING OLD
THAT'S A NICE TRICK! TO SNEAK BACK AND GO SWIMMING WITHOUT ME! WELL, GO AHEAD AND ENJOY YOURSELF--- I'M GOING FOR A HIKE!
!
7-22
WALT DISNEY

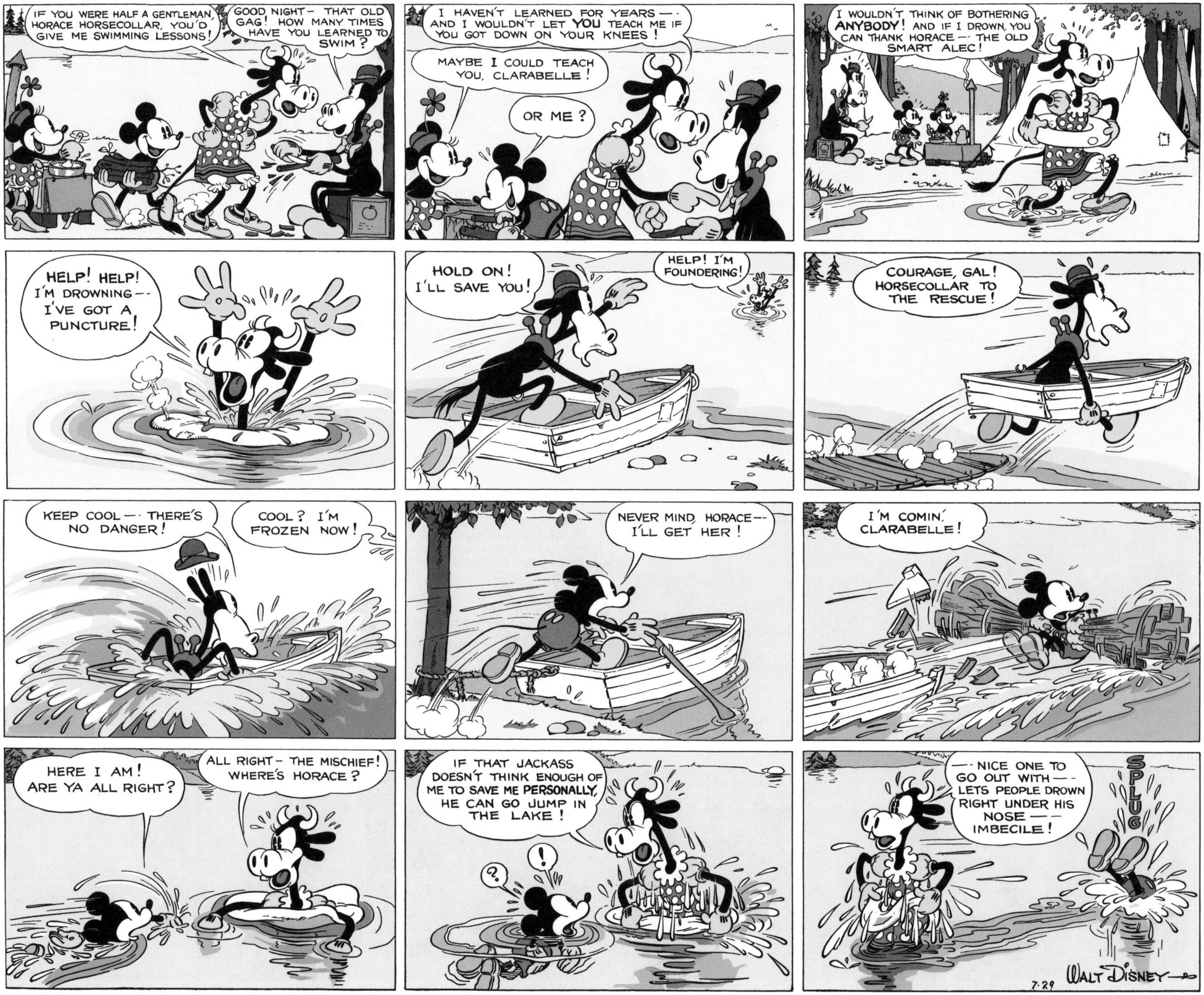
IF YOU WERE HALF A GENTLEMAN, HORACE HORSECOLLAR, YOU'D GIVE ME SWIMMING LESSONS!
GOOD NIGHT— THAT OLD GAG! HOW MANY TIMES HAVE YOU LEARNED TO SWIM?
I HAVEN'T LEARNED FOR YEARS—AND I WOULDN'T LET YOU TEACH ME IF YOU GOT DOWN ON YOUR KNEES!
MAYBE I COULD TEACH YOU, CLARABELLE!
OR ME?
I WOULDN'T THINK OF BOTHERING ANYBODY! AND IF I DROWN, YOU CAN THANK HORACE—THE OLD SMART ALEC!
HELP! HELP! I'M DROWNING—I'VE GOT A PUNCTURE!
HOLD ON! I'LL SAVE YOU!
HELP! I'M FOUNDERING!
COURAGE, GAL! HORSECOLLAR TO THE RESCUE!
KEEP COOL—THERE'S NO DANGER!
COOL? I'M FROZEN NOW!
NEVER MIND, HORACE—I'LL GET HER!
I'M COMIN', CLARABELLE!
HERE I AM! ARE YA ALL RIGHT?
ALL RIGHT— THE MISCHIEF! WHERE'S HORACE?
IF THAT JACKASS DOESN'T THINK ENOUGH OF ME TO SAVE ME PERSONALLY, HE CAN GO JUMP IN THE LAKE!
?
!
—NICE ONE TO GO OUT WITH—LETS PEOPLE DROWN RIGHT UNDER HIS NOSE—IMBECILE!
SPLUG
WALT DISNEY
7-29

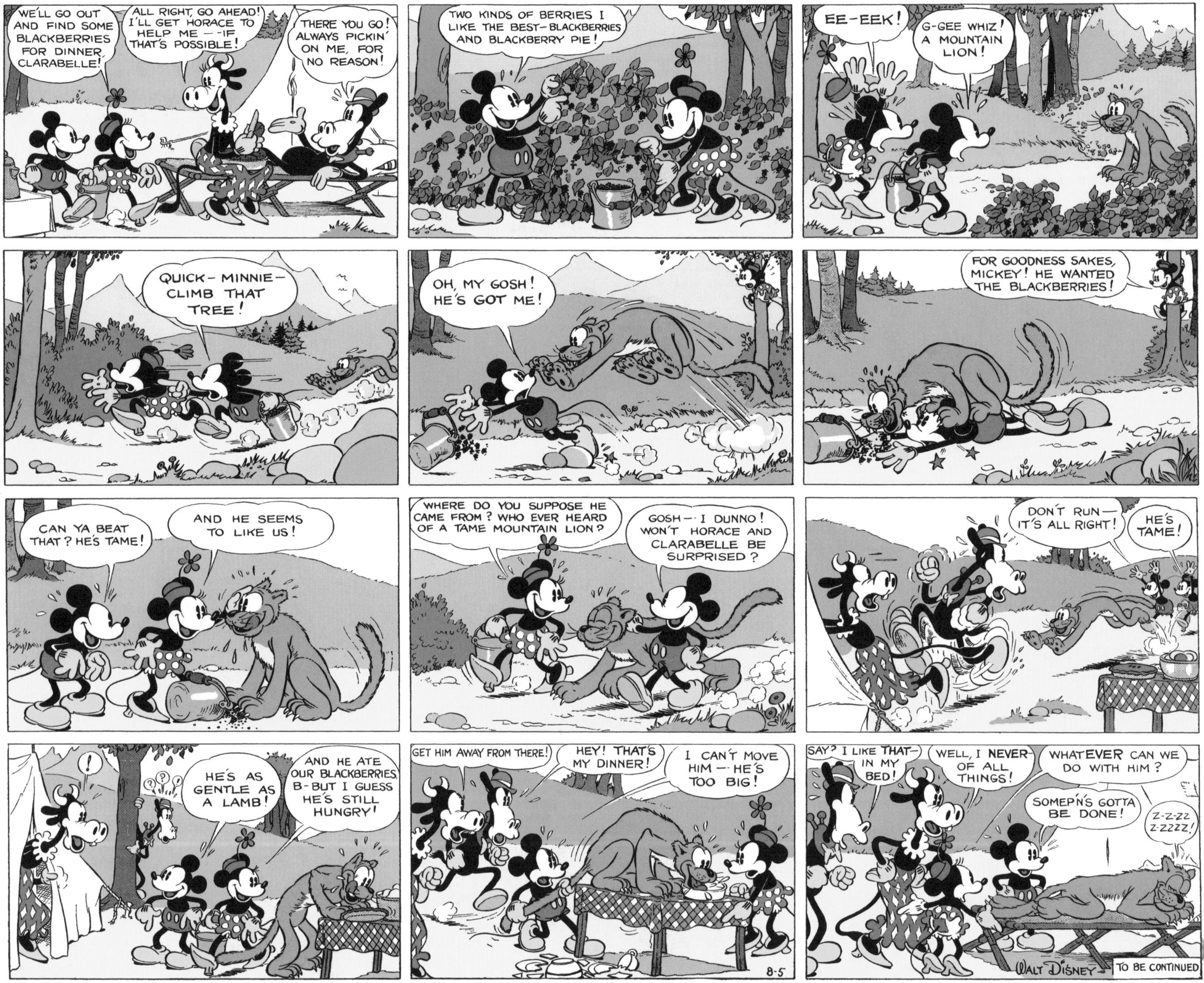
WE'LL GO OUT AND FIND SOME BLACKBERRIES FOR DINNER, CLARABELLE!
ALL RIGHT, GO AHEAD! I'LL GET HORACE TO HELP ME — -IF THAT'S POSSIBLE!
THERE YOU GO! ALWAYS PICKIN' ON ME, FOR NO REASON!
TWO KINDS OF BERRIES I LIKE THE BEST- BLACKBERRIES AND BLACKBERRY PIE!
EE-EEK!
G-GEE WHIZ! A MOUNTAIN LION!
QUICK- MINNIE- CLIMB THAT TREE!
OH, MY GOSH! HE'S GOT ME!
FOR GOODNESS SAKES, MICKEY! HE WANTED THE BLACKBERRIES!
CAN YA BEAT THAT? HE'S TAME!
AND HE SEEMS TO LIKE US!
WHERE DO YOU SUPPOSE HE CAME FROM? WHO EVER HEARD OF A TAME MOUNTAIN LION?
GOSH- · I DUNNO! WON'T HORACE AND CLARABELLE BE SURPRISED?
DON'T RUN— IT'S ALL RIGHT!
HE'S TAME!
!
?? !
HE'S AS GENTLE AS A LAMB!
AND HE ATE OUR BLACKBERRIES, B-BUT I GUESS HE'S STILL HUNGRY!
GET HIM AWAY FROM THERE!
HEY! THAT'S MY DINNER!
I CAN'T MOVE HIM — HE'S TOO BIG!
8-5
SAY? I LIKE THAT— IN MY BED!
WELL, I NEVER- OF ALL THINGS!
WHATEVER CAN WE DO WITH HIM?
SOMEP'N'S GOTTA BE DONE!
Z-Z-ZZ Z-ZZZZ!
WALT DISNEY
TO BE CONTINUED

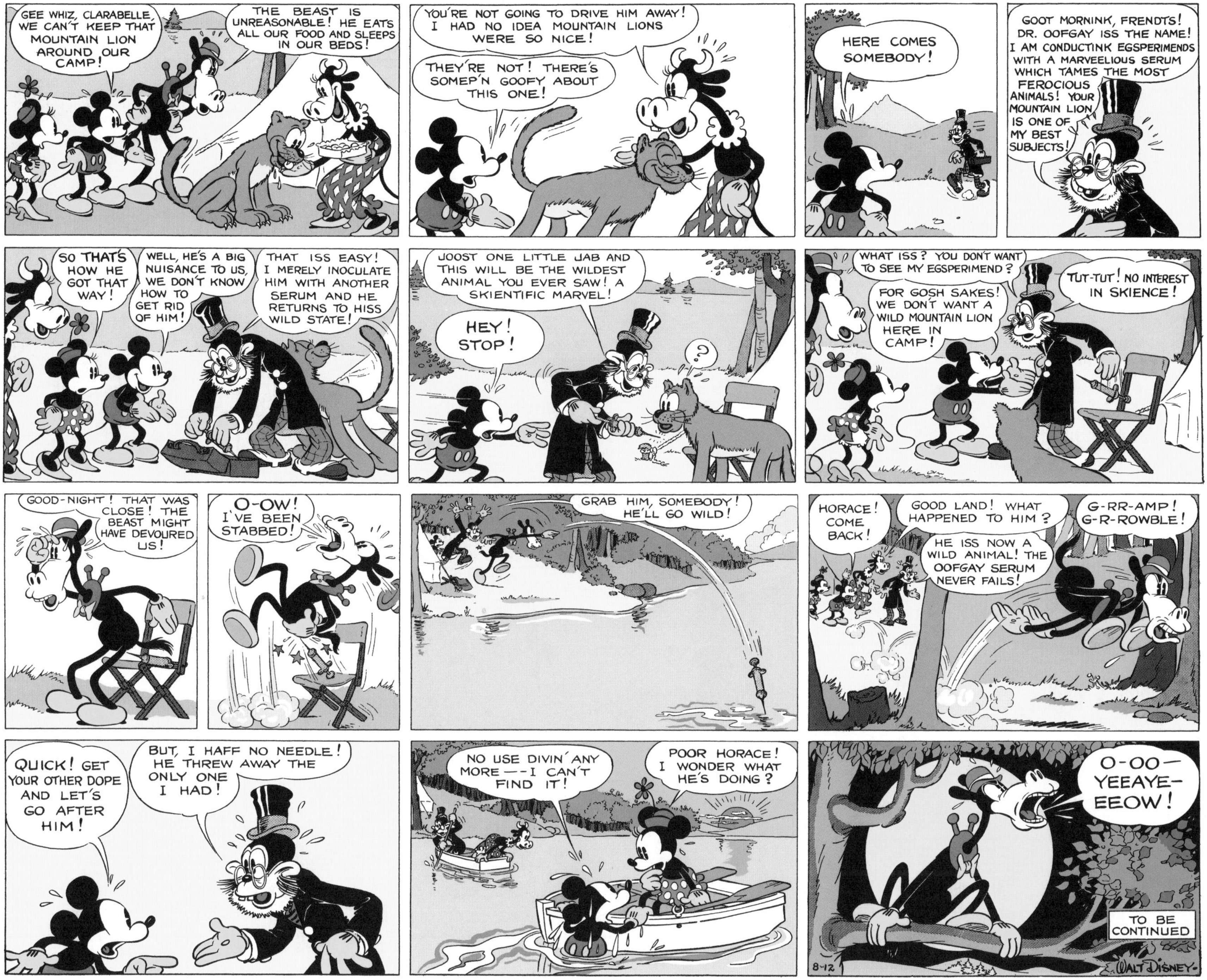
GEE WHIZ, CLARABELLE, WE CAN'T KEEP THAT MOUNTAIN LION AROUND OUR CAMP!
THE BEAST IS UNREASONABLE! HE EATS ALL OUR FOOD AND SLEEPS IN OUR BEDS!
YOU'RE NOT GOING TO DRIVE HIM AWAY! I HAD NO IDEA MOUNTAIN LIONS WERE SO NICE!
THEY'RE NOT! THERE'S SOMEP'N GOOFY ABOUT THIS ONE!
HERE COMES SOMEBODY!
GOOT MORNINK, FRENDTS! DR. OOFGAY ISS THE NAME! I AM CONDUCTINK EGSPERIMENDS WITH A MARVEELIOUS SERUM WHICH TAMES THE MOST FEROCIOUS ANIMALS! YOUR MOUNTAIN LION IS ONE OF MY BEST SUBJECTS!
SO THAT'S HOW HE GOT THAT WAY!
WELL, HE'S A BIG NUISANCE TO US, WE DON'T KNOW HOW TO GET RID OF HIM!
THAT ISS EASY! I MERELY INOCULATE HIM WITH ANOTHER SERUM AND HE RETURNS TO HISS WILD STATE!
JOOST ONE LITTLE JAB AND THIS WILL BE THE WILDEST ANIMAL YOU EVER SAW! A SKIENTIFIC MARVEL!
HEY! STOP!
?
WHAT ISS? YOU DON'T WANT TO SEE MY EGSPERIMEND?
FOR GOSH SAKES! WE DON'T WANT A WILD MOUNTAIN LION HERE IN CAMP!
TUT-TUT! NO INTEREST IN SKIENCE!
GOOD-NIGHT! THAT WAS CLOSE! THE BEAST MIGHT HAVE DEVOURED US!
O-OW! I'VE BEEN STABBED!
GRAB HIM, SOMEBODY! HE'LL GO WILD!
HORACE! COME BACK!
GOOD LAND! WHAT HAPPENED TO HIM?
HE ISS NOW A WILD ANIMAL! THE OOFGAY SERUM NEVER FAILS!
G-RR-AMP! G-R-ROWBLE!
QUICK! GET YOUR OTHER DOPE AND LET'S GO AFTER HIM!
BUT, I HAFF NO NEEDLE! HE THREW AWAY THE ONLY ONE I HAD!
NO USE DIVIN' ANY MORE — - I CAN'T FIND IT!
POOR HORACE! I WONDER WHAT HE'S DOING?
O-OO— YEEAYE— EEOW!
TO BE CONTINUED
8-12
WALT DISNEY

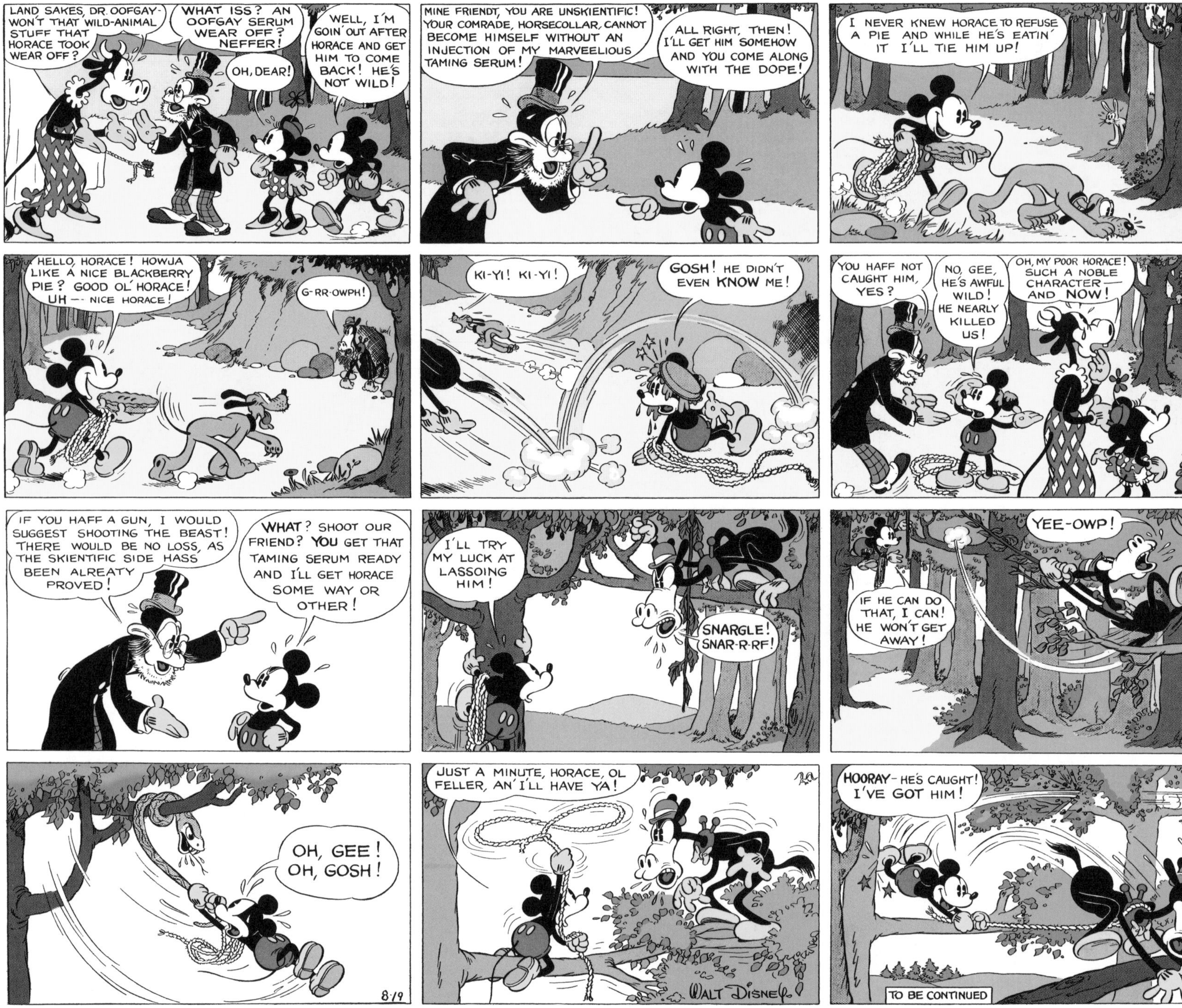
LAND SAKES, DR. OOFGAY- WON'T THAT WILD-ANIMAL STUFF THAT HORACE TOOK WEAR OFF?
WHAT ISS? AN OOFGAY SERUM WEAR OFF? NEFFER!
OH, DEAR!
WELL, I'M GOIN' OUT AFTER HORACE AND GET HIM TO COME BACK! HE'S NOT WILD!
MINE FRIENDT, YOU ARE UNSKIENTIFIC! YOUR COMRADE, HORSECOLLAR, CANNOT BECOME HIMSELF WITHOUT AN INJECTION OF MY MARVEELIOUS TAMING SERUM!
ALL RIGHT, THEN! I'LL GET HIM SOMEHOW AND YOU COME ALONG WITH THE DOPE!
I NEVER KNEW HORACE TO REFUSE A PIE AND WHILE HE'S EATIN' IT I'LL TIE HIM UP!
HELLO, HORACE! HOWJA LIKE A NICE BLACKBERRY PIE? GOOD OL' HORACE! UH -- NICE HORACE!
G-RR-OWPH!
KI-YI! KI-YI!
GOSH! HE DIDN'T EVEN KNOW ME!
YOU HAFF NOT CAUGHT HIM, YES?
NO, GEE, HE'S AWFUL WILD! HE NEARLY KILLED US!
OH, MY POOR HORACE! SUCH A NOBLE CHARACTER— AND NOW!
IF YOU HAFF A GUN, I WOULD SUGGEST SHOOTING THE BEAST! THERE WOULD BE NO LOSS, AS THE SKIENTIFIC SIDE HASS BEEN ALREATY PROVED!
WHAT? SHOOT OUR FRIEND? YOU GET THAT TAMING SERUM READY AND I'LL GET HORACE SOME WAY OR OTHER!
I'LL TRY MY LUCK AT LASSOING HIM!
SNARGLE! SNAR-R-RF!
YEE-OWP!
IF HE CAN DO THAT, I CAN! HE WON'T GET AWAY!
OH, GEE! OH, GOSH!
8-19
JUST A MINUTE, HORACE, OL FELLER, AN' I'LL HAVE YA!
WALT DISNEY
HOORAY- HE'S CAUGHT! I'VE GOT HIM!
TO BE CONTINUED

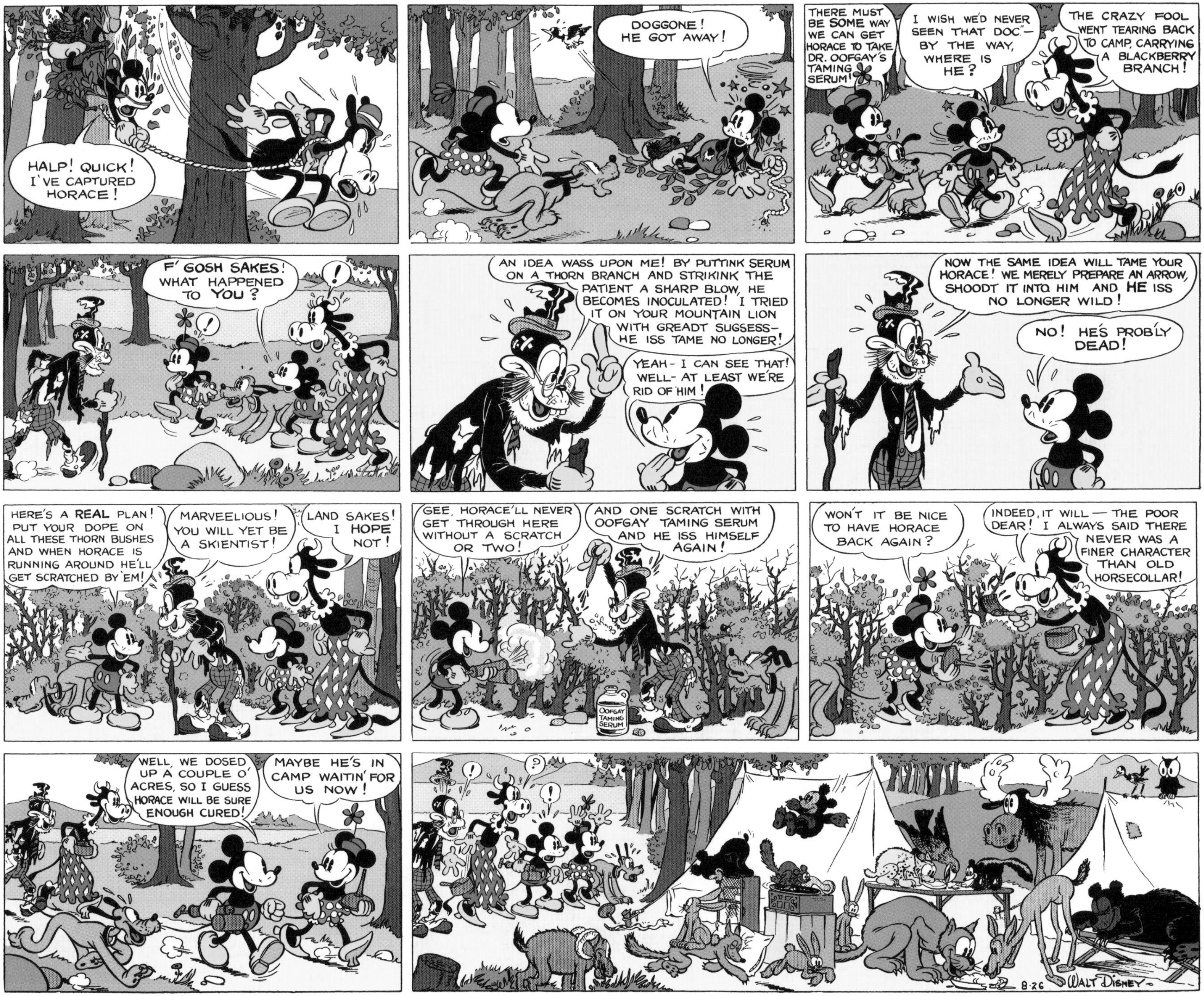
HALP! QUICK! I'VE CAPTURED HORACE!
DOGGONE! HE GOT AWAY!
THERE MUST BE SOME WAY WE CAN GET HORACE TO TAKE DR. OOFGAY'S TAMING SERUM!
I WISH WE'D NEVER SEEN THAT DOC"— BY THE WAY, WHERE IS HE?
THE CRAZY FOOL WENT TEARING BACK TO CAMP, CARRYING A BLACKBERRY BRANCH!
F' GOSH SAKES! WHAT HAPPENED TO YOU?
!
!
AN IDEA WASS UPON ME! BY PUTTINK SERUM ON A THORN BRANCH AND STRIKINK THE PATIENT A SHARP BLOW, HE BECOMES INOCULATED! I TRIED IT ON YOUR MOUNTAIN LION WITH GREADT SUGSESS— HE ISS TAME NO LONGER!
YEAH— I CAN SEE THAT! WELL— AT LEAST WE'RE RID OF HIM!
NOW THE SAME IDEA WILL TAME YOUR HORACE! WE MERELY PREPARE AN ARROW, SHOODT IT INTO HIM AND HE ISS NO LONGER WILD!
NO! HE'S PROB'LY DEAD!
HERE'S A REAL PLAN! PUT YOUR DOPE ON ALL THESE THORN BUSHES AND WHEN HORACE IS RUNNING AROUND HE'LL GET SCRATCHED BY 'EM!
MARVEELIOUS! YOU WILL YET BE A SKIENTIST!
LAND SAKES! I HOPE NOT!
GEE, HORACE'LL NEVER GET THROUGH HERE WITHOUT A SCRATCH OR TWO!
AND ONE SCRATCH WITH OOFGAY TAMING SERUM AND HE ISS HIMSELF AGAIN!
OOFGAY TAMING SERUM
WON'T IT BE NICE TO HAVE HORACE BACK AGAIN?
INDEED, IT WILL — THE POOR DEAR! I ALWAYS SAID THERE NEVER WAS A FINER CHARACTER THAN OLD HORSECOLLAR!
WELL, WE DOSED UP A COUPLE O' ACRES, SO I GUESS HORACE WILL BE SURE ENOUGH CURED!
MAYBE HE'S IN CAMP WAITIN' FOR US NOW!
!
?
!
8·26
WALT DISNEY

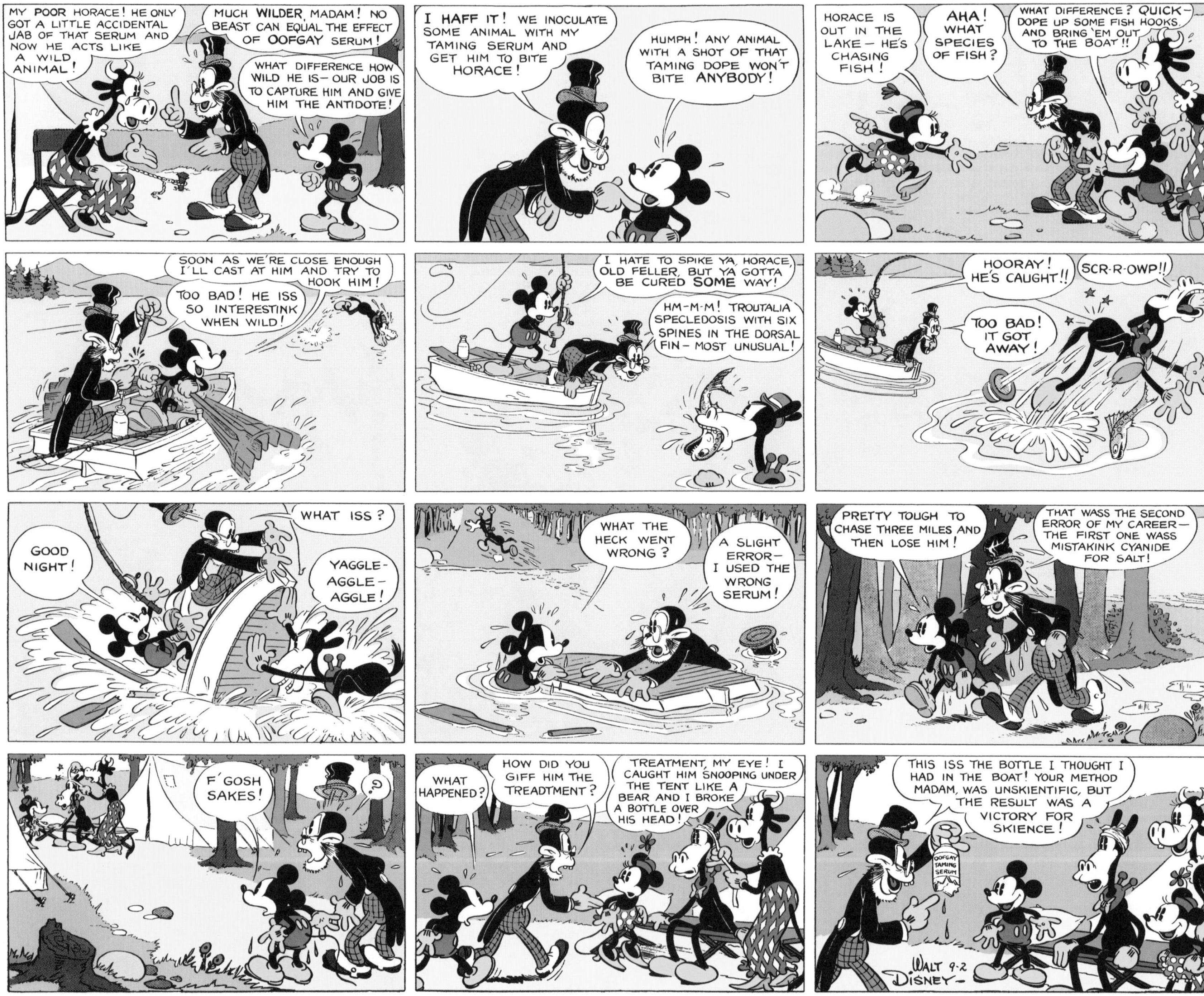
MY POOR HORACE! HE ONLY GOT A LITTLE ACCIDENTAL JAB OF THAT SERUM AND NOW HE ACTS LIKE A WILD ANIMAL!
MUCH WILDER, MADAM! NO BEAST CAN EQUAL THE EFFECT OF OOFGAY SERUM!
WHAT DIFFERENCE HOW WILD HE IS— OUR JOB IS TO CAPTURE HIM AND GIVE HIM THE ANTIDOTE!
I HAFF IT! WE INOCULATE SOME ANIMAL WITH MY TAMING SERUM AND GET HIM TO BITE HORACE!
HUMPH! ANY ANIMAL WITH A SHOT OF THAT TAMING DOPE WON'T BITE ANYBODY!
HORACE IS OUT IN THE LAKE— HE'S CHASING FISH!
AHA! WHAT SPECIES OF FISH?
WHAT DIFFERENCE? QUICK— DOPE UP SOME FISH HOOKS AND BRING 'EM OUT TO THE BOAT!!
SOON AS WE'RE CLOSE ENOUGH I'LL CAST AT HIM AND TRY TO HOOK HIM!
TOO BAD! HE ISS SO INTERESTINK WHEN WILD!
I HATE TO SPIKE YA, HORACE, OLD FELLER, BUT YA GOTTA BE CURED SOME WAY!
HM-M-M! TROUTALIA SPECLEDOSIS WITH SIX SPINES IN THE DORSAL FIN— MOST UNUSUAL!
HOORAY! HE'S CAUGHT!!
SCR-R-OWP!!
TOO BAD! IT GOT AWAY!
GOOD NIGHT!
WHAT ISS?
YAGGLE-AGGLE-AGGLE!
WHAT THE HECK WENT WRONG?
A SLIGHT ERROR— I USED THE WRONG SERUM!
PRETTY TOUGH TO CHASE THREE MILES AND THEN LOSE HIM!
THAT WASS THE SECOND ERROR OF MY CAREER— THE FIRST ONE WASS MISTAKINK CYANIDE FOR SALT!
F'GOSH SAKES!
?
WHAT HAPPENED?
HOW DID YOU GIFF HIM THE TREADTMENT?
TREATMENT, MY EYE! I CAUGHT HIM SNOOPING UNDER THE TENT LIKE A BEAR AND I BROKE A BOTTLE OVER HIS HEAD!
THIS ISS THE BOTTLE I THOUGHT I HAD IN THE BOAT! YOUR METHOD MADAM, WAS UNSKIENTIFIC, BUT THE RESULT WAS A VICTORY FOR SKIENCE!
OOFGAY TAMING SERUM
WALT DISNEY 9-2

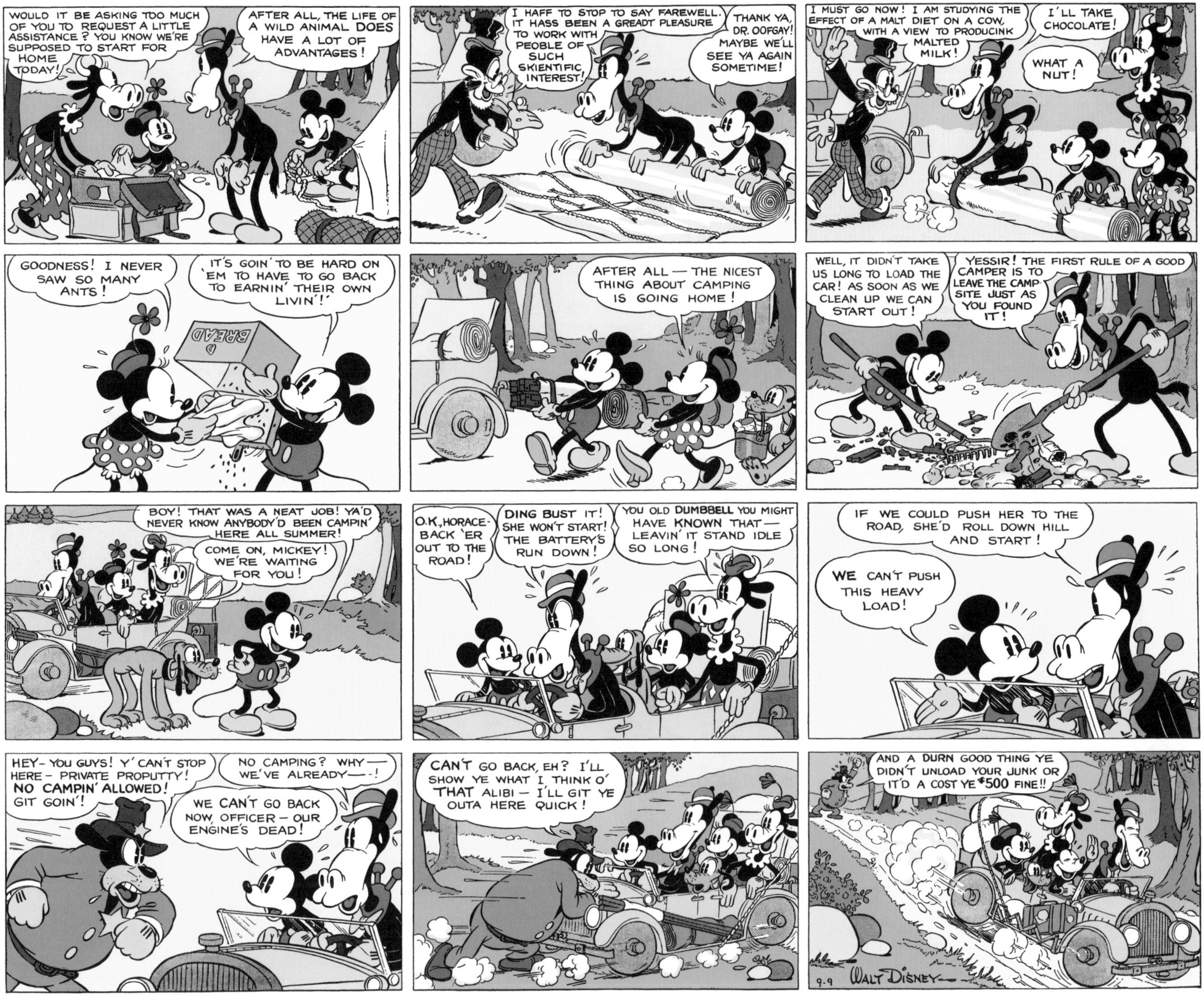
WOULD IT BE ASKING TOO MUCH OF YOU TO REQUEST A LITTLE ASSISTANCE? YOU KNOW WE'RE SUPPOSED TO START FOR HOME TODAY!
AFTER ALL, THE LIFE OF A WILD ANIMAL DOES HAVE A LOT OF ADVANTAGES!
I HAFF TO STOP TO SAY FAREWELL. IT HASS BEEN A GREADT PLEASURE TO WORK WITH PEOBLE OF SUCH SKIENTIFIC INTEREST!
THANK YA, DR. OOFGAY! MAYBE WE'LL SEE YA AGAIN SOMETIME!
I MUST GO NOW! I AM STUDYING THE EFFECT OF A MALT DIET ON A COW, WITH A VIEW TO PRODUCINK MALTED MILK!
I'LL TAKE CHOCOLATE!
WHAT A NUT!
GOODNESS! I NEVER SAW SO MANY ANTS!
IT'S GOIN' TO BE HARD ON 'EM TO HAVE TO GO BACK TO EARNIN' THEIR OWN LIVIN'!
BREAD
AFTER ALL — THE NICEST THING ABOUT CAMPING IS GOING HOME!
WELL, IT DIDN'T TAKE US LONG TO LOAD THE CAR! AS SOON AS WE CLEAN UP WE CAN START OUT!
YESSIR! THE FIRST RULE OF A GOOD CAMPER IS TO LEAVE THE CAMP SITE JUST AS YOU FOUND IT!
BOY! THAT WAS A NEAT JOB! YA'D NEVER KNOW ANYBODY'D BEEN CAMPIN' HERE ALL SUMMER!
COME ON, MICKEY! WE'RE WAITING FOR YOU!
O.K., HORACE- BACK 'ER OUT TO THE ROAD!
DING BUST IT! SHE WON'T START! THE BATTERY'S RUN DOWN!
YOU OLD DUMBBELL YOU MIGHT HAVE KNOWN THAT— LEAVIN' IT STAND IDLE SO LONG!
IF WE COULD PUSH HER TO THE ROAD, SHE'D ROLL DOWN HILL AND START!
WE CAN'T PUSH THIS HEAVY LOAD!
HEY- YOU GUYS! Y' CAN'T STOP HERE- PRIVATE PROPUTTY! NO CAMPIN' ALLOWED! GIT GOIN'!
NO CAMPING? WHY— WE'VE ALREADY——!
WE CAN'T GO BACK NOW, OFFICER – OUR ENGINE'S DEAD!
CAN'T GO BACK, EH? I'LL SHOW YE WHAT I THINK O' THAT ALIBI – I'LL GIT YE OUTA HERE QUICK!
AND A DURN GOOD THING YE DIDN'T UNLOAD YOUR JUNK OR IT'D A COST YE $500 FINE!!
9-9
WALT DISNEY

INTRODUCING
MICKEY MOUSE MOVIES
by WALT DISNEY
I'VE GOT SOMETHIN' NEW TO SHOW YA, PLUTO — IT'S A STUNT WHERE THE KIDS CAN MAKE THEIR OWN MOVIES!
PASTE
TO START WITH, THEY JUST PASTE THIS MOVIE WHEEL ON CARDBOARD, CUT OUT THE WHEEL AND PAINT THE BACK OF IT BLACK!
THE NEXT THING IS TO CUT OUT THE LITTLE SLITS AROUND THE EDGE — ARE YA LISTENIN' PLUTO?
PASTE
NOW ALL THEY HAFTA DO IS TO STICK A PIN THROUGH THAT DOT IN THE CENTER AN' PUT THE PIN INTO THE ERASER END OF A PENCIL — — LIKE THIS — SEE!
TO RUN THE MOVIE JUS' STAND BEFORE A MIRROR, SHUT ONE EYE AN' SPIN THE CARD WITH THE BLACK SIDE TOWARD YA — — AN' WATCH TH' PICTURES THRU' THE SLITS — SEE, PLUTO! I'M JUMPIN' ROPE!
PASTE
I'M GOING TO GIVE THE KIDS A DIFFERENT MOVIE ON THIS PAGE EVERY SUNDAY — AN' IF THEY'RE TOO LAZY TO MAKE 'EM, THEY'LL MISS A LOTTA FUN! AN' ANY KID THAT HAS A DOG, I HOPE HE BEHAVES BETTER'N YOU DO!
MICKEY MOUSE MOVIES
MICKEY MOUSE MOVIES
- INSTRUCTIONS -
PASTE MOVIE WHEEL ON CARDBOARD, CUT OUT WHEEL AND PAINT BACK OF IT BLACK. CUT OUT SLITS, STICK A PIN THROUGH DOT IN CENTER AND PUT PIN INTO ERASER END OF PENCIL. TO OPERATE: — STAND BEFORE A MIRROR AND SPIN WHEEL WITH BLACK SIDE TOWARD YOU. CLOSE ONE EYE AND WATCH IMAGE THROUGH SLITS!
6·24

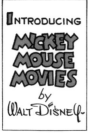

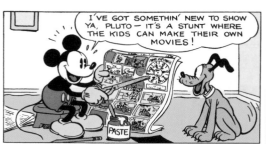

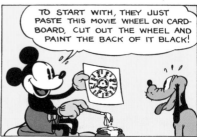

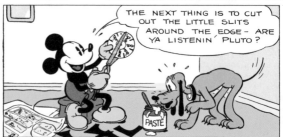

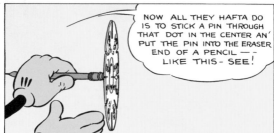

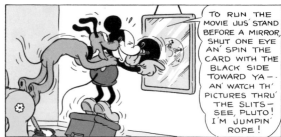

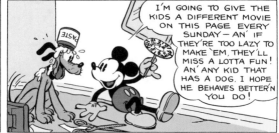

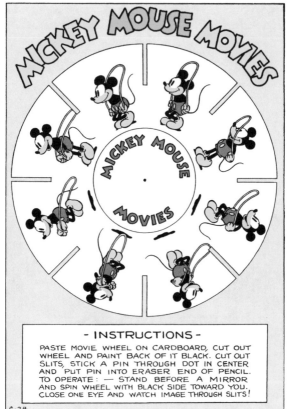

ABOVE: Gottfredson's Sunday *Mickey Mouse* was usually accompanied by a *Silly Symphony* top strip. But for one time only—on June 24, 1934—Mickey starred in his own special topper, announcing a new "premium" that would accompany subsequent Sunday pages.

While Gottfredson penciled this introductory strip, the actual "Mickey Mouse Movies" phenakistocope wheels were drawn by others. The "Movies" appeared on and off alongside the *Silly Symphony* strip through March 24, 1935.

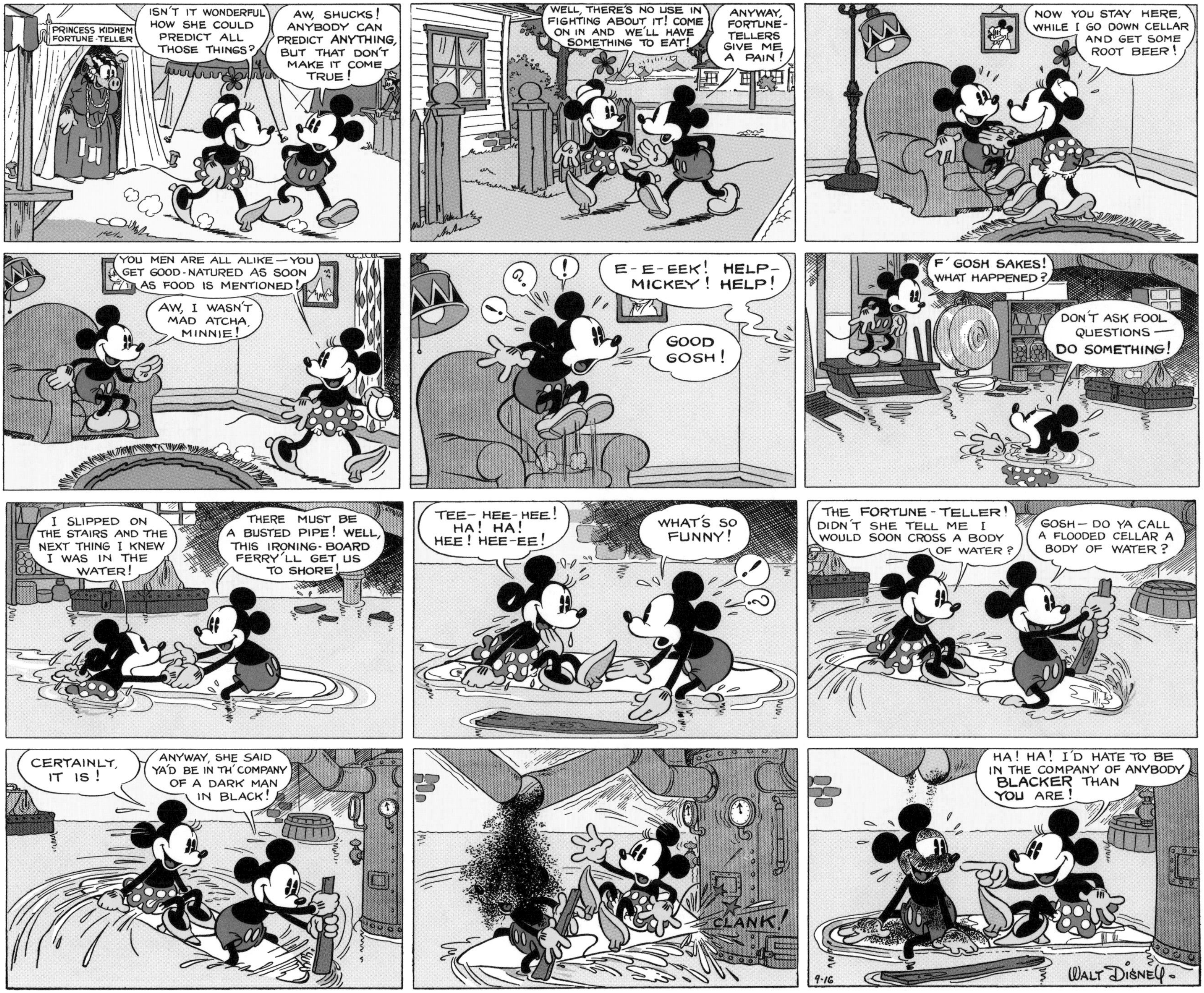
PRINCESS KIDHEM FORTUNE-TELLER
ISN'T IT WONDERFUL HOW SHE COULD PREDICT ALL THOSE THINGS?
AW, SHUCKS! ANYBODY CAN PREDICT ANYTHING, BUT THAT DON'T MAKE IT COME TRUE!
WELL, THERE'S NO USE IN FIGHTING ABOUT IT! COME ON IN AND WE'LL HAVE SOMETHING TO EAT!
ANYWAY, FORTUNE-TELLERS GIVE ME A PAIN!
NOW YOU STAY HERE, WHILE I GO DOWN CELLAR AND GET SOME ROOT BEER!
YOU MEN ARE ALL ALIKE—YOU GET GOOD-NATURED AS SOON AS FOOD IS MENTIONED!
AW, I WASN'T MAD ATCHA, MINNIE!
E-E-EEK! HELP-MICKEY! HELP!
GOOD GOSH!
F' GOSH SAKES! WHAT HAPPENED?
DON'T ASK FOOL QUESTIONS—DO SOMETHING!
I SLIPPED ON THE STAIRS AND THE NEXT THING I KNEW I WAS IN THE WATER!
THERE MUST BE A BUSTED PIPE! WELL, THIS IRONING-BOARD FERRY'LL GET US TO SHORE!
TEE-HEE-HEE! HA! HA! HEE! HEE-EE!
WHAT'S SO FUNNY!
THE FORTUNE-TELLER! DIDN'T SHE TELL ME I WOULD SOON CROSS A BODY OF WATER?
GOSH—DO YA CALL A FLOODED CELLAR A BODY OF WATER?
CERTAINLY, IT IS!
ANYWAY, SHE SAID YA'D BE IN TH' COMPANY OF A DARK MAN IN BLACK!
CLANK!
HA! HA! I'D HATE TO BE IN THE COMPANY OF ANYBODY BLACKER THAN YOU ARE!
9-16
WALT DISNEY

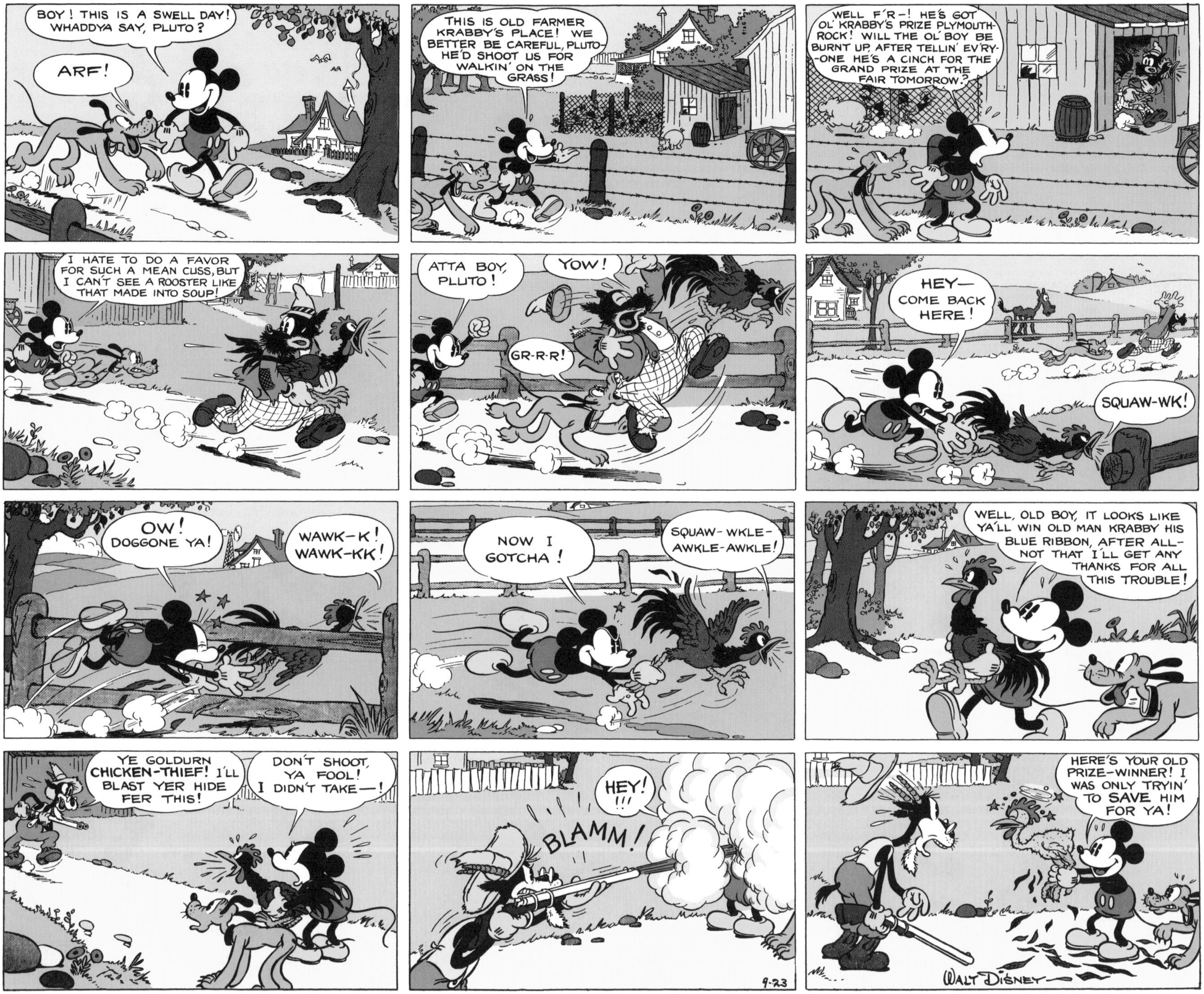
BOY! THIS IS A SWELL DAY! WHADDYA SAY, PLUTO?
ARF!
THIS IS OLD FARMER KRABBY'S PLACE! WE BETTER BE CAREFUL, PLUTO—HE'D SHOOT US FOR WALKIN' ON THE GRASS!
WELL F'R—! HE'S GOT OL' KRABBY'S PRIZE PLYMOUTH-ROCK! WILL THE OL' BOY BE BURNT UP, AFTER TELLIN' EV'RY-ONE HE'S A CINCH FOR THE GRAND PRIZE AT THE FAIR TOMORROW?
I HATE TO DO A FAVOR FOR SUCH A MEAN CUSS, BUT I CAN'T SEE A ROOSTER LIKE THAT MADE INTO SOUP!
ATTA BOY, PLUTO!
YOW!
GR-R-R!
HEY— COME BACK HERE!
SQUAW-WK!
OW! DOGGONE YA!
WAWK-K! WAWK-KK!
NOW I GOTCHA!
SQUAW-WKLE-AWKLE-AWKLE!
WELL, OLD BOY, IT LOOKS LIKE YA'LL WIN OLD MAN KRABBY HIS BLUE RIBBON, AFTER ALL—NOT THAT I'LL GET ANY THANKS FOR ALL THIS TROUBLE!
YE GOLDURN CHICKEN-THIEF! I'LL BLAST YER HIDE FER THIS!
DON'T SHOOT, YA FOOL! I DIDN'T TAKE—!
HEY! !!!
BLAMM!
9-23
HERE'S YOUR OLD PRIZE-WINNER! I WAS ONLY TRYIN' TO SAVE HIM FOR YA!
WALT DISNEY

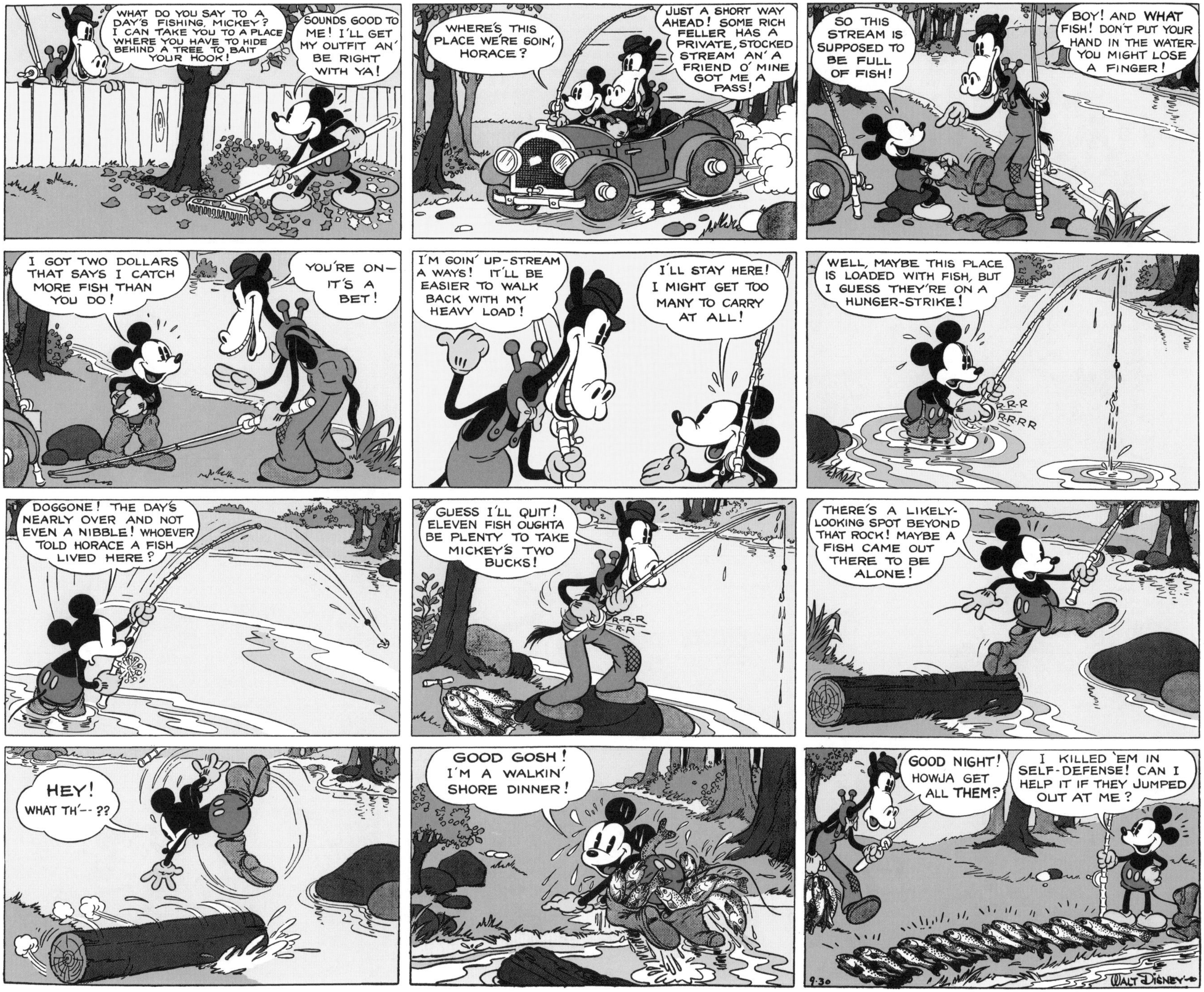
WHAT DO YOU SAY TO A DAY'S FISHING, MICKEY? I CAN TAKE YOU TO A PLACE WHERE YOU HAVE TO HIDE BEHIND A TREE TO BAIT YOUR HOOK!
SOUNDS GOOD TO ME! I'LL GET MY OUTFIT AN' BE RIGHT WITH YA!
WHERE'S THIS PLACE WE'RE GOIN', HORACE?
JUST A SHORT WAY AHEAD! SOME RICH FELLER HAS A PRIVATE, STOCKED STREAM AN' A FRIEND O' MINE GOT ME A PASS!
SO THIS STREAM IS SUPPOSED TO BE FULL OF FISH!
BOY! AND WHAT FISH! DON'T PUT YOUR HAND IN THE WATER- YOU MIGHT LOSE A FINGER!
I GOT TWO DOLLARS THAT SAYS I CATCH MORE FISH THAN YOU DO!
YOU'RE ON- IT'S A BET!
I'M GOIN' UP-STREAM A WAYS! IT'LL BE EASIER TO WALK BACK WITH MY HEAVY LOAD!
I'LL STAY HERE! I MIGHT GET TOO MANY TO CARRY AT ALL!
WELL, MAYBE THIS PLACE IS LOADED WITH FISH, BUT I GUESS THEY'RE ON A HUNGER-STRIKE!
R-R-R
R-R-R-R
DOGGONE! THE DAY'S NEARLY OVER AND NOT EVEN A NIBBLE! WHOEVER TOLD HORACE A FISH LIVED HERE?
GUESS I'LL QUIT! ELEVEN FISH OUGHTA BE PLENTY TO TAKE MICKEY'S TWO BUCKS!
R-R-R
R-R
THERE'S A LIKELY-LOOKING SPOT BEYOND THAT ROCK! MAYBE A FISH CAME OUT THERE TO BE ALONE!
HEY!
WHAT TH'-- ??
GOOD GOSH! I'M A WALKIN' SHORE DINNER!
GOOD NIGHT! HOWJA GET ALL THEM?
I KILLED 'EM IN SELF-DEFENSE! CAN I HELP IT IF THEY JUMPED OUT AT ME?
9-30
WALT DISNEY

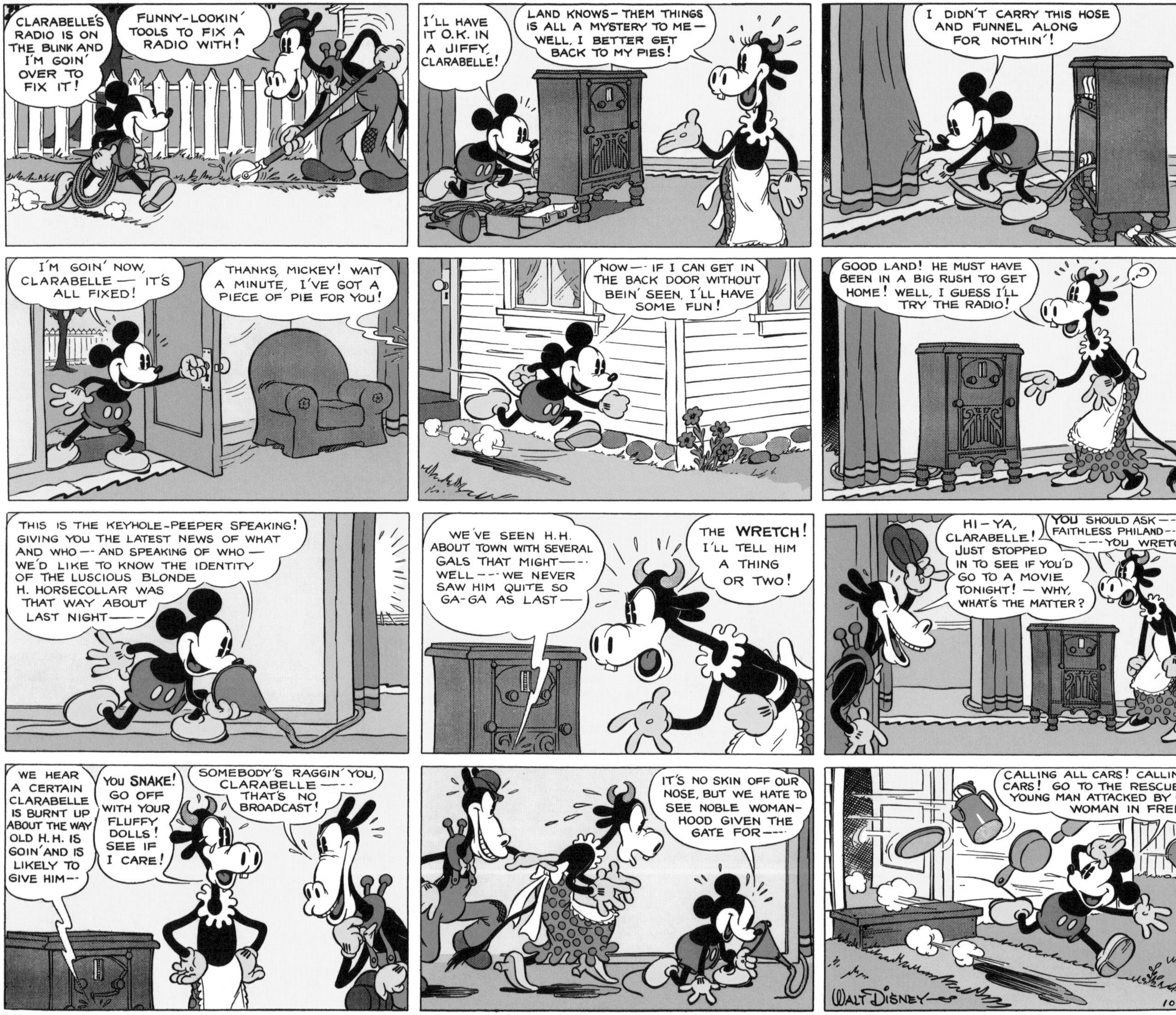
CLARABELLE'S RADIO IS ON THE BLINK AND I'M GOIN' OVER TO FIX IT!
FUNNY-LOOKIN' TOOLS TO FIX A RADIO WITH!
I'LL HAVE IT O.K. IN A JIFFY, CLARABELLE!
LAND KNOWS—THEM THINGS IS ALL A MYSTERY TO ME—WELL, I BETTER GET BACK TO MY PIES!
I DIDN'T CARRY THIS HOSE AND FUNNEL ALONG FOR NOTHIN'!
I'M GOIN' NOW, CLARABELLE—IT'S ALL FIXED!
THANKS, MICKEY! WAIT A MINUTE, I'VE GOT A PIECE OF PIE FOR YOU!
NOW—IF I CAN GET IN THE BACK DOOR WITHOUT BEIN' SEEN, I'LL HAVE SOME FUN!
GOOD LAND! HE MUST HAVE BEEN IN A BIG RUSH TO GET HOME! WELL, I GUESS I'LL TRY THE RADIO!
THIS IS THE KEYHOLE-PEEPER SPEAKING! GIVING YOU THE LATEST NEWS OF WHAT AND WHO—AND SPEAKING OF WHO—WE'D LIKE TO KNOW THE IDENTITY OF THE LUSCIOUS BLONDE H. HORSECOLLAR WAS THAT WAY ABOUT LAST NIGHT——
WE'VE SEEN H.H. ABOUT TOWN WITH SEVERAL GALS THAT MIGHT——WELL——WE NEVER SAW HIM QUITE SO GA-GA AS LAST——
THE WRETCH! I'LL TELL HIM A THING OR TWO!
HI-YA, CLARABELLE! JUST STOPPED IN TO SEE IF YOU'D GO TO A MOVIE TONIGHT!—WHY, WHAT'S THE MATTER?
YOU SHOULD ASK——YOU FAITHLESS PHILAND—ER, PHIL———YOU WRETCH!
WE HEAR A CERTAIN CLARABELLE IS BURNT UP ABOUT THE WAY OLD H.H. IS GOIN' AND IS LIKELY TO GIVE HIM—
YOU SNAKE! GO OFF WITH YOUR FLUFFY DOLLS! SEE IF I CARE!
SOMEBODY'S RAGGIN' YOU, CLARABELLE——THAT'S NO BROADCAST!
IT'S NO SKIN OFF OUR NOSE, BUT WE HATE TO SEE NOBLE WOMANHOOD GIVEN THE GATE FOR———
CALLING ALL CARS! CALLING ALL CARS! GO TO THE RESCUE OF YOUNG MAN ATTACKED BY CRAZY WOMAN IN FRENZY!
WALT DISNEY
10-7

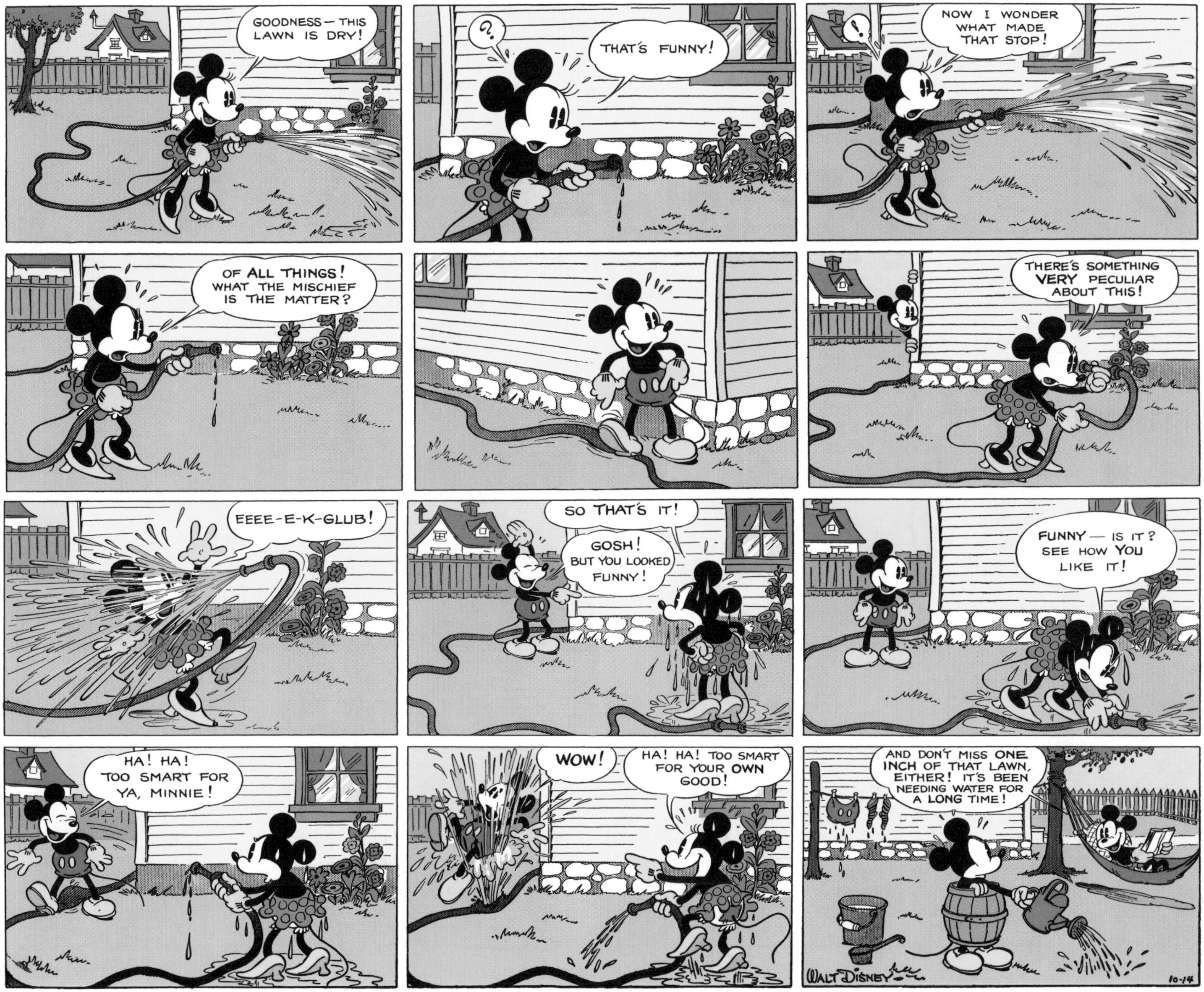
GOODNESS — THIS LAWN IS DRY!
?
THAT'S FUNNY!
!
NOW I WONDER WHAT MADE THAT STOP!
OF ALL THINGS! WHAT THE MISCHIEF IS THE MATTER?
THERE'S SOMETHING VERY PECULIAR ABOUT THIS!
EEEE-E-K-GLUB!
SO THAT'S IT!
GOSH! BUT YOU LOOKED FUNNY!
FUNNY — IS IT? SEE HOW YOU LIKE IT!
HA! HA! TOO SMART FOR YA, MINNIE!
WOW!
HA! HA! TOO SMART FOR YOUR OWN GOOD!
AND DON'T MISS ONE INCH OF THAT LAWN, EITHER! IT'S BEEN NEEDING WATER FOR A LONG TIME!
WALT DISNEY
10-14

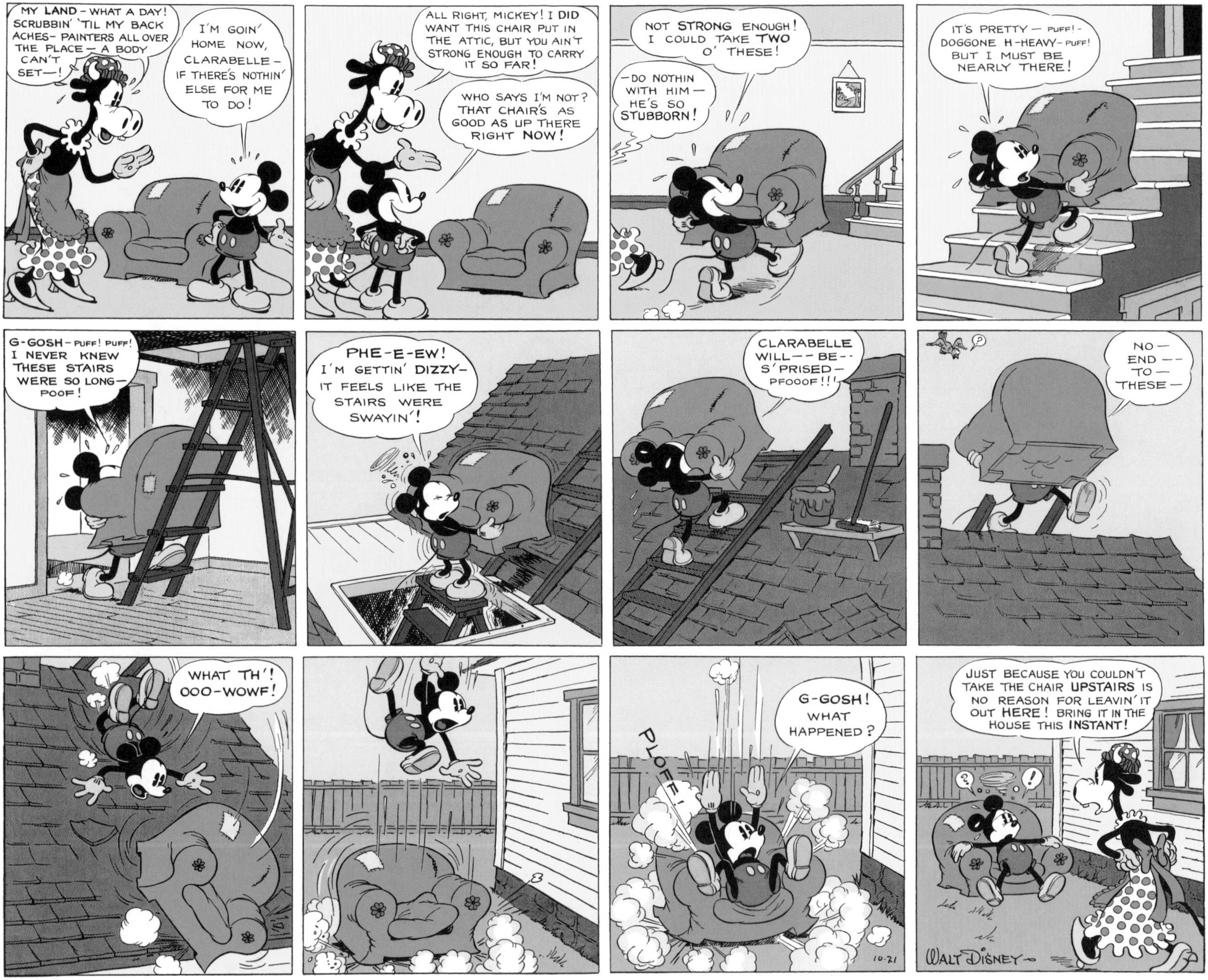
MY LAND - WHAT A DAY! SCRUBBIN' 'TIL MY BACK ACHES- PAINTERS ALL OVER THE PLACE - A BODY CAN'T SET—!
I'M GOIN' HOME NOW, CLARABELLE - IF THERE'S NOTHIN' ELSE FOR ME TO DO!
ALL RIGHT, MICKEY! I DID WANT THIS CHAIR PUT IN THE ATTIC, BUT YOU AIN'T STRONG ENOUGH TO CARRY IT SO FAR!
WHO SAYS I'M NOT? THAT CHAIR'S AS GOOD AS UP THERE RIGHT NOW!
NOT STRONG ENOUGH! I COULD TAKE TWO O' THESE!
—DO NOTHIN WITH HIM— HE'S SO STUBBORN!
IT'S PRETTY — PUFF! - DOGGONE H-HEAVY - PUFF! BUT I MUST BE NEARLY THERE!
G-GOSH - PUFF! PUFF! I NEVER KNEW THESE STAIRS WERE SO LONG - POOF!
PHE-E-EW! I'M GETTIN' DIZZY- IT FEELS LIKE THE STAIRS WERE SWAYIN'!
CLARABELLE WILL - - BE - - S'PRISED - PFOOOF!!!
NO — END - - TO — THESE —
WHAT TH'! OOO-WOWF!
PLOFF!
G-GOSH! WHAT HAPPENED?
JUST BECAUSE YOU COULDN'T TAKE THE CHAIR UPSTAIRS IS NO REASON FOR LEAVIN' IT OUT HERE! BRING IT IN THE HOUSE THIS INSTANT!
10-21
WALT DISNEY

174. "CHAIR" DID IT GO?

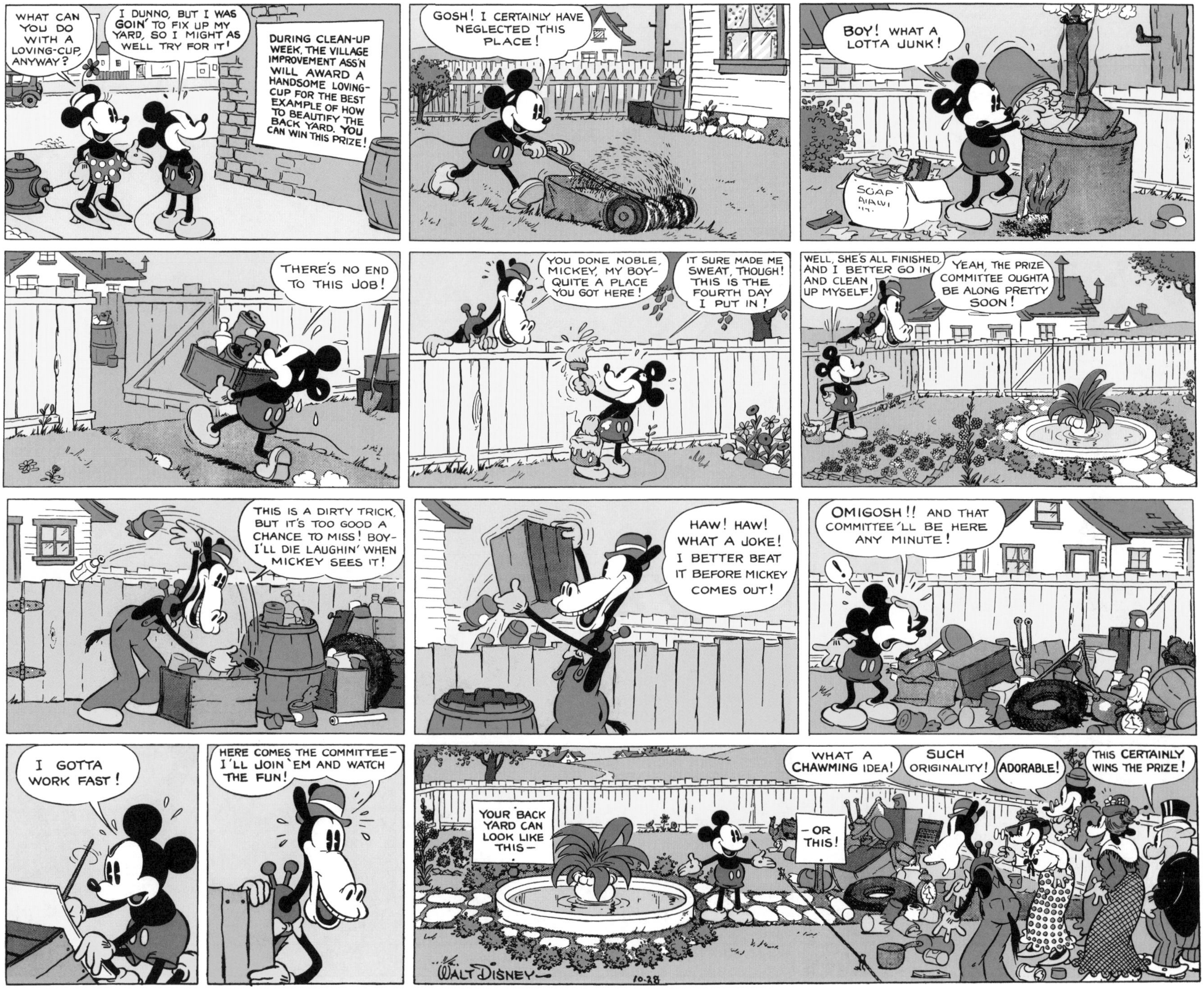
WHAT CAN YOU DO WITH A LOVING-CUP, ANYWAY?
I DUNNO, BUT I WAS GOIN' TO FIX UP MY YARD, SO I MIGHT AS WELL TRY FOR IT!
DURING CLEAN-UP WEEK, THE VILLAGE IMPROVEMENT ASS'N WILL AWARD A HANDSOME LOVING-CUP FOR THE BEST EXAMPLE OF HOW TO BEAUTIFY THE BACK YARD. YOU CAN WIN THIS PRIZE!
GOSH! I CERTAINLY HAVE NEGLECTED THIS PLACE!
BOY! WHAT A LOTTA JUNK!
SOAP
THERE'S NO END TO THIS JOB!
YOU DONE NOBLE, MICKEY, MY BOY-QUITE A PLACE YOU GOT HERE!
IT SURE MADE ME SWEAT, THOUGH! THIS IS THE FOURTH DAY I PUT IN!
WELL, SHE'S ALL FINISHED, AND I BETTER GO IN AND CLEAN UP MYSELF!
YEAH, THE PRIZE COMMITTEE OUGHTA BE ALONG PRETTY SOON!
THIS IS A DIRTY TRICK, BUT IT'S TOO GOOD A CHANCE TO MISS! BOY-I'LL DIE LAUGHIN' WHEN MICKEY SEES IT!
HAW! HAW! WHAT A JOKE! I BETTER BEAT IT BEFORE MICKEY COMES OUT!
OMIGOSH!! AND THAT COMMITTEE'LL BE HERE ANY MINUTE!
!
I GOTTA WORK FAST!
HERE COMES THE COMMITTEE-I'LL JOIN 'EM AND WATCH THE FUN!
YOUR BACK YARD CAN LOOK LIKE THIS-
-OR THIS!
WHAT A CHAWMING IDEA!
SUCH ORIGINALITY!
ADORABLE!
THIS CERTAINLY WINS THE PRIZE!
WALT DISNEY
10-28

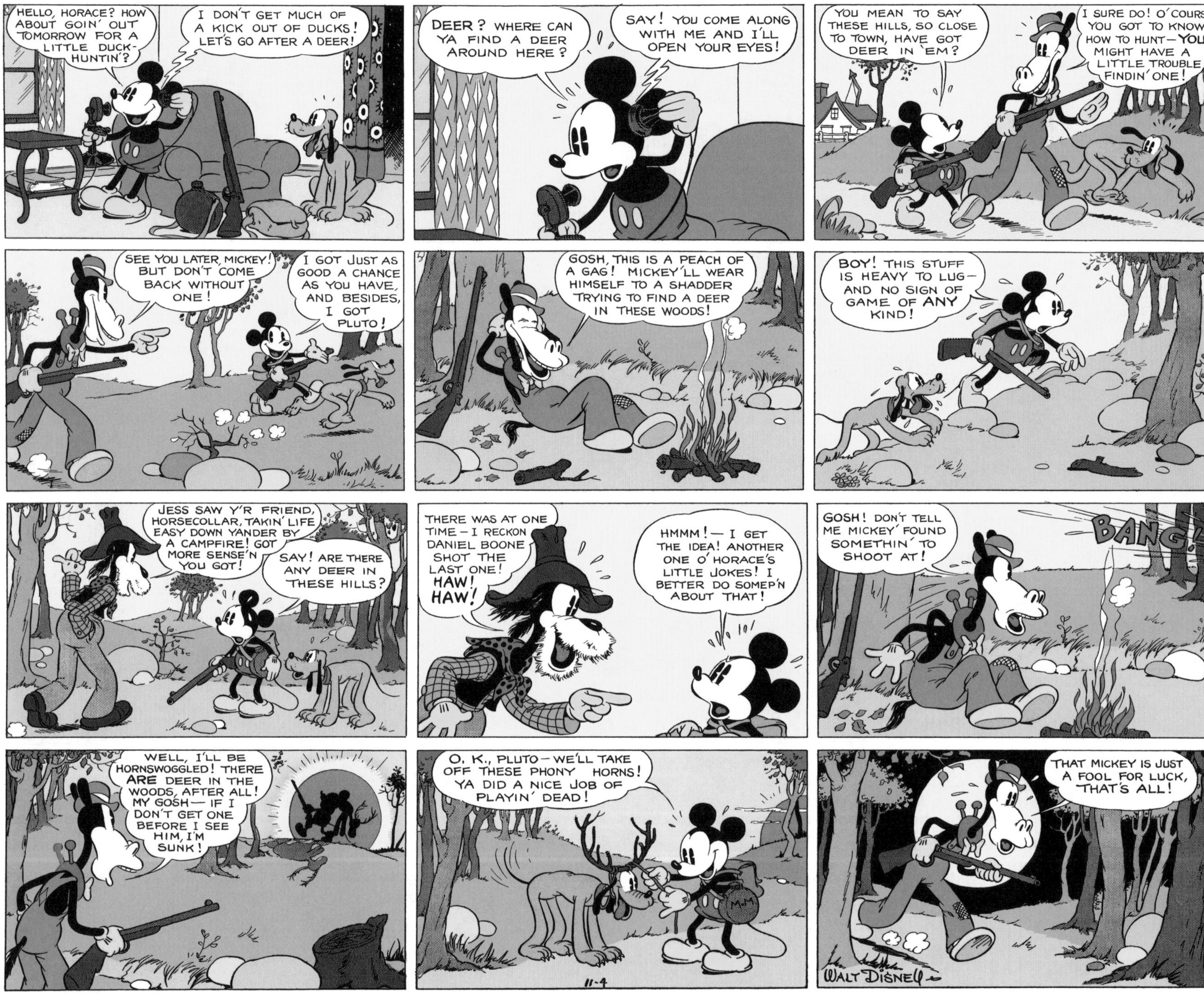
HELLO, HORACE? HOW ABOUT GOIN' OUT TOMORROW FOR A LITTLE DUCK-HUNTIN'?
I DON'T GET MUCH OF A KICK OUT OF DUCKS! LET'S GO AFTER A DEER!
DEER? WHERE CAN YA FIND A DEER AROUND HERE?
SAY! YOU COME ALONG WITH ME AND I'LL OPEN YOUR EYES!
YOU MEAN TO SAY THESE HILLS, SO CLOSE TO TOWN, HAVE GOT DEER IN 'EM?
I SURE DO! O'COURSE, YOU GOT TO KNOW HOW TO HUNT—YOU MIGHT HAVE A LITTLE TROUBLE FINDIN' ONE!
SEE YOU LATER, MICKEY! BUT DON'T COME BACK WITHOUT ONE!
I GOT JUST AS GOOD A CHANCE AS YOU HAVE, AND BESIDES, I GOT PLUTO!
GOSH, THIS IS A PEACH OF A GAG! MICKEY'LL WEAR HIMSELF TO A SHADDER TRYING TO FIND A DEER IN THESE WOODS!
BOY! THIS STUFF IS HEAVY TO LUG— AND NO SIGN OF GAME OF ANY KIND!
JESS SAW Y'R FRIEND, HORSECOLLAR, TAKIN' LIFE EASY DOWN YANDER BY A CAMPFIRE! GOT MORE SENSE'N YOU GOT!
SAY! ARE THERE ANY DEER IN THESE HILLS?
THERE WAS AT ONE TIME—I RECKON DANIEL BOONE SHOT THE LAST ONE! HAW! HAW!
HMMM!—I GET THE IDEA! ANOTHER ONE O' HORACE'S LITTLE JOKES! I BETTER DO SOMEP'N ABOUT THAT!
GOSH! DON'T TELL ME MICKEY FOUND SOMETHIN' TO SHOOT AT!
BANG!
WELL, I'LL BE HORNSWOGGLED! THERE ARE DEER IN THE WOODS, AFTER ALL! MY GOSH—IF I DON'T GET ONE BEFORE I SEE HIM, I'M SUNK!
O.K., PLUTO—WE'LL TAKE OFF THESE PHONY HORNS! YA DID A NICE JOB OF PLAYIN' DEAD!
11-4
THAT MICKEY IS JUST A FOOL FOR LUCK, THAT'S ALL!
WALT DISNEY

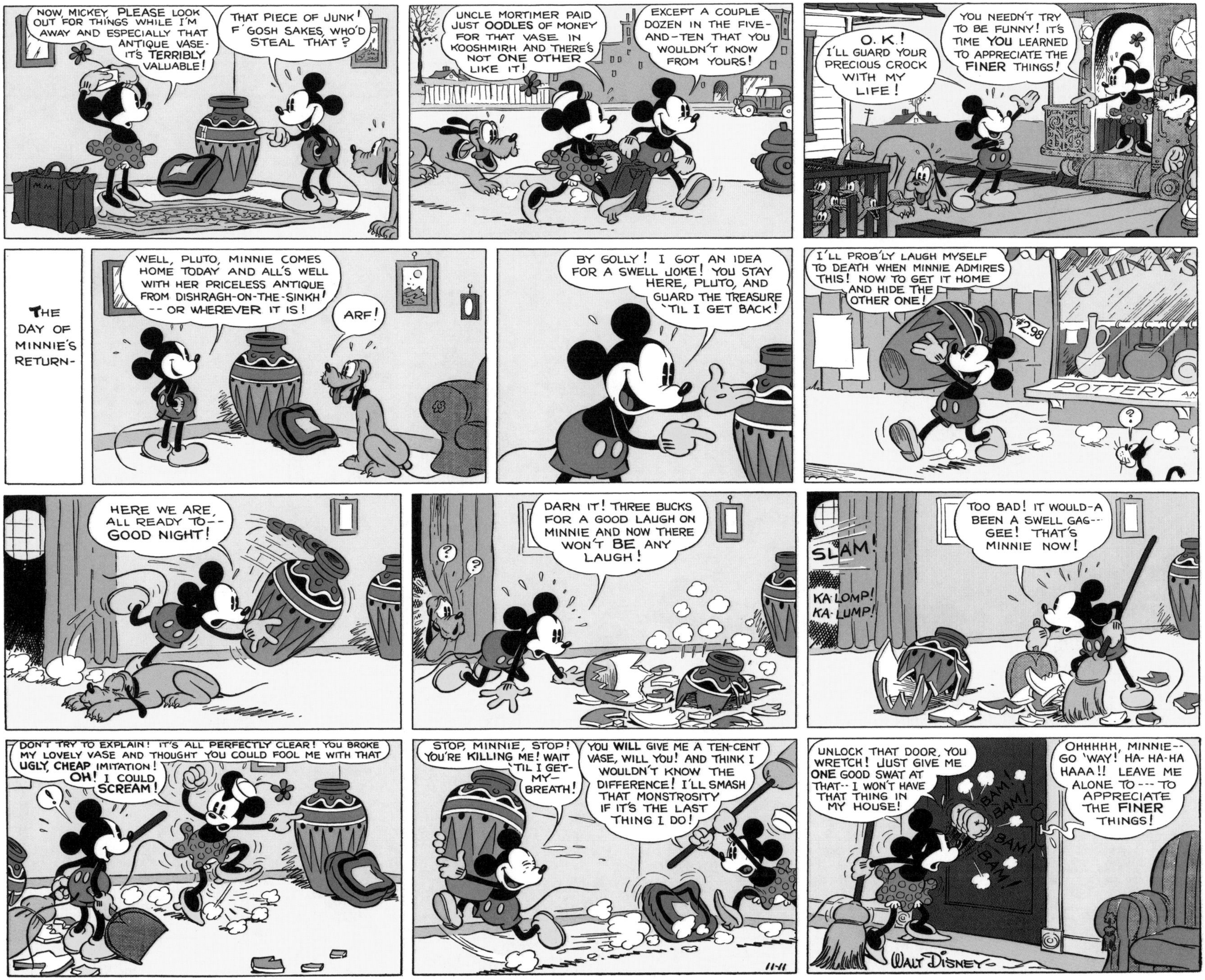
NOW, MICKEY, PLEASE LOOK OUT FOR THINGS WHILE I'M AWAY AND ESPECIALLY THAT ANTIQUE VASE-IT'S TERRIBLY VALUABLE!
THAT PIECE OF JUNK! F'GOSH SAKES, WHO'D STEAL THAT?
UNCLE MORTIMER PAID JUST OODLES OF MONEY FOR THAT VASE IN KOOSHMIRH AND THERE'S NOT ONE OTHER LIKE IT!
EXCEPT A COUPLE DOZEN IN THE FIVE-AND-TEN THAT YOU WOULDN'T KNOW FROM YOURS!
O.K.! I'LL GUARD YOUR PRECIOUS CROCK WITH MY LIFE!
YOU NEEDN'T TRY TO BE FUNNY! IT'S TIME YOU LEARNED TO APPRECIATE THE FINER THINGS!
THE DAY OF MINNIE'S RETURN-
WELL, PLUTO, MINNIE COMES HOME TODAY AND ALL'S WELL WITH HER PRICELESS ANTIQUE FROM DISHRAGH-ON-THE-SINKH! -- OR WHEREVER IT IS!
ARF!
BY GOLLY! I GOT AN IDEA FOR A SWELL JOKE! YOU STAY HERE, PLUTO, AND GUARD THE TREASURE 'TIL I GET BACK!
I'LL PROB'LY LAUGH MYSELF TO DEATH WHEN MINNIE ADMIRES THIS! NOW TO GET IT HOME AND HIDE THE OTHER ONE!
$2.98
CHINA'S
POTTERY AN
HERE WE ARE, ALL READY TO-- GOOD NIGHT!
DARN IT! THREE BUCKS FOR A GOOD LAUGH ON MINNIE AND NOW THERE WON'T BE ANY LAUGH!
SLAM!
KA-LOMP! KA-LUMP!
TOO BAD! IT WOULD-A BEEN A SWELL GAG-- GEE! THAT'S MINNIE NOW!
DON'T TRY TO EXPLAIN! IT'S ALL PERFECTLY CLEAR! YOU BROKE MY LOVELY VASE AND THOUGHT YOU COULD FOOL ME WITH THAT UGLY, CHEAP IMITATION! OH! I COULD SCREAM!
STOP, MINNIE, STOP! YOU'RE KILLING ME! WAIT 'TIL I GET-MY-BREATH!
YOU WILL GIVE ME A TEN-CENT VASE, WILL YOU! AND THINK I WOULDN'T KNOW THE DIFFERENCE! I'LL SMASH THAT MONSTROSITY IF IT'S THE LAST THING I DO!
11-11
UNLOCK THAT DOOR, YOU WRETCH! JUST GIVE ME ONE GOOD SWAT AT THAT-- I WON'T HAVE THAT THING IN MY HOUSE!
BAM! BAM! BAM! BAM!
OHHHHH, MINNIE-- GO 'WAY! HA-HA-HA HAAA!! LEAVE ME ALONE TO--- TO APPRECIATE THE FINER THINGS!
WALT DISNEY

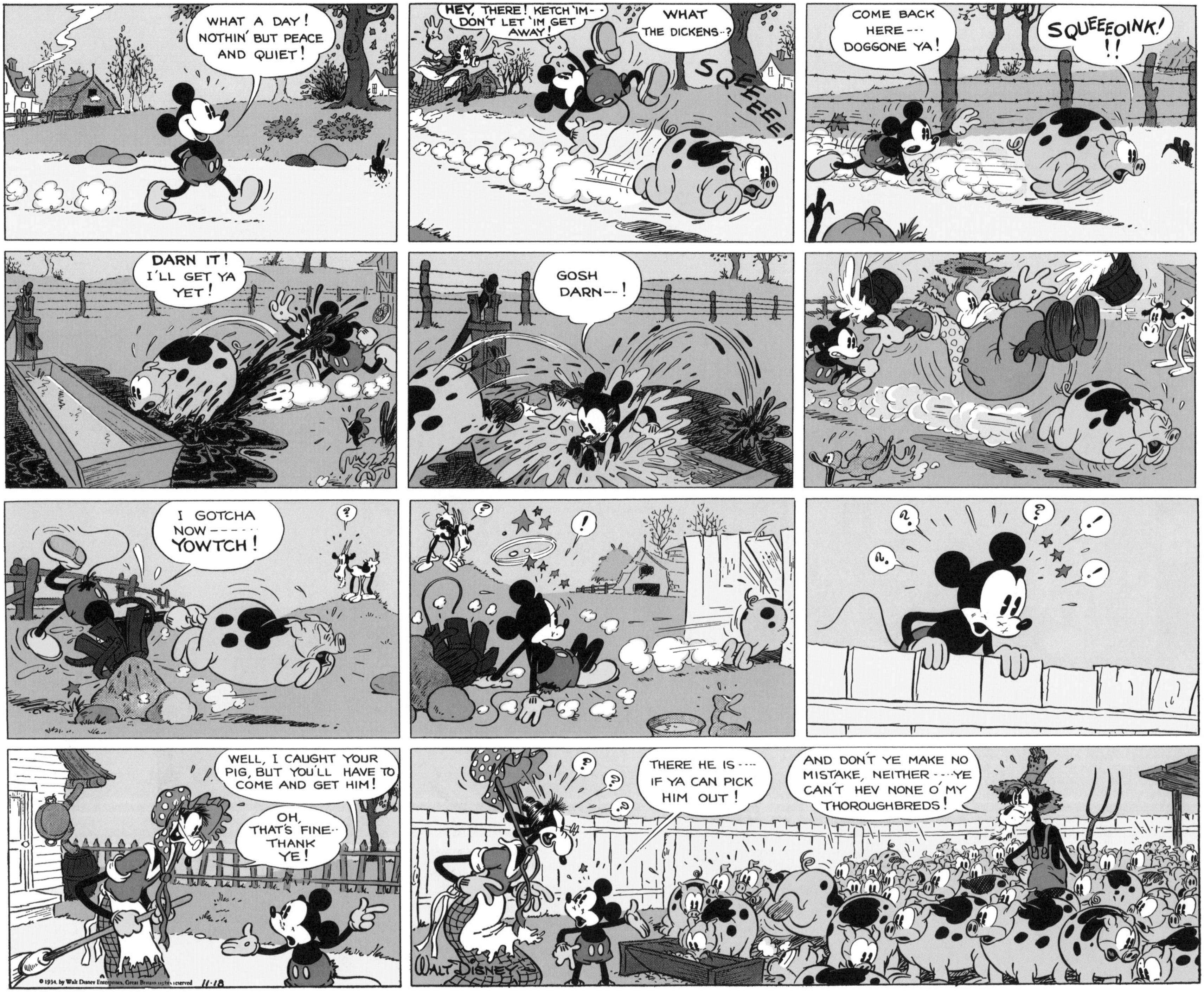
WHAT A DAY! NOTHIN' BUT PEACE AND QUIET!
HEY, THERE! KETCH 'IM-- DON'T LET 'IM GET AWAY!
WHAT THE DICKENS--?
SQUEEEEE!
COME BACK HERE--- DOGGONE YA!
SQUEEEEOINK! !!
DARN IT! I'LL GET YA YET!
GOSH DARN--!
I GOTCHA NOW------ YOWTCH!
WELL, I CAUGHT YOUR PIG, BUT YOU'LL HAVE TO COME AND GET HIM!
OH, THAT'S FINE-- THANK YE!
© 1934, by Walt Disney Enterprises, Great Britain rights reserved 11-18
THERE HE IS---- IF YA CAN PICK HIM OUT!
AND DON'T YE MAKE NO MISTAKE, NEITHER----YE CAN'T HEV NONE O' MY THOROUGHBREDS!
WALT DISNEY

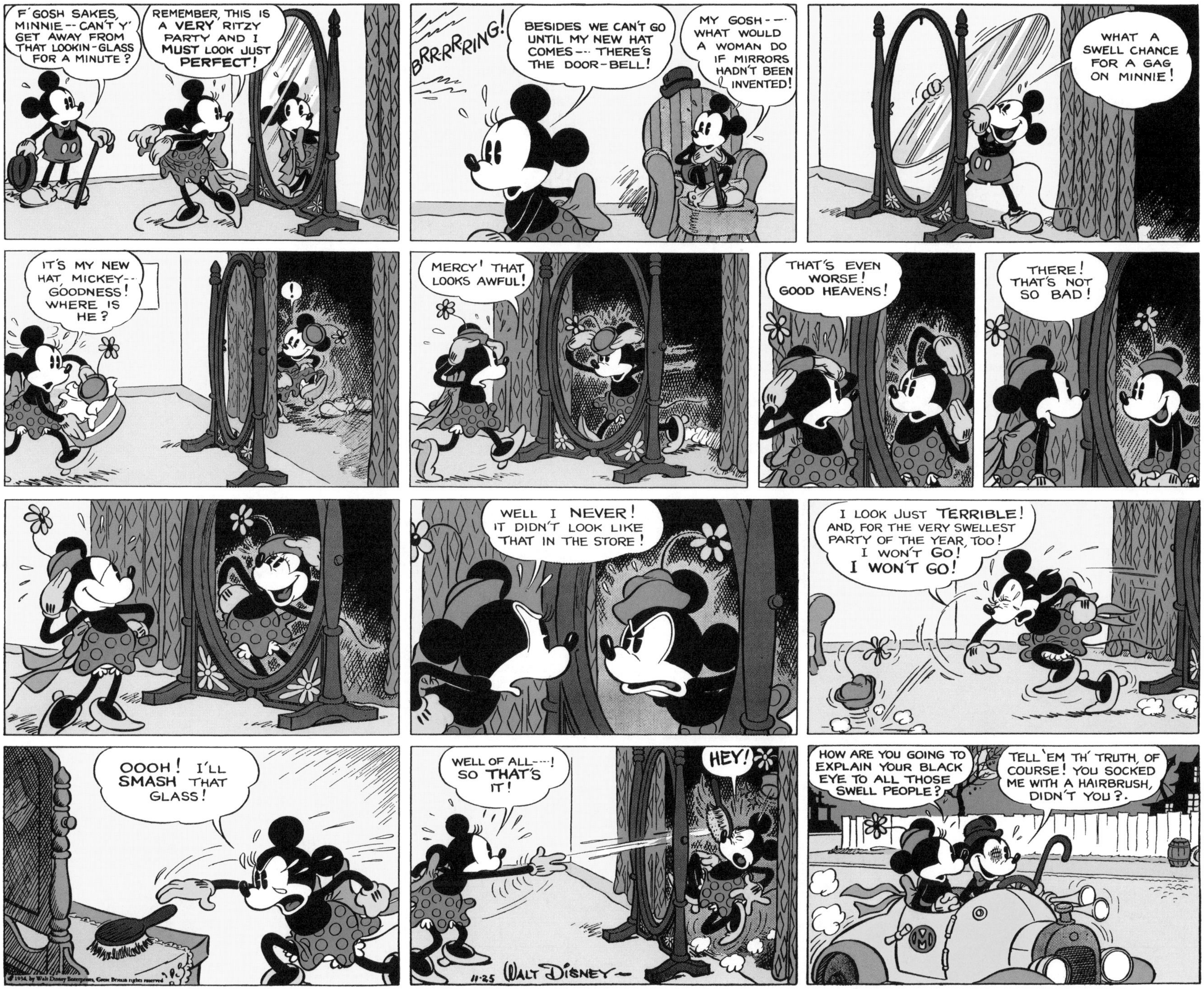
F' GOSH SAKES, MINNIE -- CAN'T Y' GET AWAY FROM THAT LOOKIN-GLASS FOR A MINUTE?
REMEMBER, THIS IS A VERY RITZY PARTY AND I MUST LOOK JUST PERFECT!
BRR-R-RRING!
BESIDES WE CAN'T GO UNTIL MY NEW HAT COMES -- THERE'S THE DOOR-BELL!
MY GOSH --- WHAT WOULD A WOMAN DO IF MIRRORS HADN'T BEEN INVENTED!
WHAT A SWELL CHANCE FOR A GAG ON MINNIE!
IT'S MY NEW HAT, MICKEY -- GOODNESS! WHERE IS HE?
!
MERCY! THAT LOOKS AWFUL!
THAT'S EVEN WORSE! GOOD HEAVENS!
THERE! THAT'S NOT SO BAD!
WELL I NEVER! IT DIDN'T LOOK LIKE THAT IN THE STORE!
I LOOK JUST TERRIBLE! AND, FOR THE VERY SWELLEST PARTY OF THE YEAR, TOO! I WON'T GO! I WON'T GO!
OOOH! I'LL SMASH THAT GLASS!
WELL OF ALL ---! SO THAT'S IT!
HEY!
11-25 WALT DISNEY
HOW ARE YOU GOING TO EXPLAIN YOUR BLACK EYE TO ALL THOSE SWELL PEOPLE?
TELL 'EM TH' TRUTH, OF COURSE! YOU SOCKED ME WITH A HAIRBRUSH, DIDN'T YOU?.

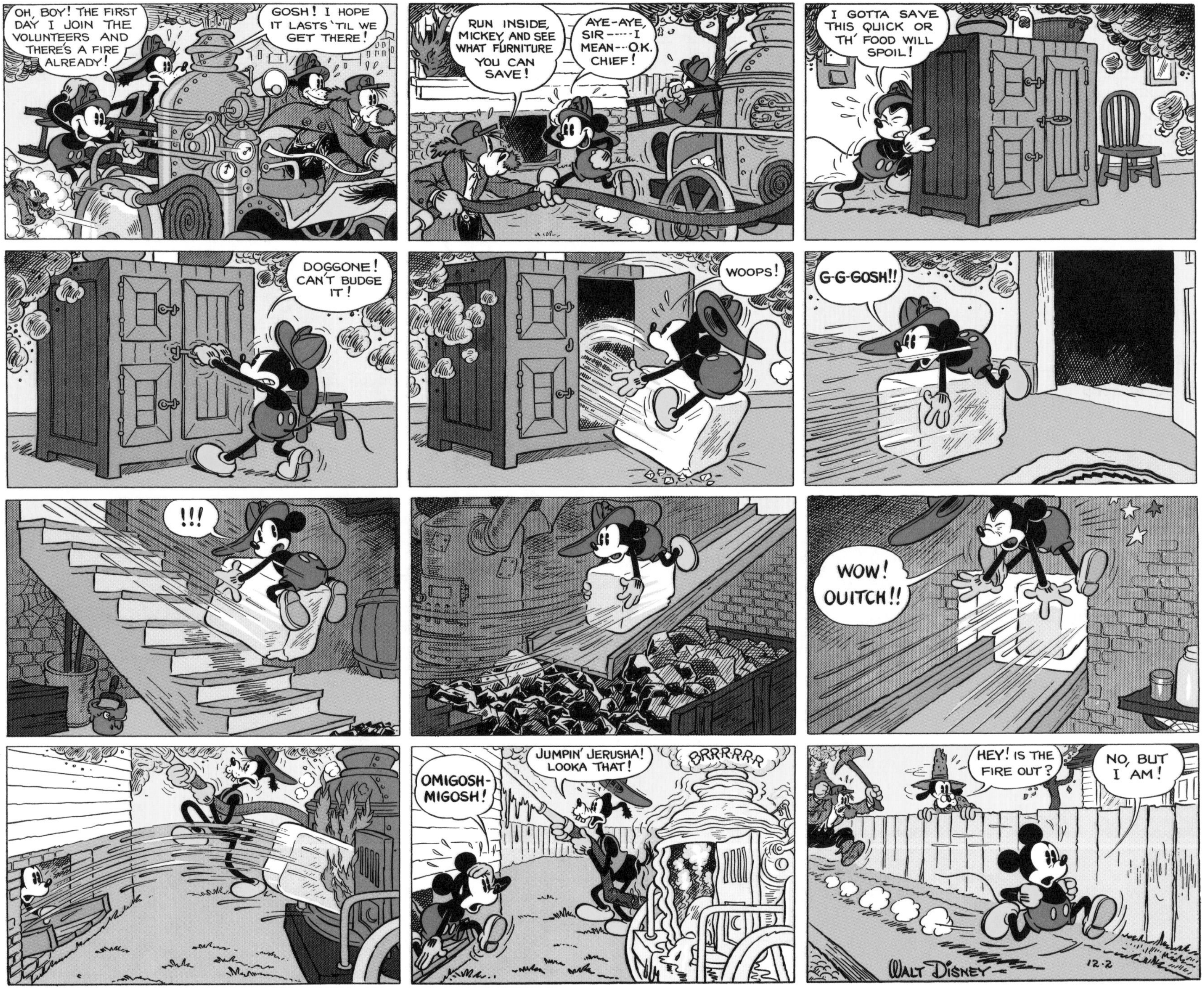
OH, BOY! THE FIRST DAY I JOIN THE VOLUNTEERS AND THERE'S A FIRE ALREADY!
GOSH! I HOPE IT LASTS 'TIL WE GET THERE!
RUN INSIDE, MICKEY, AND SEE WHAT FURNITURE YOU CAN SAVE!
AYE-AYE, SIR----I MEAN---O.K. CHIEF!
I GOTTA SAVE THIS QUICK OR TH' FOOD WILL SPOIL!
DOGGONE! CAN'T BUDGE IT!
WOOPS!
G-G-GOSH!!
!!!
WOW! OUITCH!!
OMIGOSH-MIGOSH!
JUMPIN' JERUSHA! LOOKA THAT!
BRRRRRR
HEY! IS THE FIRE OUT?
NO, BUT I AM!
WALT DISNEY
12-2

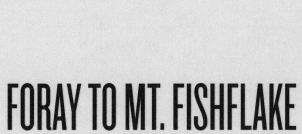

FORAY TO MT. FISHFLAKE

AND

GAG STRIPS

DECEMBER 9, 1934
–
FEBRUARY 10, 1935

MICKEY MOUSE

REGISTERED U.S. PATENT OFFICE

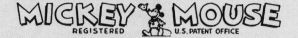

DEATH KNOCKS, FATE PESTERS

Disaster capitalism," a common term in the modern political dialogue, describes what happens when powerful, cynical oligarchs want to force profitable but unpopular ideas on their communities. Under normal conditions, one cannot easily make average citizens accept a war, a tax hike, or the privatization of public services. But in situations of duress—like a financial panic or an attack from abroad—pundits and talking heads might agree that "sacrifices" are needed, and some desperate common folk can be persuaded to accept the cynical oligarchs' ideas as answers.

The cynicism is redoubled when some oligarchs use their economic clout to create situations of duress on purpose. Induce a disaster, then push a "solution" that conveniently allows you to capitalize; from Nazis to factory bosses, many opportunistic power brokers have gone this route.

Floyd Gottfredson was no despot, but in the mid-1930s, he used something like disaster capitalism—however unwittingly—as a means of shaking up Mickey Mouse's comics world. For Mickey's other world, his world on screen, was changing. Once dominated by musicales with Horace Horsecollar and Clarabelle, Mickey's cartoon universe was becoming one ruled by Goofy, Donald Duck, and crisis-based comedy.

Late 1934's "Foray to Mount Fishflake" uses nothing less than a natural disaster to transform Mickey's strip environment accordingly. When Mickey, Minnie, Horace, and Clarabelle set out to climb a mountain, the atmosphere is reminiscent of the earlier "Dr. Oofgay's Secret Serum": two close-knit couples, bickering like family, are heading off on a grand adventure. When Dippy Dawg joins them, he takes the role of an intruder: much as in the earlier "Lair of Wolf Barker," he is a tagalong pest whose company is often unwanted. But in a telling change, Mickey wants Dippy this time—and in an even more interesting shift, a dark, dangerous night physically separates Mickey and Dippy from the rest of their cohorts. What began as a family escapade for Mickey and his older buddies becomes a pulse-pounding, one-on-one quest for Mickey and a newer friend; facing deadly peril, Mickey and Dippy grow closer together.

We are witness as Gottfredson uses his own kind of fabricated disaster to change the status quo: no lesser duress could force headstrong Horace and Clarabelle from their key co-star positions.

While Goofy—as Dippy would soon be renamed—still had some maturing to do, the seeds of his later buddy relationship were now firmly planted; the lights were literally turned out on the mood of the earlier stories. The profiting party in this feat of "comics disaster capitalism" may not have fully understood how he capitalized; but then, Goofy's understanding of things always was a bit eccentric.

As the Goof slowly became less a pest, more a pal, another pest arrived on the scene. in February 1935, an obstreperous Duck flew in with a lot of fuss and feathers—feathers oddly colored yellow at first! Turn the pages and watch as Disney history hatches before our eyes. [DG]

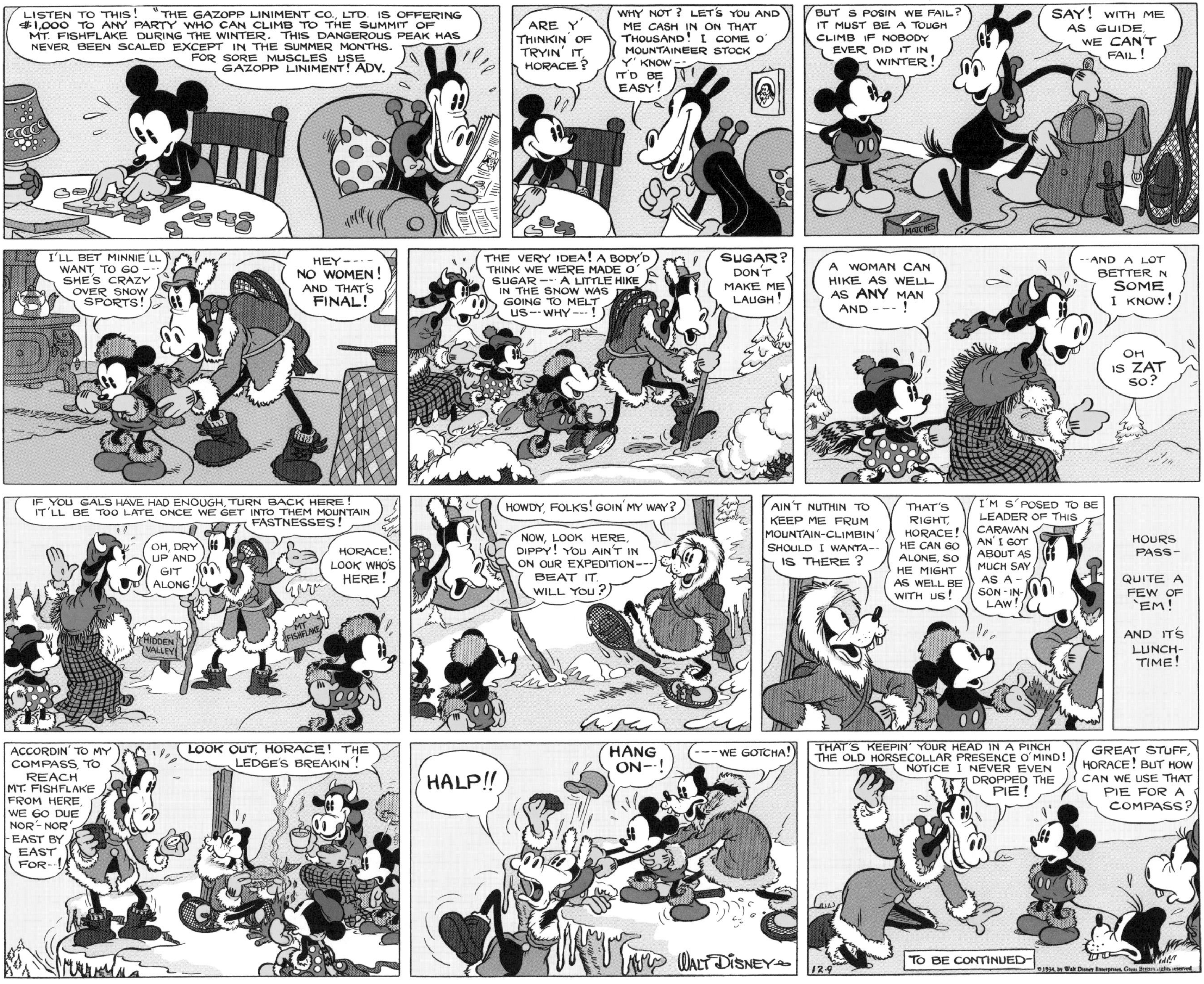
LISTEN TO THIS! "THE GAZOPP LINIMENT CO., LTD. IS OFFERING $1,000 TO ANY PARTY WHO CAN CLIMB TO THE SUMMIT OF MT. FISHFLAKE DURING THE WINTER. THIS DANGEROUS PEAK HAS NEVER BEEN SCALED EXCEPT IN THE SUMMER MONTHS. FOR SORE MUSCLES USE GAZOPP LINIMENT! ADV.
ARE Y' THINKIN' OF TRYIN' IT, HORACE?
WHY NOT? LET'S YOU AND ME CASH IN ON THAT THOUSAND! I COME O' MOUNTAINEER STOCK Y' KNOW -- IT'D BE EASY!
BUT S'POSIN WE FAIL? IT MUST BE A TOUGH CLIMB IF NOBODY EVER DID IT IN WINTER!
SAY! WITH ME AS GUIDE, WE CAN'T FAIL!
MATCHES
I'LL BET MINNIE'LL WANT TO GO --- SHE'S CRAZY OVER SNOW SPORTS!
HEY---- NO WOMEN! AND THAT'S FINAL!
THE VERY IDEA! A BODY'D THINK WE WERE MADE O' SUGAR --- A LITTLE HIKE IN THE SNOW WAS GOING TO MELT US -- WHY ---!
SUGAR? DON'T MAKE ME LAUGH!
A WOMAN CAN HIKE AS WELL AS ANY MAN AND ---!
--AND A LOT BETTER N SOME I KNOW!
OH IS ZAT SO?
IF YOU GALS HAVE HAD ENOUGH, TURN BACK HERE! IT'LL BE TOO LATE ONCE WE GET INTO THEM MOUNTAIN FASTNESSES!
OH, DRY UP AND GIT ALONG!
HORACE! LOOK WHO'S HERE!
HIDDEN VALLEY
MT FISHFLAKE
HOWDY, FOLKS! GOIN' MY WAY?
NOW, LOOK HERE, DIPPY! YOU AIN'T IN ON OUR EXPEDITION--- BEAT IT, WILL YOU?
AIN'T NUTHIN TO KEEP ME FRUM MOUNTAIN-CLIMBIN' SHOULD I WANTA-- IS THERE?
THAT'S RIGHT, HORACE! HE CAN GO ALONE, SO HE MIGHT AS WELL BE WITH US!
I'M S'POSED TO BE LEADER OF THIS CARAVAN AN' I GOT ABOUT AS MUCH SAY AS A SON-IN-LAW!
HOURS PASS- QUITE A FEW OF 'EM! AND IT'S LUNCH-TIME!
ACCORDIN' TO MY COMPASS, TO REACH MT. FISHFLAKE FROM HERE, WE GO DUE NOR'-NOR'-EAST BY EAST FOR--!
LOOK OUT, HORACE! THE LEDGE'S BREAKIN'!
HALP!!
HANG ON--!
---WE GOTCHA!
WALT DISNEY
12-9
THAT'S KEEPIN' YOUR HEAD IN A PINCH THE OLD HORSECOLLAR PRESENCE O' MIND! NOTICE I NEVER EVEN DROPPED THE PIE!
GREAT STUFF, HORACE! BUT HOW CAN WE USE THAT PIE FOR A COMPASS?
TO BE CONTINUED-
© 1934, by Walt Disney Enterprises, Great Britain rights reserved.

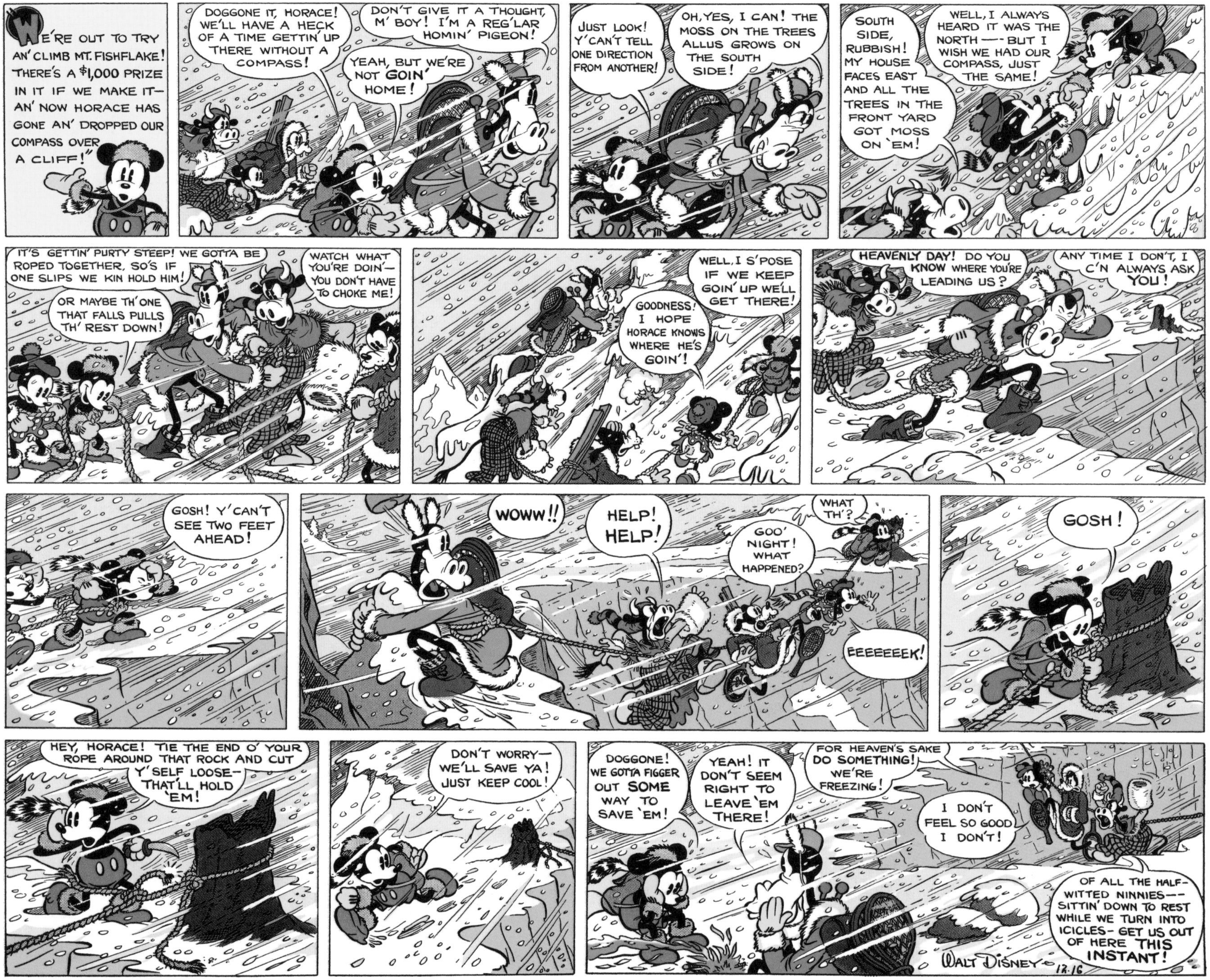
WE'RE OUT TO TRY AN' CLIMB MT. FISHFLAKE! THERE'S A $1,000 PRIZE IN IT IF WE MAKE IT— AN' NOW HORACE HAS GONE AN' DROPPED OUR COMPASS OVER A CLIFF!"
DOGGONE IT, HORACE! WE'LL HAVE A HECK OF A TIME GETTIN' UP THERE WITHOUT A COMPASS!
DON'T GIVE IT A THOUGHT, M' BOY! I'M A REG'LAR HOMIN' PIGEON!
YEAH, BUT WE'RE NOT GOIN' HOME!
JUST LOOK! Y'CAN'T TELL ONE DIRECTION FROM ANOTHER!
OH, YES, I CAN! THE MOSS ON THE TREES ALLUS GROWS ON THE SOUTH SIDE!
SOUTH SIDE, RUBBISH! MY HOUSE FACES EAST AND ALL THE TREES IN THE FRONT YARD GOT MOSS ON 'EM!
WELL, I ALWAYS HEARD IT WAS THE NORTH —- BUT I WISH WE HAD OUR COMPASS, JUST THE SAME!
IT'S GETTIN' PURTY STEEP! WE GOTTA BE ROPED TOGETHER, SO'S IF ONE SLIPS WE KIN HOLD HIM!
OR MAYBE TH' ONE THAT FALLS PULLS TH' REST DOWN!
WATCH WHAT YOU'RE DOIN'— YOU DON'T HAVE TO CHOKE ME!
WELL, I S'POSE IF WE KEEP GOIN' UP WE'LL GET THERE!
GOODNESS! I HOPE HORACE KNOWS WHERE HE'S GOIN'!
HEAVENLY DAY! DO YOU KNOW WHERE YOU'RE LEADING US?
ANY TIME I DON'T, I C'N ALWAYS ASK YOU!
GOSH! Y'CAN'T SEE TWO FEET AHEAD!
WOWW!!
HELP! HELP!
WHAT TH'?
GOO' NIGHT! WHAT HAPPENED?
EEEEEEEK!
GOSH!
HEY, HORACE! TIE THE END O' YOUR ROPE AROUND THAT ROCK AND CUT Y'SELF LOOSE— THAT'LL HOLD 'EM!
DON'T WORRY— WE'LL SAVE YA! JUST KEEP COOL!
DOGGONE! WE GOTTA FIGGER OUT SOME WAY TO SAVE 'EM!
YEAH! IT DON'T SEEM RIGHT TO LEAVE 'EM THERE!
FOR HEAVEN'S SAKE DO SOMETHING! WE'RE FREEZING!
I DON'T FEEL SO GOOD I DON'T!
OF ALL THE HALF-WITTED NINNIES— SITTIN' DOWN TO REST WHILE WE TURN INTO ICICLES— GET US OUT OF HERE THIS INSTANT!
WALT DISNEY 12.16

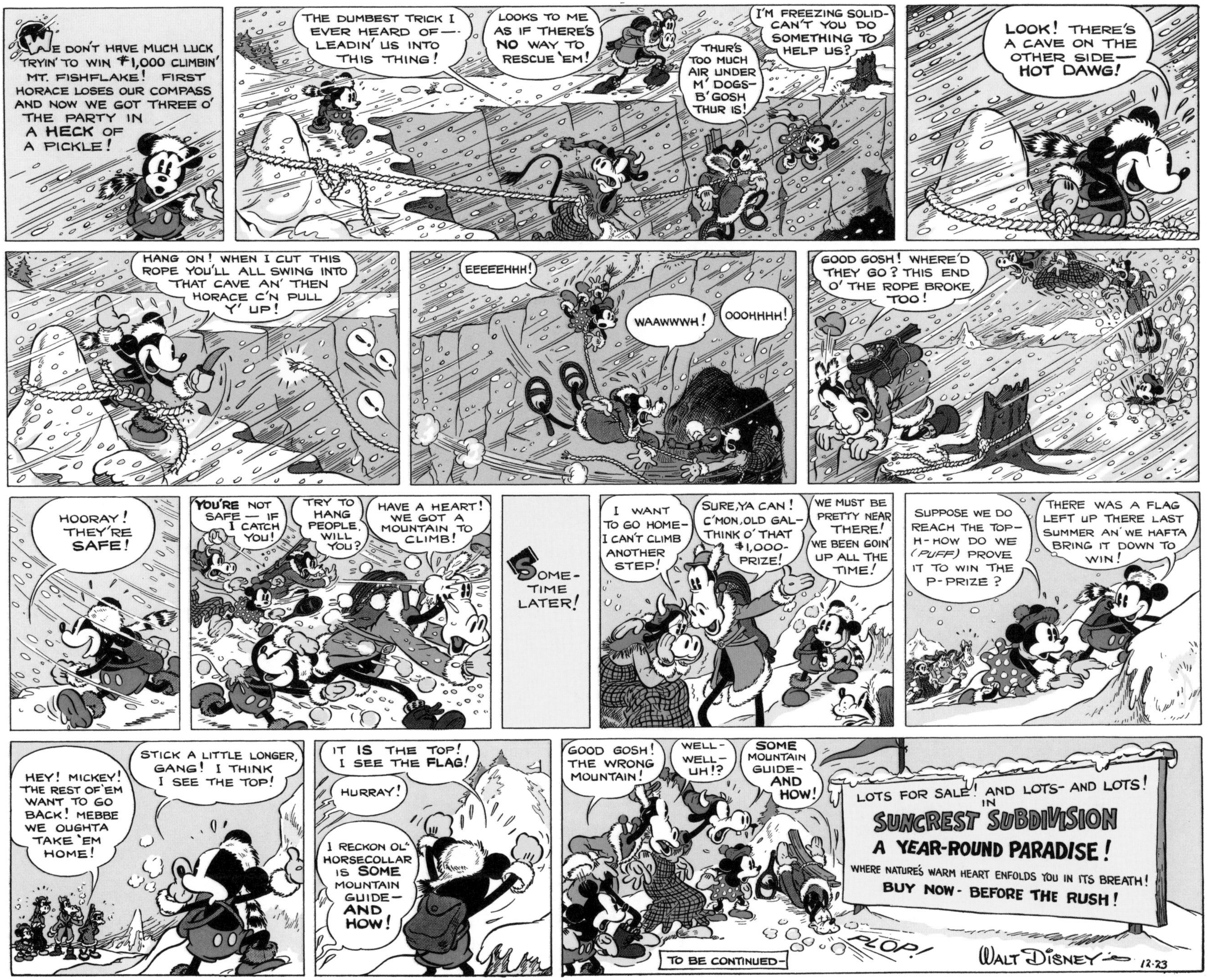
WE DON'T HAVE MUCH LUCK TRYIN' TO WIN $1,000 CLIMBIN' MT. FISHFLAKE! FIRST HORACE LOSES OUR COMPASS AND NOW WE GOT THREE O' THE PARTY IN A HECK OF A PICKLE!
THE DUMBEST TRICK I EVER HEARD OF— LEADIN' US INTO THIS THING!
LOOKS TO ME AS IF THERE'S NO WAY TO RESCUE 'EM!
I'M FREEZING SOLID— CAN'T YOU DO SOMETHING TO HELP US?
THUR'S TOO MUCH AIR UNDER M' DOGS— B'GOSH THUR IS!
LOOK! THERE'S A CAVE ON THE OTHER SIDE— HOT DAWG!
HANG ON! WHEN I CUT THIS ROPE YOU'LL ALL SWING INTO THAT CAVE AN' THEN HORACE C'N PULL Y' UP!
EEEEEHHH!
WAAWWWH!
OOOHHHH!
GOOD GOSH! WHERE'D THEY GO? THIS END O' THE ROPE BROKE, TOO!
HOORAY! THEY'RE SAFE!
YOU'RE NOT SAFE — IF I CATCH YOU!
TRY TO HANG PEOPLE, WILL YOU?
HAVE A HEART! WE GOT A MOUNTAIN TO CLIMB!
SOME-TIME LATER!
I WANT TO GO HOME— I CAN'T CLIMB ANOTHER STEP!
SURE, YA CAN! C'MON, OLD GAL— THINK O' THAT $1,000-PRIZE!
WE MUST BE PRETTY NEAR THERE! WE BEEN GOIN' UP ALL THE TIME!
SUPPOSE WE DO REACH THE TOP— H-HOW DO WE (PUFF) PROVE IT TO WIN THE P-PRIZE?
THERE WAS A FLAG LEFT UP THERE LAST SUMMER AN' WE HAFTA BRING IT DOWN TO WIN!
HEY! MICKEY! THE REST OF 'EM WANT TO GO BACK! MEBBE WE OUGHTA TAKE 'EM HOME!
STICK A LITTLE LONGER, GANG! I THINK I SEE THE TOP!
IT IS THE TOP! I SEE THE FLAG!
HURRAY!
I RECKON OL' HORSECOLLAR IS SOME MOUNTAIN GUIDE— AND HOW!
GOOD GOSH! THE WRONG MOUNTAIN!
WELL— WELL— UH!?
SOME MOUNTAIN GUIDE— AND HOW!
LOTS FOR SALE! AND LOTS— AND LOTS! IN
SUNCREST SUBDIVISION
A YEAR-ROUND PARADISE!
WHERE NATURE'S WARM HEART ENFOLDS YOU IN ITS BREATH!
BUY NOW - BEFORE THE RUSH!
PLOP!
TO BE CONTINUED—
WALT DISNEY 12-23

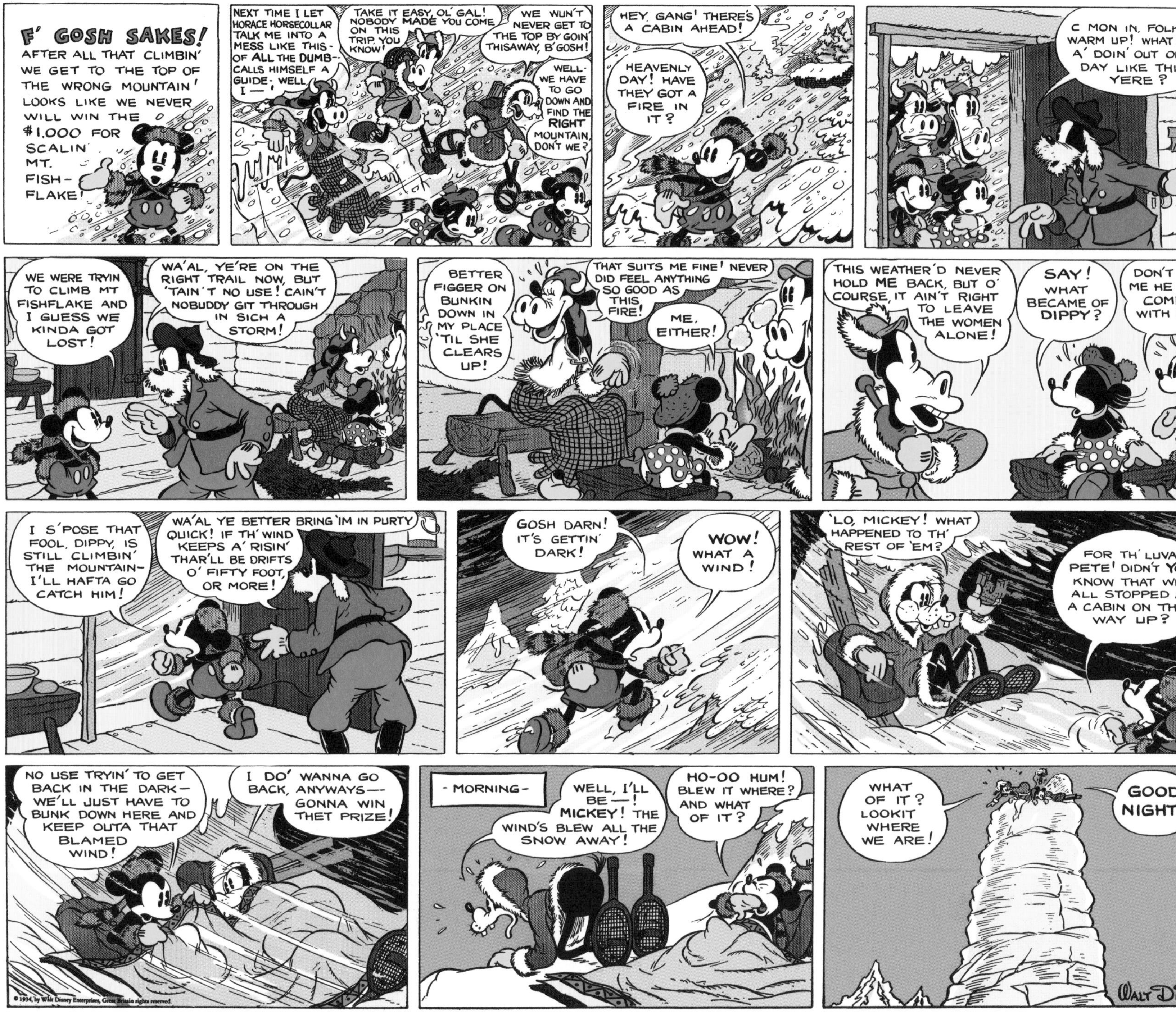
F' GOSH SAKES! AFTER ALL THAT CLIMBIN' WE GET TO THE TOP OF THE WRONG MOUNTAIN' LOOKS LIKE WE NEVER WILL WIN THE $1,000 FOR SCALIN' MT. FISH-FLAKE!
NEXT TIME I LET HORACE HORSECOLLAR TALK ME INTO A MESS LIKE THIS-OF ALL THE DUMB-CALLS HIMSELF A GUIDE-WELL, I—!
TAKE IT EASY, OL' GAL! NOBODY MADE YOU COME ON THIS TRIP, YOU KNOW!
WE WUN'T NEVER GET TO THE TOP BY GOIN' THISAWAY, B'GOSH!
WELL-WE HAVE TO GO DOWN AND FIND THE RIGHT MOUNTAIN, DON'T WE?
HEY, GANG! THERE'S A CABIN AHEAD!
HEAVENLY DAY! HAVE THEY GOT A FIRE IN IT?
C'MON IN, FOLKS, AN WARM UP! WHAT BE YE A' DOIN' OUT ON A DAY LIKE THISH YERE?
KEROS
WE WERE TRYIN TO CLIMB MT FISHFLAKE AND I GUESS WE KINDA GOT LOST!
WA'AL, YE'RE ON THE RIGHT TRAIL NOW, BUT 'TAIN'T NO USE! CAIN'T NOBUDDY GIT THROUGH IN SICH A STORM!
BETTER FIGGER ON BUNKIN DOWN IN MY PLACE 'TIL SHE CLEARS UP!
THAT SUITS ME FINE! NEVER DID FEEL ANYTHING SO GOOD AS THIS FIRE!
ME, EITHER!
THIS WEATHER'D NEVER HOLD ME BACK, BUT O' COURSE, IT AIN'T RIGHT TO LEAVE THE WOMEN ALONE!
SAY! WHAT BECAME OF DIPPY?
DON'T TELL ME HE DIDN'T COME IN WITH US!
I S'POSE THAT FOOL, DIPPY, IS STILL CLIMBIN' THE MOUNTAIN-I'LL HAFTA GO CATCH HIM!
WA'AL YE BETTER BRING 'IM IN PURTY QUICK! IF TH' WIND KEEPS A' RISIN' THAR'LL BE DRIFTS O' FIFTY FOOT, OR MORE!
GOSH DARN! IT'S GETTIN' DARK!
WOW! WHAT A WIND!
'LO, MICKEY! WHAT HAPPENED TO TH' REST OF 'EM?
FOR TH' LUVA PETE! DIDN'T YOU KNOW THAT WE ALL STOPPED AT A CABIN ON THE WAY UP?
NO USE TRYIN' TO GET BACK IN THE DARK-WE'LL JUST HAVE TO BUNK DOWN HERE AND KEEP OUTA THAT BLAMED WIND!
I DO' WANNA GO BACK, ANYWAYS-GONNA WIN THET PRIZE!
© 1934, by Walt Disney Enterprises, Great Britain rights reserved.
-MORNING-
WELL, I'LL BE—! MICKEY! THE WIND'S BLEW ALL THE SNOW AWAY!
HO-OO HUM! BLEW IT WHERE? AND WHAT OF IT?
WHAT OF IT? LOOKIT WHERE WE ARE!
GOOD NIGHT!
12-30
WALT DISNEY

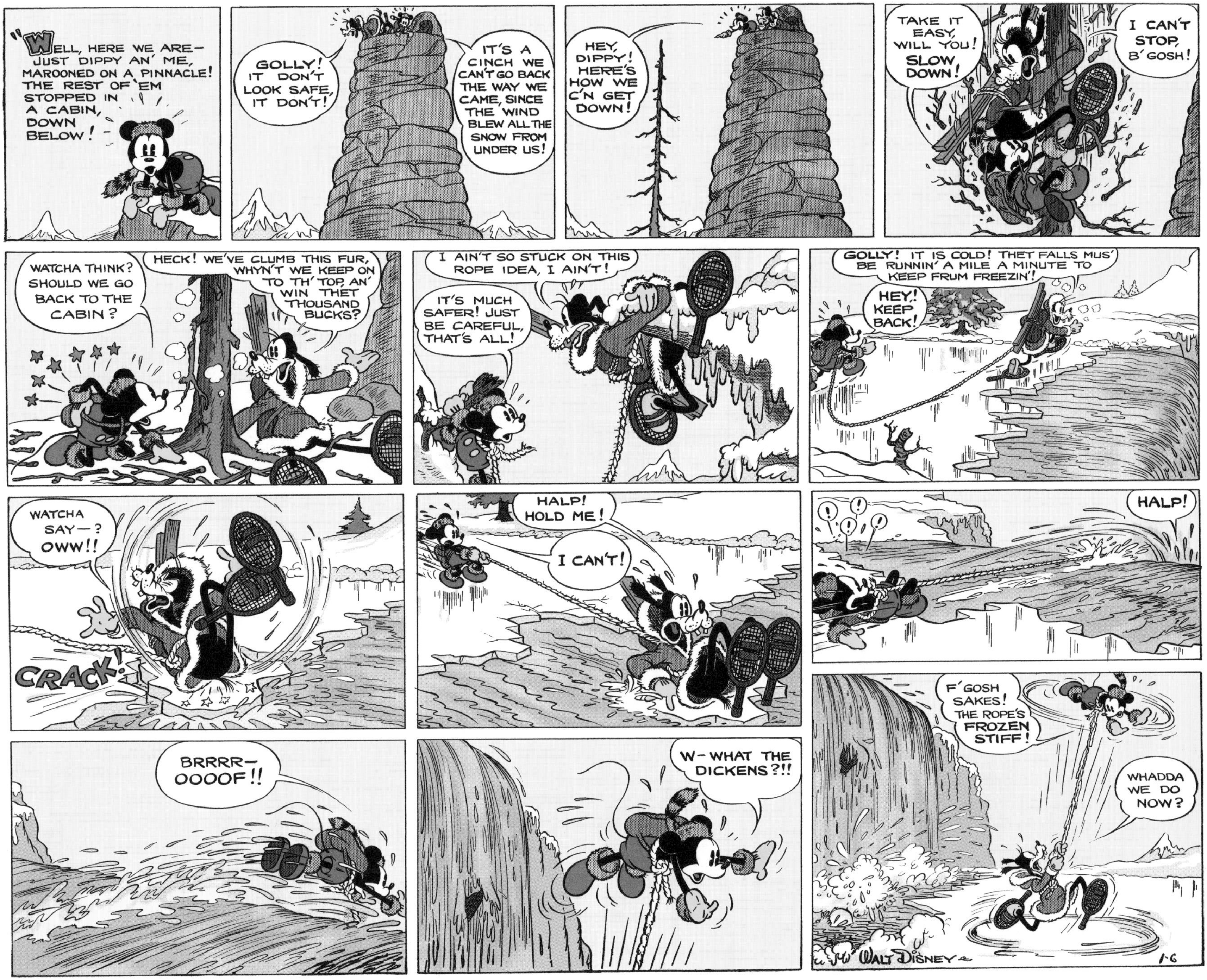
"WELL, HERE WE ARE— JUST DIPPY AN' ME, MAROONED ON A PINNACLE! THE REST OF 'EM STOPPED IN A CABIN, DOWN BELOW!
GOLLY! IT DON'T LOOK SAFE, IT DON'T!
IT'S A CINCH WE CAN'T GO BACK THE WAY WE CAME, SINCE THE WIND BLEW ALL THE SNOW FROM UNDER US!
HEY, DIPPY! HERE'S HOW WE C'N GET DOWN!
TAKE IT EASY, WILL YOU! SLOW DOWN!
I CAN'T STOP, B'GOSH!
WATCHA THINK? SHOULD WE GO BACK TO THE CABIN?
HECK! WE'VE CLUMB THIS FUR, WHYN'T WE KEEP ON TO TH' TOP, AN' WIN THET THOUSAND BUCKS?
I AIN'T SO STUCK ON THIS ROPE IDEA, I AIN'T!
IT'S MUCH SAFER! JUST BE CAREFUL, THAT'S ALL!
GOLLY! IT IS COLD! THET FALLS MUS' BE RUNNIN' A MILE A MINUTE TO KEEP FRUM FREEZIN'!
HEY! KEEP BACK!
WATCHA SAY—? OWW!!
CRACK!
HALP! HOLD ME!
I CAN'T!
HALP!
BRRRR— OOOOF!!
W-WHAT THE DICKENS?!!
F'GOSH SAKES! THE ROPE'S FROZEN STIFF!
WHADDA WE DO NOW?
WALT DISNEY
1-6

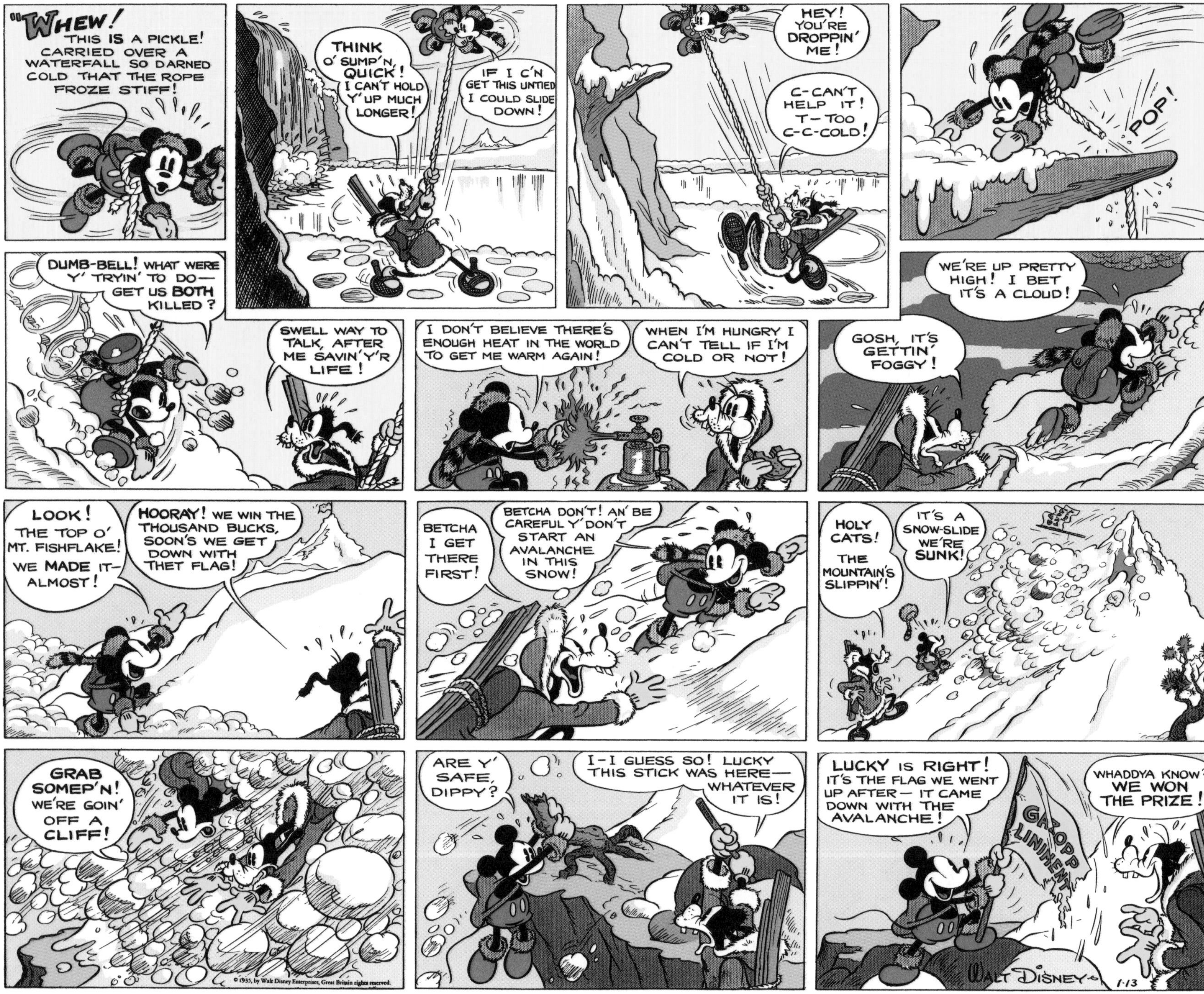
"WHEW! THIS IS A PICKLE! CARRIED OVER A WATERFALL SO DARNED COLD THAT THE ROPE FROZE STIFF!
THINK O' SUMP'N, QUICK! I CAN'T HOLD Y' UP MUCH LONGER!
IF I C'N GET THIS UNTIED I COULD SLIDE DOWN!
HEY! YOU'RE DROPPIN' ME!
C-CAN'T HELP IT! T-TOO C-C-COLD!
POP!
DUMB-BELL! WHAT WERE Y' TRYIN' TO DO— GET US BOTH KILLED?
SWELL WAY TO TALK, AFTER ME SAVIN' Y'R LIFE!
I DON'T BELIEVE THERE'S ENOUGH HEAT IN THE WORLD TO GET ME WARM AGAIN!
WHEN I'M HUNGRY I CAN'T TELL IF I'M COLD OR NOT!
WE'RE UP PRETTY HIGH! I BET IT'S A CLOUD!
GOSH, IT'S GETTIN' FOGGY!
LOOK! THE TOP O' MT. FISHFLAKE! WE MADE IT— ALMOST!
HOORAY! WE WIN THE THOUSAND BUCKS, SOON'S WE GET DOWN WITH THET FLAG!
BETCHA I GET THERE FIRST!
BETCHA DON'T! AN' BE CAREFUL Y' DON'T START AN AVALANCHE IN THIS SNOW!
HOLY CATS! THE MOUNTAIN'S SLIPPIN'!
IT'S A SNOW-SLIDE WE'RE SUNK!
GRAB SOMEP'N! WE'RE GOIN' OFF A CLIFF!
© 1935, by Walt Disney Enterprises, Great Britain rights reserved.
ARE Y' SAFE, DIPPY?
I-I GUESS SO! LUCKY THIS STICK WAS HERE— WHATEVER IT IS!
LUCKY IS RIGHT! IT'S THE FLAG WE WENT UP AFTER — IT CAME DOWN WITH THE AVALANCHE!
GAZOPP LINIMENT
WHADDYA KNOW? WE WON THE PRIZE!
WALT DISNEY
1-13

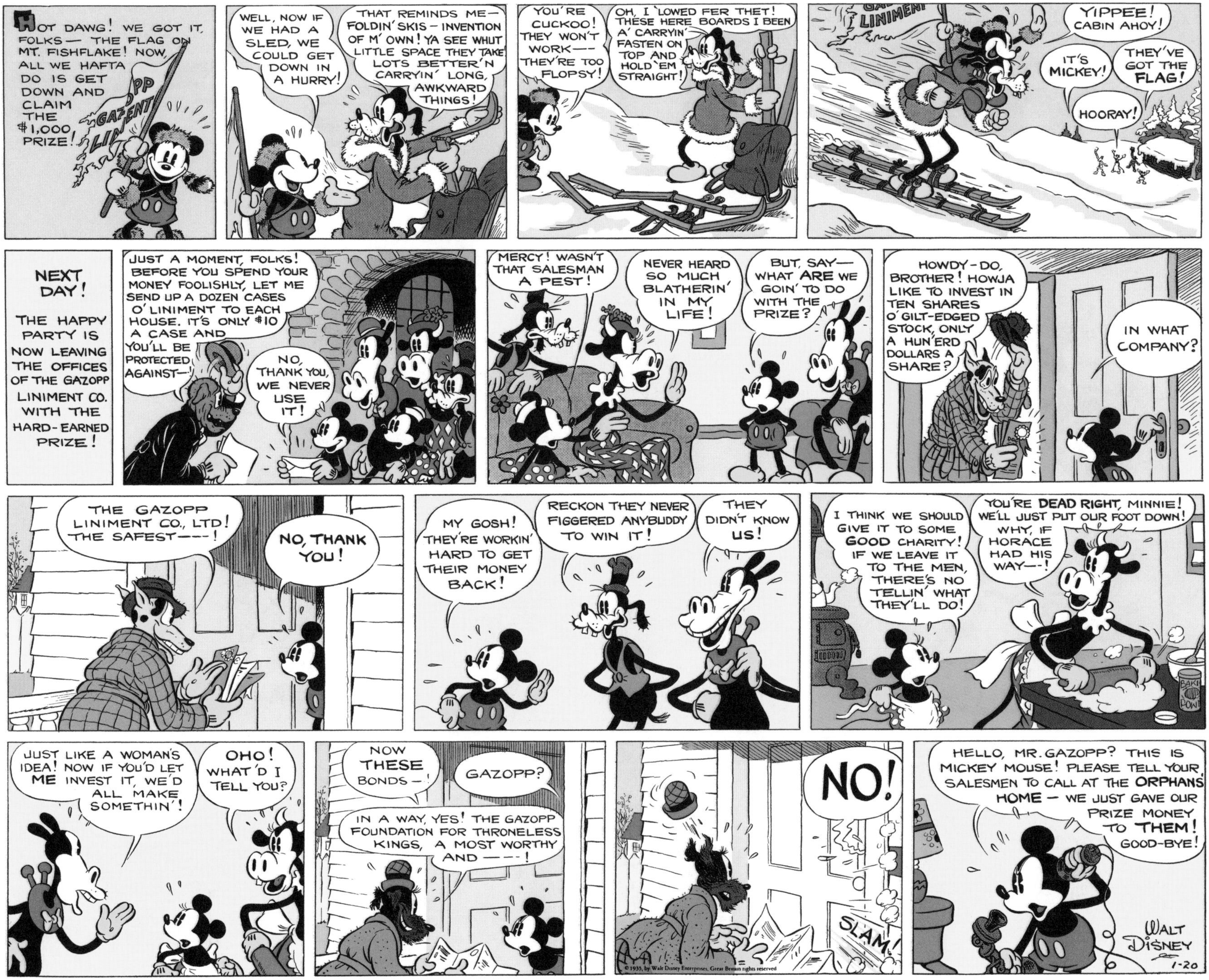
HOT DAWG! WE GOT IT, FOLKS — THE FLAG ON MT. FISHFLAKE! NOW, ALL WE HAFTA DO IS GET DOWN AND CLAIM THE $1,000 PRIZE!
GAZOPP LINIMENT
WELL, NOW IF WE HAD A SLED, WE COULD GET DOWN IN A HURRY!
THAT REMINDS ME— FOLDIN' SKIS – INVENTION OF M' OWN! YA SEE WHUT LITTLE SPACE THEY TAKE! LOTS BETTER'N CARRYIN' LONG, AWKWARD THINGS!
YOU'RE CUCKOO! THEY WON'T WORK——THEY'RE TOO FLOPSY!
OH, I 'LOWED FER THET! THESE HERE BOARDS I BEEN A' CARRYIN' FASTEN ON TOP AND HOLD 'EM STRAIGHT!
LINIMENT
YIPPEE! CABIN AHOY!
IT'S MICKEY!
THEY'VE GOT THE FLAG!
HOORAY!
NEXT DAY!
THE HAPPY PARTY IS NOW LEAVING THE OFFICES OF THE GAZOPP LINIMENT CO. WITH THE HARD-EARNED PRIZE!
JUST A MOMENT, FOLKS! BEFORE YOU SPEND YOUR MONEY FOOLISHLY, LET ME SEND UP A DOZEN CASES O' LINIMENT TO EACH HOUSE. IT'S ONLY $10 A CASE AND YOU'LL BE PROTECTED AGAINST—!
NO, THANK YOU, WE NEVER USE IT!
MERCY! WASN'T THAT SALESMAN A PEST!
NEVER HEARD SO MUCH BLATHERIN' IN MY LIFE!
BUT, SAY— WHAT ARE WE GOIN' TO DO WITH THE PRIZE?
HOWDY-DO, BROTHER! HOWJA LIKE TO INVEST IN TEN SHARES O' GILT-EDGED STOCK, ONLY A HUN'ERD DOLLARS A SHARE?
IN WHAT COMPANY?
THE GAZOPP LINIMENT CO., LTD! THE SAFEST———!
NO, THANK YOU!
MY GOSH! THEY'RE WORKIN' HARD TO GET THEIR MONEY BACK!
RECKON THEY NEVER FIGGERED ANYBUDDY TO WIN IT!
THEY DIDN'T KNOW US!
I THINK WE SHOULD GIVE IT TO SOME GOOD CHARITY! IF WE LEAVE IT TO THE MEN, THERE'S NO TELLIN' WHAT THEY'LL DO!
YOU'RE DEAD RIGHT, MINNIE! WE'LL JUST PUT OUR FOOT DOWN! WHY, IF HORACE HAD HIS WAY—!
JUST LIKE A WOMAN'S IDEA! NOW IF YOU'D LET ME INVEST IT, WE'D ALL MAKE SOMETHIN'!
OHO! WHAT'D I TELL YOU?
NOW THESE BONDS—!
GAZOPP?
IN A WAY, YES! THE GAZOPP FOUNDATION FOR THRONELESS KINGS, A MOST WORTHY AND ———!
NO!
SLAM!
© 1933, by Walt Disney Enterprises, Great Britain rights reserved
HELLO, MR. GAZOPP? THIS IS MICKEY MOUSE! PLEASE TELL YOUR SALESMEN TO CALL AT THE ORPHANS' HOME — WE JUST GAVE OUR PRIZE MONEY TO THEM! GOOD-BYE!
WALT DISNEY
1-20

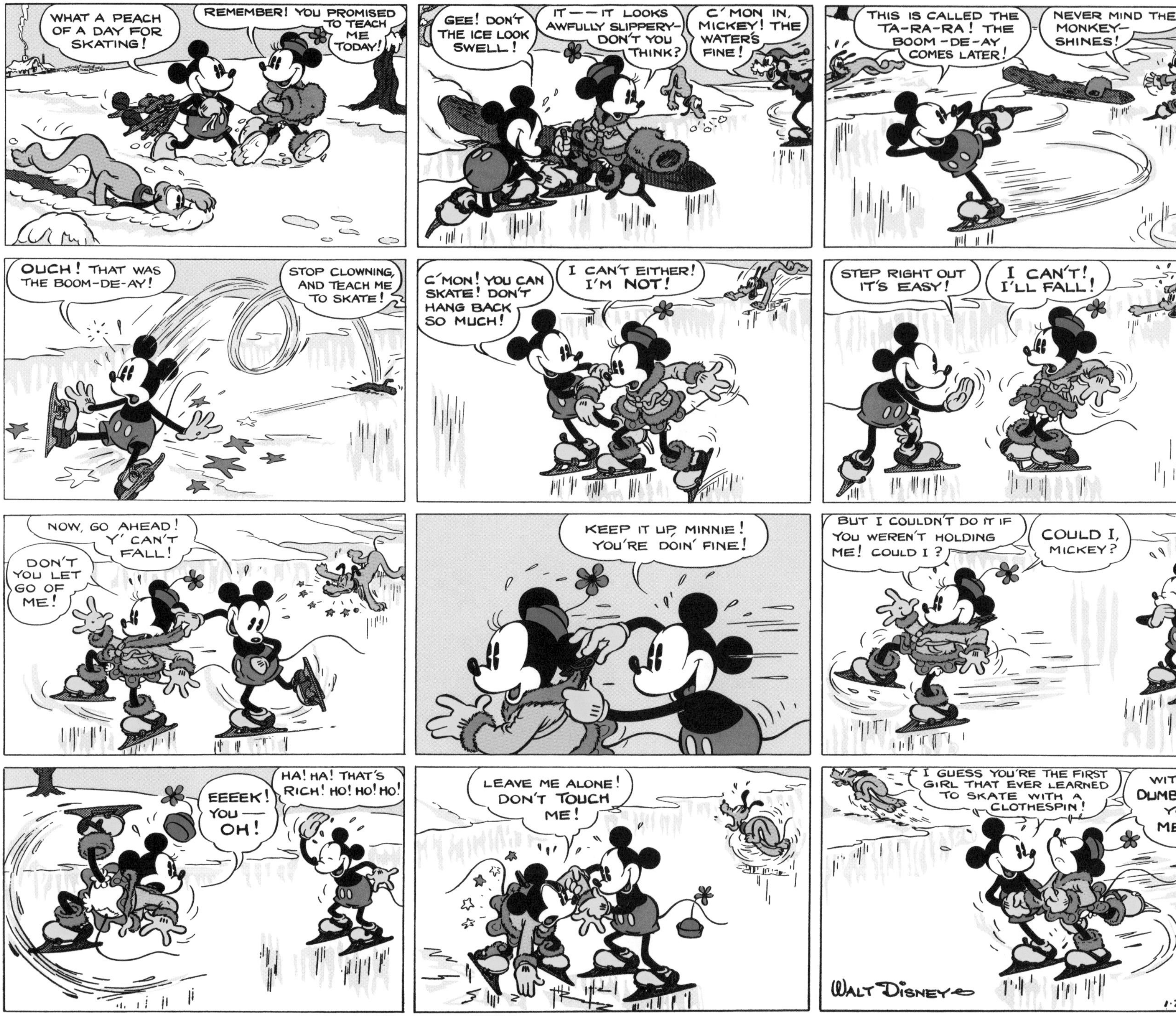
WHAT A PEACH OF A DAY FOR SKATING!
REMEMBER! YOU PROMISED TO TEACH ME TODAY!
GEE! DON'T THE ICE LOOK SWELL!
IT — — IT LOOKS AWFULLY SLIPPERY- DON'T YOU THINK?
C'MON IN, MICKEY! THE WATER'S FINE!
THIS IS CALLED THE TA-RA-RA! THE BOOM-DE-AY COMES LATER!
NEVER MIND THE MONKEY-SHINES!
OUCH! THAT WAS THE BOOM-DE-AY!
STOP CLOWNING, AND TEACH ME TO SKATE!
C'MON! YOU CAN SKATE! DON'T HANG BACK SO MUCH!
I CAN'T EITHER! I'M NOT!
STEP RIGHT OUT IT'S EASY!
I CAN'T! I'LL FALL!
NOW, GO AHEAD! Y' CAN'T FALL!
DON'T YOU LET GO OF ME!
KEEP IT UP, MINNIE! YOU'RE DOIN' FINE!
BUT I COULDN'T DO IT IF YOU WEREN'T HOLDING ME! COULD I?
COULD I, MICKEY?
EEEEK! YOU — OH!
HA! HA! THAT'S RICH! HO! HO! HO!
LEAVE ME ALONE! DON'T TOUCH ME!
I GUESS YOU'RE THE FIRST GIRL THAT EVER LEARNED TO SKATE WITH A CLOTHESPIN!
WITH A DUMB-BELL, YOU MEAN!
WALT DISNEY
1·27

190. MINNIE TAKES MICKEY DOWN A PEG

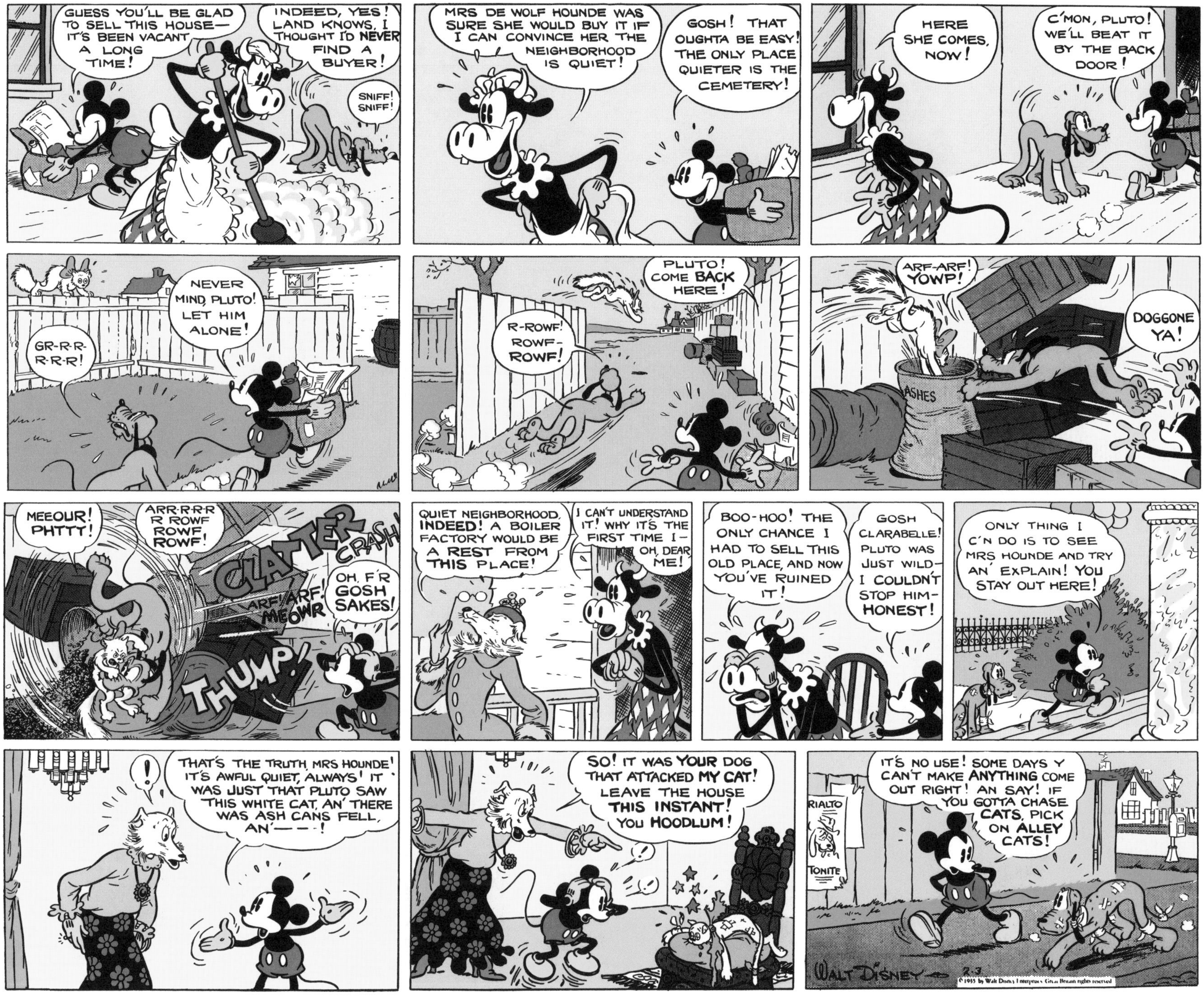
GUESS YOU'LL BE GLAD TO SELL THIS HOUSE— IT'S BEEN VACANT A LONG TIME!
INDEED, YES! LAND KNOWS, I THOUGHT I'D NEVER FIND A BUYER!
SNIFF! SNIFF!
MRS DE WOLF HOUNDE WAS SURE SHE WOULD BUY IT IF I CAN CONVINCE HER THE NEIGHBORHOOD IS QUIET!
GOSH! THAT OUGHTA BE EASY! THE ONLY PLACE QUIETER IS THE CEMETERY!
HERE SHE COMES, NOW!
C'MON, PLUTO! WE'LL BEAT IT BY THE BACK DOOR!
GR-R-R R-R-R!
NEVER MIND, PLUTO! LET HIM ALONE!
PLUTO! COME BACK HERE!
R-ROWF! ROWF- ROWF!
ARF-ARF! YOWP!
DOGGONE YA!
ASHES
MEEOUR! PHTTT!
ARR-R-R-R R ROWF ROWF! ROWF!
CLATTER
CRASH!
ARF! ARF!
MEOWR
THUMP!
OH, F'R GOSH SAKES!
QUIET NEIGHBORHOOD, INDEED! A BOILER FACTORY WOULD BE A REST FROM THIS PLACE!
I CAN'T UNDERSTAND IT! WHY IT'S THE FIRST TIME I— OH, DEAR ME!
BOO-HOO! THE ONLY CHANCE I HAD TO SELL THIS OLD PLACE, AND NOW YOU'VE RUINED IT!
GOSH CLARABELLE! PLUTO WAS JUST WILD— I COULDN'T STOP HIM— HONEST!
ONLY THING I C'N DO IS TO SEE MRS HOUNDE AND TRY AN' EXPLAIN! YOU STAY OUT HERE!
!
THAT'S THE TRUTH, MRS HOUNDE! IT'S AWFUL QUIET, ALWAYS! IT WAS JUST THAT PLUTO SAW THIS WHITE CAT, AN' THERE WAS ASH CANS FELL, AN'———!
SO! IT WAS YOUR DOG THAT ATTACKED MY CAT! LEAVE THE HOUSE THIS INSTANT! YOU HOODLUM!
IT'S NO USE! SOME DAYS Y CAN'T MAKE ANYTHING COME OUT RIGHT! AN SAY! IF YOU GOTTA CHASE CATS, PICK ON ALLEY CATS!
RIALTO
TONITE
WALT DISNEY
2-3

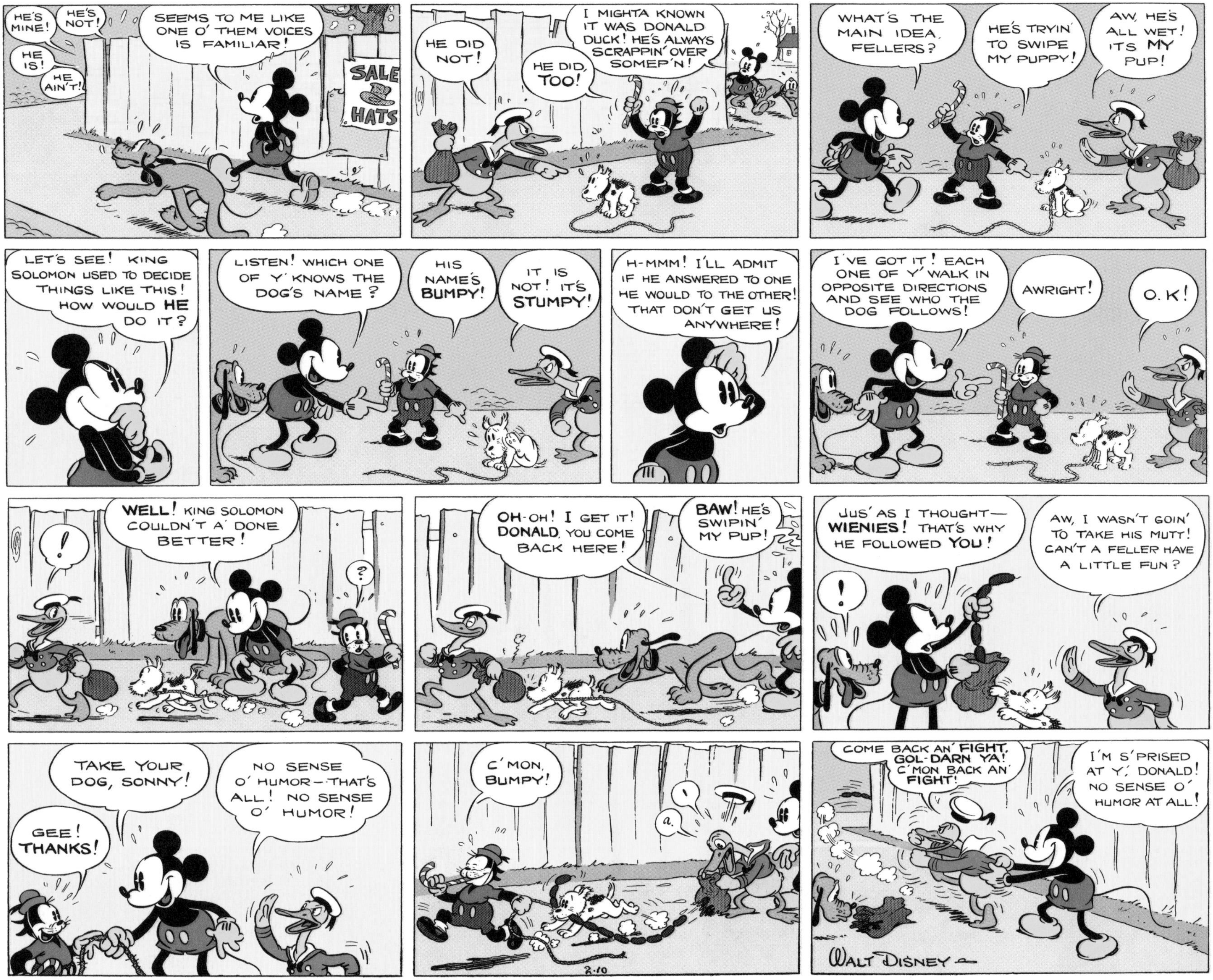
HE'S MINE!
HE'S NOT!
HE IS!
HE AIN'T!
SEEMS TO ME LIKE ONE O' THEM VOICES IS FAMILIAR!
SALE HATS
HE DID NOT!
HE DID, TOO!
I MIGHTA KNOWN IT WAS DONALD DUCK! HE'S ALWAYS SCRAPPIN' OVER SOMEP'N!
WHAT'S THE MAIN IDEA, FELLERS?
HE'S TRYIN' TO SWIPE MY PUPPY!
AW, HE'S ALL WET! IT'S MY PUP!
LET'S SEE! KING SOLOMON USED TO DECIDE THINGS LIKE THIS! HOW WOULD HE DO IT?
LISTEN! WHICH ONE OF Y' KNOWS THE DOG'S NAME?
HIS NAME'S BUMPY!
IT IS NOT! IT'S STUMPY!
H-MMM! I'LL ADMIT IF HE ANSWERED TO ONE HE WOULD TO THE OTHER! THAT DON'T GET US ANYWHERE!
I'VE GOT IT! EACH ONE OF Y' WALK IN OPPOSITE DIRECTIONS AND SEE WHO THE DOG FOLLOWS!
AWRIGHT!
O.K!
!
WELL! KING SOLOMON COULDN'T A' DONE BETTER!
?
OH-OH! I GET IT! DONALD, YOU COME BACK HERE!
BAW! HE'S SWIPIN' MY PUP!
!
JUS' AS I THOUGHT— WIENIES! THAT'S WHY HE FOLLOWED YOU!
AW, I WASN'T GOIN' TO TAKE HIS MUTT! CAN'T A FELLER HAVE A LITTLE FUN?
TAKE YOUR DOG, SONNY!
GEE! THANKS!
NO SENSE O' HUMOR—THAT'S ALL! NO SENSE O' HUMOR!
C'MON, BUMPY!
2-10
COME BACK AN' FIGHT, GOL-DARN YA! C'MON BACK AN' FIGHT!
I'M S'PRISED AT Y', DONALD! NO SENSE O' HUMOR AT ALL!
WALT DISNEY

192. DONALD THINKS IT'S A DOG'S LIFE

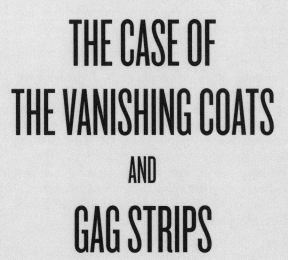

THE CASE OF
THE VANISHING COATS
AND
GAG STRIPS

FEBRUARY 17, 1935

–

JULY 21, 1935

MICKEY MOUSE
REGISTERED U.S. PATENT OFFICE

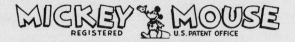

BENEATH THE OVERCOAT

Nothin' doin!" Donald shouts at Mickey. "I ain't nobody's uncle, I ain't!" Donald is abashed at the very idea of a non-relation treating him as family. But that doesn't stop Morty and Ferdie from coining the phrase "Unca Donald" in the strip for April 7, 1935. Indeed, Donald himself is not above childishly branding Mr. Zoup—his de facto landlord—with the familial pet name "Uncle Amos."

An immature duck dominates Donald's early gag strip appearances, and the same portrayal takes center stage in "The Case of the Vanishing Coats." Donald had only made his screen debut one year previous, so some infantile behavior seems appropriate. His fluctuation between schoolboy prankster and stubborn adult was simply part of the Disney developmental process—"growing pains," so to speak, as artists determined what kind of character they wanted this mallard to be.

Donald's rowdiness would gradually be toned down as he became the regular central character of the *Silly Symphony* Sunday feature and his own daily strip. In time, Donald would acquire his own biological nephews—though social scientists would likely argue that they did little to improve his behavior or personality.

"Vanishing Coats" itself is played for light-hearted laughs, showcasing the ineptitude of Donald's detective antics; but a bit of sinister seriousness seems to cross over from the grittier Mickey daily strip. As we are reminded each week, the thieving of Uncle Amos' coat supply is ruining his livelihood. He'll have to close shop if the perpetrator isn't caught. But the police consider Amos' woes a joke; Pluto lets the burglar get away; and even Mickey's shrewdness isn't providing any leads. After nearly five weeks of thievery, all Mickey can surmise is that "there's somep'n *mighty* peculiar about how these clothes get away!"

Had "Vanishing Coats" been a daily continuity, Gottfredson might have enlarged upon the potential of this psychological mystery. Indeed, the secret behind the coats' disappearance is a dilemma "for which there is no scientific cure." So what is the solution? Naturally, Mickey uses a remedy that is comically *unscientific*—even crass, by 1935 standards—to save Uncle Amos and his store.

After "Vanishing Coats'" swift, happy conclusion, there still remains one unsolved mystery: at story's start, who blackjacked Amos to steal the very first coat, and why the blazes *was* he so desperate? Perhaps this is an even darker scenario than we thought...

— THAD KOMOROWSKI

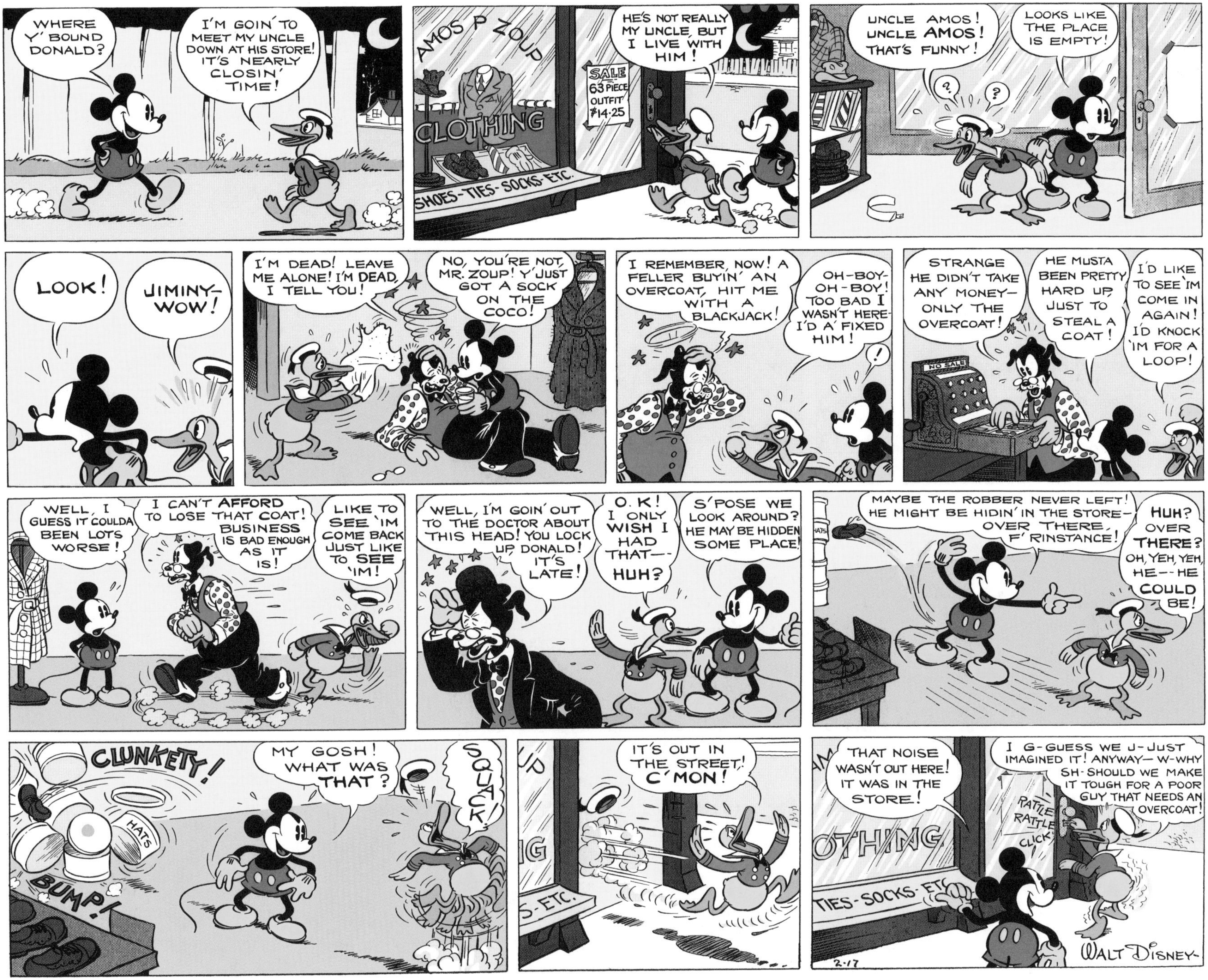
WHERE Y' BOUND DONALD?
I'M GOIN' TO MEET MY UNCLE DOWN AT HIS STORE! IT'S NEARLY CLOSIN' TIME!
AMOS P ZOUP
CLOTHING
SHOES-TIES-SOCKS-ETC.
SALE 63 PIECE OUTFIT $14.25
HE'S NOT REALLY MY UNCLE, BUT I LIVE WITH HIM!
UNCLE AMOS! UNCLE AMOS! THAT'S FUNNY!
LOOKS LIKE THE PLACE IS EMPTY!
LOOK!
JIMINY-WOW!
I'M DEAD! LEAVE ME ALONE! I'M DEAD, I TELL YOU!
NO, YOU'RE NOT, MR. ZOUP! Y' JUST GOT A SOCK ON THE COCO!
I REMEMBER, NOW! A FELLER BUYIN' AN OVERCOAT, HIT ME WITH A BLACKJACK!
OH-BOY-OH-BOY! TOO BAD I WASN'T HERE-I'D A' FIXED HIM!
STRANGE HE DIDN'T TAKE ANY MONEY-ONLY THE OVERCOAT!
NO SALE
HE MUSTA BEEN PRETTY HARD UP, JUST TO STEAL A COAT!
I'D LIKE TO SEE 'IM COME IN AGAIN! I'D KNOCK 'IM FOR A LOOP!
WELL, I GUESS IT COULDA BEEN LOTS WORSE!
I CAN'T AFFORD TO LOSE THAT COAT! BUSINESS IS BAD ENOUGH AS IT IS!
LIKE TO SEE 'IM COME BACK JUST LIKE TO SEE 'IM!
WELL, I'M GOIN' OUT TO THE DOCTOR ABOUT THIS HEAD! YOU LOCK UP, DONALD! IT'S LATE!
O.K! I ONLY WISH I HAD THAT---
HUH?
S'POSE WE LOOK AROUND? HE MAY BE HIDDEN SOME PLACE!
MAYBE THE ROBBER NEVER LEFT! HE MIGHT BE HIDIN' IN THE STORE-OVER THERE, F' RINSTANCE!
HUH? OVER THERE? OH, YEH, YEH, HE--HE COULD BE!
CLUNKETY!
BUMP!
HATS
MY GOSH! WHAT WAS THAT?
SQUACK!
IT'S OUT IN THE STREET! C'MON!
S-ETC.
THAT NOISE WASN'T OUT HERE! IT WAS IN THE STORE!
I G-GUESS WE J-JUST IMAGINED IT! ANYWAY- W-WHY SH-SHOULD WE MAKE IT TOUGH FOR A POOR GUY THAT NEEDS AN OVERCOAT!
RATTLE RATTLE CLICK
OTHING
TIES-SOCKS-ETC
2-17
WALT DISNEY

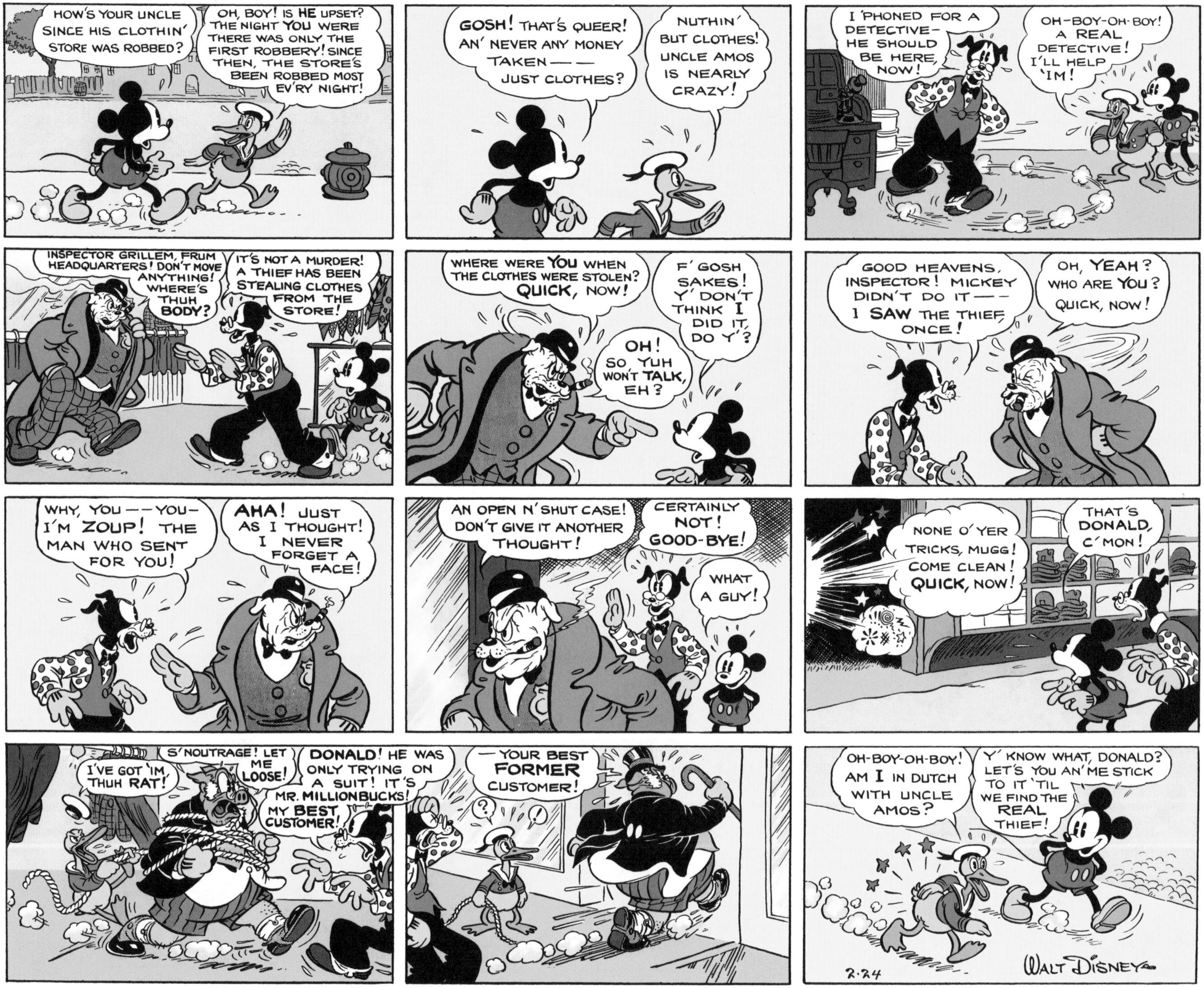
HOW'S YOUR UNCLE SINCE HIS CLOTHIN' STORE WAS ROBBED?
OH, BOY! IS HE UPSET? THE NIGHT YOU WERE THERE WAS ONLY THE FIRST ROBBERY! SINCE THEN, THE STORE'S BEEN ROBBED MOST EV'RY NIGHT!
GOSH! THAT'S QUEER! AN' NEVER ANY MONEY TAKEN — — JUST CLOTHES?
NUTHIN' BUT CLOTHES! UNCLE AMOS IS NEARLY CRAZY!
I 'PHONED FOR A DETECTIVE— HE SHOULD BE HERE, NOW!
OH-BOY-OH-BOY! A REAL DETECTIVE! I'LL HELP 'IM!
INSPECTOR GRILLEM, FRUM HEADQUARTERS! DON'T MOVE ANYTHING! WHERE'S THUH BODY?
IT'S NOT A MURDER! A THIEF HAS BEEN STEALING CLOTHES FROM THE STORE!
WHERE WERE YOU WHEN THE CLOTHES WERE STOLEN? QUICK, NOW!
F' GOSH SAKES! Y' DON'T THINK I DID IT, DO Y'?
OH! SO YUH WON'T TALK, EH?
GOOD HEAVENS, INSPECTOR! MICKEY DIDN'T DO IT — — I SAW THE THIEF, ONCE!
OH, YEAH? WHO ARE YOU? QUICK, NOW!
WHY, YOU — — YOU— I'M ZOUP! THE MAN WHO SENT FOR YOU!
AHA! JUST AS I THOUGHT! I NEVER FORGET A FACE!
AN OPEN N' SHUT CASE! DON'T GIVE IT ANOTHER THOUGHT!
CERTAINLY NOT! GOOD-BYE!
WHAT A GUY!
NONE O' YER TRICKS, MUGG! COME CLEAN! QUICK, NOW!
THAT'S DONALD, C'MON!
I'VE GOT 'IM, THUH RAT!
S'NOUTRAGE! LET ME LOOSE!
DONALD! HE WAS ONLY TRYING ON A SUIT! IT'S MR. MILLIONBUCKS! MY BEST CUSTOMER!
—YOUR BEST FORMER CUSTOMER!
?
!
OH-BOY-OH-BOY! AM I IN DUTCH WITH UNCLE AMOS?
Y' KNOW WHAT, DONALD? LET'S YOU AN' ME STICK TO IT 'TIL WE FIND THE REAL THIEF!
2-24
WALT DISNEY

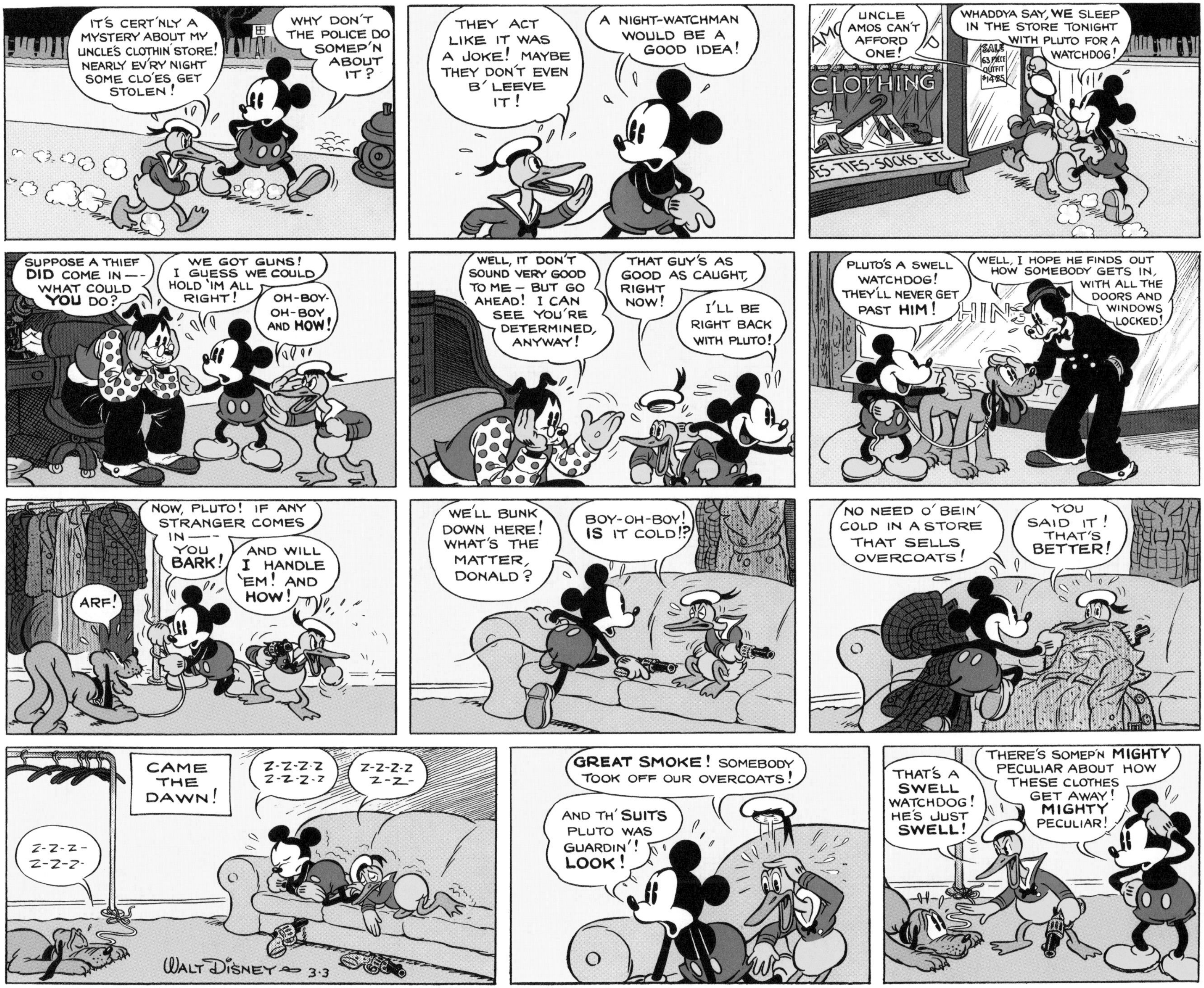
IT'S CERT'NLY A MYSTERY ABOUT MY UNCLE'S CLOTHIN' STORE! NEARLY EV'RY NIGHT SOME CLO'ES GET STOLEN!
WHY DON'T THE POLICE DO SOMEP'N ABOUT IT?
THEY ACT LIKE IT WAS A JOKE! MAYBE THEY DON'T EVEN B'LEEVE IT!
A NIGHT-WATCHMAN WOULD BE A GOOD IDEA!
UNCLE AMOS CAN'T AFFORD ONE!
WHADDYA SAY, WE SLEEP IN THE STORE TONIGHT WITH PLUTO FOR A WATCHDOG!
CLOTHING
SALE 63 PIECE OUTFIT $14.25
-IES-TIES-SOCKS-ETC.
SUPPOSE A THIEF DID COME IN— WHAT COULD YOU DO?
WE GOT GUNS! I GUESS WE COULD HOLD 'IM ALL RIGHT!
OH-BOY-OH-BOY AND HOW!
WELL, IT DON'T SOUND VERY GOOD TO ME — BUT GO AHEAD! I CAN SEE YOU'RE DETERMINED, ANYWAY!
THAT GUY'S AS GOOD AS CAUGHT, RIGHT NOW!
I'LL BE RIGHT BACK WITH PLUTO!
PLUTO'S A SWELL WATCHDOG! THEY'LL NEVER GET PAST HIM!
WELL, I HOPE HE FINDS OUT HOW SOMEBODY GETS IN, WITH ALL THE DOORS AND WINDOWS LOCKED!
NOW, PLUTO! IF ANY STRANGER COMES IN— YOU BARK!
AND WILL I HANDLE 'EM! AND HOW!
ARF!
WE'LL BUNK DOWN HERE! WHAT'S THE MATTER, DONALD?
BOY-OH-BOY! IS IT COLD!?
NO NEED O' BEIN' COLD IN A STORE THAT SELLS OVERCOATS!
YOU SAID IT! THAT'S BETTER!
CAME THE DAWN!
Z-Z-Z-Z Z-Z-Z-Z
Z-Z-Z-Z Z-Z-
Z-Z-Z- Z-Z-Z-
WALT DISNEY 3·3
GREAT SMOKE! SOMEBODY TOOK OFF OUR OVERCOATS!
AND TH' SUITS PLUTO WAS GUARDIN'! LOOK!
THAT'S A SWELL WATCHDOG! HE'S JUST SWELL!
THERE'S SOMEP'N MIGHTY PECULIAR ABOUT HOW THESE CLOTHES GET AWAY! MIGHTY PECULIAR!

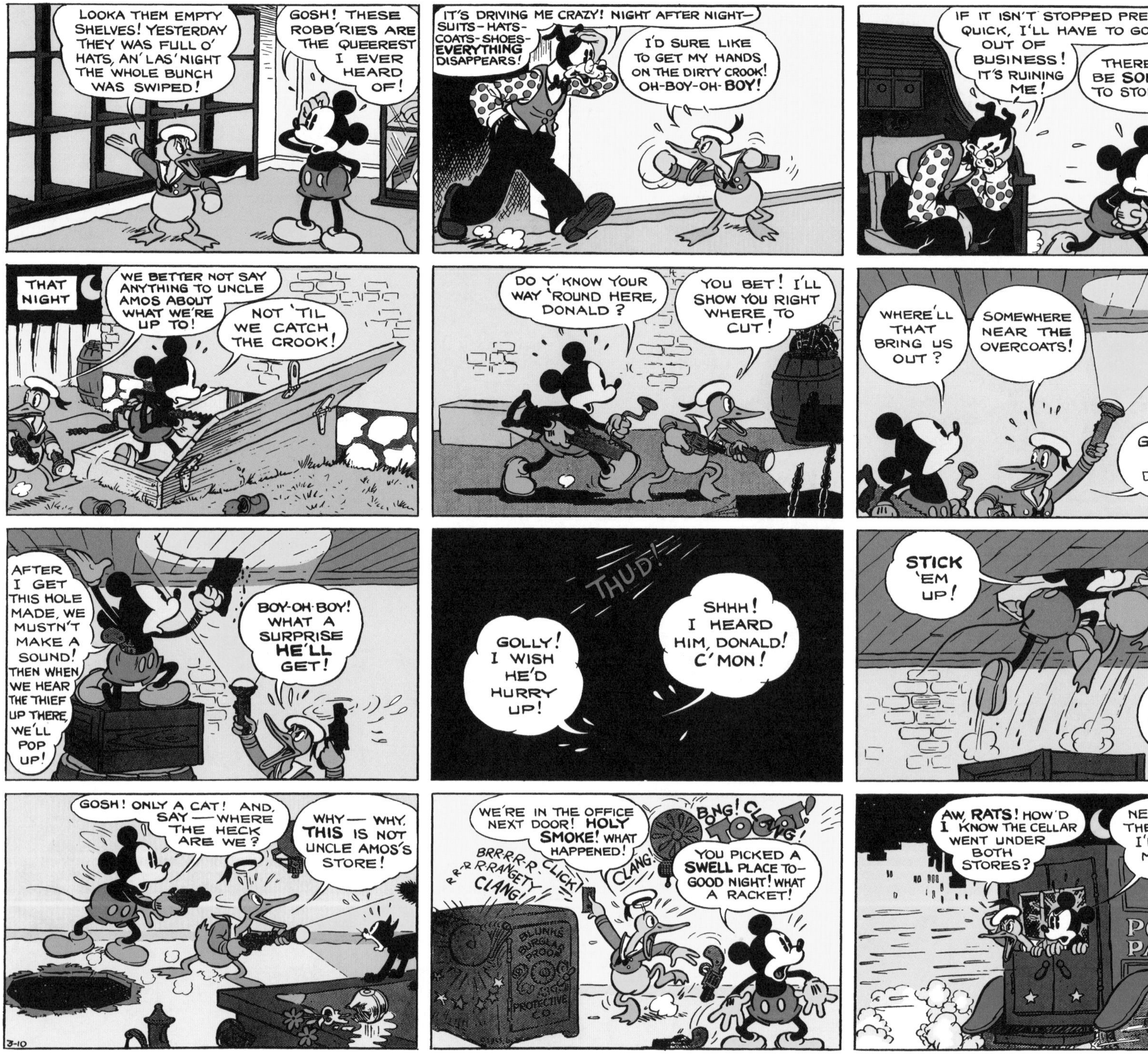
LOOKA THEM EMPTY SHELVES! YESTERDAY THEY WAS FULL O' HATS, AN' LAS' NIGHT THE WHOLE BUNCH WAS SWIPED!
GOSH! THESE ROBB'RIES ARE THE QUEEREST I EVER HEARD OF!
IT'S DRIVING ME CRAZY! NIGHT AFTER NIGHT— SUITS—HATS— COATS—SHOES— EVERYTHING DISAPPEARS!
I'D SURE LIKE TO GET MY HANDS ON THE DIRTY CROOK! OH-BOY-OH-BOY!
IF IT ISN'T STOPPED PRETTY QUICK, I'LL HAVE TO GO OUT OF BUSINESS! IT'S RUINING ME!
THERE MUST BE SOME WAY TO STOP IT!
THAT NIGHT
WE BETTER NOT SAY ANYTHING TO UNCLE AMOS ABOUT WHAT WE'RE UP TO!
NOT 'TIL WE CATCH THE CROOK!
DO Y' KNOW YOUR WAY 'ROUND HERE, DONALD?
YOU BET! I'LL SHOW YOU RIGHT WHERE TO CUT!
WHERE'LL THAT BRING US OUT?
SOMEWHERE NEAR THE OVERCOATS!
GOLLY! IT'S DARK!
AFTER I GET THIS HOLE MADE, WE MUSTN'T MAKE A SOUND! THEN WHEN WE HEAR THE THIEF UP THERE, WE'LL POP UP!
BOY-OH-BOY! WHAT A SURPRISE HE'LL GET!
THUD!
GOLLY! I WISH HE'D HURRY UP!
SHHH! I HEARD HIM, DONALD! C'MON!
STICK 'EM UP!
WE GOTCHA!
GOSH! ONLY A CAT! AND, SAY—WHERE THE HECK ARE WE?
WHY— WHY, THIS IS NOT UNCLE AMOS'S STORE!
3-10
WE'RE IN THE OFFICE NEXT DOOR! HOLY SMOKE! WHAT HAPPENED!
BRR-R-R-R CLICK!
R-R-R-R-RANGETY CLANG!
CLANG!
YOU PICKED A SWELL PLACE TO— GOOD NIGHT! WHAT A RACKET!
BLUNK'S BURGLAR PROOF
PROTECTIVE CO.
AW, RATS! HOW'D I KNOW THE CELLAR WENT UNDER BOTH STORES?
NEXT TIME I GO THERE WITH YOU I'LL BRING A MAP WITH ME!
POLICE PATROL

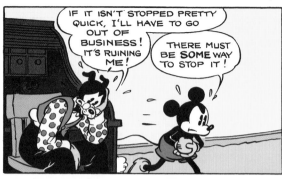

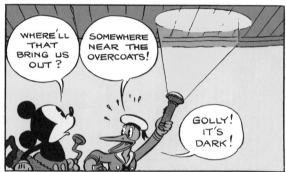

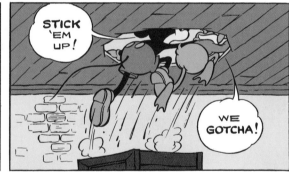

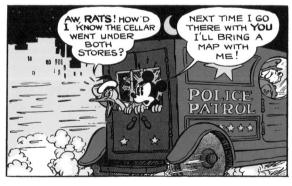

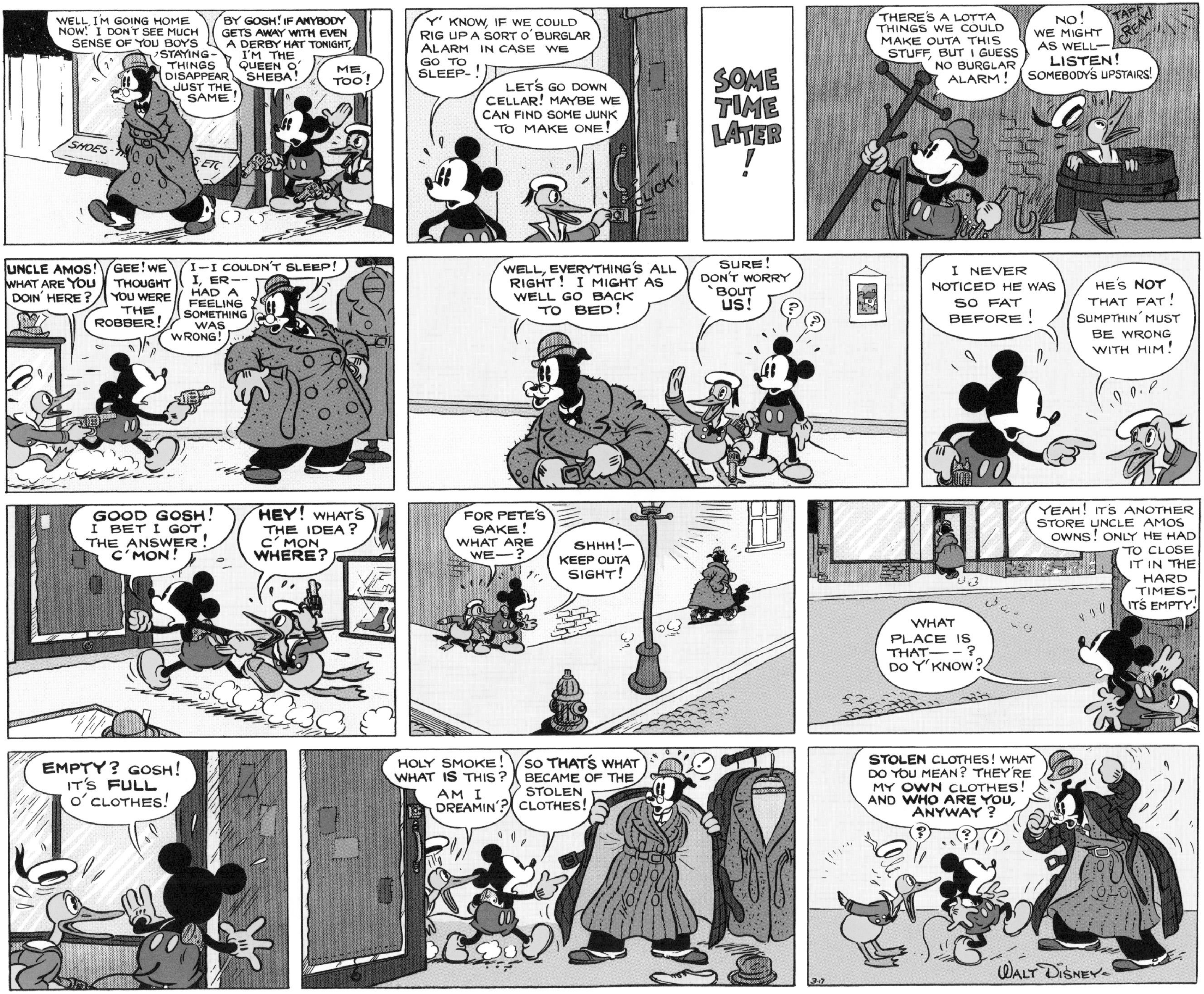

WELL, I'M GOING HOME NOW! I DON'T SEE MUCH SENSE OF YOU BOYS STAYING-
THINGS DISAPPEAR JUST THE SAME!
BY GOSH! IF ANYBODY GETS AWAY WITH EVEN A DERBY HAT TONIGHT, I'M THE QUEEN O' SHEBA!
ME, TOO!
SHOES
S ETC
Y' KNOW, IF WE COULD RIG UP A SORT O' BURGLAR ALARM IN CASE WE GO TO SLEEP-!
LET'S GO DOWN CELLAR! MAYBE WE CAN FIND SOME JUNK TO MAKE ONE!
CLICK!
SOME TIME LATER!
THERE'S A LOTTA THINGS WE COULD MAKE OUTA THIS STUFF, BUT I GUESS NO BURGLAR ALARM!
NO! WE MIGHT AS WELL— LISTEN! SOMEBODY'S UPSTAIRS!
TAP! CREAK!
UNCLE AMOS! WHAT ARE YOU DOIN' HERE?
GEE! WE THOUGHT YOU WERE THE ROBBER!
I—I COULDN'T SLEEP! I, ER-- HAD A FEELING SOMETHING WAS WRONG!
WELL, EVERYTHING'S ALL RIGHT! I MIGHT AS WELL GO BACK TO BED!
SURE! DON'T WORRY 'BOUT US!
I NEVER NOTICED HE WAS SO FAT BEFORE!
HE'S NOT THAT FAT! SUMPTHIN' MUST BE WRONG WITH HIM!
GOOD GOSH! I BET I GOT THE ANSWER! C'MON!
HEY! WHAT'S THE IDEA? C'MON WHERE?
FOR PETE'S SAKE! WHAT ARE WE—?
SHHH!— KEEP OUTA SIGHT!
YEAH! IT'S ANOTHER STORE UNCLE AMOS OWNS! ONLY HE HAD TO CLOSE IT IN THE HARD TIMES- IT'S EMPTY!
WHAT PLACE IS THAT— -? DO Y'KNOW?
EMPTY? GOSH! IT'S FULL O' CLOTHES!
HOLY SMOKE! WHAT IS THIS? AM I DREAMIN'?
SO THAT'S WHAT BECAME OF THE STOLEN CLOTHES!
STOLEN CLOTHES! WHAT DO YOU MEAN? THEY'RE MY OWN CLOTHES! AND WHO ARE YOU, ANYWAY?
3-17
WALT DISNEY

200. THE CASE OF THE VANISHING COATS

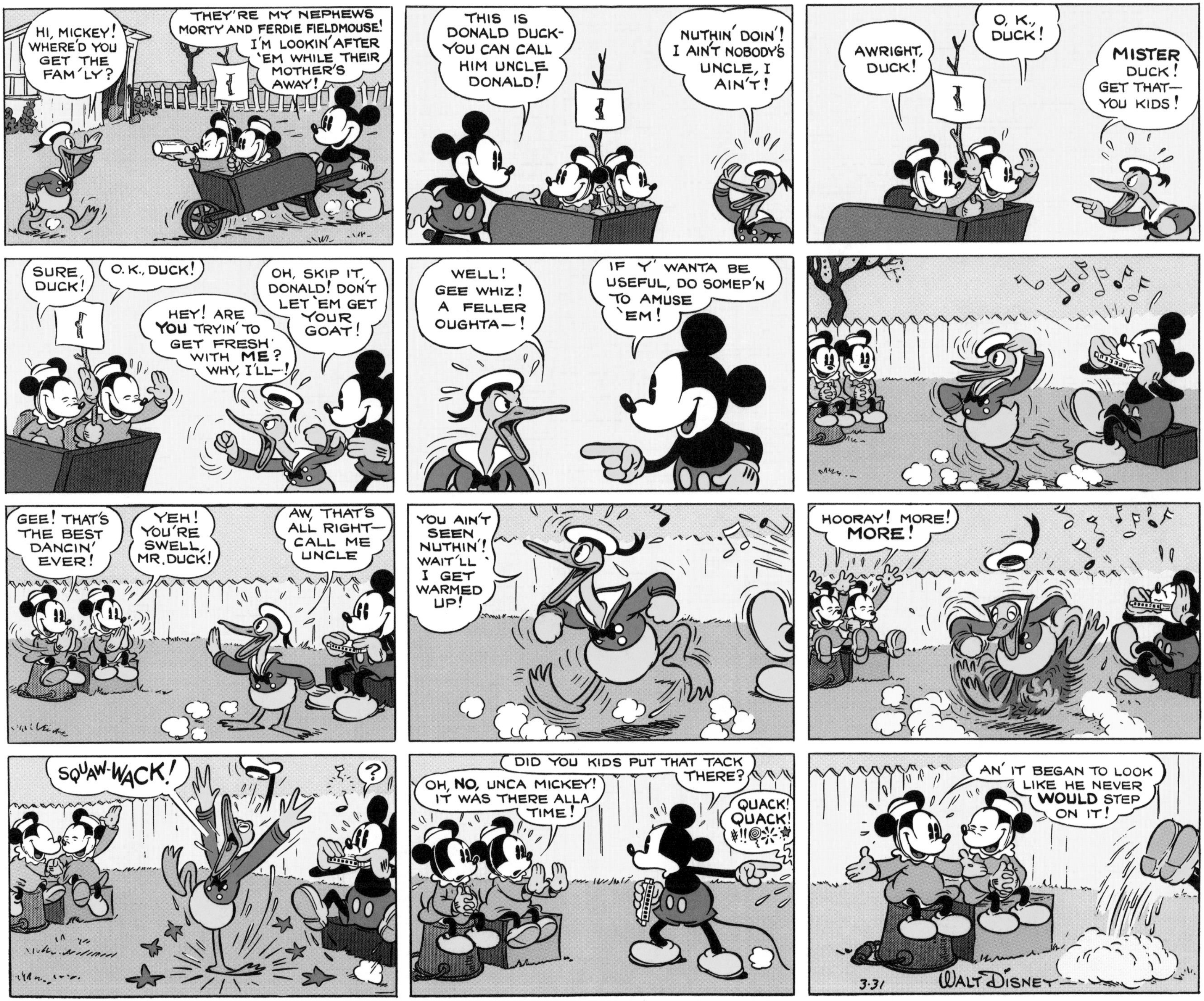
HI, MICKEY! WHERE'D YOU GET THE FAM'LY?
THEY'RE MY NEPHEWS MORTY AND FERDIE FIELDMOUSE! I'M LOOKIN' AFTER 'EM WHILE THEIR MOTHER'S AWAY!
THIS IS DONALD DUCK-YOU CAN CALL HIM UNCLE DONALD!
NUTHIN' DOIN'! I AIN'T NOBODY'S UNCLE, I AIN'T!
AWRIGHT, DUCK!
O, K., DUCK!
MISTER DUCK! GET THAT—YOU KIDS!
SURE, DUCK!
O. K., DUCK!
HEY! ARE YOU TRYIN' TO GET FRESH WITH ME? WHY, I'LL—!
OH, SKIP IT, DONALD! DON'T LET 'EM GET YOUR GOAT!
WELL! GEE WHIZ! A FELLER OUGHTA—!
IF Y' WANTA BE USEFUL, DO SOMEP'N TO AMUSE 'EM!
GEE! THAT'S THE BEST DANCIN' EVER!
YEH! YOU'RE SWELL, MR. DUCK!
AW, THAT'S ALL RIGHT—CALL ME UNCLE
YOU AIN'T SEEN NUTHIN'! WAIT'LL I GET WARMED UP!
HOORAY! MORE! MORE!
SQUAW-WACK!
?
DID YOU KIDS PUT THAT TACK THERE?
OH, NO, UNCA MICKEY! IT WAS THERE ALLA TIME!
QUACK! QUACK!
AN' IT BEGAN TO LOOK LIKE HE NEVER WOULD STEP ON IT!
3-31
WALT DISNEY

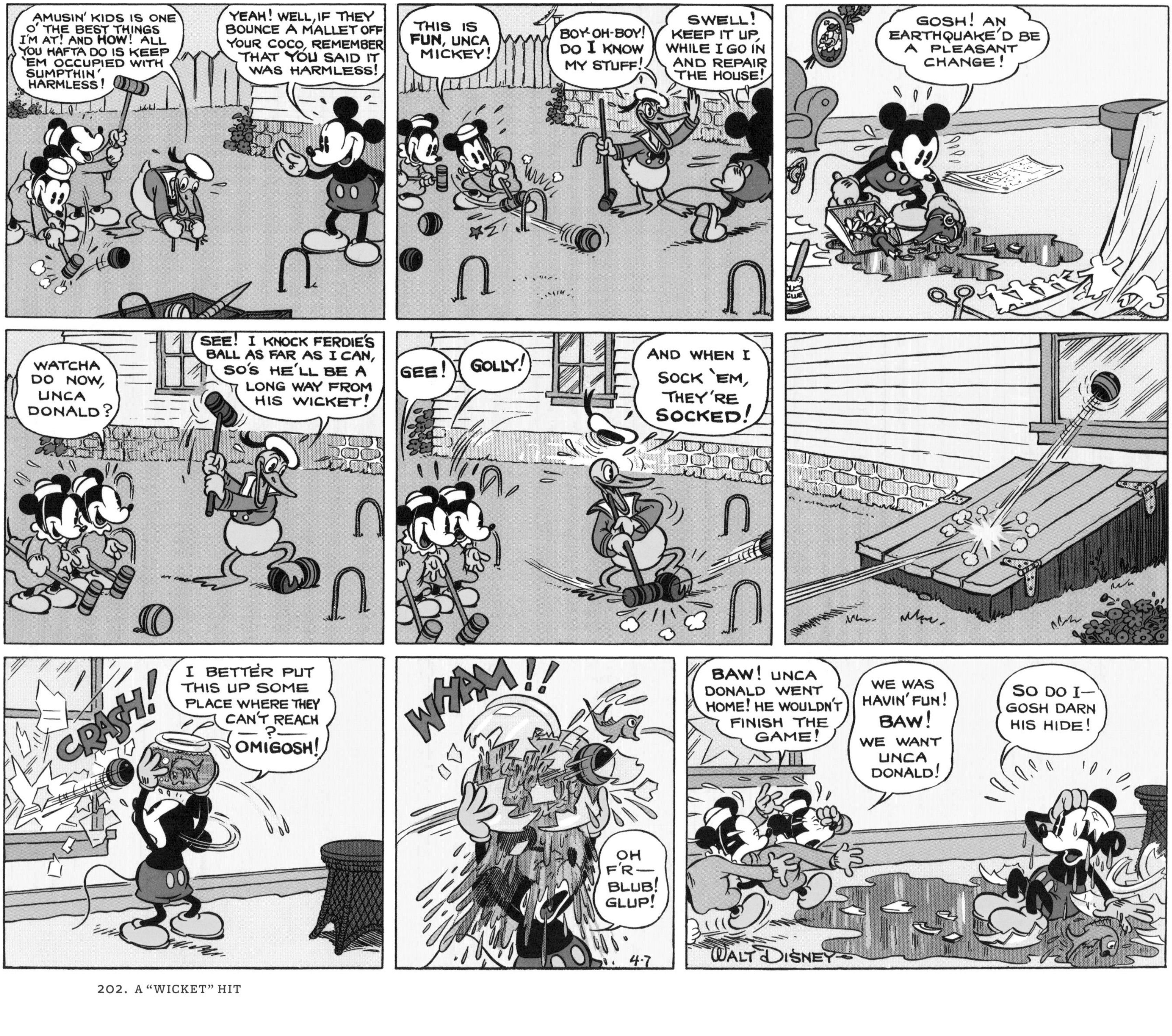
AMUSIN' KIDS IS ONE O' THE BEST THINGS I'M AT! AND HOW! ALL YOU HAFTA DO IS KEEP 'EM OCCUPIED WITH SUMPTHIN' HARMLESS!
YEAH! WELL, IF THEY BOUNCE A MALLET OFF YOUR COCO, REMEMBER THAT YOU SAID IT WAS HARMLESS!
THIS IS FUN, UNCA MICKEY!
BOY-OH-BOY! DO I KNOW MY STUFF!
SWELL! KEEP IT UP, WHILE I GO IN AND REPAIR THE HOUSE!
GOSH! AN EARTHQUAKE'D BE A PLEASANT CHANGE!
WATCHA DO NOW, UNCA DONALD?
SEE! I KNOCK FERDIE'S BALL AS FAR AS I CAN, SO'S HE'LL BE A LONG WAY FROM HIS WICKET!
GEE!
GOLLY!
AND WHEN I SOCK 'EM, THEY'RE SOCKED!
CRASH!
I BETTER PUT THIS UP SOME PLACE WHERE THEY CAN'T REACH —?— OMIGOSH!
WHAM!!
OH F'R— BLUB! GLUP!
4-7
BAW! UNCA DONALD WENT HOME! HE WOULDN'T FINISH THE GAME!
WE WAS HAVIN' FUN! BAW! WE WANT UNCA DONALD!
SO DO I— GOSH DARN HIS HIDE!
WALT DISNEY

202. A "WICKET" HIT

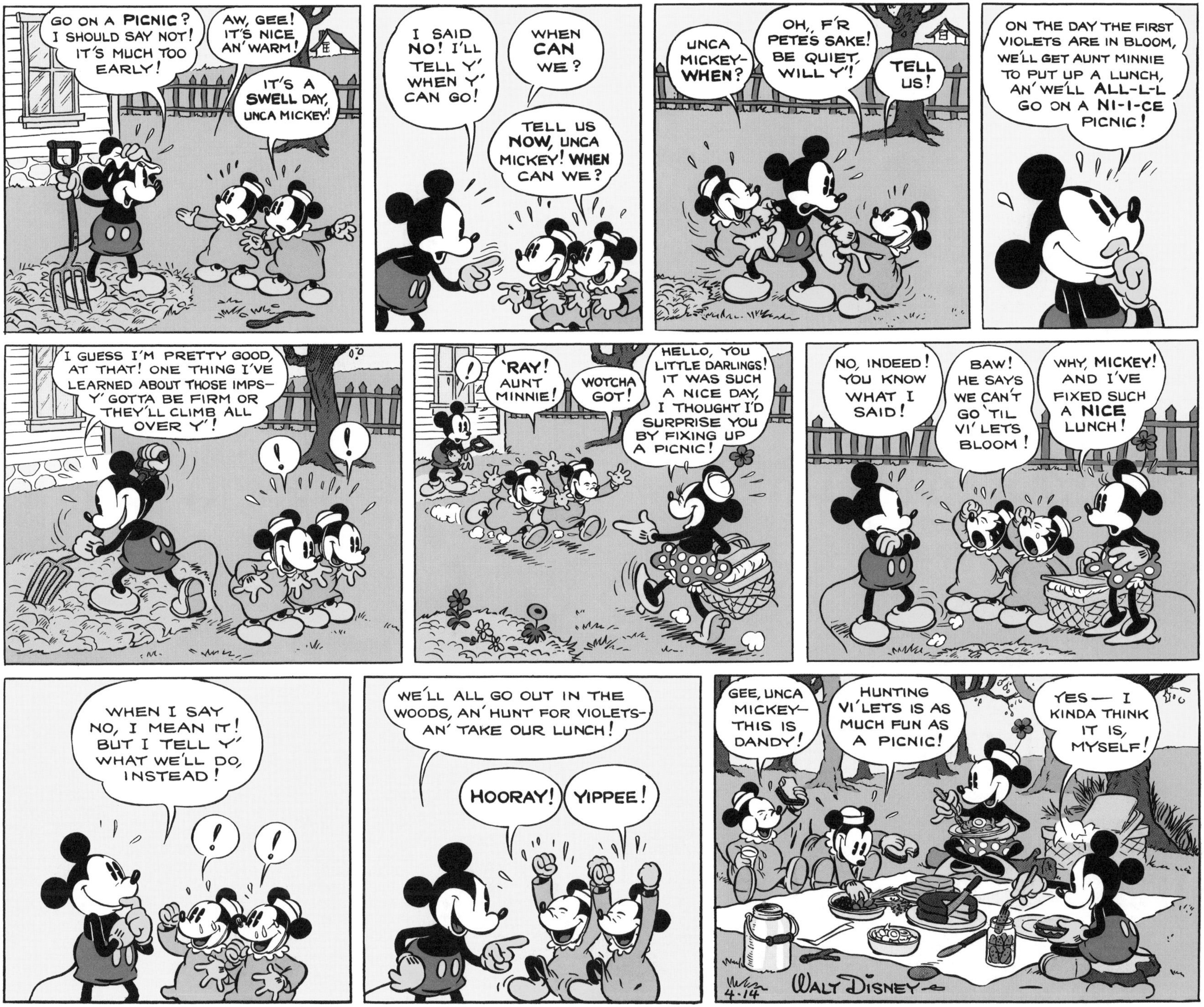
GO ON A PICNIC? I SHOULD SAY NOT! IT'S MUCH TOO EARLY!
AW, GEE! IT'S NICE AN' WARM!
IT'S A SWELL DAY, UNCA MICKEY!
I SAID NO! I'LL TELL Y' WHEN Y' CAN GO!
WHEN CAN WE?
TELL US NOW, UNCA MICKEY! WHEN CAN WE?
UNCA MICKEY- WHEN?
OH, F'R PETE'S SAKE! BE QUIET, WILL Y'!
TELL US!
ON THE DAY THE FIRST VIOLETS ARE IN BLOOM, WE'LL GET AUNT MINNIE TO PUT UP A LUNCH, AN' WE'LL ALL-L-L GO ON A NI-I-CE PICNIC!
I GUESS I'M PRETTY GOOD, AT THAT! ONE THING I'VE LEARNED ABOUT THOSE IMPS- Y' GOTTA BE FIRM OR THEY'LL CLIMB ALL OVER Y'!
'RAY! AUNT MINNIE!
WOTCHA GOT!
HELLO, YOU LITTLE DARLINGS! IT WAS SUCH A NICE DAY, I THOUGHT I'D SURPRISE YOU BY FIXING UP A PICNIC!
NO, INDEED! YOU KNOW WHAT I SAID!
BAW! HE SAYS WE CAN'T GO 'TIL VI'LETS BLOOM!
WHY, MICKEY! AND I'VE FIXED SUCH A NICE LUNCH!
WHEN I SAY NO, I MEAN IT! BUT I TELL Y' WHAT WE'LL DO, INSTEAD!
WE'LL ALL GO OUT IN THE WOODS, AN' HUNT FOR VIOLETS- AN' TAKE OUR LUNCH!
HOORAY!
YIPPEE!
GEE, UNCA MICKEY- THIS IS DANDY!
HUNTING VI'LETS IS AS MUCH FUN AS A PICNIC!
YES— I KINDA THINK IT IS, MYSELF!
4-14
WALT DISNEY

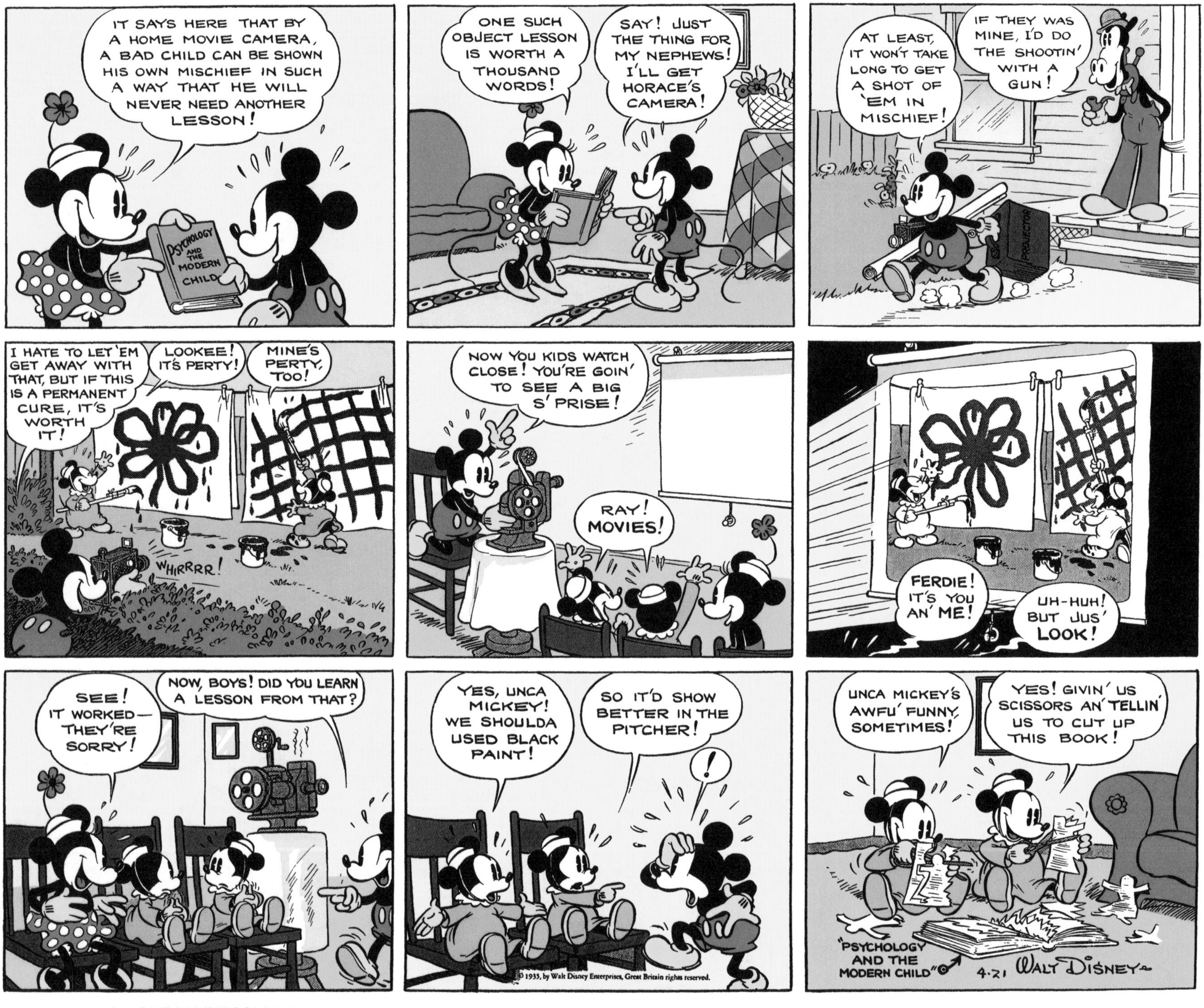
IT SAYS HERE THAT BY A HOME MOVIE CAMERA, A BAD CHILD CAN BE SHOWN HIS OWN MISCHIEF IN SUCH A WAY THAT HE WILL NEVER NEED ANOTHER LESSON!
PSYCHOLOGY AND THE MODERN CHILD
ONE SUCH OBJECT LESSON IS WORTH A THOUSAND WORDS!
SAY! JUST THE THING FOR MY NEPHEWS! I'LL GET HORACE'S CAMERA!
AT LEAST, IT WON'T TAKE LONG TO GET A SHOT OF 'EM IN MISCHIEF!
IF THEY WAS MINE, I'D DO THE SHOOTIN' WITH A GUN!
PROJECTOR
I HATE TO LET 'EM GET AWAY WITH THAT, BUT IF THIS IS A PERMANENT CURE, IT'S WORTH IT!
LOOKEE! IT'S PERTY!
MINE'S PERTY, TOO!
WHIRRRR!
NOW YOU KIDS WATCH CLOSE! YOU'RE GOIN' TO SEE A BIG S'PRISE!
RAY! MOVIES!
FERDIE! IT'S YOU AN' ME!
UH-HUH! BUT JUS' LOOK!
SEE! IT WORKED— THEY'RE SORRY!
NOW, BOYS! DID YOU LEARN A LESSON FROM THAT?
YES, UNCA MICKEY! WE SHOULDA USED BLACK PAINT!
SO IT'D SHOW BETTER IN THE PITCHER!
!
© 1933, by Walt Disney Enterprises, Great Britain rights reserved.
UNCA MICKEY'S AWFU' FUNNY SOMETIMES!
YES! GIVIN' US SCISSORS AN' TELLIN' US TO CUT UP THIS BOOK!
"PSYCHOLOGY AND THE MODERN CHILD"
4·21 WALT DISNEY

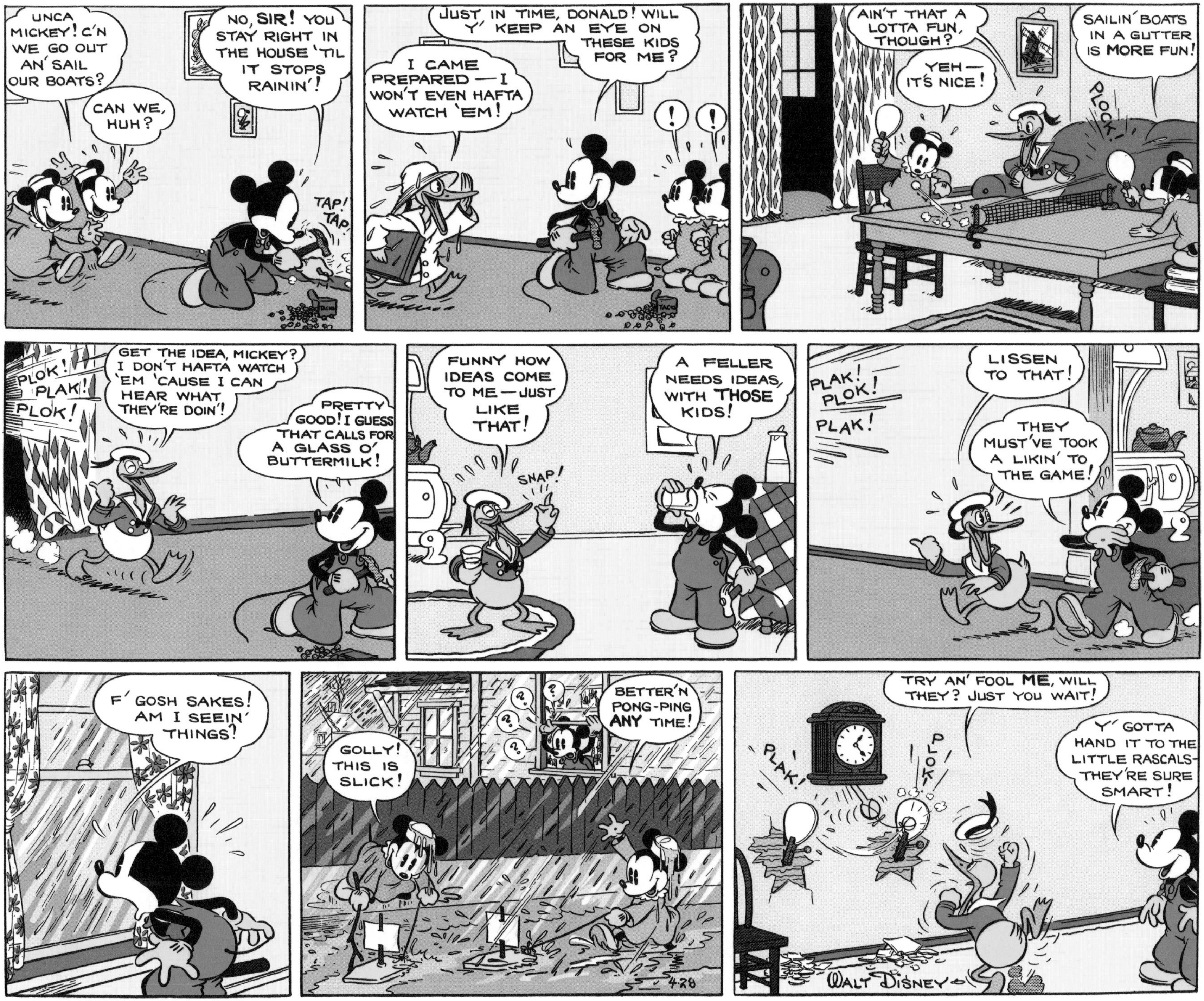
UNCA MICKEY! C'N WE GO OUT AN' SAIL OUR BOATS?
CAN WE, HUH?
NO, SIR! YOU STAY RIGHT IN THE HOUSE 'TIL IT STOPS RAININ'!
TAP! TAP
JUST IN TIME, DONALD! WILL Y' KEEP AN EYE ON THESE KIDS FOR ME?
I CAME PREPARED — I WON'T EVEN HAFTA WATCH 'EM!
!
!
AIN'T THAT A LOTTA FUN, THOUGH?
YEH — IT'S NICE!
SAILIN' BOATS IN A GUTTER IS MORE FUN!
PLOCK!
PLOK! PLAK! PLOK!
GET THE IDEA, MICKEY? I DON'T HAFTA WATCH 'EM 'CAUSE I CAN HEAR WHAT THEY'RE DOIN'!
PRETTY GOOD! I GUESS THAT CALLS FOR A GLASS O' BUTTERMILK!
FUNNY HOW IDEAS COME TO ME — JUST LIKE THAT!
SNAP!
A FELLER NEEDS IDEAS, WITH THOSE KIDS!
PLAK! PLOK! PLAK!
LISSEN TO THAT!
THEY MUST'VE TOOK A LIKIN' TO THE GAME!
F' GOSH SAKES! AM I SEEIN' THINGS?
BETTER'N PONG-PING ANY TIME!
GOLLY! THIS IS SLICK!
4-28
TRY AN' FOOL ME, WILL THEY? JUST YOU WAIT!
Y' GOTTA HAND IT TO THE LITTLE RASCALS — THEY'RE SURE SMART!
PLAK!
PLOK!
WALT DISNEY

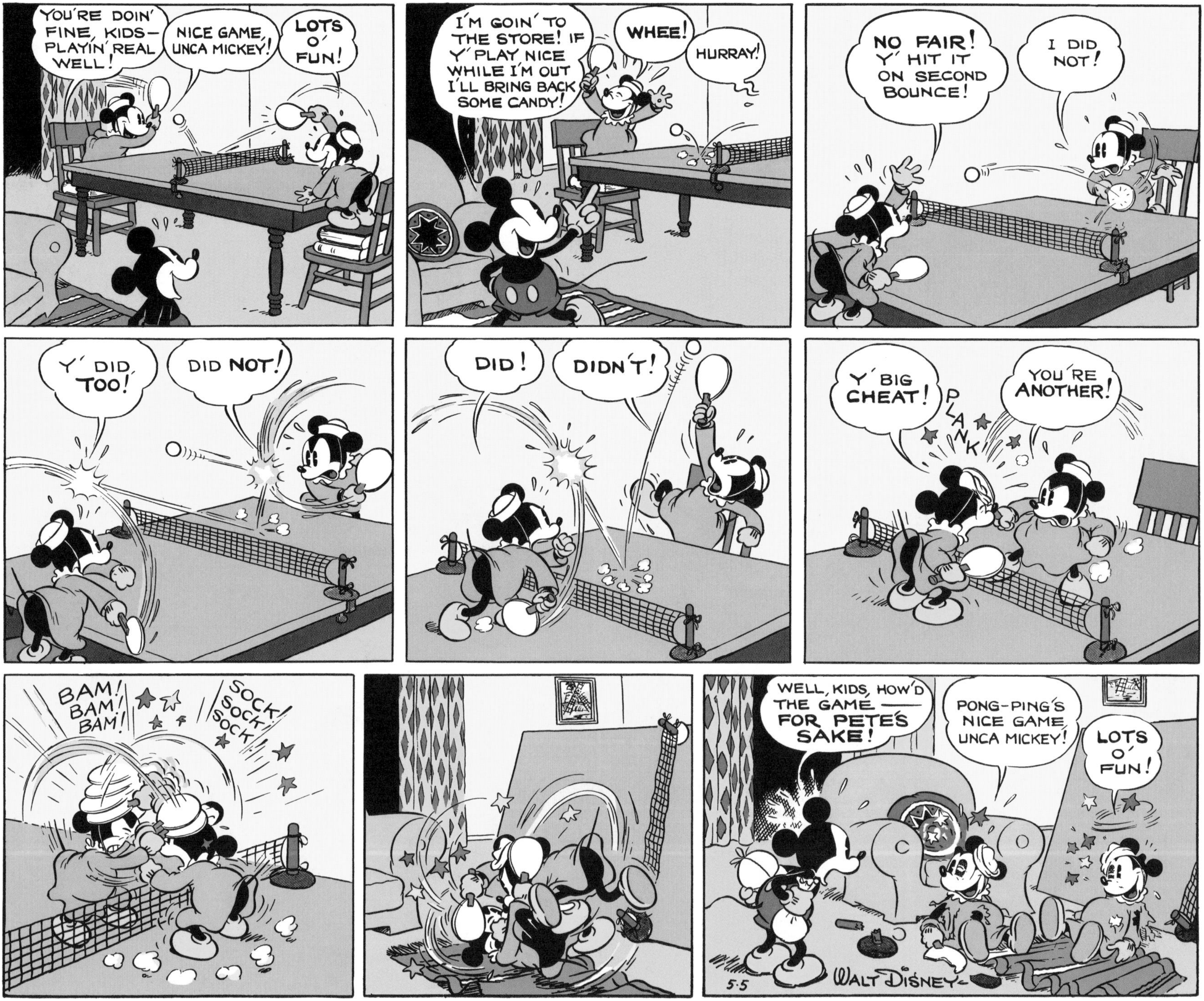
YOU'RE DOIN' FINE, KIDS— PLAYIN' REAL WELL!
NICE GAME, UNCA MICKEY!
LOTS O' FUN!
I'M GOIN' TO THE STORE! IF Y' PLAY NICE WHILE I'M OUT I'LL BRING BACK SOME CANDY!
WHEE!
HURRAY!
NO FAIR! Y' HIT IT ON SECOND BOUNCE!
I DID NOT!
Y' DID TOO!
DID NOT!
DID!
DIDN'T!
Y' BIG CHEAT!
PLANK
YOU'RE ANOTHER!
BAM! BAM! BAM!
SOCK! SOCK! SOCK!
WELL, KIDS, HOW'D THE GAME —— FOR PETE'S SAKE!
PONG-PING'S NICE GAME UNCA MICKEY!
LOTS O' FUN!
5·5
WALT DISNEY

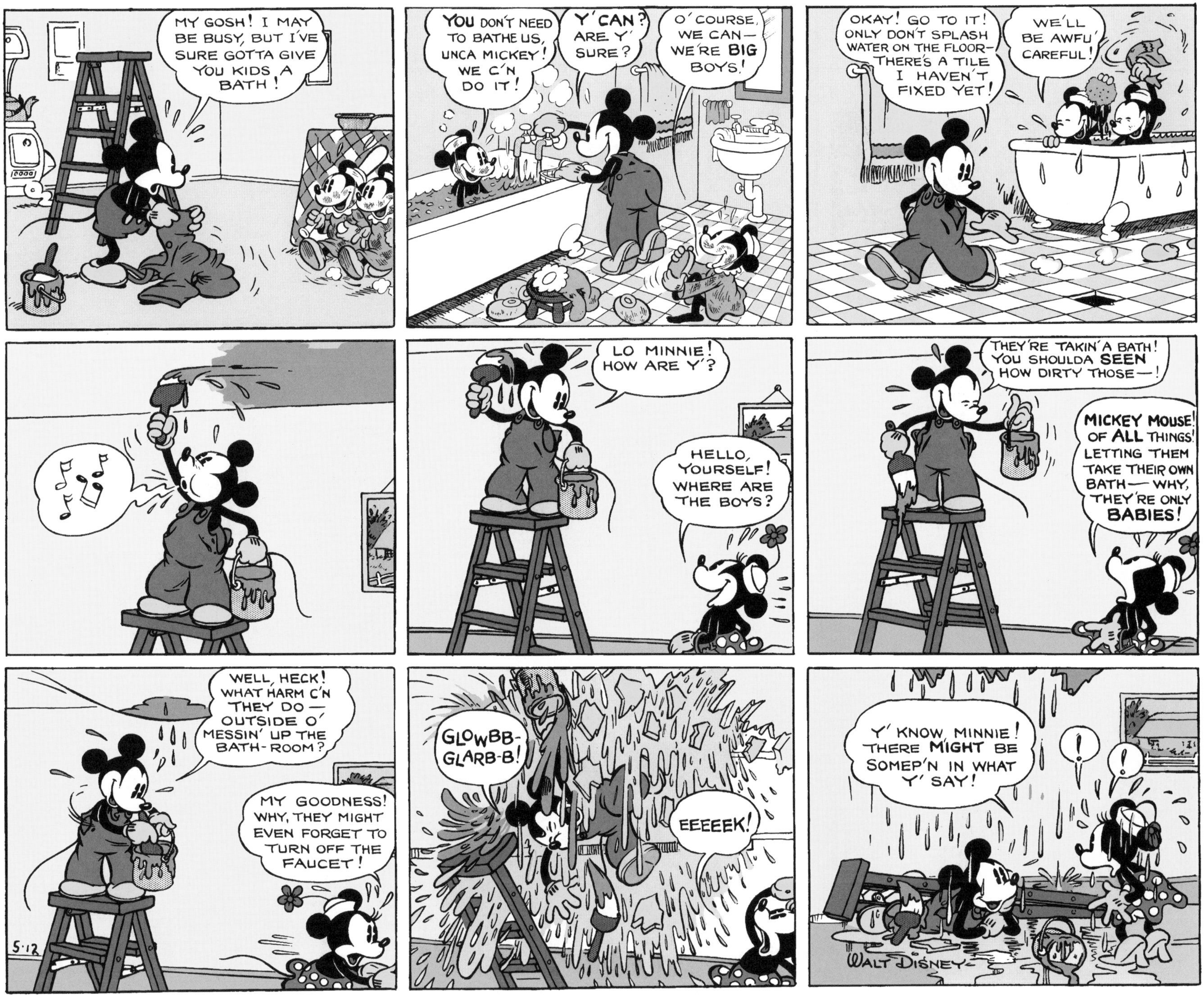
MY GOSH! I MAY BE BUSY, BUT I'VE SURE GOTTA GIVE YOU KIDS A BATH!
YOU DON'T NEED TO BATHE US, UNCA MICKEY! WE C'N DO IT!
Y' CAN? ARE Y' SURE?
O' COURSE, WE CAN— WE'RE BIG BOYS!
OKAY! GO TO IT! ONLY DON'T SPLASH WATER ON THE FLOOR— THERE'S A TILE I HAVEN'T FIXED YET!
WE'LL BE AWFU' CAREFUL!
LO MINNIE! HOW ARE Y'?
HELLO, YOURSELF! WHERE ARE THE BOYS?
THEY'RE TAKIN' A BATH! YOU SHOULDA SEEN HOW DIRTY THOSE—!
MICKEY MOUSE! OF ALL THINGS! LETTING THEM TAKE THEIR OWN BATH— WHY, THEY'RE ONLY BABIES!
WELL, HECK! WHAT HARM C'N THEY DO— OUTSIDE O' MESSIN' UP THE BATH-ROOM?
MY GOODNESS! WHY, THEY MIGHT EVEN FORGET TO TURN OFF THE FAUCET!
5·12
GLOWBB-GLARB-B!
EEEEEK!
Y' KNOW, MINNIE! THERE MIGHT BE SOMEP'N IN WHAT Y' SAY!
!
!
WALT DISNEY

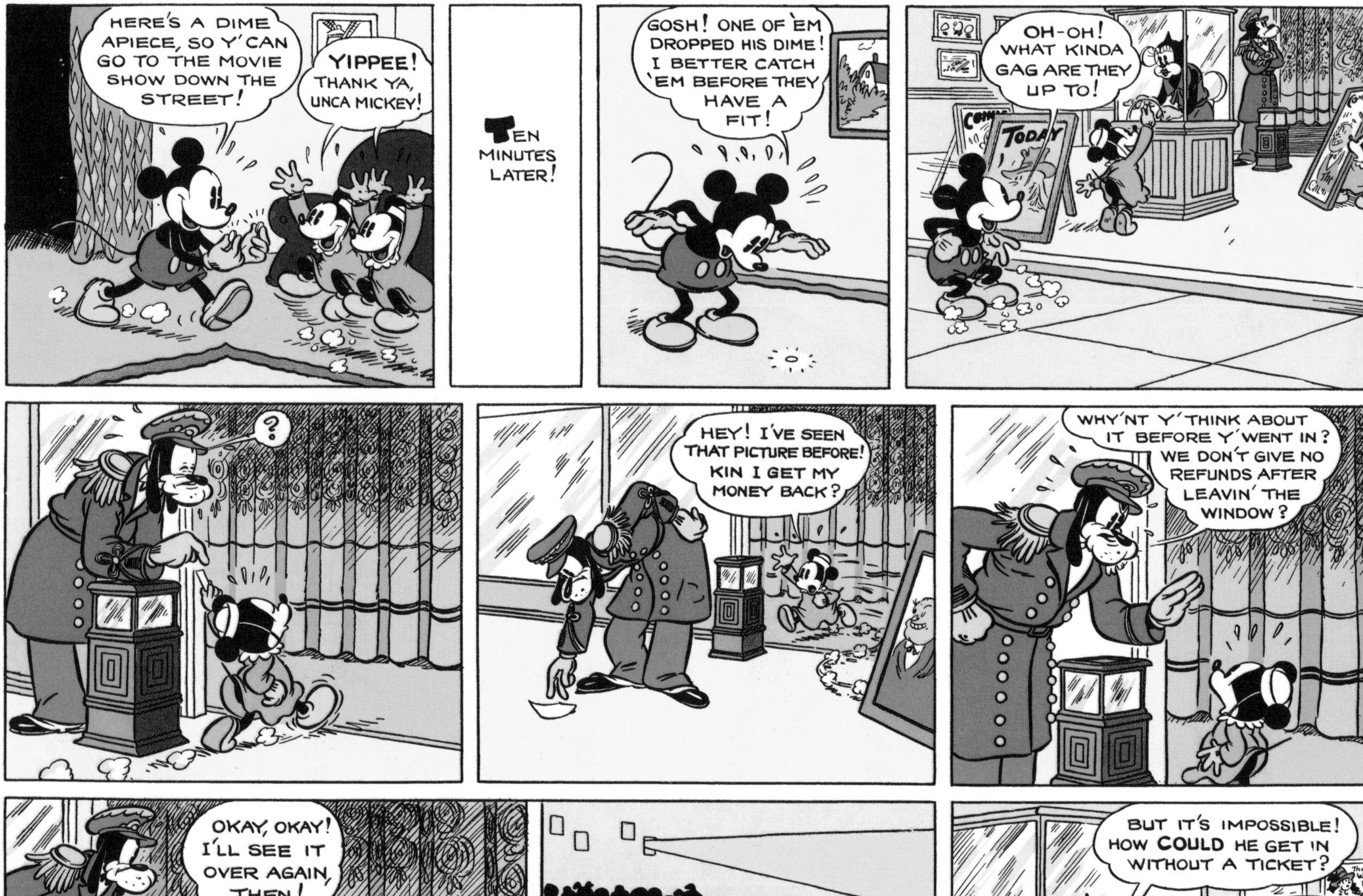
HERE'S A DIME APIECE, SO Y'CAN GO TO THE MOVIE SHOW DOWN THE STREET!
YIPPEE! THANK YA, UNCA MICKEY!
TEN MINUTES LATER!
GOSH! ONE OF 'EM DROPPED HIS DIME! I BETTER CATCH 'EM BEFORE THEY HAVE A FIT!
OH-OH! WHAT KINDA GAG ARE THEY UP TO!
TODAY
?
HEY! I'VE SEEN THAT PICTURE BEFORE! KIN I GET MY MONEY BACK?
WHY'NT Y'THINK ABOUT IT BEFORE Y'WENT IN? WE DON'T GIVE NO REFUNDS AFTER LEAVIN' THE WINDOW?
OKAY, OKAY! I'LL SEE IT OVER AGAIN, THEN!
5-19
BUT IT'S IMPOSSIBLE! HOW COULD HE GET IN WITHOUT A TICKET?
HERE'S HIS DIME, LADY! IF Y'KNEW MY NEPHEWS Y'WOULDN'T ASK FOOLISH QUESTIONS!
WALT DISNEY

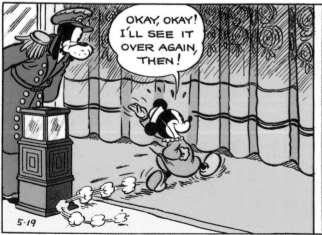

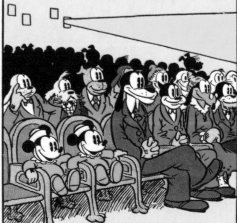

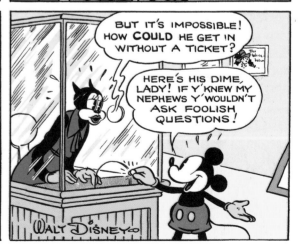

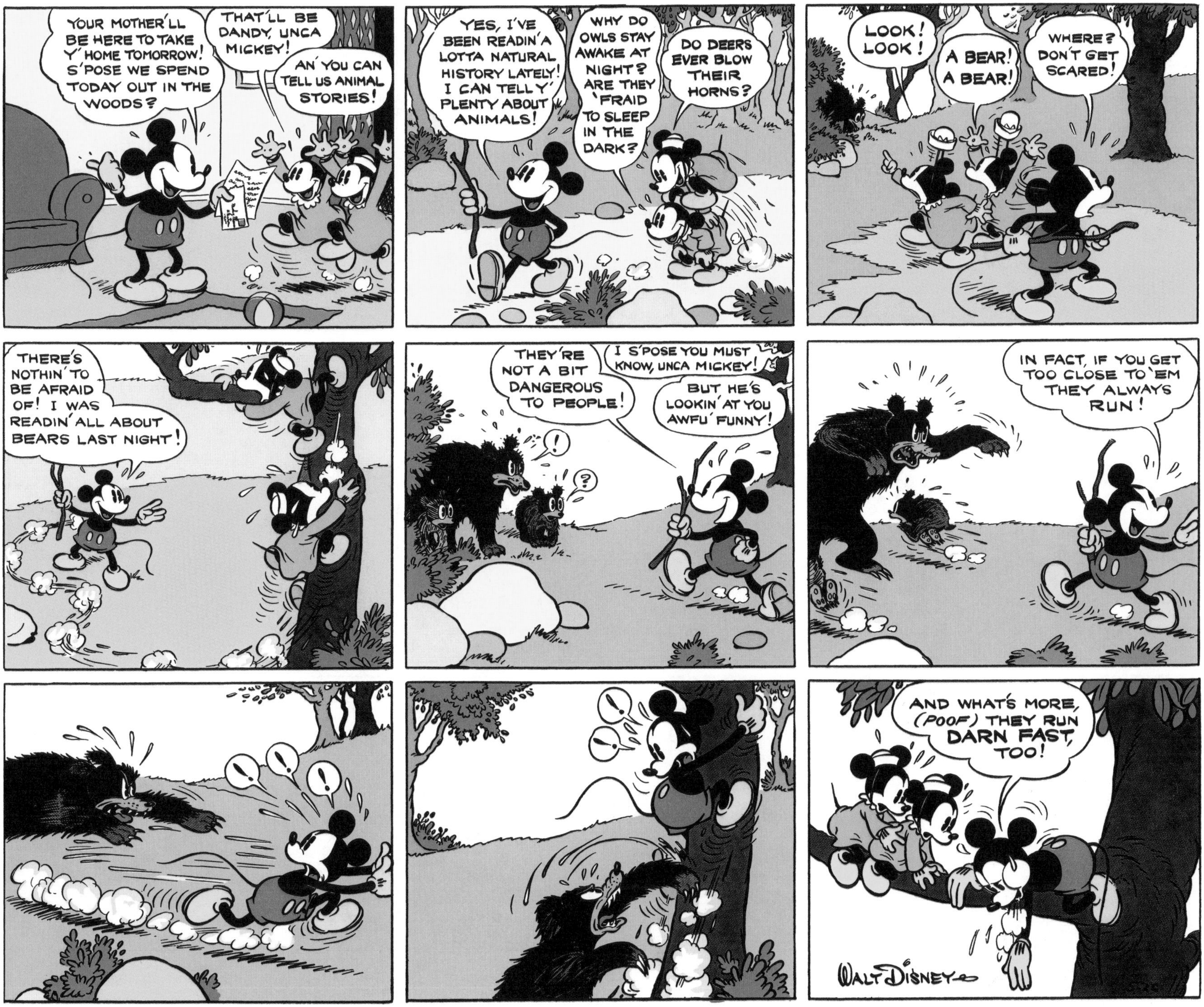
YOUR MOTHER'LL BE HERE TO TAKE Y' HOME TOMORROW! S'POSE WE SPEND TODAY OUT IN THE WOODS?
THAT'LL BE DANDY, UNCA MICKEY!
AN' YOU CAN TELL US ANIMAL STORIES!
YES, I'VE BEEN READIN' A LOTTA NATURAL HISTORY LATELY! I CAN TELL Y' PLENTY ABOUT ANIMALS!
WHY DO OWLS STAY AWAKE AT NIGHT? ARE THEY 'FRAID TO SLEEP IN THE DARK?
DO DEERS EVER BLOW THEIR HORNS?
LOOK! LOOK!
A BEAR! A BEAR!
WHERE? DON'T GET SCARED!
THERE'S NOTHIN' TO BE AFRAID OF! I WAS READIN' ALL ABOUT BEARS LAST NIGHT!
THEY'RE NOT A BIT DANGEROUS TO PEOPLE!
I S'POSE YOU MUST KNOW, UNCA MICKEY!
BUT HE'S LOOKIN' AT YOU AWFU' FUNNY!
IN FACT, IF YOU GET TOO CLOSE TO 'EM THEY ALWAYS RUN!
AND WHAT'S MORE, (POOF) THEY RUN DARN FAST, TOO!
WALT DISNEY

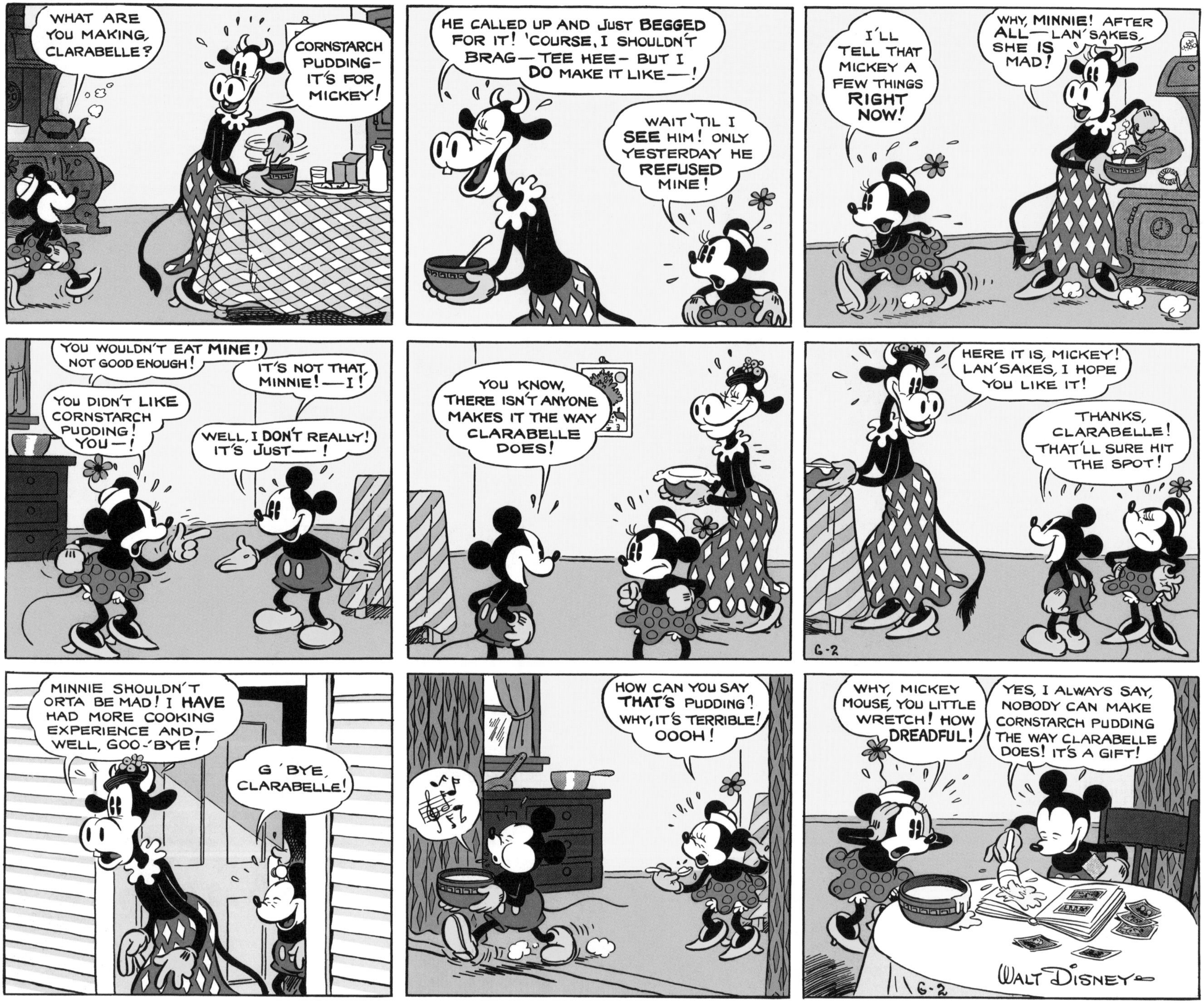
WHAT ARE YOU MAKING, CLARABELLE?
CORNSTARCH PUDDING— IT'S FOR MICKEY!
HE CALLED UP AND JUST BEGGED FOR IT! 'COURSE, I SHOULDN'T BRAG— TEE HEE— BUT I DO MAKE IT LIKE—!
WAIT 'TIL I SEE HIM! ONLY YESTERDAY HE REFUSED MINE!
I'LL TELL THAT MICKEY A FEW THINGS RIGHT NOW!
WHY, MINNIE! AFTER ALL— LAN' SAKES, SHE IS MAD!
YOU WOULDN'T EAT MINE! NOT GOOD ENOUGH!
YOU DIDN'T LIKE CORNSTARCH PUDDING! YOU—!
IT'S NOT THAT, MINNIE!—I!
WELL, I DON'T REALLY! IT'S JUST—!
YOU KNOW, THERE ISN'T ANYONE MAKES IT THE WAY CLARABELLE DOES!
HERE IT IS, MICKEY! LAN' SAKES, I HOPE YOU LIKE IT!
THANKS, CLARABELLE! THAT'LL SURE HIT THE SPOT!
G-2
MINNIE SHOULDN'T ORTA BE MAD! I HAVE HAD MORE COOKING EXPERIENCE AND— WELL, GOO-'BYE!
G 'BYE, CLARABELLE!
HOW CAN YOU SAY THAT'S PUDDING? WHY, IT'S TERRIBLE! OOOH!
WHY, MICKEY MOUSE, YOU LITTLE WRETCH! HOW DREADFUL!
YES, I ALWAYS SAY, NOBODY CAN MAKE CORNSTARCH PUDDING THE WAY CLARABELLE DOES! IT'S A GIFT!
WALT DISNEY
G-2

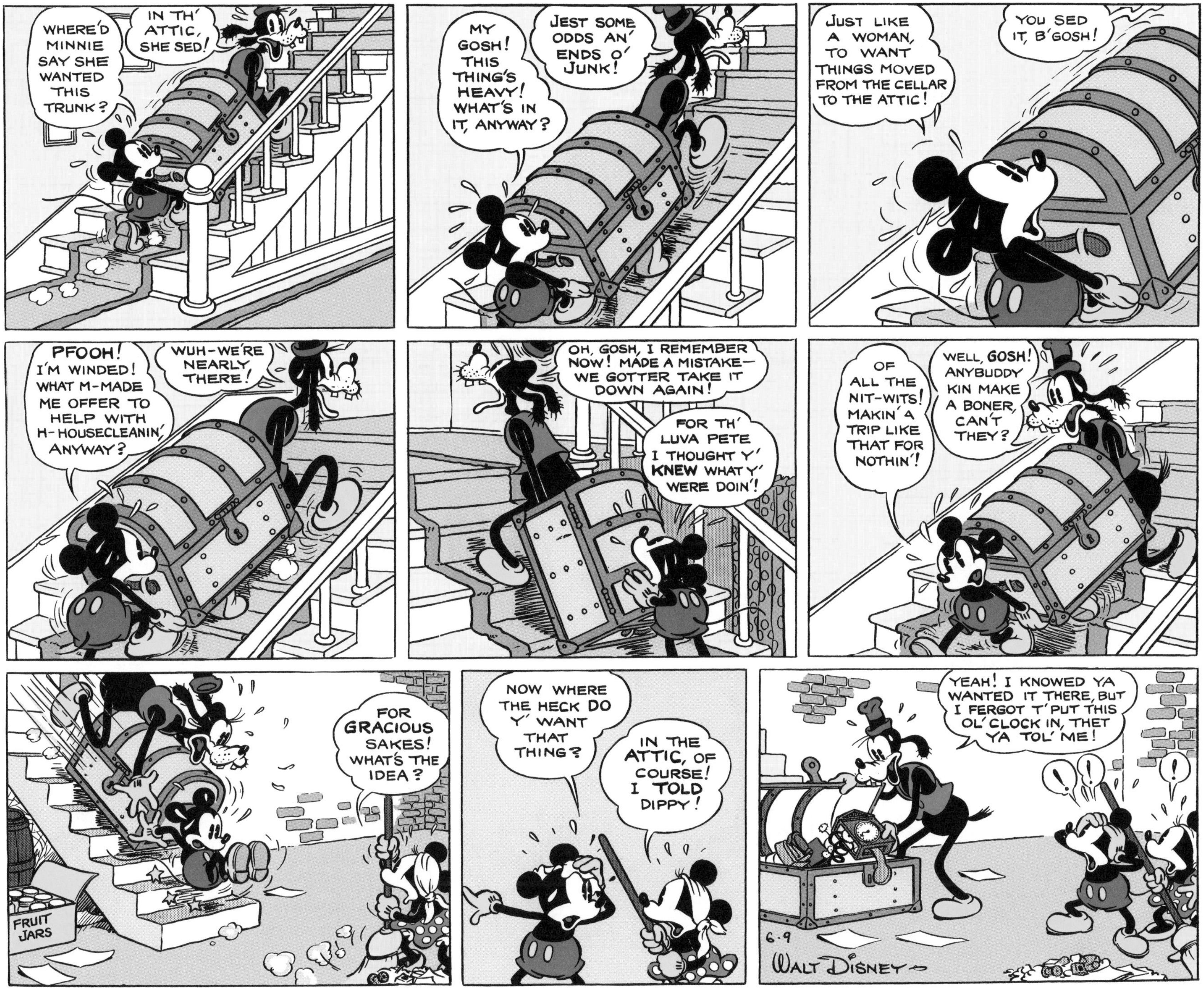
WHERE'D MINNIE SAY SHE WANTED THIS TRUNK?
IN TH' ATTIC, SHE SED!
MY GOSH! THIS THING'S HEAVY! WHAT'S IN IT, ANYWAY?
JEST SOME ODDS AN' ENDS O' JUNK!
JUST LIKE A WOMAN, TO WANT THINGS MOVED FROM THE CELLAR TO THE ATTIC!
YOU SED IT, B'GOSH!
PFOOH! I'M WINDED! WHAT M-MADE ME OFFER TO HELP WITH H-HOUSECLEANIN' ANYWAY?
WUH-WE'RE NEARLY THERE!
OH, GOSH, I REMEMBER NOW! MADE A MISTAKE— WE GOTTER TAKE IT DOWN AGAIN!
FOR TH' LUVA PETE I THOUGHT Y' KNEW WHAT Y' WERE DOIN'!
OF ALL THE NIT-WITS! MAKIN' A TRIP LIKE THAT FOR NOTHIN'!
WELL, GOSH! ANYBUDDY KIN MAKE A BONER, CAN'T THEY?
FOR GRACIOUS SAKES! WHAT'S THE IDEA?
FRUIT JARS
NOW WHERE THE HECK DO Y' WANT THAT THING?
IN THE ATTIC, OF COURSE! I TOLD DIPPY!
YEAH! I KNOWED YA WANTED IT THERE, BUT I FERGOT T' PUT THIS OL' CLOCK IN, THET YA TOL' ME!
! ! !
6-9
WALT DISNEY

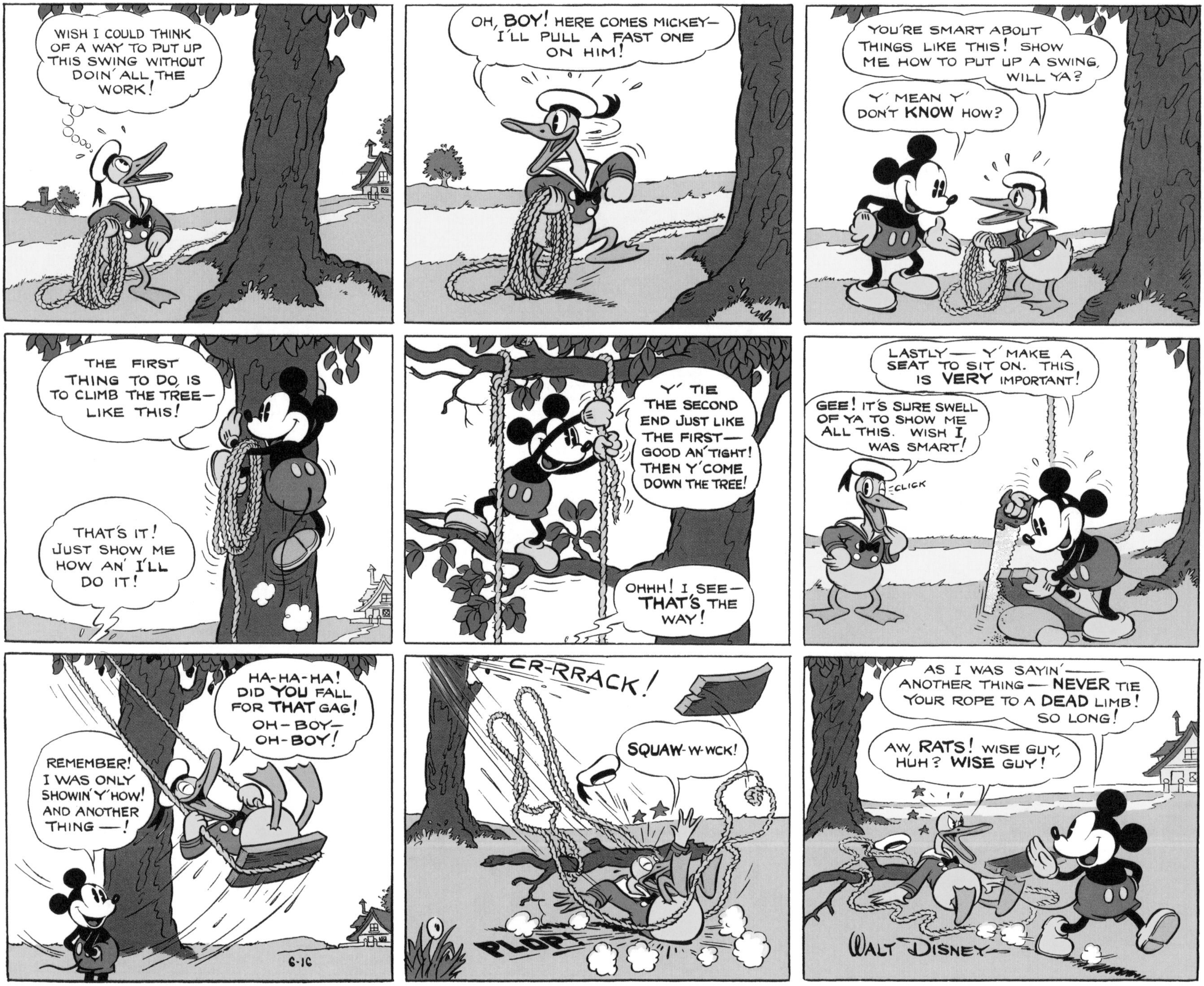
WISH I COULD THINK OF A WAY TO PUT UP THIS SWING WITHOUT DOIN' ALL THE WORK!
OH, BOY! HERE COMES MICKEY— I'LL PULL A FAST ONE ON HIM!
YOU'RE SMART ABOUT THINGS LIKE THIS! SHOW ME HOW TO PUT UP A SWING, WILL YA?
Y' MEAN Y' DON'T KNOW HOW?
THE FIRST THING TO DO, IS TO CLIMB THE TREE— LIKE THIS!
THAT'S IT! JUST SHOW ME HOW AN' I'LL DO IT!
Y' TIE THE SECOND END JUST LIKE THE FIRST— GOOD AN' TIGHT! THEN Y' COME DOWN THE TREE!
OHHH! I SEE— THAT'S THE WAY!
LASTLY— Y' MAKE A SEAT TO SIT ON. THIS IS VERY IMPORTANT!
GEE! IT'S SURE SWELL OF YA TO SHOW ME ALL THIS. WISH I WAS SMART!
CLICK
HA-HA-HA! DID YOU FALL FOR THAT GAG! OH-BOY-OH-BOY!
REMEMBER! I WAS ONLY SHOWIN' Y' HOW! AND ANOTHER THING—!
6-16
CR-RRACK!
SQUAW-W-WCK!
PLOP!
AS I WAS SAYIN'— ANOTHER THING— NEVER TIE YOUR ROPE TO A DEAD LIMB! SO LONG!
AW, RATS! WISE GUY, HUH? WISE GUY!
WALT DISNEY

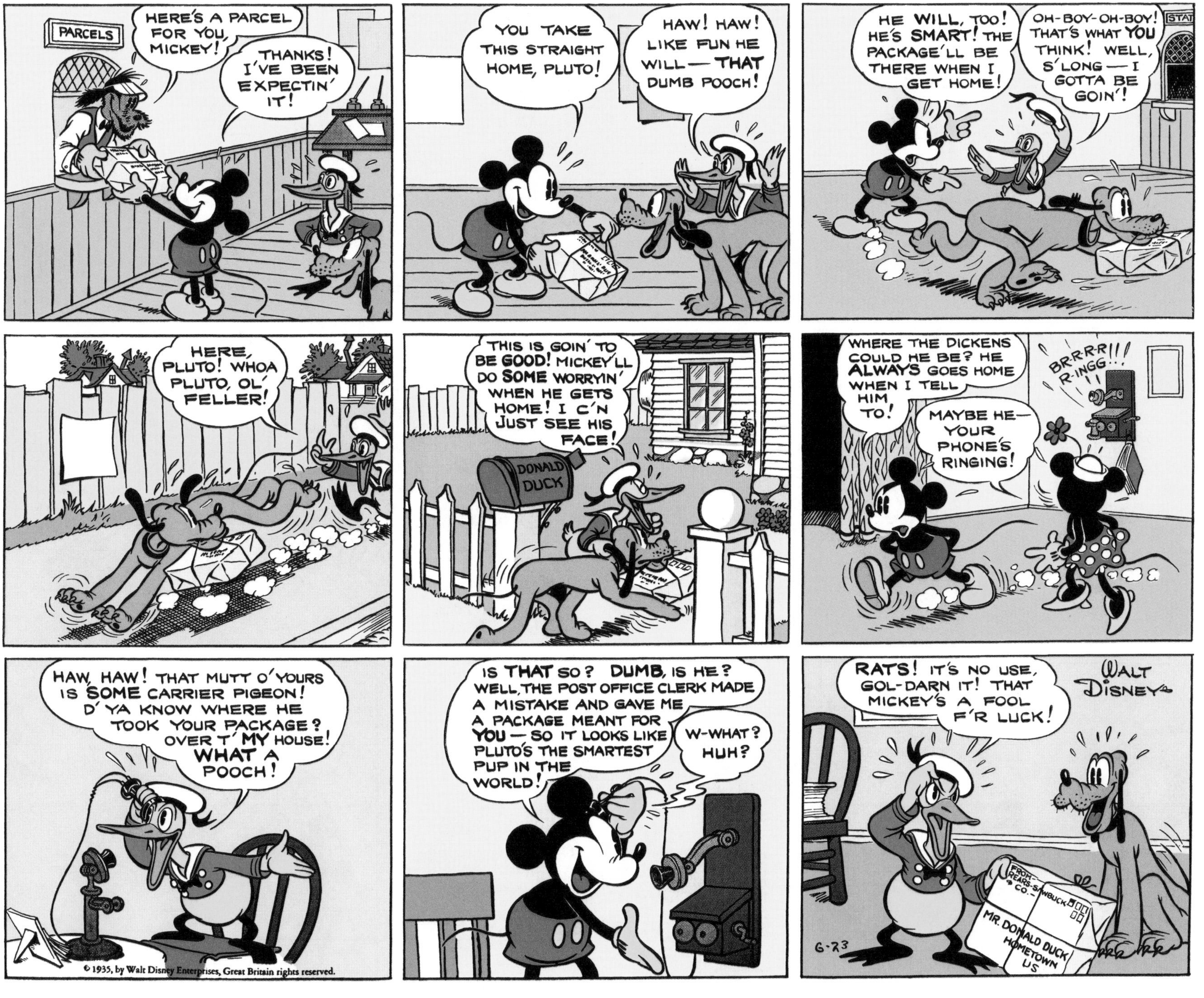
PARCELS
HERE'S A PARCEL FOR YOU, MICKEY!
THANKS! I'VE BEEN EXPECTIN' IT!
YOU TAKE THIS STRAIGHT HOME, PLUTO!
HAW! HAW! LIKE FUN HE WILL — THAT DUMB POOCH!
HE WILL, TOO! HE'S SMART! THE PACKAGE'LL BE THERE WHEN I GET HOME!
OH-BOY-OH-BOY! THAT'S WHAT YOU THINK! WELL, S'LONG — I GOTTA BE GOIN'!
HERE, PLUTO! WHOA PLUTO, OL' FELLER!
THIS IS GOIN' TO BE GOOD! MICKEY'LL DO SOME WORRYIN' WHEN HE GETS HOME! I C'N JUST SEE HIS FACE!
DONALD DUCK
WHERE THE DICKENS COULD HE BE? HE ALWAYS GOES HOME WHEN I TELL HIM TO!
BR-R-R-R!!! R-INGG!!!
MAYBE HE— YOUR PHONE'S RINGING!
HAW, HAW! THAT MUTT O' YOURS IS SOME CARRIER PIGEON! D' YA KNOW WHERE HE TOOK YOUR PACKAGE? OVER T' MY HOUSE! WHAT A POOCH!
IS THAT SO? DUMB, IS HE? WELL, THE POST OFFICE CLERK MADE A MISTAKE AND GAVE ME A PACKAGE MEANT FOR YOU — SO IT LOOKS LIKE PLUTO'S THE SMARTEST PUP IN THE WORLD!
W-WHAT? HUH?
RATS! IT'S NO USE, GOL-DARN IT! THAT MICKEY'S A FOOL F'R LUCK!
WALT DISNEY
FROM- REARS-SAWBUCK & CO.
MR. DONALD DUCK HOMETOWN US
6-23

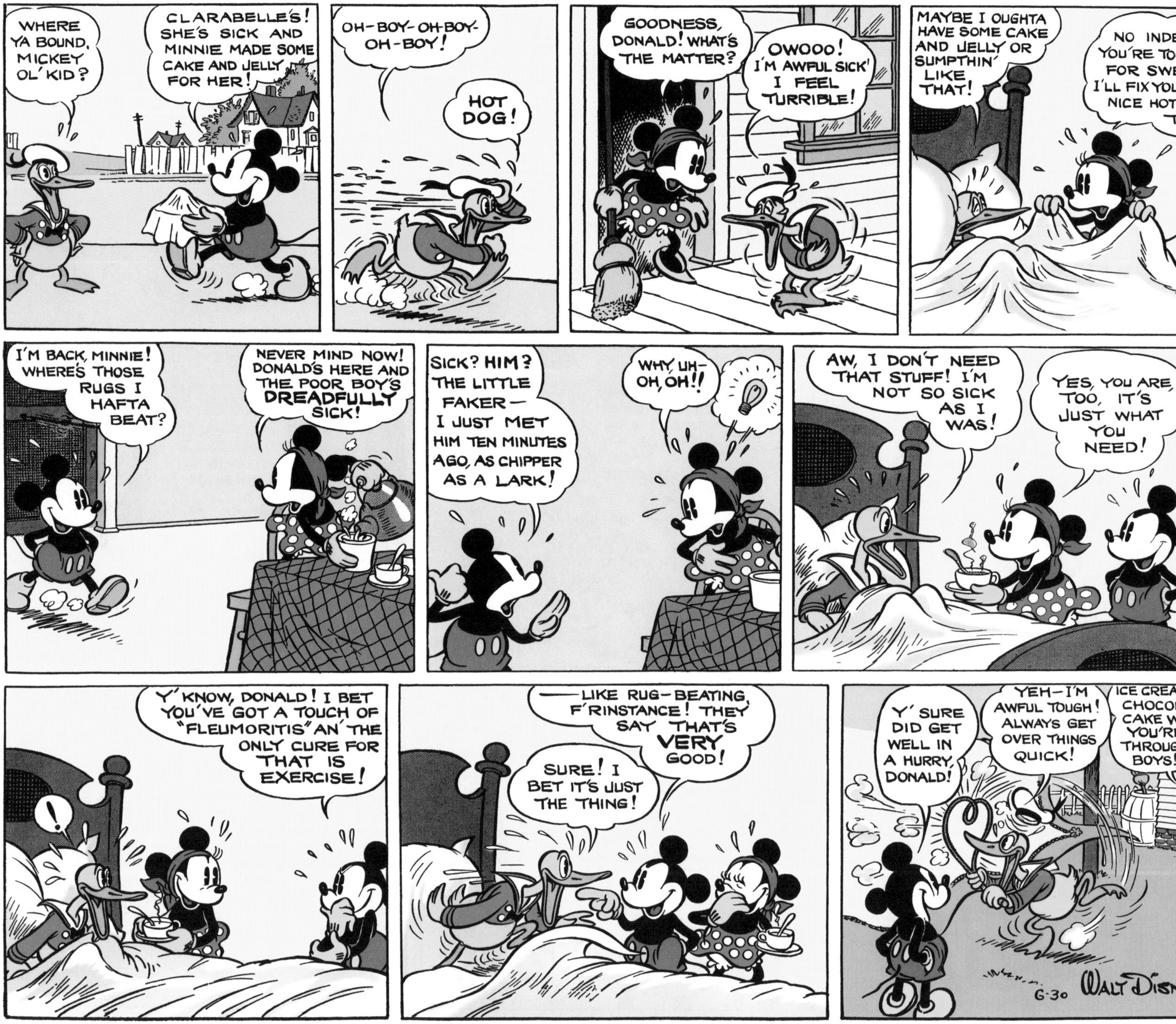
WHERE YA BOUND, MICKEY OL' KID?
CLARABELLE'S! SHE'S SICK AND MINNIE MADE SOME CAKE AND JELLY FOR HER!
OH-BOY-OH-BOY-OH-BOY!
HOT DOG!
GOODNESS, DONALD! WHAT'S THE MATTER?
OWOOO! I'M AWFUL SICK! I FEEL TURRIBLE!
MAYBE I OUGHTA HAVE SOME CAKE AND JELLY OR SUMPTHIN' LIKE THAT!
NO INDEED! YOU'RE TOO SICK FOR SWEETS! I'LL FIX YOU SOME NICE HOT SAGE TEA!
I'M BACK, MINNIE! WHERE'S THOSE RUGS I HAFTA BEAT?
NEVER MIND NOW! DONALD'S HERE AND THE POOR BOY'S DREADFULLY SICK!
SICK? HIM? THE LITTLE FAKER — I JUST MET HIM TEN MINUTES AGO, AS CHIPPER AS A LARK!
WHY, UH-OH, OH!!
AW, I DON'T NEED THAT STUFF! I'M NOT SO SICK AS I WAS!
YES, YOU ARE, TOO, IT'S JUST WHAT YOU NEED!
Y'KNOW, DONALD! I BET YOU'VE GOT A TOUCH OF "FLEUMORITIS" AN' THE ONLY CURE FOR THAT IS EXERCISE!
!
—LIKE RUG-BEATING, F'RINSTANCE! THEY SAY THAT'S VERY GOOD!
SURE! I BET IT'S JUST THE THING!
Y'SURE DID GET WELL IN A HURRY, DONALD!
YEH-I'M AWFUL TOUGH! ALWAYS GET OVER THINGS QUICK!
ICE CREAM AND CHOCOLATE CAKE WHEN YOU'RE THROUGH, BOYS!
6-30
WALT DISNEY

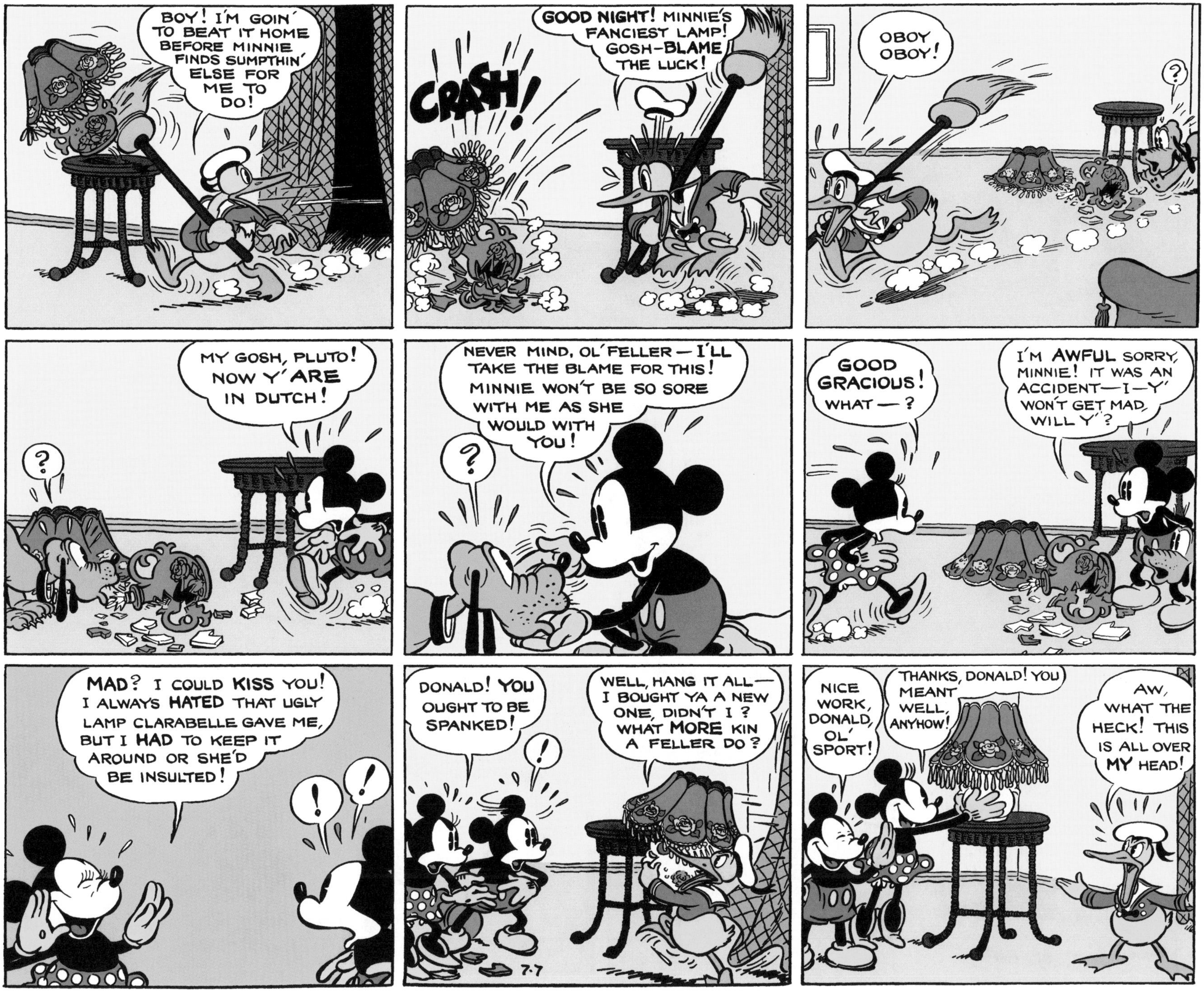
BOY! I'M GOIN' TO BEAT IT HOME BEFORE MINNIE FINDS SUMPTHIN' ELSE FOR ME TO DO!
CRASH!
GOOD NIGHT! MINNIE'S FANCIEST LAMP! GOSH-BLAME THE LUCK!
OBOY OBOY!
?
MY GOSH, PLUTO! NOW Y'ARE IN DUTCH!
?
NEVER MIND, OL' FELLER — I'LL TAKE THE BLAME FOR THIS! MINNIE WON'T BE SO SORE WITH ME AS SHE WOULD WITH YOU!
?
GOOD GRACIOUS! WHAT — ?
I'M AWFUL SORRY, MINNIE! IT WAS AN ACCIDENT — I — Y' WON'T GET MAD, WILL Y'?
MAD? I COULD KISS YOU! I ALWAYS HATED THAT UGLY LAMP CLARABELLE GAVE ME, BUT I HAD TO KEEP IT AROUND OR SHE'D BE INSULTED!
!
!
DONALD! YOU OUGHT TO BE SPANKED!
!
WELL, HANG IT ALL — I BOUGHT YA A NEW ONE, DIDN'T I? WHAT MORE KIN A FELLER DO?
7-7
NICE WORK, DONALD, OL' SPORT!
THANKS, DONALD! YOU MEANT WELL, ANYHOW!
AW, WHAT THE HECK! THIS IS ALL OVER MY HEAD!

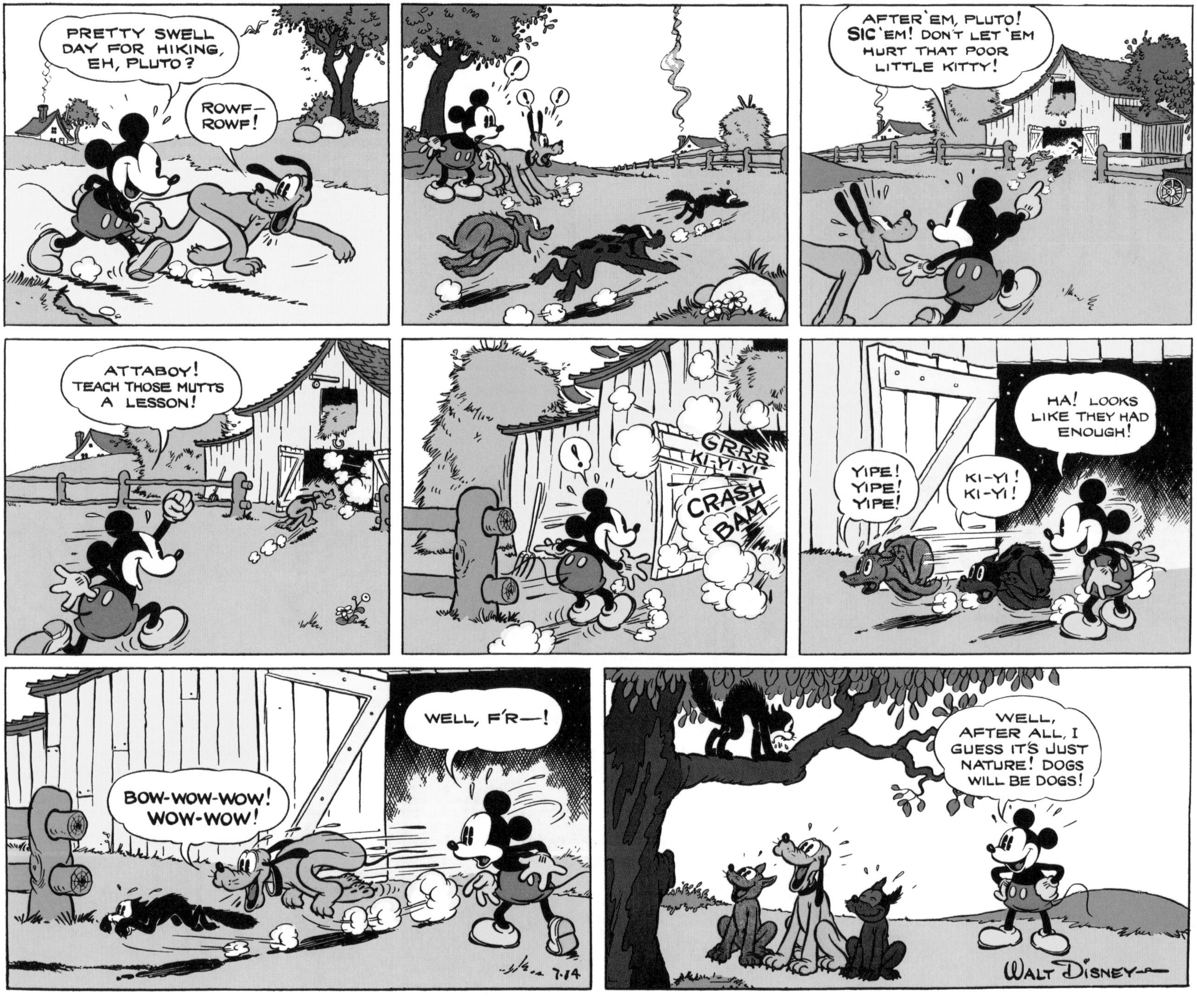
PRETTY SWELL DAY FOR HIKING, EH, PLUTO?
ROWF–ROWF!
!
!
!
AFTER 'EM, PLUTO! SIC 'EM! DON'T LET 'EM HURT THAT POOR LITTLE KITTY!
ATTABOY! TEACH THOSE MUTTS A LESSON!
!
GRR-R
KI-YI-YI
CRASH
BAM
YIPE! YIPE! YIPE!
KI-YI! KI-YI!
HA! LOOKS LIKE THEY HAD ENOUGH!
WELL, F'R—!
BOW-WOW-WOW! WOW-WOW!
7-14
WELL, AFTER ALL, I GUESS IT'S JUST NATURE! DOGS WILL BE DOGS!
WALT DISNEY

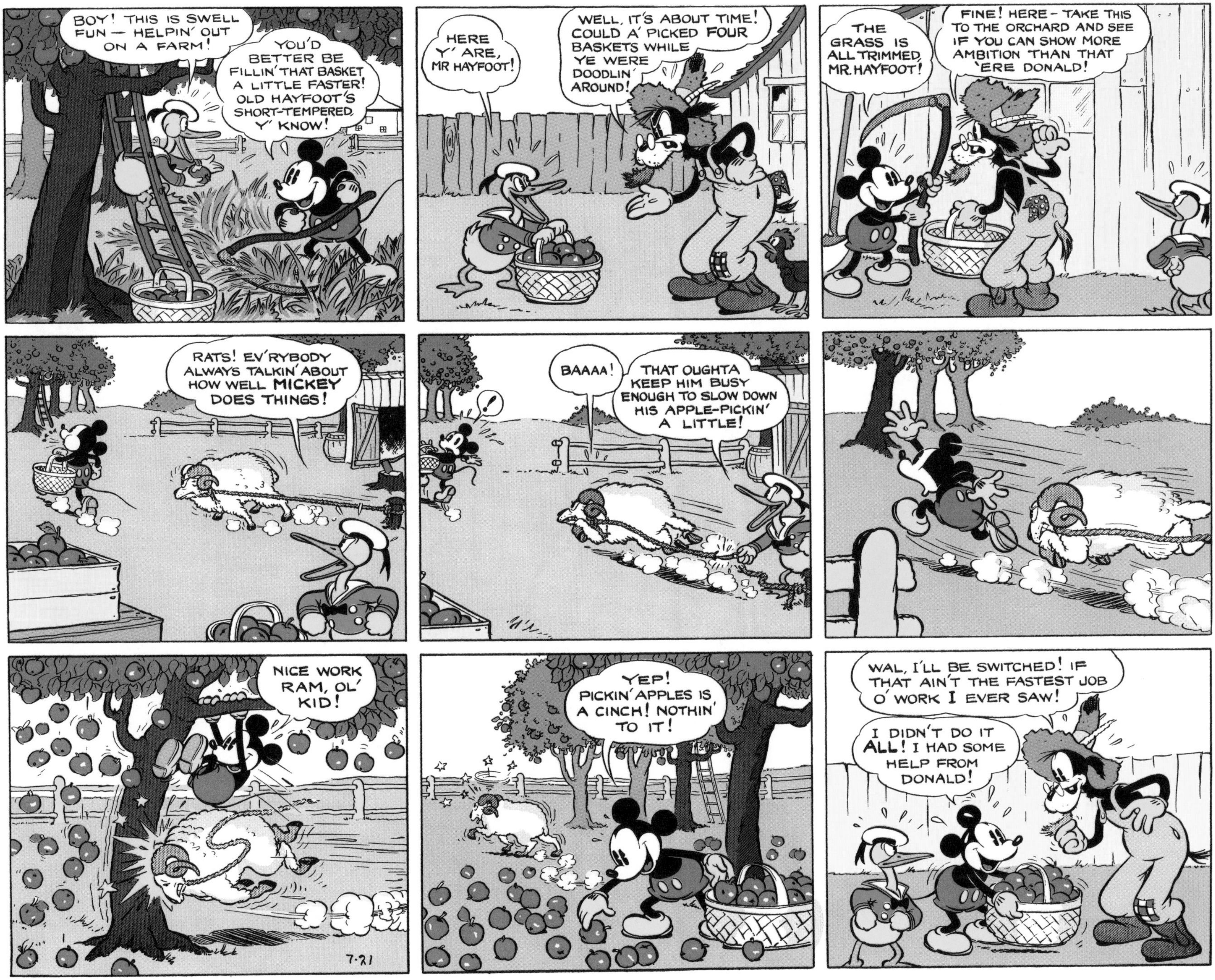
BOY! THIS IS SWELL FUN — HELPIN' OUT ON A FARM!
YOU'D BETTER BE FILLIN' THAT BASKET A LITTLE FASTER! OLD HAYFOOT'S SHORT-TEMPERED, Y' KNOW!
HERE Y' ARE, MR HAYFOOT!
WELL, IT'S ABOUT TIME! COULD A' PICKED FOUR BASKETS WHILE YE WERE DOODLIN' AROUND!
THE GRASS IS ALL TRIMMED, MR. HAYFOOT!
FINE! HERE - TAKE THIS TO THE ORCHARD AND SEE IF YOU CAN SHOW MORE AMBITION THAN THAT 'ERE DONALD!
RATS! EV'RYBODY ALWAYS TALKIN' ABOUT HOW WELL MICKEY DOES THINGS!
BAAAA!
THAT OUGHTA KEEP HIM BUSY ENOUGH TO SLOW DOWN HIS APPLE-PICKIN' A LITTLE!
!
NICE WORK RAM, OL' KID!
7-21
YEP! PICKIN' APPLES IS A CINCH! NOTHIN' TO IT!
WAL, I'LL BE SWITCHED! IF THAT AIN'T THE FASTEST JOB O' WORK I EVER SAW!
I DIDN'T DO IT ALL! I HAD SOME HELP FROM DONALD!

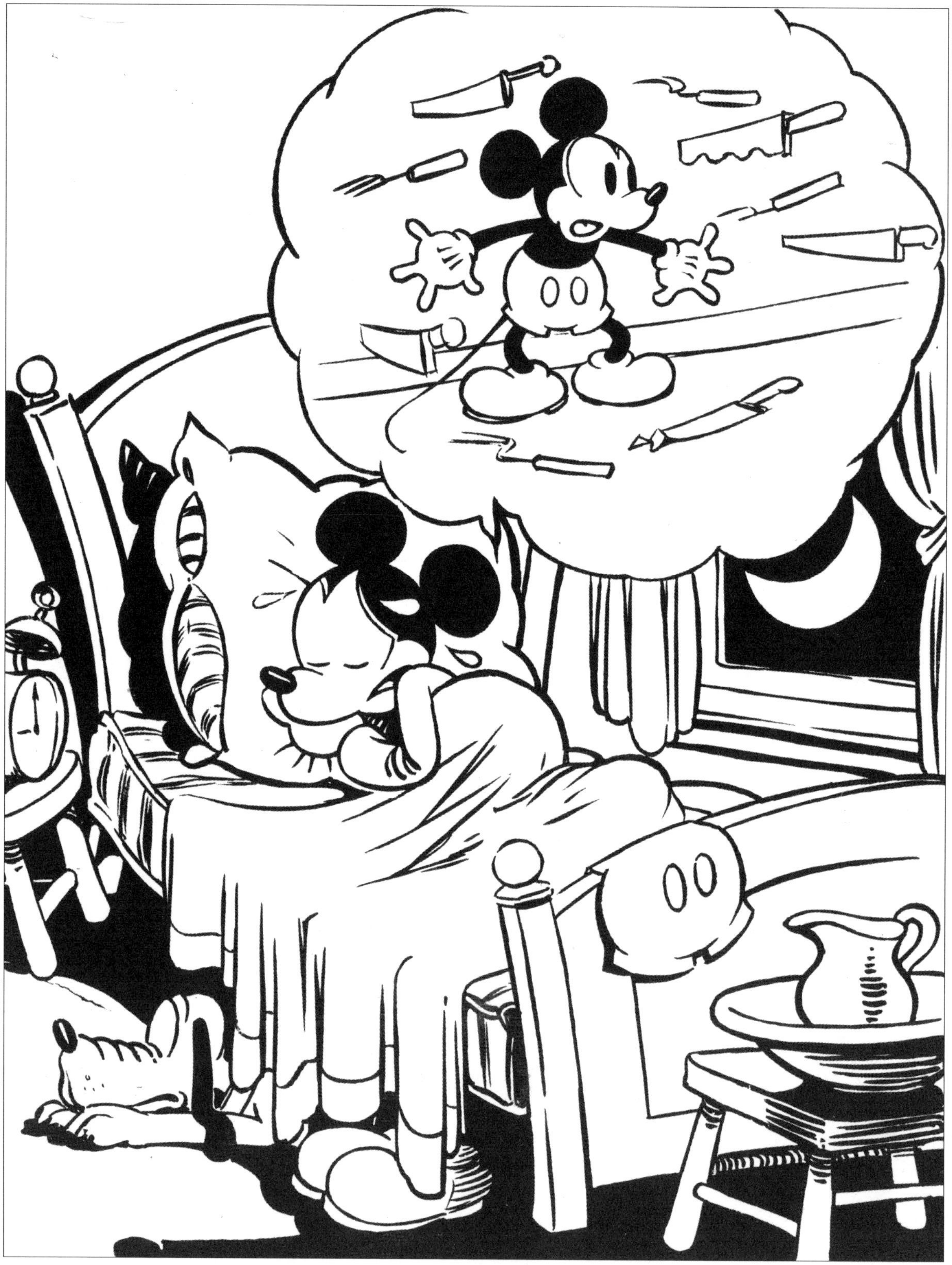

Mickey's nephews made Sunday strip mayhem in 1935—but not as much as Mickey faced from their "ancestors," the multiple mouselings in *Mickey's Nightmare* (1932; see page 253 for details). Poor Mickey envisions the kids' circus knife-throwing act in this *Nightmare* publicity drawing. Art attributed to Floyd Gottfredson (pencils) and Tom Wood (inks); image courtesy Walt Disney Photo Library.

HOPPY THE KANGAROO

AND

GAG STRIPS

JULY 28, 1935

–

DECEMBER 29, 1935

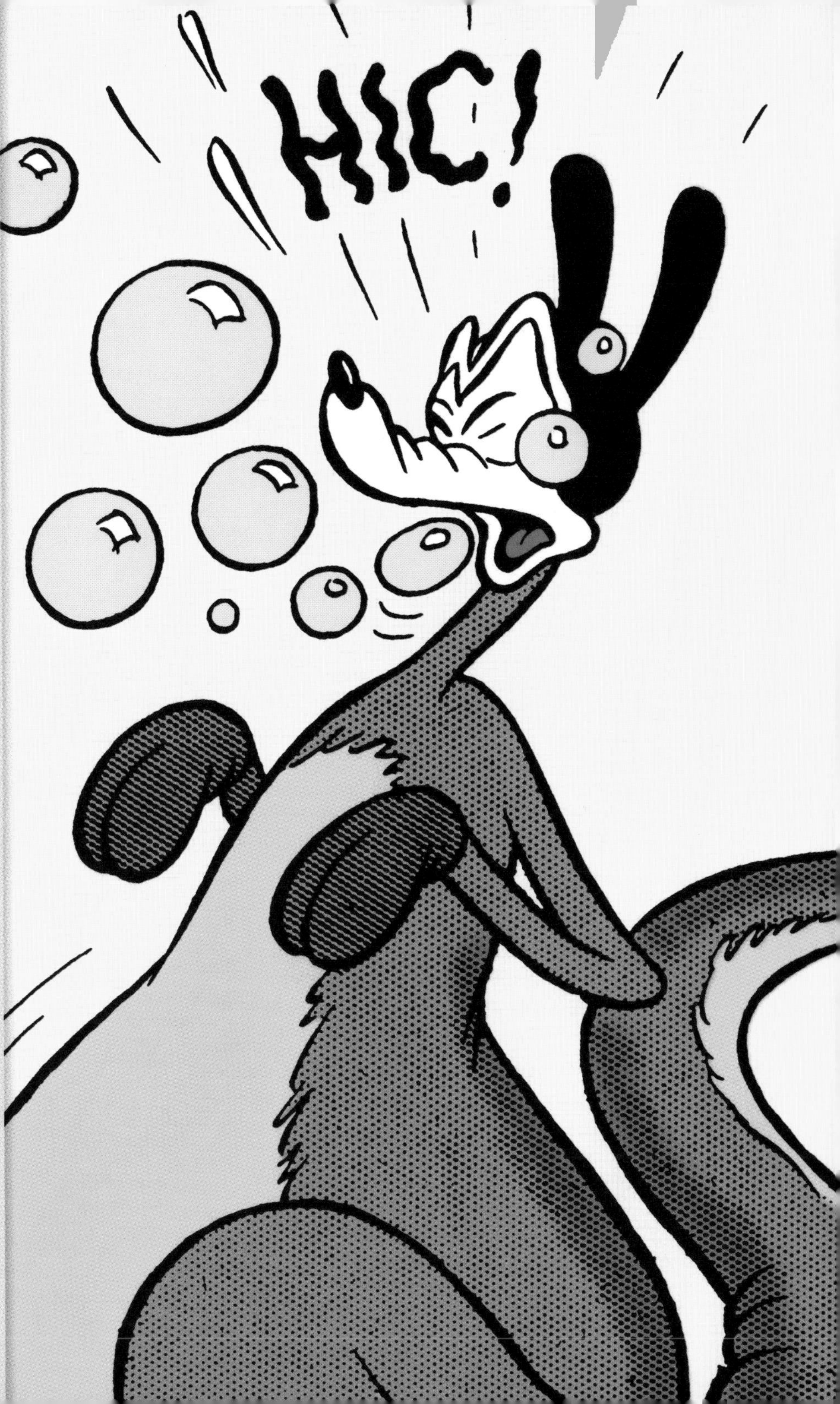
HIC!

MICKEY MOUSE
REGISTERED U.S. PATENT OFFICE

HOPPY THE AMBASSADOR

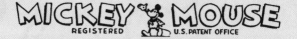

Numerous Mickey Mouse cartoons, comics, and marketing initiatives have been based on current events. Lindbergh's famous flight inspired the cartoon *Plane Crazy* (1928) and the comics continuity "Lost on a Desert Island" (1930). A national vogue for horse races led to the cartoon *The Steeplechase* (1933); the popularity of Depression-era science fiction inspired Gotfredson's "Island in the Sky" (1936-37).

"Hoppy the Kangaroo," on the other hand, was a whole different animal. Would you believe—a comics continuity inspired by a *wine tycoon*?

The "Hoppy" backstory began inauspiciously in early 1933, when the Disney studio circulated an outline for a proposed Mickey short called "The Station Agent." Mickey was to be "station master and freight agent of a one-horse depot," where he and Pluto would be pestered by a shipment of three boxing kangaroos.[1] It's easy to see why kangaroos seemed like ideal subjects for animation; with their jumping, fighting, and comical physiques, the animals would seem to be naturally funny. But perhaps the humor didn't flow as quickly as expected. After some on-and-off development, "Station Agent" evolved into the saga of a different big, bumptious critter—*Donald's Ostrich* (1937)—and kangaroos were left back out in the outback.

But not for long.

Mickey Mouse and Disney cartoons were popular from the start in Australia; and in August 1934, major Sydney wine exporter Leo Buring (1876-1961) decided to express his personal admiration. Buring sent a special gift to the Disney studio: three live wallabies, who—given the Marx Brothers-inspired names Poucho, Leapo, and Hoppo—spent awhile as popular office pets.[2] Their presence revived the notion of an Aussie-themed Mickey cartoon: *Mickey's Kangaroo* (1935) moved quickly into production.

No longer set at a train station, the plot was now staged at Mickey's home, to which two crated kangaroos were sent by Buring himself (!). Rather basic hijinks followed: Mickey boxed with mother 'roo Hoppy while Pluto battled her pouch-borne joey. The story was made unusual only by the technique of voicing Pluto's thoughts in a growly voice; otherwise, *Mickey's Kangaroo* offered little that was out of the ordinary.

In Australia, however, this didn't matter. The Down Under nation boasted little local animation presence; its greatest cartoon celebrity was expatriate Pat Sullivan, a New York-based producer who claimed to have created 1920s studio star Felix the Cat.[3] But since then, nothing, leaving *Mickey's Kangaroo* to fill a kind of vacuum. "This cartoon... will concentrate the minds of millions throughout the world on our portion of the globe," one Aussie newspaper gushed.[4]

Hoppy's tale didn't end there. Newspapers next had the honor of publishing Gottfredson's "Hoppy the Kangaroo" Sunday serial, in which the mama 'roo became a male; the baby was excised; and the cartoon's simple plot was spiced up immeasurably by the addition of Pegleg Pete and a gorilla. Formulaic conflict between Mouse and pets now became a classic grudge match between timeless foes.

We like to think Leo Buring raised his glass in a toast. [DG]

---

1 Walt Disney, et al. ""The Station Agent." Story outline, 1933.

2 Alice Pardoe West, "Drama Interest Kept Alive by Club's Activity." *The Ogden Standard-Examiner*, 12 August 1934. Buring only meant to send two animals, a grown male and female; but their baby was unexpectedly born in transit.

3 Decades later, after the Sullivan estate sold off the character, studio staffers could safely credit director Otto Messmer with Felix's creation.

4 "Mickey's Kangaroo." *The West Australian*, 12 July 1935.

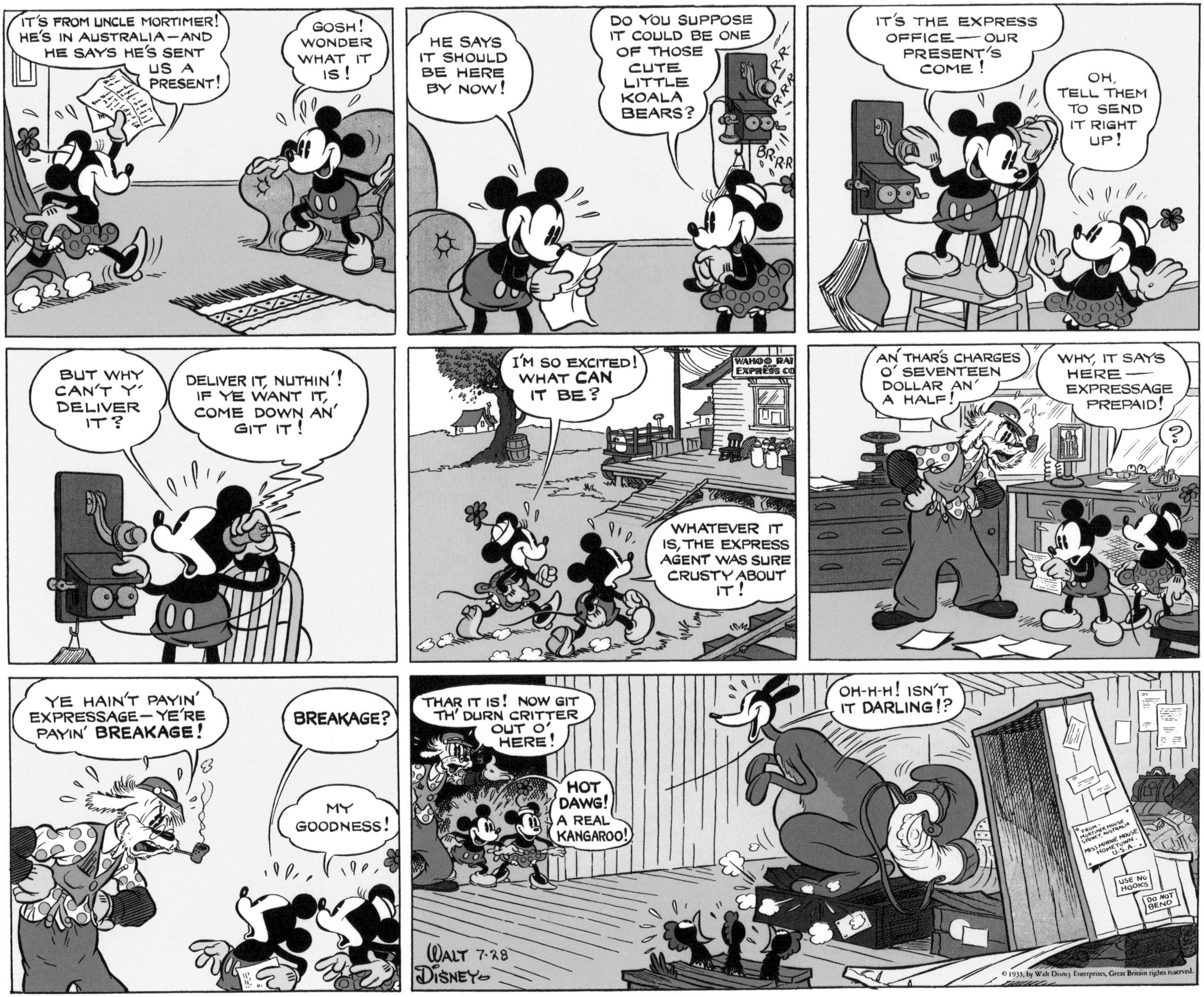
IT'S FROM UNCLE MORTIMER! HE'S IN AUSTRALIA—AND HE SAYS HE'S SENT US A PRESENT!
GOSH! WONDER WHAT IT IS!
HE SAYS IT SHOULD BE HERE BY NOW!
DO YOU SUPPOSE IT COULD BE ONE OF THOSE CUTE LITTLE KOALA BEARS?
R-R-R-R-R
BR-R-R
IT'S THE EXPRESS OFFICE—OUR PRESENT'S COME!
OH, TELL THEM TO SEND IT RIGHT UP!
BUT WHY CAN'T Y' DELIVER IT?
DELIVER IT, NUTHIN'! IF YE WANT IT, COME DOWN AN' GIT IT!
I'M SO EXCITED! WHAT CAN IT BE?
WAHOO RAI AND EXPRESS CO
WHATEVER IT IS, THE EXPRESS AGENT WAS SURE CRUSTY ABOUT IT!
AN' THAR'S CHARGES O' SEVENTEEN DOLLAR AN' A HALF!
WHY, IT SAYS HERE—EXPRESSAGE PREPAID!
?
YE HAIN'T PAYIN' EXPRESSAGE—YE'RE PAYIN' BREAKAGE!
BREAKAGE?
MY GOODNESS!
THAR IT IS! NOW GIT TH' DURN CRITTER OUT O' HERE!
HOT DAWG! A REAL KANGAROO!
OH-H-H! ISN'T IT DARLING!?
FROM—MORTIMER MOUSE SYDNEY, AUSTRALIA MISS MINNIE MOUSE HOMETOWN, U.S.A.
USE NO HOOKS
DO NOT BEND
WALT DISNEY 7-28
© 1935, by Walt Disney Enterprises, Great Britain rights reserved.

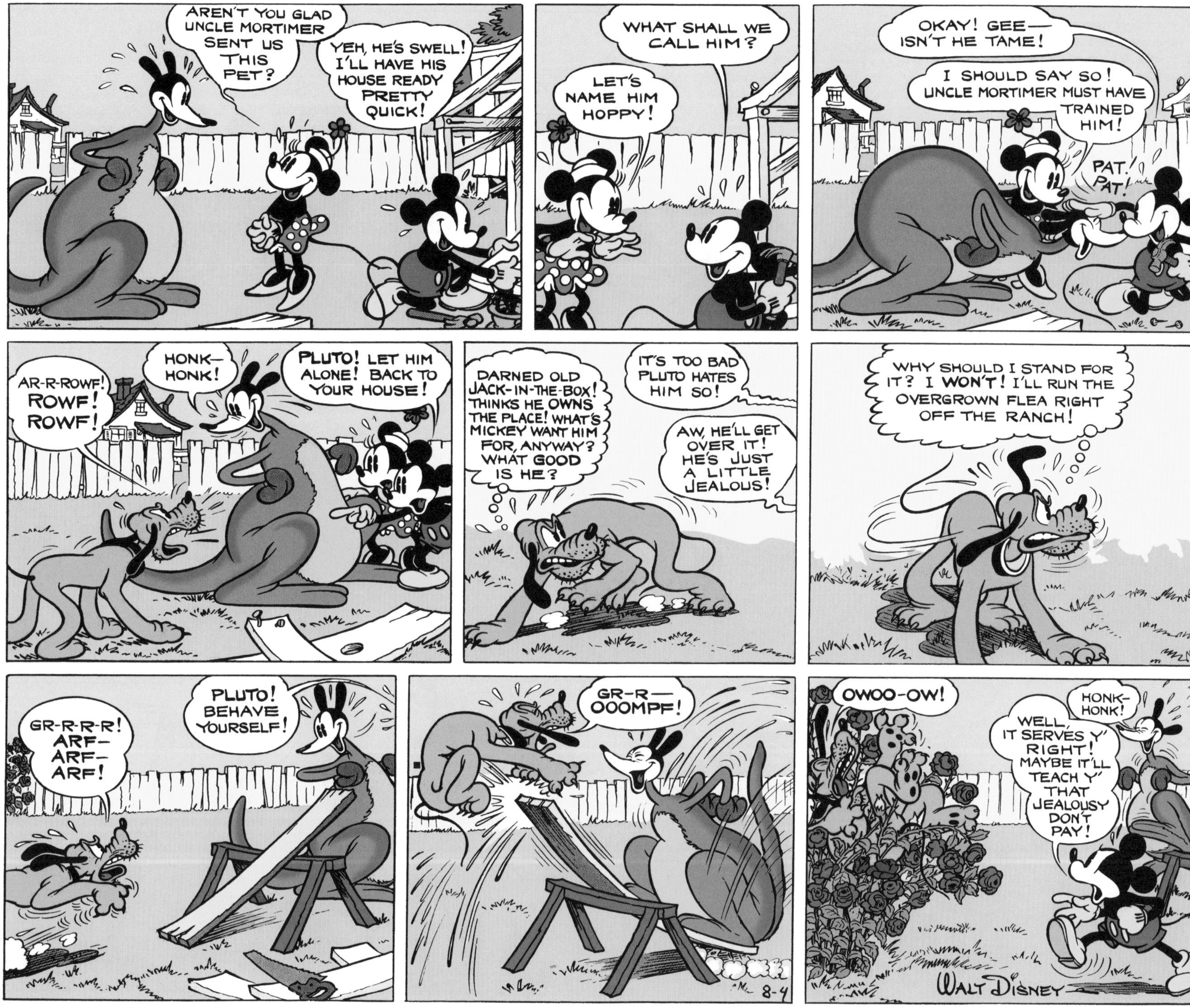
AREN'T YOU GLAD UNCLE MORTIMER SENT US THIS PET?
YEH, HE'S SWELL! I'LL HAVE HIS HOUSE READY PRETTY QUICK!
WHAT SHALL WE CALL HIM?
LET'S NAME HIM HOPPY!
OKAY! GEE— ISN'T HE TAME!
I SHOULD SAY SO! UNCLE MORTIMER MUST HAVE TRAINED HIM!
PAT! PAT!
AR-R-ROWF! ROWF! ROWF!
HONK-HONK!
PLUTO! LET HIM ALONE! BACK TO YOUR HOUSE!
DARNED OLD JACK-IN-THE-BOX! THINKS HE OWNS THE PLACE! WHAT'S MICKEY WANT HIM FOR, ANYWAY? WHAT GOOD IS HE?
IT'S TOO BAD PLUTO HATES HIM SO!
AW, HE'LL GET OVER IT! HE'S JUST A LITTLE JEALOUS!
WHY SHOULD I STAND FOR IT? I WON'T! I'LL RUN THE OVERGROWN FLEA RIGHT OFF THE RANCH!
GR-R-R-R! ARF-ARF-ARF!
PLUTO! BEHAVE YOURSELF!
GR-R— OOOMPF!
8-4
OWOO-OW!
HONK-HONK!
WELL, IT SERVES Y' RIGHT! MAYBE IT'LL TEACH Y' THAT JEALOUSY DON'T PAY!
WALT DISNEY

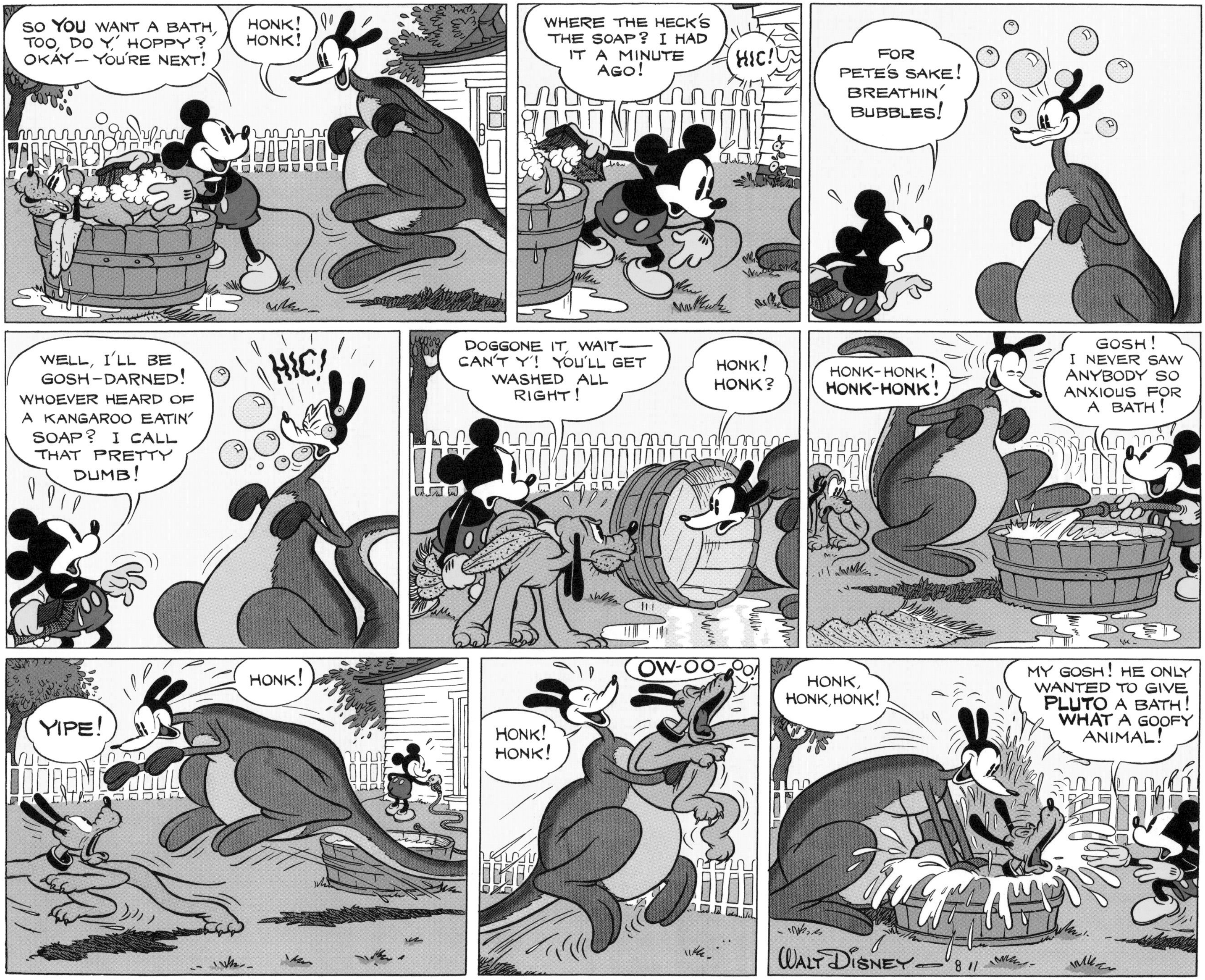

SO YOU WANT A BATH, TOO, DO Y', HOPPY? OKAY— YOU'RE NEXT!
HONK! HONK!
WHERE THE HECK'S THE SOAP? I HAD IT A MINUTE AGO!
HIC!
FOR PETE'S SAKE! BREATHIN' BUBBLES!
WELL, I'LL BE GOSH-DARNED! WHOEVER HEARD OF A KANGAROO EATIN' SOAP? I CALL THAT PRETTY DUMB!
HIC!
DOGGONE IT, WAIT— CAN'T Y'! YOU'LL GET WASHED ALL RIGHT!
HONK! HONK?
HONK-HONK! HONK-HONK!
GOSH! I NEVER SAW ANYBODY SO ANXIOUS FOR A BATH!
YIPE!
HONK!
HONK! HONK!
OW-OO-OO!
HONK, HONK, HONK!
MY GOSH! HE ONLY WANTED TO GIVE PLUTO A BATH! WHAT A GOOFY ANIMAL!
WALT DISNEY 8 11

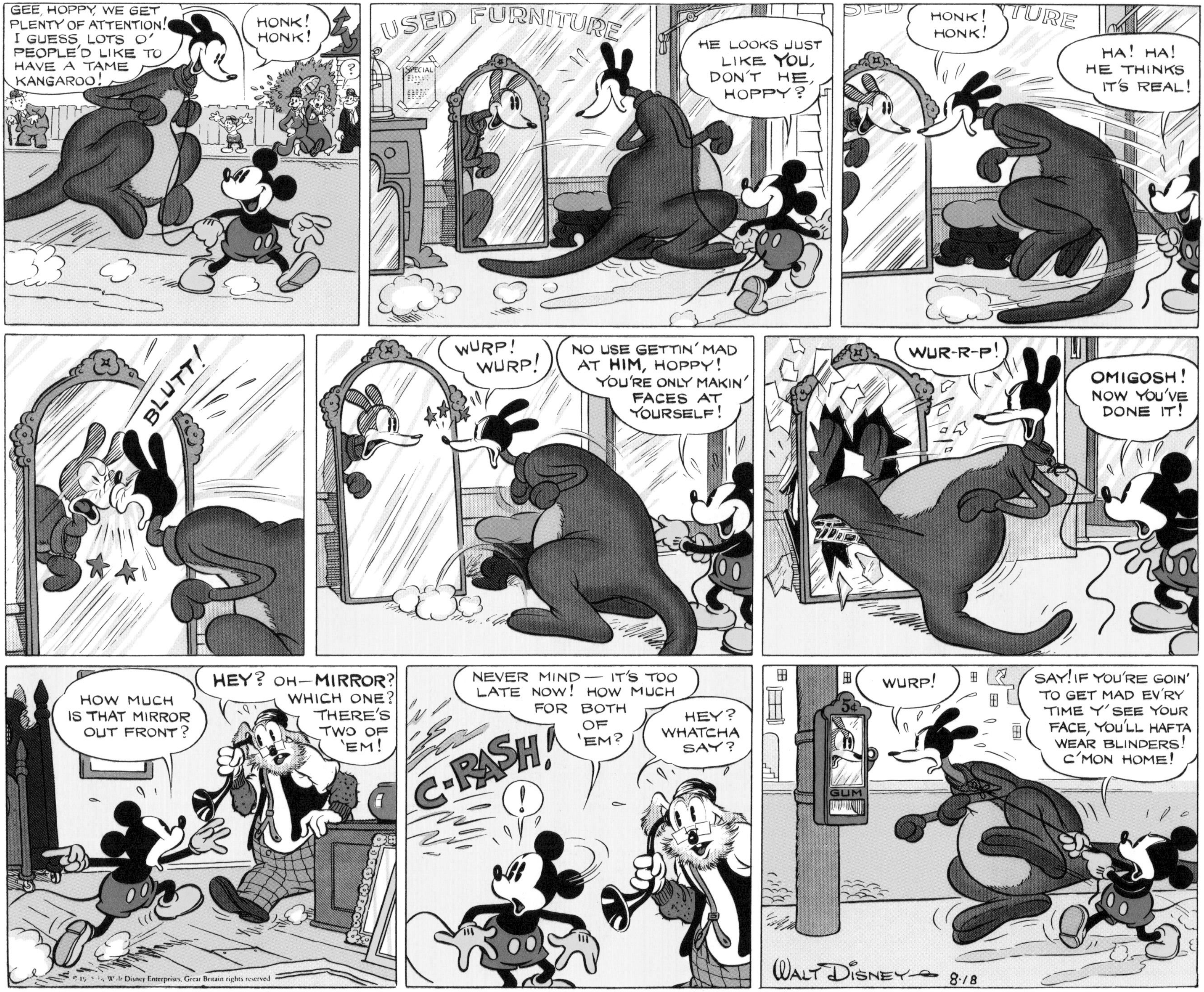
GEE, HOPPY, WE GET PLENTY OF ATTENTION! I GUESS LOTS O' PEOPLE'D LIKE TO HAVE A TAME KANGAROO!
HONK! HONK!
?
USED FURNITURE
SPECIAL
HE LOOKS JUST LIKE YOU, DON'T HE, HOPPY?
HONK! HONK!
HA! HA! HE THINKS IT'S REAL!
BLUTT!
WURP! WURP!
NO USE GETTIN' MAD AT HIM, HOPPY! YOU'RE ONLY MAKIN' FACES AT YOURSELF!
WUR-R-P!
OMIGOSH! NOW YOU'VE DONE IT!
HOW MUCH IS THAT MIRROR OUT FRONT?
HEY? OH—MIRROR? WHICH ONE? THERE'S TWO OF 'EM!
Disney Enterprises, Great Britain rights reserved
C-RASH!
NEVER MIND— IT'S TOO LATE NOW! HOW MUCH FOR BOTH OF 'EM?
!
HEY? WHATCHA SAY?
5¢
GUM
WURP!
SAY! IF YOU'RE GOIN' TO GET MAD EV'RY TIME Y' SEE YOUR FACE, YOU'LL HAFTA WEAR BLINDERS! C'MON HOME!
WALT DISNEY 8·18

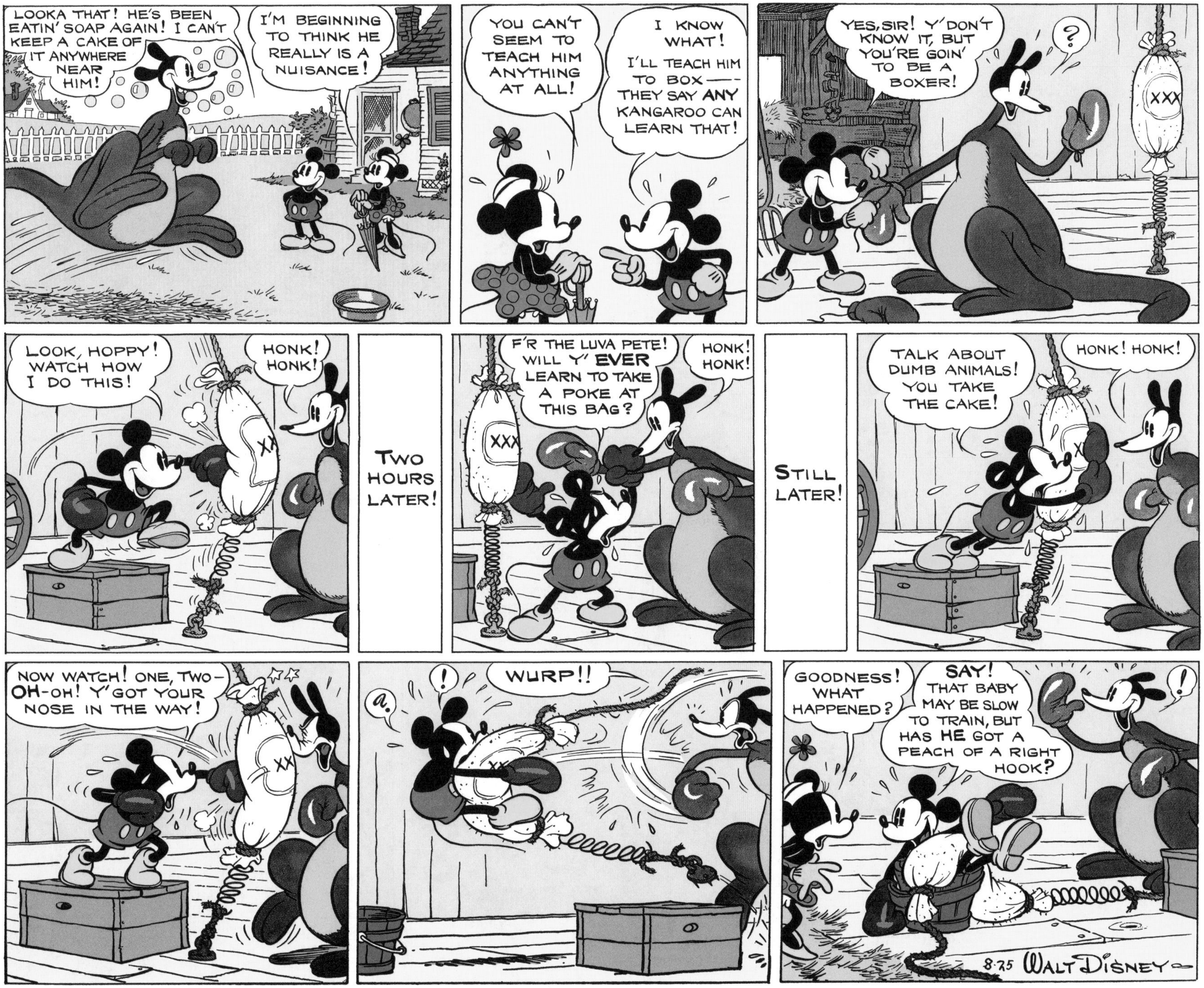
LOOKA THAT! HE'S BEEN EATIN' SOAP AGAIN! I CAN'T KEEP A CAKE OF IT ANYWHERE NEAR HIM!
I'M BEGINNING TO THINK HE REALLY IS A NUISANCE!
YOU CAN'T SEEM TO TEACH HIM ANYTHING AT ALL!
I KNOW WHAT! I'LL TEACH HIM TO BOX—— THEY SAY ANY KANGAROO CAN LEARN THAT!
YES, SIR! Y'DON'T KNOW IT, BUT YOU'RE GOIN' TO BE A BOXER!
?
XXX
LOOK, HOPPY! WATCH HOW I DO THIS!
HONK! HONK!
TWO HOURS LATER!
F'R THE LUVA PETE! WILL Y' EVER LEARN TO TAKE A POKE AT THIS BAG?
HONK! HONK!
STILL LATER!
TALK ABOUT DUMB ANIMALS! YOU TAKE THE CAKE!
HONK! HONK!
NOW WATCH! ONE, TWO— OH-OH! Y'GOT YOUR NOSE IN THE WAY!
a.
!
WURP!!
GOODNESS! WHAT HAPPENED?
SAY! THAT BABY MAY BE SLOW TO TRAIN, BUT HAS HE GOT A PEACH OF A RIGHT HOOK?
!
8·25 WALT DISNEY

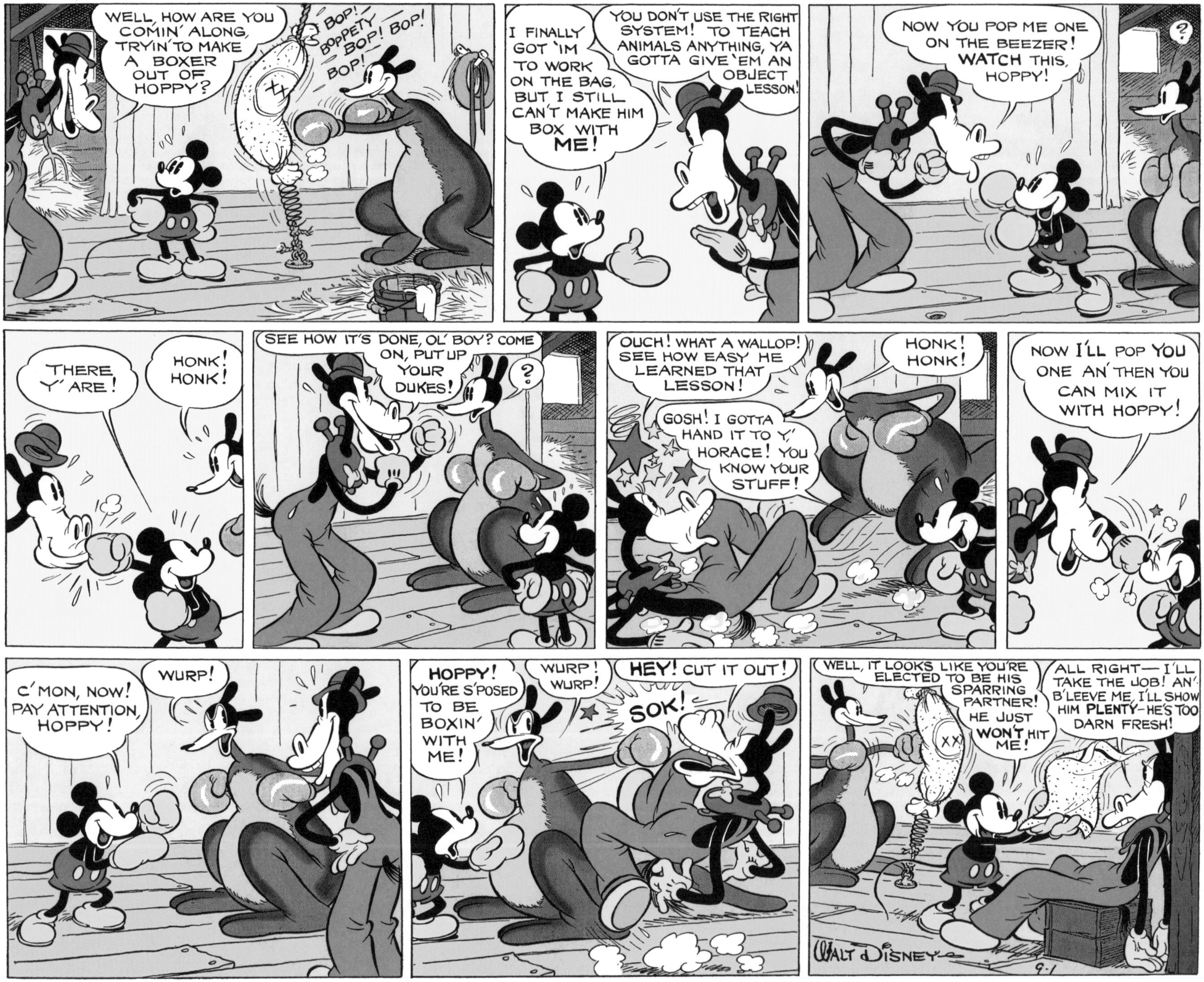
WELL, HOW ARE YOU COMIN' ALONG, TRYIN' TO MAKE A BOXER OUT OF HOPPY?
BOP! BOPPETY BOP! BOP! BOP!
I FINALLY GOT 'IM TO WORK ON THE BAG, BUT I STILL CAN'T MAKE HIM BOX WITH ME!
YOU DON'T USE THE RIGHT SYSTEM! TO TEACH ANIMALS ANYTHING, YA GOTTA GIVE 'EM AN OBJECT LESSON!
NOW YOU POP ME ONE ON THE BEEZER! WATCH THIS, HOPPY!
?
THERE Y' ARE!
HONK! HONK!
SEE HOW IT'S DONE, OL' BOY? COME ON, PUT UP YOUR DUKES!
?
OUCH! WHAT A WALLOP! SEE HOW EASY HE LEARNED THAT LESSON!
HONK! HONK!
GOSH! I GOTTA HAND IT TO Y', HORACE! YOU KNOW YOUR STUFF!
NOW I'LL POP YOU ONE AN' THEN YOU CAN MIX IT WITH HOPPY!
C'MON, NOW! PAY ATTENTION, HOPPY!
WURP!
HOPPY! YOU'RE S'POSED TO BE BOXIN' WITH ME!
WURP! WURP!
HEY! CUT IT OUT!
SOK!
WELL, IT LOOKS LIKE YOU'RE ELECTED TO BE HIS SPARRING PARTNER! HE JUST WON'T HIT ME!
ALL RIGHT— I'LL TAKE THE JOB! AN' B'LEEVE ME, I'LL SHOW HIM PLENTY—HE'S TOO DARN FRESH!
WALT DISNEY
9-1

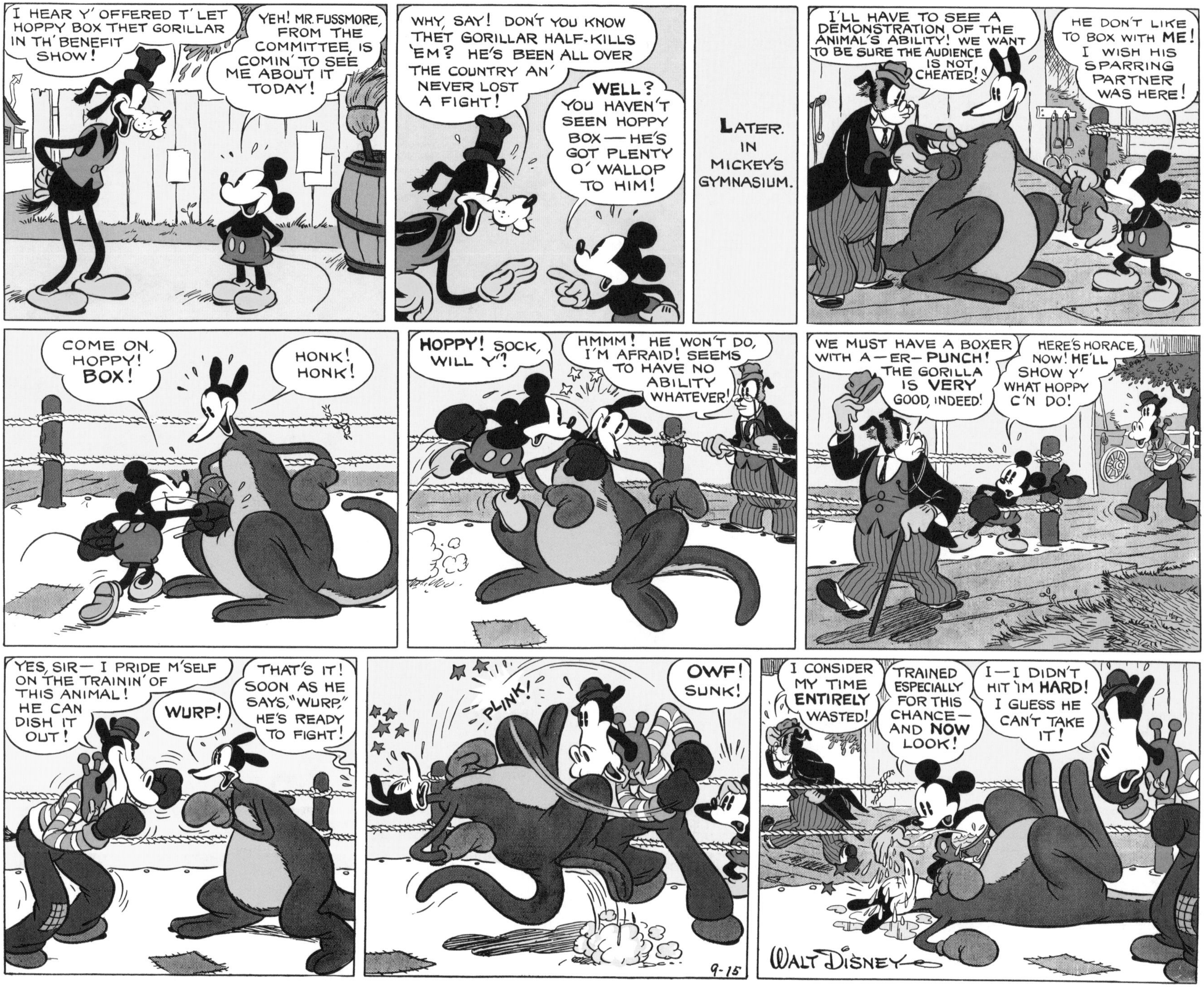
I HEAR Y' OFFERED T' LET HOPPY BOX THET GORILLAR IN TH' BENEFIT SHOW!
YEH! MR. FUSSMORE, FROM THE COMMITTEE, IS COMIN' TO SEE ME ABOUT IT TODAY!
WHY, SAY! DON'T YOU KNOW THET GORILLAR HALF-KILLS 'EM? HE'S BEEN ALL OVER THE COUNTRY AN' NEVER LOST A FIGHT!
WELL? YOU HAVEN'T SEEN HOPPY BOX—HE'S GOT PLENTY O' WALLOP TO HIM!
LATER. IN MICKEY'S GYMNASIUM.
I'LL HAVE TO SEE A DEMONSTRATION OF THE ANIMAL'S ABILITY! WE WANT TO BE SURE THE AUDIENCE IS NOT CHEATED!
HE DON'T LIKE TO BOX WITH ME! I WISH HIS SPARRING PARTNER WAS HERE!
COME ON, HOPPY! BOX!
HONK! HONK!
HOPPY! SOCK, WILL Y'?
HMMM! HE WON'T DO, I'M AFRAID! SEEMS TO HAVE NO ABILITY WHATEVER!
WE MUST HAVE A BOXER WITH A—ER—PUNCH! THE GORILLA IS VERY GOOD, INDEED!
HERE'S HORACE, NOW! HE'LL SHOW Y' WHAT HOPPY C'N DO!
YES, SIR— I PRIDE M'SELF ON THE TRAININ' OF THIS ANIMAL! HE CAN DISH IT OUT!
WURP!
THAT'S IT! SOON AS HE SAYS, "WURP," HE'S READY TO FIGHT!
PLINK!
OWF! SUNK!
9-15
I CONSIDER MY TIME ENTIRELY WASTED!
TRAINED ESPECIALLY FOR THIS CHANCE— AND NOW LOOK!
I—I DIDN'T HIT 'IM HARD! I GUESS HE CAN'T TAKE IT!
WALT DISNEY

230. HOPPY THE KANGAROO

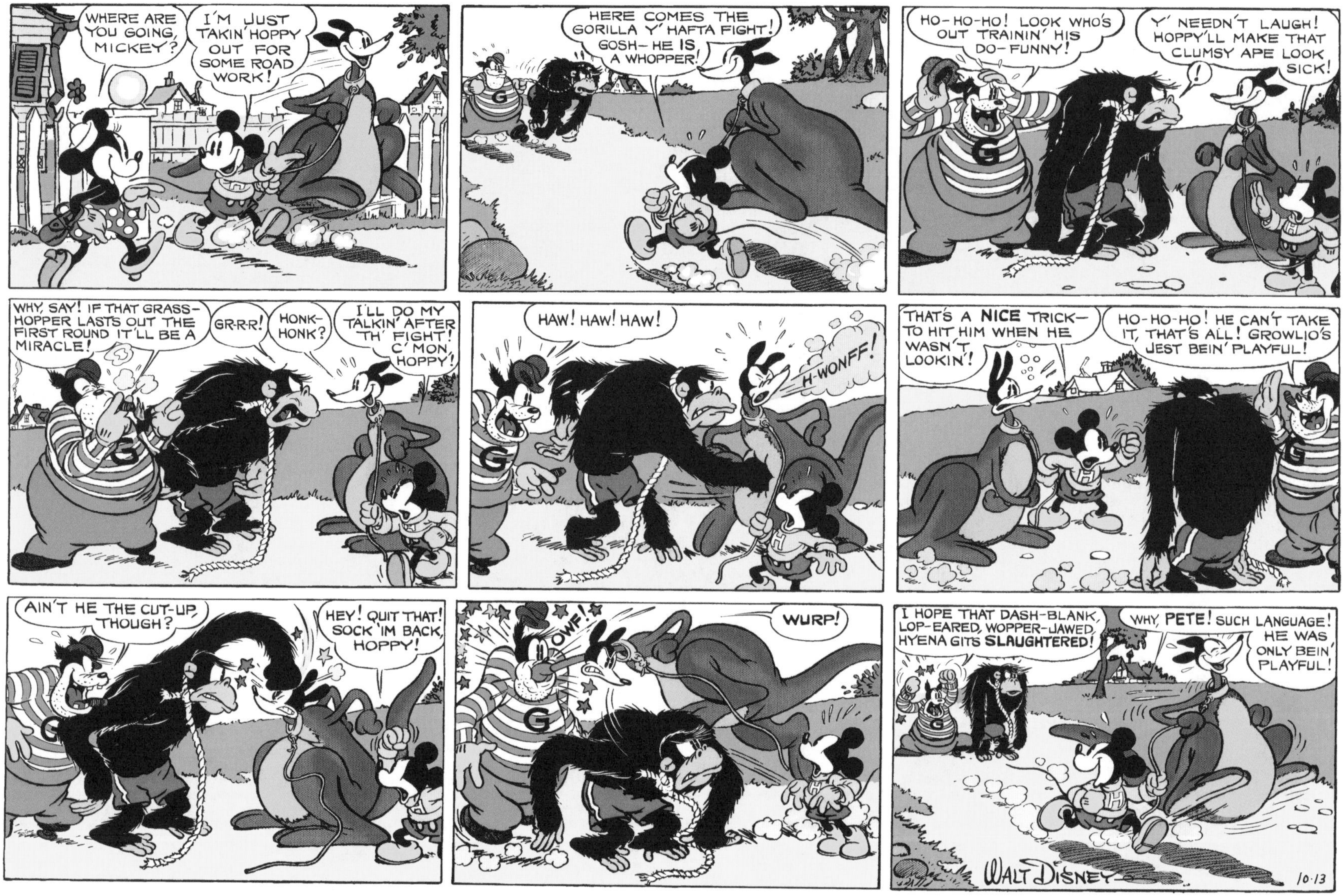
WHERE ARE YOU GOING, MICKEY?
I'M JUST TAKIN' HOPPY OUT FOR SOME ROAD WORK!
HERE COMES THE GORILLA Y' HAFTA FIGHT! GOSH– HE IS A WHOPPER!
HO-HO-HO! LOOK WHO'S OUT TRAININ' HIS DO-FUNNY!
Y' NEEDN'T LAUGH! HOPPY'LL MAKE THAT CLUMSY APE LOOK SICK!
!
WHY, SAY! IF THAT GRASS-HOPPER LASTS OUT THE FIRST ROUND IT'LL BE A MIRACLE!
GR-R-R!
HONK-HONK?
I'LL DO MY TALKIN' AFTER TH' FIGHT! C'MON, HOPPY!
HAW! HAW! HAW!
H-WONFF!
THAT'S A NICE TRICK– TO HIT HIM WHEN HE WASN'T LOOKIN'!
HO-HO-HO! HE CAN'T TAKE IT, THAT'S ALL! GROWLIO'S JEST BEIN' PLAYFUL!
AIN'T HE THE CUT-UP, THOUGH?
HEY! QUIT THAT! SOCK 'IM BACK, HOPPY!
OWF!
WURP!
I HOPE THAT DASH-BLANK LOP-EARED, WOPPER-JAWED HYENA GITS SLAUGHTERED!
WHY, PETE! SUCH LANGUAGE! HE WAS ONLY BEIN' PLAYFUL!
WALT DISNEY
10·13

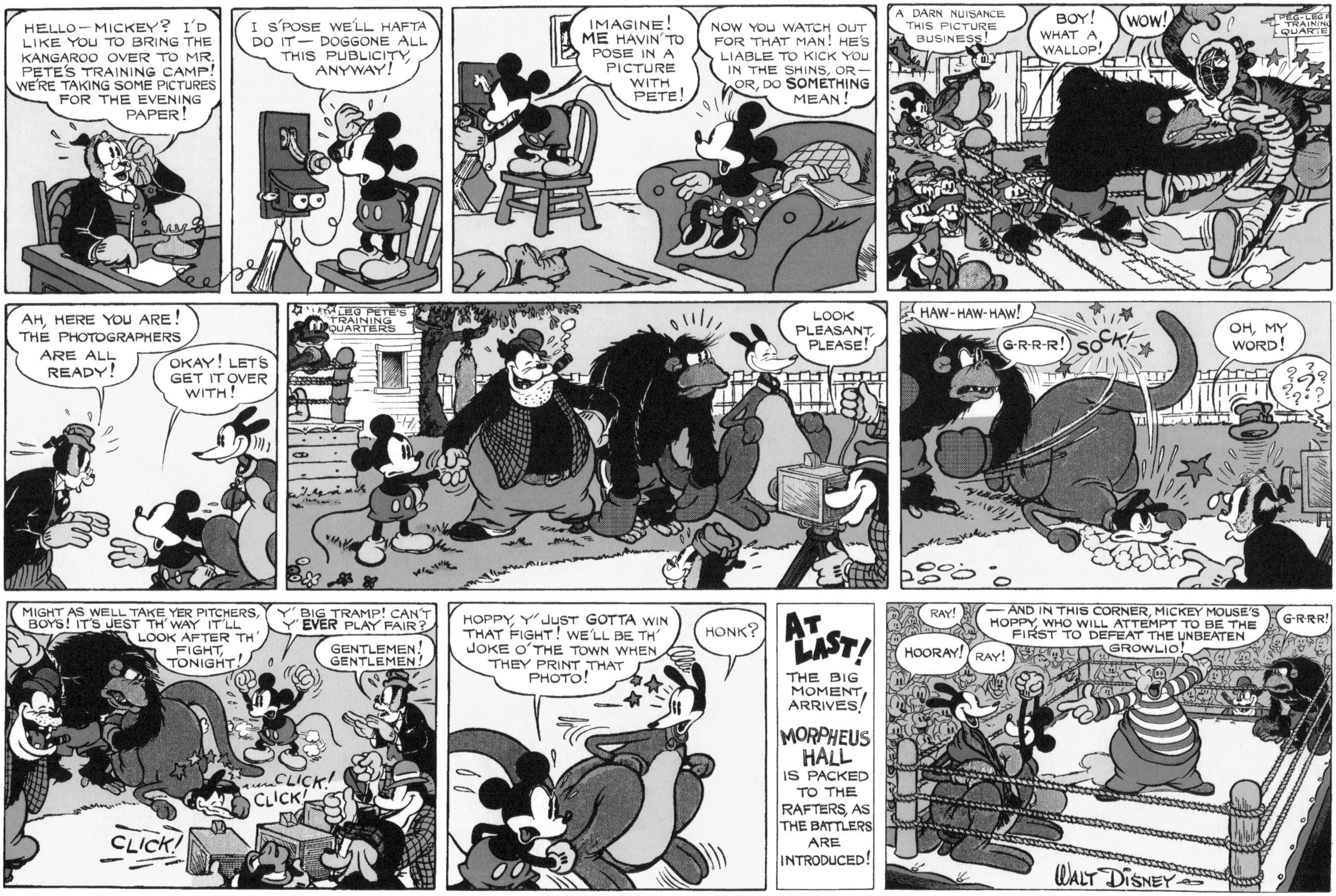
HELLO—MICKEY? I'D LIKE YOU TO BRING THE KANGAROO OVER TO MR. PETE'S TRAINING CAMP! WE'RE TAKING SOME PICTURES FOR THE EVENING PAPER!
I S'POSE WE'LL HAFTA DO IT—DOGGONE ALL THIS PUBLICITY, ANYWAY!
IMAGINE! ME HAVIN' TO POSE IN A PICTURE WITH PETE!
NOW YOU WATCH OUT FOR THAT MAN! HE'S LIABLE TO KICK YOU IN THE SHINS, OR—OR, DO SOMETHING MEAN!
A DARN NUISANCE THIS PICTURE BUSINESS!
BOY! WHAT A WALLOP!
WOW!
AH, HERE YOU ARE! THE PHOTOGRAPHERS ARE ALL READY!
OKAY! LET'S GET IT OVER WITH!
LEG PETE'S TRAINING QUARTERS
LOOK PLEASANT, PLEASE!
HAW-HAW-HAW!
G-R-R-R!
SOCK!
OH, MY WORD!
MIGHT AS WELL TAKE YER PITCHERS, BOYS! IT'S JEST TH' WAY IT'LL LOOK AFTER TH' FIGHT, TONIGHT!
Y' BIG TRAMP! CAN'T Y' EVER PLAY FAIR?
GENTLEMEN! GENTLEMEN!
CLICK!
CLICK!
CLICK!
HOPPY, Y' JUST GOTTA WIN THAT FIGHT! WE'LL BE TH' JOKE O' THE TOWN WHEN THEY PRINT THAT PHOTO!
HONK?
AT LAST! THE BIG MOMENT ARRIVES! MORPHEUS HALL IS PACKED TO THE RAFTERS, AS THE BATTLERS ARE INTRODUCED!
RAY!
HOORAY!
RAY!
—AND IN THIS CORNER, MICKEY MOUSE'S HOPPY, WHO WILL ATTEMPT TO BE THE FIRST TO DEFEAT THE UNBEATEN GROWLIO!
G-R-R-R!
WALT DISNEY

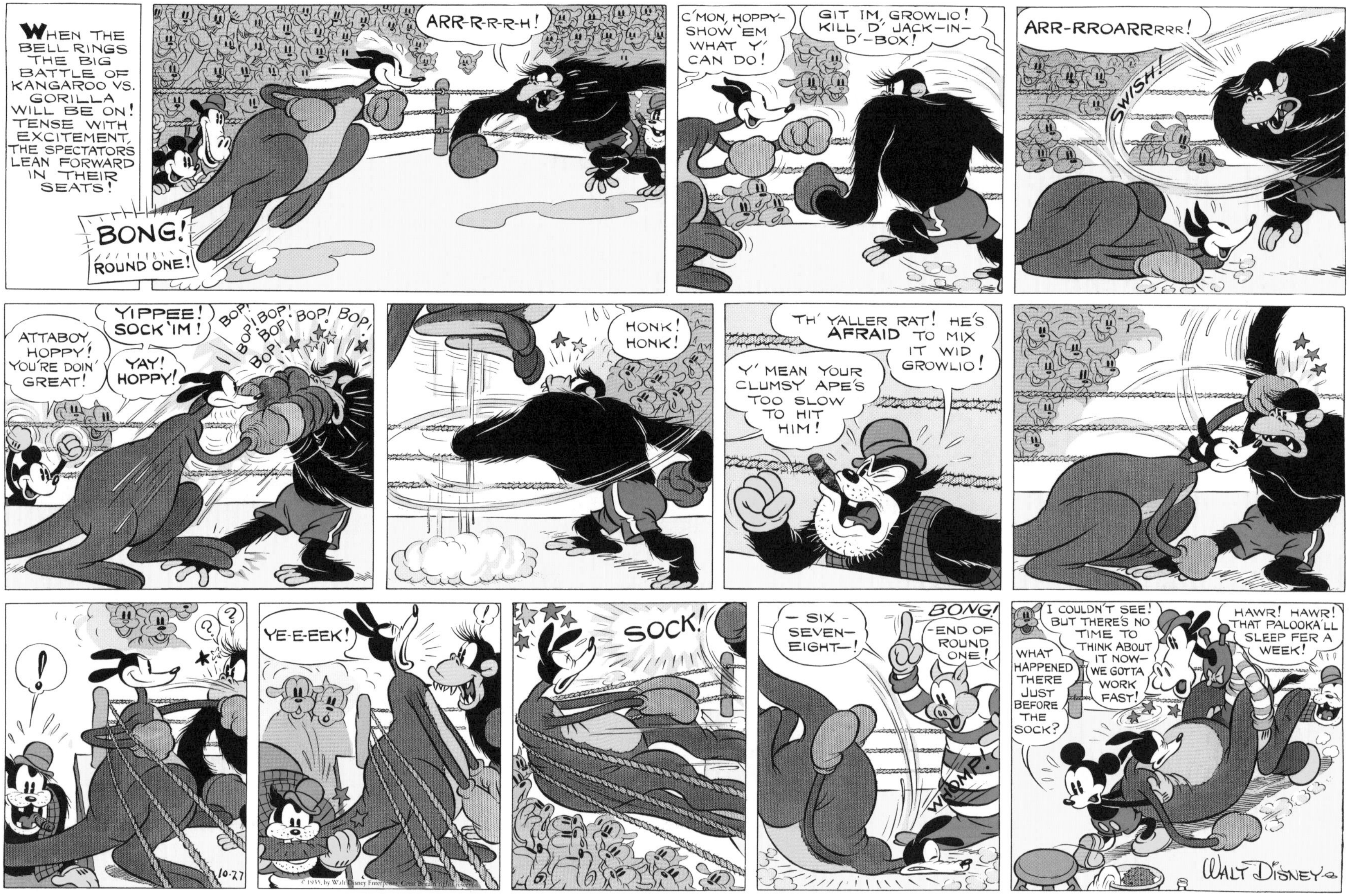
WHEN THE BELL RINGS THE BIG BATTLE OF KANGAROO VS. GORILLA WILL BE ON! TENSE WITH EXCITEMENT, THE SPECTATORS LEAN FORWARD IN THEIR SEATS!
ARR-R-R-R-H!
BONG!
ROUND ONE!
C'MON, HOPPY-SHOW 'EM WHAT Y' CAN DO!
GIT IM, GROWLIO! KILL D' JACK-IN-D'-BOX!
ARR-RROARRRRR!
SWISH!
ATTABOY, HOPPY! YOU'RE DOIN' GREAT!
YIPPEE! SOCK 'IM!
YAY! HOPPY!
BOP! BOP! BOP! BOP! BOP! BOP!
HONK! HONK!
TH' YALLER RAT! HE'S AFRAID TO MIX IT WID GROWLIO!
Y' MEAN YOUR CLUMSY APE'S TOO SLOW TO HIT HIM!
!
?
10-27
YE-E-EEK!
!
© 1935, by Walt Disney Enterprises. Great Britain rights reserved.
SOCK!
— SIX — SEVEN — EIGHT —!
BONG!
-END OF ROUND ONE!
WHOMP!
WHAT HAPPENED THERE JUST BEFORE THE SOCK?
I COULDN'T SEE! BUT THERE'S NO TIME TO THINK ABOUT IT NOW— WE GOTTA WORK FAST!
HAWR! HAWR! THAT PALOOKA'LL SLEEP FER A WEEK!
WALT DISNEY

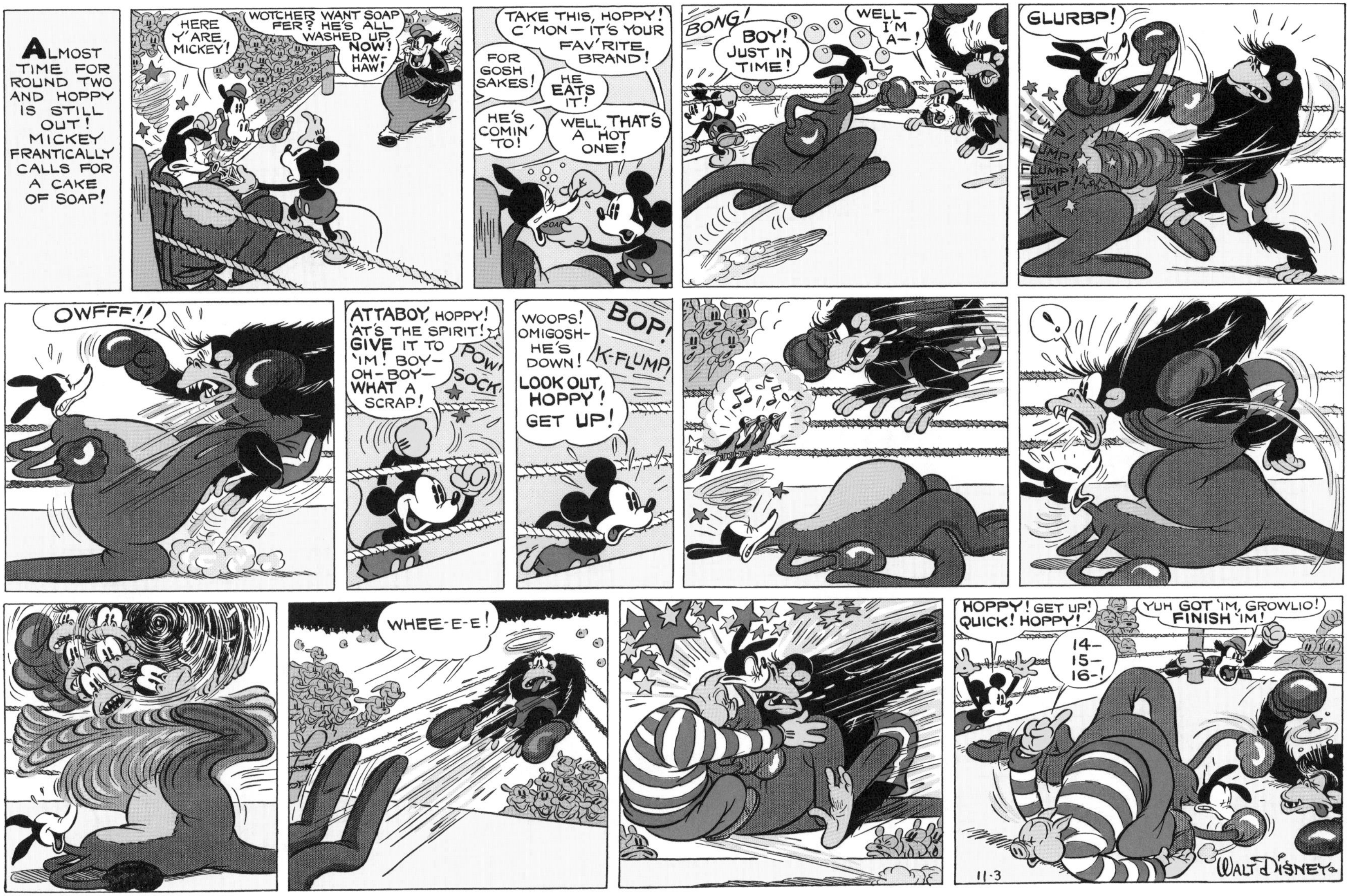
ALMOST TIME FOR ROUND TWO AND HOPPY IS STILL OUT! MICKEY FRANTICALLY CALLS FOR A CAKE OF SOAP!
HERE Y'ARE, MICKEY!
WOTCHER WANT SOAP FER? HE'S ALL WASHED UP NOW! HAW-HAW!
SOAP
TAKE THIS, HOPPY! C'MON — IT'S YOUR FAV'RITE BRAND!
FOR GOSH SAKES!
HE EATS IT!
HE'S COMIN' TO!
WELL, THAT'S A HOT ONE!
SOAP
BONG!
BOY! JUST IN TIME!
WELL — I'M A—!
GLURBP!
FLUMP! FLUMP! FLUMP! FLUMP!
OWFFF!!
ATTABOY, HOPPY! 'AT'S THE SPIRIT! GIVE IT TO 'IM! BOY-OH-BOY— WHAT A SCRAP!
POW! SOCK!
WOOPS! OMIGOSH— HE'S DOWN!
BOP!
K-FLUMP!
LOOK OUT, HOPPY! GET UP!
!
WHEE-E-E!
HOPPY! GET UP! QUICK! HOPPY!
YUH GOT 'IM, GROWLIO! FINISH 'IM!
14— 15— 16—!
11-3
WALT DISNEY

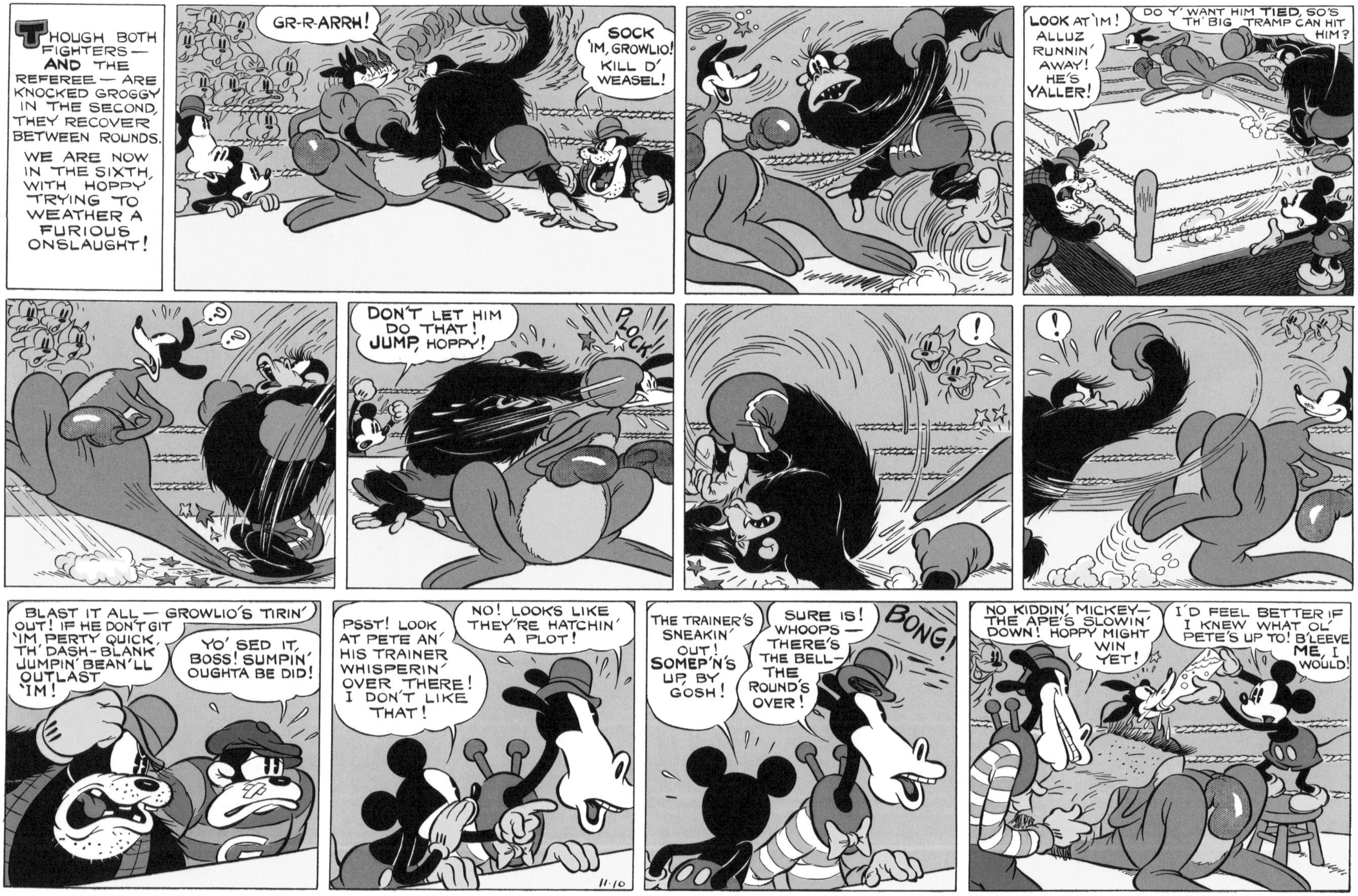
THOUGH BOTH FIGHTERS— AND THE REFEREE— ARE KNOCKED GROGGY IN THE SECOND, THEY RECOVER BETWEEN ROUNDS.
WE ARE NOW IN THE SIXTH, WITH HOPPY TRYING TO WEATHER A FURIOUS ONSLAUGHT!
GR-R-ARRH!
SOCK 'IM, GROWLIO! KILL D' WEASEL!
LOOK AT 'IM! ALLUZ RUNNIN' AWAY! HE'S YALLER!
DO Y' WANT HIM TIED, SO'S TH' BIG TRAMP CAN HIT HIM?
DON'T LET HIM DO THAT! JUMP, HOPPY!
PLOCK!
!
!
BLAST IT ALL — GROWLIO'S TIRIN' OUT! IF HE DON'T GIT 'IM PERTY QUICK, TH' DASH-BLANK JUMPIN' BEAN'LL OUTLAST 'IM!
YO' SED IT, BOSS! SUMPIN' OUGHTA BE DID!
PSST! LOOK AT PETE AN' HIS TRAINER WHISPERIN' OVER THERE! I DON'T LIKE THAT!
NO! LOOKS LIKE THEY'RE HATCHIN' A PLOT!
11·10
THE TRAINER'S SNEAKIN' OUT! SOMEP'N'S UP, BY GOSH!
SURE IS! WHOOPS — THERE'S THE BELL— THE ROUND'S OVER!
BONG!
NO KIDDIN', MICKEY— THE APE'S SLOWIN' DOWN! HOPPY MIGHT WIN YET!
I'D FEEL BETTER IF I KNEW WHAT OL' PETE'S UP TO! B'LEEVE ME, I WOULD!

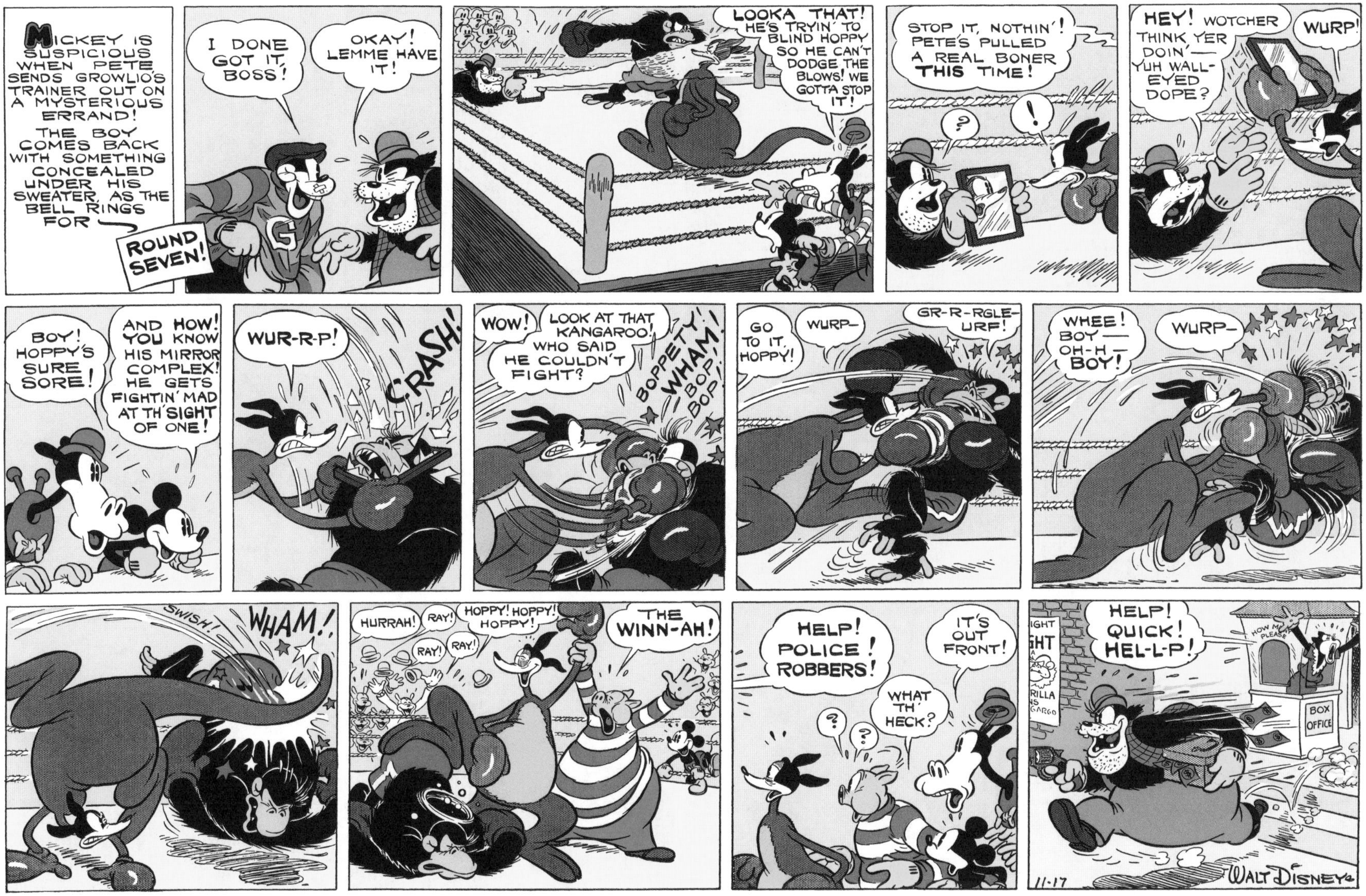
MICKEY IS SUSPICIOUS WHEN PETE SENDS GROWLIO'S TRAINER OUT ON A MYSTERIOUS ERRAND!
THE BOY COMES BACK WITH SOMETHING CONCEALED UNDER HIS SWEATER, AS THE BELL RINGS FOR
ROUND SEVEN!
I DONE GOT IT, BOSS!
OKAY! LEMME HAVE IT!
LOOKA THAT! HE'S TRYIN' TO BLIND HOPPY SO HE CAN'T DODGE THE BLOWS! WE GOTTA STOP IT!
STOP IT, NOTHIN'! PETE'S PULLED A REAL BONER THIS TIME!
?
!
HEY! WOTCHER THINK YER DOIN'— YUH WALL-EYED DOPE?
WURP!
BOY! HOPPY'S SURE SORE!
AND HOW! YOU KNOW HIS MIRROR COMPLEX! HE GETS FIGHTIN' MAD AT TH' SIGHT OF ONE!
WUR-R-P!
CRASH!
WOW!
LOOK AT THAT KANGAROO! WHO SAID HE COULDN'T FIGHT?
BOPPETY WHAM! BOP BOP!
GO TO IT, HOPPY!
WURP—
GR-R-RGLE-URF!
WHEE! BOY— OH-H BOY!
WURP—
SWISH!
WHAM!
HURRAH!
RAY!
HOPPY! HOPPY! HOPPY!
RAY!
RAY!
THE WINN-AH!
HELP! POLICE! ROBBERS!
IT'S OUT FRONT!
?
?
WHAT TH' HECK?
HELP! QUICK! HEL-L-P!
BOX OFFICE
11-17
WALT DISNEY

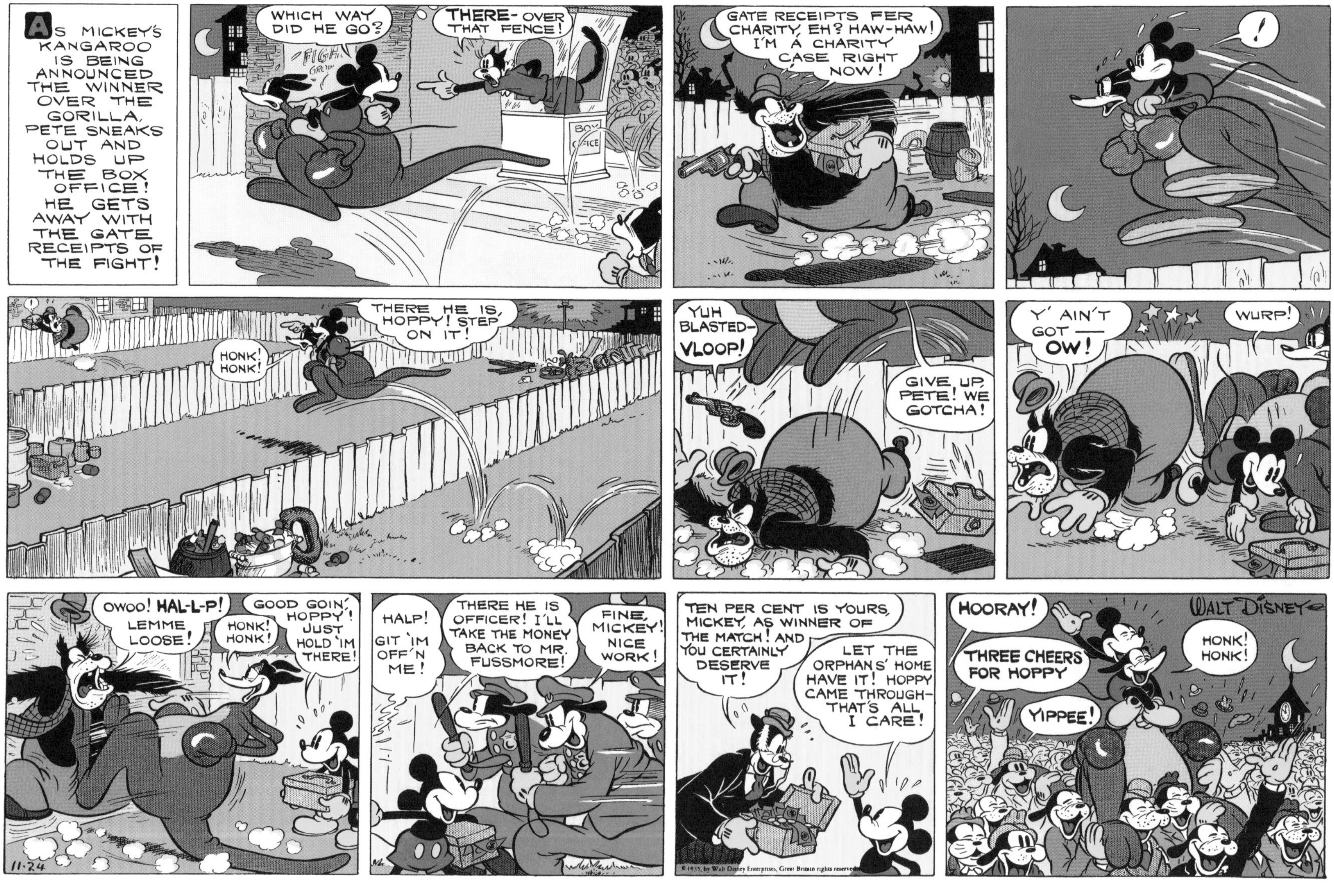
AS MICKEY'S KANGAROO IS BEING ANNOUNCED THE WINNER OVER THE GORILLA, PETE SNEAKS OUT AND HOLDS UP THE BOX OFFICE! HE GETS AWAY WITH THE GATE RECEIPTS OF THE FIGHT!
WHICH WAY DID HE GO?
THERE- OVER THAT FENCE!
BOX OFFICE
GATE RECEIPTS FER CHARITY, EH? HAW-HAW! I'M A CHARITY CASE RIGHT NOW!
!
THERE HE IS, HOPPY! STEP ON IT!
HONK! HONK!
YUH BLASTED- VLOOP!
GIVE UP, PETE! WE GOTCHA!
Y' AIN'T GOT — OW!
WURP!
OWOO! HAL-L-P! LEMME LOOSE!
HONK! HONK!
GOOD GOIN', HOPPY! JUST HOLD 'IM THERE!
11-24
HALP! GIT 'IM OFF'N ME!
THERE HE IS OFFICER! I'LL TAKE THE MONEY BACK TO MR. FUSSMORE!
FINE, MICKEY! NICE WORK!
TEN PER CENT IS YOURS, MICKEY, AS WINNER OF THE MATCH! AND YOU CERTAINLY DESERVE IT!
LET THE ORPHANS' HOME HAVE IT! HOPPY CAME THROUGH- THAT'S ALL I CARE!
© 1935, by Walt Disney Enterprises, Great Britain rights reserved
HOORAY!
WALT DISNEY
THREE CHEERS FOR HOPPY
HONK! HONK!
YIPPEE!

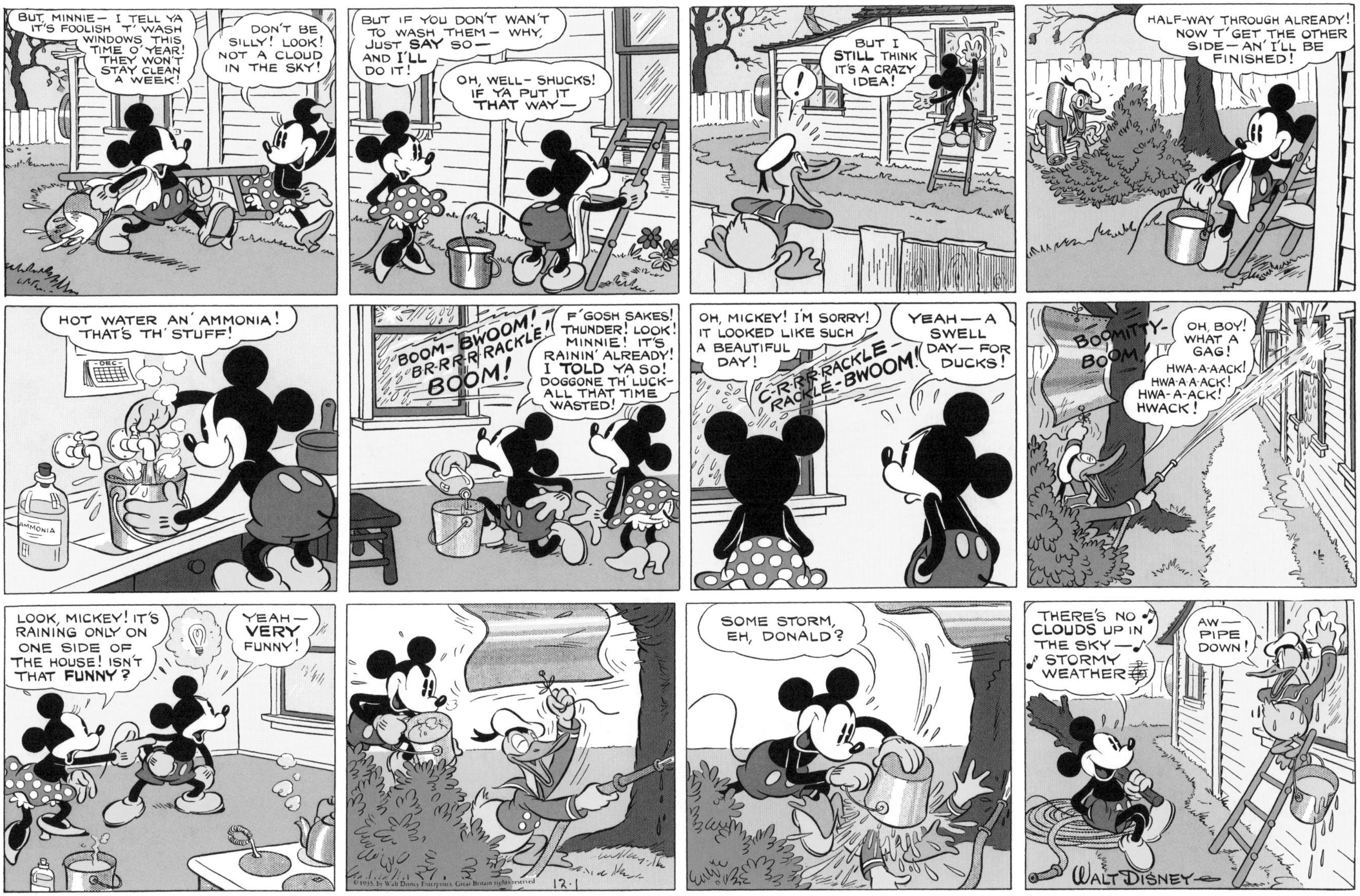
BUT, MINNIE— I TELL YA IT'S FOOLISH T' WASH WINDOWS THIS TIME O' YEAR! THEY WON'T STAY CLEAN A WEEK!
DON'T BE SILLY! LOOK! NOT A CLOUD IN THE SKY!
BUT IF YOU DON'T WAN'T TO WASH THEM— WHY, JUST SAY SO— AND I'LL DO IT!
OH, WELL- SHUCKS! IF YA PUT IT THAT WAY—
!
BUT I STILL THINK IT'S A CRAZY IDEA!
HALF-WAY THROUGH ALREADY! NOW T' GET THE OTHER SIDE— AN' I'LL BE FINISHED!
HOT WATER AN' AMMONIA! THAT'S TH' STUFF!
-DEC-
AMMONIA
BOOM-BWOOM! BR-RR-RACKLE! BOOM!
F'GOSH SAKES! THUNDER! LOOK! MINNIE! IT'S RAININ' ALREADY! I TOLD YA SO! DOGGONE TH' LUCK- ALL THAT TIME WASTED!
OH, MICKEY! I'M SORRY! IT LOOKED LIKE SUCH A BEAUTIFUL DAY!
C-R-R-R-RACKLE-RACKLE-BWOOM!
YEAH— A SWELL DAY— FOR DUCKS!
BOOMITTY-BOOM!
OH, BOY! WHAT A GAG! HWA-A-AACK! HWA-A-A-ACK! HWA-A-ACK! HWACK!
LOOK, MICKEY! IT'S RAINING ONLY ON ONE SIDE OF THE HOUSE! ISN'T THAT FUNNY?
YEAH— VERY FUNNY!
© 1935, by Walt Disney Enterprises. Great Britain rights reserved
12·1
SOME STORM, EH, DONALD?
THERE'S NO CLOUDS UP IN THE SKY— STORMY WEATHER
AW— PIPE DOWN!
WALT DISNEY

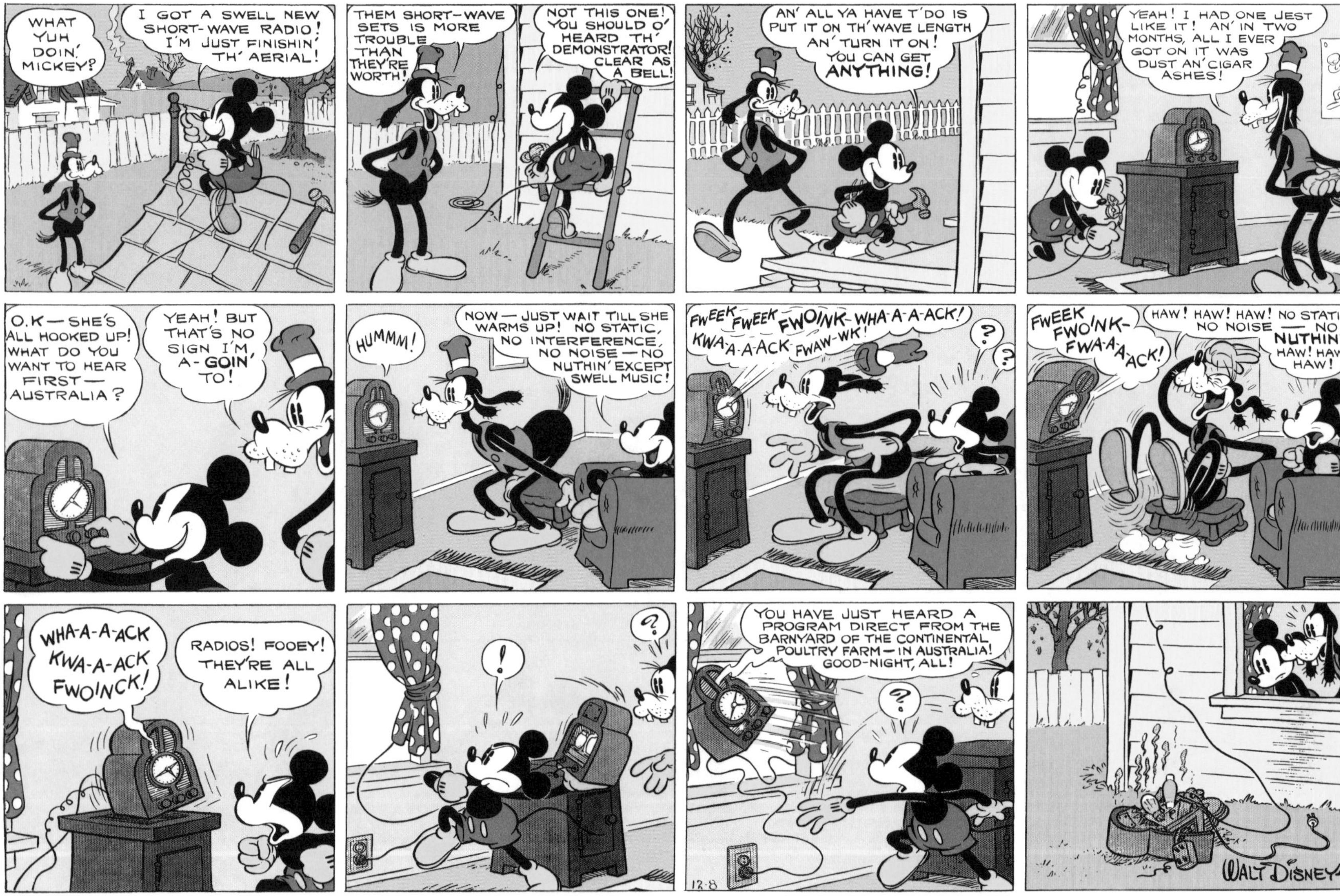
WHAT YUH DOIN' MICKEY?
I GOT A SWELL NEW SHORT-WAVE RADIO! I'M JUST FINISHIN' TH' AERIAL!
THEM SHORT-WAVE SETS IS MORE TROUBLE THAN THEY'RE WORTH!
NOT THIS ONE! YOU SHOULD O' HEARD TH' DEMONSTRATOR! CLEAR AS A BELL!
AN' ALL YA HAVE T'DO IS PUT IT ON TH' WAVE LENGTH AN' TURN IT ON! YOU CAN GET ANYTHING!
YEAH! I HAD ONE JEST LIKE IT! AN' IN TWO MONTHS, ALL I EVER GOT ON IT WAS DUST AN' CIGAR ASHES!
O.K — SHE'S ALL HOOKED UP! WHAT DO YOU WANT TO HEAR FIRST — AUSTRALIA?
YEAH! BUT THAT'S NO SIGN I'M A-GOIN' TO!
HUMMM!
NOW — JUST WAIT TILL SHE WARMS UP! NO STATIC, NO INTERFERENCE, NO NOISE — NO NUTHIN' EXCEPT SWELL MUSIC!
FWEEK FWEEK FWOINK-WHA-A-A-ACK! KWA-A-A-ACK FWAW-WK!
?
?
FWEEK FWO'INK-FWA-A-A-ACK!
HAW! HAW! HAW! NO STATIC, NO NOISE — NO NUTHIN'! HAW! HAW! HAW!
WHA-A-A-ACK KWA-A-ACK FWOINCK!
RADIOS! FOOEY! THEY'RE ALL ALIKE!
!
?
YOU HAVE JUST HEARD A PROGRAM DIRECT FROM THE BARNYARD OF THE CONTINENTAL POULTRY FARM — IN AUSTRALIA! GOOD-NIGHT, ALL!
?
12-8
WALT DISNEY

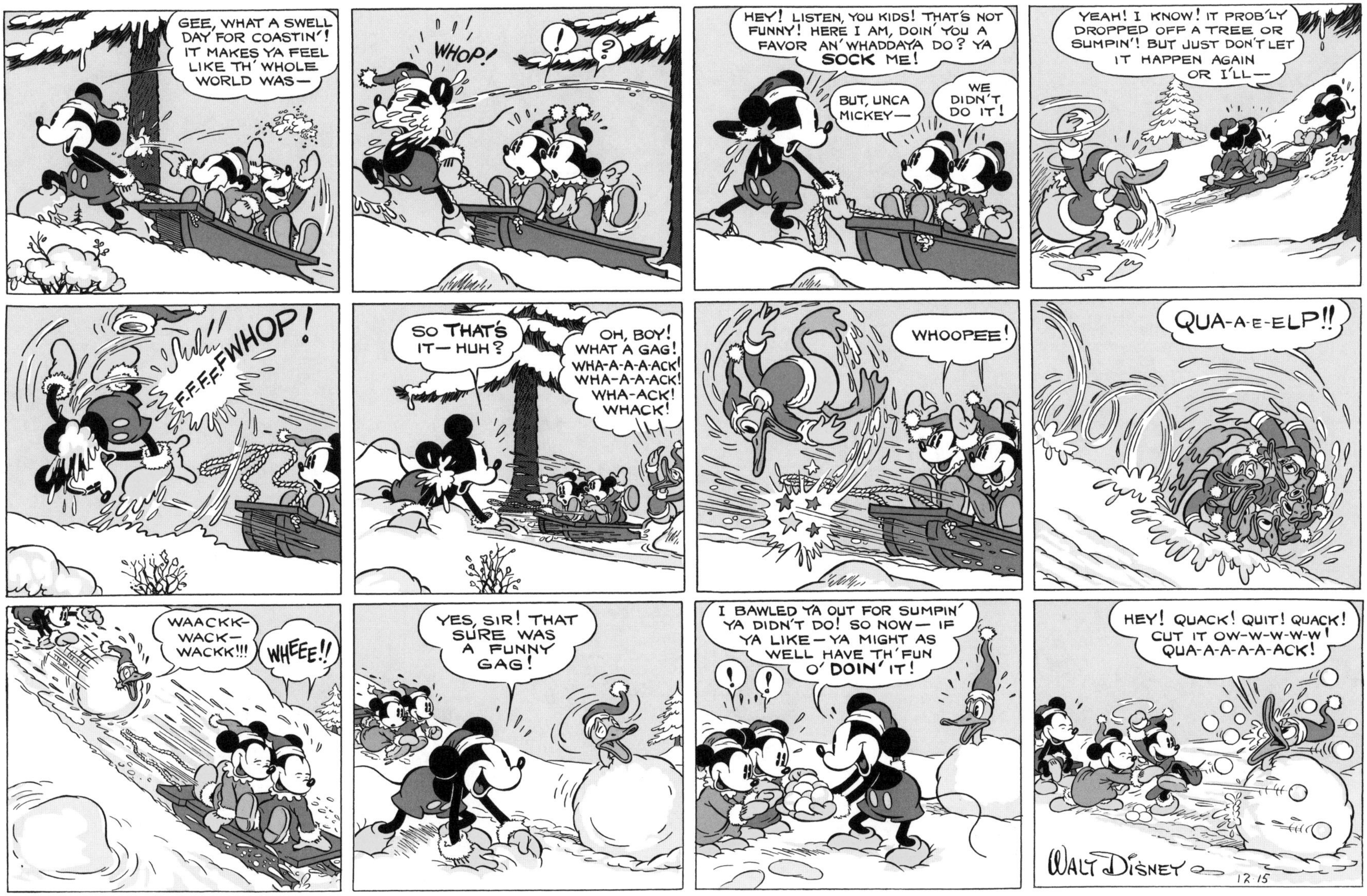
GEE, WHAT A SWELL DAY FOR COASTIN'! IT MAKES YA FEEL LIKE TH' WHOLE WORLD WAS—
WHOP!
!
?
HEY! LISTEN, YOU KIDS! THAT'S NOT FUNNY! HERE I AM, DOIN' YOU A FAVOR AN' WHADDAYA DO? YA SOCK ME!
BUT, UNCA MICKEY—
WE DIDN'T DO IT!
YEAH! I KNOW! IT PROB'LY DROPPED OFF A TREE OR SUMPIN'! BUT JUST DON'T LET IT HAPPEN AGAIN OR I'LL—
F-F-F-F-FWHOP!
SO THAT'S IT— HUH?
OH, BOY! WHAT A GAG! WHA-A-A-A-ACK! WHA-A-A-ACK! WHA-ACK! WHACK!
WHOOPEE!
QUA-A-E-ELP!!
WAACKK-WACK-WACKK!!!
WHEEE!!
YES, SIR! THAT SURE WAS A FUNNY GAG!
I BAWLED YA OUT FOR SUMPIN' YA DIDN'T DO! SO NOW— IF YA LIKE— YA MIGHT AS WELL HAVE TH' FUN O' DOIN' IT!
! !
HEY! QUACK! QUIT! QUACK! CUT IT OW-W-W-W-W! QUA-A-A-A-ACK!
WALT DISNEY
12-15

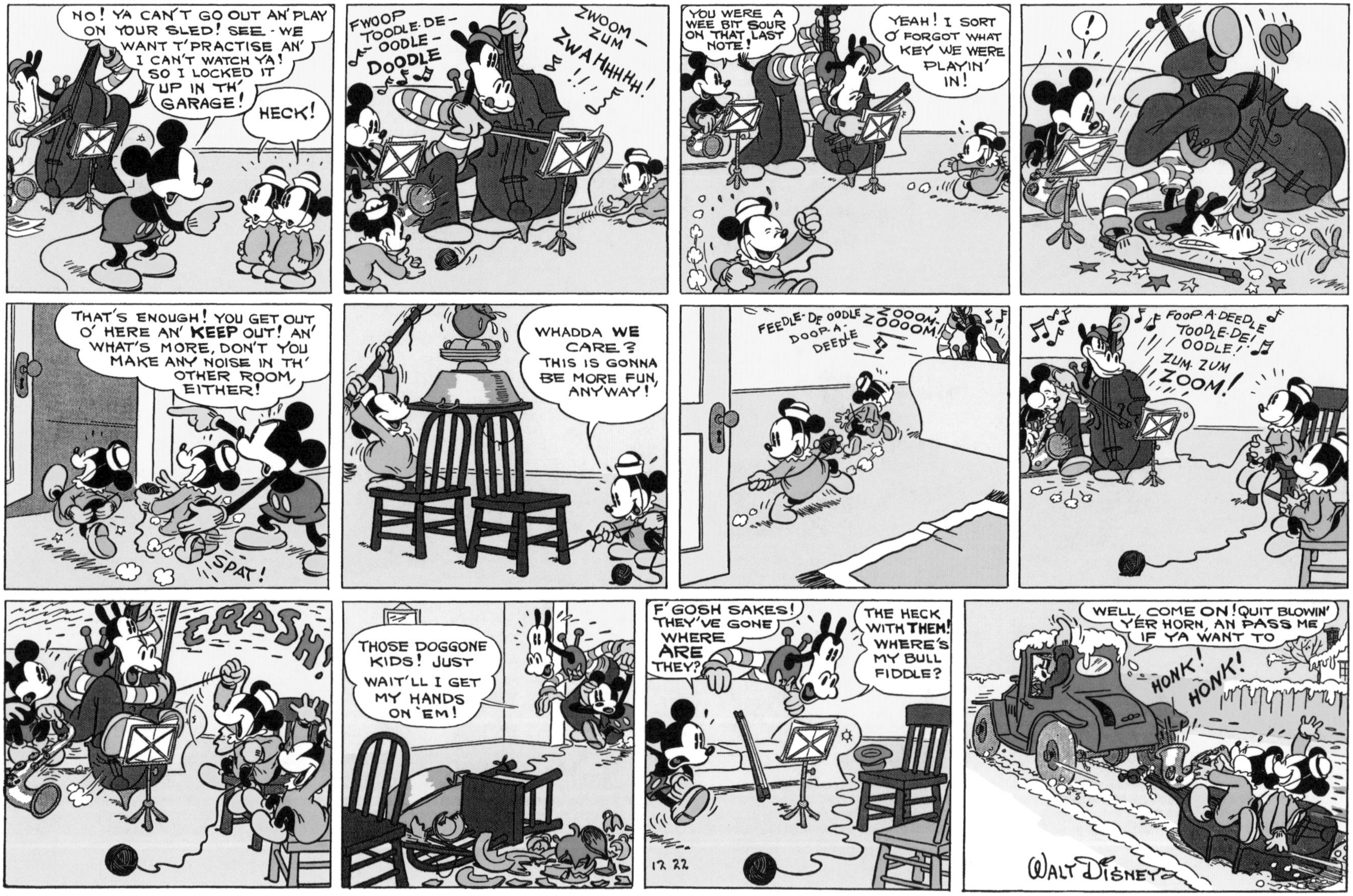
NO! YA CAN'T GO OUT AN' PLAY ON YOUR SLED! SEE - WE WANT T'PRACTISE AN' I CAN'T WATCH YA! SO I LOCKED IT UP IN TH' GARAGE!
HECK!
FWOOP TOODLE-DE-OODLE-DOODLE
ZWOOM-ZUM ZWAHHHHH!
YOU WERE A WEE BIT SOUR ON THAT LAST NOTE!
YEAH! I SORT O' FORGOT WHAT KEY WE WERE PLAYIN' IN!
!
THAT'S ENOUGH! YOU GET OUT O' HERE AN' KEEP OUT! AN' WHAT'S MORE, DON'T YOU MAKE ANY NOISE IN TH' OTHER ROOM, EITHER!
SPAT!
WHADDA WE CARE? THIS IS GONNA BE MORE FUN, ANYWAY!
FEEDLE-DE OODLE DOOP-A-DEEDLE
ZOOOM-ZOOOOM!
FOOP-A-DEEDLE TOODLE-DE-OODLE!
ZUM-ZUM ZOOM!
CRASH!
THOSE DOGGONE KIDS! JUST WAIT'LL I GET MY HANDS ON 'EM!
12 22
F' GOSH SAKES! THEY'VE GONE WHERE ARE THEY?
THE HECK WITH THEM! WHERE'S MY BULL FIDDLE?
WELL, COME ON! QUIT BLOWIN' YER HORN, AN PASS ME IF YA WANT TO
HONK! HONK!
WALT DISNEY

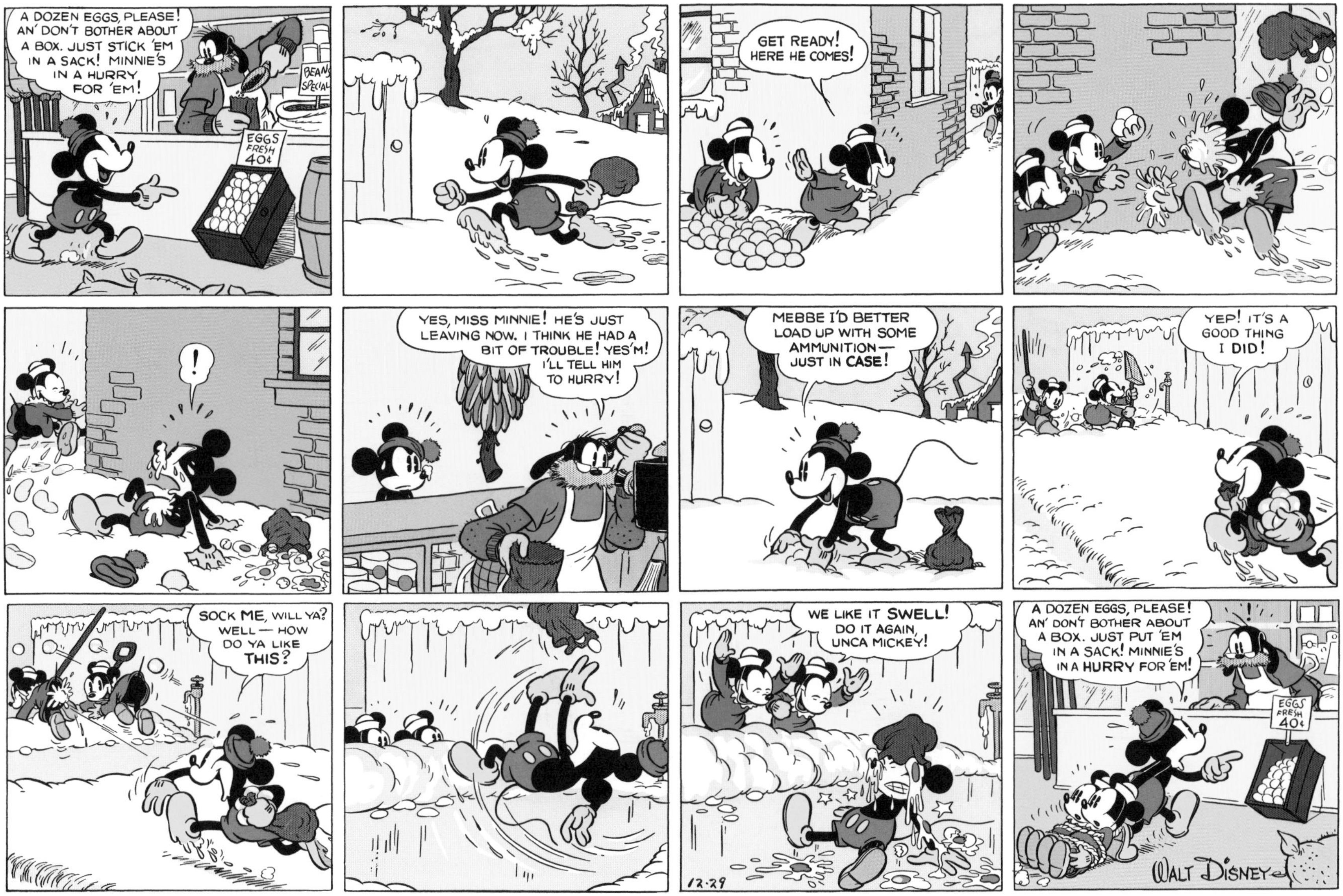
A DOZEN EGGS, PLEASE! AN' DON'T BOTHER ABOUT A BOX. JUST STICK 'EM IN A SACK! MINNIE'S IN A HURRY FOR 'EM!
EGGS FRESH 40¢
GET READY! HERE HE COMES!
!
YES, MISS MINNIE! HE'S JUST LEAVING NOW. I THINK HE HAD A BIT OF TROUBLE! YES'M! I'LL TELL HIM TO HURRY!
MEBBE I'D BETTER LOAD UP WITH SOME AMMUNITION— JUST IN CASE!
YEP! IT'S A GOOD THING I DID!
SOCK ME, WILL YA? WELL— HOW DO YA LIKE THIS?
WE LIKE IT SWELL! DO IT AGAIN, UNCA MICKEY!
12-29
A DOZEN EGGS, PLEASE! AN' DON'T BOTHER ABOUT A BOX. JUST PUT 'EM IN A SACK! MINNIE'S IN A HURRY FOR 'EM!
!
EGGS FRESH 40¢
WALT DISNEY

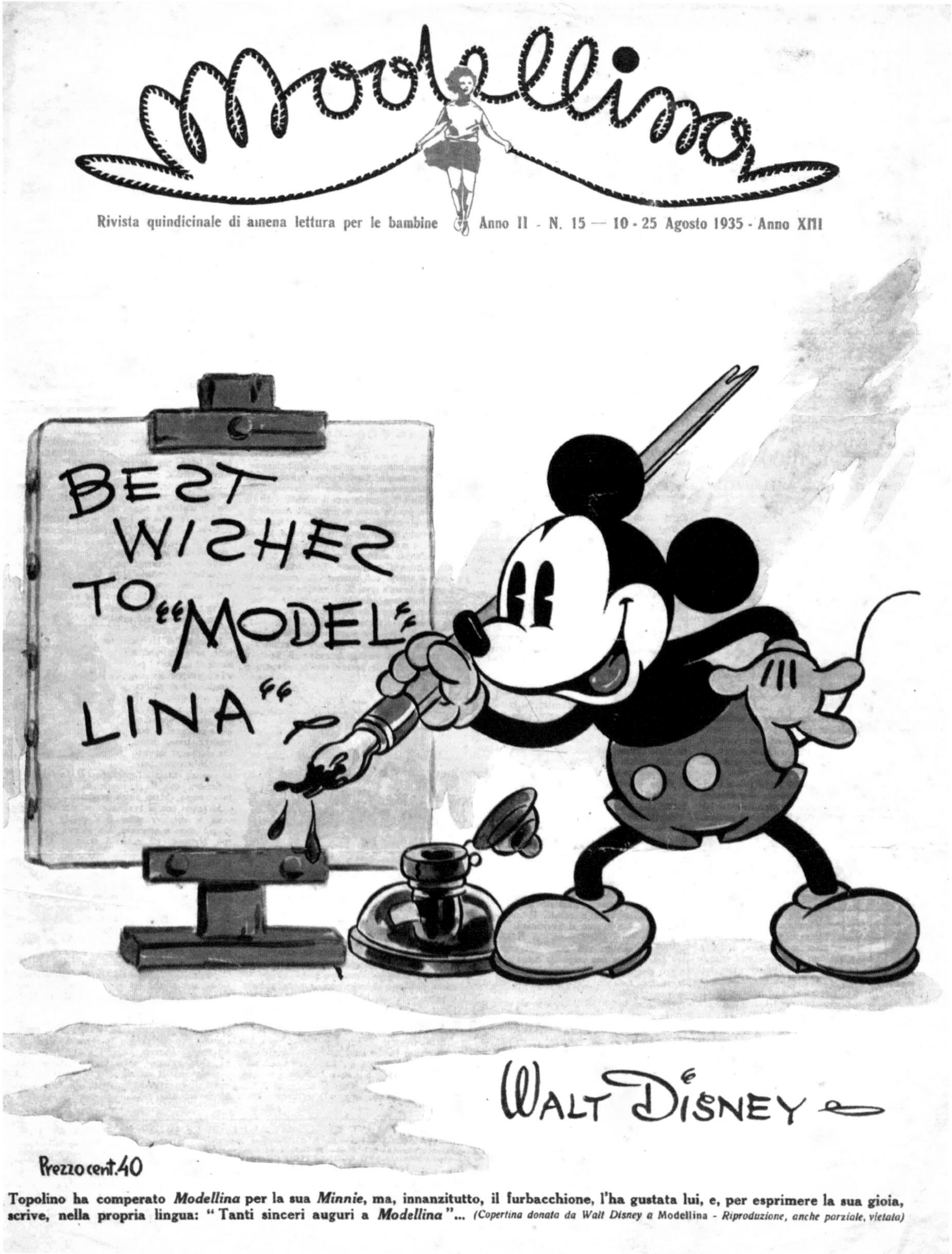
Modellina
Rivista quindicinale di amena lettura per le bambine Anno II - N. 15 — 10 - 25 Agosto 1935 - Anno XIII

BEST WISHES TO "MODEL-LINA"
WALT DISNEY
Prezzo cent. 40

Topolino ha comperato *Modellina* per la sua *Minnie*, ma, innanzitutto, il furbacchione, l'ha gustata lui, e, per esprimere la sua gioia, scrive, nella propria lingua: "Tanti sinceri auguri a *Modellina*"... *(Copertina donata da Walt Disney a* Modellina *- Riproduzione, anche parziale, vietata)*

Mickey's widespread popularity in Europe led to special publicity tie-ups, many of them handled by our domestic Comic Strip Department. The Italian children's magazine *Modellina* received this special cover in 1935; layout by Floyd Gottfredson, finished pencils and inks by Tom Wood. Image courtesy Sergio Lama.

THE GOTTFREDSON ARCHIVES

Essays and
Special Features

The Monthly "Sundays"

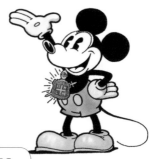

» BY DAVID GERSTEIN AND JIM KORKIS

DEMOLAY INTERNATIONAL is a Masonic youth group for boys aged 12-21, aimed at building civic awareness, leadership skills, and personal responsibility.[1] The original aims of DeMolay—named for Jacques DeMolay, 14th century Knights Templar leader—also included providing "inspiration and direction" to children left fatherless by World War I. DeMolay founder Frank S. Land earned his enduring nickname, "Dad," through his early mentoring of these troubled youths.

Land was called a "grand humanitarian" by Walt Disney, who joined DeMolay one year after the organization's 1919 founding.[2] The 19-year-old Walt became the 107th member of the original Mother Chapter of DeMolay in Kansas City, Missouri, and his fellow members remembered him as hardworking and extremely imaginative.[3]

Belief in one Supreme Being was a basic requirement for young DeMolay members. But the seriousness of religion was offset by the fun of secret passwords, handshakes, and other kid-oriented club rituals, which appealed to young boys as well as building a feeling of fraternity.

Group activities emphasized the seven cardinal virtues: love of parents, reverence for sacred things, courtesy, comradeship (friendship), fidelity (faithfulness), cleanness, and patriotism. In 1965, Walt stated that DeMolay's "precepts have been beyond value in making decisions, in facing dilemmas and crises... I am proud, indeed, still to retain my bond with DeMolay..."

TOP RIGHT: In the early 1930s, Walt Disney gave DeMolay founder Frank Land this special Mickey drawing, penciled by Les Clark. Mickey wears the 1919 DeMolay badge that Disney himself wore as a member. Image courtesy of Dale Dietzman, Past State Chapter Dad of Florida DeMolay; used with permission.

RIGHT: From Gottfredson's "Mickey Mouse and the Ransom Plot" (July 30, 1931). Since DeMolay is a boys' organization, the DeMolay remake (page 251) swaps Clarabelle and Minnie out for male bit player Percy Pig.

HURRY, MICKEY= WE GOTTA BE GOIN!
COMIN, HORACE=SOON AS I TIE PLUTO UP= I DON'T WANT TO LOSE HIM WHILE WE'RE GONE
DON'T FEEL BAD, MICKEY=HE'LL BE ALL RIGHT WHILE WE'RE GONE
7-30

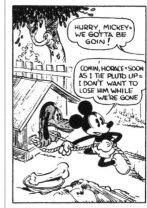

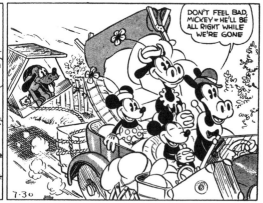

In 1931, Walt Disney was given the DeMolay Legion of Honor, an award representing outstanding leadership in civic, professional, fraternal, or spiritual endeavors. As a gesture of thanks, one year later, Walt asked studio animator Fred Spencer—also a DeMolay alumnus—to create a comics feature for the *International DeMolay Cordon* newsletter: nothing less than a companion series to the *Mickey Mouse* newspaper strip.

The monthly "Mickey Mouse Chapter" installments, resembling slightly shortened *Mickey* Sunday episodes, began in the December 1932 *Cordon* and ran through May 1933, skipping March. The May installment promised more strips in September, but more never came. We are pleased to reprint the five published episodes here, starting on the next page.

It is unknown whether Spencer worked directly with Floyd Gottfredson's team on "Mickey Mouse Chapter," but the May segment is effectively an expanded remake of Gottfredson's July 30, 1931 daily strip. •

The authors wish to thank Didier Ghez and Paul F. Anderson for additional background research. Strips courtesy Chancellor Robert R. Livingston Masonic Library of Grand Lodge, with thanks to Director Thomas M. Savini.

1 Most information about DeMolay and Frank S. Land: DeMolay International, "What is DeMolay?" Demolay International website, http://www.demolay.org/aboutdemolay (accessed April 14, 2011).

2 All Walt Disney quotes: Paul F. Anderson, "Special DHI Guest Essay on DeMolay," Disney History Institute (blog), entry posted March 21, 2011, http://www.disneyhistoryinstitute.com/2011/03/mickey-mouse-chapter-of-demolay.html (accessed December 19, 2012).

3 "Creator Grooms Mickey Mouse for Full-Length Features on Screen." *Kansas City Star*, 6 July 1936.

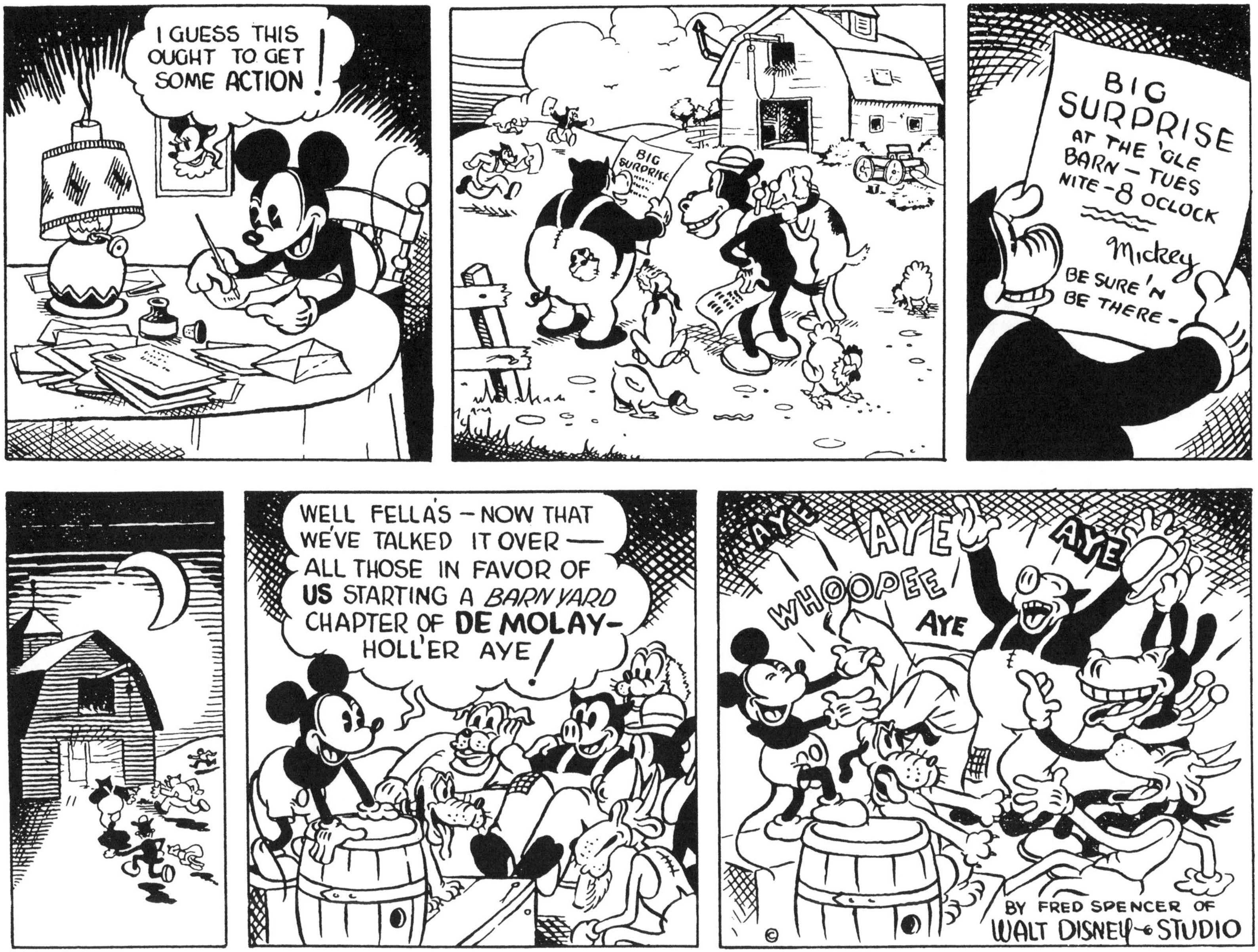
I GUESS THIS OUGHT TO GET SOME ACTION!
BIG SURPRISE
BIG SURPRISE AT THE 'OLE BARN – TUES NITE – 8 OCLOCK
Mickey
BE SURE 'N BE THERE –
WELL FELLA'S – NOW THAT WE'VE TALKED IT OVER — ALL THOSE IN FAVOR OF US STARTING A BARNYARD CHAPTER OF DE MOLAY – HOLL'ER AYE!
AYE
AYE
AYE
WHOOPEE
AYE
BY FRED SPENCER OF WALT DISNEY STUDIO

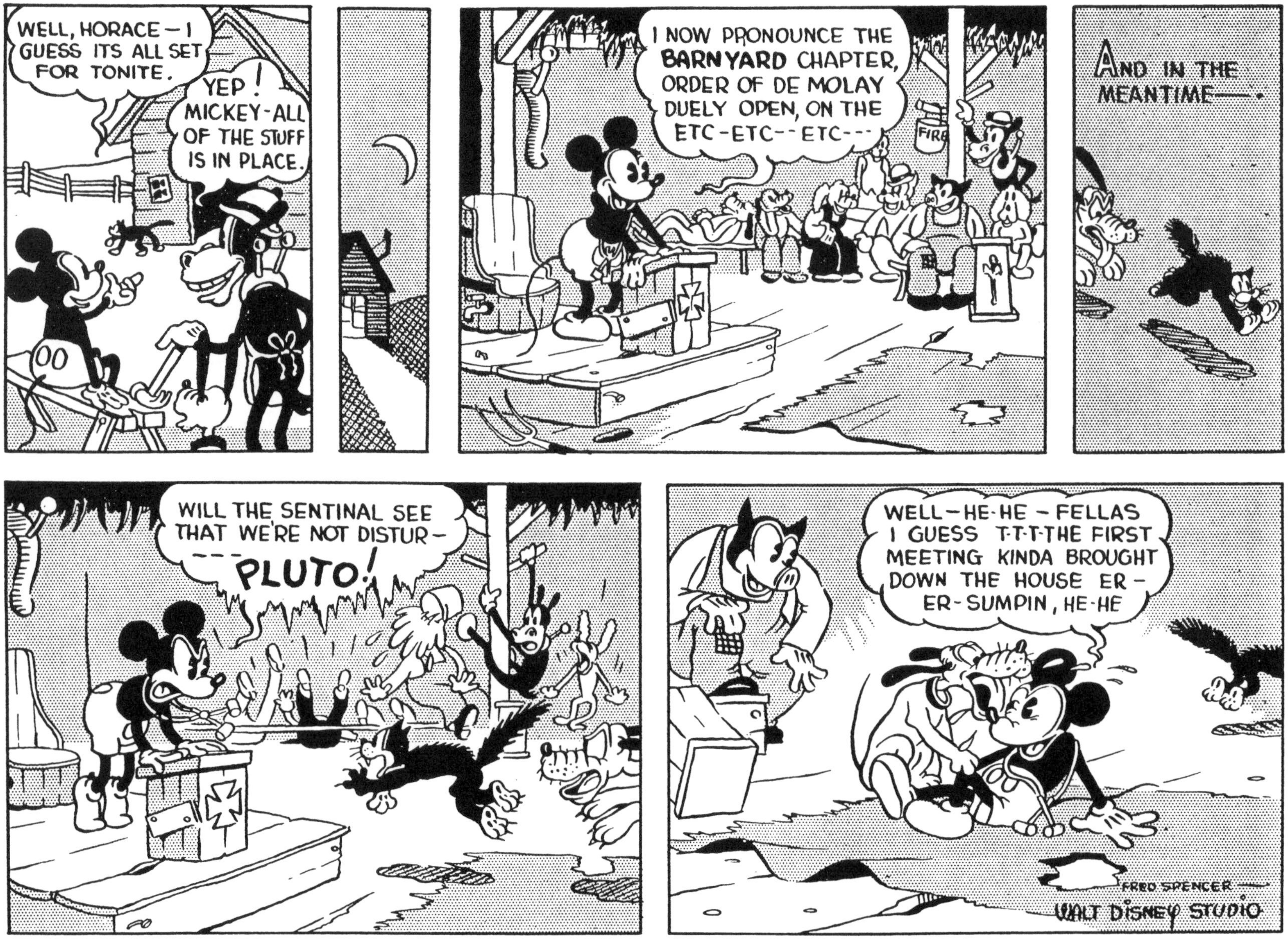
WELL, HORACE — I GUESS ITS ALL SET FOR TONITE.
YEP! MICKEY-ALL OF THE STUFF IS IN PLACE.
I NOW PRONOUNCE THE BARNYARD CHAPTER, ORDER OF DE MOLAY DUELY OPEN, ON THE ETC-ETC--ETC---
FIRE
AND IN THE MEANTIME—.
WILL THE SENTINAL SEE THAT WE'RE NOT DISTUR- ---PLUTO!
WELL—HE-HE—FELLAS I GUESS T-T-T-THE FIRST MEETING KINDA BROUGHT DOWN THE HOUSE ER-ER-SUMPIN, HE-HE
FRED SPENCER —
WALT DISNEY STUDIO

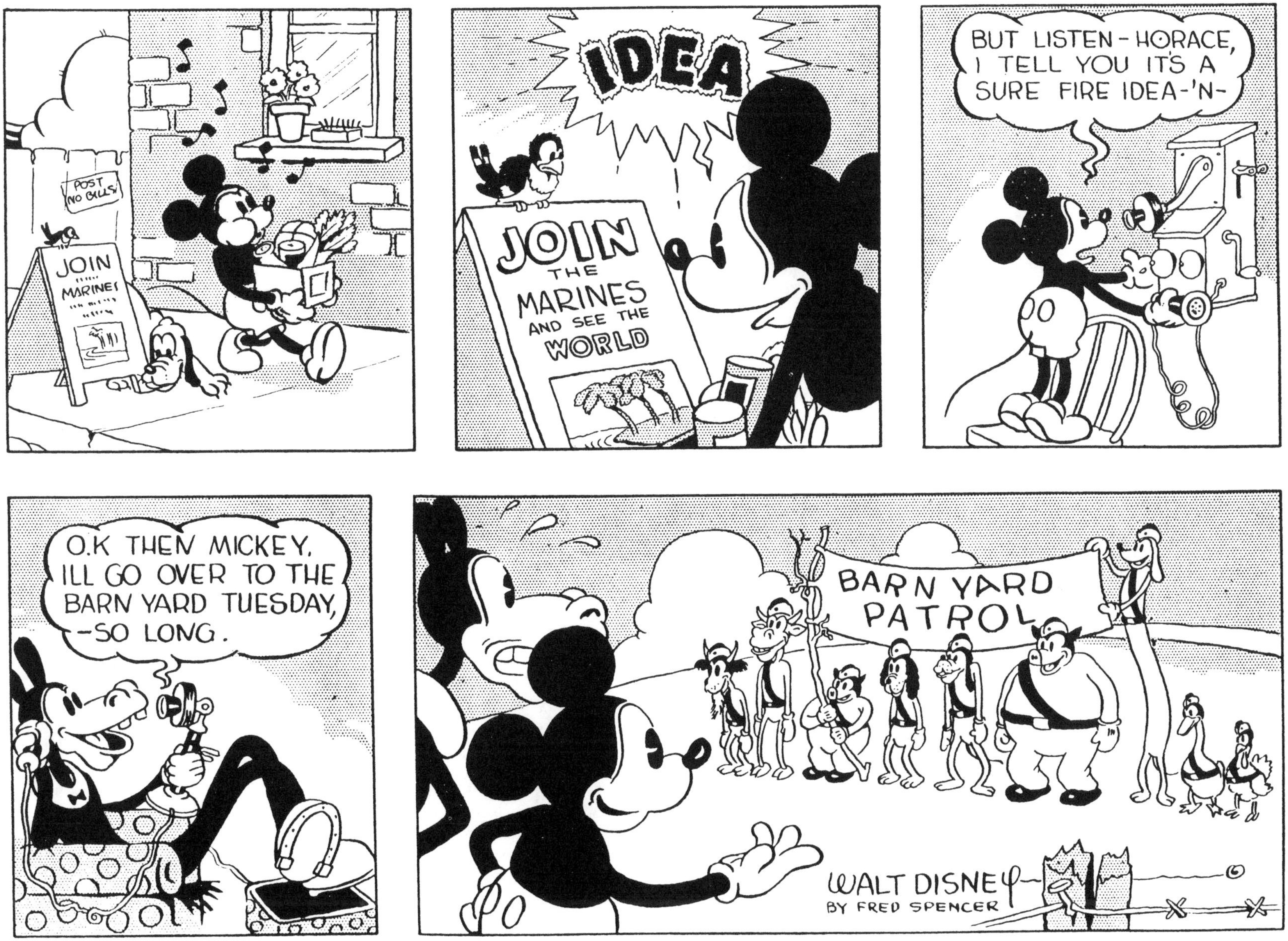
POST NO BILLS
JOIN
MARINES
IDEA
JOIN THE MARINES AND SEE THE WORLD
BUT LISTEN - HORACE, I TELL YOU IT'S A SURE FIRE IDEA-'N-
O.K THEN MICKEY, ILL GO OVER TO THE BARN YARD TUESDAY, -SO LONG.
BARN YARD PATROL
WALT DISNEY
BY FRED SPENCER

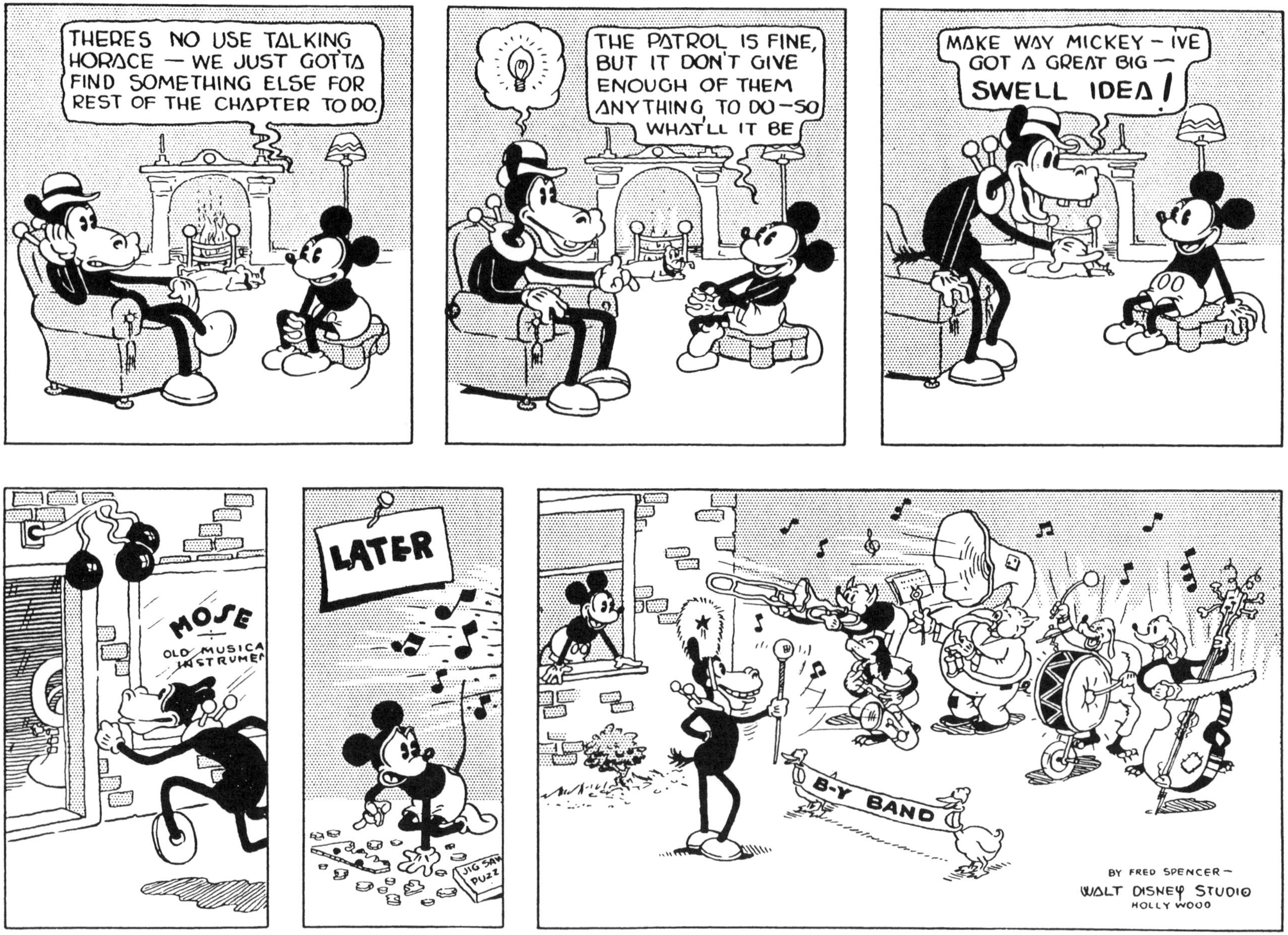
THERES NO USE TALKING HORACE — WE JUST GOT'TA FIND SOMETHING ELSE FOR REST OF THE CHAPTER TO DO.
THE PATROL IS FINE, BUT IT DON'T GIVE ENOUGH OF THEM ANYTHING TO DO—SO WHAT'LL IT BE
MAKE WAY MICKEY — IVE GOT A GREAT BIG — SWELL IDEA!
MOSE
OLD MUSICA INSTRUMEN
LATER
JIG SAW PUZZ
B-Y BAND
BY FRED SPENCER —
WALT DISNEY STUDIO
HOLLYWOOD

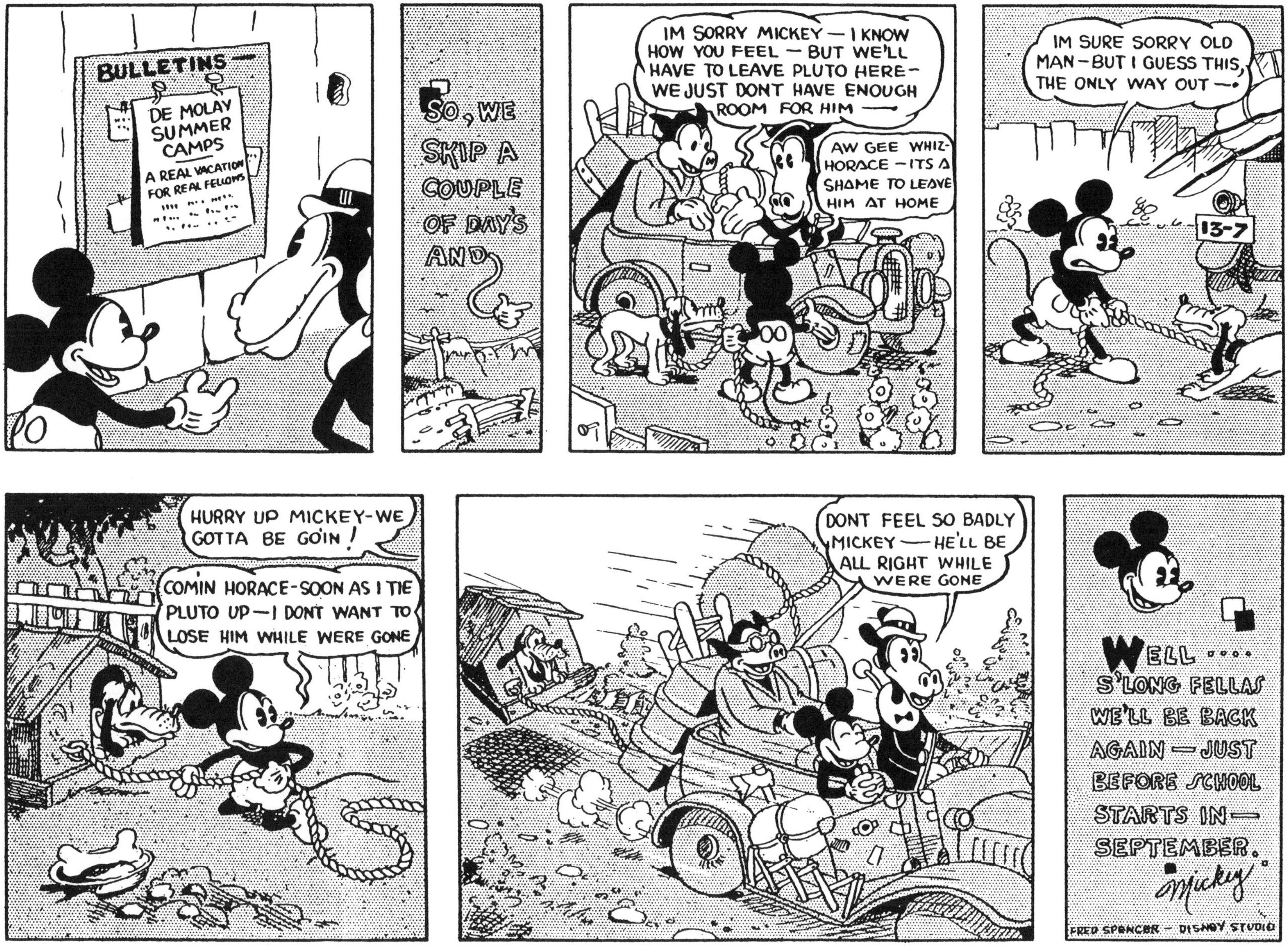
BULLETINS
DE MOLAY SUMMER CAMPS
A REAL VACATION FOR REAL FELLOWS
SO, WE SKIP A COUPLE OF DAY'S AND
IM SORRY MICKEY — I KNOW HOW YOU FEEL — BUT WE'LL HAVE TO LEAVE PLUTO HERE — WE JUST DONT HAVE ENOUGH ROOM FOR HIM —
AW GEE WHIZ — HORACE — ITS A SHAME TO LEAVE HIM AT HOME
IM SURE SORRY OLD MAN — BUT I GUESS THIS, THE ONLY WAY OUT —
13-7
HURRY UP MICKEY - WE GOTTA BE GO'IN !
COMIN HORACE - SOON AS I TIE PLUTO UP — I DONT WANT TO LOSE HIM WHILE WERE GONE
DONT FEEL SO BADLY MICKEY — HE'LL BE ALL RIGHT WHILE WERE GONE
WELL .... S'LONG FELLAS WE'LL BE BACK AGAIN — JUST BEFORE SCHOOL STARTS IN — SEPTEMBER.
Mickey
FRED SPENCER - DISNEY STUDIO

Every country that loves Mickey Mouse has had its own edition—or editions—of Floyd Gottfredson's epics. And each country's Disney comics publisher has tried to make its own version unique, usually by asking homegrown talent to create their own covers or vignettes based on the stories.

In this series we're proud to anthologize these images, both foreign and domestic, old and new—and give you a sense of how far Gottfredson's classic adventures have traveled over the years. We'll start with two covers under which "Dan the Dogcatcher" was reprinted... though the bullying Dan only dared to show his face on one. [DG]

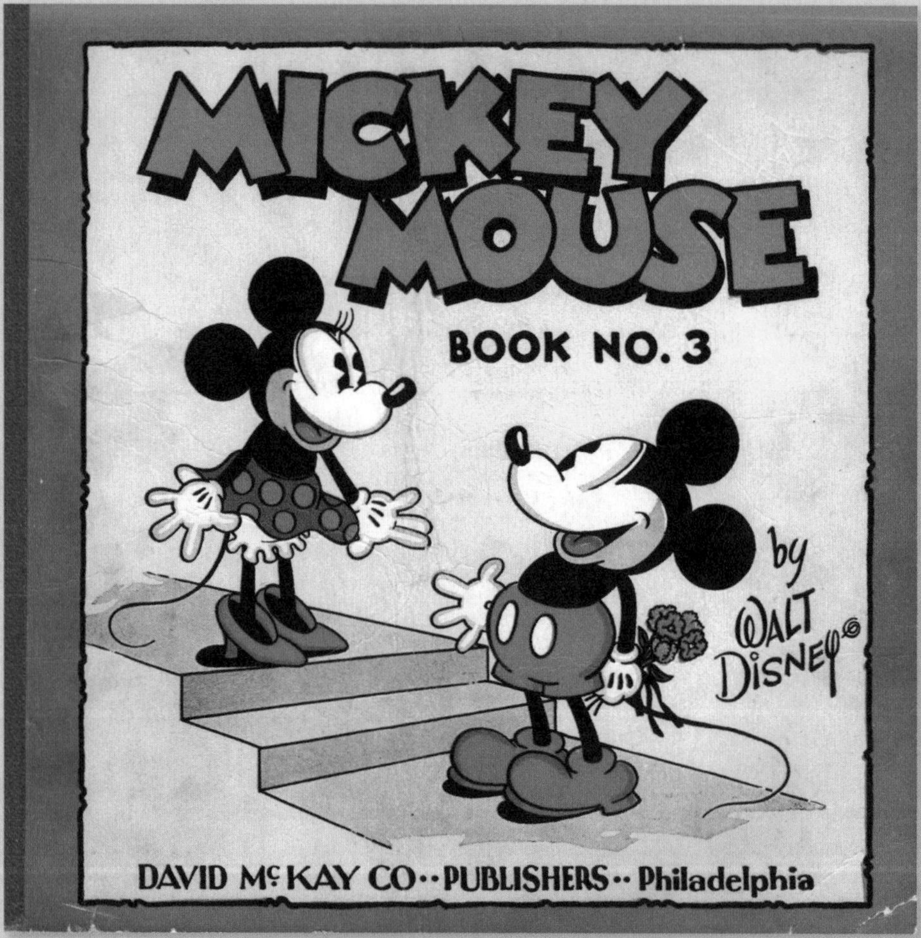
MICKEY MOUSE
BOOK NO. 3
by WALT DISNEY
DAVID McKAY CO.. PUBLISHERS.. Philadelphia

LEFT: David McKay's *Mickey Mouse Series* 3 (1933), pencils by Floyd Gottfredson. This was the first Disney comic book to consist entirely of Sunday strips—and the first to be printed entirely in color. Image courtesy Thomas Jensen.

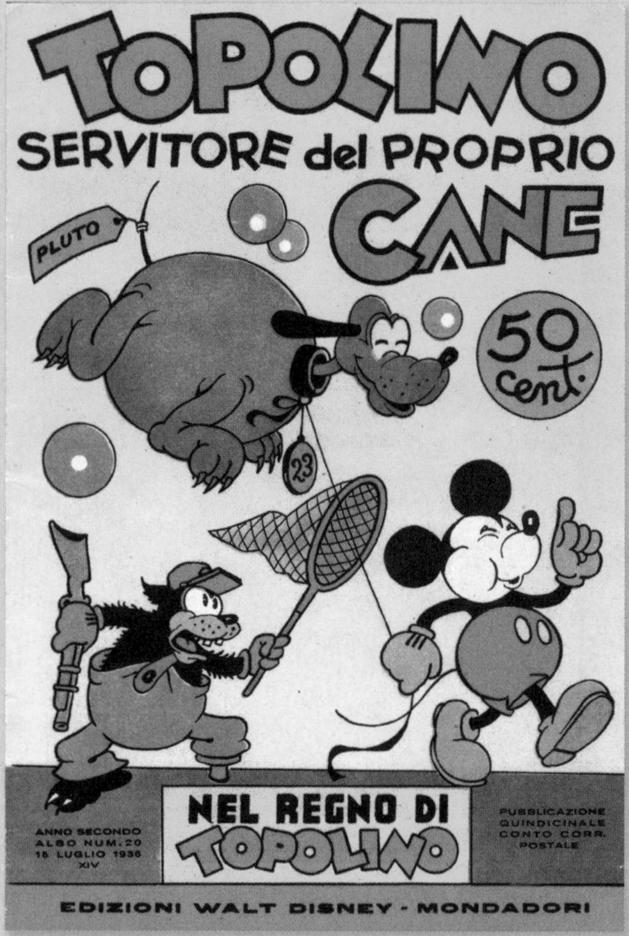
TOPOLINO
SERVITORE del PROPRIO
CANE
PLUTO
50 cent.
23
NEL REGNO DI
TOPOLINO
ANNO SECONDO
ALBO NUM. 20
15 LUGLIO 1936
XIV
PUBBLICAZIONE
QUINDICINALE
CONTO CORR.
POSTALE
EDIZIONI WALT DISNEY - MONDADORI

RIGHT: Italian *Nel Regno di Topolino* 20 (1936). Art by Antonio Rubino; image courtesy Leonardo Gori.

Mickey's nephews started with a rabbit.

Well, perhaps that's a rather obvious statement. Mickey Mouse would not exist had Walt Disney not lost control of his earlier hit character, Oswald the Lucky Rabbit. So had there been no Oswald, there would be no Mickey—and thus, naturally, no Morty and Ferdie Fieldmouse.

But in fact, the pesky twins actually owe Oswald a special, separate debt apart from Mickey's own.

To understand why, we must jump back to 1927—to the cartoon *Poor Papa*, the first Oswald storyline to go into production. "Already the father of a large family,"[1] the rabbit sees red when storks bring him fifteen new Bunny Kids, with hundreds more to follow. After bathing mobs of babies in a churn and drying them on a clothesline, angry Oswald fends off further stork deliveries by taking to the roof with a shotgun.

When distributor Charles Mintz screened *Poor Papa*—its title borrowed from a 1926 pop tune about a harried husband—he got angry, too. Mintz wanted his new cartoon star to be a sympathetic youngster; Oswald was a middle-aged, unpleasant dad.[2] Mintz shelved *Papa*, then demanded Walt Disney and Ub Iwerks de-age Oswald immediately. And a younger hero, it seemed, had little need for babies: the Bunny Kids disappeared a few films later.

But perhaps they deserved a second chance. For in 1928, when *Poor Papa* was belatedly released, it got reviews as positive as any other Oswald short. This seems to have set Walt to thinking. Maybe the *Papa* plot could be remade without *Papa*'s flaws—and with a different kind of star character.

Mickey's Nightmare (1932) was the result, framing the stork invasion as a dream. While some scenes directly copied *Papa*—Minnie, like Oswald's Fanny, lying in bed with a row of kids on either side—the comedy now grew from bewilderment, not anger. Whereas Oswald had been a grown-up grump, at war with the storks and his children, Mickey is a youngster forced to play parent; comically embarrassed and endearingly sympathetic.

Walt Disney apparently loved the result—enough to bring back the dream kids as orphans in later cartoons.[3] He also asked Gottfredson to introduce two of them as nephews in the comics. In their debut story, "Mortimer" and Ferdie are the children of "Mrs. Fieldmouse," seemingly a neighbor. But the tall lady mouse is ret-conned into a de facto sister several weeks later, when Mickey begins introducing her boys as his relatives.

JOSEPH M. SCHENCK
presents
WALT DISNEY'S
MICKEY MOUSE
'The STEAMROLLER'
UNITED ARTISTS
PICTURE

Gottfredson's early uses of Morty and Ferdie reflect *Mickey's Nightmare*; but show traces of *Poor Papa* too. The twins are mischievous to the point of anarchy, making Mickey more sympathetic by default. But should Mickey react with bossy anger—as he sometimes does—then the unsympathetic Oswald of *Papa* hops back into view. While Gottfredson never spoke of it later, his team evidently faced a balancing act: how parental could Mickey get while remaining a likeable underdog?

By 1935 a satisfying middle ground was achieved, with Mickey portrayed less as a parent, more as a big brother. We find him caught between his nephews, Minnie, and third parties in comedies of manners; he is more adult than the boys, yet still tempted to engage them on their childish level.

We're quite some ways from blasting storks off the roof. [DG]

LEFT: Morty and Ferdie's ancestors: Oswald gets even with the Bunny Kids in *Trolley Troubles* (1927). The Kids would later return as video game foes in *Disney Epic Mickey* (2010).

RIGHT: For all their comics popularity, Mickey's nephews only made a few screen appearances; *Mickey's Steamroller* (1934) was the first. Art by Tom Wood; image courtesy Walt Disney Archives.

1 Walt Disney et al. "Poor Papa: Synopsis, Gags and Situations." Studio reference document, 1928.

2 Charles Mintz, telegram to Walt Disney, April 15, 1927.

3 The cartoons run from *Giantland* (1933) to *Pluto's Party* (1952); when *Giantland* was adapted to this volume's "Rumplewatt the Giant" (1934), the orphans made their comics debut.

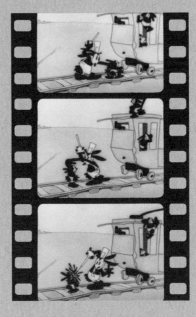

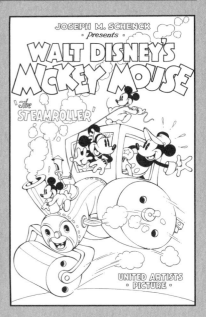

Behind the Scenes: MINNIE'S YOO-HOO

READING THE *MICKEY MOUSE* Sunday strip of October 16, 1932, the modern fan might miss the significance of the moment. As carefree Mickey paints his hencoop, he sings a silly song about barnyard noise. "Th' cows an' th' chickens, they all sound like th' dickens/When I hear my little Minnie's *yoo-hoo!*" At first, the tune seems little different from other comic songs sung in the *Mickey Mouse* Sunday, many of them written by Gottfredson himself.

But there was something different about "Minnie's Yoo-Hoo": across the United States, a million kids were singing it with Mickey.

The backstory takes us to 1929, when sound cartoons were new. Rival studios were toying with synchronized speech, an innovation Disney had yet to perfect. Early Mickey cartoons had featured more clucks than words. But Disney had resolved to change this in a big, publicity-worthy way. Let other funny animals talk; the Mouse would roar. *Sing*, that is.

I'M THE GUY THEY CALL LITTLE MICKEY MOUSE!
I'LL JUST PLUNGE INTO WORK—THAT'LL KEEP MY MIND OFF MINNIE AND THAT SLICKER SHE FELL FOR!
MICKEY MOUSE'S MINIATURE GOLF

"The theme song [concept] seems to have passed to the studios of motion comic strips," the *Los Angeles Times* reported. "Mickey's voice will ring out clear and true for the total time space of one minute... 700 drawings will be required [to get] the song out of his system. These muscular movements of the throat and body must occur in such a fashion that they synchronize perfectly..."[1]

The resulting cartoon, *Mickey's Follies* (1929), shows that its animators had carefully analyzed the throat and body. Maybe *too* much so—or maybe it was on purpose: in singing his song, Mickey contorts into some of the funniest poses he ever struck. And the lyrics of "Minnie's Yoo-Hoo," written by Walt Disney and studio composer Carl Stalling, only helped him along.

Not surprisingly, *Mickey's Follies* was a hit; no less surprisingly, the new theme song had a long life ahead. Summer 1929 saw the launch of the Mickey Mouse Clubs: no relation to the later TV series, but rather a nationwide group of Disney-sponsored theatre clubs for kids. Boasting over a million members by 1932,[2] the Clubs featured games, contests, a "Mickey Mouse Club yell"... and a theme song. At each matinee meeting, the uniformed Song Leader led young "Mickey Mice" in singing "Minnie's Yoo-Hoo." A special sing-along film, adapted from *Mickey's Follies*, rang in theatres' rafters for years.

The music didn't stop there. Until 1933, "Yoo-Hoo" was also the theme song of Mickey's screen cartoons. Then it returned in later decades for *The Mouse Factory* TV variety show (1972) and the animated *Mickey Mouse Works* (1999). It's easy to see why Floyd Gottfredson should have picked up the song; it's amazing he didn't use it *more* often.

That said, Gottfredson faced the music often enough to engage in a playful dig at its ubiquity. In the daily strip of October 28, 1930, Mickey doesn't sing "Minnie's Yoo-Hoo" while he works; he has a radio on hand to sing it for him! At the time—in our world—a cover by bandmaster Leo Zollo was just about to come out. [DG]

1 Muriel Babcock, "Talkie Idea Strikes Animated Cartoons and Film Antics Turn Vocal." *Los Angeles Times*, 11 August 1929. By the time this article saw print, *Mickey's Follies* had already been released.

2 Cecil Munsey, *Disneyana: Walt Disney Collectibles* (New York: Hawthorn Books, Inc.), p. 102.

MICKEY MOUSE CLUB
MICKEY MOUSE "THEME SONG"
MINNIE'S YOO HOO
"Minnie's Yoo Hoo!"
MICKEY MOUSE
THEME SONG
AS SUNG BY— WALT DISNEY'S WORLD FAMOUS CARTOON CHARACTER MICKEY MOUSE

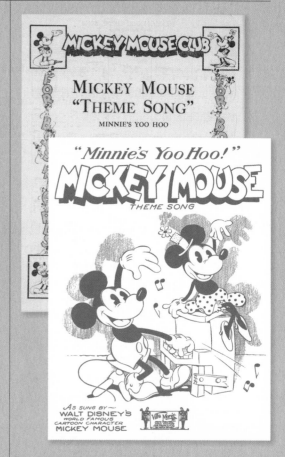

LEFT: From "Mr. Slicker and the Egg Robbers" (October 28, 1930). The Mickey Mouse Club campaign book stated that "The King Features Syndicate... releases a Mickey Mouse comic strip for newspapers, which is being used in some of the best newspapers in the world. Work up a cooperative proposition with them..."

ABOVE: "Minnie's Yoo-Hoo" as both Mickey Mouse Club theme song and standalone hit: sheet music, 1930. Piano-playing image penciled by Les Clark, inked by Win Smith; images courtesy Hake's Americana.

OPPOSITE: Mickey "getting the song out of his system" in *Minnie's Yoo-Hoo* (1930), the Club sing-along film. Animation repurposed from *Mickey's Follies* (1929).

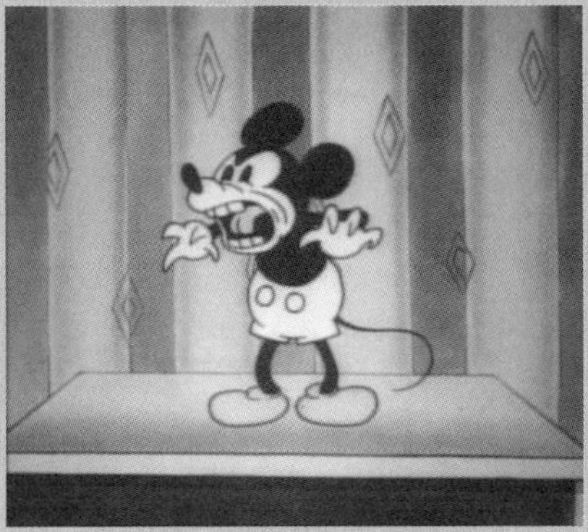

Oh! the old tom cat
With his meow meow meow

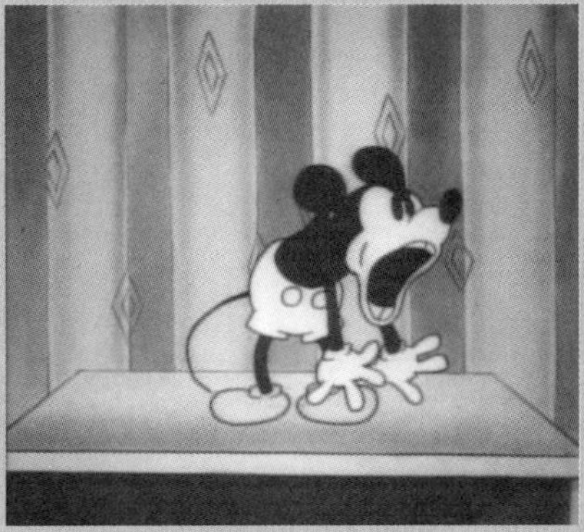

Old houn' dog
With his bow wow wow,

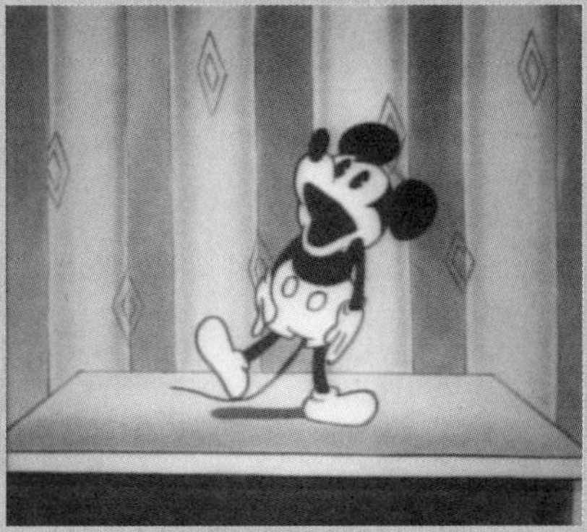

The crow's caw caw
And the mule's hee haw

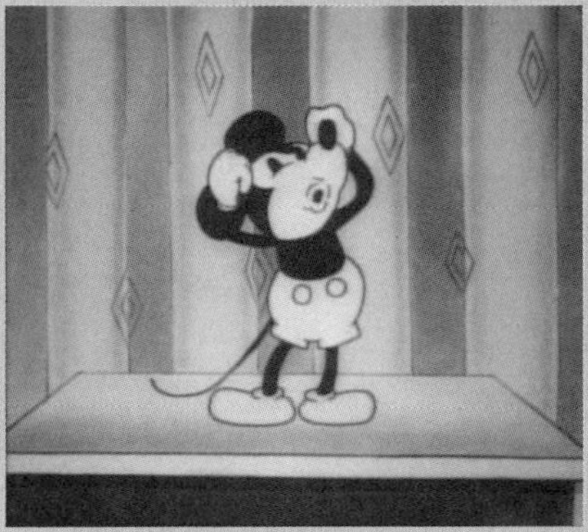

Gosh, what a racket
Like an old buzz saw

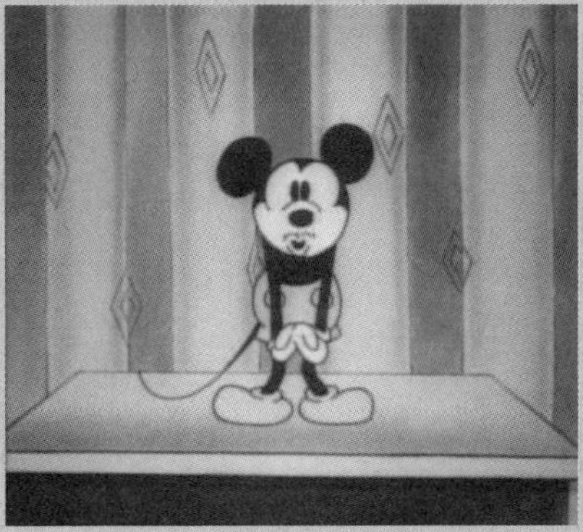

I have listened to the cuckoo
'Kuke' his cuckoo

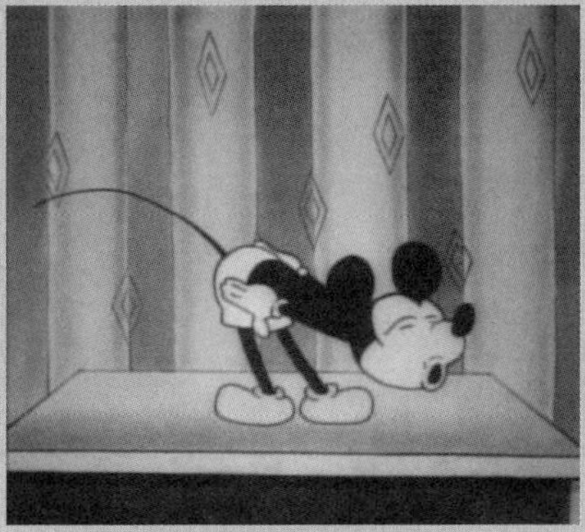

And I've heard the rooster
Cock his doodle doo-oo

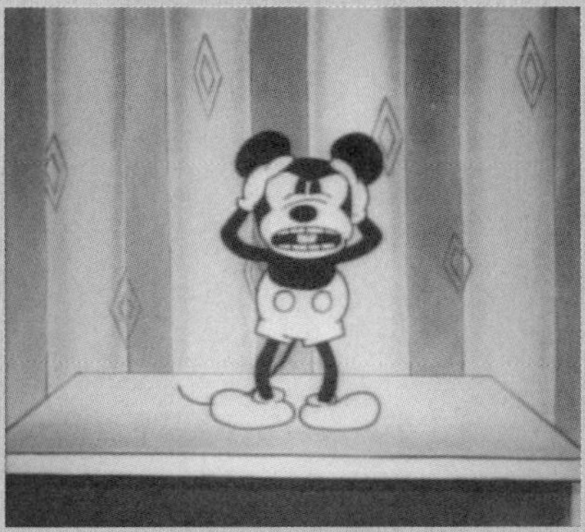

With the cows and the chickens
They all sound like the dickens

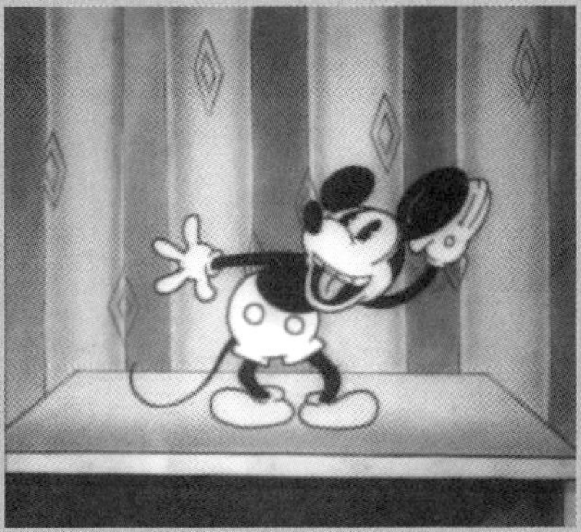

When I hear my little Minnie

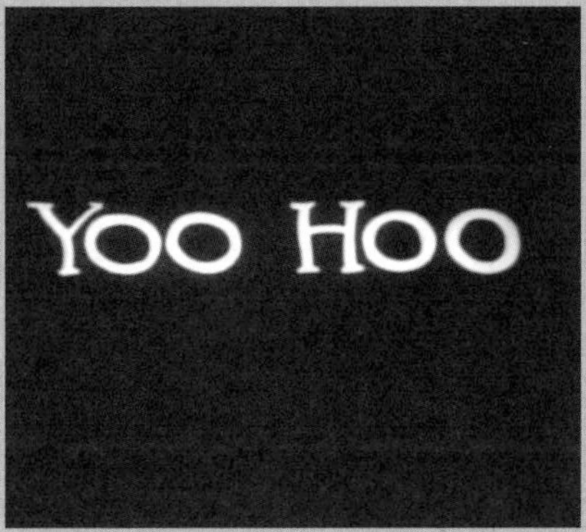
YOO HOO

Mischievous Morty and Ferdie have invaded hundreds of Disney comics covers over the years. Their debut, oddly enough, only got a front cover to itself in one country. But *what* a cover it was.

Upon landing on Italy's *Topolino* 7 (1933), the October 30, 1932 strip from "Mickey's Nephews" became the first-ever Gottfredson work to be published in Italy—displacing cruder Mickey strips drawn by local talent. While some of those cruder strips had actually been Gottfredson-inspired (see page *271*), there proved to be no substitute for the real thing.

Eighty years later, there still isn't. [DG]

Italian *Topolino* 7 (1933). Strip art by Floyd Gottfredson and Ted Thwaites; image courtesy David Gerstein.

Italian *Nel Regno di Topolino* 22 (1936; story title translates roughly to "Unca Mickey's new agonies"!). Gottfredson art reinked by Antonio Rubino; image courtesy Leonardo Gori.

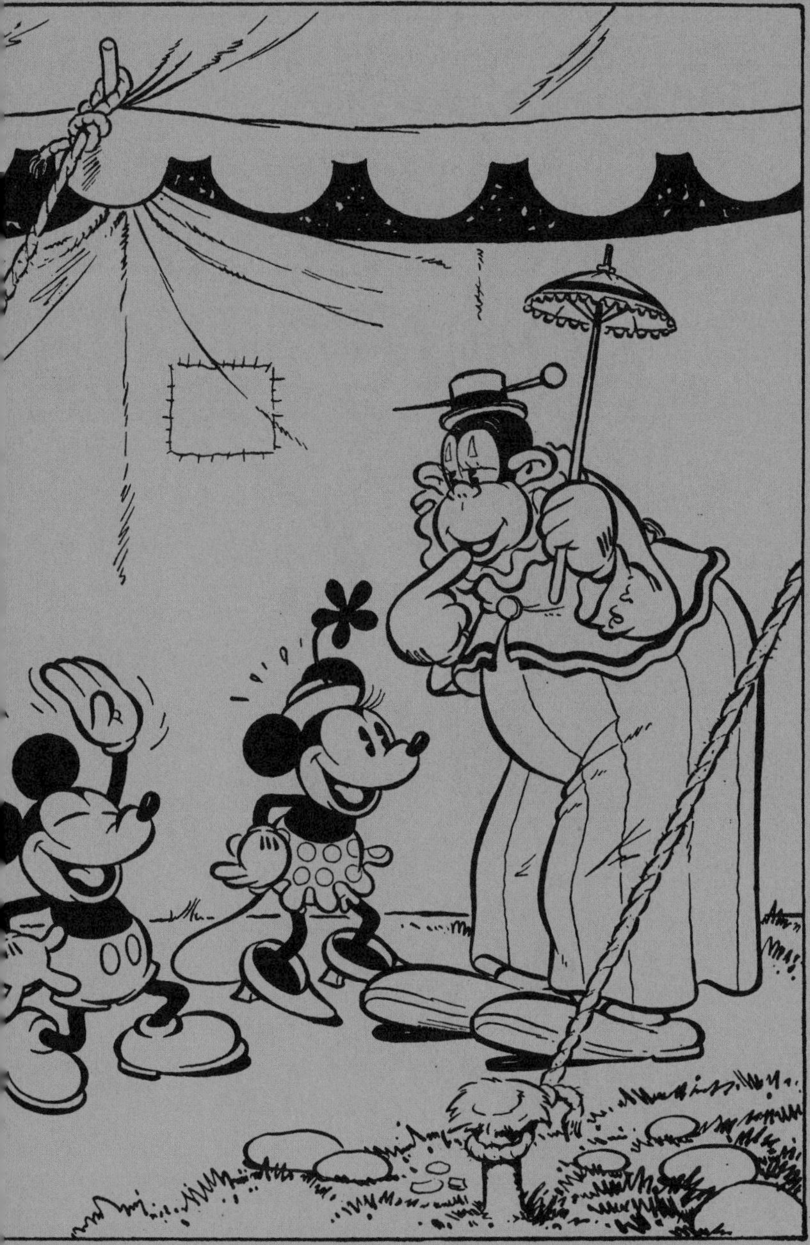

The Comics Dept. at Work: THE MOUSETON POPS

1933 found Floyd Gottfredson, Al Taliaferro, and inker Ted Thwaites moving from strength to strength. The *Mickey Mouse* daily and Sunday strips were both going strong; so was the *Silly Symphony* topper feature. And in Gottfredson's spare time—as manager of the Comic Strip Department—he supervised Tom Wood's studio publicity art. Soon afterward, Publicity would split off to become a separate branch of Disney entirely.

Before that happened, however, Gottfredson, Taliaferro, and Thwaites joined Wood for one last noncomics hurrah. The occasion was Mickey's first foray into a new kind of kids' product: pop-up books, just then recently brought to America by New York licensee Blue Ribbon Publishing. Blue Ribbon founder Harold Lentz, a pioneer in paper engineering, actually created the term "pop-up" to characterize his titles. Like "Kleenex" and "Hoover," it has since become a handy generic—applied even to other publishers' versions of the product.

Blue Ribbon's 1933 *Pop-Up Mickey Mouse* featured a cover inked by Wood. Wood seems to have drawn the *Pop-Up Minnie Mouse* cover from start to finish, along with all of the actual pop-up spreads in both books.

But only a few spreads in each book actually popped up. The rest of the art, save just one page in *Minnie*, was visibly inked by Taliaferro and Ted Thwaites—and penciled by Gottfredson and Taliaferro. Some drawings represented all-new Gottfredson pencil work; other times, Gottfredson's poses were mined from Sunday serials such as "Lair of Wolf Barker."

Reprinted on the next few pages are those vignettes that, to our eyes, show the greatest degree of Gottfredson's involvement. Read on to check out two of the strangest children's stories ever told...

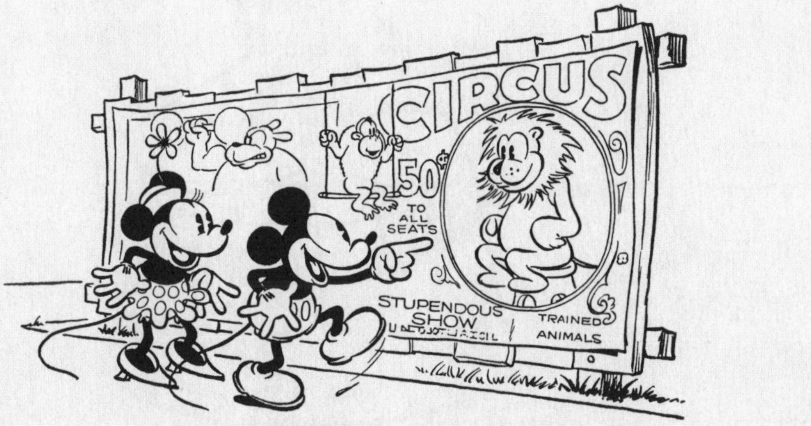
CIRCUS
50¢
TO ALL SEATS
STUPENDOUS SHOW
TRAINED ANIMALS

In *The Pop-Up Mickey Mouse*, the circus is coming to Mouseton—until the tents, animal trainers and caretakers are suddenly blown away by a huge windstorm! The circus animals are left unemployed and alone, and it's up to Mickey and Minnie to give them shelter. "The poor things would have to swim oceans, and walk thousands and thousands and thousands of miles to get back to their own countries," Minnie exclaims.

Mickey and Minnie swiftly turn their farm into a makeshift zoo. But how to fund the animals' eventual journey home? Thinking hard, our heroes utilize the critters' special talents to create giraffe butter, camel milk, and other salable taste treats. Mouseton citizens are scared to buy the odd foods—until the Mayor gives them a tasty endorsement. Soon enough money is made that a Noah-like ark can be built. Bon voyage, beasties.

"La-dies and gentlemen," he began. "Minnie and I are not going to let you go hungry and homeless for long."

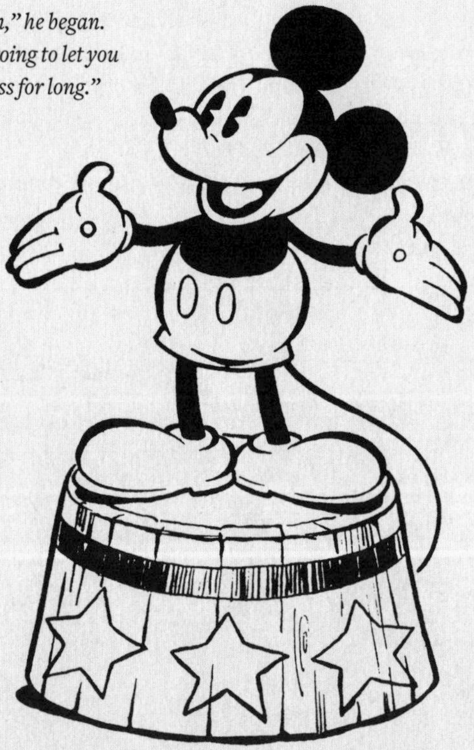

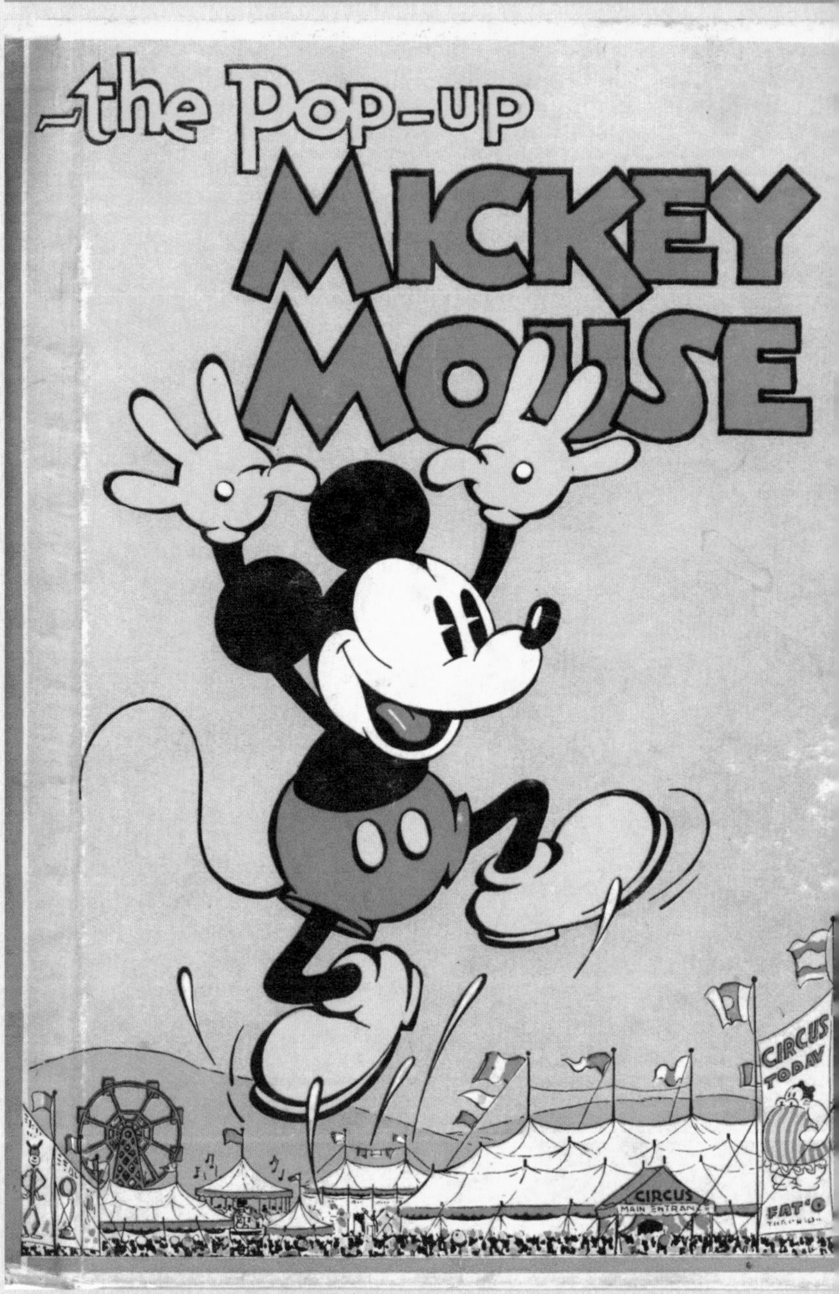
the Pop-up
MICKEY
MOUSE
CIRCUS TODAY
CIRCUS
MAIN ENTRANCE

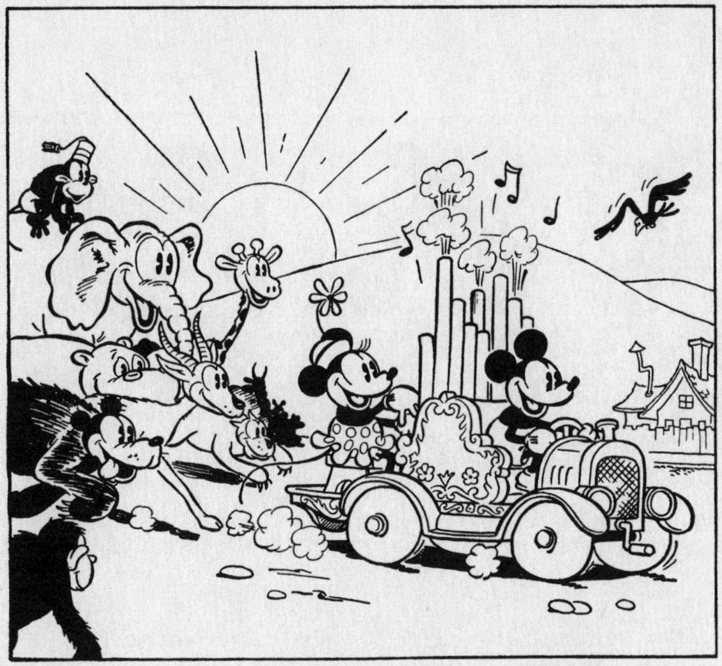

They marched in alphabetical order as follows: antelope, bear, camel, duck, elephant, fleas, giraffe, hippopotamus, ibex, jaguar, kangaroo, leopard, and lion, miscellaneous.

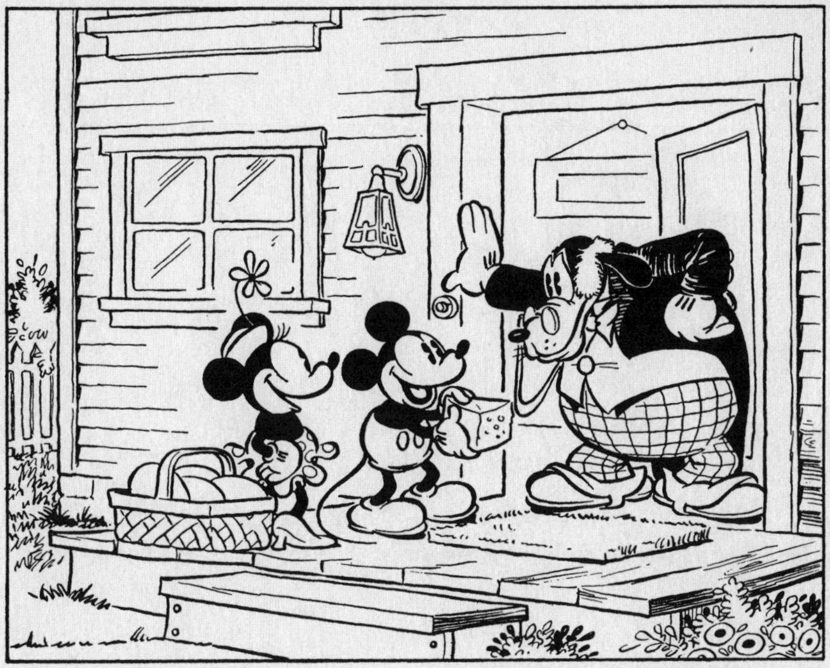

"Taste it," urged Mickey. "Elephant's cheese is very rare, and nobody ever tasted anything like it."

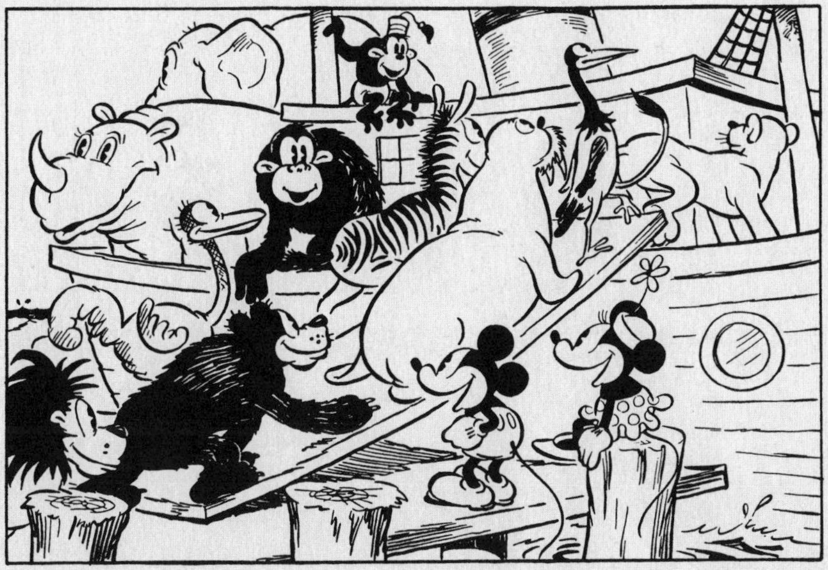

They named it "Mickey's Ark," and they all marched on board in alphabetical order.

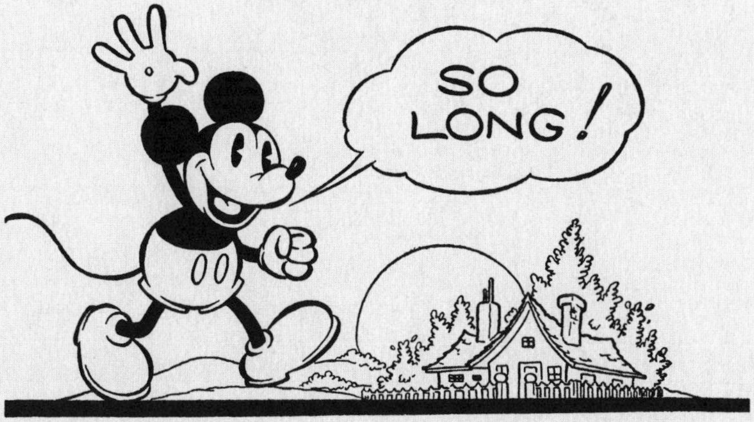
SO LONG!

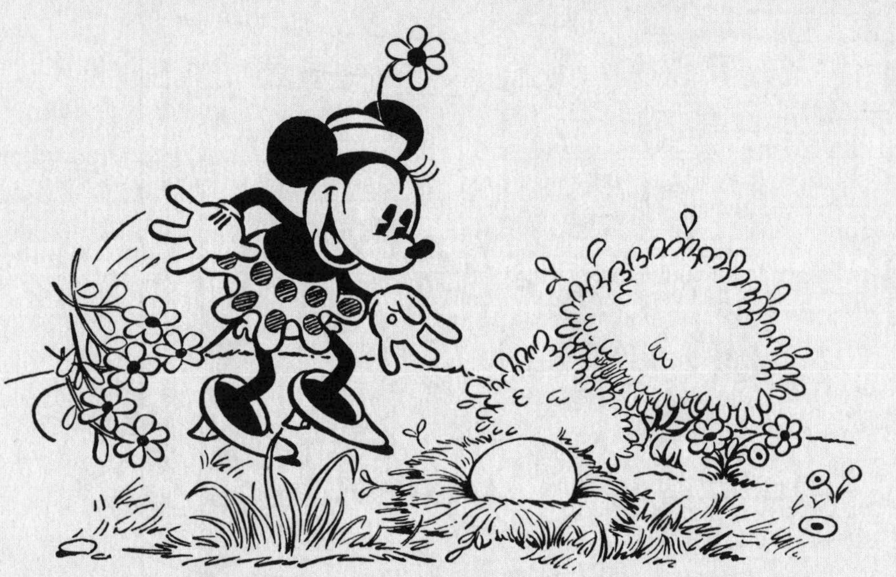

"Ohhhhh!" breathed Minnie, and her "Ohhhhh!" was very soft and round and gentle.

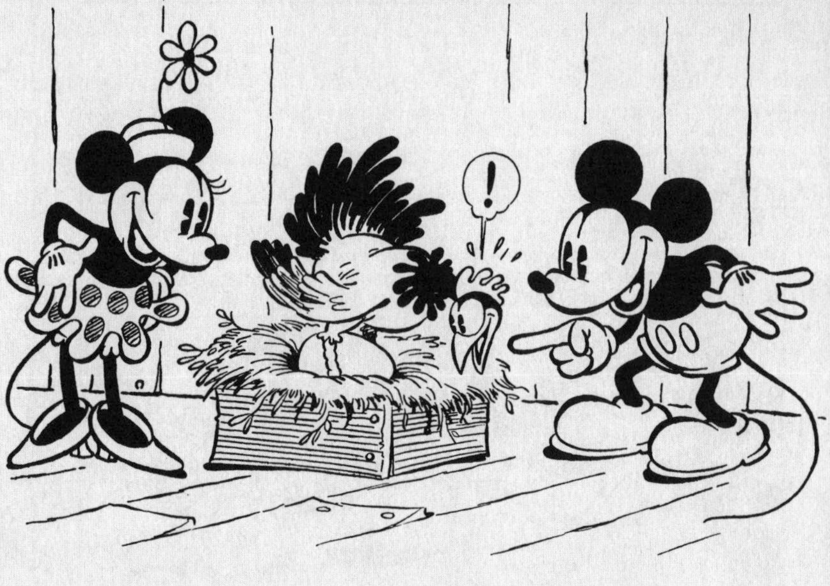

"Clara Cluck, of course," replied Minnie. "That hen can hatch anything."
"Except doorknobs," interrupted Mickey.

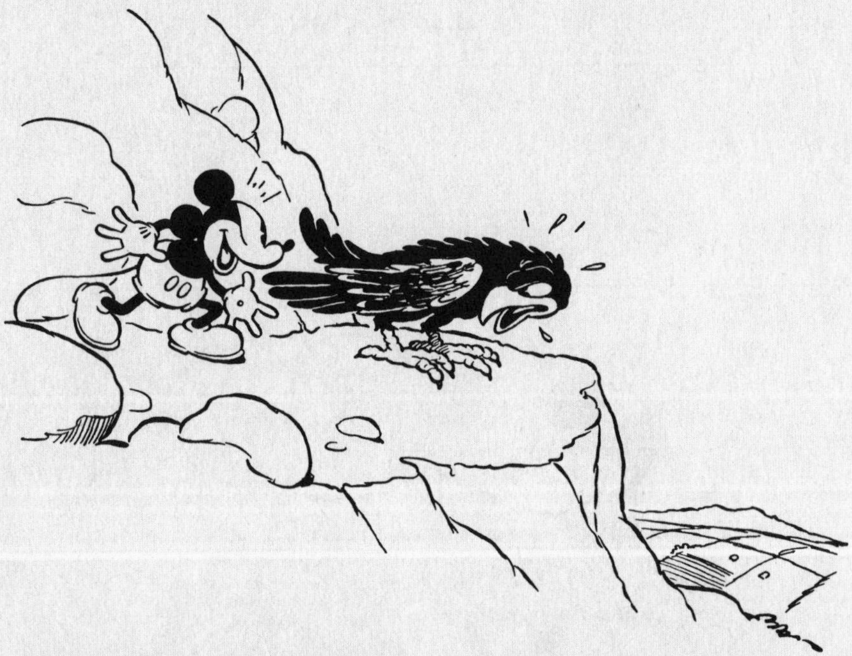

"Go home," screamed Clutch. "Go home before I kill you. I saw the brown egg first. The egg was mine. And Moby Duck is mine."

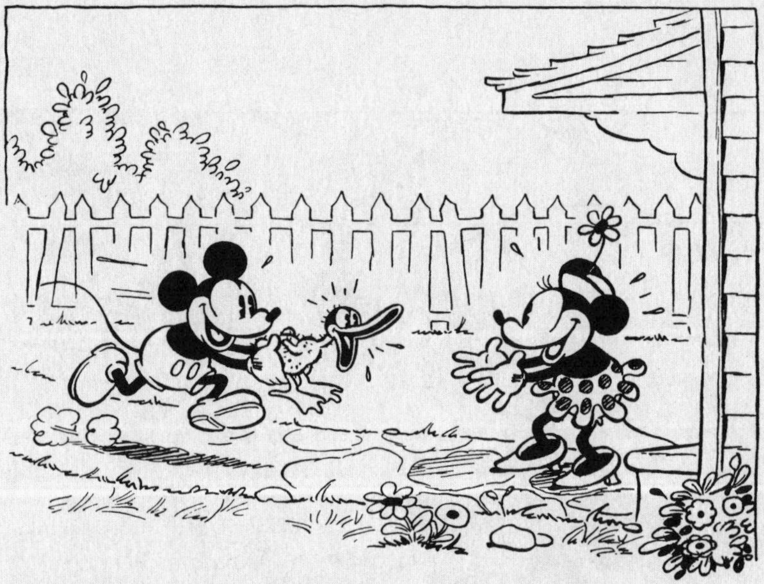

"Oh, Moby," she cried, "I thought we'd never, never see you again."

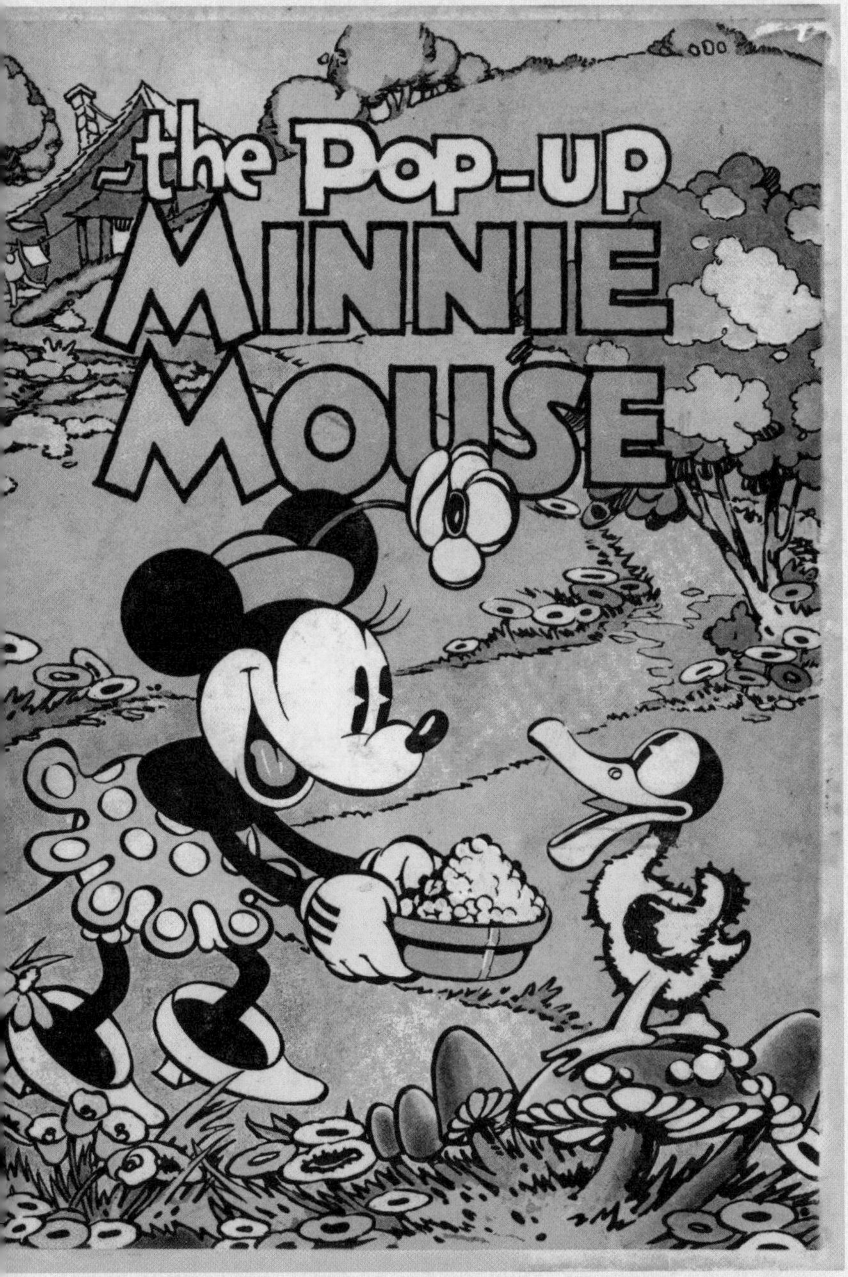
the Pop-up
MINNIE
MOUSE

Minnie's pop-up book finds our heroine and Mickey saving an orphan egg from a fearsome she-hawk named Clutch. Back home, Minnie's hen Clara Cluck (no relation to the later Disney character) hatches the egg, giving birth to a duckling named Moby Duck (no relation to... etc. etc.). But Clutch invades Minnie's farm, swearing revenge. She might have missed out on the egg—but there's nothing she'd like better than a nice duck for dinner!

When Clutch swoops down and kidnaps Moby, Mickey trails her to foreboding Bleak Mountain, where he tricks the hawk and snatches back the hatchling. But the villain still pursues them, trying to maul both Mouse and mallard! Luckily, friendly fauna rally to their rescue. Even Pluto's fleas get into the act, biting Clutch and distracting her till the hawk is hog-tied. In the end, our forest friends formally evict the bad bird. [DG]

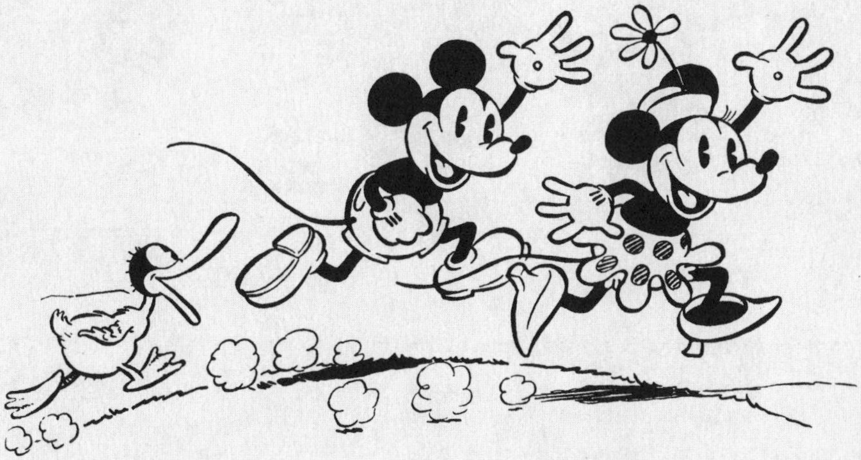

Gottfredson's World: EARLY EPICS

Mickey's first blockbuster color adventures, "The Lair of Wolf Barker" and "Rumplewatt the Giant," have received a lot of fan attention over the years. They've also received extra-classic cover art from the likes of Dutch master Daan Jippes—and Gottfredson's own comic strip team.

But "Rumplewatt" and "Wolf" haven't totally overshadowed their gag-strip and short story contemporaries. In Europe, even Mickey's mishap with a dentist (!) got a toothsome cover of its own. [DG]

GLADSTONE
WALT DISNEY'S
MICKEY MOUSE
3
"the LAIR of WOLF BARKER"

TOPOLINO
E IL BAULE MAGICO
60 CENT.
QUESTO ALBO CONTIENE 2 FIGURINE OMAGGIO TOPOLINO
ANNO III - ALBO N. 45
25 SETTEMBRE 1937-XV
Pubblicazione quindicinale
NEL REGNO DI TOPOLINO
EDIZIONI WALT DISNEY • MONDADORI • MILANO

TOPOLINO
E IL VAMPIRO DELLA PRATERIA
ALBO D'ORO N. 110
36 PAGINE - 50 LIRE

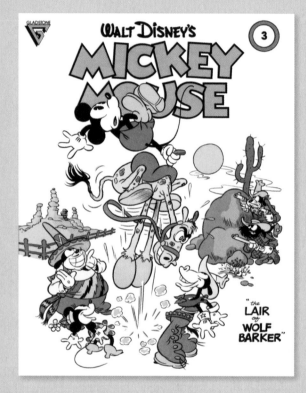

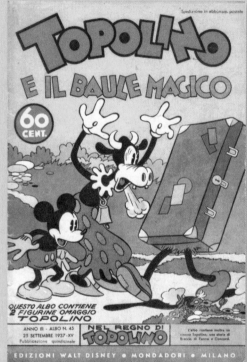

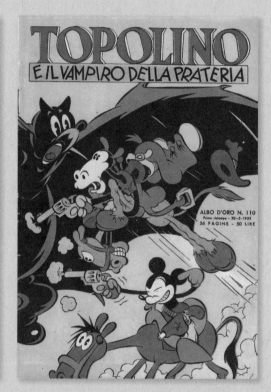

Gladstone Comic Album 3 (1987). Art by Daan Jippes; image courtesy Mike Matei.

Italian *Nel Regno Topolino* 45 (1937), illustrating "Lair of Wolf Barker." Art partly reinked from Gottfredson by Antonio and Michele Rubino; image courtesy Leonardo Gori.

Italian *Albo d'Oro* 48110 (1953), illustrating a mixed-up combination of "Lair of Wolf Barker" and Gottfredson's later "Bat Bandit of Inferno Gulch." Art by Floyd Gottfredson and Ambrogio Vergani; image courtesy The Walt Disney Company.

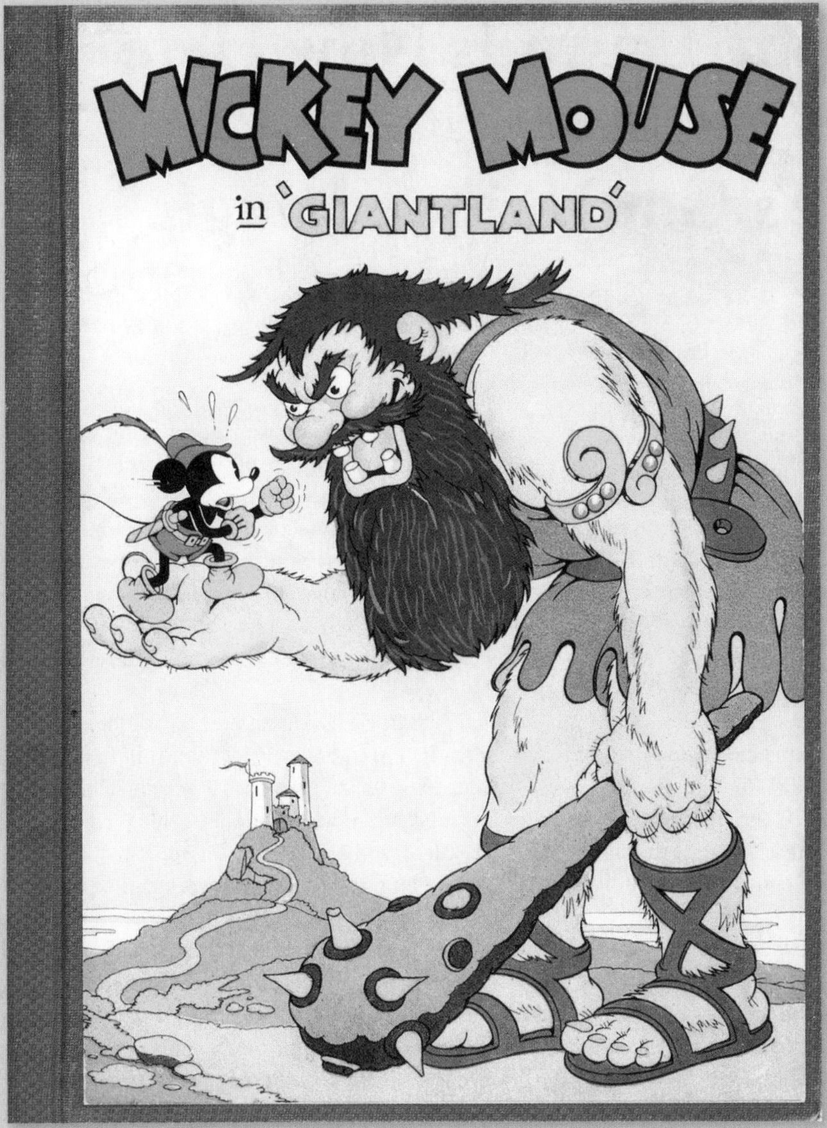
MICKEY MOUSE
in 'GIANTLAND'

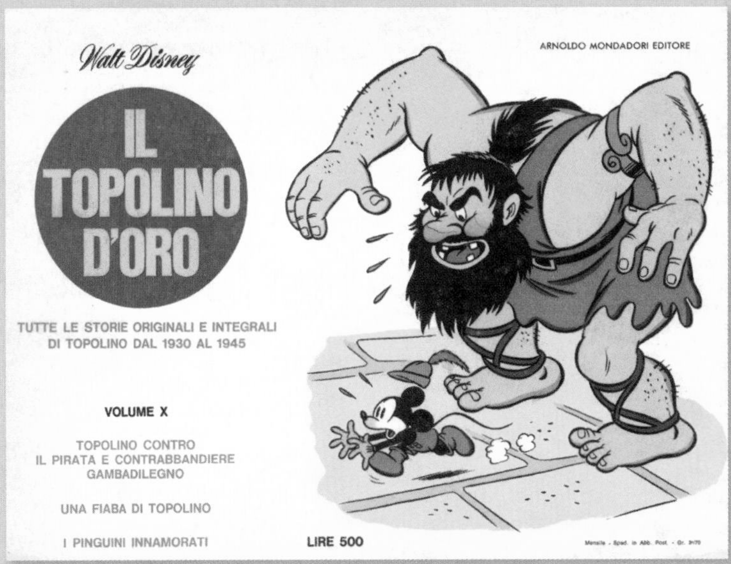
Walt Disney
ARNOLDO MONDADORI EDITORE
IL TOPOLINO D'ORO
TUTTE LE STORIE ORIGINALI E INTEGRALI
DI TOPOLINO DAL 1930 AL 1945
VOLUME X
TOPOLINO CONTRO
IL PIRATA E CONTRABBANDIERE
GAMBADILEGNO
UNA FIABA DI TOPOLINO
I PINGUINI INNAMORATI
LIRE 500

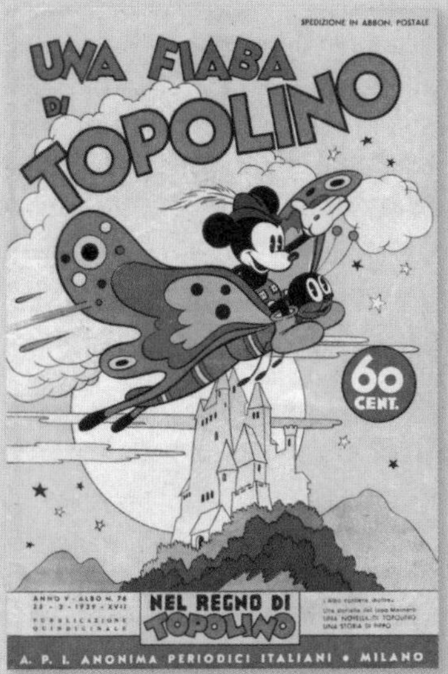
SPEDIZIONE IN ABBON. POSTALE
UNA FIABA DI TOPOLINO
60 CENT.
NEL REGNO DI TOPOLINO
A. P. I. ANONIMA PERIODICI ITALIANI • MILANO

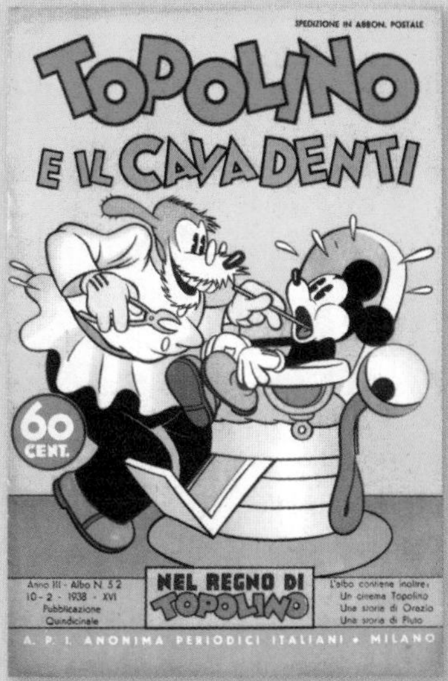
SPEDIZIONE IN ABBON. POSTALE
TOPOLINO E IL CAVADENTI
60 CENT.
Anno III - Albo N. 52
10 - 2 - 1938 - XVI
Pubblicazione
Quindicinale
NEL REGNO DI TOPOLINO
L'albo contiene inoltre:
Un cinema Topolino
Una storia di Orazio
Una storia di Pluto
A. P. I. ANONIMA PERIODICI ITALIANI • MILANO

David McKay hardback (1934), illustrating "Rumplewatt the Giant." Pencils attributed to Floyd Gottfredson, inks by Tom Wood.

Italian *Topolino d'oro* 10 (1971), illustrating "Rumplewatt the Giant." Art by Marco Rota; image courtesy Leonardo Gori.

Italian *Nel Regno Topolino* 76 (1939), illustrating "Rumplewatt the Giant." Art reinked from Gottfredson by Michele Rubino; image courtesy Leonardo Gori.

Italian *Nel Regno Topolino* 52 (1938), illustrating November 12, 1933 gag strip. Art reinked from Gottfredson by Michele Rubino; image courtesy Leonardo Gori.

Dippy Dawg Is Now Here

* * * * * *Joins Mickey Mouse* * * * * *

He's Got Unique Laugh

By IRENE CAVANAUGH

From the Los Angeles Illustrated Daily News, *June 3, 1932*

The Gottfredson Gang in "Their Own" Words

MICKEY AND HIS FRIENDS were box-office gold in the 1930s—thanks largely to their innovative character animation and sound. In the comics, however, Mickey had neither motion nor music. Popularity instead grew out of character complexity.

Case in point: when Dippy Dawg debuted in the funnies, he was cast as a pest full of eccentric hobbies and way-out ideas. On screen, by contrast, the future Goofy was just… goofy. He laughed; he acted yokel-like; but he would not gain depth for awhile.

How, then, to bridge the disparity between cartoons and comics? The answer lay in a masterful press campaign. Disney invited journalists to write mock-interviews with Mickey's gang, chronicling their more complex "private" lives: for instance, telling moviegoers that the offscreen Dippy was more nuanced than he looked. Then Gottfredson's strip could easily include those nuances.

1930s mock-interviews also invoked another Gottfredsonian nuance: Mickey's inability to get cultured. In the piece excerpted here, his trip to a celebrity astrologer leaves both parties seeing stars. [DG]

HARUMPH, harumph, harumph, harumph, harumph-hhh!"

If you hear a chorus of small boys disturbing the cinema capital with deep-throated and raucous laughter in this vein, do not imagine there is an epidemic of whooping cough on.

They are simply practicing the latest razz, the Dippy Dawg laugh, originated at the Walt Disney studios, which has already caught the fancy of the younger generation.

The laugh came into being with the creation of a new character in Mickey Mouse's hilarious company, which Walt Disney has christened Dippy Dawg.

But let's have Mickey Mouse himself tell us about this new aspirant for fame in sound cartoonland.

"Frequently of late we have been disturbed during our rehearsals preliminary to actual shooting by an unearthly laugh from the audience of animals that always assembles on such occasions," stated Mickey.

"Clarabelle Cow was greatly annoyed by it, and vainly tried to trace it to Horse Collar Horace, whom, as you doubtless know, came from the farm and has not yet lost all his uncouth ways, in spite of Clarabelle's efforts to reform him.

"But we soon decided Horse Collar was innocent, as I put my sweetheart, Minnie Mouse, to watch [him under] observation on the set.[1]

"When members of the company [found the real culprit, approached] him when he was not actually [expecting it, and] dragged him into the open, he began to laugh. Such a guffaw you never heard before. It seemed to come direct from his Adam's apple. It was just such a laugh as you would expect from an ignorant country bumpkin, the village cutup, in other words.

"Mr. Disney, always on the outlook for new talent for our company, baited him into trying out his comedy on us. As proud of his accomplishments as any rube, he showed us how he could pitch peanuts into the air and catch them in his mouth.

"He was such a perfect specimen of the small town pest who thinks he is funny that Mr. Disney decided to give him a role in my company. You know the breed, the yapp that is always annoying the girls; the kind who wears a flower in his buttonhole with a tube attached to a squirt bulb in his pocket, or puts mucilage on the chairs at the country store.

"So Dippy Dawg is with us permanently. He is making his sound cartoon debut in our latest feature cartoon, titled *Mickey's Revue*." ●

1 Due to a printing error, several sentences in this article originally appeared incomplete. We have approximated the missing content as seems appropriate.

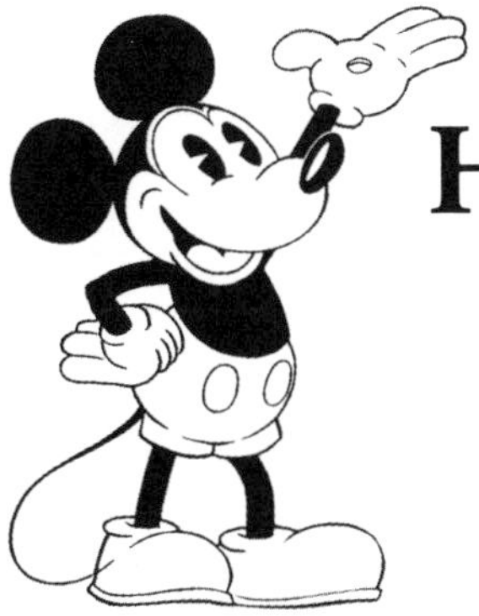

Here's My Horoscope, Folks!

* * * *

says Mickey Mouse

* * * *

Yes, Evangeline Adams does a real horoscope of Mickey, the boy wonder

Excerpted from Screenland *Vol. XXV No. 3, January 1933*

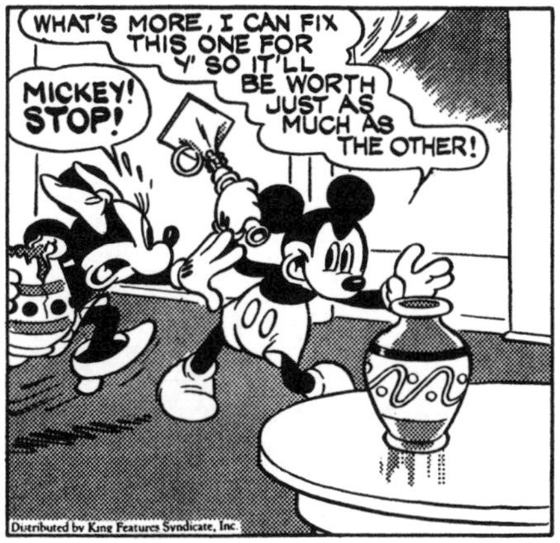
MICKEY! STOP!
WHAT'S MORE, I CAN FIX THIS ONE FOR Y' SO IT'LL BE WORTH JUST AS MUCH AS THE OTHER!
Distributed by King Features Syndicate, Inc.

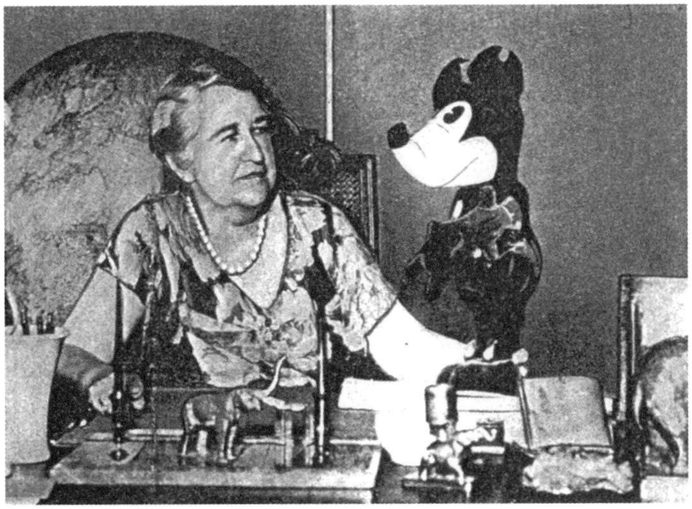

WHEN i was a youngster of two and a half or so, it was all right for me to live a gay, flibberty-gibbet sort of life, going out on all-night crumb-hunting parties, running around with kitchen-mousettes, and so on. But I reached my fourth birthday last October 1, and when a fellow gets to be four it's time he began to take life seriously.

I decided it would be a good idea to have my horoscope read, and find out just where I stood. Naturally I went to see Evangeline Adams, the famous astrologer, about it, so as to be sure of having it done right. Well, she went right to work to look up my stars; and it certainly is remarkable the way that lady can find out things about you! Talking about my popularity with the fans, Miss Adams said:

"While the fairies and Santa Claus have filled so important a part in the lives of children in the past, the trend of modern thinking is to discourage anything which does not have a physical form, and you are fortunate in being able to take the place of all the traditions of the past, as you have a very original, attractive and concrete form with which to meet the demands of the modern age."

Well, that's just about what I try to do in my work—to translate the fairy tale into modern terms, to be a sort of new "Puss in Boots" adapted to the jazz age. Take those "curiouser and curiouser" things that happened to Alice in Wonderland—wouldn't it have been even more exciting to see these fantastic things happen right before your eyes in the movies?

But I'm getting away from Miss Adams' reading. "There is everything to indicate that your influence will be felt in the far corners of the world," she continued, "and that you can be of far greater power than any of your rivals in the fable world."

All right with me! But say, wait a minute—aren't the stars going to smile on my romantic hopes? I'm engaged to Minnie Mouse, you know, and that little gal means more to me than anything else in the world. But listen to what Evangeline Adams says about that:

"Your father (meaning Walt Disney, of course) has shown great wisdom in not allowing you to become involved in anything matrimonial. For the position of Mars would bring you disaster unless you travel in single harness."

Oh, yeah? Well, we'll see about that! Career or no career, I'm going to have my Minnie some day, and if anybody tries to stop us you'll be reading about one of those airplane elopements to Yuma, Arizona. Meaning no disrespect to Miss Adams, of course; but if the stars don't encourage my romance it'll have to get along without their encouragement, that's all. •

LEFT: Evangeline Adams (1868-1932), "America's first astrological superstar," passed away shortly before her Mickey tie-in appeared. This photo was specially arranged for *Screenland*.

ABOVE: Just as Mickey lost patience with Adams' highfalutin advice, he reaches his limit with Minnie's antiques expertise in Gottfredson's "Miracle Master" (September 14, 1939).

Mickey's 1934 Sunday sagas took him deep into the Mouseton hinterlands—where North American cover artists feared to tread, but Disney's Italian talent bravely forged ahead. From mad science with Dr. Oofgay to cliff-climbing calamities, everything was covered. [DG]

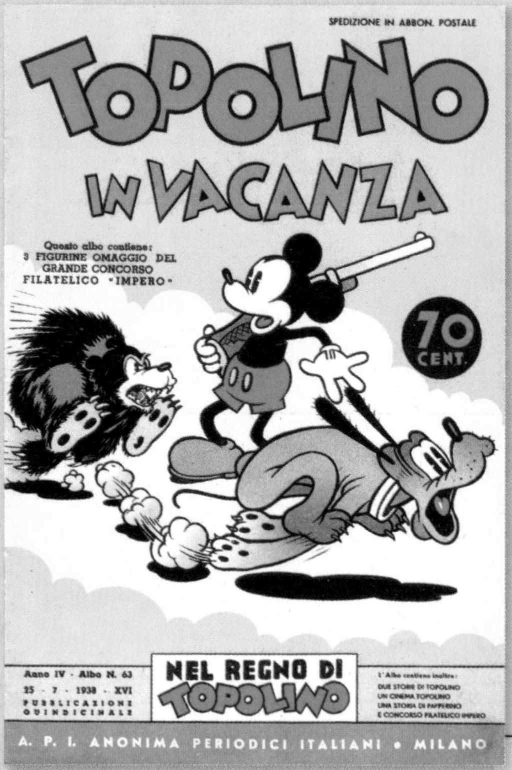
SPEDIZIONE IN ABBON. POSTALE
TOPOLINO
IN VACANZA
Questo albo contiene:
3 FIGURINE OMAGGIO DEL
GRANDE CONCORSO
FILATELICO "IMPERO"
70 CENT.
Anno IV - Albo N. 63
25 - 7 - 1938 - XVI
PUBBLICAZIONI QUINDICINALI
NEL REGNO DI TOPOLINO
L'Albo contiene inoltre:
DUE STORIE DI TOPOLINO
UN CINEMA TOPOLINO
UNA STORIA DI PAPPERINO
E CONCORSO FILATELICO IMPERO
A. P. I. ANONIMA PERIODICI ITALIANI • MILANO

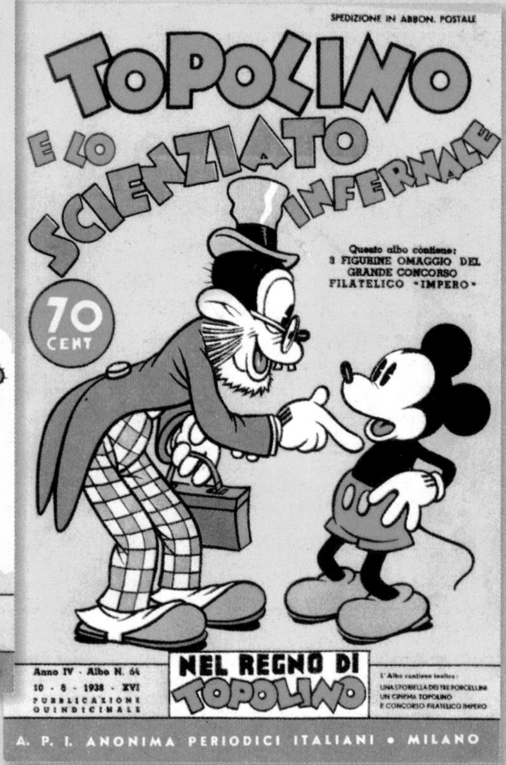
SPEDIZIONE IN ABBON. POSTALE
TOPOLINO
E LO SCIENZIATO INFERNALE
Questo albo contiene:
3 FIGURINE OMAGGIO DEL
GRANDE CONCORSO
FILATELICO "IMPERO"
70 CENT.
Anno IV - Albo N. 64
10 - 8 - 1938 - XVI
PUBBLICAZIONI QUINDICINALI
NEL REGNO DI TOPOLINO
L'Albo contiene inoltre:
UNA STORIELLA DEI TRE PORCELLINI
UN CINEMA TOPOLINO
E CONCORSO FILATELICO IMPERO
A. P. I. ANONIMA PERIODICI ITALIANI • MILANO

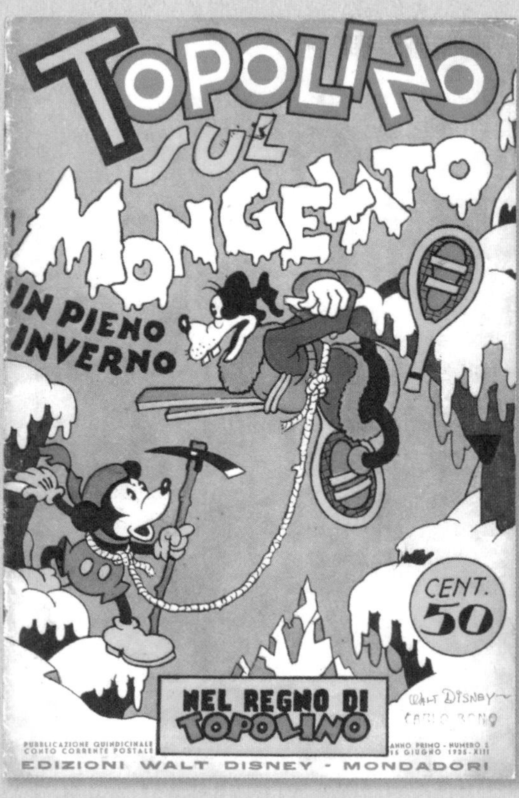
TOPOLINO
SUL MONGELATO
IN PIENO INVERNO
CENT. 50
NEL REGNO DI TOPOLINO
PUBBLICAZIONE QUINDICINALE
CONTO CORRENTE POSTALE
ANNO PRIMO - NUMERO 2
16 GIUGNO 1935-XIII
EDIZIONI WALT DISNEY - MONDADORI

LEFT: Italian *Nel Regno di Topolino* 63 and 64 (1938), illustrating "Dr. Oofgay's Secret Serum." Art reinked from Gottfredson by Michele Rubino; images courtesy Leonardo Gori.

RIGHT: Italian *Nel Regno di Topolino* 2 (1935), illustrating "Foray to Mount Fishflake." Art by Antonio Rubino; image courtesy Leonardo Gori.

Behind the Scenes: INTERIOR DECORATORS

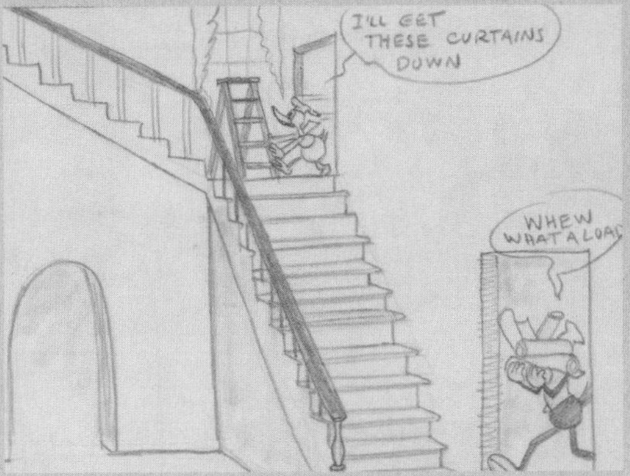

I'LL GET THESE CURTAINS DOWN
WHEW WHAT A LOAD

As J. B. Kaufman explains in this volume's foreword, Disney's unfinished cartoon "Spring Cleaning" inspired several *Mickey Mouse* Sunday strips. With "Interior Decorators"—a spin-off short that was also shelved—the creative process went the other way.

Here's how story man Homer Brightman planned to turn the October 21, 1934 *Mickey* strip (see page 174) into a Goofy gag for "Decorators." It's an intriguing look at the creative process—because retooling a Mickey scene for Goofy involved more than just trading one character for another.

Mickey, after all, is an intent, focused mouse. In the strip, he makes a clumsy mistake less because he's a klutz, more because he's a little *too* driven and focused on his task. Goofy, by contrast, plays the gag as the klutz to end all klutzes. Walking through a windowpane... gawrsh!

Images courtesy Walt Disney Feature Animation Research Library; special thanks to Fox Carney. [DG]

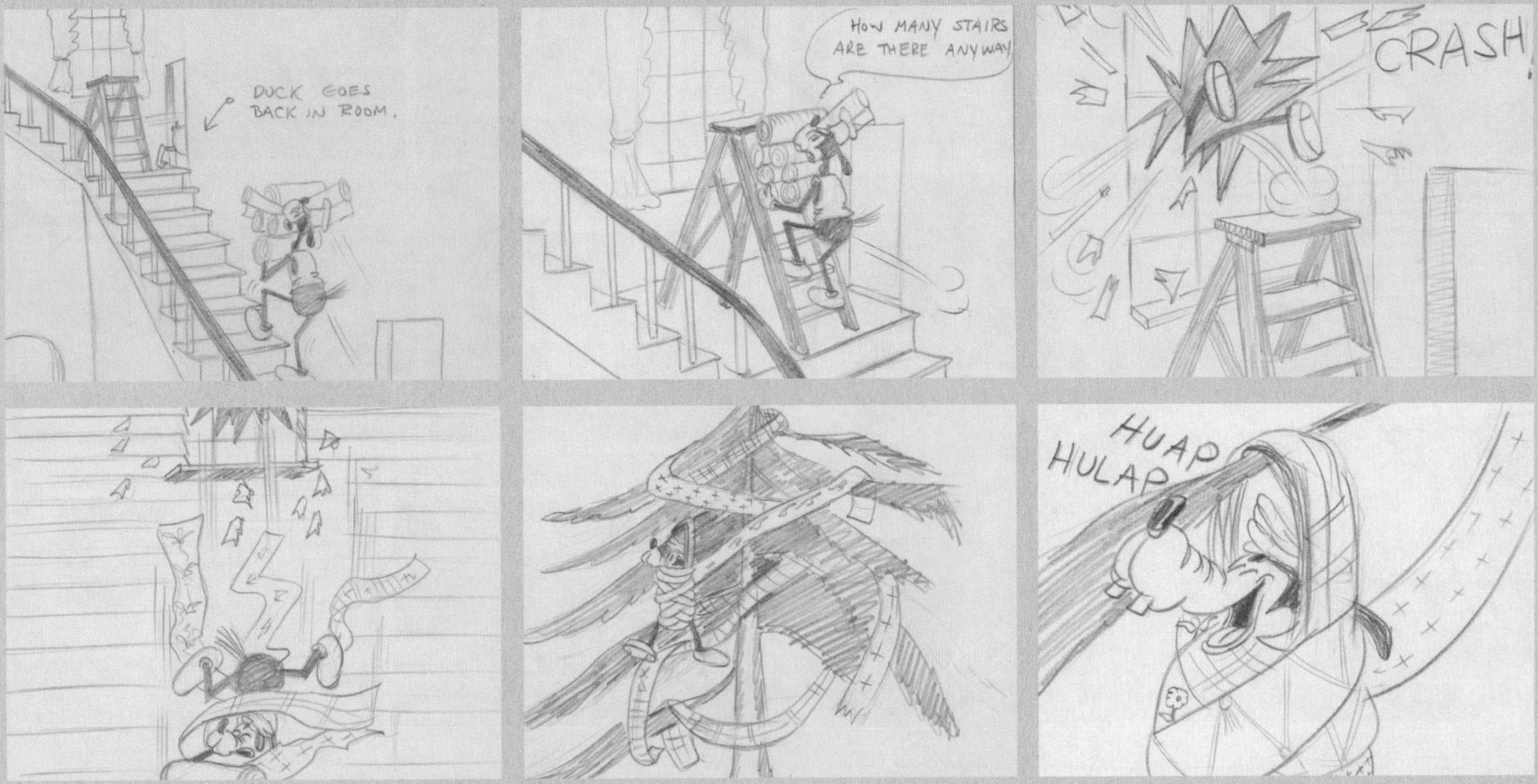

DUCK GOES BACK IN ROOM.
HOW MANY STAIRS ARE THERE ANYWAY
CRASH
HUAP
HULAP

"*Wrapping Up*" THE CASE OF THE VANISHING COATS

As one of Gottfredson's few major Mickey/Donald team-ups, "Case of the Vanishing Coats" (1935) has seen many a reprint over the years. In *Donald Duck* 286 (1994), Donald's 60th birthday issue, "Coats" and other Duck-centric classics were wrapped in a new frame story by William Van Horn. It it, "Birthday Boy" Donald experiences the vintage tales as nightmares after too many ice cream sundaes! Here's how "Vanishing Coats" was interpolated—complete with a rare in-story reference to Donald's evolving beak length. [DG]

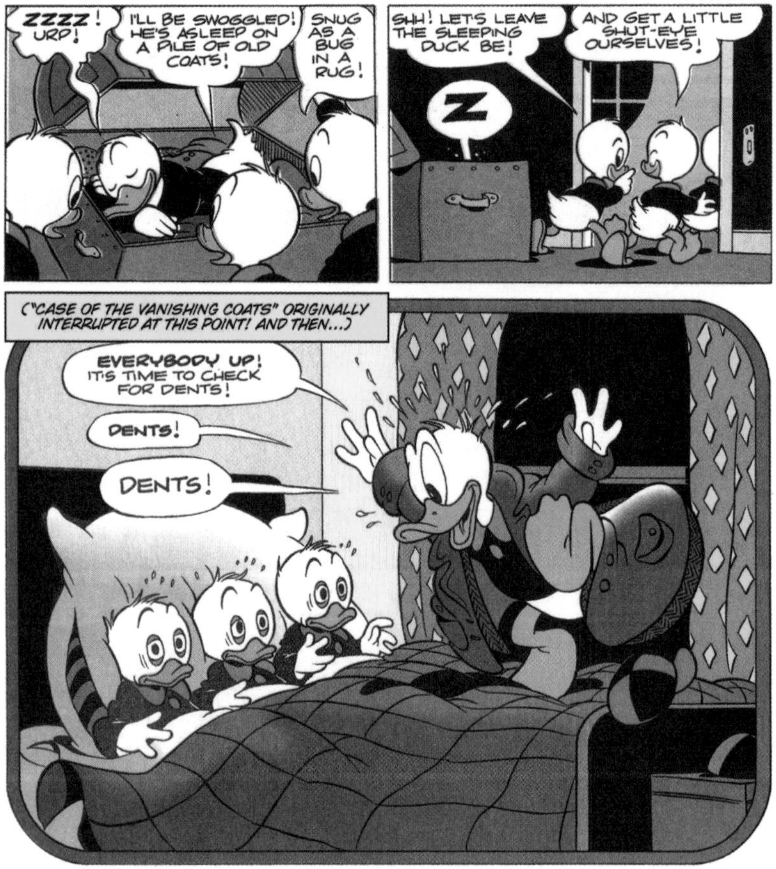
ZZZZ! URP!
I'LL BE SWOGGLED! HE'S ASLEEP ON A PILE OF OLD COATS!
SNUG AS A BUG IN A RUG!
SHH! LET'S LEAVE THE SLEEPING DUCK BE!
AND GET A LITTLE SHUT-EYE OURSELVES!
Z
("CASE OF THE VANISHING COATS" ORIGINALLY INTERRUPTED AT THIS POINT! AND THEN...)
EVERYBODY UP! IT'S TIME TO CHECK FOR DENTS!
DENTS!
DENTS!

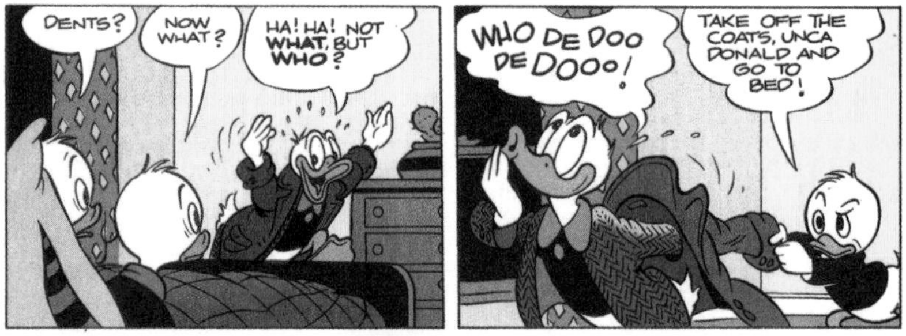
DENTS?
NOW WHAT?
HA! HA! NOT WHAT, BUT WHO?
WHO DE DOO DE DOOO!
TAKE OFF THE COATS, UNCA DONALD AND GO TO BED!

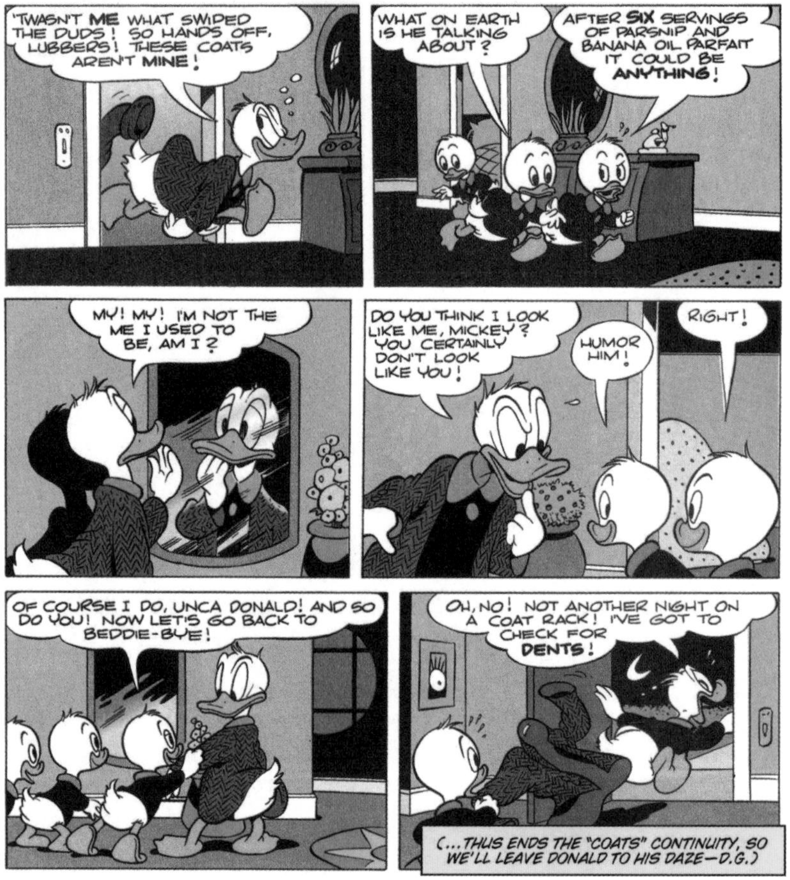
'TWASN'T ME WHAT SWIPED THE DUDS! SO HANDS OFF, LUBBERS! THESE COATS AREN'T MINE!
WHAT ON EARTH IS HE TALKING ABOUT?
AFTER SIX SERVINGS OF PARSNIP AND BANANA OIL PARFAIT IT COULD BE ANYTHING!
MY! MY! I'M NOT THE ME I USED TO BE, AM I?
DO YOU THINK I LOOK LIKE ME, MICKEY? YOU CERTAINLY DON'T LOOK LIKE YOU!
HUMOR HIM!
RIGHT!
OF COURSE I DO, UNCA DONALD! AND SO DO YOU! NOW LET'S GO BACK TO BEDDIE-BYE!
OH, NO! NOT ANOTHER NIGHT ON A COAT RACK! I'VE GOT TO CHECK FOR DENTS!
(...THUS ENDS THE "COATS" CONTINUITY, SO WE'LL LEAVE DONALD TO HIS DAZE—D.G.)

"The Case of the Vanishing Coats" has been a comic book perennial—but very few magazines have reflected its inclusion on the cover. On a similarly odd note, another early magazine featured vintage 1935 Donald strips... but treated Morty and Ferdie as the cover stars. Maybe the mischievous nephews simply tricked Donald into standing "off-camera"? [DG]

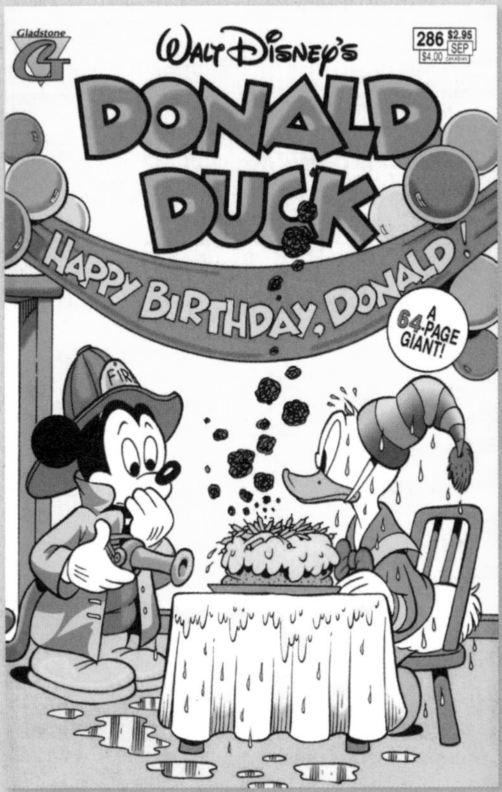
Gladstone
WALT DISNEY'S
DONALD DUCK
286
$2.95
SEP
$4.00
HAPPY BIRTHDAY, DONALD!
A 64-PAGE GIANT!

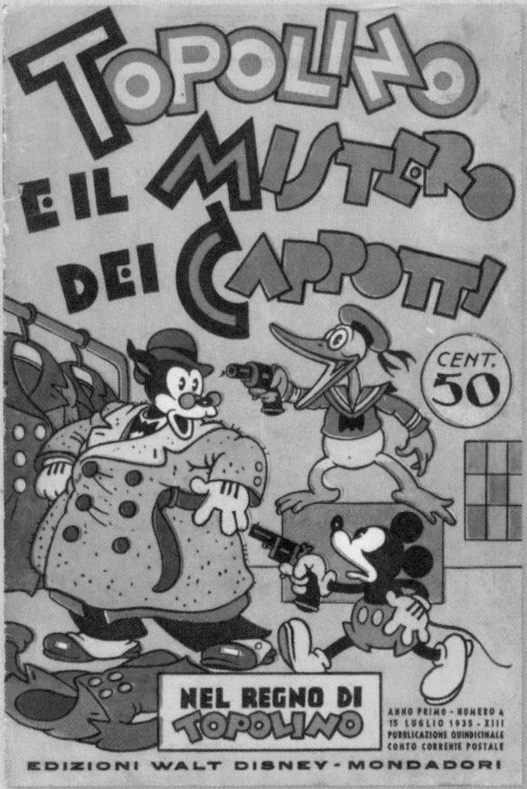
TOPOLINO E IL MISTERO DEI CAPPOTTI
CENT. 50
NEL REGNO DI TOPOLINO
ANNO PRIMO - NUMERO 4
15 LUGLIO 1935 - XIII
PUBBLICAZIONE QUINDICINALE
CONTO CORRENTE POSTALE
EDIZIONI WALT DISNEY - MONDADORI

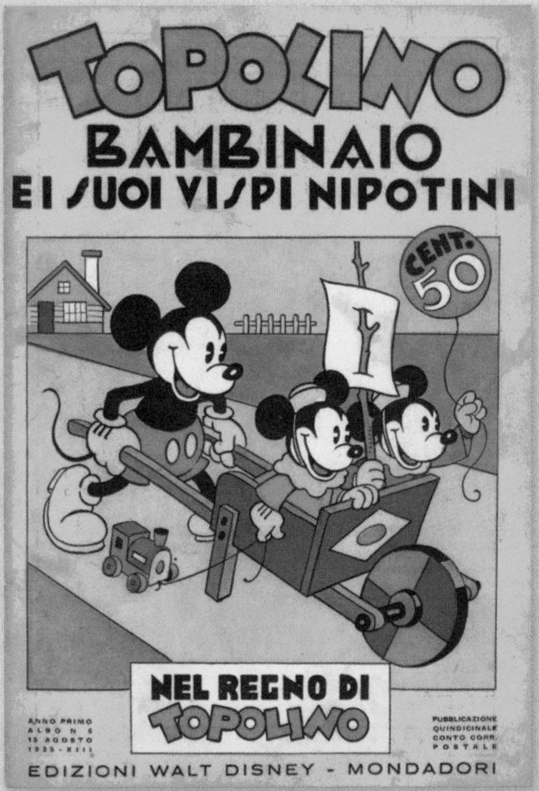
TOPOLINO
BAMBINAIO
E I SUOI VISPI NIPOTINI
CENT. 50
NEL REGNO DI TOPOLINO
EDIZIONI WALT DISNEY - MONDADORI

LEFT: Donald Duck 286 (1994), illustrating "Case of the Vanishing Coats" and its modern frame story (see opposite). Art by William Van Horn; image courtesy Thomas Jensen.

MIDDLE: Italian *Nel Regno di Topolino* 4 (1935), illustrating "Case of the Vanishing Coats." Art by Antonio Rubino; image courtesy Leonardo Gori.

RIGHT: Italian *Nel Regno di Topolino* 6 (1935), illustrating the March 31, 1935 gag strip. Art by Antonio Rubino; image courtesy Leonardo Gori.

A marsupial—er, *super serial* like "Hoppy" was destined to receive a super bunch of dedicated cobbers... uh, *covers*. As local reprints piled up, fans got *bushed* trying to grab them all for a *fair dinkum*—er, a fair *price*. (Whew.)

The 'roo's most prized reprint was his first one, published in his biological country of origin: Australia! Disney's kangaroo "star" was so popular down under that he received Mickey's first story-specific comic book cover in that country.

The art shows Hoppy having such a *g'day* that he doesn't even notice the mysterious joey in his pouch—a character from the *Mickey's Kangaroo* (1935) cartoon who isn't actually in Gottfredson's comic! [DG]

MICKEY'S KANGAROO
by WALT DISNEY.
© COPYRIGHT WALT DISNEY
PRINTED & PUBLISHED BY JOHN SANDS LTD., SYDNEY

GLADSTONE
WALT DISNEY'S
GLADSTONE COMIC ALBUM SERIES
8
MICKEY MOUSE
"HOPPY THE KANGAROO"

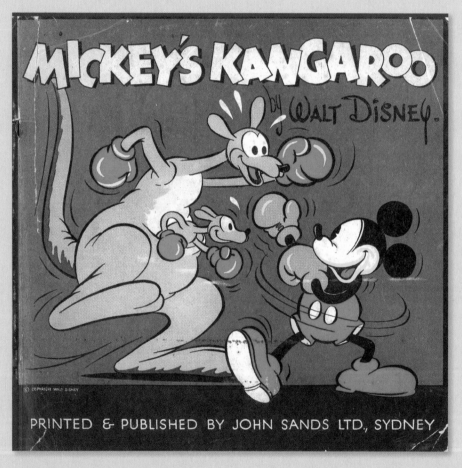

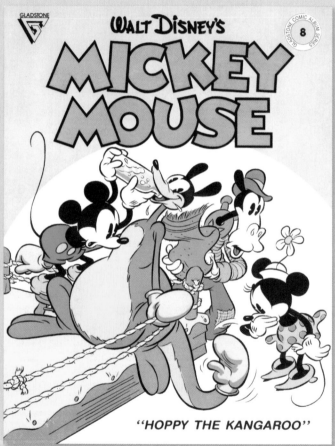

LEFT: Australian *Mickey Mouse* unnumbered issue (1935: the fourth Disney comic by publisher John Sands). Image courtesy Ricky Turner and Kosta Labropoulos.

RIGHT: *Gladstone Comic Album* 8 (1987). Art by Daan Jippes; image courtesy Thomas Jensen.

THE HEIRS OF GOTTFREDSON:

TOPOLINO

» *by* SERGIO LAMA *and* DAVID GERSTEIN

FLOYD GOTTFREDSON didn't create his first *Mickey Mouse* Sunday pages until 1932; yet as early as 1931, he was exerting a major, exciting influence on long-form, weekly Mickey Mouse comic strips. But how?

The answer becomes clear when we look at the strips' target market: Italy. In Italy, Disney's publishing activities bloomed faster than in the United States; in Italy, Gottfredson managed to affect local audiences *before* they had actually seen his work. For in Italy, and Italy alone, Gottfredson's "heirs"—local talents who carried on his style—actually beat him to a spot on the newsstand! This is their fascinating story.

Mickey Mouse was a film character first. Over his initial few years in Italian cinemas, Disney's big-eared star found ever-growing popularity, thanks in no small part to Sunday matinee shows for children. The same story was playing out in theatres around the world. The cartoons themselves were becoming increasingly sophisticated, and their success could be defined as global.

The same cannot be said for Mickey's comics debut. When January 1930 brought the first daily strips into print, they initially appeared in just a small number of American newspapers. That number would increase exponentially after May, when Gottfredson began work on the series. But until then, King Features Syndicate—and its magnate CEO William Randolph Hearst—almost had to force client papers to jump on the bandwagon.

RIGHT: From Guglielmo Guastaveglia's first *Topolino* strip (Italian *Il Popolo di Roma*, April 16, 1931). Image courtesy The Walt Disney Company.

The strip had a similarly rough start in Italy. Lorenzo Gigli, an editor with the *Gazzetta del Popolo* ("People's Gazette") newspaper, published "Lost on a Desert Island" (1930), the initial pre-Gottfredson serial. It was Gigli who gave Mickey his famous Italian name of *Topolino* ("little mouse"). But Gigli dulled the serial's impact by printing the strips out of order and only once a week. After 1930, Gigli dropped *Topolino* from the *Gazzetta* entirely. Perhaps he considered the strip a flop; regardless, he never gave Gottfredson a chance to make his debut.

What next? After being dumped by the *Gazzetta*, *Mickey Mouse* might have been hard for King to resell elsewhere in Italy—Gottfredson notwithstanding. Unless, perhaps, the strip was rebooted as a totally different-looking product. But how different could it become? Quite a bit, actually...

From April 16 to August 13, 1931, the newspaper *Il Popolo di Roma* ("The People of Rome") published a weekly, long-form Mickey Mouse comic strip on its children's page. But it was not the American *Mickey*. This new product was created for *Il Popolo* by **Guglielmo Guastaveglia** (1889-1984), a well-known

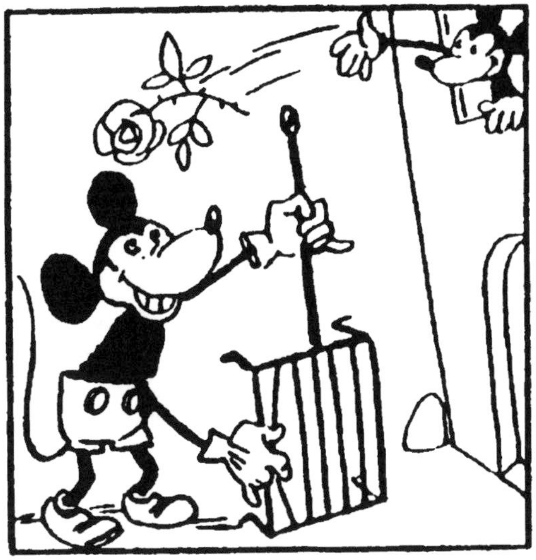

Mickey sings for Minnie's sake
An aria sweet as chocolate cake.
While Minnie, poised at window, rests
And dreams of love's togetherness.

local gag cartoonist. Yet it was nevertheless authorized by Disney via King Features, as indicated by an "exclusively for Italy" notice beneath each strip.[1]

Guglielmo Guastaveglia brought decades of comics training to *Il Popolo* and Mickey. He had earlier been an editor, writer, and director for various popular humor journals; he worked a twenty-year stretch with *Travaso delle Idee* ("The Transfer of Ideas"), a comic weekly launched at the turn of the century.

Guastaveglia's first Mickey pages took an artisanal approach that reflected this past experience. Settings were typically Italian in design. Rhyming narration—another Italian tradition—usually replaced voice balloon dialogue. Gags showed Mickey outwitting a black cat reminiscent of Felix the Cat; the Otto Messmer character, while not a Disney brand, was another King-licensed property.[2]

Three weeks in, someone evidently cried foul. Either Disney or Italian King representative

Guglielmo Emanuel sacked the faux Felix, then supplied Guastaveglia with Gottfredson and Win Smith photostats for future reference use.[3] Details of Guastaveglia's later Disney strips—a character pose here, a borrowed gag there—reveal that the artist carefully studied these American dailies, none yet published in Italy. Then he combined their flavor with his own.

The results seem to have been a success. *Il Popolo* gave Mickey a short run similar to the *Gazzetta*—but devoted far more space to him, suggesting greater acceptance. More importantly, in a land where no one knew "real" Gottfredson, Guastaveglia gave readers their first taste of Gottfredson's style. Guastaveglia's Mickey still cavorted though Italian backdrops, including soccer

games (May 28) and a deli selling Parmesan cheese (May 21). But Mickey's peers were now Gottfredson-style dogs and pigs; his new enemy was Kat Nipp, a formidable foe from 1931 Gottfredson daily strips.[4] And their ensuing hijinks actually did Gottfredson one better. Guastaveglia began to feature escalating gags and fairly complicated setups: the kind that Gottfredson, in 1931, could not have put across in a four-panel daily strip.

In his antiquated, rhyming, Rome-centric way, Guglielmo Guastaveglia directly anticipated the Gottfredson Sunday strips to come.

Guastaveglia also anticipated later Italian events. In fall 1932, *Il Popolo*'s run had long since ended; and for the moment, there was no Disney comics presence in the country. A new publisher, Florence-based Casa Editrice Nerbini, decided to issue an entire Mickey *magazine* without Disney or King Features involvement—and without, as it happened, Gottfredson inspiration. Nerbini's *Topolino* 1 (1932) paired Mickey not with Minnie or Kat Nipp, but with a nonhumanized elephant that he mercilessly pranked. Some Guastaveglia influence was visible; Gottfredson influence was not.

The elephant-fighting Mickey, drawn by **Giove Toppi** (1888-1942), never got to evolve like Guastaveglia's. King and Disney understandably

objected to the unlicensed magazine. In an effort to avoid further offense, Nerbini briefly replaced Topolino with "Topo Lino" ("Lino Mouse"), an entirely different-looking rodent.

Then a deal was struck. Nerbini became an authorized King Features partner, allowing the legitimate use of Mickey. Disney took ownership of Nerbini's earlier mouse material—even Topo Lino—and all its original Disney content going forward. Toppi and colleague **Angelo Burattini** (1891-1969) continued to draw occasional Mickey strips for Nerbini. But the "main" Disney artist in *Topolino* was now Gottfredson, who at last had a regular Italian showcase for his work—starting with many of this volume's Sunday strips.

Guglielmo Guastaveglia was Gottfredson's first Italian "heir"; Toppi and Burattini functioned more like stepping stones to later, greater successors. Yet oddly important stepping stones they were. For without their efforts, famous future heirs like Romano Scarpa might have had no Disney comics line to work for! •

1 Mark Johnson (Archivist, King Features Syndicate), conversations with David Gerstein, December 2012. Period documentation does not survive at King, but the pattern matches King's sublicensing of other comics features in Europe at the time.

2 Perhaps Guastaveglia mistook Felix for a Disney character; the somewhat Felixlike Julius the Cat was a featured player in silent era Disney cartoons. The 2005 American edition of one Guastaveglia Mickey strip interprets Guastaveglia's cat as Julius.

3 Johnson to Gerstein, *ibid.*

4 Kat Nipp, called *Maramao* by Guastaveglia, would wait five years before Italian audiences saw him in Gottfredson's hand (in *Nel Regno di Topolino* 17, 1936).

MICKEY MOUSE

DO NOT TOUCH
PULL HARD

Making house calls, Dr. Bear
Has come upon an illness rare.
"Arthritic tail—see how it squirms;
The very latest thing in germs."

Through a peephole in his flat
Leo sticks his tail, so that
The sickly part can get some sun.
That's Doctor's treatment number one.

Kat Nipp, Mickey's foe of fable,
Hates him like Cain hated Abel.
Turning 'round the warning sign,
He hopes our hero to malign.

PULL HARD
PULL HARD

"Tasty-looking wienie, Nipp!
Was it pricey?" "Not a bit;
Leo's sharing them for free!
Ring his bell; have one on me!"

Following the sign, our mouse
Yanks the "bell-pull" of the house
With strength to make a lion proud!
He's also got a lion cowed...

But Mickey doesn't know that yet;
Until the "bell-pull" shakes and frets
And disappears into the wall!
Mickey takes a messy fall.

!

Leo goes on such a tear
He wrecks his house and doesn't care!
"I'm a goner," Mick surmises.
Then the lion realizes...

Mickey's hard yank cured his tail!
No more does Leo weep and wail;
Instead he gives, with grateful eyes,
A wienie as a thank-you prize!

Kat Nipp sees the tasty meal.
"Leo's sharing food for real?
And here I thought I fooled you fine!
Some day, Mouse, revenge is mine!"

(Esclusività per l'Italia).

(Riproduzione vietata)

MICKEY MOUSE

PARTS
BIKE STORE

Eager little mouselings sweet
Howl as one for grub to eat—
And sadly strike poor Mickey dumb;
For Mickey can't afford a crumb.

Nearby butcher Percy Pig
Displays a ham that's awf'ly big
And Parmesan so ripe and soft
That folks can smell it miles off.

Hunger fires up the brain—
Our Mickey Mouse discovers, when
He spots an advertising sign
And hatches an idea fine.

HAM!
Yeek!

"Hey Percy! See that fellow there?
He's a glutton millionaire
Who's buying foodstuff by the bale!
Tell him what you have for sale!"

...suggests the prideful boar.
Kat Nipp gives an angry roar
Just like a tiger on the track:
"So, *I'm* a ham? You take that back!"

The pig's off like the wind,
Fueled by terrified chagrin.
Kat Nipp yells, "Insulting cad—
I'll collar you and beat you bad!"

BIKE STORE

Once the chase leads pig and cat
A long way off, we notice that
Our cunning little hero may
Have money-saving plans in play...

First in war! First in peace!
First to build a bike of *cheese*
And fastest man to ride one, too;
That's our Mickey. Toodle-loo!

Reaching home with cocky feeling
Mickey finishes "free-wheeling."
Parmesan means kids won't know
That hungry feeling down below!

(Riproduzione vietata)

(Esclusività per l'Italia)

—Continued on Page 276

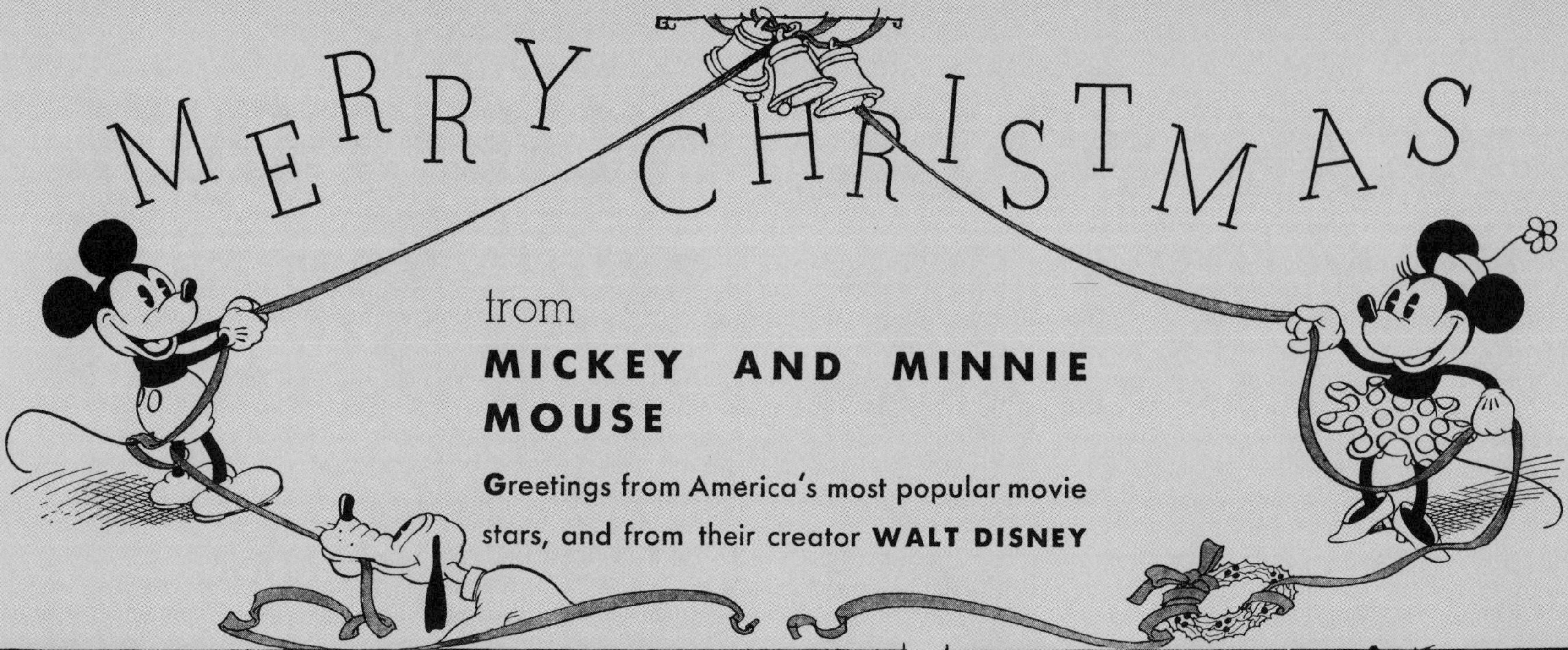
MERRY CHRISTMAS
from
MICKEY AND MINNIE MOUSE
Greetings from America's most popular movie stars, and from their creator WALT DISNEY

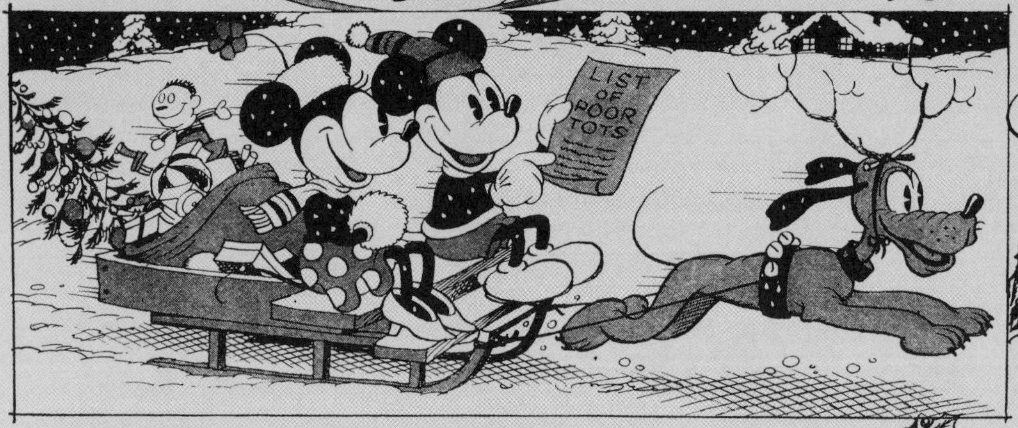
LIST OF POOR TOTS

1. "See, Minnie," said Mickey, "I've made up a list
Of children that Santa Claus probably missed!"

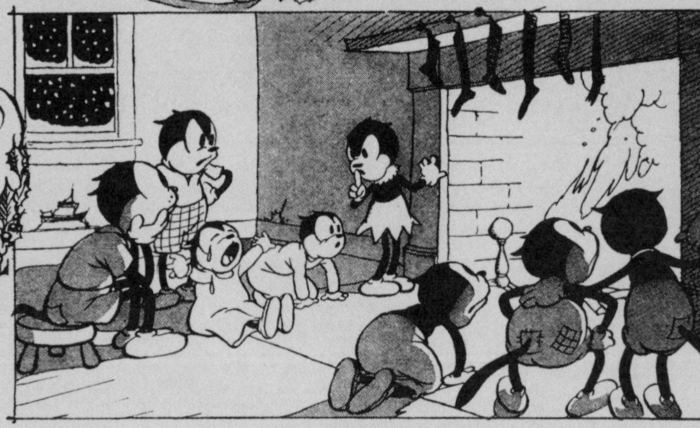

2. Tattered and starved, at the end of their rope,
These poor kids had naught in their tummies but—hope!

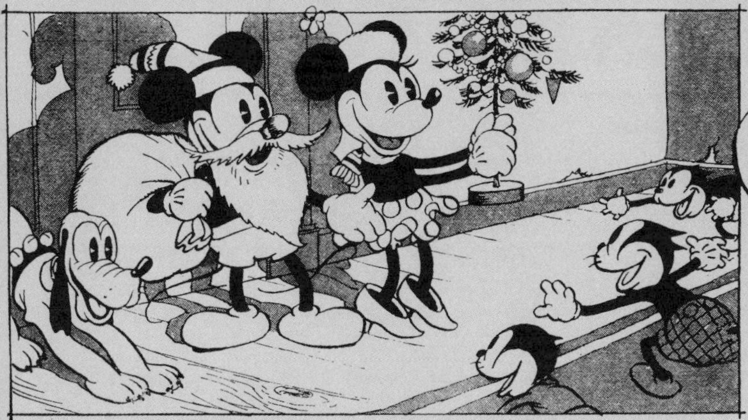

3. When suddenly, laughing and shouting, "SURPRISE!"
Mickey and Minnie appeared in disguise.

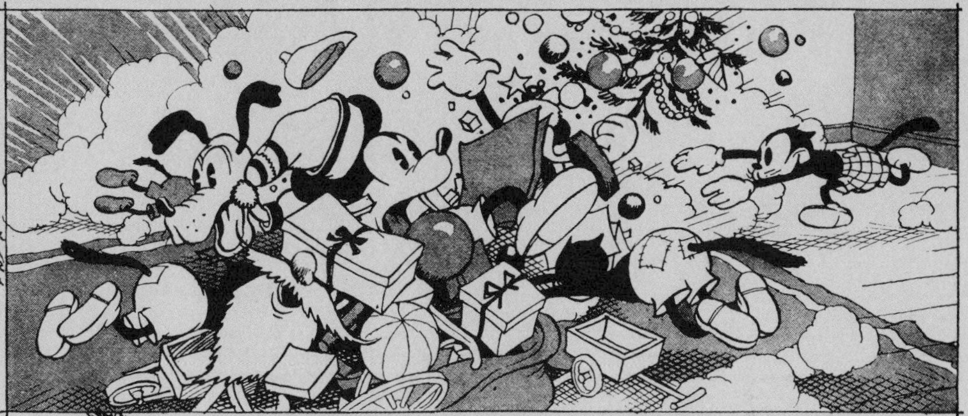

4. "Whoopee!" "It's Santa Claus!" "Look at the toys!"
And they were submerged by a deluge of boys.

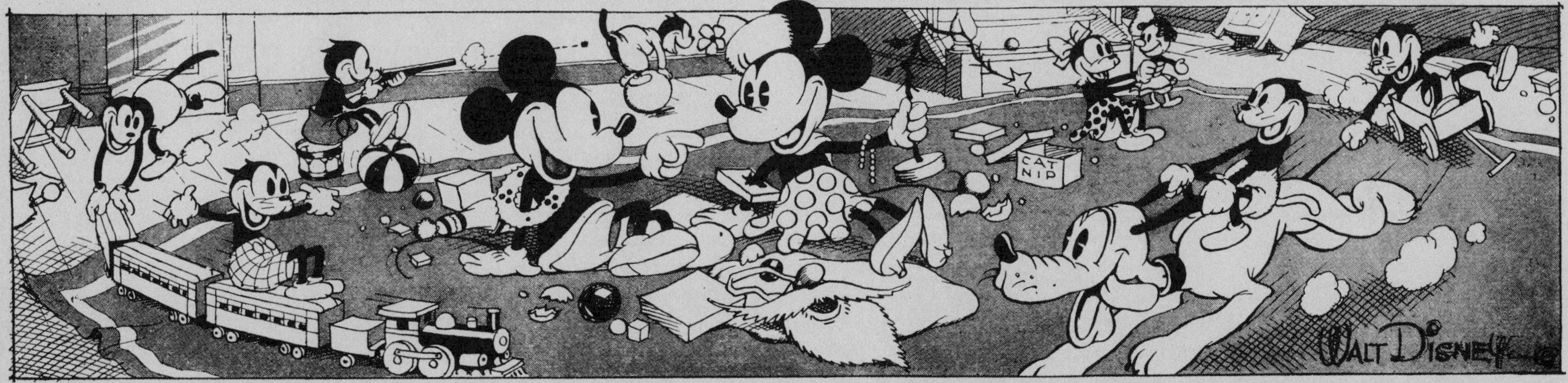
CAT NIP
WALT DISNEY

5. Said Mickey: "This proves it! I really believe
That it is more blessed to give than receive."

6. "These toys will be wrecked and forgotten, I'll bet,
But the pleasure WE'VE had, we will NEVER forget!"

Turnabout is fair play. American Disney staffers mimicked the Italian comics style—complete with text under the panels!—when Gottfredson's Comic Strip Department produced this special Christmas strip for *The Delineator* magazine (1932). Image courtesy David Gerstein.

MICKEY MOUSE

HO-HO-HUM!

Nasty Kat Nipp's sleeping sweet
As Mick sneaks in, and for a treat
Snips off his tail—as payback "thanks"
For many weeks of wicked pranks!

The dozing villain slumbers on
Till wakened by his clock alarm.
He stirs and yawns with happy heart,
Not knowing of his missing part.

Then he sees. Is his face *red!*
He'd caterwaul to wake the dead
Except it might let Mickey know
He'd got him good—the so-and-so!

Instead, it's smarter to pretend
That Nipp prefers his lower end
Without that ugly tail there.
Perfect! Look at Mickey stare!

Next—another plan that's cute.
How about a substitute?
A tail of wienies, freshly fried;
Although the butcher's price is high.

Mickey spots the hot new look
And knows he's just been made a schnook.
"I've gotta get back at this cat;
And with a clever scheme, at that."

LOOK, WIENIES!
BON VOYAGE!

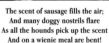

Our hero whistles up a crowd
Of hungry dogs, berserk and loud
And closely packed as canned sardines.
Let's see what their presence means.

The scent of sausage fills the air;
And many doggy nostrils flare
As all the hounds pick up the scent
And on a wienie meal are bent!

On top of this, we also know
That dogs are cats' eternal foe.
"Shoo!" says Nipp, "or get in line!
I'll take your bites one at a time!"

MICKEY MOUSE

DYNAMITE
Mr. Mickey Mouse
To: Kat Nipp

A fudge cake, exquisite to see,
Is not the place for TNT—
But into this café's choicest round
Kat Nipp pours powder by the pound.

Then he orders Baker Mutt:
"Deliver one cake to my hut;
The other goes to Mickey Mouse."
He hopes to blow him up, the louse!

But spying Mickey's seen it all.
"Nipp will never make me fall!
A thousand times he'll try for naught,"
He taps his forehead at the thought.

Mr. Mickey Mouse
To: Kat Nipp

In haste to circumvent the cat
Our hero grabs a bowler hat
And paintpot, so that he can start
To render some fantastic art.

Three strokes later, look who's here:
The portrait of a buccaneer.
"I'll go fool that baker now;
He'll think I'm Nipp. Meow! Meow!"

"Hey, baker-man! Kat Nipp—that's me!
I've come back here, as you can see
To switch those namecards 'round, for I
Want each to go to the other guy."

YOUR CAKE, SIR!

Soon enough, to Kat Nipp's pad
Comes baker's boy with cake in bag.
He brings it out, still warm and sticky;
Now the other goes to Mickey.

"What a tender, tasty treat!
This dessert's got others beat!
And any minute, Mickey might
Cut into his—and die of fright!"

Kaboom! A blast from out the sweet
Throws Kat Nipp forehead-over-feet.
As he tumbles back to earth
Our Mickey laughs for all he's worth!

MICKEY MOUSE

CHUG!

"What's your answer, Minnie girl:
Is any cyclist in the world
As safe and fast and slick as me?
Ha! Such a biker couldn't be!"

"The rocky road may dip and slope;
But on my bike you needn't mope.
Sit back and laugh—enjoy the sights.
My leather seat will hold you tight!"

"Then again, Toots, maybe we
Have had too much frivolity.
Why don't we stop and rest awhile
While you congratulate my style?"

"Sorry, Minnie; my mistake—
But one that any ace could make.
A pedal-master I remain;
Such boo-boos will not come again!"

"In fact, I'll help you to forget
That spill you took. Hang on, don't fret;
Watch my speed just knock 'em dead
As I zip past that car ahead!"

"Milord, Sir Pedal-Master? I
Would love to stay, but I must fly.
A far more modest, skilled chauffeur
Is what I'd honestly prefer."

MICKEY MOUSE

Minnie

Kat Nipp's got it in his head
To kidnap Minnie Mouse;
But her beloved has a plan
To save his future spouse.

These extra shoes are needed to
Protect our hero's mate.
But pending that, the wicked cat
First has to take the bait!

"Minnie, no!" our Mickey shouts.
"Don't drown yourself, my dear!
You needn't end it all like this
Just 'cause Kat Nipp is near."

The villain thinks the girl is lost!
He dives into the drink
To rescue her—so why is Mickey
Smiling, do you think?

Nipp had yearned to capture
Minnie's kisses, you can bet;
But now, a prisoner of love,
He's captured in this net.

A wicked fate for Nipp: to hang
Immobilized like this
While Mick and Min sit down below
And share a comfy kiss!

MICKEY MOUSE

Mickey takes a reckless dare,
Forgetting that it's quite unfair

To toss a rock at Jumbo's dome.
He should leave well enough alone.

Jumbo, smarting at the whack,
Bursts out of his cul-de-sac.

It looks like he'll lay Mickey low.
(And don't forget, we told him so.)

Run, run, Mickey—speedy mite!
Jumbo grabs his tail tight;

But Mickey lets the end break free
And scrambles for security.

Run, run, Mickey—find a goal!
Down the way he sees a hole

Beneath a nearby city wall.
Could it be salvation's call?

Mickey squirms in with a pop.
Elephant's too fast to stop;

Chugging like a streamline train,
He gets brickwork on the brain.

Dizzy Jumbo lies at rest
Feeling very second-best.

Mickey grins, "I may be small,
But I can save myself; that's all!"

A DEMANDING DIRECTOR

"Look sharp! Sit straight! Act resolute—
And get that grimace off your snoot!"
A bossy cameraman's demands
Bring shivers to poor Mickey's hands.

Stepping much too near the ledge,
The movie-man falls off the edge
And doesn't grab the wall in time,
So tumbles downward toward the brine.

He hits the flimsy boat, and knocks
It on its side to face the dock;
Tossing Mickey all asunder,
Toward the camera, quick as thunder.

While waiting for the puffed-up louse
To save himself, our playful mouse
Reverses roles: "Act resolute—
And get that grimace off your snoot!"

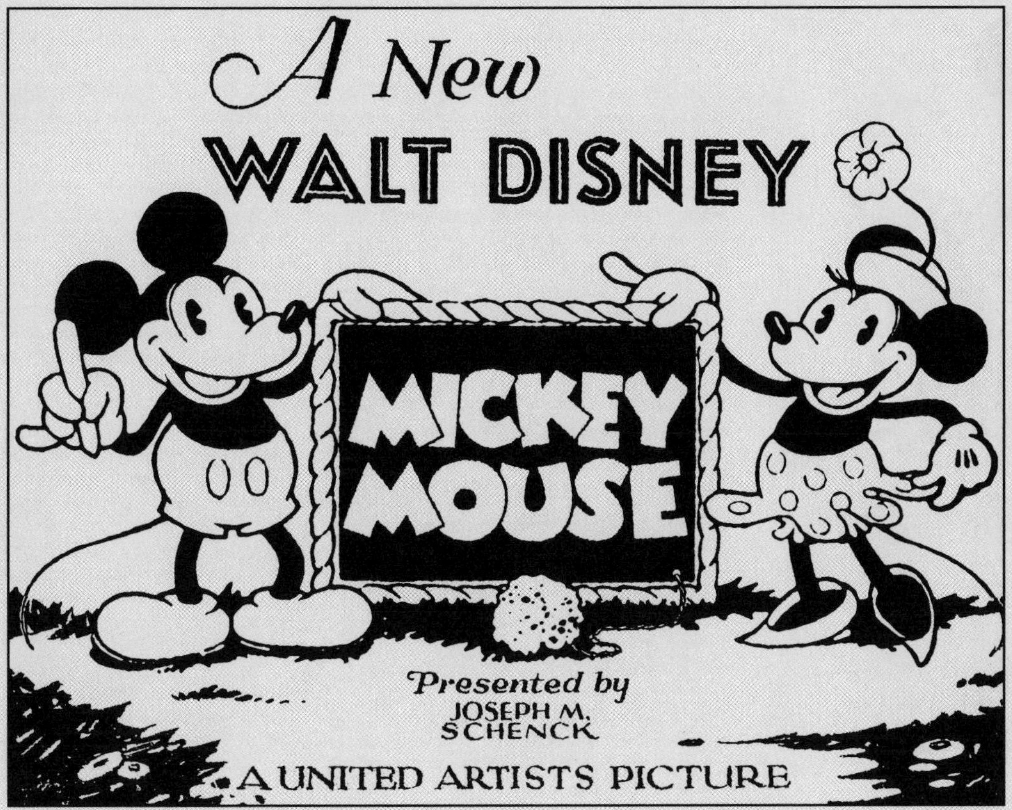
A New
WALT DISNEY
MICKEY
MOUSE
Presented by
JOSEPH M.
SCHENCK
A UNITED ARTISTS PICTURE

"Any time you can tell your story visually, do it. Leave [words] out if you can, or tell it in action as much as you can. Use the word to complement the drawing... your writing has to be fairly pithy... to make the point as briefly as possible... [but] once you get it down there, it's even a more perfect medium than your television or whatever, because it's there. [Readers] can go back to it if they're puzzled."

— Floyd Gottfredson to Arn Saba, 1979

LEFT: This rare 1932 lantern slide design, attributed to Gottfredson, once promoted new Mickey cartoons in cinemas. Slight distortion to the image originates with its source, a Disney exhibitors' catalog; we know no surviving examples of the slide itself. The Mickey/Minnie concept and poses are similar to, but not quite the same as, the design used for contemporary cartoons' main titles. Image courtesy Hake's Americana.

SINCERELY YOURS –
MICKEY MOUSE,
MINNIE MOUSE
AND
Walt Disney

working extensively with the Walt Disney Company and its licensees. Gerstein's published work includes *Mickey and the Gang: Classic Stories in Verse*; *Walt Disney Treasures – Disney Comics: 75 Years of Innovation*; and *The Katzenjammer Kids: 100 Years in Norway*. He has also worked with Disney to preserve the *Mickey Mouse* newspaper strips seen in this volume.

GARY GROTH co-founded Fantagraphics Books and *The Comics Journal* in 1976. And he is still at it.

J. B. KAUFMAN is a film historian on the staff of the Walt Disney Family Foundation. He is the author of *The Fairest One of All: The Making of Walt Disney's Snow White and the Seven Dwarfs* and *South of the Border With Disney*, and the coauthor—with Russell Merritt—of *Walt in Wonderland: The Silent Films of Walt Disney* and *Walt Disney's Silly Symphonies: A Companion to the Classic Cartoon Series*.

KEVIN HUIZENGA has published books and comics with Drawn & Quarterly, Fantagraphics and others. He also self-published mini-comics for over ten years. Many of his stories feature the character Glenn Ganges and sweatles. His most recent books are *Gloriana* and *Amazing Facts and Beyond! with Leon Beyond*. He lives in St. Louis with his wife, cat, and two snakes.

LEONARDO GORI is a comics scholar and collector specializing in Italian Disney authors and syndicated 1930s newspaper strips. With Frank Stajano and others, he has written many books on Italian "fumetti" and American comics in Italy. He has also written thrillers, which have been translated into Spanish, Portuguese, and Korean.

FRANCESCO ("Frank") STAJANO was imprinted on Disney comics at preschool age and never grew out of it: the walls of his house are covered in bookshelves and many of them hold comics. He has often written about Disney comics, particularly with Leonardo Gori. In real life he is an associate professor at the University of Cambridge in England.

JOE TORCIVIA is a comics historian renowned for decades of Disney, Warner Bros, Hanna-Barbera, and DC Comics scholarship. He has also worked as a dialogue writer for American editions of European Disney comics. He maintains the blog "The Issue At Hand" (*tiahblog.blogspot. com*), featuring a lighthearted look at pop culture. Torcivia has also read every retelling and/or redrawing of Gottfredson's "Island in the Sky" (1936)—and lived to tell about it.

THAD KOMOROWSKI began his professional association with Disney comics as a teenager, writing character dialogue for American editions of European *Uncle Scrooge* stories. Today a historian and archivist, Komorowski maintains the blog *whataboutthad.com*, devoted to the art of animation, comics, and live-action film. He is the author of *Sick Little Monkeys: The Unauthorized Ren & Stimpy Story*.

JIM KORKIS has been an active historian of the worlds of Disney for over three decades. He has written hundreds of articles and several books on the Walt Disney Company. He worked for nearly fifteen years at Disney in a variety of capacities including performer, animation instructor, facilitator, and writer. As an approved freelance contractor, he continues to provide research and writing for Disney today.

SERGIO LAMA was born in Florence in 1936. Since childhood he has been involved in comics as an avid reader, collector and scholar. In the 1970s he became a columnist for some of the first Italian comics fanzines, including *Exploit Comics*; later, he would also write essays on early Italian magazines. With Fabio Gadducci and Leonardo Gori, he authored *Eccetto Topolino*, the seminal book on American syndicated comics in Italy during the 1930s and 1940s. Lama's research into early 20th century Italian comic artists has helped to create a serious database of their significant, previously neglected works.